PLUTARCH

MORALIA

XIV

LCL 428

PLUTARCH

MORALIA

VOLUME XIV

WITH AN ENGLISH TRANSLATION BY

BENEDICT EINARSON

AND

PHILLIP H. DE LACY

HARVARD UNIVERSITY PRESS

CAMBRIDGE, MASSACHUSETTS

LONDON, ENGLAND

First published 1967

LOEB CLASSICAL LIBRARY® is a registered trademark
of the President and Fellows of Harvard College

ISBN 978-0-674-99472-0

*Printed on acid-free paper and bound by
The Maple-Vail Book Manufacturing Group*

CONTENTS

PREFACE

WE retain the moveable ν before consonants wherever the MSS. allow us to do so, and we follow their nearly unanimous usage in the treatment of elision and the accentuation of ἐστι.

Of the superior figures and letters attached to the symbols for MSS. 1 indicates the first hand, 2 the second, and so forth ; c indicates a correction by the first hand, ac the reading thus corrected ; r indicates an erasure, ar the reading before erasure ; t indicates a reading in the text, ss a superscribed reading, m a reading in the margin ; and s indicates a part of the MS. supplied by a later hand.

We have collated from photographs all MSS. known to us. A list follows ; the dating is that of the catalogues and later studies. An asterisk is appended to letters that here indicate a different MS. from the MS. they indicated in volume VII.

A 1671 in the national library at Paris ; A.D. 1296.
B 1675 in the national library at Paris ; 15th century.
C 1955 in the national library at Paris ; 11th–12th century.
D* 1374 in the Vatican library ; 15th–16th century.
E 1672 in the national library at Paris ; written shortly after A.D. 1302.

F* 2365 in the Vatican library ; 16th century.

G* 101 in the Angelican library ; 16th century.

H   283 in the Palatine library at Heidelberg ; 11th–12 century.

J* III C 1 in the national library at Naples ; 14th–15th century.

K* R-I-5 in the library of the Escorial; 16th century.

L   69, 13 in the Laurentian library ; 10th century.

M* VI in the appendix to the library of St. Mark ; 12th–13th century.

N* III C 3 in the national library at Naples ; 15th century.

P   2425 in the national library at Paris ; A.D. 1537.

Q   173 in the national library at Munich ; 16th century.

R* 977 in the Rossi collection at Rome ; 16th century ; written by Johannes Honorios.

S* Φ-II-5 in the library of the Escorial; 16th century.

T   2456 in the national library at Paris ; 16th century ; written by Michael Damascenus.

U   97 in the Urbino collection at the Vatican ; 10th–11th century.

V* 186 in the Vatican library ; 13th century.

W* 192 in the Vatican library ; 13th–14th century.

X   250 in the library of St. Mark ; 11th century. Xᵇ supplied missing parts in the 15th century.

Z* 215 in the national library at Munich ; 15th century.

a* 59, 1 in the Laurentian library ; 14th century.

b* 2048 in the University library at Bologna ; 16th century.

c   5692 in the Harleian collection at the British Museum ; 15th century.

d   56, 2 in the Laurentian library ; 15th century.
     The missing conclusion of the *Non posse suaviter
     vivi secundum Epicurum* has been supplied by d^s
     (the same as d^2) from κ.

e*   152 in the Este library at Modena ; 15th–16th
     century.

f*   III 40 in the collection of the *Acquisiti* in the
     Laurentian library ; 15th–16th century.

g   170 in the Palatine collection at the Vatican ;
     15th century.

h*   322 in the library of St. Mark ; probably A.D.
     1449.

j*   265 in the Barberini collection at the Vatican ;
     written by Johannes Honorios in A.D. 1543 (*cf.*
     R. da Rios, *Aristoxeni Elementa Harmonica*, Rome,
     1954, p. xxxvii n. 2).

k*   221 in the Vatican library ; written by Johannes
     Honorios ; a copy of j*.

n   350 III E 28 in the national library at Naples
     and 1676 in the Vatican library ; 15th century.

o   2700 in the University library at Bologna ; 15th–
     16th century.

q*   58, 29 in the Laurentian library ; 15th cen-
     tury.

r   41 in the Rehdiger collection at Wrocław Univer-
     sity ; 16th century.

s*   2451 in the national library at Paris ; 15th
     century.

t   100 in the Urbino collection at the Vatican ;
     A.D. 1402.

u   99 in the Urbino collection at the Vatican ; 15th
     century.

v*   176 in the collection of Greek philosophy in the
     national library at Vienna ; 14th century.

x   200 in the collection of the *Miscellanei* in the Bodleian library ; 16th century.

y   1009 in the Vatican library ; 14th century.

α   C 126 inf. (859) in the Ambrosian library ; A.D. 1294–1295.

β   1013 in the Vatican library ; 14th century.

γ   139 in the Vatican library ; written shortly after A.

δ   80 in the collection of Queen Christina at the Vatican ; 15th century.

ε   4690 in the national library at Madrid ; 14th century.

κ   80, 5 in the Laurentian library ; 14th century.

λ   80, 30 in the Laurentian library ; 15th–16th century.

μ   80, 21 in the Laurentian library ; 15th century.

π   80, 22 in the Laurentian library ; 14th century.

σ   248 in the library of St. Mark ; A.D. 1455.

s   Excerpts in MS. Φ-III-11 of the library of the Escorial ; 16th century.

τ   51 in the cathedral at Toledo ; 15th–16th century.

ψ   25 (B 120) in the Vallicella library ; 16th century. A copy of Stephanus' edition.

517 in the library of St. Mark ; 15th century ; see p. 188.

429 in the national library at Munich ; 15th century ; see pp. 11 and 188.

Ald.[2] indicates manuscript conjectures found in certain copies of the Aldine edition of 1509.

It is a pleasure to acknowledge scholarly help received from Professors W. D. Anderson, D. Feaver, C. Finch and H. Lloyd-Jones ; the many courtesies

PREFACE

of the custodians of the MSS.; and the generosity of the trustees of the Loeb Foundation and of the University of Chicago in defraying expenses.

BENEDICT EINARSON
The University of Chicago

PHILLIP H. DE LACY
Cornell University

THAT EPICURUS ACTUALLY MAKES A PLEASANT LIFE IMPOSSIBLE

(NON POSSE SUAVITER VIVI SECUNDUM EPICURUM)

INTRODUCTION

As a Platonist Plutarch often polemizes against both the Stoics and the Epicureans. In nine titles he mentions Chrysippus or the Stoics by name, in eight Epicurus or the Epicureans, and to the eight we may add the *Reply to Colotes* and the discussion of the precept " Live Unknown." [a] One title, *Selections and Refutations of the Stoics and Epicureans* (No. 148 in the Catalogue of Lamprias), has a place on both lists. Three of the anti-Epicurean works bear titles parallel to those of anti-Stoic works :

> *On the Contradictions of the Epicureans* (No. 129)
> *On the Contradictions of the Stoics*
> *That the Epicureans Speak More Paradoxically than the Poets* (No. 143)
> *That the Stoics Speak More Paradoxically than the Poets* (No. 79)
> *On Free Will in Reply to Epicurus* (No. 133)
> *On Free Will in Reply to the Stoics* (No. 154).

The titles of the remaining lost anti-Epicurean writings are *A Reply to Epicurus' Lecture(s) On the Gods* (No. 80), *On Superstition in Reply to Epicurus* (No. 155), and *On Lives in Reply to Epicurus* (No. 159).[b]

Most of the polemical essays were no doubt written

---

[a] *Cf.* K. Ziegler in Pauly-Wissowa, *s.v.* " Plutarchos," vol. xxi. 1 (1951), coll. 704. 65–705. 15.

[b] Epicurus wrote a work in four books *On Lives* (Diogenes Laert. x. 28).

after Plutarch had set up his school. The *Reply to Colotes in Defence of the Other Philosophers* is the report of a lecture by Plutarch in the school, while the essay on the impossibility of a pleasant life reports a discussion that took place after the lecture.

The two essays are widely separated in the two mss., E and B, that contain them both, and in the Aldine and Basle editions.[a] Ferron first brought them together in his translation (Lyons, 1555) ; but failing to notice that the essay on the pleasant life refers to the *Reply to Colotes* at 1086 c-d,[b] he retained the order of the Basle edition, merely omitting the essays that intervene. This arrangement was taken over by R. Estienne (1572), and passed from his edition to all subsequent editions, including the present.

In the first work Plutarch is the principal speaker, in the second he yields to Aristodemus and Theon. The first is dedicated to Saturninus, the second has no dedication, which is natural enough, as the discussion in the second is carried on by Theon and Aristodemus. The tone of the first is noticeably sharper. In the second it has become a good deal milder, no doubt in deference to certain criticisms (for which see 1086 e and 1096 e with the note). There is a strong hint that the end of the second essay (1104 c—1107 c) is taken from a previous lecture of Plutarch's.

[a] Thirty essays intervene in E, fourteen in B, and forty-eight in the Aldine and its copy, the Basle edition.

[b] It is noted by Gassendi, who cites the *Reply to Colotes* (1119 f) as " the first of the two books against Colotes " (priore in Coloten libro) in his *Animadversiones in Decimum Librum Diogenis Laertii, Qui est de Vita, Moribus, Placitisque Epicuri* (Lyons, 1649), p. 116.

The scene of the dialogue is a gymnasium (1086 D) near Plutarch's school, presumably at Chaeronea.

The speakers are Aristodemus and Theon, and a few words are spoken by Zeuxippus and by Plutarch himself. Theon is represented as reluctant to speak (1104 A ; *cf.* 1087 B) ; Aristodemus is an enthusiast. We may suppose that some of the students are also present, ready to intervene if Theon's memory should fail (1104 A).

It will be convenient to state the Epicurean position first, and then observe how Plutarch attacks it.

Pleasure, according to the Epicureans, is the highest good ; it is the ultimate aim of all our activities past, present, and future. It is of two kinds, pleasure of a settled state, and pleasure in motion. The settled pleasure is the same as the absence of pain ; indeed only those pleasures in movement are chosen that are incidental to the riddance of pain.

Such are the pleasures of the body. Pleasure of the mind is a reflection of these. Absence of perturbation (*ataraxia*) corresponds to the settled pleasures of the body, and animation (*euphrosynê*) at the anticipation or remembrance of a pleasure in movement of the body is a pleasure in movement of the mind. Because it is not limited to the present but draws also on past and future, pleasure of the mind admits of greater stability and permanence than pleasure of the body ; it is thus the proper object of the philosophical life.

After a short introduction (chapters i-ii) the essay on the pleasant life falls into two main sections, divided by the dramatic interruption at the beginning of chapter xx.

I. The first section has three parts, corresponding

to Plato's threefold division of the soul and Aristotle's three kinds of lives (*Eth. Nic.* i. 5 [1095 b 17-19]).

A. (chapters iii-viii). The life of pleasure, as the Epicureans proclaim it, is dedicated to those pleasures that originate in the body and have meaning only by reference to the body. Such pleasure is of little consequence ; it is more limited, both spatially and temporally, than pain, and it has no existence apart from pain, as the removal of pain is its upper limit (chapter iii). The pleasures of the mind, which on this view consist solely of the memory and expectation of physical pleasures, must be even less substantial than the bodily sensations from which they rise (chapters iv-v) ; nor does such a precarious good free the mind from the fears and anxieties which on the Epicurean view form the chief obstacle to the pleasant life (chapter vi). This narrow concept of the good destroys the more exalted features of human life and reduces men to the level of, or even below, the animals (chapters vii-viii).

B. (chapters ix-xiv). The contemplative life, which the Epicureans reject, affords pleasures that are free from any admixture of pain and are truly congenial to the mind. These include the pleasures of art, literature, history (chapters ix-x), and mathematics (chapter xi), which are far more substantial than the recollection of physical pleasures (chapter xii) ; here belongs also musical theory, which " makes even the lover forget " (chapter xiii). The intellectual pleasures give due recognition to the higher aspects of man's nature and the ascendancy of mind over body (chapter xiv).

C. (chapters xv-xix). Finally, the active life, which confers benefits that lead to public recognition and gratitude, brings far greater pleasures than the trivial activities of the Epicureans in their garden. Even ordinary persons, as well as the very greatest, show by their conduct a preference for glory over self-indulgence (chapters xv-xvii). The memory of glorious actions is also more pleasant than that of physical pleasures (chapter xviii). Nor was Epicurus himself insensitive to the pleasures of fame, and his failure to obtain them by legitimate means must have been a source of pain to him (chapter xix).

II. The discussion now turns to the dismal prospect presented by the Epicurean attitude toward (A) the gods and (B) the afterlife. The argument is not that the Platonic or Stoic views are true ; it is that the Platonic or Stoic view yields greater pleasure than the Epicurean.

A. Aristodemus (chapters xx-xxiii) points out that the Epicureans, in their effort to remove the anxiety caused by superstitious fear of the gods, replace fear by insensibility and so destroy also the pleasure attendant on a belief in divine benevolence (chapter xx). For evil persons religious belief acts as a restraint and so makes their lives more peaceful ; for ordinary persons the pleasure derived from religious belief outweighs the fear ; whereas to Epicurus, who goes through the motions of worship through fear of public censure and has no compensating hopes, religion is a painful constraint (chapter xxi). For truly good men the belief that the gods love and reward virtue is a source of indescribable joy (chapter xxii). But the Epicureans, who look to nothing evil or good from the gods, can offer no recourse in misfortune except complete annihilation (chapter xxiii).

A PLEASANT LIFE IMPOSSIBLE

B. This last point leads to the discussion of the afterlife (chapters xxv-xxx), and Theon replaces Aristodemus as speaker. Recalling that for Epicurus the fear of punishment is the only deterrent of vice, Theon argues that on this premise it would be advantageous for the wicked to fear punishment after death (chapter xxv); in ordinary persons the childish fear of the afterlife is overwhelmed by the pleasure they derive from the thought that existence does not come to an end in death, while they are indeed made anxious by the fear that death may mean extinction (chapter xxvi)—an anxiety which Epicurus intensifies by his teaching (chapter xxvii). Epicurus thus robs life of one of its greatest pleasures, the expectation of a better life to come (chapter xxviii); an expectation which is equally pleasant whether one's life in this world has been happy or wretched, whereas the contrary Epicurean view brings hopelessness to the miserable and despair to the fortunate (chapter xxix). For if death is annihilation it is indeed a fearful prospect (chapter xxx). Such then are the pleasures, of continued existence, of divine benevolence, of learning, of ambition, which Epicurus excludes when he ties the soul to the body and limits good to the escape from evil (chapter xxxi).

The essay illuminates the relation of Epicurus' hedonism to the thought of Plato and Aristotle. Plato in the *Philebus* (53 c 5) had placed pleasure under " becoming " rather than " being," and had argued (53 E—54 D) that as " becoming " is always for some end (*heneka tou*), it cannot be the *hou heneka*, the highest good. Aristotle did not accept this Platonic position, asserting that not all pleasures are " becomings," but some are activities (*energeiai*) and

7

therefore ends (*Eth. Nic.* vii. 12 [1153 a 9-10]).[a] To be
sure, Aristotle does not admit pleasure as the highest
end, but he recognizes that it accompanies that virtuous activity which he identifies with happiness. Epicurus holds that the highest pleasure is not a " becoming " : it is not a " settling down " (*katastasis*;
cf. Philebus, 42 D 6), as Plato had described it, but the
" settled condition " (*katastēma*; *Mor.* 1089 D) that
constitutes the final limit of the removal of all causes
of disturbance. The *Magna Moralia* (ii. 7 [1205 b
20-24]) takes a similar position.

The " settled condition " of the physical organism
presupposes that the " necessary " desires, primarily
those for food and drink, are satisfied ; hence the
prominence of the " pleasures of the belly " in Epicurean thought. But that the " motions " by which
these needs are satisfied should themselves be pleasant is an unnecessary elaboration, for the body does
not require expensive fare ; such pleasures of motion,
however, are acceptable, so long as they do not
exceed the limits of nature.[b]

The " settled condition of the flesh " is a state of
peace and tranquillity [c]; the pleasure it affords is
not a source of disquietude, as Plato had said of
pleasure (*tarattousāi*, *Philebus*, 63 D 6). With Aristotle
(*Eth. Nic.* vii. 14 [1154 b 27-28]), Epicurus held that
pleasure is more to be found in rest than in motion.
Pleasure is not limitless (*Philebus*, 27 E, 28 A), nor is
it characterized by that madness (*Philebus*, 63 D 6),
brutishness, and violence which in Plato's view

---

[a] *Cf. Magna Mor.* ii. 7 (1204 b 6-7, 19-23, 1205 b 34-37).

[b] See V. Brochard, *Études de philosophie ancienne et
philosophie moderne* (Paris, 1912), p. 273.

[c] *Cf.* Brochard (*op. cit.* pp. 258-260), who contrasts the
Cyrenaic view, that pleasures require motion.

(*Philebus*, 67 B) set it at odds with reason and intellect ; it is rather the ultimate end of virtue and wisdom, without which it cannot be realized. For it is by imposing limits on the desires that the mind, with the aid of philosophy, brings about the tranquillity on which the pleasant life depends.[a]

It is of course all-important for Epicurus to establish the role of the mind in the pursuit of pleasure. Plato had already set up in the *Philebus* (36 c) a correlation between false opinions and false pleasures ; and whereas Epicurus would doubtless (with Theophrastus) [b] deny that a pleasure can be " false," he most emphatically affirms that a pleasant life can be secured only if one's opinions about the gods, the physical world, the soul, and good and evil are true, since false opinions are the principal cause of fear and anxiety.

Another important contribution of the mind to the pursuit of pleasure lies in the role of memory and anticipation. Plato had stated (*Philebus*, 32 B-C, 33 C— 36 B, 47 D 1-2) that desire is attended by a memory of past satisfactions and a corresponding hope for the future ; and Plato set up the opposition of memory and desire as one of soul and body. Epicurus sees in this opposition a means of escaping from bondage to the feelings of the moment (*Mor.* 1088 B), such as characterizes the life of brutes and slaves. For the mind has at its command both past and future, and by dwelling on pleasures remembered and anticipated it may achieve a high measure of independence from the hazards of the present.[c]

---

[a] See Brochard, *op. cit.* p. 280.

[b] Frag. 85 (ed. Wimmer), from Damascius, *Lectures on the Philebus*, §§ 167-168 (ed. Westerink, p. 81).

[c] *Cf.* Brochard, *op. cit.* p. 284.

Thus Epicurus, without relinquishing bodily sensation as the basis of all pleasure,[a] established his claim that pleasure is (in the terms with which Aristotle describes happiness) the highest in the hierarchy of ends (*akrotaton*, *Eth. Nic.* i. 4 [1095 a 16]; cf. *Mor.* 1089 D), that it is something to be prized (*timion*, *Eth. Nic.* i. 12 [1102 a 1, 4]; cf. *Mor.* 1088 E), divine (*theion*, *Eth. Nic.* i. 12 [1102 a 4]), lasting (*monimos*, *Eth. Nic.* i. 10 [1100 b 2]), secure (*bebaiotês*, *Eth. Nic.* i. 10 [1100 b 13]; cf. *Mor.* 1097 E), complete (*teleios*, *Eth. Nic.* i. 7 [1097 a 29]; cf. *Mor.* 1088 E), needing nothing further (*autarkes*, *Eth. Nic.* i. 7 [1097 b 8]; cf. the *Letter to Menoeceus*, 130), not easily altered (*mêdamôs eumetabolon*, *Eth. Nic.* i. 10 [1100 b 2-3]), and requiring the cultivation of man's highest faculties (*Eth. Nic.* i. 7 [1098 a 3-18]; cf. the *Letter to Menoeceus*, 132).

Plutarch's answer to Epicurus rests on a combination of the Platonic position that the pleasure attendant on the removal of pain is impure, slavish, and insignificant, with the Aristotelian view that the highest activities of the soul are attended by the highest pleasures. He is especially critical of the role Epicurus assigns to the mind, arguing that memory and anticipation cannot remedy the instability of physical pleasure, that the opinions about things which the Epicureans accept as true are less able to dispel mental anguish than certain of those they reject as false, and that the reference of all activities of the mind back to the body destroys the whole upper level of human life.

---

[a] It should of course be remembered that pleasures of the body are not limited to taste and touch, but include all the senses. Thus, conversations with his friends (that is, philosophical discussions) were among the pleasures that Epicurus remembered on his deathbed.

10

A PLEASANT LIFE IMPOSSIBLE

Twenty-one mss. of the essay are known to us : X *a* nBrAγπσκτβμQKδE g cd. In X the first part of the essay (slightly less than half, through ἦ γὰρ 1096 c at the bottom of folio 307ᵛ) is by the earlier hand (loss of a double leaf of four pages has carried away -νων εἶναι—σοφοκλέους 1091 E—1093 D). The missing end has been supplied on supplementary leaves by Xˢ (which we do not cite) from a derivative of *a*. Q breaks off at 1103 F, after καὶ δεῖ ; g in the middle of a line, after ἔδοξας (1104 A) ; c after φθόνος (1102 D) ; d after κατελθεῖν (1097 c), dˢ supplying the rest from κ. A passage of some five lines (ὁ θάνατος—ἀφαιρεῖται 1106 B) is found in ms. 429 of the national library at Munich, an anthology of the 14th century. It contains no significant variants.

The mss. are related as shown on the following page.[a]

[a] Our present view of the relation of X *a* gc—the better readings of gc being due to corruption and conjecture, and not to tradition—was reached when it was too late to change the order and spacing of the sigla, which should have been *a* X gc. The second hand of β has taken readings from a ms. closely connected with g ; we therefore cite β². Xˢ presents a scholar's text with wilful changes. Xˢ begins at 1096 c ; c ends at 1102 D, g at 1104 A. In these passages agreement of Xˢ with c or g is very slight. At 1098 c ἀμφέθηκέ Xˢᵃᶜ gc have ἀντέθηκέ ; at 1098 c Xˢ gc (and β E¹) have ἦ, the rest ἤ ; at 1103 c Xˢ g (and αγτ²) have διοσκόρους, the rest διοσκούρους ; at 1103 F Xˢ g have τῶν, but g alone has λόγων against λόγον of Xˢ and the rest. Conceivably Xˢ derives from a connexion of g into which readings from a Planudean ms. were imported wholesale. Thus Xˢ has ὅταν at 1100 c for ὁ gc and ὅτι the rest. It would have been easier to misread ι as the compendium for αν if -τι had been superscribed or squeezed in after ὁ.

In the present essay γ is the principal and perhaps the only source of κ ; and the same holds in the *De Latenter Vivendo*, the *De Musica*, and the following essays contained in vol. vii : *De Cupiditate Divitiarum, De Invidia et Odio,*

11

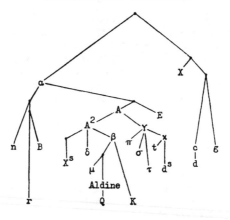

We regularly cite the readings of X α gc.

The following renderings can be mentioned :

ARNOLDUS FERRONUS, *Plutarchi Liber Contra Coloten.**
    Quo id suscipitur probandum, Ne uiuere quidem
    iucundè quenquam qui sectam sequatur Epicuri.
    Lyons, 1555.

WILLIAM BAXTER, " That it is not possible to live
    pleasurably according to the Doctrine of *Epi-
    curus.*" In *Plutarch's Morals*, vol. ii, Fifth
    Edition, London, 1718. We cite a number of
    conjectures from " The *Translator*'s Emendations
    and Remarks " (*ibid.*, pp. 193-216).

De Laude Ipsius, De Fato, and *De Exilio.* In the *De Sera
Numinis Vindicta* κ derives from A but not through γ ; in
the *De Cupiditate Divitiarum* and in the *Consolatio ad Uxorem* there is a connexion between κ and γ, but κ also shows
the influence of another Planudean, perhaps A. Our stemma
of the *De Invidia et Odio* (*Class. Philol.* vol. liii, p. 223)
should be corrected to show κ as a descendant of γ.

A PLEASANT LIFE IMPOSSIBLE

L'ABBÉ LAMBERT, " Examen du système d'Épicure."
In *Nouvelle traduction de divers morceaux des
Œuvres morales de Plutarque*, Paris, 1763.

MARCELLO ADRIANI, " Che non si può viver lietamente
secondo la dottrina di Epicuro." In *Opuscoli di
Plutarco*, vol. vi, Milan, 1829, pp. 123-175.

J. J. HARTMAN, " Het betoog dat de Leer van Epicurus zelfs het levensgenot opheft." In *De
Avondzon des Heidendoms*[2], part 2, Leiden, 1912,
pp. 235-291.

OTTO APELT, " Beweis, dass man nach Epikur über-
haupt nicht vergnügt leben kann." In *Plutarch,
Moralische Schriften*, Erstes Bändchen, Leipzig,
1926, pp. 56-110.

B. SNELL, " Man kann nach Epikurs Grundsätzen
nicht glücklich werden." In *Plutarch, Von der
Ruhe des Gemütes und andere philosophische Schriften*, Zürich, 1948, pp. 52-74.

The dialogue is No. 82 in the Catalogue of Lamprias.

ΟΤΙ ΟΥΔΕ ΖΗΝ ΕΣΤΙΝ
ΗΔΕΩΣ[1] ΚΑΤ' ΕΠΙΚΟΥΡΟΝ

1. Κωλώτης[2] ὁ Ἐπικούρου συνήθης βιβλίον ἐξέδωκεν ἐπιγράψας " ὅτι κατὰ τὰ[3] τῶν ἄλλων φιλο-
D σόφων δόγματα οὐδὲ ζῆν ἐστιν."[4] ὅσα τοίνυν ἡμῖν
ἐπῆλθεν εἰπεῖν πρὸς αὐτὸν ὑπὲρ τῶν φιλοσόφων
ἐγράφη πρότερον. ἐπεὶ δὲ καὶ τῆς σχολῆς διαλυθείσης ἐγένοντο λόγοι[5] πλείονες[6] ἐν τῷ περιπάτῳ
πρὸς τὴν αἵρεσιν, ἔδοξέ μοι καὶ τούτους ἀναλαβεῖν,
εἰ καὶ δι' ἄλλο μηθὲν ἀλλ' ἐνδείξεως ἕνεκα τοῖς
εὐθύνουσιν ἑτέρους[7] ὅτι δεῖ τοὺς λόγους ἕκαστον ὧν
ἐλέγχει καὶ τὰ γράμματα μὴ παρέργως διελθεῖν,
μηδὲ φωνὰς ἀλλαχόθεν ἄλλας ἀποσπῶντα[8] καὶ ῥήμασιν ἄνευ πραγμάτων[9] ἐπιτιθέμενον[10] παρακρούεσθαι[11] τοὺς ἀπείρους.

2. Προελθόντων γὰρ ἡμῶν εἰς τὸ γυμνάσιον
ὥσπερ εἰώθειμεν ἐκ τῆς[12] διατριβῆς, Ζεύξιππος,

---

[1] οὐδὲ ζῆν ἐστιν ἡδέως a and Catalogue of Lamprias : οὐδὲ
ἡδέως ζῆν X ; οὐδὲ ἡδέως (g¹ omits δὲ ἡ-) ζῆν ἐστι g³ c.
[2] κωλώτης X g c (and so throughout) : κολώτης a (and so
throughout).
[3] τὰ X³a g c : X¹ omits.
[4] ἐστιν (-ὶν X¹)a g c : ἐστὶν ἡδέως X³.
[5] λόγοι added here by Meziriacus, after περιπάτῳ by Ald.³.
[6] πλείονες Xa g : πλείους c.
[7] ἑτέρους a : -ως X g c.
[8] ἀποσπῶντα X꜀a g c : -αι Xᵃᶜ.

14

THAT EPICURUS ACTUALLY MAKES A PLEASANT LIFE IMPOSSIBLE

1. Epicurus' disciple Colotes brought out a book entitled " That Conformity to the Doctrines of the Other Philosophers Actually makes Life Impossible." What I was prompted to reply to him in defence of the philosophers has already been put in writing.[a] But since after the session was over a number of further arguments were brought against the sect [b] in the course of the promenade, I determined to record them like the rest, if for no other reason, at least to show persons who undertake to set others right that they must each study with care the arguments and books of the men they impugn, and must not mislead the inexperienced by detaching expressions from different contexts [c] and attacking mere words apart from the things to which they refer.

2. When we had gone on to the gymnasium, as was our custom after the lecture, Zeuxippus said :

[a] 1107 D—1127 E, infra.
[b] The Epicureans.
[c] Cf. 1108 D, infra, and Mor. 548 c.

9 πραγμάτων σ²⁸⁶ (nulla re subiecta Ferronus) : γραμμάτων Xα g c.
10 ἐπιτιθέμενον Xα c : -οι g.
11 παρακρούεσθαι Xylander : ἀποκρούεσθαι Xα g c.
12 τῆς X g c β² : α omits.

(1086)

E " ἐμοὶ μέν," ἔφη, " δοκεῖ πολὺ[1] τῆς προσηκούσης
ὁ λόγος εἰρῆσθαι παρρησίας μαλακώτερον· ἀπίασι
δ᾽[2] ἡμῖν ἐγκαλοῦντες οἱ περὶ Ἡρακλείδην ὡς[3] τοῦ
Ἐπικούρου καὶ τοῦ Μητροδώρου[4] μηδὲν αἰτίων
ὄντων θρασύτερον καθαψαμένοις."[5] καὶ ὁ Θέων,
" εἶτα οὐκ ἔλεγες," εἶπεν, " ὅτι τοῖς ἐκείνων ὁ
Κωλώτης παραβαλλόμενος εὐφημότατος[6] ἀνδρῶν
φαίνεται; τὰ γὰρ ἐν ἀνθρώποις αἴσχιστα ῥήματα—βωμολοχίας, ληκυθισμούς, ἀλαζονείας, ἑται-
ρήσεις, ἀνδροφονίας, βαρυστόνους, πολυφθόρους,
βαρυεγκεφάλους—συναγαγόντες Ἀριστοτέλους καὶ
Σωκράτους καὶ Πυθαγόρου καὶ Πρωταγόρου καὶ
F Θεοφράστου καὶ Ἡρακλείδου καὶ Ἱππαρχίας[7] καὶ
τίνος γὰρ οὐχὶ τῶν ἐπιφανῶν κατεσκέδασαν, ὥστε
εἰ καὶ τἆλλα πάντα σοφῶς εἶχεν αὐτοῖς, διὰ τὰς
βλασφημίας ταύτας καὶ κακηγορίας[8] πορρωτάτω
σοφίας ἂν εἴργεσθαι· ' φθόνος γὰρ ἔξω θείου χοροῦ '
καὶ ζηλοτυπία δι᾽ ἀσθένειαν ἀποκρύψαι μὴ δυνα-

---

[1] πολὺ X^2a g c : πολλοὶ X^1.
[2] ἀπίασι δ᾽ XA^2E g c : ἀπίασιν aA^1.
[3] ὡς added by Stegmann.
[4] After Μητροδώρου Dübner omits ἡμῶν.
[5] καθαψαμένοις X^1 g c $β^2$: -άμενοι X^2a.
[6] εὐφημότατος Xa c(-όττ) : εὐφημότης g.
[7] ἱππαρχίας X g c : ἱππάρχου a.
[8] κακηγορίας Ald.[2] : κατηγορίας Xa g c.

---

[a] Otherwise unknown.
[b] Theon was probably Plutarch's assistant in the school :
cf. 1087 A, *infra*, and Pohlenz' note (p. 123).
[c] Epicurus, Frag. 237 (ed. Usener).
[d] There are eight insults and seven eminent names. Socrates was the charlatan (*cf.* 1117 D, *infra*), Hipparchia
doubtless the prostitute, and Aristotle (possibly with Theophrastus) among the " heroes of many misadventures," as

16

" I, for one, think that the statement of the argument fell far short of the plain speech that was required. Yet Heracleides [a] has gone off charging us with undue vehemence in our attack on the unoffending Epicurus and Metrodorus." Here Theon [b] put in : "And you didn't reply that by their standard [c] Colotes looks like a paragon of measured speech ? For they made a collection of the most disgraceful terms to be found anywhere—' buffoonery,' ' hollow booming,' ' charlatanism,' ' prostitution,' ' assassin,' ' groaner,' ' hero of many a misadventure,' ' nincompoop,' [d]—and showered it [e] on Aristotle, Socrates, Pythagoras, Protagoras, Theophrastus, Heracleides, Hipparchia—indeed what eminent name have they spared ? Thus, even if they had done wisely in everything else, this abusive and defamatory language would have put a great distance between them and wisdom, since ' envy has no place in the choir divine ' [f] nor jealousy so feeble that it is powerless to conceal its mortification."

Epicurus called the dialecticians (Diogenes Laert. x. 8). Heracleides of Aenus, a pupil of Plato, murdered Cotys (1126 c, *infra*). " Hollow booming " was suited to tragic declamation (*cf.* Pearson on Sophocles, Frag. 1063), and thus might have been assigned to Pythagoras. Perhaps Hipparchia the Cynic was the buffoon. Epicurus used *barystonoi* (" deep groaners," a derisive term applied to tragic actors) in Frag. 114 (ed. Usener) of persons who would take him for a pupil of Nausiphanes. Of the persons in the list who were then alive or could have been (the fragment comes from a letter to his friends in Mytilenê, and would be dated 310 or later) Hipparchia was not a lecturer and Heracleides was inactive ; thus Theophrastus is the only person to whom the term could refer. This leaves " nincompoop " for Protagoras.

[e] Plutarch has in mind an *heôlokrasia*, a collection of leavings which at rowdy banquets was dumped on guests who had fallen asleep.

[f] Plato, *Phaedrus*, 247 A.

(1086) μένη[1] τὸ ἀλγοῦν.'' ὑπολαβὼν οὖν ὁ 'Αριστόδημος,[2]
'' 'Ηρακλείδης οὖν,'' ἔφη, '' γραμματικὸς ὢν ἀντὶ
1087 τῆς ' ποιητικῆς τύρβης ' ὡς ἐκεῖνοι[3] λέγουσιν καὶ
τῶν ' 'Ομήρου μωρολογημάτων ' ἀποτίνει[4] ταύτας
'Επικούρῳ χάριτας ἢ ὅ τι[5] Μητρόδωρος ἐν γράμμασι τοσούτοις τῷ[6] ποιητῇ λελοιδόρηκεν. ἀλλ'
ἐκείνους μὲν ἐῶμεν, ὦ Ζεύξιππε· τὸ δὲ ἐν ἀρχῇ τῶν
λόγων ῥηθὲν πρὸς τοὺς ἄνδρας, ὡς οὐκ ἔστιν εὖ[7]
ζῆν κατ' αὐτούς, τί οὐ[8] μᾶλλον, ἐπεὶ κέκμηκεν[9]
οὗτος,[10] αὐτοὶ δι' αὐτῶν[11] περαίνομεν[12] ἅμα καὶ
Θέωνα παραλαβόντες;'' καὶ ὁ Θέων πρὸς αὐτόν,
'' ἀλλ' ' οὗτος μέν,' '' ἔφη, '' ὁ ' ἆθλος ' ἑτέροις ' ἐκ-
τετέλεσται ' πρὸ[13] ἡμῶν·

νῦν αὖτε[14] σκυπὸν ἄλλον

εἰ δοκεῖ θέμενοι τοιαύτῃ τινὶ δίκῃ μετίωμεν ὑπὲρ
B τῶν φιλοσόφων τοὺς ἄνδρας· ἀποδεῖξαι γάρ, ἄπερ
ἢ δυνατόν, ἐπιχειρήσωμεν[15] ὅτι μηδὲ ζῆν ἡδέως
ἐστὶν κατ' αὐτούς.'' '' παπαῖ,''[16] εἶπον[17] ἔγωγε γελάσας,[18] '' εἰς τὴν γαστέρα τοῖς ἀνδράσιν ἔοικας[19]

---

[1] ζηλοτυπία . . . δυναμένη X[2](-ης X[1])A[2]E g c : ζηλοτυπίας
. . . δυναμένης aA[1].
[2] ἀριστόδημος g c : ἀριστοτέλης Xa.
[3] ἐκεῖνοι (-εί- X[2])a g c : ἐκείνοις X[1].
[4] ἀποτίνει Xa[r] c : -τείνει a[ar] g.
[5] ὅ τι nos : ὅτι Xa g c.   [6] τῷ added by Emperius.
[7] εὖ added by Wilamowitz.   [8] οὐ a : συ X ; σοι g c.
[9] ἐπεὶ κέκμηκεν a : ἐπικέκμηκεν X g c.
[10] οὗτος Xa g : αὐτοὺς c.
[11] αὐτῶν a (αυ- X) : ἑαυτῶν g c.
[12] περαίνομεν Xa g : -ωμεν c.
[13] πρὸ (προ X)a[r] g c : πρὸς a[ar].
[14] αὖτε (-τω X[1]?)a g c : αὖ τὸν X[3].
[15] ἐπιχειρήσωμεν X[1]a g : -ομεν X[2]? c.
[16] παπαῖ Usener (παπαι X g c) : παῦσαι a.

18

A PLEASANT LIFE IMPOSSIBLE, 1086–1087

Aristodemus interposed : " Heracleides then, a student of literature, is repaying his debt to Epicurus [a] for such favours of theirs as ' rabble of poets ' and ' Homer's idiocies ' and the variety of abuse that Metrodorus [b] has in so many writings heaped upon the poet. But enough, Zeuxippus, of Heracleides and his set. Why do we not instead take the point made against these gentlemen [c] at the outset of the discussion,[d] that they make a good life impossible, and since our friend here [e] is spent, develop it by ourselves, enlisting Theon to help us ? " To this Theon said : " But ' This task has been accomplished ' by others before us [f] ; ' now another mark ' [g] let us set up, if you agree, and avenge the philosophers by visiting on these gentlemen the punishment I proceed to describe : let us set out to prove, if proved it can be, that they actually make a pleasurable life impossible." " Oho ! " I said laughing. " It looks as if you are going to hop on their ' belly ' [h] and make

[a] Epicurus, Frag. 228 (ed. Usener).
[b] Metrodorus, Frag. 24 (ed. Körte).
[c] The Epicureans.
[d] *Reply to Colotes*, 1108 c, *infra*.
[e] Plutarch, who had just delivered the *Reply to Colotes*.
[f] The " others " are no doubt Plutarch, and the reference may be to the lost work *On Lives in Reply to Epicurus*.
[g] Homer, *Od.* xxii. 5-6. After stringing the bow and sending the arrow through the axes, Odysseus says to the suitors

> " This task has been accomplished harmlessly ;
> Now at another mark, not hit before,
> I try my hand "

and proceeds to shoot them.
[h] A proverb : *cf. Life of Lucullus*, chap. xi. 2 (498 c).

---

[17] εἶπον a g c : -εν X.
[18] γελάσας X¹a g c : ἐγγελάσας X²ʳᵐ (now erased ?).
[19] ἔοικας Xa g : -εν c.

19

(1087) ἐναλεῖσθαι[1] καὶ τὸν[2] περὶ[3] τῶν κρεῶν ἐπάξειν,
ἀφαιρούμενος ἡδονὴν ἀνθρώπων βοώντων

οὐ γὰρ πυγμάχοι[4] εἰμὲν[5] ἀμύμονες

οὐδὲ ῥήτορες οὐδὲ προστάται δήμων οὐδὲ ἄρχοντες,

ἀεὶ δ᾽ ἡμῖν δαίς τε φίλη

καὶ πᾶσα διὰ σαρκὸς ἐπιτερπὴς κίνησις ἐφ᾽ ἡδονήν
τινα καὶ χαρὰν ψυχῆς ἀναπεμπομένη.[6] δοκεῖς οὖν
μοι μὴ τὸ ἔαρ[7] ἐξαιρεῖν,[8] ὥς φασιν, ἀλλὰ τὸ ζῆν
ἀφαιρεῖσθαι τοὺς ἄνδρας εἰ τὸ ζῆν ἡδέως μὴ ἀπο-
C λείψεις[9] αὐτοῖς." "τί οὖν," εἶπεν ὁ Θέων, " εἰ
δοκιμάζεις τὸν λόγον, αὐτὸς οὐ χρῇ[10] παρόν; "[11]
" χρήσομαι," εἶπον,[12] " ἀκροώμενος καὶ ἀποκρινόμενος,[13] ἂν δέησθε· τὴν δὲ ἡγεμονίαν ὑμῖν[14] παρα-
δίδωμι." μικρὰ δὴ προφασισαμένου τοῦ Θέωνος
᾽Αριστόδημος, " ὡς σύντομον," ἔφη, " καὶ λείαν
ἔχων ὁδὸν ἀπετάφρευσας ἡμῖν πρὸς τὸν λόγον, οὐκ
ἐάσας περὶ[15] τοῦ καλοῦ πρότερον εὐθύνας ὑποσχεῖν
τὴν αἵρεσιν. ἀνθρώπους γὰρ ἡδονὴν ὑποτιθεμένους
τέλος οὐκ ἔστιν ἐξελάσαι[16] τοῦ ἡδέως ζῆν ῥάδιον·

---

[1] ἐναλεῖσθαι Xa c : ἐνδιαλεῖσθαι g.
[2] τὸν a^c : τῶν Xa^ac ; τὴν g c. [3] περὶ Xa c : παρὰ g.
[4] πυγμάχοι X g c : πύγμαχοι a.
[5] εἰμὲν X^1 ?(or εἴμεν) g c : εἶμεν X^2a^2 ; ἦμεν a^1.
[6] ἀναπεμπομένη A^3 and Reiske : -ης Xa g c.
[7] ἔαρ X g c : ἡδὺ a.
[8] ἐξαιρεῖν Bern. : ἐξαίρειν Xa g c.
[9] ἀπολείψεις X^2A^2 : -ης X^1a g c.
[10] οὐ χρῇ σ^2 and Amyot : οὐ χρὴ Xa g c ; οὐχὶ A^2 ; οὐ
χρεία β^2.
[11] παρόν Pohlenz : παρόντι Xa ; παρ᾽ ὧν τι g c.
[12] εἶπον g c : εἶπεν Xa.

them run for their ' flesh ' [a] when you take pleasure away from people who shout

> No manly boxers we

or orators or champions of the commonwealth or magistrates ;

> We ever hold the table dear instead [b]

and ' every agreeable stirring of the flesh that is transmitted upward to give some pleasure and delight to the mind.' [c] So I think you are not ' removing the springtime from their year,' [d] as the saying goes, but depriving these men of life, if you are not going to leave them the possibility of living pleasurably." " Then why," said Theon, " if you approve the subject, do you not follow it up yourself, now that the opportunity offers ? " " I will follow it up," I answered, " by being a listener, and, if you desire it, by answering questions ; but I leave the conduct of the discussion to you and the rest." After Theon had made a few excuses, Aristodemus exclaimed : " What a short and easy approach to the topic you had ! Yet you barred us from it when you forbade [e] us to examine first their view of the good life. For it is not easy to dislodge from a pleasant life men who hold the position that pleasure is the highest good ;

---

[a] A proverb : *cf. Mor.* 555 c, note.
[b] Homer, *Od.* viii. 246, 248.
[c] Epicurus, Frag. 433, 552 (ed. Usener).
[d] Proverbial : *cf.* Herodotus, vii. 162. 1 and Aristotle, *Rhetoric*, i. 7 (1365 a 33).   [e] 1087 A, *supra.*

---

[13] ἀποκρινόμενος g c : -άμενος Xa.
[14] ὑμῖν Xa c : ἡμῖν g.   [15] περὶ Xa : ὑπὲρ g c.
[16] ἐξελάσαι Ald.[2] : ἐξετάσαι X[1]a g c ; ἐξετάσαντας X[2] ? (erased ?).

(1087) τοῦ δὲ καλῶς ἐκπεσόντες[1] ἅμ᾽ ἂν[2] καὶ τοῦ ἡδέως
συνεξέπιπτον, ἐπεὶ[3] τὸ ἡδέως ζῆν ἄνευ τοῦ καλῶς
ἀνύπαρκτόν ἐστιν, ὡς αὐτοὶ λέγουσιν."

3. Καὶ ὁ Θέων, " ἀλλὰ τοῦτο μέν," εἶπεν, " ἂν
D δόξῃ, τοῦ λόγου προϊόντος ἀναθησόμεθα· νῦν[4] δὲ
χρησώμεθα[5] τοῖς διδομένοις ὑπ᾽ αὐτῶν. οἴονται δὲ
περὶ γαστέρα τἀγαθὸν εἶναι καὶ τοὺς ἄλλους πόρους
τῆς σαρκὸς ἅπαντας δι᾽ ὧν ἡδονὴ καὶ μὴ ἀλγηδὼν
ἐπεισέρχεται· καὶ πάντα τὰ[6] καλὰ καὶ σοφὰ ἐξευρήματα τῆς περὶ γαστέρα ἡδονῆς ἕνεκα[7] γεγονέναι καὶ
τῆς ὑπὲρ ταύτης ἐλπίδος ἀγαθῆς, ὡς ὁ σοφὸς εἴρηκε
Μητρόδωρος. αὐτόθεν μὲν οὖν, ὦ ἑταῖρε, φαίνονται
γλίσχρον τι καὶ σαθρὸν[8] καὶ οὐ βέβαιον αἴτιον τοῦ
ἀγαθοῦ λαμβάνοντες, ἀλλὰ τοῖς πόροις τούτοις δι᾽
ὧν ἡδονὰς ἐπεισάγονται καὶ πρὸς ἀλγηδόνας ὁμοίως
E κατατετρημένον,[9] μᾶλλον δὲ ἡδονὴν μὲν ὀλίγοις ἀλγηδόνα δὲ πᾶσι τοῖς μορίοις δεχόμενον. πόση[10] γὰρ
ἡδονὴ περὶ ἄρθρα καὶ νεῦρα καὶ πόδας καὶ χεῖρας,
οἷς ἐνοικίζεται πάθη δεινὰ[11] καὶ σχέτλια, ποδαγρικὰ
καὶ ῥευματικὰ[12] καὶ φαγεδαινικὰ καὶ διαβρώσεις καὶ
ἀποσήψεις; ὀσμῶν δὲ καὶ χυμῶν τὰ ἥδιστα προσ-

---

[1] ἐκπεσόντες a g c : -ος X.
[2] ἅμ᾽ ἂν Bern. : ἅμα Xa g c.
[3] ἐπεὶ Xa c : ἐπεὶ δὲ g.
[4] νῦν Xa g : αὐτῷ c.
[5] χρησώμεθα X g[c] c : -όμεθα a g[ac].
[6] τὰ added by Bern.
[7] ἕνεκα a : ἔνοικα X g c.
[8] σαθρὸν Döhner : σαπρὸν Xa g c.
[9] κατατετρημένον g c : κατατετριμμένον Xa.
[10] πόση nos (ποία Kronenberg ; πῶς Schellens) : πᾶσα Xa g c.
[11] πάθη δεινὰ Meziriacus : τὰ πάθη δεινὰ Xa ; τὰ δεινὰ πάθη g c.
[12] ποδαγρικὰ καὶ ῥευματικὰ g c : ποδαγρικαὶ καὶ ῥεύματι X ; ποδαγρικὰ ῥεύματα a.

whereas once we had driven them out of the possession of a good life, they would at the same time be
driven from that of a pleasant one, since, as they say
themselves,[a] a pleasant life has no existence apart
from a good one."

3. To this Theon said : " Well, if we so decide, we
shall reverse that decision as the discussion proceeds ;
for the present, let us make the most of what they
offer us. They believe that the good is found in the
belly [b] and all other passages of the flesh through
which pleasure and non-pain [c] make their entrance,
and that all the notable and brilliant inventions of
civilization were devised for this belly-centred pleasure
and for the good [d] expectation of this pleasure, as the
sage Metrodorus [e] has said. So it is at once evident,
my friend, that they take as their foundation of good
a thing narrow, flimsy, and unstable,[f] one that by
these passages through which they let pleasures in
is equally open to pains as well ; or rather, one that
receives pleasure in few of its parts, but pain in all.
For what degree of pleasure is found in the joints,
the tendons, the feet and the hands, where lodge
grievous and cruel afflictions, the gout and rheuma-
tisms and ulcers that eat through the flesh and cause
it to putrefy and drop off ? Present to the body the

[a] Epicurus, *Letter to Menoeceus*, 132 ; *Cardinal Tenet* v ;
Cicero, *De Finibus*, i. 18 (57).

[b] Epicurus, Frag. 409 (ed. Usener) ; *cf.* 1125 A, *infra*.

[c] *Cf.* Diogenes Laert. x. 137.

[d] That is, secure or confident : *cf.* πιστὸν ἔλπισμα (1089 D,
infra) and πίστις βέβαιος (*Letter to Pythocles*, 85).

[e] Frag. 7 (ed. Körte) ; *cf.* 1125 B, *infra*.

[f] The Epicureans contended that their highest good was
stable and secure : *cf.* 1089 D, *infra*.

(1087) ἀγαγὼν τῷ σώματι[1] μικρὸν εὑρήσεις χωρίον ἐν
αὑτῷ παντάπασι τὸ κινούμενον λείως καὶ προσηνῶς,
τὰ δ' ἄλλα πολλάκις δυσχεραίνει καὶ ἀγανακτεῖ.
πυρὶ δὲ καὶ σιδήρῳ καὶ δήγματι[2] καὶ ὑστριχίσιν
οὐδὲν[3] ἀπαθὲς οὐδὲ ἀναίσθητον ἀλγηδόνος, ἀλλὰ
καὶ καῦμα καὶ ῥῖγος εἰς ἅπαντα καταδύεται καὶ
F πυρετός, αἱ δὲ ἡδοναὶ καθάπερ αὖραι πρὸς ἑτέραις[4]
ἕτεραι[5] τοῦ σώματος ἄκραις ἐπιγελῶσαι[6] διαχέον-
ται. καὶ χρόνος[7] ὁ μὲν τούτων οὐ πολὺς ἀλλ'
ὥσπερ οἱ διάττοντες ἔξαψιν ἅμα καὶ σβέσιν ἐν τῇ
σαρκὶ λαμβάνουσιν, ἐκεῖ[8] δὲ τοῦ πόνου μάρτυς[9] ὁ[10]
Αἰσχύλου Φιλοκτήτης ἱκανός·

οὐ γὰρ δακὼν[11] (φησὶν) ἀνῆκεν, ἀλλ' ἐνώκισε[12]
δεινὴν στομωτὸν[13] ἔμφυσιν,[14] ποδὸς λαβήν.[15]

1088 οὐκ ὀλισθηρὰ γὰρ[16] ἀλγηδὼν οὐδὲ ἕτερα τοιαῦτα
κνῶσα[17] καὶ γαργαλίζουσα τοῦ σώματος· ἀλλ' ὥσπερ
τὸ τῆς μηδικῆς σπέρμα πολυκαμπὲς καὶ σκαληνὸν[18]
ἐμφύεται τῇ γῇ καὶ διαμένει πολὺν χρόνον ὑπὸ
τραχύτητος, οὕτως ὁ πόνος ἄγκιστρα καὶ ῥίζας δια-
σπείρων καὶ συμπλεκόμενος[19] τῇ σαρκὶ καὶ παραμέ-

---

[1] τῷ σώματι Xa g : τὰ σώματα c.
[2] δήγματι Xa c : δόγματι g.
[3] οὐδὲν] οὐ μόνον οὐδὲν Post.
[4] ἑτέραις a g c : ἑτέρους X.
[5] ἕτεραι X²a g c : ἕταιρε X^{ac} ; ἕταιρας X^c.
[6] ἐπιγελῶσαι a : -ώσαις X g c.
[7] χρόνος X g c : ὁ χρόνος a.
[8] ἐκεῖ nos (ἐκείνων Pohlenz ; εἰς Bern.) : ἐκ Xa[t] g c : ὁ a^{3m}.
[9] μάρτυς a g c : μάντις X.   [10] ὁ a : X g c omit.
[11] δακών Hirschig : ὁ δράκων Xa g c.
[12] ἐνώκισε a : ἐνώκησε X g c.
[13] στομωτόν G. Hermann : στομάτων Xa g c.
[14] ἔμφυσιν X g c : ἔκφυσιν a.
[15] λαβήν Amyot : λαβεῖν Xa g c(-έν).

24

most delightful odours and savours and you will find that the area which experiences a ' smooth and gentle motion '[a] is extremely small, whereas the effect on the rest is often disagreeable and irritating ; but no area is immune to fire, a stab, a sting, or the lash of a whip, or insensible to pain : indeed heat too and cold penetrate everywhere, as does fever, while the pleasures, like breezes, as they refresh the heights of the body, now one and now another, are dissipated. And the duration of these is not long, but like shooting stars they are no sooner kindled in the flesh than they expire ; whereas the pain that is found in those other regions is sufficiently attested by the Philoctetes of Aeschylus [b] :

> Once it had struck, the snake
> Did not release its hold, but lodged in me
> Its fangs of tempered steel, that grip my foot.

For there is nothing smooth and gliding in pain, nor does its scratching and tickling propagate an answering smoothness in the body. No, just as the seed of lucerne, which is jagged and irregular, is so rough that it lodges in the soil and remains there a long time, so pain broadcasts its hooks and roots and entangles itself in the flesh, lasting not only for the

---

[a] Epicurus, Frag. 411 (ed. Usener).
[b] From the *Philoctetes* of Aeschylus, Nauck, *Trag. Graec. Frag.*, Aesch. 252 ; H. J. Mette, *Die Frag. d. Aisch.* (Berlin, 1959), no. 396. The example of Philoctetes is also cited against the Epicureans by Cicero, *De Fin.* ii. 29 (94) and *Tusc. Disput.* ii. 7 (19).

---

[16] οὐκ ὀλισθηρὰ γὰρ nos (οὐ γὰρ ὀλισθηρὸν ἡ Emperius) : ὀλίσθη X ; ὀλισθείη a ; ὀλισθη and a blank of 5 letters g c.
[17] κνῶσα nos : κινοῦσα Xa g c.
[18] σκαληνὸν Xa : σκληρὸν g c.
[19] συμπλεκόμενος a g c : συνεμπλεκόμενος X.

25

(1088) νων οὐχ ἡμέρας οὐδὲ νύκτας[1] μόνον ἀλλὰ καὶ ὥρας
ἐτῶν ἐνίοις[2] καὶ περιόδους ὀλυμπιακὰς[3] μόλις ὑπ'
ἄλλων πόνων ὥσπερ ἥλων σφοδροτέρων ἐκκρουό-
μενος ἀπαλλάττεται. τίς γὰρ ἔπιε[4] χρόνον τοσοῦτον ἢ ἔφαγεν ὅσον[5] διψῶσιν οἱ πυρέττοντες καὶ
B πεινῶσιν οἱ πολιορκούμενοι; ποῦ δέ ἐστιν ἄνεσις
καὶ συνουσία[6] μετὰ φίλων ἐφ' ὅσον κολάζουσι καὶ
στρεβλοῦσι τύραννοι; καὶ γὰρ τοῦτο[7] τῆς τοῦ σώματος φαυλότητος καὶ ἀφυΐας πρὸς τὸ ἡδέως ζῆν
ἐστιν, ὅτι τοὺς πόνους ὑπομένει μᾶλλον ἢ τὰς
ἡδονὰς καὶ πρὸς[8] ἐκείνους ἔχει ῥώμην καὶ δύναμιν,[9]
ἐν δὲ ταύταις ἀσθενές ἐστι[10] καὶ ἀψίκορον. τὸ δὲ
ἡδέως ζῆν[11] εἰς τὴν ἀπονίαν ἀνάπτοντες[12] πλείονα
περὶ τούτου λέγειν οὐκ ἐῶσιν ἡμᾶς, ὁμολογοῦντες
αὐτοὶ[13] μικρὸν εἶναι τὸ τῆς σαρκὸς ἡδύ, μᾶλλον δὲ
ἀκαρές, εἴ γε δὴ μὴ κενολογοῦσι[14] μηδὲ ἀλαζονεύον-
ται,[15] Μητρόδωρος μὲν λέγων ὅτι ' πολλάκις προσ-
επτύσαμεν ταῖς τοῦ σώματος ἡδοναῖς,' Ἐπίκουρος

[1] νύκτας Amyot : νυκτὸς Xa g c.
[2] ἐνίοις X g c : ἐνίους a.
[3] ὀλυμπιακὰς X²(from ὅ-) g c : -ῶν a.
[4] ἔπιε X²(apparently with a superscribed β, perhaps to indicate transposition with ἔφαγεν, which however has no superscribed a)a g c : ἔπιαιν X¹ ?
[5] ὅσον Xa c : ὅσων g.
[6] συνουσία X¹(-αι X^{ar})a : κοινωνία (κιν- g) c.
[7] τοῦτο] τοῦτο τεκμήριον Post.
[8] καὶ πρὸς Xa g : c omits in a blank of 12 letters.
[9] καὶ δύναμιν Xa g : c omits.
[10] ἐστι X²(ε superscribed ; ἔστι Baxter) : τι X¹a g c.
[11] καὶ ἀψίκορον—ζῆν Xa g : c omits in a blank of 28 letters.
[12] εἰς τὴν ἀπονίαν ἀνάπτοντες Diano: ἀνάπτωνται X ; ἂν ἅπτων-
ται a g c.
[13] αὐτοὶ Xa g : c omits in a blank of 12 letters.

space of days and nights,[a] but in some persons for
whole seasons and olympiads, and is barely got rid
of when new pains thrust it out, like nails more
strongly driven.[b] For who has ever spent the time
drinking or eating that victims of fever spend in
thirst [c] or the people of a beleaguered city spend in
hunger? Where can we find a gathering of friends who
meet for the pleasure of each other's company that
is prolonged to the length of time to which tyrants
protract their punishment and torture ? Indeed here
is another aspect of the body's incapacity and in-
aptitude for a pleasant life, that it can better sustain
pain than pleasure and shows strength and endurance
in confronting the one, but in the midst of pleasures
is a weakling and soon has had enough. But by
attaching the pleasurable life to painlessness they
preclude us from dwelling longer on the point, since
they admit themselves that the pleasure of the flesh
is a slight or rather an infinitesimal thing—that is, if
this is not mere empty and pretentious talk—[d] Metrodorus [e] when he says ' I have often spat on the
pleasures of the body ' and Epicurus [f] who asserts

---

[a] Epicurus (*Cardinal Tenet* iv) had said that extreme pain
is the briefest, and pain only great enough to outweigh
pleasure lasts only a few days. To this Cicero (*De Fin.* ii.
29 [94]) makes much the same reply as Plutarch.
[b] *Cf.* the proverb, " one nail drives out another," Leutsch
and Schneidewin, *Paroem. gr.* i, pp. 253, 363, ii, p. 116.
[c] *Cf.* Plato, *Philebus*, 45 B 6.
[d] *Cf.* 1090 A and 1114 A, *infra*. The charge was often
made by the Epicureans themselves : *cf. Cardinal Tenet*
xxxvii ; Frags. 69 and 511 (ed. Usener) ; and 1124 c, *infra*.
[e] Frag. 62 (ed. Körte). [f] Frag. 600 (ed. Usener).

---

[14] κενολογοῦσι Χ a² g c : καινολογοῦσι a¹.
[15] μηδὲ ἀλαζο(-ω- Χ¹)νεύονται (-ωνται Χ¹ g) Χ²⁸⁸a g : c omits
in a blank of 16 letters.

C δὲ καὶ γελᾶν φησι ταῖς ὑπερβολαῖς τοῦ περὶ τὸ
σῶμα νοσήματος πολλάκις κάμνοντα[1] τὸν σοφόν.
οἷς οὖν οἱ πόνοι[2] τοῦ σώματος οὕτως[3] εἰσὶν ἐλαφροὶ
καὶ ῥᾴδιοι πῶς ἔνεστί τι[4] ταῖς ἡδοναῖς ἀξιόλογον ;
καὶ[5] γὰρ εἰ μὴ χρόνῳ μηδὲ[6] μεγέθει τῶν πόνων
ἀποδέουσιν, ἀλλὰ περὶ πόνους ἔχουσιν, καὶ πέρας
αὐταῖς κοινὸν Ἐπίκουρος τὴν παντὸς[7] τοῦ ἀλγοῦν-
τος ὑπεξαίρεσιν ἐπιτέθεικεν, ὡς[8] τῆς φύσεως ἄχρι
τοῦ λῦσαι τὸ ἀλγεινὸν αὐξούσης[9] τὸ ἡδύ, περαιτέρω
δὲ προελθεῖν οὐκ ἐώσης[10] κατὰ[11] μέγεθος, ἀλλὰ
ποικιλμούς τινας οὐκ ἀναγκαίους ὅταν ἐν[12] τῷ μὴ
πονεῖν γένηται[13] δεχομένης· ἡ δὲ ἐπὶ τοῦτο μετ᾽
ὀρέξεως πορεία, μέτρον ἡδονῆς[14] οὖσα, κομιδῇ βρα-
D χεῖα καὶ σύντομος.[15] ὅθεν αἰσθόμενοι[16] τῆς ἐνταῦθα
γλισχρότητος ὥσπερ ἐκ χωρίου λυπροῦ[17] τοῦ σώματος μεταφέρουσι[18] τὸ τέλος[19] εἰς τὴν ψυχήν, ὡς[20]
ἐκεῖ νομὰς[21] καὶ λειμῶνας[22] ἀμφιλαφεῖς[23] ἡδονῶν
ἔξοντες,[24]

ἐν δὲ Ἰθάκῃ οὔτ᾽ ἂρ δρόμοι εὐρέες οὔτε

---

[1] κάμνοντα Xa g : κά and a blank of 8 letters c.
[2] οἷς οὖν (ἂν for οὖν g) οἱ πόνοι Xa g : a blank of 12 letters
and πόνων c.   [3] οὕτως Xa g : ἵνα c.
[4] ἔνεστί τι g c : ἔνεστι X ; ἂν ἔστί τι a.   [5] καὶ Xa g : ὁ c.
[6] χρόνῳ μηδὲ (καὶ for μηδὲ g) Xa g : c omits in a blank of
13 letters.
[7] καὶ πέρας—παντὸς Xa g(αὐτοῖς for αὐταῖς) : c omits in a
blank of 58 letters.
[8] ὡς Xa g : c omits.   [9] αὐξούσης Xa g : ἀξιούσης c.
[10] προελθεῖν οὐκ ἐώσης Xa : μὴ ἐώσης προελθεῖν g c.
[11] κατὰ a (κὰ τὰ X[c] from καὶ τὰ): κατὰ τὸ g c.
[12] ἐν γ[ac] and Amyot : οὐκ ἐν Xa g c.
[13] γένηται Xa c : g omits.
[14] ἡδονῆς Xa g : ἥδο and a blank of 5 letters c.
[15] σύντομος a g c : σύντονος X.
[16] αἰσθόμενοι Xa : αἰσθόμενος g c.

28

that in illness the sage often actually laughs at the
paroxysms of the disease.[a] Then how can men for
whom the pains of the body are so slight and easy
to bear find anything appreciable in its pleasures ?
Indeed, even supposing that the pleasures do not fall
short of the pains either in duration or in magnitude,
they are nevertheless bound up with pains, and Epicurus [b] has imposed on them a limit that applies to
all of them alike : the removal of all pain. For he
believes that our nature adds to pleasure only up to
the point where pain is abolished and does not allow
it any further increase in magnitude (although the
pleasure, when the state of painlessness is reached,
admits of certain unessential variations [c]). But to
proceed to this point, accompanied by desire, is our
stint of pleasure, and the journey is indeed short and
quick. Hence it is that becoming aware of the poverty
here they transfer their final good from the body, as
from an unproductive piece of land, to the soul, persuaded that there they will find pastures and meadows
lush with pleasures ;

> Whereas in Ithaca no coursing grounds
> Are there, nor yet [d]

[a] See 1090 A, *infra*.
[b] Frag. 417 (ed. Usener) ; *cf. Cardinal Tenet* iii and 1091
A, *infra*.
[c] *Cf.* Epicurus, *Cardinal Tenet* xviii.
[d] Homer, *Od.* iv. 605.

---

[17] ἐκ χωρίου λυπροῦ Xa g : c omits in a blank of 20 letters.
[18] μεταφέρουσι Xa g : μεταφέρουσα c.
[19] τὸ τέλος X g c : τοῦ τέλους a.   [20] ὡς Xa : g c omit.
[21] ἐκεῖ νομὰς Xylander : ἐκεῖνο ἡμᾶς Xa g c.
[22] λειμῶνας Xa g : λειμῶνες c.
[23] ἀμφιλαφεῖς Xa : a blank of 5 letters and φεῖς g ; a blank
of 21 letters and ἐφ' c.
[24] ἔξοντες Reiske : ἔξοντας X g c : ἀέξοντας a.

(1088) ' λείη '¹ περὶ τὸ σαρκίδιον ἡ ἀπόλαυσις ἀλλὰ τρα-
χεῖα, μεμιγμένη πρὸς πολὺ² τὸ ἀλλότριον καὶ
σφυγματῶδες.''

4. Ὑπολαβὼν οὖν ὁ Ζεύξιππος, '' εἶτα οὐ καλῶς,'' ἔφη,³ '' δοκοῦσί σοι ποιεῖν οἱ ἄνδρες, ἀρχό-
μενοι μὲν ἀπὸ τοῦ σώματος, ἐν ᾧ πρῶτον ἐφάνη
γένεσις, ἐπὶ δὲ⁴ τὴν ψυχὴν ὡς βεβαιοτέραν καὶ τὸ
E πᾶν ἐν αὐτῇ τελειοῦσαν ἰόντες ; ''⁵ '' καλῶς νὴ
Δία,'' ἔφη Θέων,⁶ '' καὶ κατὰ φύσιν, εἴ τι⁷ κρεῖττον
ἐνταῦθα⁸ μετιόντες καὶ τελειότερον⁹ ἀληθῶς ἀνευρί-
σκουσιν¹⁰ ὥσπερ οἱ θεωρητικοὶ καὶ πολιτικοὶ τῶν
ἀνδρῶν. εἰ δὲ ἀκούεις αὐτῶν μαρτυρομένων¹¹ καὶ
βοώντων ὡς ἐπ' οὐδενὶ ψυχὴ τῶν ὄντων πέφυκε
χαίρειν καὶ γαληνίζειν πλὴν ἐπὶ σώματος ἡδοναῖς
παρούσαις ἢ προσδοκωμέναις, καὶ τοῦτο αὐτῆς τὸ
ἀγαθόν ἐστιν, ἆρα οὐ δοκοῦσί σοι διεράματι¹² τοῦ
σώματος χρῆσθαι τῇ ψυχῇ, καὶ¹³ καθάπερ οἶνον ἐκ
πονηροῦ¹⁴ καὶ μὴ στέγοντος ἀγγείου τὴν ἡδονὴν δια-
χέοντες ἐνταῦθα καὶ παλαιοῦντες οἴεσθαι¹⁵ σεμνό-
τερόν τι ποιεῖν καὶ τιμιώτερον ; καίτοι γε οἶνον

¹ ἐν δὲ ἰθάκῃ οὐ γὰρ (οὔτ' ἄρ Victorius) δρόμοι εὐρέες οὔτε
λείη Χα : ἐν δ (a blank of 2 letters) άκη (a blank of 4 letters)
δρόμοι εὐρέες οὔτε λείη g ; a blank of 39 letters and ἡ c.
² πρὸς πολὺ Χα : τι (a blank of 2 letters) πολὺ g ; κατα-
πολὺ c.
³ καλῶς ἔφη Χα g : κ and a blank of 8 letters c.
⁴ ἐπὶ δὲ a : ἐπὶ Χ g c (εἶτ' ἰόντες ἐπὶ Bern.; ἡδονῆς, εἶτα
μεταφέροντες τὴν ἕδραν αὐτῆς ἐπὶ Pohlenz).
⁵ αὐτῇ τελειοῦσαν ἰόντες nos : ταύτῃ (αὐτῇ a) τελειοῦντες Χα
g c.
⁶ ἔφη Θέων Patzig : ἔφην ἐγὼ Χα g c.
⁷ εἴ τι Xylander : ἔτι Χα g c.
⁸ ἐνταῦθα Χα g : ἐντεῦθεν c.
⁹ τελειότερον Χα : τελειότητα g ; τελειότατον c(-ότ⁷).
¹⁰ ἀνευρίσκουσιν Χα c : εὑρίσκουσιν g.

30

A PLEASANT LIFE IMPOSSIBLE, 1088

anything ' smooth '^a in the path of fruition in our
little piece of flesh: it is ' rugged,'^b with a goodly admixture of aches and pains."

4. Here Zeuxippus interposed : " Why, do you not
hold that the gentlemen ^c do well to begin with the
body, where pleasure first appears, and then pass to
the soul as having more stability and bringing everything to perfection within itself ? " " They do well
indeed," said Theon, " and follow the natural course,
if in passing to the soul they really discover there
something better and more final, as do those men who
follow the intellectual and active lives. But when
you hear their ^d loud protest that the soul is so constituted as to find joy and tranquillity in nothing in
the world but pleasures of the body either present
or anticipated, and that this is its good, do they not
appear to you to be using the soul as a decanter of
the body, and to imagine that by decanting pleasure,
like wine, from a worthless and leaky vessel ^e and
leaving it to age in its new container, they are turning
it into something more respectable and precious ?

^a Hesiod, *Works and Days*, 288.
^b Used of Ithaca in Homer, *Od.* ix. 27.
^e Epicurus, Frag. 417 (ed. Usener). *Cf.* Seneca, *De Otio*,
7. 2 : " nec ille tertius [that is, Epicurus] . . . voluptatem
inertem probat, sed eam quam ratione efficit firmam sibi."
^d Frag. 429 (ed. Usener) ; *cf.* Frag. 425.
^e *Cf.* 1089 D, *infra.* The Epicureans had themselves used
the comparison of the leaky vessel : Lucretius, iii. 936, 1009,
vi. 20 f. See also *Mor.* 473 D, *Life of Marius*, chap. xlvi. 3
(433 B), and Seneca, *Ep.* 99. 5.

---

¹¹ μαρτυρομένων ΧΑ²Ε g c : μαρτυρουμένων aA¹.
¹² διεράματι g c (διεραματι Χ) : διέραμά τι a.
¹³ καί added by Wyttenbach.
¹⁴ οἶνον ἐκ πονηροῦ Χa g : ἐκ πονηροῦ οἶνον c.
¹⁵ οἴεσθαι Χ²a g c : οἴεσθε Χ¹.

31

(1088)

F μὲν χρόνῳ διαλυθέντα τηρεῖ καὶ συνηδύνει, τῆς δὲ
ἡδονῆς ἡ ψυχὴ παραλαβοῦσα τὴν μνήμην ὥσπερ
ὀσμὴν ἄλλο δὲ οὐδὲν φυλάσσει· ζέσασα γὰρ ἐπὶ
σαρκὶ κατασβέννυται, καὶ τὸ μνημονευόμενον αὐτῆς
ἀμαυρόν ἐστι καὶ κνισῶδες, ὥσπερ ἑώλων[1] ὧν τις
1089 ἔφαγεν ἢ ἔπιεν[2] ἀποτιθεμένου[3] καὶ ταμιεύοντος ἐπινοίας[4] ἐν αὑτῷ[5] καὶ χρωμένου δηλονότι ταύταις
προσφάτων[6] μὴ παρόντων. ὅρα δὲ ὅσῳ μετριώτερον
οἱ Κυρηναϊκοί, καίπερ ἐκ μιᾶς οἰνοχόης Ἐπικούρῳ
πεπωκότες, οὐδὲ ὁμιλεῖν ἀφροδισίοις οἴονται δεῖν
μετὰ φωτὸς ἀλλὰ σκότος προθεμένους, ὅπως μὴ τὰ
εἴδωλα τῆς πράξεως ἀναλαμβάνουσα διὰ τῆς ὄψεως
ἐναργῶς[7] ἡ διάνοια πολλάκις ἀνακαίηται[8] τὴν ὄρε-
ξιν. οἱ δὲ τούτῳ μάλιστα τὸν σοφὸν ἡγούμενοι
διαφέρειν, τῷ[9] μνημονεύειν ἐναργῶς καὶ συνέχειν
ἐν αὑτῷ[10] τὰ[11] περὶ τὰς ἡδονὰς φάσματα καὶ πάθη
B καὶ κινήσεις, εἰ μὲν οὐθὲν[12] ἄξιον σοφίας παρεγ-
γυῶσιν, ὥσπερ ἐν ἀσώτων[13] οἰκίᾳ τῇ ψυχῇ τοῦ
σοφοῦ τὰ τῆς ἡδονῆς ἐκκλύσματα[14] μένειν[15] ἐῶντες,
μὴ λέγωμεν· ὅτι δὲ[16] οὐκ ἔστιν ἀπὸ τούτων ἡδέως

[1] ἑώλων a : σόλων X g c.
[2] ἔφαγεν ἢ ἔπιεν X (-ιε a) : ἔπιεν ἢ ἔφαγε g c.
[3] ἀποτιθεμένου Reiske : τιθεμένου.
[4] ἐπινοίας Reiske : ἐπινοίαις.
[5] αὑτῷ X²a (αὐτῷ X¹) : ἑαυτῷ g c.
[6] προσφάτων a : πρὸς φίλων X g c.
[7] ἐναργῶς X g c : ἐναργῶς ἐν αὐτῇ a¹ (αὐ- a²).
[8] ἀνακαίηται X (-κάηται g) c : ἀνακαίη a.
[9] τῷ a g c : τὸ X¹ ; τὸ μὴ X² (now erased).
[10] αὑτῷ a² (αὐ- X¹a¹) : ἑαυτῷ X² (now erased) g c.
[11] τὰ Xa c : τὰς g.
[12] οὐθὲν X g c : οὐδὲν a.
[13] ἐν ἀσώτων Castiglioni (ἀσώτων ἐν Michael) : σωμάτων
Xa g c.

32

Yet there is a difference : the new vessel preserves the wine that has settled *a* in the course of time and improves its flavour, whereas in the case of pleasure the soul takes over and preserves the memory of it, as it were the bouquet, and nothing else ; for the pleasure effervesces in the flesh and then goes flat, and what is left of it in recollection is faint and greasy, as though a man were to lay away and store up in himself the thoughts of yesterday's stale food and drink, resorting to these, we must suppose, when nothing fresh is at hand. Observe the greater moderation of the Cyrenaics, though they have tippled from the same jug as Epicurus *b* : they even think it wrong to indulge in sexual commerce when there is a light, and instead provide for a cover of darkness, so that the mind may not, by receiving the images of the act in full clarity through the sense of sight, repeatedly rekindle the desire.*c* Whether the other set *d* who hold that the superiority of the sage lies above all in this, in vividly remembering and keeping intact in himself the sights and feelings and movements associated with pleasure, are thus recommending a practice unworthy the name of wisdom by allowing the slops of pleasure to remain in the soul of the sage as in the house of a wastrel, let us not say ; but that this sort of thing cannot sustain a pleasurable

---

a The wine separates into liquid and sediment.

b Usener, *Epicurea*, p. 293 ; perhaps an echo of Aristophanes, *Knights*, 1289. *Cf.* also Kock, *Com. Att. Frag.* iii, Adesp. 465.

c *Cf. Mor.* 654 D, 705 A-B (as emended by Döhner).

d Epicurus, Frag. 579 (ed. Usener).

---

¹⁴ ἐκκλύσματα X¹a g c : ἐκκυλύσματα X³.
¹⁵ μένειν Xa g : c omits.
¹⁶ δὲ XA²E g c : aA¹ omit.

(1089) ζῆν αὐτόθεν πρόδηλον.[1] οὐ γὰρ εἰκὸς[2] εἶναι μέγα[3]
τῆς ἡδονῆς τὸ μνημονευόμενον εἰ μικρόν γ᾽ ἐδόκει[4]
τὸ παρόν, οὐδὲ οἷς συνεφέρετο[5] μετρίως[6] γινομένοις
ὑπερχαίρειν[7] γενομένων, ὅπου γ᾽[8] οὐδὲ τοῖς ἐκπε-
πληγμένοις τὰ σωματικὰ καὶ θαυμάζουσιν ἐμμένει
τὸ χαίρειν παυσαμένοις,[9] ἀλλὰ σκιά τις ὑπολείπεται
καὶ ὄναρ ἐν τῇ ψυχῇ τῆς ἡδονῆς[10] ἀποπταμένης, οἷον
ὑπέκκαυμα τῶν ἐπιθυμιῶν, ὥσπερ ἐν ὕπνοις[11] διψῶντος ἢ ἐρῶντος[12] ἀτελεῖς ἡδοναὶ καὶ ἀπολαύσεις
C δριμύτερον ἐγείρουσι[13] τὸ ἀκόλαστον. οὔτε δὴ τούτοις ἐπιτερπὴς ἡ μνήμη τῶν ἀπολελαυσμένων,[14] ἀλλ᾽
ἐξ ὑπολείμματος[15] ἡδονῆς ἀμυδροῦ καὶ διακένου πολὺ
τὸ οἰστρῶδες καὶ νύττον ἐναργοῦς[16] ἀναφέρουσα τῆς
ὀρέξεως, οὔτε τοὺς μετρίους καὶ σώφρονας εἰκὸς
ἐνδιατρίβειν τῇ ἐπινοίᾳ τῶν τοιούτων οὐδὲ ἅπερ
ἔσκωπτε τὸν Ἐπίκουρον[17] Καρνεάδης[18] πράττοντας[19]
οἷον ἐξ ἐφημερίδων ἀναλέγεσθαι ᾽ ποσάκις[20] ῾Ηδείᾳ
καὶ Λεοντίῳ συνῆλθον; ᾽ ἢ ῾ ποῦ[21] Θάσιον ἔπιον; ᾽ ἢ[22]

---

[1] πρόδηλον a : τὸ πρόδηλον X g c.
[2] εἰκὸς Reiske : ἴσον X g c : ἴσως a.
[3] μέγα Reiske : μετὰ Xa g c.
[4] γ᾽ ἐδόκει Bern. (ἐδόκει Wyttenbach) : τε δοκεῖ Xa g c.
[5] συνεφέρετο g c : συνέφερε (-ν X) τὸ Xa ; συνεξεφέρετο Pohlenz.   [6] μετρίως Wyttenbach : μετρίοις Xa g c.
[7] ὑπερχαίρειν XA²ʸ ʳβ¹ʸ ʳE¹ʸ ʳ (ὑποχαίρειν β²ʸ ʳ [ὑπο super-
scribed]) g : ὑποχωρεῖν a ; ὑπερεξαίρειν c.
[8] γ᾽ added by Stegmann.
[9] τὰ σωμ.—παυσαμένοις XA²ᵐ E g c : aA¹ omit.
[10] τῆς ἡδονῆς Xa : τῇ and a blank of 9 letters in g, 12 in c.
[11] ὕπνοις X g c : ὕπνω a.
[12] διψῶντος ἢ ἐρῶντος Victorius in Q : διψῶντες ἢ ὁρῶντες
X g c ; διψῶντες ἢ ἐρῶντες a.
[13] ἐγείρουσι Xa : ἐγείρουσιν g c.
[14] ἀπολελαυσμένων Xa g : ἀπολελαυμένων c.
[15] ἐξ ὑπολείμματος (-ξυ- X)a : ἐξ ἐλλείματος g ; ἐξελλείμματος c.
[16] ἐναργοῦς a : ἐναργῶς X g c.

life is immediately evident. For it is unlikely that
what is remembered of the pleasure should be great
when what was present of it was considered small, or
that a man who took a passing interest in the thing
when it occurred should experience rapture when it
was over. Why even in persons who are enthralled
by the works of the body and whole-heartedly admire
them, the delight does not last when the experience
is over, but only a sort of shadow or dream [a] is left
behind in the soul after the pleasure has fled—
embers, as it were, to kindle desire, just as in the
dreams of sleep the unconsummated pleasures and
fruitions of thirst or love serve to arouse the more
sharply our lusting for fulfilment. Not only, then, do
these men get no joy from the memory of their in-
dulgences, which brings them instead from a faint
and unsubstantial remnant of pleasure the great
heat and prodding of a vividly conceived lust; it is
also quite unlikely that persons of moderation and
temperance should dwell on such thoughts and do
the sort of thing with which Carneades twitted Epicurus [b]—gather as from an official journal statistics
about ' how often I had a meeting with Hedeia or
Leontion,' [c] or ' where I drank Thasian wine ' or ' on

---

[a] Cf. Mor. 565 e.
[b] Cf. Epicurus, Frag. 436 (ed. Usener).
[c] On the women in Epicurus' school see 1097 d-e, 1129 b,
infra; Diogenes Laert. x. 4, 7, 23; Sbordone, Philodemi
Adversus [Sophistas], pp. 89, 137-139.

---

[17] Ἐπίκουρον added by Bern.
[18] Καρνεάδης Wyttenbach: καρνεάδην X[2] g; κορνιάδην X[1]a;
καρνέα c.
[19] πράττοντας Pohlenz: πράττοντα Xa g c (Wilamowitz
would omit). [20] ποσάκις Basle ed. of 1542: πολλάκις Xa gc.
[21] ἢ ποῦ a: ἢ που X; ἢ που g c.
[22] ἢ added by Usener: a blank of one letter X; a g c omit.

(1089) ' ποίας εἰκάδος[1] ἐδείπνησα[2] πολυτελέστατα; ' δεινὴν γὰρ ἐμφαίνει καὶ θηριώδη περὶ τὰ γινόμενα καὶ προσδοκώμενα τῆς ἡδονῆς ἔργα ταραχὴν καὶ λύσσαν ἡ τοσαύτη πρὸς ἀναμνήσεις βάκχευσις αὐτῆς D τῆς ψυχῆς καὶ πρόστηξις.

" Ὅθεν αὐτοί μοι δοκοῦσιν τούτων αἰσθόμενοι τῶν ἀτοπιῶν[3] εἰς τὴν ἀπονίαν καὶ τὴν εὐστάθειαν ὑποφεύγειν τῆς σαρκός, ὡς ἐν τῷ ταύτην ἐπινοεῖν περί τινας[4] ἐσομένην καὶ γεγενημένην τοῦ ἡδέως ζῆν ὄντος[5]· τὸ γὰρ εὐσταθὲς σαρκὸς[6] κατάστημα καὶ τὸ περὶ ταύτης πιστὸν ἔλπισμα τὴν ἀκροτάτην χαρὰν καὶ βεβαιοτάτην ἔχειν[7] τοῖς ἐπιλογίζεσθαι δυναμένοις. (5.) ὅρα δὴ πρῶτον μὲν οἷα ποιοῦσι, τὴν εἴτε ἡδονὴν ταύτην εἴτε ἀπονίαν ἢ[8] εὐστάθειαν[9] ἄνω καὶ κάτω μετερῶντες[10] ἐκ τοῦ σώματος εἰς τὴν ψυχήν, E εἶτα πάλιν ἐκ ταύτης εἰς ἐκεῖνο τῷ μὴ στέγειν ἀπορρέουσαν καὶ περιολισθάνουσαν[11] ἀναγκαζόμενοι τῇ ἀρχῇ συνάπτειν, καὶ ' τὸ μὲν ἡδόμενον ' ὥς φησι ' τῆς σαρκὸς τῷ χαίροντι τῆς ψυχῆς ' ὑπερείδοντες, αὖθις δ' ἐκ[12] τοῦ χαίροντος εἰς τὸ ἡδόμενον τῇ ἐλπίδι τελευτῶντες. καὶ πῶς οἷόν τε τῆς βάσεως

---

[1] εἰκάδος Bern. : εἰκάδας X[c] (from ἤκαδας) ; εἰκάδας a g c.
[2] ἐδείπνησα a : ἐδείπνησαν X g c.
[3] ἀτοπιῶν Xa : ἀτοπημάτων g c.
[4] τινας a : τινος X g c (ἡμᾶς Emperius).
[5] ὄντος X[r]a g c : -ως X[ar].
[6] σαρκὸς Xa g : τῆς σαρκὸς c.
[7] ἔχειν X g c : ἔχει a.
[8] ἢ Xa g : καὶ c.
[9] εὐστάθειαν K and Xylander : εὐπάθειαν Xa g c.
[10] μετερῶντες Dübner : μεταίροντες Xa g c.
[11] περιολισθάνουσαν X[1]a (-αίν- X[2]) : διολισθαίνουσαν g c.

36

what twentieth of the month I had the most sumptuous dinner.'[a] For it betrays a grave and brutish unsettling and derangement of spirit about the actual business of pleasure, present and prospective, when the mind by itself revels with such passionate attachment in the business of recollection.

" It is this, I believe, that has driven them,[b] seeing for themselves the absurdities to which they were reduced, to take refuge in the ' painlessness ' and the 'stable condition of the flesh,' supposing that the pleasurable life is found in thinking of this state as about to occur in people or as being achieved ; for the ' stable and settled condition of the flesh ' and the ' trustworthy expectation ' of this condition contain, they say, the highest and the most assured delight for men who are able to reflect. (5.) Now first observe their conduct here, how they [c] keep decanting this ' pleasure ' or ' painlessness ' or ' stable condition ' of theirs back and forth, from body to mind and then once more from mind to body, compelled, since pleasure is not retained in the mind but leaks and slips away,[d] to attach it to its source, shoring up ' the pleasure of the body with the delight of the soul,' as Epicurus puts it, but in the end passing once more by anticipation from the delight to the pleasure. And how is it possible, when the founda-

---

[a] A dinner was held on the twentieth of each month in honour of Metrodorus, and after Epicurus' death, in his own honour as well : Diogenes Laert. x. 18. *Cf.* Festugière, *Epicurus and his Gods* (trans. Chilton), p. 23.

[b] Epicurus, Frag. 68 (ed. Usener).

[c] Epicurus, Frag. 431 (ed. Usener).

[d] *Cf.* Plato, *Gorgias*, 493 A—494 B, and the note on 1088 E, *supra.*

---

[12] δ' ἐκ Reiske : δὲ Χα g c.

(1089) τιναττομένης μὴ συντινάττεσθαι[1] τὸ ἐπὸν[2] ἢ βέβαιον ἐλπίδα καὶ χαρὰν ἀσάλευτον εἶναι περὶ πρά-
γματος σάλον ἔχοντος τοσοῦτον καὶ μεταβολὰς[3] ὅσαι
σφάλλουσι[4] τὸ σῶμα, πολλαῖς μὲν ἔξωθεν ὑποκείμενον ἀνάγκαις καὶ πληγαῖς, ἐν αὐτῷ δὲ ἔχον ἀρχὰς
κακῶν ἃς οὐκ ἀποτρέπει λογισμός ; οὐδὲ γὰρ ἂν[5]
προσέπιπτεν ἀνδράσι νοῦν ἔχουσι στραγγουρικὰ
F πάθη καὶ δυσεντερικὰ καὶ[6] φθίσεις καὶ ὕδρωπες, ὧν
τοῖς μὲν αὐτὸς Ἐπίκουρος συνηνέχθη, τοῖς δὲ
Πολύαινος,[7] τὰ δὲ Νεοκλέα καὶ Ἀγαθόβουλον ἐξ-
ήγαγεν. καὶ ταῦτα οὐκ ὀνειδίζομεν, εἰδότες καὶ
Φερεκύδην[8] καὶ Ἡράκλειτον ἐν νόσοις χαλεπαῖς
γενομένους, ἀλλ' ἀξιοῦμεν αὐτοὺς εἰ[9] τοῖς πάθεσι
1090 βούλονται τοῖς ἑαυτῶν ὁμολογεῖν καὶ μὴ κεναῖς
φωναῖς θρασυνόμενοι καὶ δημαγωγοῦντες ἀλαζο-
νείαν προσοφλισκάνειν, ἢ μὴ λαμβάνειν χαρᾶς ἀρχὴν
ἁπάσης τὴν τῆς[10] σαρκὸς εὐστάθειαν ἢ μὴ φάναι
χαίρειν καὶ ὑβρίζειν τοὺς ἐν πόνοις ὑπερβάλλουσι
καὶ νόσοις γινομένους.[11] κατάστημα μὲν γὰρ εὐσταθὲς σαρκὸς γίνεται πολλάκις, ἔλπισμα δὲ πιστὸν
ὑπὲρ σαρκὸς καὶ βέβαιον οὐκ ἔστιν ἐν ψυχῇ νοῦν

---

[1] τιναττομένης μὴ συντινάττεσθαι a : -σσ- μὴ -ττ- Χ ; -σσ-
μὴ -σσ- g c.
[2] ἐπὸν van Herwerden : ἐνὸν Χ[r]a (ἐμὸν Χ[ar]) ; βαῖνον g c.
[3] μεταβολὰς Χa g : -αῖς c.
[4] ὅσαι σφάλλουσι Wyttenbach : ὅσαις (ὅσαι a) φυλάττουσι Χa
g ; ὅσαις ἔχουσι c.
[5] ἂν a : Χ g c omit ; Pohlenz places it before ἀνδράσι.
[6] δυσεντερικὰ καὶ Χa[2]A g c : a[1] omits.
[7] πολύαινος Χa : πολύβιος g c.
[8] φερεκύδην Χa : φενεκύδην g c.
[9] εἰ Χa[c]A[2]E g c : ἐν a[ac]A[1].
[10] τὴν τῆς Usener : τῆς Χa g c.
[11] γινομένους Χa[2] g c : γενομένους a[1].

38

tion totters, that the superstructure should not totter as well, or that there should be either firm expectation or unfluctuating delight over a thing exposed to all the tossing and changes that bring down the body, which is not only subject to many external compulsions and impacts, but also contains in itself sources of evil that no reasoning can avert ? Could reason avert them, reasonable men would never be afflicted with strangury, dysentery, consumption and the dropsy, with some of which Epicurus [a] himself had to contend, Polyaenus with others, while others were fatal to Neocles and Agathobulus.[b] I am not flinging this in their teeth, since I know that both Pherecydes and Heracleitus were visited with terrible diseases,[c] but my judgement is that if they [d] would take a tone more in keeping with their own bitter experience and not incur in addition the odium of ranting, by courting applause with a bold display of hollow words, they ought either to refrain from taking the position [e] that the ' stable condition of the flesh ' is the source of all delight, or from asserting that persons in the throes of an excruciating disease feel delight and treat the affliction with insolent contempt. For whereas a ' stable condition of the flesh ' [f] occurs frequently enough, no certain and firm expectation where the flesh is concerned can arise in a reasonable

[a] Strangury and dysentery : cf. Frag. 138 (ed. Usener).
[b] Probably a slip of Plutarch's for Aristobulus, a brother of Epicurus (see Usener's index, s.v.). Usener supposes Polyaenus died of consumption, Neocles and Aristobulus of the dropsy.
[c] Heracleitus died of the dropsy, Pherecydes from an outgrowth of lice : cf. Mor. 1064 A.
[d] Epicurus, Frag. 600 (ed. Usener).
[e] Epicurus, Frag. 424 (ed. Usener).
[f] Epicurus, Frag. 68 (ed. Usener).

(1090) ἐχούσῃ γενέσθαι· ἀλλ' ὥσπερ ἐν θαλάττῃ[1] κατ'
Αἰσχύλον

ὠδῖνα τίκτει[2] νὺξ κυβερνήτῃ[3] σοφῷ

καὶ γαλήνη[4] (τὸ γὰρ μέλλον ἄδηλον), οὕτως ἐν
B σώματι ψυχὴν εὐσταθοῦντι καὶ ταῖς περὶ σώματος
ἐλπίσι τἀγαθὸν θεμένην[5] οὐκ ἔστιν ἄφοβον καὶ
ἀκύμονα[6] διεξαγαγεῖν. οὐ γὰρ ἔξωθεν μόνον, ὥσπερ
ἡ θάλασσα,[7] χειμῶνας ἴσχει καὶ καταιγισμοὺς τὸ
σῶμα, πλείονας δὲ ταραχὰς ἐξ ἑαυτοῦ καὶ μείζονας
ἀναδίδωσιν· εὐδίαν δὲ χειμερινὴν μᾶλλον ἄν τις ἢ
σαρκὸς ἀβλάβειαν ἐλπίσειεν αὐτῷ παραμενεῖν[8] βε-
βαίως. τὸ γὰρ ἐφήμερα τὰ ἡμέτερα[9] καλεῖν καὶ
ἀβέβαια καὶ ἀστάθμητα φύλλοις τε γινομένοις ἔτους
ὥρα καὶ φθίνουσιν εἰκάζειν τὸν βίον τί παρέσχηκεν
ἄλλο τοῖς ποιηταῖς ἢ[10] τὸ τῆς σαρκὸς ἐπίκηρον καὶ
πολυβλαβὲς καὶ νοσῶδες, ἧς δὴ[11] καὶ τὸ ἄκρον ἀγα-
C θὸν δεδιέναι καὶ κολούειν παρεγγυῶσιν· ' σφαλερὸν
γὰρ ἡ ἐπ' ἄκρον εὐεξία,'[12] φησὶν Ἱπποκράτης,

ὁ δ' ἄρτι θάλλων σαρκὶ[13] διοπετὴς ὅπως
ἀστὴρ ἀπέσβη[14]

κατὰ τὸν Εὐριπίδην· ὑπὸ δὲ βασκανίας καὶ φθόνου

---

[1] θαλάττῃ X g c : θαλάσσῃ a.
[2] ὠδῖνα τίκτει Victorius in Q : ὦ (ὦ X β²) δεινὰ (aA¹ have ὠδινὰ) τῇ πόλει Xa g c.   [3] κυβερνήτῃ a g c : κυβερνήτης X.
[4] γαλήνη X g c : γαλήνῃ a ; γαληνὴ Reiske.
[5] θεμένην Xa c : τιθεμένην g.
[6] ἀκύμονα Cobet : ἄκυμον Xa g c.
[7] θάλασσα Xa g : θάλαττα c.
[8] παραμενεῖν Hartman : παραμένειν Xa g c.
[9] θημέτερα added by Kronenberg.
[10] ἢ Xa g : καὶ c.   [11] δὴ X²a g c : δὲ X¹.
[12] ἡ (ἡ X) ἐπ' ἄκρον (ἔπακρον X¹) εὐεξία Xa (cf. Mor. 682 E):
αἱ εἰς ἄκρον εὐεξίαι g c (αἱ ἐπ' ἄκρον εὐεξίαι Hippocrates).

40

mind, but as at sea, to quote Aeschylus,[a]

> Night brings forth travail for a practised skipper

—and so too does a calm, the future being uncertain— so the mind that has stowed the ultimate good in a body that is in a stable condition and in expectations for the body [b] cannot continue to the end without fear and the prospect of high weather. For the body, unlike the sea, suffers not only from storms and claps of wind that assail it from without, but brings forth from itself a greater number of more serious disturbances ; and you could better count on a winter spell of fair weather to be lasting than an immunity of the flesh from harm. For what else has led poets to call our condition ephemeral and uncertain and incalculable [c] and to compare our life to the leaves that are put forth in the spring and perish [d] than the frailty, vulnerability, and morbidity of the flesh ? Indeed, we are warned to dread and curtail even its greatest good, for Hippocrates [e] asserts that ' extreme excellence of the constitution is precarious ' and Euripides [f] says

> He who but now
> Flourished in health, has like a shooting star
> Vanished.

And men suppose that the young and handsome are

---

[a] *The Suppliant Women*, 770 ; quoted also in *Mor.* 619 E.
[b] Epicurus, Frag. 413 (ed. Usener).
[c] Euripides, *Orestes*, 981.
[d] Homer, *Il.* vi. 146 ; quoted also in *Mor.* 560 c.
[e] *Aphorisms*, i. 3 ; quoted also in *Mor.* 682 E.
[f] Nauck, *Trag. Graec. Frag.*, Eur. 971 ; quoted also in *Mor.* 416 D.

---

[13] σαρκὶ X a g c : σάρκα *Mor.* 416 D.
[14] ἀπέσβη a g c : ἀπεστη X.

(1090) βλάπτεσθαι προσορωμένους[1] οἴονται τοὺς καλούς,
ὅτι τάχιστα τὸ ἀκμάζον ἴσχει μεταβολὴν τοῦ σώματος δι' ἀσθένειαν.

6. '' "Ὅτι δὲ ὅλως μοχθηρὰ[2] τὰ πράγματα καὶ[3]
πρὸς βίον ἄλυπόν ἐστιν αὐτοῖς, σκόπει καὶ ἀφ' ὧν
πρὸς ἑτέρους[4] λέγουσιν. τοὺς γὰρ ἀδικοῦντας καὶ
παρανομοῦντας[5] ἀθλίως[6] φησὶ[7] καὶ περιφόβως ζῆν
τὸν πάντα χρόνον ὅτι κἂν[8] λαθεῖν δύνωνται[9] πίστιν
D περὶ τοῦ λαθεῖν λαβεῖν ἀδύνατόν ἐστιν· ὅθεν ὁ[10] τοῦ
μέλλοντος ἀεὶ[11] φόβος ἐγκείμενος οὐκ ἐᾷ χαίρειν
οὐδὲ θαρρεῖν ἐπὶ τοῖς παροῦσιν.[12] ταῦτα δὲ καὶ
πρὸς ἑαυτοὺς εἰρηκότες[13] λελήθασιν· εὐσταθεῖν μὲν
γάρ ἐστι[14] καὶ ὑγιαίνειν τῷ σώματι πολλάκις, πίστιν
δὲ λαβεῖν περὶ τοῦ διαμένειν[15] ἀμήχανον· ἀνάγκη[16]
δὴ ταράττεσθαι καὶ ὠδίνειν ἀεὶ πρὸς τὸ μέλλον
ὑπὲρ[17] τοῦ σώματος, ἣν[18] περιμένουσιν ἐλπίδα πιστὴν
ἀπ'[19] αὐτοῦ[20] καὶ βέβαιον[21] οὐδέπω[22] κτήσασθαι δυναμένους.[23] τὸ δὲ μηδὲν ἀδικεῖν οὐδέν ἐστι πρὸς τὸ
θαρρεῖν· οὐ γὰρ τὸ δικαίως παθεῖν ἀλλὰ τὸ παθεῖν
φοβερόν, οὐδὲ συνεῖναι μὲν αὐτὸν ἀδικίαις[24] ἀνιαρόν,[25]

[1] προσορωμένους Xylander : προορωμένους Xa g c.
[2] ὅλως μοχθηρὰ Xa g : c omits in a blank of 18 letters.
[3] καὶ X[1] g c : καὶ οὗ X[2] ; a omits.
[4] ἑτέρους Xa g : τοῖς c.
[5] παρανομοῦντας Xa g : παρασυροῦντας c.
[6] ἀθλίως Xa c : ἀθλίους g.
[7] φησὶ XaA[1] : φασὶ A[2]β[2]E g c.
[8] -φόβως (-φόβους g)—κἂν Xa g : c omits in a blank of 26
letters.   [9] δύνωνται Xa : δύναιντο g c.
[10] ὅθεν ὁ Xa[c] (a[ac] omits ὁ) : a blank of 7 letters and ὡς g ;
ἦ c.   [11] ἀεὶ Xa g : ἀ c.
[12] τοῖς παροῦσι (-ιν X) a g : τῆς παρουσίας c.
[13] εἰρηκότες Xa g : ἑστηκότες c.
[14] ἐστι Xa g : c omits.
[15] διαμένειν Xa g c : διαμενεῖ Usener (but cf. 1090 c-D).
[16] ἀνάγκη Xa g : c omits in a blank of 17 letters.

injured when they are gazed on, because of the evil
eye of envy,[a] since whatever is at its peak in the
body is the more quickly apt to change, owing to the
body's weakness.

6. " That their general prospects are poor even
for a life without mental anguish you may also judge
in the light of the remarks they address to others.
Criminals and transgressors of the laws, says Epicurus,[b] pass their entire lives in misery and apprehension, since even though they may succeed in
escaping detection, they can have no assurance of
doing so ; in consequence fear for the next moment
lies heavy on them and precludes any delight or confidence in their present situation. In these words
without knowing it they[c] have also replied to themselves : we can often enjoy in the body a ' stable
condition,' that is, health, but there is no way to
acquire any assurance that it will last. Hence they
cannot but suffer constant dismay and anguish for
the body in facing the future, since it has never
yet provided them with that ' secure and steadfast
hope ' that they keep waiting for. To do no wrong
does nothing to bring assurance ; it is not suffering de-
servedly, but suffering at all that is dreaded, and that

---

[a] Cf. Theocritus, *Idyll* vi. 39, with Gow's note.
[b] *Cardinal Tenets* xxxiv and xxxv ; cf. Frag. 532, 582 (ed.
Usener). [c] Epicurus, Frag. 68 (ed. Usener).

---

[17] ὑπὲρ ΧΑ²Ε g c : ὑπὸ aΑ¹.
[18] ἦν Wyttenbach : ἢ τί Χ (η τί Χ¹)a g c.
[19] ἀπ' Χa g c : περί Post.
[20] αὐτοῦ Χa g : a blank of 19 letters and οὐ c.
[21] βέβαιον Χa (cf. *Letter to Pythocles*, 85) : βεβαίαν g c.
[22] οὐδέπω Χa g c : οὐδέποτε Bern. ; οὐδέ πως ? Post.
[23] δυναμένους Χ¹a : δυνάμενοι Χ² c ; διαμένοι g¹ (δυναμένοι g²).
[24] ἀδικίαις Χa g : c omits in a blank of 11 letters.
[25] ἀνιαρὸν Χa g : ἀνιαρὰ c.

(1090)

E περιπεσεῖν δὲ ταῖς ἄλλων οὐ χαλεπόν· ἀλλ' εἰ μὴ
μεῖζον, οὐκ ἔλαττόν γε τὸ[1] κακὸν ἦν Ἀθηναίοις ἢ[2]
Λαχάρους[3] καὶ Συρακοσίοις[4] ἡ Διονυσίου χαλεπότης
ἤπερ αὐτοῖς ἐκείνοις[5]· ταράττοντες γὰρ ἐταράττοντο
καὶ πείσεσθαι κακῶς προσεδόκων ἐκ τοῦ προαδικεῖν
καὶ προλυμαίνεσθαι[6] τοὺς ἐντυγχάνοντας.[7] ὄχλων
δὲ θυμοὺς καὶ λῃστῶν ὠμότητας καὶ κληρονόμων
ἀδικίας, ἔτι δὲ λοιμοὺς ἀέρων καὶ θαλάσσης ἄμπωτιν,[8] ὑφ' ἧς[9] Ἐπίκουρος ὀλίγον ἐδέησε κατα-
ποθῆναι πλέων εἰς Λάμψακον,[10] ὡς γράφει, τί ἂν
λέγοι τις; ἀρκεῖ γὰρ ἡ φύσις τῆς σαρκός, ὕλην
F ἔχουσα νόσων[11] ἐν αὑτῇ καὶ τοῦτο δὴ τὸ παιζόμενον
'ἐκ τοῦ βοὸς τοὺς ἱμάντας' λαμβάνουσα τὰς ἀλγηδόνας ἐκ τοῦ σώματος, ὁμοίως τοῖς[12] τε φαύλοις καὶ
τοῖς ἐπιεικέσι τὸν βίον ἐπισφαλῆ[13] ποιεῖν[14] καὶ φοβερόν, ἄνπερ ἐπὶ σαρκὶ καὶ τῇ περὶ σάρκα ἐλπίδι
1091 μάθωσιν, ἄλλῳ δὲ μηθενὶ[15] χαίρειν καὶ θαρρεῖν, ὡς
Ἐπίκουρος ἔν τε[16] ἄλλοις πολλοῖς γέγραφε καὶ τούτοις ἅ ἐστι περὶ τέλους.

[1] τὸ] τότε ?   [2] ἡ Χ^ca (ἡ Χ^{ac}) : ἢ g c.
[3] λαχάρους a : λαχάρου Χ g c.
[4] Συρακοσίοις Bern. : συρρακουσίοις Χ c ; συρακουσίοις a ;
συρακουσσίοις g.
[5] ἤπερ (so a ; ἢ παρ' Χ g) αὐτοῖς ἐκείνοις Χa g : c omits.
[6] προλυμαίνεσθαι Reiske : κυμαίνεσθαι Χa g c (λυμαίνεσθαι
Α²E).
[7] ἐντυγχάνοντας B : προεντυγχάνοντας Χa g ; προστυγχάνον-
τας c.
[8] θαλάσσης ἄμπωτιν nos : θάλασσαν εὐβραγκὴν Χ(θ. εὐβράγ-
κην a ; θ. εὐκράγκην β² ; θ. εὐράγκην β²⁹⁰) g c (θάλασσαν Εὐβοϊ-
κὴν Post).   [9] ἧς B : αἷς Χa g c.
[10] λάμψακον Χa g² : λάψακον g¹ c.
[11] νόσων Χ²a g c : νόσον Χ¹.
[12] τοῖς Χa : g c omit.
[13] ἐπισφαλῆ Χ²a g c : -εῖ Χ¹.
[14] ποιεῖν aΑ¹ g² : ποιεῖ ΧΑ²E g¹ c.

44

it is misery to live with your own crimes on your head
does not mean that there is no hardship in exposure
to the crimes of others. Indeed for the Athenians
the savagery of Lachares, and for the Syracusans
that of Dionysius, if it was not a greater, was certainly
no less an evil than it was for Lachares and Dionysius
themselves ; for these felt disquiet because they
caused it, and their anticipations of being made to
suffer sprang from previous crimes and outrages per-
petrated on those who had come within their reach.
And what need to mention the fury of mobs,[a] the
savagery of bandits, the crimes of inheritors,[b] and
again the pestilences of the air and the reflux of the
sea that came near to engulfing Epicurus [c] on his
voyage to Lampsacus, as he writes ? For the nature
of the flesh possesses in itself the raw material of
diseases, and as in the jesting proverb we speak of
getting the whip from the ox's hide,[d] so it gets the
pains of the body from the body, and suffices to make
life precarious and full of fears for criminals and
honest men alike, once they have been taught to
let their delight and trust depend on the body and
on expectation for the body and on nothing else, as
Epicurus [e] teaches in his treatise *On the Highest Good*
and in many other passages as well.

[a] Bignone (*L'Aristotele perduto*, vol. ii, pp. 143-147) supposes that Epicurus was threatened by a mob at Mytilenê.
[b] The Athenian cleruchs at Samos, including Epicurus'
family, were dispossessed in favour of the displaced Samians
and their heirs in 322.   [c] Frag. 189 (ed. Usener).
[d] *Cf.* Leutsch and Schneidewin, *Paroem. Gr.*, vol. i, p.
402 and vol. ii, p. 162 ; see also Kock, *Com. Att. Frag.*, vol.
iii, p. 496 and Marx on Lucilius, 326.
[e] Frag. 68 (ed. Usener).

[15] μηθενὶ ΧΑ²Ε : μηδενὶ g c.
[16] σάρκα—ἔν τε ΧΑ²Ε g c : aΑ¹ omit.

(1091)   7. " Οὐ μόνον τοίνυν ἄπιστον καὶ ἀβέβαιον ἀρχὴν λαμβάνουσι τοῦ ἡδέως ζῆν ἀλλὰ καὶ παντάπασιν εὐκαταφρόνητον καὶ μικράν, εἴπερ αὐτοῖς
κακῶν ἀποφυγῇ[1] τὸ χαρτόν ἐστι καὶ τὸ ἀγαθόν,
ἄλλο δὲ οὐδὲν διανοεῖσθαί φασιν, οὐδὲ ὅλως τὴν
φύσιν ἔχειν[2] ὅποι[3] θήσεται[4] τὸ ἀγαθὸν εἰ μὴ μόνον
ὅθεν ἐξελαύνεται τὸ κακὸν αὐτῆς, ὥς φησι Μητρόδωρος ἐν τοῖς πρὸς τοὺς σοφιστάς· ' ὥστε τοῦτο
αὐτὸ τὸ ἀγαθόν[5] ἐστι, τὸ φυγεῖν τὸ κακόν· ἔνθα
γὰρ τεθήσεται τἀγαθὸν οὐκ ἔστιν ὅταν μηθὲν ἔτι
B ὑπεξίῃ[6] μήτε ἀλγεινὸν μήτε λυπηρόν.' ὅμοια δὲ
καὶ τὰ Ἐπικούρου λέγοντος τὴν τοῦ ἀγαθοῦ φύσιν
ἐξ αὐτῆς τῆς φυγῆς τοῦ κακοῦ καὶ τῆς μνήμης καὶ
ἐπιλογίσεως καὶ χάριτος ὅτι τοῦτο[7] συμβέβηκεν
αὐτῷ[8] γεννᾶσθαι· ' τὸ γὰρ ποιοῦν,'[9] φησίν, ' ἀνυπέρ-
βλητον γῆθος τὸ παρ' αὐτὸ[10] πεφυγμένον μέγα
κακόν· καὶ αὕτη φύσις ἀγαθοῦ, ἄν τις ὀρθῶς ἐπιβάλῃ[11] ἔπειτα σταθῇ καὶ μὴ κενῶς περιπατῇ περὶ
ἀγαθοῦ θρυλῶν.' φεῦ τῆς μεγάλης ἡδονῆς τῶν
ἀνδρῶν καὶ μακαριότητος ἣν καρποῦνται χαίροντες
ἐπὶ τῷ μὴ κακοπαθεῖν μηδὲ λυπεῖσθαι μηδὲ ἀλγεῖν.

[1] ἀποφυγῇ X²a g : ἀποφύγῃ X¹ c.
[2] ἔχειν a g c : ἔχει X.
[3] ὅποι (ὅ-X¹) Xa c : ὅπῃ g.
[4] θήσεται X g c : τεθήσεται a.
[5] τἀγαθόν Usener : ἀγαθόν.
[6] ὑπεξίῃ X²a : ὑπεξείῃ X¹ g c.
[7] τοῦτο X g c : τούτῳ a.
[8] αὐτῷ a g c : αὐτὸ X.   [9] ποιοῦν Xa g : ποιόν c.
[10] παρ' αὐτὸ a : παρ' αὐτὸν X ; παρ' αὐτῶν g c (πάραυτα
Usener ; παρὰ λόγον Pohlenz).
[11] ἐπιβάλῃ X g c : ἐπιβάλλῃ a (ἐπιβαλὼν? Post).

7. " To pursue : not only is the basis that they assume for the pleasurable life untrustworthy and insecure, it is quite trivial and paltry as well, inasmuch as their ' thing delighted in ' *a*—their Good— is an escape from ills, and they say that they can conceive of no other, and indeed that our nature has no place at all in which to put its good except the place left when its evil is expelled, as Metrodorus *b* asserts in his *Reply to the Sophists* : ' Hence this very thing is the Good, escape from the evil ; for there is nowhere for the Good to be put when nothing painful to the body or distressing to the mind is any longer making way for it.' Epicurus *c* too makes a similar statement to the effect that the Good is a thing that arises out of your very escape from evil and from your memory and reflexion and gratitude *d* that this has happened to you. His words are these : ' For what produces a jubilation unsurpassed is the contrast of the great evil escaped ; and this is the nature of good, if you apply your mind rightly and then stand firm and do not stroll about *e* prating meaninglessly about good.' Oh the great pleasure and blessed state this company *f* enjoy, as they revel in suffering no hardship or anxiety or pain ! Is this

a For the word *cf.* Epicurus, *On Nature*, Frag. 31. 18. 4, p. 329 (ed. Arrighetti).

b Frag. 28 (ed. Körte).

c Frag. 423 (ed. Usener).

d Epicurus uses *charis* (gratitude) in the sense of " grateful recollection " in the *Letter to Menoeceus*, 122 ; *Gnom. Vat.* 17 (where see the note in Bailey's *Epicurus*, p. 378) ; for the thought see also Cicero, *De Fin.* i. 17 (57), 19 (62).

e A jibe at the Peripatetics.

f Frag. 419 (ed. Usener). The Epicureans used the term *makarios* (" blessed ") of the gods and of themselves. They may, like Aristotle (*Eth. Nic.* vii. 11 [1152 b 7 f.]), have associated the word with *chairein* (" to delight ").

(1091) ἆρ' οὐκ ἄξιόν ἐστιν ἐπὶ τούτοις καὶ φρονεῖν καὶ
C λέγειν ἃ λέγουσιν, ἀφθάρτους καὶ ἰσοθέους ἀποκαλοῦντες αὑτοὺς καὶ δι' ὑπερβολὰς καὶ ἀκρότητας
ἀγαθῶν[1] εἰς βρόμους καὶ ὀλολυγμοὺς ἐκβακχεύοντες
ὑφ'[2] ἡδονῆς ὅτι τῶν ἄλλων περιφρονοῦντες ἐξευρή-
κασι μόνοι θεῖον ἀγαθὸν καὶ μέγα,[3] τὸ μηθὲν[4] ἔχειν
κακόν; ὥστε μήτε[5] συῶν ἀπολείπεσθαι μήτε προ-
βάτων εὐδαιμονίᾳ,[6] τὸ τῇ σαρκὶ καὶ τῇ ψυχῇ περὶ[7]
τῆς σαρκὸς ἱκανῶς ἔχειν μακάριον τιθεμένους.[8]
ἐπεὶ τοῖς γε κομψοτέροις καὶ γλαφυρωτέροις τῶν
ζῴων οὐκ ἔστι φυγὴ[9] κακοῦ τέλος,[10] ἀλλὰ καὶ πρὸς
ᾠδὰς ἀπὸ[11] κόρου τρέπεται καὶ νήξεσι χαίρει καὶ
πτήσεσι καὶ ἀπομιμεῖσθαι[12] παίζοντα[13] φωνάς τε
D παντοδαπὰς καὶ ψόφους ὑφ' ἡδονῆς καὶ γαυρότητος
ἐπιχειρεῖ[14] καὶ πρὸς ἄλληλα χρῆται φιλοφροσύναις
καὶ σκιρτήσεσιν, ὅταν ἐκφύγῃ τὸ κακὸν τἀγαθὸν[15]
πεφυκότα ζητεῖν, μᾶλλον δὲ ὅλως[16] πᾶν τὸ ἀλγεινὸν
καὶ τὸ ἀλλότριον ὡς ἐμποδὼν ὄντα τῇ διώξει τοῦ
οἰκείου καὶ κρείττονος ἐξωθοῦντα τῆς φύσεως.
8. '' Τὸ γὰρ ἀναγκαῖον οὐκ ἀγαθόν ἐστιν ἀλλ'
ἐπέκεινα τῆς φυγῆς τῶν κακῶν κεῖται τὸ ἐφετὸν
καὶ τὸ αἱρετὸν καὶ νὴ Δία τὸ[17] ἡδὺ καὶ οἰκεῖον, ὡς

[1] ἀγαθῶν Xa c : παθῶν g.
[2] ὑφ' Xa : ὑπὸ (ἀπὸ c) τῆς g c.   [3] μέγα g c : μετὰ Xa.
[4] τὸ (τὸν Xar) μηθὲν Xa[1] (τοῦ μηθὲν a²A) : τὸ μηδὲν g c.
[5] μήτε XA²E g c : μὴ aA[1].
[6] εὐδαιμονίᾳ Reiske : εὐδαιμονίαν Xa g c.
[7] περὶ Xa : παρὰ g c.
[8] μακάριον τιθεμένους XA g c : μακάριόν τι θεμένους a (but
the second acute may be later).
[9] φυγὴ μ² and Victorius (φύσει φυγὴ Xylander) : φύσει Xar
(from φύσεῖ) g c.   [10] τέλος Xr g c βr : τέλους Xara.
[11] ἀπὸ Kronenberg : ὑπὸ Xa g c.
[12] ἀπομιμεῖσθαι Xa : ἀπομιμεῖται g c.
[13] παίζοντα a : παίζοντας X g c.

not a thing to make them proud and use the language they do,[a] when they style themselves 'imperishable'[b] and 'equal to the gods'[c] and from excess and pre-eminence of blessings explode in their pleasure into wild cries of rapture and ecstasy because they alone, scorning all other blessings, have discovered one as great as it is godlike, to wit, not to suffer any ill? Therefore in felicity they are no whit inferior to swine or sheep, since they count it blessedness for everything to go well with the flesh and with the mind in its concern for the flesh. Actually for the cleverer and more graceful animals the escape from evil is not the highest end; rather, when they have had their fill they turn to song, or revel in swimming or in flight, or for pure joy and high spirits take up a playful imitation of words and sounds of every kind, and greet one another with caresses and gambols, since once they have escaped evil they instinctively seek out the good, or better, let us say that they expel from their nature everything painful or alien to it as an impediment to the pursuit of what belongs to that nature and is a higher good.

8. " For what is imposed by necessity is not good; the object of our aspiration and choice lies beyond the escape from ills; yes, and so too does what is pleasant and in harmony with our nature, as Plato[d]

---

[a] *Cf.* Metrodorus, Frag. 38 (ed. Körte) and Epicurus, Frag. 141, note (ed. Usener).
[b] *Cf.* Epicurus' letter to his mother (Frag. 65. 1. 23-40, ed. Arrighetti), translated in note *b* on p. 250, *infra*.
[c] *Cf.* Epicurus, Frag. 165 (ed. Usener).
[d] *Republic*, ix, 584 B—585 A, 586 A.

---

[14] γαυρότητος ἐπιχειρεῖ Xa : γαυρόττ (-τητας g) ἐπιτελεῖ g c.
[15] τὸ κακὸν τἀγαθὸν a : τἀγαθὸν τὸ κακὸν X g c.
[16] ὅλως Xa g : ἐστιν ὡς c.   [17] τὸ Xa g : καὶ c.

PLUTARCH'S MORALIA

(1091) Πλάτων ἔλεγε, καὶ ἀπηγόρευεν τὰς λυπῶν καὶ
πόνων ἀπαλλαγὰς ἡδονὰς μὴ νομίζειν, ἀλλ' οἷόν
τινα σκιαγραφίαν[1] ἢ μῖξιν οἰκείου καὶ ἀλλοτρίου,
καθάπερ λευκοῦ καὶ μέλανος,[2] ἀπὸ τοῦ κάτω πρὸς
E τὸ μέσον ἀναφερομένων, ἀπειρίᾳ δὲ τοῦ ἄνω[3] καὶ
ἀγνοίᾳ τὸ μέσον ἄκρον ἡγουμένων[4] εἶναι καὶ πέρας·
ὥσπερ Ἐπίκουρος ἡγεῖται καὶ Μητρόδωρος, οὐσίαν
τἀγαθοῦ[5] καὶ ἀκρότητα τὴν τοῦ κακοῦ φυγὴν τιθέμενοι καὶ χαίροντες ἀνδραπόδων τινὰ χαρὰν ἢ δε-
σμίων ἐξ εἱργμοῦ λυθέντων, ἀσμένως ἀλειψαμένων
καὶ ἀπολουσαμένων μετ' αἰκίας καὶ[6] μάστιγας,
ἐλευθέρας δὲ καὶ καθαρᾶς καὶ ἀμιγοῦς καὶ ἀμωλωπίστου[7] χαρᾶς ἀγεύστων καὶ ἀθεάτων.[8] οὐ γὰρ εἰ
τὸ ψωριᾶν τὴν σάρκα καὶ λημᾶν τὸν ὀφθαλμὸν
ἀλλότριον ἤδη καὶ τὸ κνᾶσθαι καὶ τὸ[9] ἀπομάττεσθαι
F θαυμάσιον· οὐδ' εἰ τὸ ἀλγεῖν καὶ φοβεῖσθαι τὰ θεῖα
καὶ ταράττεσθαι τοῖς ἐν Ἅιδου κακὸν ἡ τούτων
ἀποφυγὴ μακάριον καὶ ζηλωτόν. ἀλλὰ μικρόν τινα
τόπον καὶ γλίσχρον ἀποφαίνουσι τῆς χαρᾶς ἐν ᾧ
στρέφεται καὶ κυλινδεῖται, μέχρι τοῦ μὴ ταράττεσθαι τοῖς ἐν Ἅιδου κακοῖς ἡ τούτων[10] παρὰ τὰς
κενὰς δόξας προϊοῦσα καὶ τοῦτο ποιουμένη τῆς
1092 σοφίας τέλος ὃ δόξειεν ἂν[11] αὐτόθεν ὑπάρχειν τοῖς

[1] σκιαγραφίαν ΧΑ²Ε g c : σκιο- αΑ¹.
[2] After μέλανος Döhner supposes a lacuna, which Pohlenz
would fill somewhat as follows : τοὺς δὲ τὸ μὴ ἀλγεῖν ἡδονὴν
νομίζοντας οὐδὲν διαφέρειν τῶν.
[3] ἄνω Victorius in Q : κάτω Χα g c.
[4] ἡγουμένων] -νων through Σοφοκλέους (1093 D) is wanting
in X through the loss of two leaves (eight pages).
[5] τἀγαθοῦ a g : ἀγαθοῦ c.
[6] μετ' αἰκίας καὶ aᶜΑ : μετ' ἀδικίας καὶ aᵃᶜ : μετὰ τὰς ἀδικίας
καὶ τὰς g c.
[7] ἀμωλωπίστου Bern. : ἀπουλωτίστου a g c.
[8] ἀθεάτων a g : ἀθεμίτων c.   [9] τὸ g c : a omits.

50

said, who forbade us to regard riddance from pain
and discomfort as pleasure, but as instead some trick
of perspective as it were or blend of what is in harmony with our nature with what is alien to it, like a
blend of white and black, which occurs when people
ascend from a lower to a middle region, and suppose,
in their lack of any experience or knowledge of the
higher region, that the middle is the summit and the
end. So Epicurus[a] supposes and Metrodorus[b] too,
when they take the position that escape from ill is
the reality and upper limit of the good; and thus
their delight is that of slaves or prisoners released
from confinement, overjoyed to be anointed and
bathed after the cruel usage and the flogging, but
knowing neither the taste nor the vision of a free
man's delight, pure, untainted, and bearing no welts
from the lash. For it does not follow that if an itching
of the skin or a rheumy flux in the eye is foreign to
our nature, scratching the skin and wiping the eye
are on that account a glorious experience ; nor does
it follow that if pain, fear of the supernatural and
terror about the hereafter are evil, escape from them
is godlike and bliss beyond compare.[c] No ; these
men coop up their delight in quarters that are small
and cramped, and there it circles about and wallows,
advancing no farther, this delight of theirs, than to
escape the anxiety about the ills of the hereafter that
comes from false notions, and taking as the final goal
of wisdom a state with which, it would appear, the

---

[a] Frag. 423 (ed. Usener).
[b] Frag. 28 (ed. Körte).
[c] Epicurus, Frag. 384 (ed. Usener).

---

[10] ἡ (ἦ g c) τούτων a g c : Wyttenbach would omit.
[11] ἂν added by Bern.

(1092) ἀλόγοις. εἰ γὰρ πρὸς τὴν ἀπονίαν[1] τοῦ σώματος
οὐ διαφέρει πότερον δι' αὐτὸν[2] ἢ φύσει τοῦ πονεῖν
ἐκτός ἐστιν, οὐδὲ πρὸς τὴν ἀταραξίαν[3] μεῖζόν ἐστι
τὸ δι' αὐτὸν[4] ἢ κατὰ φύσιν οὕτως[5] ἔχειν ὥστε μὴ
ταράττεσθαι. καίτοι φήσειεν ἄν τις οὐκ ἀλόγως
ἐρρωμενεστέραν εἶναι διάθεσιν τὴν φύσει μὴ δεχο-
μένην τὸ ταράττον ἢ τὴν ἐπιμελείᾳ καὶ λόγῳ δια-
φεύγουσαν. ἔστω δὲ ἔχειν ἐπίσης· καὶ γὰρ οὕτως
φανοῦνται τῶν θηρίων πλέον οὐδὲν ἔχοντες ἐν τῷ
μὴ ταράττεσθαι τοῖς ἐν "Αιδου καὶ τοῖς[6] περὶ θεῶν
λεγομένοις μηδὲ προσδοκᾶν λύπας μηδὲ ἀλγηδόνας
B ὅρον οὐκ[7] ἐχούσας. αὐτὸς γοῦν Ἐπίκουρος εἰπὼν
ὡς ' εἰ[8] μηδὲν ἡμᾶς αἱ ὑπὲρ τῶν μετεώρων ὑποψίαι
ἠνώχλουν ἔτι τε[9] τὰ περὶ θανάτου καὶ ἀλγηδόνων,
οὐκ ἄν ποτε προσεδεόμεθα φυσιολογίας ' εἰς τοῦτο[10]
ἄγειν ἡμᾶς οἴεται τὸν λόγον ἐν ᾧ τὰ θηρία φύσει
καθέστηκεν[11]· οὔτε γὰρ ὑποψίας ἔχει φαύλας περὶ
θεῶν οὔτε δόξαις κεναῖς[12] ἐνοχλεῖται περὶ τῶν μετὰ[13]
θάνατον οὐδὲ ὅλως ἐπινοεῖ τι δεινὸν ἐν τούτοις οὐδὲ
οἶδε. καίτοι εἰ μὲν ἐν τῇ προλήψει τοῦ θεοῦ τὴν
πρόνοιαν ἀπέλιπον ἐφαίνοντο ἂν ἐλπίσι χρησταῖς

---

[1] ἀπονίαν a[2]A g c : ἀπόνοιαν a[1].
[2] αὐτὸν c : αὐτὸν g ; αὐτό a[2] (from αὐτό).
[3] ἀταραξίαν g c : ἀταραξίαν τῆς ψυχῆς a.
[4] αὐτὸν c : αὐτὸν g ; αὐτὸ a (αὐτὴν Bern. ; αὐτὴν Reiske).
[5] οὕτως g c : ὡς οὕτως a.
[6] τοῖς added by Pohlenz.
[7] οὐκ added by Reiske (exitum non habentes Ferronus).
[8] εἰ g c β[2] : a omits.
[9] τε g c : a omits.
[10] τοῦτο a g[ac] c : τοῦτον g[css].
[11] ἄγειν—καθέστηκεν g c : a omits.

brutes begin. For if it makes no difference in the
freedom of the body from pain whether it has got
free by your own efforts or by a natural process, so
too in peace of mind the unperturbed condition
achieved by your own efforts has no advantage over
the condition when it is that of nature. Indeed it
might be urged with some reason that there is greater
strength in the condition that is naturally imperturb-
able than in one that escapes disturbing influences
by exercising care and taking thought. But let us
grant that the two states are equally unperturbed,
since even so these gentlemen will be seen to be no
better off than the brutes in this matter of not being
disturbed by the hereafter and by tales about the gods
and of not anticipating endless anxiety and pain.
Thus Epicurus [a] himself, when he says ' If we were not
troubled with misgivings about celestial phenomena
and again about death and pain, we should never have
stood in need of natural philosophy,' [b] imagines that
his system leads us to the state in which the brutes
are permanently placed by nature. For the brutes
have no wrong-headed misgivings about the gods and
are not troubled with baseless notions about what
awaits them after death ; indeed they have no idea
or knowledge whatever of anything to fear on either
score. Yet if the Epicureans had left room for providence in their conception of God men of intelligence
would then be seen to be better equipped for a

---

[a] *Cardinal Tenet* xi.

[b] The Epicureans described their system as *physiologia*
(" natural philosophy ") and called themselves *physiologoi*
(" natural philosophers ") : *cf.* 1098 D, 1100 A, 1117 B, *infra* ;
Cicero, *De Nat. Deor.* i. 8 (20) with Pease's note.

---

[12] δόξαις κεναῖς Madvig : δόξας αἷς a ; δόξας ἐν αἷς g c.
περὶ τῶν μετὰ Reiske : τῶν μετὰ g c : μετὰ τὸν a.

(1092) πλέον ἔχοντες οἱ φρόνιμοι τῶν θηρίων πρὸς τὸ
ἡδέως ζῆν· ἐπεὶ δὲ τέλος ἦν τοῦ περὶ θεῶν λόγου
τὸ μὴ φοβεῖσθαι θεὸν ἀλλὰ παύσασθαι ταραττο-
C μένους, βεβαιότερον οἶμαι τοῦτο ὑπάρχειν τοῖς ὅλως
μὴ νοοῦσι θεὸν ἢ τοῖς νοεῖν μὴ βλάπτοντα μεμαθηκόσιν. οὐ γὰρ ἀπήλλακται δεισιδαιμονίας ἀλλ'
οὐδὲ περιπέπτωκεν, οὐδὲ ἀποτέθειται[1] τὴν ταράτ-
τουσαν ἔννοιαν περὶ θεῶν[2] ἀλλ' οὐδ' εἴληφε. τὰ δὲ
αὐτὰ καὶ[3] περὶ τῶν ἐν Ἅιδου λεκτέον· τὸ[4] μὲν γὰρ
ἐλπίζειν χρηστὸν[5] ἀπ' ἐκείνων οὐδετέροις[6] ὑπάρχει,
τοῦ[7] δ' ὑποπτεύειν καὶ φοβεῖσθαι τὰ[8] μετὰ[9] θάνατον
ἧττον μέτεστιν οἷς οὐ γίνεται[10] θανάτου πρόληψις
ἢ τοῖς προλαμβάνουσιν ὡς οὐδὲν πρὸς ἡμᾶς ὁ θάνατος. πρὸς μέν γε τούτους ἔστιν, ἐφ' ὅσον περὶ
αὐτοῦ[11] διαλογίζονται[12] καὶ σκοποῦσι, τὰ δὲ ὅλως
D ἀπήλλακται τοῦ φροντίζειν τῶν οὐ πρὸς ἑαυτά,
πληγὰς δὲ φεύγοντα καὶ τραύματα καὶ φόνους[13]
τοῦτο τοῦ θανάτου δέδοικεν ὃ καὶ τούτοις φοβερόν
ἐστιν.

9. "Ἃ μὲν οὖν λέγουσιν αὐτοῖς[14] ὑπὸ σοφίας
παρεσκευασμένα τοιαῦτά ἐστιν· ὧν δὲ αὐτοὺς[15] ἀφαι-
ροῦνται καὶ ἀπελαύνουσιν[16] ἤδη σκοπῶμεν. τὰς μὲν
γὰρ ὑπὲρ σαρκὸς καὶ ἐπὶ σαρκὸς[17] εὐπαθείᾳ τῆς

---

[1] ἀποτέθειται a: ὑποτέθειται g c. [2] θεῶν a: τῶν θεῶν g c.
[3] καὶ a: g c omit. [4] τὸ a[c] (διὸ a[ac]?) c: τοῦτο g.
[5] χρηστὸν a g c: τι χρηστὸν Meziriacus.
[6] οὐδετέροις o[2] and Ald.[2]: οὐδέτερον a g c. [7] τοῦ g c: τὸ a.
[8] τὰ added by Meziriacus. [9] μετὰ g c: μετὰ τὸν a.
[10] οὐ γίνεται] οὐδ' ἐγγίνεται Castiglioni.
[11] ἐφ' ὅσον περὶ αὐτοῦ a: ἐφόσον g c.
[12] διαλογίζονται a: -αί τι g c. [13] φόνους g c: φθόνους a.
[14] αὐτοῖς Ald.[2] (αὑτοῖς g c): αὐτοὺς a.
[15] δὲ αὐτοὺς a: δ' ἑαυτοὺς g c.
[16] ἀπελαύνουσιν a: ἀπολαύουσιν g c.

pleasurable life than the brutes because they could hope; since, however, the aim of their theology [a] is to have no fear of God, but instead to be rid of our anxieties, I should think that this condition is more securely in the possession of creatures that have no faintest notion of God than of those who have been taught to think of him as injuring no one. Of these the former have not been delivered from superstition, since they have never even been its victims; nor have they put aside the notion about the gods that is disturbing, but have never even adopted it. The same is to be said of the hereafter: neither creature expects any good of it, but misgiving and dread of what comes after death is less the portion of those who have no conception of death than of those who conceive that death is no concern of ours.[b] Death *is* a concern of these men to the extent that they reason about it and subject it to inquiry [c]; but the brutes are relieved of any concern whatever for what is nothing to them, and when they avoid blows and wounds and being killed they fear that in death which the Epicureans fear as well.

9. "Such then are the improvements upon nature with which they say wisdom has provided [d] them. Let us now consider what they deprive themselves of and banish themselves from. As for the melting away of the mind that occurs in the expectation or

---

[a] Frag. 384 (ed. Usener).
[b] For this famous Epicurean phrase see the *Letter to Menoeceus*, 124, 125, *Cardinal Tenet* ii, and Lucretius, iii. 830.   [c] *Cf.* 1106 E, *infra*.
[d] For the phrase *cf. Cardinal Tenet* xxvii: ὧν ἡ σοφία παρασκευάζεται.

---

[17] ὑπὲρ σαρκὸς καὶ ἐπὶ σαρκὸς nos (ἐπὶ σαρκὶ καὶ σαρκὸς Victorius): ἐπὶ σαρκὸς καὶ σαρκὸς a; ἐπὶ σαρκὸς g c.

(1092) ψυχῆς διαχύσεις, ἐὰν ὦσι μέτριαι, μηθὲν[1] ἐχούσας
μέγα[2] μηδὲ ἀξιόλογον, ἂν[3] δὲ ὑπερβάλλωσι,[4] πρὸς
τῷ κενῷ καὶ ἀβεβαίῳ φορτικὰς φαινομένας καὶ
θρασείας, οὐδὲ ψυχικὰς ἄν τις οὐδὲ χαράς,[5] ἀλλὰ
σωματικὰς ἡδονὰς καὶ[6] οἷον ἐπιμειδιάσεις καὶ συν-
E επιθρύψεις προσείποι τῆς ψυχῆς. ἃς δὲ ἄξιον καὶ
δίκαιον εὐφροσύνας καὶ χαρὰς νομίζεσθαι[7] καθαραὶ[8]
μέν εἰσι τοῦ ἐναντίου καὶ σφυγμὸν[9] οὐδένα κεκραμένον οὐδὲ δηγμὸν οὐδὲ μετάνοιαν ἔχουσιν, οἰκεῖον
δὲ τῇ ψυχῇ καὶ ψυχικὸν ἀληθῶς καὶ γνήσιον καὶ
οὐκ ἐπείσακτον αὐτῶν τἀγαθόν ἐστιν οὐδὲ ἄλογον
ἀλλ' εὐλογώτατον[10] ἐκ τοῦ θεωρητικοῦ καὶ φιλο-
μαθοῦς ἢ πρακτικοῦ[11] καὶ φιλοκάλου τῆς διανοίας
φυόμενον. ὧν ὅσας[12] ἑκάτερον καὶ ἡλίκας ἡδονὰς
ἀναδίδωσιν οὐκ ἄν τις ἀνύσειε διελθεῖν προθυμού-
μενος· ὑπομνῆσαι δὲ βραχέως αἵ[13] τε ἱστορίαι πάρ-
εισι πολλὰς μὲν ἐπιτερπεῖς διατριβὰς ἔχουσαι, τὸ
F δὲ ἐπιθυμοῦν ἀεὶ τῆς ἀληθείας[14] ἀκόρεστον καταλείπουσαι[15] καὶ ἄπληστον ἡδονῆς· δι' ἣν οὐδὲ τὸ ψεῦδος
ἀμοιρεῖ χάριτος, ἀλλὰ καὶ πλάσμασι καὶ ποιήμασι
τοῦ πιστεύεσθαι μὴ προσόντος ἔνεστιν ὅμως τὸ

---

[1] μηθὲν a g : μηδὲν c.
[2] μέγα a c : g omits.
[3] ἂν a c : ἐὰν g.
[4] ὑπερβάλλωσι a g : ὑπερβάλωσι c.
[5] χαρὰς Reiske : χάριτας a g c.
[6] καὶ g c : a omits.
[7] νομίζεσθαι a : κομίζεσθαι g : εἰσκομίζεσθαι c.
[8] καθαραὶ a g : καθαρὰ c.
[9] σφυγμὸν a : σφιγμὸν g ; σφηγμὸν c.
[10] εὐλογώτατον a g : εὐλ and a blank of 6 letters and τατον c.
[11] πρακτικοῦ a : τραγικοῦ g c β[288].
[12] ὧν ὅσας a g : c omits in a blank of 12 letters.
[13] Before αἵ Pohlenz would add αἵ τε μαθήσεις, Reiske ἥ τε πεῖρα.
[14] ἀληθείας a g c : ἀληθοῦς Hartman.
[15] καταλείπουσαι g c : ἀπολείπουσαι a.

on the occasion of fleshly enjoyment, this when moderate has nothing about it that is great or appreciable, and when extreme is not only unfounded and unstable but strikes us as coarse and immodest ; and a man would refuse to term it so much as ' mental ' or a ' delight,' but rather a ' physical pleasure of the mind ' as it beams, as it were, upon the body and humours it.[a] But what properly deserves to be considered ' animation '[b] and ' delight ' is pure of any taint of its opposite, has no element of aching or stabbing pain, and brings with it no regret[c] ; the good in it is proper to the mind and really ' mental ' and authentic and not adventitious or irrational but rational in the truest sense, since it comes from the speculative and philosophical or else the active and honourable part of the mind.[d] The pleasures yielded by each of these two parts are so many and so great that with the best in the world no one could tell the whole story. For a brief reminder, however, we can appeal first to history, providing as it does many hours of agreeable pastime, but yet leaving us with our thirst for more and still more truth insatiable and unblunted with pleasure ; a pleasure moreover which lends to fiction a power to charm, and the purest fabrications and poetic inventions, to which no belief is accorded, have none the less the winning

[a] Frag. 410 (ed. Usener).

[b] "Animation" renders *euphrosynê*, a word for joy that owing to its etymology (from *phrên*, " mind ") was often applied to the pleasures of the mind : *cf.* Plato, *Protagoras*, 337 c.

[c] *Cf. Mor.* 476 F.

[d] For the Platonist all pleasure is of the mind, none of the body ; but the pleasure can be of the highest or philosophical part of the mind, of the next part, the spirited and enterprising, or of the lowest part, the desiderative.

1093 πεῖθον. (10.) ἐννόει γὰρ ὡς δακνόμενοι τὸν Πλάτωνος ἀναγινώσκομεν Ἀτλαντικὸν καὶ τὰ τελευταῖα
τῆς Ἰλιάδος, οἷον ἱερῶν κλειομένων ἢ θεάτρων
ἐπιποθοῦντες τοῦ μύθου τὸ λειπόμενον. αὐτῆς δὲ
τῆς ἀληθείας ἡ μάθησις οὕτως ἐράσμιόν ἐστι καὶ
ποθεινὸν ὡς[1] τὸ ζῆν καὶ τὸ εἶναι διὰ τὸ γινώσκειν·
τοῦ δὲ θανάτου τὰ σκυθρωπότατα λήθη καὶ ἄγνοια
καὶ σκότος. ἦ[2] καὶ νὴ Δία μάχονται τοῖς φθείρουσι
τῶν ἀποθανόντων τὴν αἴσθησιν ὀλίγου δεῖν ἅπαντες,
ὡς ἐν μόνῳ τῷ αἰσθανομένῳ καὶ γινώσκοντι τῆς
ψυχῆς τιθέμενοι τὸ ζῆν καὶ τὸ εἶναι καὶ τὸ χαίρειν.
B ἔστι γὰρ καὶ τοῖς ἀνιῶσι τὸ μεθ' ἡδονῆς τινος
ἀκούεσθαι· καὶ ταραττόμενοι πολλάκις ὑπὸ τῶν
λεγομένων καὶ κλαίοντες ὅμως λέγειν κελεύομεν,[3]
ὥσπερ οὗτος·

—οἴμοι πρὸς αὐτῷ γ' εἰμὶ τῷ δεινῷ λέγειν.
—κἄγωγ'[4] ἀκούειν· ἀλλ' ὅμως[5] ἀκουστέον.

ἀλλὰ τοῦτο μὲν ἔοικε τῆς περὶ τὸ πάντα γινώσκειν
ἡδονῆς ἀκρασία τις εἶναι καὶ ῥύσις ἐκβιαζομένη
τὸν λογισμόν. ὅταν δὲ μηδὲν ἔχουσα βλαβερὸν ἢ
λυπηρὸν[6] ἱστορία καὶ διήγησις ἐπὶ πράξεσι καλαῖς
καὶ μεγάλαις προσλάβῃ λόγον ἔχοντα δύναμιν καὶ
χάριν, ὡς τὸν[7] Ἡροδότου τὰ Ἑλληνικὰ καὶ τὰ[8]

---

[1] ὡς g c : εἰς a.
[2] ἦ g c β[2] : ἦ a.
[3] κελεύομεν g c : κελεύοντες a.
[4] κἄγωγ' a : καὶ ὥστε g c.
[5] ἀλλ' ὅμως a : ἄλλοτε g c.
[6] βλαβερὸν ἢ λυπηρὸν g c : λυπηρὸν ἢ βλαβερὸν a.
[7] τὸν a : τῶν g c.   [8] τὰ g c : a omits.

grace of truth.[a] (10.) Thus reflect how keenly we are stirred as we read Plato's tale of Atlantis [b] and the last part of the *Iliad* ; we regret as much to miss the rest of the story as if it were some temple or theatre for which the hour of closing had come. But to learn the truth itself is a thing as dear to us and desirable as to live and be, because it brings us knowledge, and the most dismal part of death is oblivion and ignorance and darkness. Indeed it is for this that well nigh the whole of mankind are opposed to those who deny all awareness to the dead, showing in this that they take living and being and the feeling of delight to be found only in the part of the soul that is aware and knows.[c] For even those who bring us painful news are nevertheless listened to with a certain pleasure,[d] and although it often happens that we are disturbed by what is said and weep, we nevertheless bid them speak on, as in the play [e] :

—Ah ! Now I come to what I dread to utter.
—And I to hear ; yet hear the thing I must.

Here, however, it appears that somehow the delight we take in knowing the whole story gets out of hand and a strong current of passion overpowers our reason. But when the story and the telling involves no harm or pain, and to its theme of splendid and great actions it adds the power and charm of eloquence, as when Greek history is told by Herodotus

[a] *Cf.* Pindar, *Olympian Odes*, i. 1. 30 f.
[b] The *Critias*.
[c] *Cf.* Aristotle, *Protrepticus*, Frag. 7, p. 37 (ed. Ross) and *Eudemian Ethics*, vii. 12 (1245 a 9-10).
[d] *Cf.* Plato, *Philebus*, 48 A 5-6 and Aristotle, *Poetics*, 4 (1448 b 10-19).
[e] Sophocles, *Oedipus the King*, 1169-1170 ; quoted also in *Mor.* 522 c.

(1093) Περσικὰ τὸν[1] Ξενοφῶντος,

ὅσσα[2] τε[3] Ὅμηρος ἐθέσπισε θέσκελα εἰδώς

C ἢ ἃς[4] Περιόδους[5] Εὔδοξος ἢ Κτίσεις[6] καὶ Πολιτείας
Ἀριστοτέλης ἤ[7] Βίους ἀνδρῶν Ἀριστόξενος ἔ-
γραψεν, οὐ μόνον μέγα καὶ πολὺ τὸ εὐφραῖνον ἀλλὰ
καὶ καθαρὸν καὶ ἀμεταμέλητόν ἐστι. τίς δ᾽ ἂν
φάγοι πεινῶν καὶ πίοι[8] διψῶν τὰ[9] Φαιάκων ἥδιον
ἢ[10] διέλθοι τὸν Ὀδυσσέως ἀπόλογον τῆς πλάνης;
τίς δ᾽ ἂν ἡσθείη συναναπαυσάμενος τῇ καλλίστῃ
γυναικὶ μᾶλλον ἢ προσαγρυπνήσας οἷς γέγραφε
περὶ Πανθείας[11] Ξενοφῶν ἢ περὶ Τιμοκλείας Ἀριστόβουλος ἢ Θήβης[12] Θεόπομπος;[13]

11. " Ἀλλὰ ταύτας τῆς ψυχῆς ἐξωθοῦσιν,[14] ἐξω-
D θοῦσι δὲ καὶ τὰς ἀπὸ τῶν μαθημάτων.[15] καίτοι
ταῖς μὲν ἱστορίαις ἁπλοῦν τι καὶ λεῖόν ἐστιν· αἱ δέ[16]
ἀπὸ γεωμετρίας καὶ ἀστρολογίας καὶ ἁρμονικῆς
δριμὺ καὶ ποικίλον ἔχουσαι τὸ[17] δέλεαρ οὐθὲν τῶν

[1] τὸν a : τῶν g c.
[2] ὅσσα Dübner : ὅσα a g c.
[3] τε g (τὲ c) : δὲ a.
[4] ἃς Pohlenz : τῆς a ; τὰς g c β².
[5] περιόδους g c β² : πε a.
[6] κτίσεις a : κτήσεις g c.
[7] ἤ a : g c omit.
[8] πίοι a : πίη g c.
[9] τὰ a : τῶν g c.
[10] ἢ a : εἰ g ; ἢ εἰ c.
[11] πανθείας a : πανθίας g c.
[12] θήβης g c : θήσβης aA¹ ; θίσβης A²E.
[13] θεόπομπος g c : θεόπεμπτος a.
[14] ταύτας τῆς ψυχῆς ἐξωθοῦσιν nos (ταύτας τε τῆς ψυχῆς ἐξω-
θοῦσι τὰς ἡδονὰς Bern. ; ταύτας μὲν τὰς ἡδονὰς ἐξωθοῦσιν οὗτοι
τῆς ψυχῆς Westman) : ταῦτα τῆς ψυχῆς a g c.
[15] μαθημάτων a c : παθημάτων g.
[16] δὲ a g : γὰρ c.
[17] τὸ β² : καὶ a g c.

and Persian by Xenophon,[a] or as with

> The wondrous word inspired Homer sang [b]

or Eudoxus' *Description of the World*,[c] Aristotle's *Foundations* and *Constitutions of Cities*,[d] or Aristoxenus' *Lives*,[e] the joy it gives is not only great and abundant, but untainted as well and attended with no regret. Who would take greater pleasure in stilling his hunger or quenching his thirst with Phaeacian good cheer [f] than in following Odysseus' tale of his wanderings ? [g] Who would find greater pleasure in going to bed with the most beautiful of women than in sitting up with Xenophon's story of Pantheia,[h] Aristobulus' of Timocleia,[i] or Theopompus' of Thebê ? [j]

11. " But all these pleasures they banish from the mind, and they also banish those that come from mathematics.[k] Yet the attraction in the histories is of a uniform and equable nature ; whereas the pleasures of geometry and astronomy and harmonics have a pungent and multifarious enticement that gives

---

[a] In the *Education of Cyrus*.

[b] Unidentified ; Schneider cites it as no. 385 of the *Fragmenta Anonyma* in his *Callimachea*.

[c] *Cf. Mor.* 353 c.

[d] Aristotle is said to have written 158 such constitutions. Of these one has been largely recovered, the *Constitution of Athens* ; the fragments of the rest are printed in Rose, pp. 303-367 (Frags. 472-603). These *Constitutions* contained accounts of historical developments and would naturally include the foundations.　　[e] Frag. 10a (ed. Wehrli).

[f] *Cf.* Homer, *Od.* ix. 5-11.　　[g] Homer, *Od.* ix-xii.

[h] *Education of Cyrus*, iv. 6. 11, v. 1. 2-18, vi. 1. 31-51, 4. 2-11, vii. 3. 3-16.

[i] Jacoby, *Frag. Gr. Hist.* 139 f 2 ; *cf. Mor.* 259 d, *Life of Alexander*, chap. xii (670 e—671 b).

[j] Jacoby, *Frag. Gr. Hist.* 115 f 337 ; *cf. Mor.* 194 d, 256 a, and *Life of Pelopidas*, chaps. xxviii (293 a–c) and xxxv (297 d—298 a).　　[k] *Cf.* Frag. 229[a] (ed. Usener).

61

(1093) ἀγωγίμων¹ ἀποδέουσιν, ἕλκουσαι καθάπερ ἴυγξι
τοῖς διαγράμμασιν· ὧν ὁ γευσάμενος, ἄνπερ ἔμπειρος ᾖ, τὰ Σοφοκλέους περίεισιν² ᾄδων

> μουσομανεῖ δὲ λάφθην³ δακέτῳ⁴ ποτὶ δειράν.⁵
> ἔχομαι δ' ἔκ τε⁶ λύρας ἔκ τε νόμων
> οὓς Θαμύρας⁷ περίαλλα⁸ μουσοποιεῖ

καὶ νὴ Δία Εὔδοξος καὶ Ἀρίσταρχος καὶ Ἀρχιμή-
δης. ὅπου γὰρ οἱ φιλογραφοῦντες οὕτως ἄγονται
E τῇ πιθανότητι τῶν ἔργων ὥστε Νικίαν⁹ γράφοντα
τὴν Νέκυιαν¹⁰ ἐρωτᾶν πολλάκις τοὺς οἰκέτας εἰ
ἠρίστηκεν,¹¹ Πτολεμαίου¹² δὲ τοῦ βασιλέως ἑξή-
κοντα τάλαντα τῆς γραφῆς συντελεσθείσης¹³ πέμ-
ψαντος αὐτῷ μὴ λαβεῖν μηδὲ ἀποδόσθαι¹⁴ τὸ ἔργον,
τίνας οἰόμεθα καὶ πηλίκας ἡδονὰς ἀπὸ γεωμετρίας
δρέπεσθαι καὶ ἀστρολογίας Εὐκλείδην γράφοντα τὰ
διοπτικά¹⁵ καὶ Φίλιππον¹⁶ ἀποδεικνύντα περὶ τοῦ

---

¹ τῶν ἀγωγίμων Reiske : ἀγώγιμον a g c.
² With περίεισιν X resumes.
³ δὲ λάφθην X ; δε (δὲ c) λαφθήν g c ; δ' ἐλάμφθην a.
⁴ δακέτῳ Brunck : δαν καὶ το (τὸ for το X) X g c ; δ' ἂν καὶ
τῷ (τῶ from τὸ) aᶜ.
⁵ ποτὶ δειρὰν A²E : ποτιδειραν X ; ποτιδειρὰν aA¹ : ποτί-
δειραν g c.
⁶ ἔχομαι (so Blaydes ; εὔχομαι X g ; ἔρχομαι a) δ' ἔκ τε
Xa g : c omits in a blank of 20 letters.
⁷ οὓς Θαμύρας Porson : οὐ θαμοίρας (or οὐθαμοίρας) X g c :
οὐ θαμύρας a.
⁸ περίαλλα X c : περίαλα g ; περὶ ἄλλα a.
⁹ νικίαν a g c : νεικίαν X.
¹⁰ Νέκυιαν Bern. : νεκυίαν Xa ; νεηνίαν g c.
¹¹ ἠρίστηκε (ἠρίστηκεν X)a : ἠρίστησε g ; ἠρίστευσε c.

them all the potency of a love-charm as they draw
us with the strong compulsion of their theorems. But
taste of that potion, if you are an adept, and you will
go about singing the lines of Sophocles [a] :

> A thing of wildest music at my throat :
> The lyre has rapt me to an ecstasy
> With glorious harmonies of Thamyras

and of Eudoxus, I will add, and Aristarchus and Archimedes. For if men who love to paint are so taken
with the seductiveness of a canvas that when Nicias [b]
was painting the Visit to the Dead [c] he frequently
asked the servants whether he had breakfasted, and
when the picture was ready and King Ptolemy [d] sent
him sixty talents, refused the sum and would not sell
the work, how exquisite and great must we suppose
the pleasures were that Euclid reaped from geometry
and astronomy when he wrote the treatise involving
the dioptra,[e] Philip when he demonstrated the shape

---

[a] Nauck, *Trag. Graec. Frag.*, Sophocles, No. 224 ; Frag.
245 (ed. Pearson).
[b] An Athenian painter of the end of the fourth century,
mentioned in *Mor.* 346 A. The anecdote is also told in *Mor.*
786 B and by Aelian (*Varia Historia*, iii. 31).
[c] Homer, *Od.* xi.
[d] Ptolemy I became satrap of Egypt in 323 and assumed
the style of king in 305. Nicias gave the painting to the
Athenians : Pliny, *N.H.* xxxv. 132.
[e] Presumably the *Phaenomena*, where the dioptra is used
in proving the first theorem. Proclus (*In Primum Euclidis
Elementorum Librum* [ed. Friedlein, Leipzig, 1873], p. 42.
4-6) lists *dioptikē* (so the MS.) as a part of astronomy.

---

[12] πτολεμαίου Xa g : a blank of 4 letters and μετά c.
[13] συντ. a g c : συντ. ἦ X.
[14] μηδὲ ἀποδόσθαι a : μη δόσθαι X ; μηδὲ δόσθαι g c.
[15] διοπτικὰ Xa g c : διοπτρικὰ Xylander.
[16] φίλιππον Xa g : τὸν φίλιππον c.

(1093) σχήματος τῆς σελήνης[1] καὶ Ἀρχιμήδην ἀνευρόντα
τῇ γωνίᾳ τὴν διάμετρον τοῦ ἡλίου τηλικοῦτον[2] τοῦ
μεγίστου κύκλου μέρος[3] οὖσαν ἡλίκον ἡ γωνία τῶν[4]
τεσσάρων ὀρθῶν, καὶ Ἀπολλώνιον καὶ Ἀρίσταρχον
F ἑτέρων[5] τοιούτων εὑρετὰς γενομένους, ὧν νῦν ἡ
θέα καὶ κατανόησις ἡδονάς τε μεγάλας καὶ φρόνημα θαυμάσιον ἐμποιεῖ τοῖς μανθάνουσιν; καὶ
οὐκ ἄξιον οὐδαμῇ τὰς ἐκ τῶν

ὀπτανίων[6] καὶ ματρυλείων[7] ἡδονὰς

1094 ἐκείνας παραβάλλοντα[8] ταύταις καταισχύνειν τὸν
Ἑλικῶνα καὶ τὰς Μούσας

ἔνθ' οὔτε ποιμὴν ἀξιοῖ φέρβειν βοτὰ
οὐδ'[9] ἦλθέ πω σίδαρος[10]·

ἀλλ' αὗται μέν εἰσιν ὡς ἀληθῶς ἀκήρατοι νομαὶ τῶν
μελιττῶν,[11] ἐκεῖνα[12] δὲ συῶν καὶ τράγων κνησμοῖς
ἔοικεν, προσαναπιμπλάντα[13] τῆς ψυχῆς τὸ παθητι-
κώτατον. ἔστι μὲν οὖν ποικίλον καὶ ἰταμὸν τὸ φιλ-

---

[1] τοῦ σχήματος τῆς σελήνης Xa g : σχήματος c.
[2] τηλικοῦτον X g c : τηλικοῦτο a.
[3] μέρος X g c : μέρους a.
[4] τῶν X[3]a[2] g c : τὸ X[1]a[1] (or τῷ ?).
[5] ἑτέρων Xa c : καὶ ἑτέρων g.
[6] ὀπτανίων r : ὁ(ὁ- X[1])πτανείων Xa g c.
[7] ματρυλείων Dübner : ματρυλλίων Xa[2] (μαντ- a[1]) g c.
[8] παραβάλλοντα Xa : παραβάλλοντας g c.
[9] οὐδ' Xa g c and Euripides : οὔτ' Orion.
[10] σίδαρος X g c : σίδηρος a and some mss. of Euripides.
[11] τῶν μελιττῶν Xa : μελισσῶν g c.
[12] ἐκεῖνα Xa : ἐκεῖνο g c.
[13] προσαναπιμπλάντα X[r] (-ανα- X[ar])a c : -πιπ- g.

---

[a] K. von Fritz (s.v. " Philippos " 42 in Pauly-Wissowa,
vol. xix. 2 [1938], cols. 2355. 52-2356. 28) credits Philip of

of the moon,[a] and Archimedes when he discovered by his quadrant that the diameter of the sun bears the same proportion to a celestial great circle as the angle intercepted by it on the quadrant bears to four right angles,[b] and Apollonius and Aristarchus when they made similar discoveries, the contemplation and understanding of which today fills students with the greatest of pleasures and a wonderful sense of mastery? And in no way may we compare those others,

The pleasures of the kitchen and the stews,[c]

with these and thus dishonour Helicon and the Muses—

No shepherd there makes bold to graze his flock; Nor ever came the cutting edge of iron.[d]

No; while these pleasures are in very truth the ' inviolate ' haunt of ' bees,'[e] the others resemble the rubbings and scrapings of swine and he-goats,[f] and add further contagion to the most easily disordered part of the soul. Our love of pleasure, to be

Opus with the proof that the moon is spherical, as the shape of the dark and illuminated parts from phase to phase can only be accounted for on that assumption.

[b] Cf. *Life of Marcellus*, chap. xix. 11 (309 A). J. L. Heiberg (*Quaestiones Archimedeae* [Copenhagen, 1879], p. 34) compares *Arenarius*, 10-11.

[c] From Menander, according to Wilamowitz (Menander, *Das Schiedsgericht (Epitrepontes)* [Berlin, 1925], p. 92).

[d] Euripides, *Hippolytus*, 75-76.

[e] Euripides, *Hippolytus*, 76-77. The bee is a cleanly creature (Aristotle, *Hist. Animal.* ix. 40 [626 a 24-25]) and was even believed to attack persons who had recently engaged in intercourse (*Mor.* 144 D; cf. also Columella, *On Agriculture*, ix. 14. 3; Aelian, *Hist. Animal.* v. 11; and *Geoponica*, xv. 2. 19).

[f] Cf. Xenophon, *Memorabilia*, i. 2. 30.

(1094) ἥδονον, οὔπω δέ τις ἐρωμένῃ πλησιάσας ὑπὸ χαρᾶς
ἐβουθύτησεν οὐδὲ ηὔξατό τις ἐμπλησθεὶς ὄψων ἢ
πεμμάτων βασιλικῶν εὐθὺς ἀποθανεῖν· Εὔδοξος δὲ[1]
B ηὔχετο παραστὰς τῷ ἡλίῳ καὶ καταμαθὼν τὸ σχῆμα τῶν ἄστρων[2] καὶ τὸ μέγεθος καὶ τὸ εἶδος[3] ὡς
ὁ Φαέθων καταφλεγῆναι, καὶ Πυθαγόρας ἐπὶ τῷ
διαγράμματι βοῦν ἔθυσεν, ὥς φησιν Ἀπολλόδωρος[4]·

ἡνίκα Πυθαγόρης τὸ περικλεὲς εὕρετο γράμμα,
κεῖν'[5] ἐφ' ὅτῳ[6] λαμπρὴν[7] ἤγαγε[8] βουθυσίην—

εἴτε περὶ τῆς ὑποτεινούσης ὡς ἴσον[9] δύναται ταῖς
περιεχούσαις τὴν ὀρθήν, εἴτε πρόβλημα περὶ τοῦ
χωρίου τῆς παραβολῆς. Ἀρχιμήδη[10] δὲ βίᾳ τῶν
διαγραμμάτων ἀποσπῶντες[11] συνήλειφον[12] οἱ θερά-
ποντες· ὁ δὲ ἐπὶ τῆς κοιλίας ἔγραφε τὰ σχήματα
C τῇ στλεγγίδι, καὶ λουόμενος ὥς φασιν ἐκ τῆς ὑπερ-
χύσεως ἐννοήσας τὴν τοῦ στεφάνου μέτρησιν οἷον
ἔκ τινος κατοχῆς ἢ ἐπιπνοίας ἐξήλατο[13] βοῶν ' εὕρηκα '[14] καὶ τοῦτο πολλάκις φθεγγόμενος ἐβάδιζεν.
οὐδενὸς δὲ ἀκηκόαμεν οὔτε[15] γαστριμάργου περι-

---

[1] δὲ (δ' X²) a g c : X¹ omits.
[2] τῶν ἄστρων X g c : τοῦ ἄστρου a.
[3] εἶδος a : ἦθος X g c.
[4] ἀπολλόδωρος X^c (-ωρ- in an erasure) g c : ἀπολλόδοτος a.
[5] κεῖν' g c (and Anth. Pal., Diogenes Laertius) : κεῖνος X²
(from κεῖνος) ; κεῖνο a (κλεινὸς Athenaeus).
[6] ὅτῳ Anth. Pal. and Diogenes Laertius : ᾧ Xa g c (and
Athenaeus).
[7] λαμπρὴν Xa g c : κλεινὴν Athenaeus, Anth. Pal., and
Diogenes Laertius.
[8] ἤγαγε Athenaeus, Anth. Pal., Diogenes Laertius : ἠγά-
γετο X g c ; ἤγετο a.
[9] ὡς ἴσον X²a g c : ω//σων X¹.
[10] ἀρχιμήδη Xa : ἀρχιμήδην g c.
[11] ἀποσπῶντες a g c : κατασπῶντες X.

66

sure, takes many forms and is enterprising enough ; but no one has so far upon having his way with the woman he loves been so overjoyed that he sacrificed an ox, nor has anyone prayed to die on the spot if he could only eat his fill of royal meat or cakes ; whereas Eudoxus prayed to be consumed in flames like Phaëthon if he could but stand next to the sun and ascertain the shape, size, and composition of the planets, and when Pythagoras discovered his theorem he sacrificed an ox in honour of the occasion, as Apollodorus [a] says :

> When for the famous proof Pythagoras
> Offered an ox in splendid sacrifice—

whether it was the theorem that the square on the hypotenuse is equal to the sum of the squares on the sides of the right angle [b] or a problem about the application of a given area.[c] His servants used to drag Archimedes [d] away from his diagrams by force to give him his rubbing down with oil ; and as they rubbed him he used to draw the figures on his belly with the scraper ; and at the bath, as the story goes, when he discovered from the overflow how to measure the crown, as if possessed or inspired, he leapt out shouting ' I have it ' and went off saying this over and over.[e] But of no glutton have we ever heard

---

[a] Cf. Cicero, De Nat. Deor. iii. 36 (88) with Pease's note.
[b] Euclid, Elements, i. 47.
[c] Cf. Mor. 720 A ; Euclid, Elements, i. 44 with Sir T. L. Heath's note.
[d] Cf. Mor. 786 c and Life of Marcellus, chap. xvii (307 E).
[e] Cf. Vitruvius, ix, praef. 10.

---

[12] συνήλειφον a[c] (συνείληφον Xa[ac]): ὑπήλειφον g c.
[13] ἐξήλατο Xa g : ἐξήλλατο c.
[14] εὕρηκα a g c : εὑρηκώς X.   [15] οὔτε a : οὐδὲ X g c.

(1094) παθῶς οὕτω ' βέβρωκα ' βοῶντος οὔτε ἐρωτικοῦ
' πεφίληκα,' μυρίων μυριάκις ἀκολάστων γεγονότων καὶ ὄντων.[1] ἀλλὰ καὶ βδελυττόμεθα τοὺς
μεμνημένους δείπνων[2] ἐμπαθέστερον ὡς ἐφ' ἡδοναῖς
μικραῖς καὶ μηδενὸς ἀξίαις ὑπερασμενίζοντας.
Εὐδόξῳ δὲ καὶ Ἀρχιμήδει[3] καὶ Ἱππάρχῳ συνεν-
θουσιῶμεν, καὶ Πλάτωνι πειθόμεθα[4] περὶ τῶν μαθη-
D μάτων ὡς ἀμελούμενα δι' ἄγνοιαν καὶ ἀπειρίαν
' ὅμως βίᾳ ὑπὸ χάριτος αὐξάνεται.'
   12. '' Ταύτας μέντοι τὰς τηλικαύτας καὶ τοσαύτας ἡδονὰς ὥσπερ ἀεννάους[5] ἐκτρέποντες οὗτοι καὶ
ἀποστρέφοντες οὐκ ἐῶσι γενέσθαι[6] τοὺς πλησιά-
σαντας αὐτοῖς, ἀλλὰ τοὺς μὲν ' ἐπαραμένους τὰ
ἀκάτια ' φεύγειν ἀπ' αὐτῶν κελεύουσι,[7] Πυθοκλέους δὲ[8] πάντες καὶ πᾶσαι δέονται δι'[9] Ἐπικούρου καὶ ἀντιβολοῦσιν ὅπως οὐ ζηλώσει[10] τὴν
ἐλευθέριον καλουμένην παιδείαν· Ἀπελλῆν δέ τινα
θαυμάζοντες καὶ ὑπερασπαζόμενοι γράφουσιν ὅτι
τῶν μαθημάτων ἀποσχόμενος ἐξ ἀρχῆς καθαρὸν
ἑαυτὸν ἐτήρησεν. περὶ δὲ τῆς ἱστορίας, ἵνα τὴν
E ἄλλην ἀνηκόαν ἐάσω, παραθήσομαι μόνα τὰ Μητροδώρου γράφοντος ἐν τοῖς περὶ ποιημάτων[11]· ' ὅθεν
μηδὲ εἰδέναι φάσκων μεθ' ὁποτέρων[12] ἦν ὁ Ἕκτωρ,

[1] γεγονότων καὶ ὄντων a g c : γέγονε τῶν καιόντων X.
[2] δείπνων Xa g : δεῖπνον c.
[3] ἀρχιμήδει X[c] g c : ἀρχιμήδη X[a]c a.
[4] πλάτωνι πειθόμεθα Xa c : πλάτωνα πειθώμεθα g.
[5] ἀεννάους X[2] g c : ἀενάους X[c] (from ἀένν before completing
the word)a.
[6] γενέσθαι XAE g c : γενέσθαι a.
[7] κελεύουσι a : καὶ κελεύουσι X(X[2m] has σημείωσαι σφάλμα
οἵμαι) g c.
[8] δὲ a : καὶ X g c.
[9] δι' Xa c : g omits.

68

that he shouted with similar rapture ' I ate it,' and of no gallant that he shouted ' I kissed her,' though sensualists unnumbered have existed in the past and are with us now. We actually have an aversion to people who recall in too lively a fashion the meals they have had, as overenthusiastic about small and trivial pleasures. But we are caught up with the rapture of Eudoxus and Archimedes and Hipparchus and find that what Plato [a] says about mathematics is true, that although it is neglected because men have no knowledge or experience of it, ' it nevertheless forces its way on, so strong is its spell.'

12. " Yet these men divert and alter the course of these pleasures, so great and numerous—that never, as it were, go dry—and cut off their disciples from the taste ; instead they tell some to ' hoist all sail '[b] to escape from them, while Pythocles is urgently implored by all, men and women alike, in the person of Epicurus,[c] not to set his heart on ' the so-called education of free men,' and in admiration and most hearty commendation of one Apelles they[d] write that from childhood he held aloof from mathematics and kept himself unspotted. As for history, not to mention their want of learning in other fields, I shall quote no more than the words of Metrodorus,[e] who writes in his book *On Poems* : ' So when you say that you do not even know on which side Hector fought,[f]

---

[a] *Republic*, vii, 528 c.

[b] Frag. 163 (ed. Usener) ; *cf. Mor.* 15 D and 662 c.

[c] Frag. 164 (ed. Usener).

[d] Frag. 117 (ed. Usener).   [e] Frag. 24 (ed. Körte).

[f] The last line of the *Iliad* (xxiv. 804) mentions Hector.

---

[10] ζηλώσει a(-ῶσι A¹) g : ζηλώσῃ ΧΑ²Ε c.

[11] ποιημάτων Gomperz : ποιητῶν Χα^c (from -ὼν) g c.

[12] μεθ' ὁποτέρων Χ² g c : μεθοποτέρων Χ¹ ; μετὰ ποτέρων a.

(1094) ἢ τοὺς πρώτους στίχους τῆς Ὁμήρου ποιήσεως, ἢ πάλιν τὰ ἐν μέσῳ, μὴ ταρβήσῃς.'[1]

" "Ὅτι τοίνυν αἱ τοῦ σώματος ἡδοναὶ καθάπερ οἱ ἐτησίαι μαραίνονται μετὰ τὴν ἀκμὴν καὶ ἀπολήγουσιν οὐ λέληθε τὸν Ἐπίκουρον· διαπορεῖ γοῦν εἰ γέρων ὁ σοφὸς ὢν καὶ μὴ δυνάμενος πλησιάζειν ἔτι ταῖς τῶν καλῶν ἀφαῖς χαίρει καὶ ψηλαφήσεσιν, οὐ τὰ αὐτὰ μὲν τῷ[2] Σοφοκλεῖ διανοούμενος ἀσμένως ἐκφυγόντι τὴν ἡδονὴν ταύτην ὥσπερ ἄγριον καὶ F λυττῶντα δεσπότην. ἀλλ' ἔδει γε τοὺς ἀπολαυστικοὺς ὁρῶντας ὅτι πολλὰς ἀφαυαίνει[3] τῶν ἡδονῶν τὸ γῆρας

ἥ τε Ἀφροδίτη τοῖς γέρουσιν ἄχθεται

1095 κατ' Εὐριπίδην ταύτας μάλιστα συνάγειν τὰς ἡδονάς, ὥσπερ εἰς πολιορκίαν ἄσηπτα σιτία καὶ ἄφθαρτα παρατιθεμένους,[4] εἶτα ἄγειν ἀφροδίσια τοῦ βίου καὶ μεθεόρτους καλὰς ἐν ἱστορίαις καὶ ποιήμασιν διατρίβοντας[5] ἢ προβλήμασι μουσικοῖς καὶ γεωμετρικοῖς.[6] οὐ γὰρ ἂν ἐπῆλθεν αὐτοῖς εἰς νοῦν βαλέσθαι τὰς τυφλὰς καὶ νωδὰς ἐκείνας ψηλαφήσεις καὶ ἐπιπηδήσεις τοῦ ἀκολάστου μεμαθηκόσιν εἰ μηδὲν ἄλλο γράφειν περὶ Ὁμήρου καὶ περὶ Εὐριπίδου, ὡς Ἀριστοτέλης καὶ Ἡρακλείδης καὶ Δικαίαρχος. ἀλλ' οἶμαι τοιούτων ἐφοδίων μὴ

---

[1] ταρβήσῃς Χ[2]a g c : παραβήσῃς Χ[1].
[2] μὲν τῷ Χa g c : μέντοι Pohlenz (μέντοι τῷ Bern.).
[3] ἀφαυαίνει Χa[c] (from -ειν) : ἀφα and a blank of 4-7 letters and νει g c.
[4] παρατιθεμένους ΧΕ g c : περι- aΑ.
[5] διατρίβοντας a g c : -ὸς Χ.
[6] γεωμετρικοῖς Χ[c]a g c : -ῆς Χa[c] ?

70

or the opening lines of Homer's poem, or again what comes between, do not be dismayed.'

" Now it has not escaped Epicurus [a] that bodily pleasures, like the etesian winds, after reaching their full force, slacken and fail ; thus he raises the problem whether the sage when old and impotent still delights in touching and fingering the fair. In this he is not of the same mind as Sophocles, who was glad to have got beyond reach of this pleasure as of a savage and furious master.[b] What men who like the sensual life should do instead, since they see that old age makes many pleasures wither away

And Aphroditê frowns upon the old

(to quote Euripides [c]) is to gather up these other pleasures most of all, as if laying in for a siege a stock of victuals that will not go bad or perish, and then, when the business of their life is done, to celebrate the holiday [d]—followed by good mornings after—by passing the hours with history and poetry or questions of music and geometry. For then that blind and toothless fingering and leaping of lustful appetite of which Epicurus [e] speaks would never have entered their heads, if they had learned enough (if nothing else) to write about Homer and Euripides, as Aristotle,[f] Heracleides [g] and Dicaearchus [h] did. But since they were never concerned (I take it) to make

[a] Frag. 21 (ed. Usener).
[b] Cf. Plato, Republic, i, 329 c and Mor. 525 A with the note.
[c] From the Aeolus of Euripides : Nauck, Trag. Graec. Frag., Eur. 23 ; quoted also in Mor. 285 B and 786 A.
[d] See p. 89, note c.
[e] Cf. Usener, Epicurea, p. 343 (addendum to Frag. 21).
[f] Aristotle wrote on Problems in Homer : Frags. 142-179 (ed. Rose).
[g] Frag. 168 (ed. Wehrli).   [h] Frag. 73 (ed. Wehrli).

(1095)

B φροντίσαντες, τῆς δ᾽ ἄλλης αὐτῶν πραγματείας
ἀτερποῦς καὶ ξηρᾶς ὥσπερ αὐτοὶ τὴν ἀρετὴν λέγουσιν οὔσης, ἥδεσθαι πάντως ἐθέλοντες, τοῦ δὲ
σώματος ἀπαγορεύοντος, αἰσχρὰ καὶ ἄωρα πράττειν ὁμολογοῦσιν, τῶν τε προτέρων ἡδονῶν ἀναμι-
μνήσκοντες ἑαυτοὺς καὶ χρώμενοι ταῖς παλαιαῖς
ἀπορίᾳ προσφάτων ὥσπερ τεταριχευμέναις, καὶ
νεκρὰς[1] ἄλλας[2] πάλιν καὶ τεθνηκυίας οἷον ἐν τέφρᾳ
ψυχρᾷ τῇ σαρκὶ κινοῦντες παρὰ φύσιν καὶ ἀναζω-
πυροῦντες, ἅτε δὴ[3] μηδὲν[4] οἰκεῖον ἡδὺ μηδὲ[5] χαρᾶς
ἄξιον ἔχοντες ἐν τῇ ψυχῇ παρεσκευασμένον.

13. "Καίτοι τἆλλα μὲν ὡς ἡμῖν[6] ἐπῆλθεν εἴ-
C ρηται· μουσικὴν δὲ ὅσας[7] ἡδονὰς καὶ χάριτας οἵας
φέρουσαν ἀποστρέφονται καὶ φεύγουσιν καὶ[8] βουλόμενος οὐκ ἂν τις ἐκλάθοιτο, δι᾽ ἀτοπίαν ὧν Ἐπίκουρος λέγει, φιλοθέωρον[9] μὲν ἀποφαίνων τὸν σοφὸν ἐν ταῖς Διαπορίαις καὶ χαίροντα παρ᾽ ὁντινοῦν
ἕτερον ἀκροάμασι καὶ θεάμασι Διονυσιακοῖς, προβλήμασι δὲ μουσικοῖς καὶ κριτικῶν[10] φιλολόγοις
ζητήμασιν οὐδὲ παρὰ πότον διδοὺς χώραν, ἀλλὰ
καὶ τοῖς φιλομούσοις τῶν βασιλέων παραινῶν στρατηγικὰ[11] διηγήματα καὶ φορτικὰς βωμολοχίας ὑπο-
μένειν μᾶλλον ἐν τοῖς συμποσίοις ἢ λόγους περὶ
μουσικῶν καὶ ποιητικῶν προβλημάτων περαινομέ-
D νους. ταυτὶ γὰρ ἐτόλμησεν[12] γράφειν ἐν τῷ περὶ

---

[1] νεκρὰς Rasmus : νεκραῖς Xa g c.
[2] ἄλλας Xa : ἄλλας δὲ g c.
[3] δὴ Xa : δὲ g c.
[4] μηδὲν a : μὴ δὲ (μὴ δε X) X g c.
[5] μηδὲ X (μὴ δὲ g c) : μετὰ a.
[6] ὡς (ὡς X) ἡμῖν Xa c : ἡμῖν ὡς g.
[7] δὲ ὅσας a : δείσας X ; δ᾽ εἰς τὰς g c.
[8] καὶ added by Bern.
[9] φιλοθέωρον β² : φιλοθεωρὸν Xa g c.

72

such provision and everything else in their system is as joyless and jejune as they for their part say virtue is,[a] and they want pleasure at all costs, but are physically unequal to it, they confess to shameful acts that do not become their years as they rehearse the memory of past pleasures and for want of fresh ones resort to those that are stale, like pickled meat, and recall to unnatural life and fan to a flame, in the cold ashes as it were of the body, pleasures lifeless and quite dead, since they have no store in their minds of what brings mental pleasure or is worthy of delight.

13. " So far I have mentioned their views just as they happened to occur to me, but no one could forget even if he wished their rejection and avoidance of music with the great pleasures and exquisite delight it brings ; the absurd discrepancy of Epicurus' [b] statements sees to that. On the one hand he says in the *Disputed Questions* that the sage is a lover of spectacles and yields to none in the enjoyment of theatrical recitals [c] and shows ; but on the other he allows no place, even over the wine, for questions about music and the enquiries of critics and scholars and actually advises a cultivated monarch to put up with recitals of stratagems and with vulgar buffooneries at his drinking parties sooner than with the discussion of problems in music and poetry. For such is the actual advice that he [d] presumed to set down in his

 [a] Frag. 505 (p. 358, ed. Usener).
[b] Frag. 20 (ed. Usener).
[c] *Cf.* Diogenes Laert. x. 120.   [d] Frag. 5 (ed. Usener).

---

[10] κριτικῶν a : -ὸν X ; -οῖς g c.
[11] στρατηγικὰ Xa g c (*cf. Mor.* 547 E) : στρατιωτικὰ Meziriacus.   [12] ἐτόλμησε (-εν X) a g : ἐτόλμησαν c.

(1095) βασιλείας, ὥσπερ Σαρδαναπάλῳ[1] γράφων ἢ Ναнάρῳ
τῷ σατραπεύσαντι Βαβυλῶνος. οὐδὲ γὰρ Ἱέρων
γ᾽ ἂν[2] οὐδὲ Ἄτταλος οὐδὲ Ἀρχέλαος[3] ἐπείσθησαν
Εὐριπίδην καὶ Σιμωνίδην καὶ Μελανιππίδην καὶ[4]
Κράτητας καὶ Διοδότους ἀναστήσαντες ἐκ τῶν
συμποσίων κατακλῖναι Κάρδακας[5] καὶ Ἀγριᾶνας
μεθ᾽ αὐτῶν[6] καὶ Καλλίας γελωτοποιοὺς καὶ Θρα-
σωνίδας τινὰς καὶ Θρασυλέοντας, ὀλολυγμοὺς καὶ
κροτοθορύβους ποιοῦντας. εἰ δὲ[7] Πτολεμαῖος ὁ
πρῶτος συναγαγὼν τὸ μουσεῖον τούτοις ἐνέτυχεν[8]
Ε τοῖς καλοῖς καὶ βασιλικοῖς παραγγέλμασιν ἆρα οὐκ
ἂν εἶπεν[9]

τοῖς Σαμίοις, ὦ Μοῦσα, τίς ὁ φθόνος;

Ἀθηναίων γὰρ οὐδενὶ πρέπει ταῖς Μούσαις οὕτως

[1] σαρδαναπάλῳ X a¹A¹E g c : -λλῳ a²A².
[2] γ᾽ ἂν Xa : γοῦν g c.
[3] ἀρχέλαος a : ἀρχέλων X g c.
[4] καὶ Xa : g c omit.
[5] κάρδακας a : κόρδακας X g c.
[6] αὐτῶν (αὐ- X) Xa : ἑαυτῶν g c.
[7] εἰ δὲ Xa c : εἶδε g.
[8] ἐνέτυχε Cobet : συνετυχεν X ; συνέτυχε a g c.
[9] εἶπεν] Madvig punctuates here ; X has no punctuation ;
a g c punctuate after σαμίοις.

[a] Cf. Jacoby, Frag. d. gr. Hist., 688 F 1, pp. 442. 19–448.
14.
[b] Cf. Jacoby, Frag. d. gr. Hist., 688 F 6, pp. 450. 31–451.
4 and 90 F 4, pp. 331. 20–335. 24.
[c] Hieron, host of Simonides, was an usurper (cf. Mor.
551 F) ; so too Archelaüs, host of Euripides. Attalus II, who
may be meant here, was cruel and suspicious (cf. Justin,
xxxvi. 4. 1-3). Diodotus is unknown ; he was presumably a
74

A PLEASANT LIFE IMPOSSIBLE, 1095

book *On Kingship*, as if he were writing to Sardanapalus [a] or Nanarus [b] the satrap of Babylon. For he
could not have persuaded even such kings as Hieron
or Attalus or Archelaüs [c] to dismiss Euripides, Simonides, or Melanippides, or yet a Crates or Diodotus, from their convivial bouts and seat as their guests
instead a set of mercenary bandits [d] or Agrianes,[e] a
buffoon like Callias,[f] or the likes of Thrasonides [g] or
Thrasyleon,[h] persons apt to break out in ' wild jubila-
tions ' and ' uproarious applause.' [i] If Ptolemy, who
founded the Museum,[j] had read these high-minded
and royal recommendations, would he not have said

Oh Muse, why do the Samians [k] wish thee ill? [l]

For it ill becomes any Athenian to quarrel with the

grammarian. Melanippides, the dithyrambic poet, died at
the court of Perdiccas, predecessor of Archelaüs.
    [d] " *Cardaces* : not a separate tribe, but barbarians serving
for hire ; so Theopompus. In general the Persians called
cardax everyone brave and thievish." So Aelius Dionysius
(ed. Erbse, *s.v.*).
    [e] A Thracian or Macedonian hill tribe who appear in the
armies of Alexander, Antigonus II, Antiochus III, and
Philip III.
    [f] Not identified.
    [g] The braggart soldier in Menander's *Rejected Lover*.
    [h] A foolish soldier who gave the title to another of Men-
ander's plays (Frags. 203-207 ed. Körte-Thierfelder).
    [i] The expressions are Epicurus': *cf.* Frag. 143 (ed.
Usener) and 1117 A, *infra*.
    [j] " Sanctuary of the Muses " ; the name of a group of
scholars and mathematicians assembled by Ptolemy I.
    [k] Epicurus was born on Samos of Athenian parentage.
    [l] Apparently a citation or parody of a verse otherwise
unknown. *Cf.* Zenodotus (*Anth. Pal.* vii. 117. 5) of Zeno of
Citium :

   εἰ δὲ πάτρα Φοίνισσα, τίς ὁ φθόνος;
   " If of Phoenician stock, why take it ill ? "

75

(1095) ἀπεχθάνεσθαι καὶ πολεμεῖν·

ὅσσα[1] δὲ μὴ πεφίληκε Ζεὺς ἀτύζονται[2] βοὰν[3]
Πιερίδων ἀίοντα.[4]

τί λέγεις, ὦ Ἐπίκουρε; κιθαρῳδῶν καὶ αὐλητῶν
ἕωθεν ἀκροασόμενος[5] εἰς τὸ θέατρον βαδίζεις, ἐν δὲ
συμποσίῳ Θεοφράστου περὶ συμφωνιῶν διαλεγομένου καὶ Ἀριστοξένου περὶ[6] μεταβολῶν καὶ Ἀριστοτέλους[7] περὶ Ὁμήρου[8] τὰ ὦτα καταλήψῃ[9] ταῖς
χερσὶ δυσχεραίνων καὶ βδελυττόμενος; εἶτα οὐκ
F ἐμμελέστερον ἀποφαίνουσι τὸν Σκύθην Ἀτέαν,[10] ὃς
Ἰσμηνίου[11] τοῦ αὐλητοῦ[12] ληφθέντος αἰχμαλώτου καὶ
παρὰ πότον αὐλήσαντος ὤμοσεν ἥδιον ἀκούειν τοῦ
ἵππου χρεμετίζοντος; οὐχ ὁμολογοῦσι δὲ τῷ καλῷ
πολεμ ῖν τὸν ἄσπονδον καὶ ἀκήρυκτον πόλεμον εἰ
μὴ καὶ[13] ἡδονὴ[14] πρόσεστι; τί[15] σεμνὸν καὶ καθάριον[16]
1096 ἀσπάζονται καὶ ἀγαπῶσιν; οὐκ ἦν δὲ πρὸς τὸ
ἡδέως ζῆν ἐπιεικέστερον μύρα καὶ θυμιάματα δυσ-
χεραίνειν ὡς κάνθαροι καὶ γῦπες ἢ κριτικῶν καὶ
μουσικῶν λαλιὰν βδελύττεσθαι καὶ φεύγειν; ποῖος

[1] ὅσσα Victorius : ὅσα Xa g c.
[2] ἀτύζονται a g c : ἀτύξονται X.
[3] βοὰν X[1] σ[2] : βοᾶν X[2]a g c.
[4] πιεριδων ἀίοντα μ[2] : περιδονέοντα Xa g c.
[5] ἀκροασόμενος Xa : ἀκροασάμενος g c.
[6] περὶ a : X g c omit.
[7] Ἀριστοτέλους Nauck : ἀριστοφάνης X ; ἀριστοφάνους a g c.
[8] ὁμήρου a g c : ὅμηρον X.
[9] καταλήψῃ a g c : καταλείψῃ X.
[10] ἀτέαν a : ἀττέαν X g c.
[11] Ἰσμηνίου Victorius : ἀμινίου X g c ; ἀμεινίου a.
[12] αὐλητοῦ a : X g c omit.
[13] μὴ καὶ nos (μηδεμία or μὴ Pohlenz) : μὴ δὲ (μη δὲ X) Xa
g c.   [14] ἡδονὴ a : ἡδονὴ X g c.
[15] πρόσεστι, τί a (no punctuation X) : πρόσεστί τι g c.
[16] καθάριον Xa : καθάριον, ἦν g c.

Muses in this fashion and make war on them; rather

> All things unloved of Zeus, what time they hear
> The cry of the Pierians, are dismayed.[a]

What's this, Epicurus? To hear singers to the cithara and performers on the flute you go to the theatre at an early hour, but when at a banquet Theophrastus[b] holds forth on concords, Aristoxenus[c] on modulations, and Aristotle[d] on Homer, you will clap your hands over your ears in annoyance and disgust? Pshaw! Do the Epicureans not make the Scyth Ateas[e] look as if he had more music in his soul—who swore, when the flute-player Hismenias[f] was a prisoner and performed at a banquet, that he found greater pleasure in the whinnying of his horse? Do they[g] not confess that they are waging war without truce or herald on all that is beautiful, so long as it is not agreeable as well? What holy and cleanly thing do they welcome and cherish? If your aim is the pleasant life, would it not have been more reasonable to shrink from perfume and incense, as do dung-beetles and vultures,[h] than to loathe and avoid the talk of students of literature and music? For what

---

[a] Pindar, *Pythian Odes*, i. 13-14; quoted also in *Mor.* 167 c and 746 B.   [b] *Cf.* Frag. 89 (ed. Wimmer).

[c] Frag. 127 (ed. Wehrli).

[d] Frag. 99 (ed. Rose). One would expect a reference to a grammarian contemporary with Epicurus. The mss. give "Aristophanes": but the famous critic was born (257 B.C.?) after Epicurus' death (270).

[e] A king of the Scythians who fell in battle against Philip II of Macedon in 339 B.C., aged over ninety. For the anecdote see also *Mor.* 174 F and 334 B.

[f] Also mentioned in *Mor.* 632 c and the *Life of Demetrius*, chap. i. 6 (889 B).   [g] Frag. 512 (ed. Usener).

[h] *Cf. Mor.* 87 c, 710 E, 1058 A, and Theophrastus, *De Causis Plantarum*, vi. 5. 1.

(1096) γὰρ ἂν αὐλὸς ἢ κιθάρα διηρμοσμένη[1] πρὸς ᾠδὴν ἢ
τίς χορὸς

εὐρύοπα κέλαδον ἀκροσόφων ἀγνύμενον[2] διὰ
στομάτων

φθεγγόμενος οὕτως εὔφρανεν[3] Ἐπίκουρον καὶ Μητρόδωρον ὡς Ἀριστοτέλη καὶ Θεόφραστον καὶ Δικαίαρχον καὶ Ἱερώνυμον[4] οἱ περὶ χορῶν λόγοι καὶ
διδασκαλιῶν[5] καὶ τὰ[6] διαύλων[7] προβλήματα καὶ
ῥυθμῶν καὶ ἁρμονιῶν; οἷον διὰ τί τῶν ἴσων
αὐλῶν ὁ στενότερος ὀξύτερον ὁ δὲ εὐρύτερος[8] βαρύ-
B τερον φθέγγεται· καὶ διὰ τί τῆς σύριγγος ἀνασπω-
μένης πᾶσιν ὀξύνεται τοῖς φθόγγοις, κλινομένης[9] δὲ
πάλιν βαρύνεται,[10] καὶ συναχθεὶς πρὸς τὸν[11] ἕτερον
βαρύτερον,[12] διαχθεὶς[13] δὲ ὀξύτερον ἠχεῖ· καὶ τί δήποτε τῶν θεάτρων ἂν ἄχυρα τῆς ὀρχήστρας κατα-
σκεδάσῃς ὁ ἦχος[14] τυφλοῦται, καὶ χαλκοῦν Ἀλέξανδρον ἐν Πέλλῃ βουλόμενον ποιῆσαι τὸ προσκήνιον
οὐκ εἴασεν ὁ τεχνίτης ὡς διαφθεροῦντα[15] τῶν ὑπο-
κριτῶν τὴν φωνήν· καὶ τί δήποτε τῶν[16] γενῶν διαχεῖ

[1] διηρμοσμένη a g c : διηρμοσμενον X.
[2] ἀγνύμενον X g c : ἀγνυμένων a.
[3] εὔφρανεν X g c : ηὔφρανεν a.
[4] ὡς ἀρ. καὶ θεόφ. καὶ δικαίαρχον καὶ ἱερώνυμον X : ὡς ἀρ. καὶ θεόφ. καὶ ἱερώνυμον καὶ δικαίαρχον a ; καὶ ἱερώνυμον g c.
[5] διδασκαλιῶν X g c : -λίαι a.
[6] τὰ a g c : τ̀ from τ' X[c].
[7] διαύλων nos (in this sense the word is not attested, but cf. μοναύλων) : δι' αὐλῶν Xa g c (αὐλῶν Pohlenz ; ἴδι' αὐλῶν R. G. Bury).
[8] ὀξύτερον ὁ δὲ εὐρύτερος added by Rasmus.
[9] κλινομένης a g c : κλινομένοις X.
[10] βαρύνεται Rasmus : βαρύνει X a g c.
[11] τὸν Xa c : g omits.
[12] βαρύτερον added by Xylander (gravius Ferronus).

flute or cithara attuned to vocal music or what chorus
sending forth

> A rolling thunder from melodious throats [a]

could so have enthralled the mind of Epicurus and
Metrodorus as the minds of Aristotle and Theophrastus and Dicaearchus [b] and Hieronymus [c] were enthralled by discussion of choruses and the production
of plays and by questions about double flutes and
rhythms and harmonies? For example : why of
flutes of equal length does the narrower have the
higher pitch, the wider the lower? And why, when
the *syrinx* [d] is drawn back, are the notes all raised in
pitch, but when it is released again, they are lowered?
And why, when one pipe is brought close to the other,
does it have a lower tone, but a higher when the pipes
are drawn apart? And why, when chaff is spread
over the orchestra of a theatre, is the resonance
muffled,[e] and when Alexander wanted to make the
proscenium at Pella of bronze, did the architect de-
mur, as he would thus have spoiled the effect of the
actors' voices? And why of the genera does the

---

[a] D. L. Page, *Poetae Melici Graeci* (Oxford, 1962), Frag.
1008 (Adesp. 90).
[b] Frag. 74 (ed. Wehrli).
[c] Frag. 26 (ed. Wehrli).
[d] *Cf.* 1138 A, *infra* with the note and Kathleen Schlesinger,
The Greek Aulos (London, 1939), pp. 62-67.
[e] *Cf.* the Aristotelian *Problems*, xi. 25 (901 b 30-35).

---

[13] διαχθεὶς (-εὶς X) Xa g : διδαχθεὶς c.
[14] ὁ ἦχος Pohlenz (ἢ χοῦν, ὁ ἦχος Reiske) : ηο χάος X ; ἢ
χοῦν ὁ λαὸς a ; κοχάος g c.
[15] διαφθεροῦντα X[ar?]a g c : διαφθερ///|τα X[r]. X[3m] has συν,
no doubt a misreading of εὐ in X[3m] (now erased), which was a
supplement of the blank below.
[16] τῶν a : a blank of 2| + 1 letters X, of 5-6 g c.

79

(1096) τὸ χρωματικόν, ἡ δὲ ἁρμονία συνίστησιν.[1] ἤθη δὲ
ποιητῶν καὶ πλάσματα καὶ[2] διαφοραὶ χαρακτήρων
C καὶ λύσεις ἀποριῶν ἐν τῷ πρέποντι καὶ γλαφυρῷ[3]
τὸ οἰκεῖον ἅμα καὶ πιθανὸν ἔχουσαι τὸ τοῦ Ξενοφῶντος ἐκεῖνό μοι δοκοῦσι καὶ τὸν ἐρῶντα[4] ποιεῖν[5]
ἐπιλανθάνεσθαι· τοσοῦτον ἡδονῇ[6] κρατοῦσιν.[7]

14. " Ἧς οὐ μέτεστι τούτοις οὐδὲ[8] φασὶν[9] οὐδὲ
βούλονται μετεῖναι· κατατείναντες δὲ[10] τὸ θεωρη-
τικὸν εἰς τὸ σῶμα καὶ κατασπάσαντες ὥσπερ μολιβδίσι[11] ταῖς τῆς σαρκὸς ἐπιθυμίαις οὐδὲν ἀπολείπουσιν ἱπποκόμων ἢ ποιμένων χόρτον ἢ καλάμην[12]
ἢ τινα πόαν προβαλλόντων,[13] ὡς ταῦτα βόσκεσθαι
καὶ τρώγειν προσῆκον αὐτῶν τοῖς θρέμμασιν. ἢ[14]
γὰρ οὐχ[15] οὕτως ἀξιοῦσι τὴν ψυχὴν ταῖς τοῦ σώματος
D ἡδοναῖς κατασυβωτεῖν, ὅσον ἐλπίσαι τι[16] περὶ σαρκὸς
ἢ παθεῖν ἢ μνημονεῦσαι χαίρουσαν, οἰκεῖον δὲ μηδὲν[17] ἡδὺ μηδὲ τερπνὸν ἐξ αὑτῆς[18] λαμβάνειν μηδὲ
ζητεῖν ἐῶντες; καίτοι τί γένοιτ᾽ ἂν ἀλογώτερον
ἢ[19] δυοῖν ὄντοιν ἐξ ὧν ὁ ἄνθρωπος πέφυκε, σώματος
καὶ ψυχῆς, ψυχῆς δὲ τάξιν ἡγεμονικωτέραν ἐχού-
σης, σώματος μὲν ἴδιόν τι καὶ κατὰ φύσιν καὶ

---

[1] συνίστησιν Xa g : συνίσταται c.
[2] πλάσματα καὶ Xa c : πλασμάτων g.
[3] γλαφυρῷ a : γλαφυρῶν X g c.
[4] ἐρῶντα Reiske : ἔρωτα Xa g c.
[5] ποιεῖν a g : πιεῖν X c.
[6] ἡδονῇ X g β² : ἡδονῆς a c.
[7] κρατοῦσιν X g c β² : κρατούσης a.
[8] οὐδὲ (οὐδὲ X)Xa c : ὡς δὲ g.
[9] φασὶν Xa : φησὶν g ; c omits in a blank of 5 letters.
[10] δὲ Xa c : g omits.
[11] μολιβδίσι aᶜ (ιβ from βι ?) g c : μολυβδίσῃ X.
[12] καλάμην AE : καλάμους X(no accent)a g c.
[13] προβαλλόντων a : προβαλόντων X g c.
[14] ἢ a (ἢ X) : ἦ g c.

chromatic relax the hearer, the enharmonic make
him tense ? As for the rendering of character in the
poets and their qualities and different levels of style,
and the discovery of solutions as specific and convin-
cing as they are apt and neat to various knotty questions, why I think that in Xenophon's [a] words they
even make the lover forget his passion, so entrancing
is the pleasure they bring.

14. " It is a pleasure in which these people have
no part and they do not claim or want any part in it
either. Instead they lay the contemplative part of
the soul flat in the body and use the appetites of the
flesh as leaden weights [b] to hold it down. In this
they [c] are no better than stable hands or shepherds,
who serve their charges with hay or straw or grass of
one kind or the other as the proper food for them to
crop and chew.[d] Do they not in similar fashion play
swineherd to the soul, feeding it only on this swill [e] of
the bodily pleasures, permitting it to delight only in
the hope or experience or recollection of some carnal
thing, and forbidding it to take or seek from itself
any pleasure or gratification of its own ? Yet what
could be more unaccountable than this : that when
there are two components of man's nature, body and
soul, the soul having the greater authority, the body
should have a good peculiar, natural, and appropriate

---

[a] *Cynegetica*, v. 33.   [b] *Cf.* Plato, *Republic*, vii, 519 B.
[c] Frag. 429 (ed. Usener).
[d] *Cf.* 1117 F, *infra*.
[e] *Cf.* Homer, *Od.* x. 241-243.

---

15 With οὐχ' X[s] begins ; we do not record its readings.
16 ἐλπίσαί τι a : ἐλπὶς ἔτι g c.
17 μηδὲν a : μὴ δὲ g c.
18 αὐτῆς Victorius : αὐτοῦ (αυ- a) g c.
19 ἢ g c : ἢ εἰ aAE.

PLUTARCH'S MORALIA

(1096) οἰκεῖον ἀγαθὸν εἶναι, ψυχῆς δὲ μηθέν,[1] ἀλλὰ τῷ[2] σώματι καθῆσθαι προσβλέπουσαν[3] αὐτὴν καὶ τοῖς μὲν[4] τοῦ σώματος πάθεσιν ἐπιμειδιῶσαν καὶ συνηδομένην καὶ συγχαίρουσαν, αὐτὴν δ' ἀκίνητον ἐξ ἀρχῆς καὶ ἀπαθῆ καὶ μηδὲν αἱρετὸν ἔχουσαν μηδὲ

E ὀρεκτὸν ὅλως μηδὲ χαρτόν; ἢ γὰρ ἁπλῶς ἀποκαλυψαμένους ἔδει σαρκοποιεῖν[5] τὸν ἄνθρωπον ὅλον, ὥσπερ ἔνιοι ποιοῦσι τὴν τῆς ψυχῆς[6] οὐσίαν ἀναιροῦντες, ἢ δύο φύσεις ἐν ἡμῖν διαφόρους ἀπολιπόντας ἴδιον ἀπολιπεῖν ἑκατέρας καὶ ἀγαθὸν καὶ κακὸν καὶ οἰκεῖον καὶ ἀλλότριον· ὥσπερ ἀμέλει καὶ τῶν αἰσθήσεων ἑκάστη[7] πρὸς ἴδιόν τι πέφυκεν αἰσθητόν, εἰ[8] καὶ πάνυ συμπαθοῦσιν[9] ἀλλήλαις. ἔστι δὲ τῆς ψυχῆς ἴδιον αἰσθητήριον ὁ νοῦς, ᾧ[10] μηθὲν οἰκεῖον ὑποκεῖσθαι, μὴ θέαμα μὴ κίνημα μὴ πάθος συγγενὲς οὗ τυγχάνουσα χαίρειν πέφυκε, πάντων ἀλογώτατόν ἐστιν· εἰ μή τι νὴ Δία λελήθασιν ἔνιοι συκοφαντοῦντες[11] τοὺς ἄνδρας.''

F 15. Κἀγὼ πρὸς αὐτόν, " οὐχ ἡμῖν γε κριταῖς,'' ἔφην, " ἀλλὰ πάσης ἀφεῖσαι τῆς ἐπηρείας, ὥστε θαρρῶν τὰ λοιπὰ τοῦ λόγου πέραινε.'' " πῶς ; "

[1] μηθέν a c : μηδέν g.
[2] τῷ a c : g omits.
[3] προσβλέπουσαν a[2] g c : προβλέπουσαν a[1].
[4] μὲν g c : a omits.
[5] σαρκοποιεῖν a g : σαρκοπό with a blank of 2 letters c.
[6] τῆς (τῆς from ψ g[c]) ψυχῆς g c : ψυχικὴν a[o] (probably from ψυχὴν).
[7] καὶ τῶν αἰσθήσεων ἑκάστη a : ἑκάστη τῶν αἰσθήσεων g c.
[8] εἰ g c : a omits.
[9] συμπαθοῦσιν β[2] : ἐμπαθοῦσιν a g c.
[10] ᾧ a g : ὧν c.
[11] λελήθασιν ἔνιοι συκοφαντοῦντες a : λέληθας συνεπισυκοφαντῶν g c (λέληθα συνεπισυκοφαντῶν Bern.).

to itself, the soul none; that the soul instead should sit idly by, looking to the body and greeting with smiles[a] the body's experiences and joining in its pleasure and delight, but should never itself initiate a movement or response nor possess an object of choice or of desire or delight at all? They should either have thrown all concealment aside and made man in his entirety a mere thing of flesh, as some[b] do who abolish the substantial character of the soul, or else, leaving in us two different natures, they should also have left to each its good and evil, what is its own and what is alien to it. This, for example, is the case with the senses: each is so constituted as to be directed toward a sense-object peculiar to it,[c] even though they respond together. Now the peculiar sense-organ of the soul is the mind; and that the mind should have no object of its own, no spectacle or movement or experience of a kindred nature at the attainment of which the soul is constituted to feel delight, is the very height of unreason—that is, if this is not an unfair charge that some persons,[d] unaware of its falsity, bring against these men."

15. " Not if you make me the judge," I answered. " You are declared not guilty of any kind of slander; therefore proceed with the rest of the argument undeterred." " How so?" he said; " is not Aristo-

[a] Frag. 410, note (ed. Usener); cf. also Mor. 672 D, and 1087 F and 1092 D, supra.

[b] As those who describe the soul as the harmony (Simmias, Dicaearchus) or mixture (Heracleides) of the body. Cf. 1112 E, 1119 A, infra, and De Libid. et Aegrit., chap. v.

[c] Cf. Lucretius, iv. 489-495; Aristotle, De Anima, iii. 1 (425 a 19 f.).

[d] Perhaps this is an answer to some objection raised against the Reply to Colotes (cf. 1086 E, supra) and " some persons " refers to Plutarch himself (cf. 1118 D-E, infra).

(1096) εἶπεν· " οὐ γὰρ Ἀριστόδημος ἡμᾶς,[1] εἰ σὺ παντάπα-
1097 σιν ἀπηγόρευκας, διαδέξεται ; " " πάνυ μὲν οὖν,"
εἶπεν ὁ Ἀριστόδημος, " ὅταν ἀποκάμῃς ὥσπερ οὗ-
τος· ἔτι δὲ ἀκμάζων, ὦ μακάριε, χρῆσαι σεαυτῷ
μὴ[2] δοκῇς ἀπομαλθακίζεσθαι."

" Καὶ μήν," ὁ Θέων εἶπεν, " πάνυ ῥᾴδιόν ἐστι
τὸ λειπόμενον· λείπεται δὲ τὸ πρακτικὸν ὅσας
ἡδονὰς ἔχει διελθεῖν. αὐτοὶ δὲ δήπου λέγουσιν
ὡς τὸ εὖ ποιεῖν ἥδιόν ἐστι τοῦ πάσχειν. εὖ δὲ
ποιεῖν ἔστι μὲν ἀμέλει καὶ διὰ λόγων, τὸ δὲ πλεῖ-
στον ἐν πράξει καὶ μέγιστον, ὡς τοὔνομα τῆς εὐ-
εργεσίας ὑφηγεῖται καὶ μαρτυροῦσιν αὐτοί.[3] μικρῷ
γὰρ ἔμπροσθεν ἠκούομεν," ἔφη,[4] " τούτου λέγοντος
οἵας[5] φωνὰς ἀφῆκεν Ἐπίκουρος, οἷα[5] δὲ γράμματα
B τοῖς φίλοις[6] ἔπεμψεν, ὑμνῶν καὶ μεγαλύνων Μητρόδωρον, ὡς εὖ τε καὶ νεανικῶς ἐξ ἄστεως[7] ἐπὶ
θάλασσαν[8] ἔβη[9] Μιθρῇ[10] τῷ Σύρῳ βοηθήσων, καὶ
ταῦτα πράξαντος οὐθὲν[11] τότε τοῦ Μητροδώρου.
τίνας οὖν οἰόμεθα καὶ πηλίκας ἡδονὰς εἶναι τὰς
Πλάτωνος ὁπηνίκα Δίων ὁρμήσας ἀπ' αὐτοῦ κατ-
έλυσε Διονύσιον καὶ Σικελίαν ἠλευθέρωσεν; τίνας
δὲ Ἀριστοτέλους ὅτε τὴν[12] πατρίδα κειμένην ἐν

[1] ἡμᾶς a c : g omits.
[2] Before μὴ Stegmann omits καὶ.
[3] αὐτοί a : αὐτοῖς g c.
[4] ἔφη a : g c omit.
[5] οἷα a : οἵας g c.
[6] γράμματα τοῖς φίλοις a : γραμμάτων φίλων g c.
[7] ἄστεως Wyttenbach and ξ[t] : ἄστεος a g c.
[8] ἐπὶ θάλασσαν nos : ἀλλὰ a g c (ἅλα Victorius [reading
κατέβη] or εἰς τὴν θάλασσαν ; εἰς Πειραιᾶ Xylander ; ἅλαδε
Wyttenbach ; εἰς Ἁλὰς Apelt).
[9] ἔβη Apelt ι συνέβη a g c (κατέβη Xylander, Wyttenbach ;
συγκατέβη Reiske).
[10] Μιθρῇ Usener (Μίθρη Victorius in Q) : μίθρω a g c.

demus to take up where I leave off, supposing that you are too spent to go on ? " " That I will do," said Aristodemus, " when you are quite exhausted like our friend here. But you are still going strong, bless your heart ; exert your powers if you don't want to be taken for a quitter."

" Indeed," said Theon, " the rest is quite easy— to recount the many pleasures of the active part of the soul. Why, the Epicureans *a* themselves assert that it is more pleasant to confer a benefit than to receive one. Now to be sure you may also convey a benefit by means of words, but you convey most and the most important by action, as the very name of ' benefaction ' *b* suggests and as they testify themselves. Thus a short while ago," he said, " we heard our friend here *c* describe the expressions Epicurus *d* gave vent to and the letters he sent to his friends as he extolled and magnified Metrodorus, telling how nobly and manfully he went from town to the coast *e* to help Mithres *f* the Syrian, and this although Metrodorus accomplished nothing on that occasion. Then how high and full must have been the pleasure Plato *g* knew when Dion, setting out from his company, overthrew Dionysius and set Sicily free ? Or Aristotle,*h* when he raised again his native city, levelled to the

---

a Frag. 544 (ed. Usener) ; *cf. Mor.* 778 c.
b *Euergesia* (benefit) contains *ergon* (deed).
c Plutarch ; the reference is to 1126 E-F of the *Reply to Colotes.*
d Frag. 194 (ed. Usener).
e From Athens to the Piraeus.
f On Mithres see 1126 E, note, *infra.*
g *Cf.* 1126 B-C, *infra.*   *h* *Cf.* 1126 F, *infra.*

---

^τ
¹¹ πράξαντος οὐθὲν a g : πράξαν and a blank of 10 letters c.
¹² ὅτε τὴν a : τὴν g ; c omits in a blank of 10 letters.

(1097) ἐδάφει πάλιν ἀνέστησε καὶ κατήγαγε τοὺς πολίτας;
τίνας δὲ Θεοφράστου καὶ Φανίου[1] τοὺς τῆς πατρίδος
ἐκκοψάντων τυράννους ; ἰδίᾳ μὲν γὰρ ὅσοις ἐβοή-
C θησαν ἀνδράσιν,[2] οὐ πυροὺς[3] διαπέμποντες οὐδὲ
ἀλφίτων μέδιμνον, ὡς Ἐπίκουρος ἐνίοις ἔπεμψεν,
ἀλλὰ φεύγοντας διαπραξάμενοι κατελθεῖν καὶ δεδε-
μένους λυθῆναι καὶ τέκνα καὶ γυναῖκας ἐστερημέ-
νους ἀπολαβεῖν, τί ἂν λέγοι[4] τις ὑμῖν ἀκριβῶς
εἰδόσιν ;[5] ἀλλὰ τὴν ἀτοπίαν οὐδὲ βουλόμενόν ἐστι
τοῦ ἀνθρώπου παρελθεῖν, τὰς[6] μὲν Θεμιστοκλέους
καὶ Μιλτιάδου πράξεις ὑπὸ πόδας[7] τιθεμένου καὶ
κατευτελίζοντος, ὑπὲρ αὑτοῦ[8] δὲ ταυτὶ τοῖς φίλοις
γράφοντος· ' δαιμονίως[9] τε καὶ μεγαλοπρεπῶς ἐπε-
μελήθητε ἡμῶν τὰ περὶ τὴν τοῦ σίτου κομιδὴν καὶ
D οὐρανομήκη σημεῖα ἐνδέδειχθε τῆς πρὸς ἐμὲ εὐ-
νοίας.' ὥστε εἴ τις ἐξεῖλε τὸ σιτάριον ἐκ τῆς ἐπι-
στολῆς τοῦ φιλοσόφου δόξαν ἂν παραστῆσαι τὰ
ῥήματα τῆς χάριτος ὡς ὑπὲρ τῆς Ἑλλάδος ὅλης ἢ
τοῦ δήμου τῶν Ἀθηναίων ἐλευθερωθέντος ἢ σω-
θέντος γραφομένης.

16. "Ὅτι μὲν οὖν καὶ πρὸς τὰς τοῦ σώματος
ἡδονὰς ἡ φύσις δεῖται χορηγίας πολυτελοῦς καὶ
οὐκ ἔστιν ἐν μάζῃ καὶ φακῇ[10] τὸ ἥδιστον, ἀλλ' ὄψα

---

[1] τίνας δὲ (τινὰς g) θεοφράστου καὶ φειδίου (φεινίου g ; Φανίου
Rasmus) a g : c omits in a blank of 25 letters.
[2] ἐβοήθησαν ἀνδράσιν a : ἐβοήθησαν ἄδραστος g ; ἐβοήθει and
a blank of 9 letters c.
[3] πυροὺς a : πῦρ g c.
[4] λέγοι a c : λέγῃ g.
[5] ἀκριβῶς εἰδόσιν a g : a blank of 11 letters and δόσιν c.
[6] τὰς a : τοῦ g c.   [7] πόδας a : πόδα g c.

ground, and restored it to his countrymen ? Or
Theophrastus [a] and Phanias,[b] who cleared away the
tyrants from their city ? In private life what need is
there to tell you, who know it well, of the many they
helped—not sending them wheat or a bushel of meal,
as Epicurus [c] did to a few, but obtaining remission of
banishment, release from prison, and restoration of
wives and children that had been taken from them ?
But even if one wished one could not pass over the
man's absurd inconsistency : he treads under foot
and belittles the actions of Themistocles and Miltiades [d] and yet writes [e] this to his friends about
himself :

> The way in which you have provided for me in the matter
> of sending the grain was godlike and munificent, and you
> have given tokens of your regard for me that reach to high
> heaven.

So if someone had taken that corn ration of his bread-
stuff from our philosopher's letter, the expressions of
gratitude would have conveyed the impression that
it was written in thanksgiving for the freedom or
deliverance of the whole Greek nation or of the
Athenian state.

16. " Now the point [f] that even for the pleasures
of the body our nature requires costly provision, and
that the most pleasant enjoyment is not to be found
in barley-cake and lentil soup, but that the appetite
of the sensualist demands succulent viands and Tha-

---

[a] Cf. 1126 f, *infra.*   [b] Cf. Frag. 7 (ed. Wehrli).
[c] Frag. 184ª (ed. Usener).   [d] Frag. 559 (ed. Usener).
[e] Frag. 183 (ed. Usener).   [f] Frag. 467 (ed. Usener).

[8] αὑτοῦ E (αὐτοῦ a) : ἑαυτοῦ g c.
[9] δαιμονίως Usener : δαῖως a ; δαίως g ; δάϊόν c.
[10] φακῇ a : φυγῇ g c.

(1097) καὶ Θάσια καὶ μύρα

καὶ πεπτὰ καὶ κροτητὰ τῆς ξουθοπτέρου
πελανῷ μελίσσης¹ ἀφθόνως δεδευμένα

ζητοῦσιν αἱ τῶν ἀπολαυστικῶν ὀρέξεις, καὶ πρός
γε τούτοις εὐπρεπεῖς καὶ νέας γυναῖκας, οἷα² Λεόν-
E τιον³ καὶ Βοίδιον⁴ καὶ ῾Ηδεῖα καὶ Νικίδιον⁵ ἐνέμοντο
περὶ τὸν κῆπον, ἀφῶμεν. ταῖς μέντοι τῆς ψυχῆς⁶
χαραῖς ὁμολογουμένως μέγεθος ὑποκεῖσθαι δεῖ
πράξεων καὶ κάλλος ἔργων ἀξιολόγων, εἰ μέλλουσι
μὴ διάκενοι μηδὲ ἀγεννεῖς καὶ κορασιώδεις ἀλλ᾽
ἐμβριθεῖς ἔσεσθαι καὶ βέβαιοι καὶ μεγαλοπρεπεῖς.
τὸ δὲ ἐκ περιττοῦ⁷ πρὸς εὐπαθείας⁸ ἐπαίρεσθαι ναυ-
τῶν⁹ δίκην ᾽Αφροδίσια ἀγόντων καὶ μέγα φρονεῖν
ὅτι ῾ νοσῶν νόσον ἀσκίτην τινὰς¹⁰ ἑστιάσεις φίλων
συνῆγε καὶ οὐκ ἐφθόνει τῆς προσαγωγῆς τοῦ ὑγροῦ
τῷ ὕδρωπι καὶ τῶν ἐσχάτων Νεοκλέους λόγων
F μεμνημένος ἐτήκετο τῇ μετὰ δακρύων ἰδιοτρόπῳ

¹ πελάνῳ (πελανῷ Liddell-Scott-Jones) μελίσσης g c : πελα-
νομελίσσης a.
² οἷα a g c : οἷαι β² (οἷαι Baxter).
³ λεόντιον a g : λεόντειον c.
⁴ βοίδιον a g : βοίδιον c.
⁵ Νικίδιον Xylander : νικήδειον a ; κνίδιον g c.
⁶ τῆς ψυχῆς a g : ταῖς ψυχαῖς c.
⁷ ἐκ περιττοῦ nos (περιττῶς Kronenberg, omitting πρὸς) :
περὶ τοῦ a g c.
⁸ εὐπαθείας a : εὐπαθῆ g c.
⁹ ναυτῶν a : αὐτῶν g c.
¹⁰ νοσῶν νόσον ἀσκίτην τινὰς (Victorius had already proposed
ἀσκίτῃ) Bern. : νόσῳ νοσῶν ἀσκεῖ τίνας a ; νοσῶν ὅσον ἀσκεῖ
τινὰς (-ὲς c) g c.

sian wine [a] and perfumes

> And cakes and jumbles richly moist
> With the oblation of the whirring bee [b]

and not only this, but young and attractive women, like Leontion, Boidion, Hedeia, and Nicidion, who ranged at will [c] in the Garden—this point let us waive. Admittedly however the delights of the soul must rest on actions of some consequence and notable accomplishments of some lustre, if they are not to be empty or vulgar and childish, but solid, abiding and impressive. But [d] for a man to go out of his way to work up an excitement about small comforts, like sailors celebrating a feast of Aphroditê, [e] and to be proud because ' when suffering from the dropsy [f] he invited friends to a number of common meals and in spite of the disease did not refuse to take liquid, and was softened, recalling Neocles' [g] last words, by the curious pleasure

---

[a] Cf. 1089 c, supra.

[b] From the end of the Cretan Women of Euripides : Nauck, Trag. Graec. Frag., Eur. 467.

[c] Boidion means " little heifer," Leontion " little lioness."

[d] Frag. 190 (ed. Usener).

[e] The word Aphrodisia (" feast of Aphroditê ") is used of any festivity celebrating the successful outcome of an enterprise. Thus Xenophon (Hell. v. 4. 4) uses the word of the banquet held by the Theban polemarchs in 379 B.C. to celebrate the end of their term of office ; Plutarch merely speaks of an " entertainment " (Mor. 577 c) or of " drinking, company, and married women " (Life of Pelopidas, chap. ix. 4 [282 B]). In our passage Plutarch uses it of sailors on a spree after a voyage ; cf. Mor. 785 E and the Life of Lucullus, chap. xliv [i]. 3 (521 B). See M. P. Nilsson, Griechische Feste von religiöser Bedeutung mit Ausschluss der Attischen (Leipzig, 1906), pp. 374 f.

[f] Metrodorus, Frag. 46 (ed. Körte). Cf. 1089 F, supra.

[g] Neocles, a brother of Epicurus, predeceased him ; cf. 1089 F, supra, and Frag. 186 (ed. Usener).

(1097) ἡδονῇ '—ταῦτα οὐδεὶς ἂν ὑγιαινόντων[1] εὐφροσύνας
ἀληθεῖς ἢ χαρὰς ὀνομάσειεν, ἀλλ' εἴ τίς ἐστι[2] καὶ
ψυχῆς Σαρδάνιος[3] γέλως, ἐν τούτοις ἐστὶ τοῖς παρα-
βιασμοῖς καὶ κλαυσιγέλωσιν.[4] εἰ δ' οὖν ταῦτα
φήσει τις εὐφροσύνας καὶ χαράς, σκόπει τὰς ὑπερβολὰς τῶν ἡδονῶν ἐκείνων·

1098 ἡμετέραις βουλαῖς Σπάρτη[5] μὲν ἐκείρατο δόξαν

καὶ

οὗτός τοι[6] 'Ρώμας[7] ὁ μέγας, ξένε,[8] πατρίδος[9]
ἀστήρ

καὶ

δίζω ἤ σε θεὸν[10] μαντεύσομαι ἢ ἄνθρωπον.

ὅταν δὲ λάβω τὰ Θρασυβούλου καὶ Πελοπίδου πρὸ
ὀφθαλμῶν κατορθώματα καὶ τὸν ἐν Πλαταιαῖς 'Αρι-
στείδην ἢ τὸν ἐν Μαραθῶνι Μιλτιάδην,[11] ' ἐνταῦθα '
κατὰ τὸν 'Ηρόδοτον ' ἐξείργομαι γνώμην ' εἰπεῖν
ὅτι τῷ πρακτικῷ βίῳ τὸ ἡδὺ πλέον ἢ τὸ καλόν
ἐστιν.[12] μαρτυρεῖ δέ μοι καὶ 'Επαμεινώνδας[13] εἰπών,
ὥς φασιν, ἥδιστον αὐτῷ γενέσθαι τὸ[14] τοὺς τεκόντας[15]

---

[1] ὑγιαινόντων g c : ὑγιαίνων a.   [2] ἐστὶ a : g c omit.
[3] Σαρδάνιος (-δώ- Victorius) Baxter : σαρδιανὸς a g c.
[4] κλαυσιγέλωσιν a : καυσιγέλωσιν g c.
[5] Σπάρτη Aristides and Pausanias : σπάρτα a g c Schol. ad
Aeschin. 3. 211.
[6] οὗτός τοι a : οὗτοι g c.
[7] ῥώμας a g c : 'Ρώμης Life of Marcellus.
[8] ξένε a : ξεῖνε g c.
[9] πατρίδος (-ας g) c Εβ[2] : πάτριδος a[c](-ρι- in an erasure)A.
[10] ἤ σε θεὸν a : ἠὲ θεόν σε g c.
[11] ἢ τὸν ἐν μαραθῶνι μιλτιάδην a : g c omit.
[12] ἐστιν c (ἔστι a g) : ἔνεστιν Cobet.
[13] ἐπαμεινώνδας a g : -μιν- c.
[14] τὸ a g c : τῷ β[2].   [15] τεκόντας g c : γονεῖς a.

that is mingled with tears ' [a] : no one would call this
the ' mental joy ' or ' delight ' of men in their sound
mind ; no, if the soul has its Sardonic laughter, [b] we
find it here, in this forced merriment and this laughter
choked with tears. And even supposing that someone should call all this ' mental joy ' and ' delight,'
consider the magnitude of pleasures like these :

> Through me was Sparta shorn of her renown [c]

or

> Here, stranger, stands Rome's mighty star, her son [d]

or

> Shall I the prophet call thee god or man ? [e]

When I set before my eyes the exploits of Thrasybulus, or Pelopidas, or picture Aristeides at Plataea
or Miltiades at Marathon, ' here ' in the words of
Herodotus [f] ' I am constrained to pronounce ' that
the pleasure of the life of action is greater than its
glory. Epameinondas bears me out, who said, we are
told, that nothing had given him more pleasure than

---

[a] Cf. Seneca, *Ep.* xcix. 25 (Metrodorus, Frag. 34, ed.
Körte) : " illud nullo modo probo, quod ait Metrodorus :
esse aliquam cognatam tristitiae voluptatem, hanc esse cap-
tandam in eiusmodi tempore " (that is, when you lose a
young son).

[b] Cf. Pausanias, x. 17. 13 : (Sardinia has no poisonous
plants with one exception). " The fatal weed resembles
parsley, and it is said that those who have eaten it perish
laughing. It is with reference to this weed that Homer [*Od.*
xx. 302] and later authors call laughter that is for no sound
reason sardonic [*i.e.* Sardinian]."

[c] Of Epameinondas : *cf.* Preger, *Inscr. Graec. Metr.*, No.
161 and Pausanias, ix. 15. 6.

[d] Of Marcellus : *cf.* Preger, *op. cit.*, No. 168 and *Life of
Marcellus*, chap. xxx. 8 (316 B).

[e] Of Lycurgus : *cf.* H. W. Parke and D. E. W. Wormell, *The
Delphic Oracle* (Oxford, 1956), vol. ii, p. 14.   [f] vii. 139. 1.

(1098)

B ζῶντας ἐπιδεῖν τὸ ἐν Λεύκτροις τρόπαιον αὐτοῦ
στρατηγοῦντος. παραβάλωμεν οὖν τῇ Ἐπαμεινώνδου[1] μητρὶ τὴν Ἐπικούρου, χαίρουσαν ὅτι τὸν υἱὸν
ἐπεῖδεν εἰς τὸ κηπίδιον ἐνδεδυκότα καὶ κοινῇ μετὰ
τοῦ Πολυαίνου παιδοποιούμενον ἐκ τῆς Κυζικηνῆς
ἑταίρας. τὴν μὲν γὰρ Μητροδώρου μητέρα καὶ τὴν
ἀδελφὴν ὡς ὑπερέχαιρον ἐπὶ τοῖς γάμοις αὐτοῦ καὶ[2]
ταῖς πρὸς τὸν ἀδελφὸν ἀντιγραφαῖς ἐκ τῶν βιβλίων
δήπου δῆλόν ἐστι. ʻ ἀλλʼ ἡδέως τε[3] βεβιωκέναι
καὶ βρυάζειν[4] καὶ καθυμνεῖν τὸν αὐτῶν[5] βίον ἐκ-
κραυγάζοντες λέγουσι.ʼ καὶ γὰρ οἱ θεράποντες
ὅταν Κρόνια δειπνῶσιν ἢ Διονύσια κατʼ ἀγρὸν
ἄγωσι περιόντες, οὐκ ἂν αὐτῶν τὸν ὀλολυγμὸν
C ὑπομείναις καὶ τὸν θόρυβον, ὑπὸ χαρμονῆς καὶ
ἀπειροκαλίας τοιαῦτα ποιούντων καὶ φθεγγομένων

τί κάθῃ;[6] πίωμεν. οὐ καὶ σιτία[7]
πάρεστιν; ὦ δύστηνε, μὴ σαυτῷ φθόνει.
οἱ δʼ[8] εὐθὺς ἠλάλαξαν,[9] ἐν δʼ ἐκίρνατο
οἶνος· φέρων δὲ στέφανον ἀμφέθηκέ[10] τις·
ὑμνεῖτο δʼ αἰσχρῶς κλῶνα[11] πρὸς καλὸν δάφνης

[1] ἐπαμεινώνδου a g : ἐπαμινώνδα c.
[2] καὶ added by Wyttenbach.
[3] τὲ a c : g omits.   [4] βρυάζειν g c : βριάζειν a.
[5] αὐτῶν Baxter (αὐτῶν a) : ἑαυτῶν g c.
[6] τί κάθῃ ∪ – (or ∪ – τί κάθῃ) Lloyd-Jones (τί κάθη Reiske):
τί κάθη καὶ a g c (κλίθητι καὶ Meineke).
[7] σιτία Bergk, Emperius : σῖτα a (σίτα g) c.
[8] οἶδʼ a (from οἶδʼ ?) : οὐδʼ g c.
[9] ἠλάλαξαν a : ἤλλαξεν g c.
[10] ἀμφέθηκέ a : ἀντέθηκέ g c.
[11] κλῶνα a : καλωνᾶ g ; βαλωνᾶ c (with an abnormal u-shaped
β).

---

[a] Cf. Mor. 193 A, 786 D ; Life of Coriolanus, chap. iv
(215 c).

his parents' living to see the trophy at Leuctra, won
when he was general.[a] Let us then compare with
Epameinondas' mother the mother of Epicurus, who
had the joy of living to see her son ensconced in his
little garden and jointly with Polyaenus procreating
a family with the hetaira from Cyzicus.[b] As for
Metrodorus'[c] mother and sister, how overjoyed they
were at his marriage and at his *Replies* to his brother[d]
is plain enough from his writings. But (it is objected)
they shout[e] that ' they have had a pleasant life,'
' revel in it '[f] and ' hymn the praises ' of their own
' way of living.' So too when slaves hold a Saturnalian feast or go about celebrating the country
Dionysia,[g] you could not endure the jubilation[h] and
din, as in their crude exultation they act and speak
like this :

' Why sit ? Let's drink. There's food too, isn't there ?
Poor devil, never cheat yourself.' At once
They raised a clamour[i] and the wine was mixed,
Then someone brought a crown and stuck it on
And to the beat of a fine branch of bay[j]
Was Phoebus vilely hymned in notes untrue,

[b] Cf. 1127 c, *infra*. Usener (*Epicurea*, p. 416, col. 1)
identifies her with Hedeia.

[c] See pp. 554 and 566 in Körte's collection of the fragments.   [d] Timocrates ; see 1098 c, *infra*.

[e] Frag. 605 (ed. Usener) ; Frag. 49 (ed. Körte).

[f] Cf. Frag. 181 (ed. Usener) : βρυάζω τῷ κατὰ τὸ σωμάτιον
ἡδεῖ and 1107 a, *infra*.

[g] Cf. *Mor.* 527 D with the note.

[h] Cf. 1091 c, *supra*.   [i] In honour of the god.

[j] Before the drinking begins the paean is sung not to the
accompaniment of the cithara or flute but to the waving of
a branch of bay. Cf. a scholium on Aristophanes, *Wasps*,
1239 : " Some assert that it was the custom for anyone who
could not sing [*i.e.*, play his own accompaniment] at a banquet
to take a branch of bay or myrtle and sing in accompaniment
to it." See also Zenobius, *Cent.* i. 19.

ὁ Φοῖβος οὐ προσῳδά· τήν τ' ἐναύλιον[1]
ὠθῶν τις[2] ἐξέκλαγξε[3] σύγκοιτον φίλην.[4]

ᾗ[5] γὰρ οὐ τούτοις ἔοικε τὰ Μητροδώρου πρὸς τὸν
ἀδελφὸν γράφοντος· ' οὐδὲν δεῖ σῴζειν τοὺς Ἕλληνας οὐδ' ἐπὶ σοφίᾳ στεφάνων παρ' αὐτῶν τυγχάνειν, ἀλλ' ἐσθίειν καὶ πίνειν οἶνον, ὦ[6] Τιμόκρατες,
D ἀβλαβῶς τῇ γαστρὶ καὶ[7] κεχαρισμένως '; καὶ πάλιν πού φησιν ἐν τοῖς αὐτοῖς γράμμασιν ὡς ' καὶ
ἐχάρην καὶ ἐθαρσυνάμην[8] ὅτι ἔμαθον παρὰ[9] Ἐπικούρου ὀρθῶς γαστρὶ χαρίζεσθαι '· καὶ ' περὶ γαστέρα γάρ, ὦ φυσιολόγε Τιμόκρατες, τὸ ἀγαθόν.'
(17.) καὶ γὰρ ὅλον[10] οἱ ἄνθρωποι τῆς[11] ἡδονῆς τὸ
μέγεθος καθάπερ κέντρῳ καὶ διαστήματι τῇ γαστρὶ
περιγράφουσι, λαμπρᾶς δὲ καὶ βασιλικῆς καὶ φρο-
νήματα ποιούσης μέγα καὶ φῶς καὶ γαλήνην ἀληθῶς
εἰς ἅπαντας ἀναχεομένην[12] χαρᾶς οὐκ ἔστι[13] μετασχεῖν βίον ἀνέξοδον καὶ ἀπολίτευτον καὶ ἀφιλάν-
θρωπον καὶ ἀνενθουσίαστον[14] εἰς τιμὴν καὶ χάριν
ἀνελομένους. οὐ γάρ τι φαῦλον ἡ ψυχὴ[15] καὶ μικρὸν

---

[1] τ' ἐναύλιον a : τε ναυλίων g c.
[2] ὠθῶν τις a : ὅθον τίς g ; ὅθον τὶς c.
[3] ἐξέκλαγξε a (-λαξε Α²Ε ; -ραξε β²⁸⁸) : ἐξέκλαζε g c.
[4] φίλην a : ἢ φίλαν g c.   [5] ᾗ a : ἢ g c.
[6] οἶνον, ὦ Dübner (from Mor. 1125 D, which has ὦ without
οἶνον) : οἶνον c g ; οἴνῳ a.
[7] καὶ a : g c omit.
[8] ἐθαρσυνάμην a : ἐθάρσυνα μὴ g c.
[9] παρὰ g c : περὶ a.
[10] γὰρ ὅλον Pohlenz (totam Ferronus ; ὅλον Victorius in Q) :
ἔωλον a (ἔ- g) c.   [11] τῆς a : καὶ τῆς g c.
[12] ἀναχεομένην a : ἀναχεομένη g c (-ης Victorius in Q).
[13] οὐκ ἔστι a : g c omit.

While someone tried to force the courtyard door,
Howling a loving summons to his wench.[a]

Metrodorus'[b] words to his brother are of a piece
with this, are they not ? He writes : ' We are not
called to save the nation or get crowned by it for
wisdom ; what is called for, my dear Timocrates, is
to eat and to drink wine, gratifying the belly without
harming it.' And in the same letters he [c] says again :
' It made me both happy and confident to have learned
from Epicurus [d] how to gratify the belly properly '
and [e] ' the belly, Timocrates my man of science, is
the region that contains the highest end.' (17.)
Indeed these people,[f] you might say, describing a
circle with the belly as centre and radius, circum-
scribe within it the whole area of pleasure,[g] whereas
delight that is magnificent and kingly and that en-
genders a high spirit and a luminous serenity that
truly [h] diffuses itself to all men is beyond the reach
of those who set up as honourable and pleasing a
cloistered life, estranged from public duty, indifferent
to human welfare, untouched by any spark of the
divine. For the soul is nothing paltry and inconsider-

[a] Nauck, *Trag. Graec. Frag.*, Adesp. 418 ; Kock, *Comi-corum Att. Frag.*, Adesp. 1203.
[b] Frag. 41 (ed. Körte) ; quoted also at 1100 D and 1125 D, *infra*.
[c] Frag. 42 (ed. Körte).   [d] Frag. 409 (ed. Usener).
[e] Frag. 40 (ed. Körte).   [f] Frag. 409 (ed. Usener).
[g] A favourite figure in Plutarch : *cf. Mor.* 513 c with the note and Euclid, *Élements* (vol. i, p. 284. 2 [ed. Heiberg]).
[h] The words χαίρω and χαρά (delight) were derived from χέω in the sense of διαχέω (to diffuse, relax) : *cf. Et. Mag.* 807. 50 and *Et. Gud.* 100. 1-2.

---

[14] ἀνενθουσίαστον a g : ἀνενθουσίωτον c.
[15] ψυχή μ[2m] and Victorius in Q : τύχη a g c.

(1098) οὐδὲ ἀγεννές ἐστιν οὐδ' ὥσπερ τὰς πλεκτάνας[1] οἱ
E πολύποδες ἄχρι τῶν ἐδωδίμων ἐκτείνει τὰς ἐπιθυμίας, ἀλλὰ ταύτην μὲν ὀξύτατος ἀποκόπτει κόρος
ἀκαρὲς ὥρας μόριον ἀκμάσασαν, τῶν[2] δὲ πρὸς τὸ
καλὸν ὁρμῶν καὶ τὴν ἐπὶ τῷ καλῷ τιμὴν καὶ χάριν
    οὐκ ἔστιν αὐτῶν μέτρον ὁ[3] τοῦ βίου χρόνος
ἀλλὰ τοῦ παντὸς αἰῶνος ἐπιδραττόμενον τὸ φιλότιμον καὶ φιλάνθρωπον ἐξαμιλλᾶται ταῖς πράξεσι καὶ
ταῖς χάρισιν ἡδονὴν ἀμήχανον[4] ἐχούσαις, ἃς οὐδὲ
φεύγοντες οἱ χρηστοὶ διαφεύγειν δύνανται, πανταχόθεν αὐτοῖς ἀπαντώσας καὶ περιχεομένας[5] ὅταν
εὐφραίνωσι πολλοὺς εὐεργετοῦντες,
    ἐρχόμενον δ' ἀνὰ ἄστυ θεὸν ὡς εἰσορόωσιν.

F ὁ γὰρ οὕτω διαθεὶς ἑτέρους ὥστε καὶ χαίρειν καὶ
γάνυσθαι[6] καὶ ποθεῖν ἅψασθαι καὶ προσαγορεῦσαι
δῆλός ἐστι καὶ τυφλῷ μεγάλας ἔχων ἐν ἑαυτῷ καὶ
1099 καρπούμενος ἡδονάς. ὅθεν οὐδὲ κάμνουσιν ὠφε-
λοῦντες οὐδὲ ἀπαγορεύουσιν, ἀλλὰ τοιαύτας αὐτῶν[7]
ἀκούομεν φωνάς
    πολλοῦ σε θνητοῖς ἄξιον τίκτει πατήρ
καὶ
    μή γε παυσώμεσθα[8] δρῶντες εὖ βροτούς.
καὶ τί δεῖ περὶ τῶν ἄκρως ἀγαθῶν λέγειν; εἰ γάρ

---

[1] τὰς πλεκτάνας added here by us (Döhner adds πλεκτάνας
after ἐπιθυμίας; Pohlenz adds πλεκτάνας τῆς before ἐπιθυμίας).
[2] ἀκμάσασαν τῶν Dübner : ἀκμασάντων a g c.
[3] ὁ g c : a omits.
[4] ἡδονὴν ἀμήχανον a : ἡδονὰς ἀμηχάνους g c.
[5] περιχεομένας β² K¹⁰⁸ : περιεχομένας a g c.
[6] γάνυσθαι van Herwerden : γάννυσθαι a g c.

96

able, or yet petty, nor does it put forth its desires, as the octopus its tentacles, only as far as there are edibles to be got; no, such appetite flourishes for the briefest fraction of an hour, and then is cut short by a most swift satiety; whereas

> The span of life is time too short to measure [a]

the mind's endeavours to achieve greatness and honour and thanks for work well done; rather the love of honour and beneficence reaches out to eternity as it strives for the crown by deeds and benefactions that bring the doer a pleasure impossible to describe. Even when he tries a good man cannot escape the thanks, which come to meet him from all sides and flock around him, as multitudes rejoice in benefits conferred

> And as he goes about the town,
> Gaze on him as a god. [b]

For one who has put others in the mood to be happy and rejoice and long to touch him and to greet him, why, even the blind can see that such a man has in himself great pleasures, and has them as the reward of what he has done. Thus such men never weary or have enough of conferring benefits, but we hear in connexion with them words like these:

> A boon to mortals did thy sire beget thee

and

> Oh, let us never cease to help mankind. [c]

Indeed, why speak of men of exceptional virtue?

[a] Kock, *Comicorum Att. Frag.*, Adesp. 1241.
[b] Homer, *Od.* viii. 173; *cf.* Hesiod, *Theogony*, 91.
[c] Nauck, *Trag. Graec. Frag.*, Adesp. 410; also quoted in *Mor.* 791 D.

---

[7] αὐτῶν a g : αὐδῶν c.
[8] παυσώμεσθα Xylander : παυσώμεθα a g c.

(1099) τινι τῶν μέσως φαύλων μέλλοντι θνῄσκειν ὁ κύριος,
ἤτοι θεὸς ἢ βασιλεύς, ὥραν ἐπιδοίη μίαν ὥστε χρησάμενον[1] αὐτῇ πρός τινα[2] καλὴν πρᾶξιν ἢ[3] πρὸς
ἀπόλαυσιν εὐθὺς τελευτᾶν, τίς[4] ἂν ἐν τῷ χρόνῳ τού-
B τῳ βούλοιτο μᾶλλον Λαΐδι συγγενέσθαι καὶ πιεῖν
οἶνον Ἀριούσιον ἢ κτείνας Ἀρχίαν[5] ἐλευθερῶσαι
τὰς Θήβας;[6] ἐγὼ μὲν οὐδένα νομίζω.[7] καὶ γὰρ
τῶν μονομάχων ὁρῶ τοὺς μὴ παντάπασι θηριώδεις
ἀλλ' Ἕλληνας ὅταν εἰσιέναι[8] μέλλωσι, προκειμένων
πολλῶν ἐδεσμάτων καὶ πολυτελῶν, ἥδιον τὰ γύναια
τοῖς φίλοις ἐν τῷ χρόνῳ τούτῳ[9] παρακατατιθε-
μένους καὶ τοὺς οἰκέτας ἐλευθεροῦντας ἢ τῇ γαστρὶ
χαριζομένους.

" 'Αλλὰ καὶ εἴ τι[10] μέγα περὶ τὰς τοῦ σώματος
ἡδονάς, κοινόν ἐστι δήπου τοῦτο τοῖς πρακτικοῖς[11]·
καὶ γὰρ ' σῖτον ἔδουσιν ' καὶ ' πίνουσιν αἴθοπα οἶνον '
καὶ μετὰ φίλων ἑστιῶνται πολύ γε οἶμαι προθυμό-
C τερον ἀπὸ τῶν ἀγώνων καὶ τῶν ἔργων, ὡς[12] Ἀλέξανδρος καὶ Ἀγησίλαος καὶ νὴ Δία καὶ[13] Φωκίων
καὶ Ἐπαμεινώνδας,[14] ἢ καθάπερ οὗτοι πρὸς πῦρ
ἀλειψάμενοι καὶ τοῖς φορείοις ἀτρέμα διασεισθέντες,[15] ἀλλὰ καταφρονοῦσι τούτων ἐν ἐκείναις ταῖς

---

[1] χρησάμενον g c : χρησόμενον a.
[2] πρός τινα Xylander (alicui Ferronus) : πρὸς τὴν a g c.
[3] ἢ a : g c omit.   [4] τίς g c β² : τί a.
[5] ἀρχίαν a : ἀργίαν g c.   [6] θήβας g c : ἀθήνας a.
[7] νομίζω a² g c : a¹ omits.
[8] εἰσιέναι a : εἰσεῖναι g c.
[9] ἐν τῷ χρόνῳ τούτῳ is put here by g c : after ἥδιον by a.
[10] εἴ τι Xylander : ἐπὶ a g c.
[11] πρακτικοῖς Castiglioni (πρακτικοῖς πᾶσι Papabasileios ;
πρακτικῶν πράγμασι Pohlenz) : πρακτικοῖς πράγμασι a g c.
[12] ὡς a : ὧν g c.   [13] καὶ a : g c omit.

For if some person of only average weakness, on the point of death, should be granted by his sovereign, whether a god or a king, an hour's grace, to use for some great action or else for a good time, and then die immediately after, who in that hour would rather lie in Laïs' arms and drink Ariusian wine [a] than slay Archias and deliver Thebes ? [b] No one, say I. Why even among the gladiators I observe that those who are not utterly bestial, but Greeks, when about to enter the arena, though many costly viands are set before them, find greater pleasure at that moment in recommending their women to the care of their friends and setting free their slaves than in gratifying their belly.[c]

"Again, any remarkable quality in the bodily pleasures is plainly enough enjoyed by men of action too. They too 'eat food' and 'drink the sparkling wine' [d] and banquet with their friends, and do so with keener zest, I think, after their struggles and exploits, for instance Alexander and Agesilaüs, yes and Phocion too and Epameinondas, than when, like these, they had done no more than rub down [e] by a fire and get exercise in the gentle jouncing of their litters [f]; but men of action regard these pleasures as inconsiderable, preoccupied as they are by other

[a] Cf. Pliny, N.H. xiv. 73 and Athenaeus, i, 32 f.
[b] The story is told in the De Genio Socratis ; see especially 597 A.
[c] Cf. 1098 c-d, supra. They made their wills.
[d] Homer, Il. v. 341.
[e] For Epicurus' anointing himself see Festugière, Epicurus and his Gods (trans. Chilton), p. 70, note 56.
[f] Epicurus' poor health caused him to use a litter (Diogenes Laert. x. 7).

[14] ἐπαμεινώνδας a g : -μιν- c.
[15] διασεισθέντες a c διαπεισθέντες g.

PLUTARCH'S MORALIA

(1099) μείζοσιν ὄντες.[1]   τί γὰρ ἂν λέγοι τις Ἐπαμεινώνδαν οὐκ ἐθελήσαντα δειπνεῖν ὡς ἑώρα πολυτελέστε-
ρον τῆς οὐσίας[2] τὸ δεῖπνον, ἀλλ' εἰπόντα πρὸς τὸν
φίλον ' ἐγώ σε ᾤμην θύειν, οὐχ ὑβρίζειν '; ὅπου
καὶ Ἀλέξανδρος ἀπεώσατο τῆς Ἄδας τοὺς μαγεί-
ρους αὐτὸς εἰπὼν ἔχειν ἀμείνονας ὀψοποιούς, πρὸς
D μὲν[3] ἄριστον τὴν νυκτοπορίαν,[4] πρὸς δὲ δεῖπνον τὴν
ὀλιγαριστίαν· Φιλόξενον δὲ γράψαντα περὶ παίδων
καλῶν εἰ πρίηται[5] μικρὸν ἐδέησε τῆς ἐπιτροπῆς
ἀποστῆσαι· καίτοι τίνι μᾶλλον ἐξῆν; ἀλλ' ὥσπερ
φησὶν Ἱπποκράτης δυεῖν[6] πόνων τὸν ἥττονα ὑπὸ
τοῦ μείζονος ἀμαυροῦσθαι, καὶ τῶν ἡδονῶν τὰς
σωματικὰς αἱ πρακτικαὶ καὶ φιλότιμοι τῷ χαίροντι
τῆς ψυχῆς δι' ὑπερβολὴν καὶ μέγεθος ἐναφανίζουσι
καὶ κατασβεννύουσιν.
   18. " Εἰ τοίνυν, ὥσπερ λέγουσι, τὸ μεμνῆσθαι
τῶν προτέρων ἀγαθῶν μέγιστόν ἐστι πρὸς τὸ ἡδέως ζῆν, Ἐπικούρῳ μὲν οὐδ' ἂν εἷς ἡμῶν πιστεύσειεν
E ὅτι ταῖς μεγίσταις ἀλγηδόσι καὶ νόσοις ἐναποθνή-
σκων ἀντιπαρεπέμπετο τῇ μνήμῃ τῶν ἀπολελαυσμένων[7] πρότερον ἡδονῶν, εἰκόνα γὰρ ὄψεως ἐν βυθῷ
συνταραχθέντι καὶ κλύδωνι μᾶλλον ἄν τις ἢ μνήμην
ἡδονῆς διαμειδιῶσαν ἐν[8] σφυγμῷ[9] τοσούτῳ καὶ

[1] ὄντες g c β[2] : ὄντων a.
[2] οὐσίας a g c : θυσίας Valckenaer.
[3] μὲν A[2]E (cf. Mor. 127 β, 180 Α, and Life of Alexander,
chap. xxii. 9 [677 c]): aA[1] g c omit.
[4] νυκτοπορίαν a : νύκτα πορίαν (-είαν c) g c.
[5] πρίηται g c : πριεῖται a° (-ρι- from -αί- ?).
[6] δυεῖν a : δυοῖν g c (δύο Hippocrates).
[7] ἀπολελαυσμένων a : ἐναπολελαυσμένων g c.
[8] ἐν a : g c omit.   [9] σφυγμῷ a g : συριγμῷ c.
100

greater ones. Thus what need to mention Epameinondas' refusal to dine when he saw that the dinner
was an extravagance for his friend, saying ' I thought
this was a sacrifice and dinner, not a scandal and outrage'? What need to mention this, when Alexander[a]
rejected Ada's cooks, saying that he had better sea-
soners himself, for his breakfast night marches, and
for his dinner light breakfasting? And when Philoxenus wrote to suggest the purchase of handsome
boys, Alexander[b] came within an ace of relieving
him from his command. Yet who had greater liberty
to do what he pleased? But as Hippocrates[c] says
that of two pains the lesser is dimmed by the greater,
so too with pleasures : those of statesmanlike action
and ambition are so radiant and splendid that in the
blaze of mental joy the bodily pleasures are obliterated and extinguished.

18. " Now suppose that, as they say,[d] the recollection of past blessings is the greatest factor in a pleasant life. For one thing, not one of us would credit
Epicurus when he[e] says that while he was dying in
the greatest pain and bodily afflictions he found com-
pensation in being escorted on his journey by the
recollection of the pleasures he had once enjoyed ;
for you could sooner imagine a face reflected in water
when the depths are stirred and the seas ride high
than a smiling memory of pleasure in so great an

[a] Cf. Mor. 127 B with Wyttenbach's note, Mor. 180 A, and
Life of Alexander, chap. xxii. 7-9 (677 B-C).
[b] Mor. 333 A, Life of Alexander, chap. xxii. 1-2 (676 F—
677 A).
[c] Aphorisms, ii. 46. Thus the greater fire destroys the less
(Theophrastus, On the Senses, 18, On Fire, 10) and the greater
light the less (cf. On the Sublime, 17. 2).
[d] Frag. 436 (ed. Usener).
[e] Frag. 138 (ed. Usener).

(1099) σπαραγμῷ σώματος[1] ἐπινοήσειε, τὰς δὲ τῶν πράξεων μνήμας οὐδεὶς ἂν οὐδὲ βουληθεὶς ἐκστήσειεν
ἑαυτοῦ. πότε[2] γὰρ ἢ πῶς οἷόν τε ἦν ἐπιλαθέσθαι
τῶν Ἀρβήλων τὸν Ἀλέξανδρον ἢ τοῦ Λεοντιάδου[3]
τὸν Πελοπίδαν ἢ τῆς Σαλαμῖνος τὸν Θεμιστοκλέα;
τὴν μὲν γὰρ ἐν[4] Μαραθῶνι μάχην ἄχρι νῦν Ἀθη-
ναῖοι καὶ τὴν ἐν Λεύκτροις Θηβαῖοι καὶ νὴ Δία
F ἡμεῖς τὴν Δαϊφάντου[5] περὶ Ὑάμπολιν[6] ἑορτάζομεν,
ὡς ἴστε, καὶ θυσιῶν καὶ τιμῶν ἡ Φωκὶς ἐμπέπλη-
σται, καὶ οὐδείς ἐστιν ἡμῶν ἐφ᾽ οἷς αὐτὸς βέβρωκε
καὶ[7] πέπωκεν οὕτως ἡδόμενος ὡς ἐφ᾽ οἷς ἐκεῖνοι
κατώρθωσαν. ἐννοεῖν[8] οὖν πάρεστι πόσῃ[9] τις εὐφρο-
σύνη καὶ χαρὰ καὶ γηθοσύνη συνεβίωσεν αὐτοῖς
τοῖς τούτων δημιουργοῖς ὧν ἐν[10] ἔτεσι πεντακοσίοις
καὶ πλείοσιν οὐκ ἀποβέβληκεν ἡ μνήμη τὸ εὐφραῖνον.

" ' Καὶ μὴν ἀπὸ δόξης γίνεσθαί τινας ἡδονὰς[11]
1100 Ἐπίκουρος ὡμολόγει.' τί δὲ οὐκ ἔμελλεν αὐτὸς
οὕτω[12] σπαργῶν περιμανῶς καὶ σφαδάζων πρὸς δόξαν[13] ὥστε μὴ μόνον ἀπολέγεσθαι τοὺς καθηγητὰς
μηδὲ Δημοκρίτῳ[14] τῷ τὰ δόγματα ῥήμασιν αὐτοῖς
ὑφαιρουμένῳ[15] ζυγομαχεῖν περὶ συλλαβῶν καὶ κε-
ραιῶν, σοφὸν δὲ μηδένα φάναι πλὴν αὐτοῦ[16] γεγονέναι καὶ τῶν μαθητῶν, ἀλλὰ γράφειν ὡς Κωλώτης[17]

[1] σώματος a c : σωμάτων g.
[2] πότε Emperius : πότερον a g c.
[3] λεοντιάδου a : λεοντίδου g c.
[4] ἐν g c : a omits.
[5] δαϊφάντου a g (with no diaeresis) : δαῖφαν᾽|τοῦ c.
[6] ὑάμπολιν aʳ (ὑ- from ὑϊ- ?): πόλιν g ; a blank of 6-7 letters and πόλιν c.
[7] -κε καὶ g c : -κεν ἢ a.
[8] ἐννοεῖν a : νοεῖν g c.
[9] πάρεστι πόσῃ g c β² : πάρεστιν ὅσῃ a.

102

aching and convulsion of the body. And for another,
no one, even if he should wish, could drive out of
himself his memory of great actions. When could
Alexander have possibly forgotten Arbela, Pelopidas
Leontiades, or Themistocles Salamis ? To this day
the Athenians celebrate with a festival the victory
at Marathon, the Thebans that at Leuctra, and we
ourselves, as you all know, that of Daïphantus at
Hyampolis, and Phocis is full of sacrifices and honours;
and none of us gets such pleasure in what he has
eaten or drunk himself at the feast as in what those
men accomplished. We may then conceive how great
was the joy and delight and rapture that in their
lifetime dwelt in the minds of the actual authors of
deeds the memory of which, after five hundred years
and more, has not lost the power to gladden the heart.

" ' But Epicurus [a] (it is objected) allowed that
some pleasures come from fame.' Of course he did ;
was he not himself [b] in such a fury of tense and pal-
pitating passion for renown that he not only disowned
his teachers, quarrelled [c] with Democritus (whose
doctrines he filched word for word) about syllables
and serifs, and said [d] that except for himself and his
pupils no one had ever been a sage, but even wrote

[a] Frag. 549 (ed. Usener).   [b] Frag. 233 (ed. Usener).
[c] *Cf.* Usener, *Epicurea*, p. 97 and Frags. 233-235.
[d] Frag. 146 (ed. Usener) ; see on 1117 c, *infra*.

[10] ἐν a : g c omit.
[11] τινὰς ἡδονὰς Usener : τινὰς a ; τὰς ἡδονὰς g c.
[12] οὗτω σ² : οὗτος a g c.
[13] πρὸς δόξαν a : g c omit.
[14] Δημοκρίτῳ Ferronus (*Democrito*) : δημοκράτει a g c.
[15] ὑφαιρουμένω a (ὑφαιρούμενος β²ˢˢ) : ἀφαιρουμένω g c.
[16] αὑτοῦ Stephanus : αὐτοῦ a g c.
[17] κωλώτης g c : κολώτης a.

(1100) μὲν αὐτὸν φυσιολογοῦντα προσκυνήσειε γονάτων
ἁψάμενος, Νεοκλῆς δὲ ὁ ἀδελφὸς εὐθὺς ἐκ παίδων
ἀποφαίνοιτο μηδένα σοφώτερον Ἐπικούρου γεγονέναι μηδὲ εἶναι, ἡ δὲ μήτηρ ἀτόμους ἔσχεν ἐν
B αὐτῇ[1] τοιαύτας[2] οἷαι συνελθοῦσαι σοφὸν ἂν ἐγέννη-
σαν; εἶτα οὐχ ὥσπερ Καλλικρατίδας[3] ἔλεγε τὸν
Κόνωνα μοιχεύειν[4] τὴν θάλασσαν,[5] οὕτως ἄν τις
εἴποι τὸν Ἐπίκουρον αἰσχρῶς καὶ κρύφα πειρᾶν
καὶ παραβιάζεσθαι τὴν δόξαν, οὐ τυγχάνοντα φανερῶς ἀλλ᾽ ἐρῶντα καὶ κατατεινόμενον; ὥσπερ γὰρ
ὑπὸ λιμοῦ τὰ σώματα τροφῆς μὴ παρούσης ἀναγκά-
ζεται παρὰ φύσιν ὑφ᾽ αὑτῶν τρέφεσθαι, τοιοῦτον ἡ
φιλοδοξία ποιεῖ κακὸν[6] ἐν ταῖς ψυχαῖς, ὅταν ἐπαίνων πεινῶντες παρ᾽ ἑτέρων[7] μὴ τυγχάνωσιν, αὐτοὺς ἑαυτοὺς[8] ἐπαινεῖν. (19.) ἀλλ᾽ οἵ γε πρὸς
ἔπαινον οὕτω καὶ δόξαν[9] ἔχοντες ἆρα οὐχ ὁμολογοῦσι μεγάλας ἡδονὰς προΐεσθαι δι᾽ ἀσθένειαν ἢ
μαλακίαν φεύγοντες ἀρχὰς καὶ[10] πολιτείας καὶ
C φιλίας βασιλέων, ἀφ᾽ ὧν τὰ μεγάλα καὶ λαμπρὰ[11]
γίνεσθαι εἰς τὸν βίον[12] ἔφη Δημόκριτος; οὐ γὰρ
ἄν τινα πείσειεν ἀνθρώπων ὁ[13] τὴν Νεοκλέους μαρ-
τυρίαν καὶ τὴν Κωλώτου[14] προσκύνησιν ἐν τοσούτῳ
λόγῳ τιθέμενος καὶ ἀγαπῶν ὡς οὐκ ἂν ὑπὸ τῶν

[1] ἐν αὑτῇ β²E : ἐν αὑτῇ a² ; ἑαυτῇ a¹ ; ἐν ἑαυτῇ g c.
[2] τοιαύτας Emperius : τοσαύτας a g c.
[3] Καλλικρατίδας Bern. : -ης a g c.
[4] μοιχεύειν a : μοιχεύσειν g c.
[5] θάλασσαν g c : θάλατταν a.
[6] ποιεῖ κακὸν a : κακὸν ποιεῖ g c.
[7] ἐπαίνων . . . ἑτέρων g c : ἐπαίνου . . . ἑτέρου a.
[8] αὑτοὺς ἑαυτοὺς g c : αὑτοὺς a.
[9] οὕτω καὶ δόξαν g c : καὶ δόξαν οὕτως a.
[10] καὶ Castiglioni : ἢ a g c.
[11] καὶ λαμπρὰ Bern. : καλὰ a ; λαμπέαν g c.
[12] γίνεσθαι εἰς τὸν βίον g c : εἰς τὸν βίον γίνεσθαι (γίγν- β²) a.

that as he was expounding natural philosophy Colotes [a] embraced his knees in an act of adoration,
and that his own brother Neocles [b] declared from
childhood that there had never been born and was
not now anyone wiser than Epicurus, and that their
mother got in herself atoms of such a sort as by their
conjunction must produce a sage? Pshaw! As Calli-
cratidas [c] said that Conon was making an adulteress
of the sea, so might not a man say that Epicurus was
shamefully and covertly attempting to seduce Renown and force her to his will, since he could not win
her openly, and yet was racked with amorous desire?
For just as in the stress of famine the human body
is reduced for want of other food to do violence to
nature and feed on itself, so the love of glory brings
about a similar perversion in the mind: when men
who are famished for praise fail to get it from others
they praise themselves.[d] (19.) But surely men so
enamoured of praise and celebrity confess their
want of ability or resolution when they let slip such
pleasures, shunning office and political activity and
the friendship of kings,[e] things which Democritus [f]
said are the fount of all that is heroic and glorious
in our life. For he [g] who made so much of Neocles'
testimony and Colotes' act of adoration and took such
satisfaction in them would never convince any man
alive that if he had been applauded by the assembled

---

[a] Frag. 141 (ed. Usener), 1117 b, *infra*.
[b] Frag. 178 (ed. Usener).
[c] Xenophon, *Hellenica*, i. 6. 15.   [d] *Cf. Mor.* 540 a.
[e] *Cf.* Frag. 557 (ed. Usener) and 1127 a, *infra*.
[f] Diels and Kranz, *Die Frag. der Vorsokratiker*, Demokritos, B 157 ; *cf.* 1126 a, *infra*.
[g] Frags. 178 and 141 (ed. Usener).

---

[13] ὁ g c : ὅτι a.   [14] κωλώτου g c : κολώτου a.

(1100) Ἑλλήνων κροτηθεὶς Ὀλυμπίασιν[1] ἐξεμάνη καὶ ἀν-
ωλόλυξε, μᾶλλον δὲ ὅλως[2] ὑπὸ χαρᾶς ἤρθη κατὰ τὸν
Σοφοκλέα

γραίας ἀκάνθης πάππος ὣς φυσώμενος.

εἴ γε μὴν τὸ εὐδοξεῖν ἡδύ, τὸ ἀδοξεῖν δήπου λυπη-
ρόν· ἀδοξότερον δὲ ἀφιλίας ἀπραξίας ἀθεότητος
ἡδυπαθείας ὀλιγωρίας οὐθέν ἐστι. ταῦτα δὲ πάντες
D ἄνθρωποι πλὴν αὐτῶν ἐκείνων τῇ αἱρέσει προσεῖναι
νομίζουσιν. 'ἀδίκως,' φήσει τις. ἀλλὰ τὴν δόξαν,
οὐ τὴν ἀλήθειαν σκοποῦμεν. καὶ βιβλία μὲν μὴ
λέγωμεν μηδὲ ψηφίσματα βλάσφημα πόλεων ὅσα
γέγραπται πρὸς αὐτούς (φιλαπεχθῆμον γάρ) εἰ δὲ
χρησμοὶ καὶ μαντικὴ καὶ θεῶν πρόνοια καὶ γονέων
πρὸς[3] ἔκγονα στοργὴ καὶ ἀγάπησις καὶ πολιτεία
καὶ ἡγεμονία καὶ τὸ ἄρχειν ἔνδοξόν ἐστι καὶ εὐ-
κλεές,[4] οὕτως[5] ἀνάγκη τοὺς λέγοντας ὡς οὐ δεῖ σῴζειν τοὺς Ἕλληνας ἀλλ' ἐσθίειν καὶ πίνειν ἀβλαβῶς
τῇ γαστρὶ καὶ κεχαρισμένως ἀδοξεῖν καὶ[6] κακοὺς
νομίζεσθαι, νομιζομένους δὲ τοιούτους ἀνιᾶσθαι[7] καὶ
ζῆν ἀτερπῶς,[8] εἴ γε δὴ τὸ καλὸν ἡδὺ καὶ τὴν εὐ-
δοξίαν ἡγοῦνται.'

---

[1] ὀλυμπίασιν Q : ὀλυμπιάσιν a g c.
[2] ὅλως Wyttenbach (ὄντως Pohlenz ; πως Post) : ὅπως a g c.
[3] πρὸς a g : c omits.
[4] ἔνδοξόν ἐστι καὶ εὐκλεὲς g c β² : ἀδοξόν ἐστι καὶ ἀκλεὲς a.
[5] οὕτως a g c : πάντως Reiske ; οὐ πᾶσ' R. G. Bury.
[6] καὶ β²E²m(?) : a g c omit.
[7] ἀνιᾶσθαι Xylander : ἀνεῖσθαι a g c.
[8] ἀτερπῶς g c : ἀπρεπῶς a.

---

[a] So Themistocles was honoured (*Life of Themistocles*, chap. xvii. 4 [120 ε]). *Cf.* also the ovation to Flamininus at the Isthmian games (*Life of Flamininus*, chap. x. 4-10 [374

Greeks at Olympia [a] he would not have lost his head and raised a shout of jubilation. Or rather let us say that he would simply have been carried away for sheer joy, as Sophocles [b] has it,

> Like down on the dry thistle at a puff.

But if celebrity is pleasant, the want of it is painful ; and nothing is more inglorious than want of friends, absence of activity, irreligion, sensuality and indifference—and such is the reputation of their sect among all mankind except for themselves. ' Unfairly,' you say.[c] But we are considering reputation, not truth. And let us not mention the books composed against them or the contumelious decrees of cities [d] of which they are the subject, for that would be invidious. But let us say : if oracles and divination and divine providence and the affection and love of parent for child [e] and political activity and leadership and holding office are honourable and of good report, so surely those [f] who say that there is no need to save Greece, but rather to eat and drink so as to gratify the belly without harming it, are bound to suffer in repute and to be regarded as bad men ; and being so regarded they are bound to be distressed and live unhappily— if, as they say, they consider virtue with the honour it brings a pleasant thing.''

ᴇ—375 ᴀ]) and the honour shown to Philopoemen at the Nemean games (*Life of Philopoemen*, chap. xi. 4 [362 ᴅ]).

[b] Nauck, *Trag. Graec. Frag.*, Sophocles, 784 ; Frag. 868 (ed. Pearson).

[c] *Cf.* Seneca, *Dial.* vii. 13. 2 : '' sed illud dico : male audit, infamis est, et immerito.''

[d] Such as Rome, Messenê, and Lyctos : *cf.* Athenaeus, xii, 547 a ; Aelian, Frag. 39 and *Varia Historia*, ix. 12.

[e] *Cf.* 1123 ᴀ, *infra*.

[f] Metrodorus, Frag. 41 (ed. Körte) ; *cf.* 1098 c, *supra*.

(1100)
E

20. Ταῦτα εἰπόντος τοῦ Θέωνος ἐδόκει κατα-
παῦσαι τὸν περίπατον, καὶ[1] καθάπερ εἰώθειμεν[2] ἐπὶ
τῶν βάθρων καθεζόμενοι πρὸς τοῖς εἰρημένοις ἦμεν
σιωπῇ χρόνον οὐ πολύν. ὁ γὰρ[3] Ζεύξιππος ἀπὸ
τῶν εἰρημένων ἐννοήσας, " τίς," ἔφη, " τὰ λειπό-
μενα τῷ λόγῳ προσαποδίδωσι; καὶ[4] γὰρ οὔπω
προσῆκον ἔχοντι[5] τέλος αὐτὸς[6] ἄρτι μαντικῆς μνησθεὶς καὶ προνοίας ὑποβέβληκε[7]· ταῦτα γὰρ οὐχ
ἥκιστά φασιν οἱ ἄνδρες[8] ἡδονὴν καὶ γαλήνην καὶ
θάρσος αὐτοῖς παρασκευάζειν εἰς τὸν βίον, ὥστε
δεῖ τι λεχθῆναι καὶ περὶ τούτων." ὑπολαβὼν δὲ ὁ[9]
Ἀριστόδημος, " ἀλλὰ περὶ ἡδονῆς μὲν εἴρηται σχε-
F δόν," εἶπεν,[10] " ὡς εὐτυχῶν καὶ κατορθῶν ὁ λόγος
αὐτῶν φόβον ἀφαιρεῖ[11] τινα καὶ δεισιδαιμονίαν, εὐφροσύνην δὲ καὶ χαρὰν[12] ἀπὸ τῶν θεῶν οὐκ ἐνδίδωσιν, ἀλλ' οὕτως ἔχειν ποιεῖ[13] πρὸς αὐτοὺς τῷ μὴ
1101 ταράττεσθαι μηδὲ χαίρειν ὡς πρὸς τοὺς Ὑρκανοὺς
ἢ Σκύθας[14] ἔχομεν, οὔτε χρηστὸν οὐθὲν οὔτε φαῦλον
ἀπ' αὐτῶν προσδοκῶντες.

" Εἰ δὲ δεῖ προσθεῖναί τι τοῖς εἰρημένοις, ἐκεῖνό
μοι δοκῶ λήψεσθαι παρ' αὐτῶν πρῶτον, ὅτι τοῖς
ἀναιροῦσι λύπας καὶ δάκρυα καὶ στεναγμοὺς ἐπὶ
ταῖς τῶν φίλων τελευταῖς μάχονται καὶ λέγουσι τὴν
εἰς τὸ ἀπαθὲς καθεστῶσαν ἀλυπίαν ἀφ'[15] ἑτέρου

---

[1] καὶ a g : c omits.
[2] εἰώθειμεν a g(-ει- rewritten ?) : εἴωθε τιμᾶν c.
[3] γὰρ a g : μὲν γὰρ c.
[4] -σι καὶ a : -σιν· οὐ g c (-σι· ὁ β²).
[5] ἔχοντι nos : ἔχει a ; ἔχων g c ; ἔχειν E²ᵐᵍ ?
[6] αὐτὸς a g c : αὐτὸς δ' Pohlenz ; αὐτὸς γὰρ Emperius ;
οὗτος γὰρ Reiske ; ἃ αὐτὸς Bern.
[7] ὑποβέβληκε a : ὑποβέβηκε g c.
[8] οἱ ἄνδρες a g : οἱ ἄνδρες οἱ c ; ἄνδρες ἀναιροῦντες Post.
[9] ὁ a c : g omits.   [10] εἶπεν a : εἴπερ g c.

108

20. When Theon had concluded we decided to break off our walk, and sat down on the benches, as was our custom,[a] in silent meditation on what he had said. But not for long. For Zeuxippus said, getting his inspiration from Theon's words, "Who is to add to the argument what is still wanting? Indeed Theon himself by his reference just now [b] to divination and providence has suggested the fitting conclusion which the argument still lacks. For the gentlemen say that their treatment of these matters is no small contribution to the pleasure, serenity and confidence of their way of life; so these points require some discussion too." Aristodemus replied: "One point, that of the pleasure they derive from these views, has, I should say, been dealt with [c]: where their theory works successfully and is right, it does remove a certain superstitious fear; but it allows no joy and delight to come to us from the gods. Instead it puts us in the same state of mind with regard to the gods, of neither being alarmed nor rejoicing, that we have regarding the Hyrcanians or Scyths. We expect nothing from them either good or evil.

" But if we are to add anything to what has already been said, I think I will first take from them the following point.[d] They disagree with those who would do away with grief and tears and lamentation at the death of friends, and say that an absence of grief that renders us totally insensible stems from

[a] Cf. Mor. 937 d.	[b] 1100 d, supra.
[c] 1091 e—1092 c, supra.	[d] Frag. 120 (ed. Usener).

---

[11] ἀφαιρεῖ a g : ἀφαιρεῖται c.
[12] χαρὰν a : χάριν g c.   [13] ποιεῖ a c : g omits.
[14] ἢ Σκύθας Xylander (ἢ ᾿Ιχθυοφάγους Pohlenz) : ἰχθῦς a g c.
[15] ἀφ᾽ Usener : ὑφ᾽ a g c.

(1101) κακοῦ μείζονος ὑπάρχειν, ὠμότητος ἢ δοξοκοπίας
ἀκράτου καὶ λύσσης· διὸ πάσχειν τι βέλτιον εἶναι
καὶ λυπεῖσθαι καὶ νὴ Δία λιπαίνειν[1] τοὺς ὀφθαλμοὺς
καὶ τήκεσθαι, καὶ ὅσα δὴ παθαινόμενοι[2] καὶ γρά-
B φοντες ὑγροί τινες εἶναι καὶ φιλικοὶ δοκοῦσι. ταῦτα
γὰρ ἐν ἄλλοις τε πολλοῖς Ἐπίκουρος εἴρηκε καὶ
περὶ τῆς Ἡγησιάνακτος τελευτῆς πρὸς Σωσίθεον[3]
γράφων τὸν πατέρα[4] καὶ Πύρσωνα τὸν ἀδελφὸν τοῦ
τεθνηκότος. ἔναγχος γὰρ κατὰ τύχην τὰς ἐπιστολὰς
διῆλθον αὐτοῦ· καὶ λέγω μιμούμενος ὡς οὐχ ἧττόν
ἐστι κακὸν ἀθεότης ὠμότητος καὶ δοξοκοπίας, εἰς
ἣν ἄγουσιν ἡμᾶς οἱ τὴν χάριν[5] ἐκ τοῦ θείου[6] μετὰ
τῆς ὀργῆς ἀναιροῦντες. βέλτιον γὰρ ἐνυπάρχειν
τι καὶ συγκεκρᾶσθαι τῇ περὶ θεῶν δόξῃ κοινὸν[7]
αἰδοῦς καὶ φόβου πάθος, ἢ που[8] τοῦτο φεύγοντας
C μήτε ἐλπίδα[9] μήτε χάριν ἑαυτοῖς μήτε θάρσος
ἀγαθῶν παρόντων μήτε τινὰ δυστυχοῦσιν ἀποστρο-
φὴν πρὸς τὸ θεῖον ἀπολείπεσθαι.[10]

21. '' Δεῖ μὲν γὰρ ἀμέλει τῆς περὶ θεῶν δόξης
ὥσπερ ὄψεως λήμην ἀφαιρεῖν τὴν δεισιδαιμονίαν·
εἰ δὲ τοῦτ''[11] ἀδύνατον, μὴ συνεκκόπτειν μηδὲ τυ-
φλοῦν τὴν πίστιν ἣν οἱ πλεῖστοι περὶ θεῶν ἔχουσιν.
αὕτη δέ ἐστιν οὐ φοβερά τις οὐδὲ σκυθρωπή,[12]
καθάπερ οὗτοι πλάττουσι,[13] διαβάλλοντες τὴν πρό-

[1] νὴ δία (νηδία g) λι(λυ- g[2])παίνειν g c : μὴ διαλιπαίνειν a.
[2] παθαινόμενοι a : πειθόμενοι g c.
[3] σωσίθεον g c : δοσίθεον a[c](from σο- ?).
[4] γράφων τὸν πατέρα a : τὸν πατέρα γράφων g c.
[5] χάριν Amyot (gratia Ferronus) : χαρὰν a g c.
[6] θείου Reiske : θεοῦ a g c.
[7] κοινὸν Victorius in Q and Xylander : καινὸν a ; κενὸν g c.
[8] ἢ που a g c (cf. Plato, Laws, 716 c) : ἢ Xylander.
[9] ἐλπίδα g c : ἐλπίδος a.
[10] ἀπολείπεσθαι a : ὑπολείπευθω g c β[2].

110

A PLEASANT LIFE IMPOSSIBLE, 1101

another greater evil: hardness or a passion for notoriety so inordinate as to be insane. Hence they say that it is better to be moved somewhat and to grieve and to melt into tears and so with all the maudlin sentiment they feel and put on paper, getting themselves the name of being soft-hearted and affectionate characters. For this is what Epicurus has said not only in many other passages, but in his letter [a] on the death of Hegesianax to Sositheüs the father and Pyrson [b] the brother of the deceased. You see I recently happened to run through his letters. I say then, taking his remarks as my model, that irreligion is no less an evil than hardness and the passion for notoriety ; and irreligion is what we come to, if we follow those who with the wrath of God deny his mercies too.[c] For it is better that our belief about the gods should include an intermixture of a certain emotion that is part reverence and part fear, than that, by trying to escape this, we should leave ourselves no hope of divine favour, no confidence in prosperity, and in adversity no refuge in God.

21. "Now we should, I grant you, remove superstition from our belief in the gods like a rheum from the eye ; but if this proves impossible, we should not cut away both together and kill the faith that most men have in the gods. This is no terrifying or grim faith, as these men [d] pretend, when they traduce

[a] Frag. 167 (ed. Usener).
[b] Perhaps to be identified with Phyrson ; see T. Gomperz, *Philodem Über Frömmigkeit*, p. 157, and Usener, *Epicurea*, p. 138, note to line 24.
[c] Cf. *Cardinal Tenet* i.   [d] Frag. 369 (ed. Usener).

---

[11] τοῦτ' a : ταῦτ' g c.   [12] σκυθρωπὴ a g : σκυθρωπική c.
[13] πλάττουσι a : πράττουσι g c.

111

(1101) νοιαν ὥσπερ παισὶν Ἔμπουσαν[1] ἢ Ποινὴν ἀλιτη-
ριώδη καὶ τραγικὴν ἐπικρεμαμένην.[2] ἀλλ'[3] ὀλίγοι
μὲν τῶν ἀνθρώπων δεδίασι τὸν θεὸν οἷς οὐκ ἄμεινον
D μὴ δεδιέναι· δεδιότες γὰρ ὥσπερ ἄρχοντα χρηστοῖς
ἤπιον ἀπεχθῆ δὲ φαύλοις ἑνὶ φόβῳ, δι' ὃν οὐκ ἀδικοῦσι,[4] πολλῶν ἐλευθεροῦνται τῶν ἐπὶ τῷ[5] ἀδικεῖν,
καὶ παρ' αὑτοῖς[6] ἀτρέμα τὴν κακίαν ἔχοντες οἷον
ἀπομαραινομένην ἧττον ταράττονται τῶν χρωμένων
αὐτῇ καὶ τολμώντων εἶτα εὐθὺς δεδιότων καὶ μεταμελομένων.[7] ἡ δὲ τῶν πολλῶν[8] καὶ ἀμαθῶν καὶ[9]
οὐ πάνυ μοχθηρῶν διάθεσις πρὸς τὸν θεὸν ἔχει μὲν
ἀμέλει τῷ σεβομένῳ καὶ τιμῶντι μεμιγμένον τινὰ
σφυγμὸν καὶ φόβον, ᾗ[10] καὶ δεισιδαιμονία κέκληται,
τούτου δὲ μυριάκις[11] πλέον ἐστὶ[12] καὶ μεῖζον αὐτῇ τὸ
εὔελπι καὶ περιχαρὲς καὶ πᾶσαν εὐπραξίας ὄνησιν
E ὡς ἐκ θεῶν οὖσαν εὐχόμενον καὶ δεχόμενον. δῆλον
δὲ τεκμηρίοις[13] τοῖς μεγίστοις· οὔτε γὰρ διατριβαὶ
τῶν ἐν ἱεροῖς οὔτε καιροὶ τῶν ἑορτασμῶν οὔτε
πράξεις οὔτε ὄψεις εὐφραίνουσιν ἕτεραι μᾶλλον ὧν
ὁρῶμεν ἢ δρῶμεν αὐτοὶ περὶ τοὺς θεούς,[14] ὀργιά-
ζοντες ἢ χορεύοντες ἢ θυσίαις παρόντες[15] ἢ τελεταῖς.
οὐ γὰρ ὡς τυράννοις τισὶν ἢ δεινοῖς κολασταῖς[16]

---

[1] Ἔμπουσαν Amyot : ἐμπίπτουσαν a ; ἐμπεσοῦσαν g c.
[2] ἐπικρεμαμένην Döhner (*impendeat* Ferronus) : ἐπιγεγραμ-
μένην a g c.   [3] After ἀλλ' Pohlenz would add οὐκ.
[4] οὐκ ἀδικοῦσι g c : οὐ δοκοῦσι a.
[5] ἐλευθεροῦνται τῶν ἐπὶ τῶ g c : ἐλευθερούντων ἐπὶ τὸ a.
[6] αὑτοῖς Stephanus : αὐτοῖς a g c.
[7] μεταμελομένων a : μεταβαλλομένων g c.
[8] πολλῶν a g c : πολλῶν ὄντων Post.
[9] καὶ g c : a omits.
[10] φόβον ᾗ γ[1] : φόβον ἢ a g ; φόβος c.
[11] τούτου δὲ μυριάκις Bern. : τούτου τὲ μυριάκις g c ; μυριάκις
δὲ a.   [12] πλέον ἐστί a : πλεῖον ἐστι g (πλεῖόν ἐστι c).
[13] τεκμηρίοις a : τεκμήριον g ; ἐκ μυρίοις c.

providence as if she were some foul witch to frighten children with or unrelenting Fury out of tragedy hanging over our heads. No; among mankind a few[a] are afraid of God who would not be better off without that fear; for since they fear him as a ruler mild to the good and hating the wicked, by this one fear, which keeps them from doing wrong, they are freed from the many that attend on crime, and since they keep their viciousness within themselves, where it gradually as it were flickers down, they are less tormented than those who make free with it and venture on overt acts, only to be filled at once with terror and regret. On the other hand the attitude toward God that we find in the ignorant but not greatly wicked majority of mankind contains no doubt along with the sense of reverence and honour an element of tremulous fear (and from this we get our term for superstition[b]); but outweighing this a thousand times is the element of cheerful hope, of exultant joy, and whether in prayer or in thanksgiving of ascribing every furtherance of felicity to the gods. This is proved by the strongest kind of evidence : no visit delights us more than a visit to a temple ; no occasion than a holy day ; no act or spectacle than what we see and what we do ourselves in matters that involve the gods, whether we celebrate a ritual or take part in a choral dance or attend a sacrifice or ceremony of initiation. For on these occasions our mind is not

[a] That is, the wicked.
[b] *Deisidaimonia* (superstition) is literally " fear of the daemons."

---

14 τοὺς θεοὺς g c (θεοὺς β²) : θεῶν a.
15 ἢ θυσίαις παρόντες a gᶜ c : written twice in gᵃᵒ.
16 κολασταῖς a g : κολακευταῖς c.

(1101) ὁμιλοῦσα τηνικαῦτα ἡ ψυχὴ περίλυπός ἐστι καὶ
ταπεινὴ καὶ δύσθυμος, ὅπερ εἰκὸς ἦν· ἀλλ' ὅπου
μάλιστα δοξάζει καὶ διανοεῖται παρεῖναι τὸν θεόν,
ἐκεῖ μάλιστα λύπας καὶ φόβους καὶ τὸ φροντίζειν
ἀπωσαμένη[1] τῷ ἡδομένῳ[2] μέχρι μέθης καὶ παιδιᾶς
F καὶ γέλωτος[3] ἀφίησιν ἑαυτήν.[4]   καὶ ἐν μὲν[5] τοῖς
ἐρωτικοῖς,[6] ὡς ὁ ποιητὴς εἴρηκε

   καί τε γέρων καὶ γρῆυς, ἐπὴν[7] χρυσῆς Ἀφρο-
     δίτης
   μνήσωνται,[8] καὶ τοῖσιν ἐπηέρθη φίλον ἦτορ·

ἐν δὲ πομπαῖς καὶ θυσίαις οὐ μόνον

        γέρων καὶ γρῆυς

οὐδὲ πένης καὶ ἰδιώτης ἀλλὰ

καὶ παχυσκελὴς ἀλετρὶς πρὸς μύλην κινουμένη

1102 καὶ οἰκότριβες καὶ θῆτες ὑπὸ γήθους καὶ χαρμοσύ-
νης ἀναφέρονται· καὶ[9] πλουσίοις τε[10] καὶ βασιλεῦσιν
ἑστιάσεις καὶ πανδαισίαι τινὲς[11] ἀεὶ[12] πάρεισιν, αἱ δ'
ἐφ' ἱεροῖς καὶ θυηπολίαις, καὶ[13] ὅταν ἔγγιστα τοῦ
θείου τῇ ἐπινοίᾳ ψαύειν δοκῶσι[14] μετὰ τιμῆς καὶ
σεβασμοῦ, πολὺ διαφέρουσαν ἡδονὴν καὶ χάριν
ἔχουσι. ταύτης οὐδὲν ἀνδρὶ μέτεστιν ἀπεγνωκότι

---

    [1] ἀπωσαμένη a g : c omits in a blank of 13 letters.
      [2] τῷ ἡδομένῳ a : τῶν ἡδομένων g c.
    [3] παιδιᾶς καὶ γέλωτος a : γέλωτος καὶ παιδιᾶς g c.
      [4] ἑαυτὴν a g : τὴν c.
    [5] καὶ ἐν μὲν Wilamowitz (ἐν μὲν Reiske) : ἐν a g c.
      [6] ἐρωτικοῖς a g : ἱερατικοῖς c.
      [7] ἐπὴν a : g c omit.
    [8] μνήσωνται a : μνήσονται g c.
       [9] καὶ added by us.
      [10] τε g (τὲ a c) : δὲ Bern.

114

plunged in anxiety or cowed and depressed, as we should expect it to be in the company of tyrants or dispensers of gruesome punishments. No, wherever it believes and conceives most firmly that the god is present, there more than anywhere else it puts away all feelings of pain, of fear and of worry, and gives itself up so far to pleasure that it indulges in a playful and merry inebriation. Now in amatory matters, as the poet [a] says

> Why even crone and gaffer, when they speak
> Of golden Aphroditê, their old hearts
> Are lifted up ;

but in processions and at sacrifices not only crone and gaffer, not only men without wealth or station, but even

> The grinder with her heavy legs, who pushes at her mill [b]

and the servants of household and farm feel the lift of high spirits and a merry heart. Rich men and kings have a constant round of one banquet or full-spread dinner after another ; but when it is a feast held on the occasion of some sacred rite or sacrifice, and when they believe that their thoughts come closest to God as they do him honour and reverence, it brings pleasure and sweetness of a far superior kind. Of this a man gets nothing if he has given up

[a] Callimachus, Frag. anon. 386 (ed. Schneider) ; not in Pfeiffer.

[b] Bergk, *Poet. Lyr. Graec.*, vol. iii[4], adesp. 21 ; Diehl, *Anth. Lyr. Graec.*[3], Frag. Iamb. Adesp. 28.

---

[11] πανδαισίαι τινὲς a : παιδιαί τινες g c.
[12] ἀεὶ added by Meziriacus after πάρεισιν, placed here by us.   [13] καὶ a g c : Wilamowitz would omit.
[14] δοκῶσι a : δοκῶ g ; δοκοῦσι c.

(1102) τῆς προνοίας. οὐ γὰρ οἴνου πλῆθος οὐδὲ ὄπτησις
κρεῶν τὸ εὐφραῖνόν ἐστιν ἐν ταῖς ἑορταῖς, ἀλλ᾽[1]
ἐλπὶς ἀγαθὴ καὶ δόξα τοῦ παρεῖναι τὸν θεὸν εὐμενῆ
καὶ δέχεσθαι τὰ γινόμενα κεχαρισμένως. αὐλὸν μὲν
B γὰρ ἐνίων[2] ἑορτῶν καὶ στέφανον ἀφαιροῦμεν, θεοῦ
δὲ θυσίᾳ μὴ παρόντος ὥσπερ ἱερῶν δοχέως[3] ἄθεόν
ἐστι καὶ ἀνεόρταστον καὶ ἀνενθουσίαστον τὸ λειπό-
μενον· μᾶλλον δὲ ὅλως[4] ἀτερπὲς αὐτῷ[5] καὶ λυπη-
ρόν· ὑποκρίνεται γὰρ εὐχὰς καὶ προσκυνήσεις οὐθὲν
δεόμενος διὰ φόβον[6] τῶν πολλῶν καὶ φθέγγεται
φωνὰς ἐναντίας οἷς φιλοσοφεῖ· καὶ θύων μὲν ὡς
μαγείρῳ παρέστηκε τῷ ἱερεῖ σφάττοντι, θύσας δὲ
ἄπεισι λέγων τὸ Μενάνδρειον[7]

  ἔθυον· οὐ προσέχουσιν οὐδέν μοι θεοῖς·

οὕτω[8] γὰρ Ἐπίκουρος οἴεται δεῖν σχηματίζεσθαι
καὶ μὴ φθονεῖν[9] μηδὲ ἀπεχθάνεσθαι τοῖς πολλοῖς,
C οἷς[10] χαίρουσιν ἕτεροι πράττοντες[11] αὐτοὺς δυσχεραίνοντας[12].

  πᾶν γὰρ ἀναγκαῖον πρᾶγμ᾽ ὀδυνηρὸν[13] ἔφυ[14]

κατὰ τὸν Εὔηνον.[15] ᾗ καὶ τοὺς δεισιδαίμονας οὐ

---

[1] ἀλλ᾽ g c : ἀλλὰ καὶ a.
[2] ἐνίων (or ἔστιν ὧν) ἑορτῶν Reiske : ἑτέρων ἑορτῶν a[c] g[c] c ;
ἑορτῶν a[ac] ? ; ἑτέρων ἑτέρων ἑορτῶν g[ac].
[3] ὥσπερ ἱερῶν δοχέως Madvig (ὅσπερ ἱερῶν δοχεύς van Herwerden) : ὥσπερ ἱερὸν δοχῆς a g c (πρὸς [or ὡς πρὸς] ἱερῶν ἀπο-
δοχὴν Pohlenz).   [4] ὅλως t[t] (τὸ ὅλον Sandbach) : ὅλον a g c.
[5] αὐτῷ a : αὐτὸ g c.   [6] φόβον a c : τὸν φόβον g.
[7] μενάνδρειον g c : μὲν ἀνδρεῖον a.
[8] οὕτω g c : οὕτω from οὔτε a[c].
[9] φθονεῖν a : φρονεῖν g c ; καταφρονεῖν Pohlenz.
[10] οἷς g c : a omits.
[11] πράττοντες a g c : πράττοντας Usener.
[12] αὐτοὺς δυσχεραίνοντας Usener : αὐτοὶ δυσχεραίνοντες a g c.

116

faith in providence. For it is not the abundance of wine or the roast meats that cheer the heart at festivals, but good hope and the belief in the benign presence of the god and his gracious acceptance of what is done. For while we leave the flutes and the crowns out of certain festivals,[a] if the god is not present at the sacrifice as master of rites (so to speak) what is left bears no mark of sanctity or holy day and leaves the spirit untouched by the divine influence ; rather let us say for such a man the occasion is distasteful and even distressing. For out of fear of public opinion[b] he goes through a mummery of prayers and obeisances that he has no use for and pronounces words that run counter to his philosophy ; when he sacrifices, the priest at his side who immolates the victim is to him a butcher ; and when it is over he goes away with Menander's[c] words on his lips :

> I sacrificed to gods who heed me not.

For this is the comedy that Epicurus thinks we should play, and not spoil the pleasure of the multitude or make ourselves unpopular with them by showing dislike ourselves for what others delight in doing. This compliance is distressing

> For all compulsion is a painful thing

as Evenus[d] said. This indeed is why they[e] imagine

---

[a] Cf. *Mor.* 132 E and Apollodorus, *Bibl.* iii. 15. 7.
[b] Cf. Usener, *Epicurea*, p. 103. Epicurus was a faithful attendant at religious ceremonies ; cf. Frag. 169 (ed. Usener).
[c] Frag. 750 (ed. Körte).
[d] Frag. 8 (ed. Diehl) ; cf. Plato, *Phaedrus*, 240 c.
[e] Cf. Usener, *Epicurea*, pp. 103, 106.

---

[13] ὀδυνηρὸν g c : ἀνιηρὸν a (and so Theognis, 472 ; ἀνιαρὸν Aristotle and Alexander).
[14] ἔφυ a c : ἔφη g. [15] εὔηνον a³ g c : εὐηνόν a¹AE.

(1102) χαίροντας ἀλλὰ φοβουμένους οἴονται θυσίαις καὶ
τελεταῖς ὁμιλεῖν, μηθὲν ἐκείνων αὐτοὶ διαφέροντες
εἴ γε[1] δὴ[2] διὰ φόβον τὰ αὐτὰ δρῶσιν, οὐδ' ἐλπίδος
χρηστῆς ὅσον ἐκεῖνοι μεταλαγχάνοντες, ἀλλὰ μόνον
δεδιότες καὶ ταραττόμενοι μὴ φανεροὶ γένωνται
τοὺς πολλοὺς παραλογιζόμενοι καὶ φενακίζοντες·
ἐφ' οὓς καὶ τὰ περὶ θεῶν καὶ ὁσιότητος[3] αὐτοῖς
βιβλία συντέτακται,

ἑλικτὰ καὶ οὐδὲν[4] ὑγιὲς ἀλλὰ πᾶν πέριξ

D ἐπαμπεχομένοις καὶ ἀποκρυπτομένοις διὰ φόβον ἃς
ἔχουσι δόξας.

22. " Καὶ μὴν μετά γε τοὺς πονηροὺς καὶ τοὺς
πολλοὺς τρίτον ἤδη σκεψώμεθα τὸ βέλτιον ἀνθρώπων[5] καὶ θεοφιλέστατον γένος ἐν ἡλίκαις ἡδοναῖς
καθεστᾶσιν καθαραῖς[6] περὶ θεοῦ δόξαις[7] συνόντες,
ὡς πάντων μὲν ἡγεμὼν ἀγαθῶν πάντων δὲ πατὴρ
καλῶν ἐκεῖνός ἐστι, καὶ φαῦλον οὐθὲν[8] ποιεῖν αὐτῷ[9]
θέμις ὥσπερ οὐδὲ πάσχειν. ' ἀγαθὸς γάρ ἐστιν,
ἀγαθῷ δὲ περὶ οὐδενὸς ἐγγίνεται φθόνος '[10] οὔτε
φόβος οὔτε[11] ὀργὴ ἢ[12] μῖσος· οὐδὲ[13] γὰρ θερμοῦ τὸ
ψύχειν ἀλλὰ τὸ[14] θερμαίνειν, ὥσπερ οὐδὲ ἀγαθοῦ τὸ
E βλάπτειν. ὀργὴ δὲ χάριτος καὶ χόλος εὐμενείας

---

[1] γε Reiske : τε a g c.   [2] δὴ g c : a omits.
[3] ὁσιότητος Cobet : θειότητος a c ; θειότητα g.
[4] οὐδὲν a : οὐθὲν g c.   [5] ἀνθρώπων a : ἀνθρώποις g c.
[6] ἡδοναῖς καθεστᾶσιν καθαραῖς Pohlenz (Meziriacus would
add εἰσὶν after ἡλίκαις) : ἡδοναῖς καθαραῖς a[c] g c ; καθαραῖς
ἡδοναῖς a[bc].   [7] δόξαις Meziriacus : δόξης a g c.
[8] οὐθὲν g c : οὐδὲν a.   [9] ποιεῖν αὐτῷ a : αὐτῷ ποιεῖν g c.
[10] With φθόνος c breaks off at the end of folio 346[r].
[11] οὔτε . . . οὔτε a g : οὐδὲ . . . οὐδὲ Stegmann.
[12] ἢ a : οὔτε g.
[13] οὐδὲ Emperius : οὔτε a g.   [14] τὸ μ : a g omit.

that the superstitious attend sacrifices and initiations not because they like to but because they are afraid. Here the Epicureans are themselves no better than they, since they do the same from fear and do not even get the measure of happy anticipation that the others have, but are merely scared and worried that this deception and fooling of the public might be found out, with an eye to whom their books on the gods and on piety [a] have been composed

In twisted spirals, slanted and askew [b]

as in fear they cover up and conceal their real beliefs.

22. " Now that we have dealt with the wicked [c] and with the majority,[d] let us proceed to consider in the third place that better class of men, the dearest to Heaven, and discover how great their pleasures are, since their beliefs about God are pure from error : that he is our guide to all blessings, the father of everything honourable, and that he may no more do than suffer anything base. ' For he is good, and in none that is good arises envy about aught ' [e] or fear or anger or hatred ; for it is as much the function of heat to chill instead of warm as it is of good to harm.[f] By its nature anger is farthest removed from favour,

---

[a] Epicurus wrote *On the Gods* and *On Piety* : *cf.* Frag. 16 (ed. Arrighetti ; pp. 103-104 Usener) and Frag. 18 (ed. Arrighetti ; pp. 106-108 Usener).

[b] Euripides, *Andromaché*, 448 ; also quoted in *Mor.* 863 E and 1073 C. The words were suggested by the *skytalê*, a cryptographic device of the Spartans. A strip of leather was rolled about a staff, then the message was inscribed on it. The recipient had a staff of the same size, and was thus able to read the message.

[c] 1101 C-D, *supra.*

[d] 1101 D—1102 C, *supra.*   [e] Plato, *Timaeus*, 29 E.

[f] *Cf.* Plato, *Republic*, i, 335 D.

PLUTARCH'S MORALIA

(1102) καὶ τοῦ φιλανθρώπου καὶ φιλόφρονος τὸ δυσμενὲς
καὶ ταρακτικὸν ἀπωτάτω τῇ φύσει τέτακται· τὰ
μὲν γὰρ ἀρετῆς καὶ δυνάμεως, τὰ δὲ ἀσθενείας ἐστὶ
καὶ φαυλότητος. οὐ τοίνυν ' ὀργαῖς '[1] καὶ ' χάρισιν '
οὐ[2] ' συνέχεται ' τὸ θεῖον, ἀλλ' ὅτι μὲν χαρίζεσθαι καὶ
βοηθεῖν πέφυκεν, ὀργίζεσθαι δὲ καὶ[3] κακῶς ποιεῖν οὐ
πέφυκεν. ἀλλ' ' ὁ μὲν μέγας ἐν οὐρανῷ Ζεὺς[4] πρῶτος πορεύεται διακοσμῶν πάντα καὶ ἐπιμελούμενος,'[5] τῶν δὲ ἄλλων θεῶν ὁ μέν ἐστιν Ἐπιδώτης,[6]
ὁ δὲ Μειλίχιος, ὁ δὲ Ἀλεξίκακος· ὁ δὲ Ἀπόλλων

κατεκρίθη θνατοῖς[7] ἀγανώτατος ἔμμεν[8]

F ὡς Πίνδαρός[9] φησι. πάντα δὲ τῶν θεῶν κατὰ τὸν
Διογένη,[10] καὶ κοινὰ τὰ[11] τῶν φίλων, καὶ φίλοι τοῖς
θεοῖς οἱ ἀγαθοί, καὶ τὸν θεοφιλῆ μή τι εὖ πράττειν
ἢ θεοφιλῆ μὴ[12] εἶναι τὸν σώφρονα καὶ δίκαιον ἀδύνατόν ἐστιν. ἆρά γε δίκης ἑτέρας οἴεσθε δεῖσθαι
1103 τοὺς ἀναιροῦντας τὴν πρόνοιαν, οὐχ ἱκανὴν ἔχειν

[1] ὀργαῖς a g : ὀργαῖς, ὅτι Pohlenz.
[2] χάρισιν οὐ nos : χάρισι a g.
[3] ὅτι μὲν ... δὲ καὶ a : ὅτι ... καὶ g.
[4] Ζεὺς nos : ζεὺς κάτω a g (Ζεὺς πτηνὸν ἅρμα ἐλαύνων Xylander). [5] ἐπιμελούμενος a and Plato : ἐπινεμόμενος g.
[6] ἐπιδώτης a : ἐπιδότης g β². [7] θνατοῖς β² : θανάτοις a g.
[8] ἔμμεν κ : ἔμμεν' a ; ἔμμεναι g.
[9] Πίνδαρός Xylander : πίνδαρος πτηνὸν ἅρμα ἐλαύνων a g. Xylander would transpose πτηνὸν ἅρμα ἐλαύνων after Ζεὺς above.
[10] διογένη a : -ην g. [11] τὰ a : g omits.
[12] μὴ added here by Xylander, after ἢ by σ².

[a] Epicurus, *Cardinal Tenet* i : " What is blessed and
imperishable neither suffers trouble itself nor brings it on
others ; hence it is not a prey to feelings of anger or of
favour, for all such feelings are found in weakness."
[b] Plato, *Phaedrus*, 246 E.
[c] A name or epithet of a daemon at Sparta (Pausanias, iii.

120

wrath from goodwill, and from love of man and kindliness, hostility and the spreading of terror ; for the one set belong to virtue and power, the other to weakness and vice. Consequently it is not true that Heaven ' is not prey to feelings of anger ' and ' favour ' [a] ; rather, because it *is* God's nature to bestow favour and lend aid, it is *not* his nature to be angry and do harm. Rather, ' great Zeus in Heaven heads the procession, ordering and caring for all things ' [b] ; and of the other gods one is ' Bestower,' [c] one ' Kindly,' [d] one ' Averter of Evil ' [e] ; and Apollo, as Pindar [f] says,

Hath been adjudged most gentle to mankind.

All things belong to the gods, as Diogenes [g] said ; among friends all property is in common ; good men are friends of the gods ; and it cannot be that one dear to the gods should fail to prosper or that the temperate and upright man should fail to be dear to the gods.[h] Do you think that deniers of providence require any other punishment, and are not adequately

17. 9), of Sleep (*ibid*. ii. 10. 2), of certain gods not further described (*ibid*. ii. 27. 6), and of Zeus (*ibid*. viii. 9. 2).

[d] An epithet of Hera ; of Dionysus (*cf. Mor.* 613 D, 994 A, and *Life of Antony*, chap. xxiv. 4 [926 A]) ; of the Roman *Fortuna Obsequens* (*cf. Mor.* 322 F) ; of Aphroditê (*cf. Mor.* 370 D) ; of the Muses (Aratus, 17) ; and of Zeus (*cf. Mor.* 1076 B).

[e] Epithet of Apollo (*cf.* Pausanias, i. 3. 4), Heracles (*cf.* Aristides, *Or.* 38 [vol. I, p. 730, ed. Dindorf]), Hermes (Aristophanes, *Peace*, 422), and of Zeus (*cf. Mor.* 1076 B).

[f] Frag. 149 (ed. Snell), 158 (ed. Turyn) ; quoted also in *Mor.* 394 B, 413 C.

[g] *Cf.* Diogenes Laert. vi. 72, where Diogenes argues as follows : everything belongs to the gods ; the gods are friends of the wise ; the property of friends is in common ; therefore everything belongs to the wise.

[h] R. M. Jones (*The Platonism of Plutarch*, p. 131) compares Plato, *Republic*, i, 352 B.

121

(1103) ἐκκόπτοντας ἑαυτῶν ἡδονὴν καὶ χαρὰν τοσαύτην
ὅση πάρεστι[1] τοῖς οὕτω διακειμένοις πρὸς τὸ δαιμόνιον; ἢ τῷ[2] μὲν Ἐπικούρῳ[3] καὶ Μητρόδωρος
καὶ Πολύαινος καὶ Ἀριστόβουλος ' ἐκθάρσημα '
καὶ ' γῆθος ' ἦσαν, ὧν τοὺς πλείστους θεραπεύων
νοσοῦντας ἢ καταθρηνῶν ἀποθνήσκοντας διετέλεσε,
Λυκοῦργος δὲ ὑπὸ τῆς Πυθίας προσαγορευθεὶς

Ζηνὶ φίλος καὶ πᾶσιν[4] Ὀλύμπια δώματ᾽ ἔχουσι

καὶ Σωκράτης οἰόμενος αὐτῷ διαλέγεσθαι τὸ δαιμόνιον[5] ὑπὸ εὐμενείας καὶ Πίνδαρος ἀκούων ὑπὸ
τοῦ Πανὸς ᾀδεσθαί τι μέλος ὧν αὐτὸς ἐποίησε με-
B τρίως[6] ἔχαιρεν; ἢ Φορμίων τοὺς Διοσκόρους ἢ τὸν
Ἀσκληπιὸν Σοφοκλῆς ξενίζειν αὐτός[7] τε πειθόμενος
καὶ τῶν ἄλλων οὕτως ἐχόντων διὰ τὴν γενομένην
ἐπιφάνειαν; ἃ δὲ Ἑρμογένης ἐφρόνει περὶ τῶν
θεῶν ἄξιόν ἐστιν αὐτοῖς ὀνόμασι διαμνημονεύειν[8]·
' οὗτοι γάρ,' φησίν, ' οἱ πάντα μὲν εἰδότες πάντα
δὲ δυνάμενοι θεοὶ οὕτω μοι φίλοι εἰσὶν ὡς[9] διὰ τὸ

---

[1] πάρεστι Baxter : γάρ ἐστι a g.
[2] ἢ τῷ Pohlenz (ἡμῖν ἢ τῷ Wyttenbach): ἡμῖν τῆς aA[1] (ἡμῖν.
τῶ A[2]E); ἡ μῆνις· τοῖς g.
[3] ἐπικούρῳ a : ἐπίκουρος g.   [4] πᾶσιν a : πάλιν g.
[5] διαλέγεσθαι τὸ δαιμόνιον g : τὸ δαιμόνιον διαλέγεσθαι a.
[6] μετρίως a : μετρίων g.   [7] αὐτός a : αὐτούς g.
[8] διαμνημονεύειν a : διαμνημονεῦσαι g.
[9] ὡς a g : ὥστε Xenophon.

---

[a] Usener, *Epicurea*, pp. 92 f.
[b] Herodotus, i. 65 ; cf. *Oracular Responses* 29 and 216
(H. W. Parke and D. E. W. Wormell, *The Delphic Oracle*
[Oxford, 1956], vol. ii, pp. 14 and 216).
[c] Cf. *Life of Numa*, chap. iv. 8 (62 c).
[d] Cf. Pausanias, iii. 16. 2-3 : " . . . Close by is a house in
which they say the sons of Tyndareüs dwelt originally, while

punished when they extirpate from themselves so great a pleasure and delight as that of men who stand in this relation to the divine ? Or were Metrodorus and Polyaenus and Aristobulus a source of ' confidence ' and ' joy ' to Epicurus *ᵃ*—most of whom he was constantly tending in illness or mourning in death—while Lycurgus, when called by the Pythia

> One dear to Zeus and all who dwell on high,*ᵇ*

and Socrates, when he believed that Heaven was so propitious that it spoke to him, and Pindar,*ᶜ* when he heard that music of his own composition was sung by Pan, were only mildly pleased ? Or Phormio *ᵈ* who was host to the Dioscuri, or Sophocles *ᵉ* who was host to Asclepius, as he was convinced himself and the rest believed with him because of the epiphany that had occurred ? Hermogenes' *ᶠ* views about the gods deserve to be remembered in his very words.

> These gods [he says] who have all knowledge and all power are such friends to me that because of their care for

some time later it was acquired by Phormio, a Spartan. The Dioscuri came to him in the likeness of strangers. They said they came from Cyrenê and asked to be lodged at his house, requesting the room they liked best when they were among men. Phormio told them to take any other part of the house they pleased, but refused them the room that they requested, as he had a maiden daughter who lived in it. The next day the maiden and all her belongings had disappeared, and in the room were found statues of the Dioscuri and a table with silphium upon it."

ᵉ Cf. *Life of Numa*, chap. iv. 9 (62 D) and the *Etymologicum Magnum*, s.v. Δεξίων : " . . . They say that after Sophocles' death the Athenians wished to show him honour and set up a hero's shrine for him, calling him Dexion, from his reception (*dexis*) of Asclepius ; for he had received the god in his own house and set up an altar to him."

ᶠ Xenophon, *Symposium*, iv. 48.

(1103) ἐπιμελεῖσθαί μου οὔποτε λήθω αὐτοὺς οὔτε νυκτὸς
οὔτε ἡμέρας ὅποι[1] ἂν ὁρμῶμαι οὔτε ὅ τι ἂν μέλλω
πράττειν· διὰ δὲ τὸ προειδέναι καὶ ὅ τι ἐξ ἑκάστου[2]
ἀποβήσεται σημαίνουσι[3] πέμποντες ἀγγέλους φήμας
καὶ ἐνύπνια καὶ οἰωνούς.'

23. '' Καλὰ μὲν οὖν εἰκὸς εἶναι καὶ τὰ γινόμενα
C παρὰ τῶν θεῶν· τὸ δὲ γίνεσθαι διὰ τῶν θεῶν ταῦτα
αὐτὸ[4] μεγάλην ἡδονὴν ποιεῖ καὶ θάρσος ἀμήχανον
καὶ φρόνημα καὶ χαρὰν οἷον αὐγὴν[5] ἐπιγελῶσαν
τοῖς ἀγαθοῖς. οἱ δὲ ἄλλως ἔχοντες τῆς μὲν εὐτυ-
χίας τὸ ἥδιστον κολούουσι,[6] ταῖς δὲ δυστυχίαις ἀπο-
στροφὴν οὐκ ἀπολείπουσιν, ἀλλ' εἰς μίαν καταφυγὴν
καὶ λιμένα πράττοντες κακῶς τὴν διάλυσιν καὶ τὴν
ἀναισθησίαν ἀποβλέπουσιν· ὥσπερ εἴ τις ἐν πελάγει
καὶ χειμῶνι θαρρύνων[7] ἐπιστὰς λέγοι[8] μήτε τινὰ
τὴν ναῦν ἔχειν κυβερνήτην μήτε τοὺς Διοσκόρους
αὐτοῖς[9] ἀφίξεσθαι

D   ἐπερχόμενόν τε μαλάξοντας βιατὰν[10]
        πόντον ὠκείας τε ἀνέμων ῥιπάς,

οὐδὲν δὲ ὅμως εἶναι δεινὸν ἀλλ' ὅσον οὐδέπω κατα-
ποθήσεσθαι τὴν ναῦν ὑπὸ τῆς θαλάττης[11] ἢ συντρι-
βήσεσθαι ταχὺ πρὸς πέτρας[12] ἐκπεσοῦσαν. οὗτος[13]
γάρ ἐστιν ὁ Ἐπικούρειος λόγος ἐν νόσοις δειναῖς
καὶ πόνοις ὑπερβάλλουσιν· ' ἐλπίζεις[14] τι χρηστὸν

---

[1] ὅποι a[c]: ὅπου g a[ac]; οὔθ' ὅποι Xenophon.
[2] ἐξ ἑκάστου a and Xenophon : ἑκάστω g.
[3] σημαίνουσι a : καὶ σημαίνουσι g ; σημαίνουσί μοι Xenophon.
[4] αὐτὸ Pohlenz : αὐτὰ a g.
[5] αὐγὴν Baxter : αὐτὴν a ; g omits.
[6] κολούουσι g : κωλύουσι a.
[7] θαρρύνων (θαρνύνων g[ac]) a g[c] : θαρρύνων Pohlenz.
[8] λέγοι a : λέγει g.

124

me they never lose me from sight, night or day, wherever I go or whatever I set out to do ; and because they also know beforehand the outcome of every act, they give indications of it, sending as their messengers prophetic utterances, dreams and omens.

23. " Now it is to be presumed that what comes from the gods is excellent as well ; but its coming as a divine gift is itself a great source of pleasure and unbounded confidence and of a pride and joy that are like a gentle radiance illuminating the good. Those who do not experience this amputate the greatest pleasure of prosperity, while in misfortune they leave themselves no source of help. They can see but one haven of refuge in adversity, dissolution and the loss of all sensation.[a] It is as if someone in a storm at sea should come and reassure us by saying that the vessel has no helmsman, that no Dioscuri will come to save us

> To still the rude invasion of the seas
> And the swift hurtling of the winds [b];

there is however no cause for alarm, since at any moment the ship will be engulfed by the sea or will soon be cast on the rocks and dashed to pieces. For this is the Epicurean [c] argument in perilous disease and excruciating pain : ' You hope for some kind

[a] Frag. 500 (ed. Usener).
[b] D. Page, *Poetae Melici Graeci*, Frag. 998 (Adesp. 80) ; quoted also in *Mor.* 426 c.
[c] Frag. 448 (ed. Usener).

---

[9] αὑτοῖς g : αὐτοὺς a.
[10] βιατάν Bergk : βίαιον a g ; βία τὸν *Mor.* 426 c.
[11] θαλάττης a : θαλάσσης g.
[12] πέτρας a : τὰς πέτρας g.
[13] οὗτος a g[ac] : οὕτως g[c].
[14] ἐλπίζεις a : ἐλπίζειν g.

(1103) παρὰ θεῶν δι' εὐσέβειαν; τετύφωσαι· "τὸ γὰρ
μακάριον καὶ ἄφθαρτον οὔτε ὀργαῖς οὔτε χάρισι
συνέχεται." βέλτιόν τι τῶν ἐν τῷ βίῳ μετὰ τὸν
βίον ἐπινοεῖς; ἐξηπάτησαι· "τὸ γὰρ διαλυθὲν[1] ἀναι-
σθητεῖ, τὸ δὲ ἀναισθητοῦν οὐδὲν πρὸς ἡμᾶς.''' 'πῶς
οὖν, ἄνθρωπε, φαγεῖν με[2] καὶ χαίρειν κελεύεις;'
E 'ὅτι νὴ Δία χειμαζομένῳ τὸ ναυάγιον ἐγγύς[3] ἐστιν·
"ὁ γὰρ πόνος ὁ ὑπερβάλλων συνάψει θανάτῳ."[4]
καίτοι νεὼς μὲν ἐκπεσὼν ἐπιβάτης διαλυθείσης ἐπ'[5]
ἐλπίδος ὀχεῖται τινος ὡς γῇ προσέξων τὸ σῶμα
καὶ[6] διανηξόμενος, τῆς δὲ τούτων φιλοσοφίας

ἔκβασις οὔ πη φαίνεθ'[7] ἁλὸς πολιοῖο θύραζε

τῇ ψυχῇ, ἀλλ' εὐθὺς ἠφάνισται καὶ διέσπαρται καὶ
προαπόλωλε[8] τοῦ σώματος· ὥστε ὑπερχαίρειν τὸ
πάνσοφον τοῦτο δόγμα καὶ θεῖον παραλαβοῦσαν,
ὅτι τοῦ κακῶς πράττειν πέρας ἐστὶν αὐτῇ τὸ ἀπολέ-
σθαι καὶ φθαρῆναι καὶ μηδὲν εἶναι.

24. "'Ἀλλὰ γάρ," ἔφη πρὸς ἐμὲ βλέψας, " εὐη-
θές ἐστι καὶ[9] περὶ τούτου λέγειν ἡμᾶς, σοῦ[10] πρῴην
F ἀκηκοότας ἱκανῶς διαλεγομένου[11] πρὸς τοὺς ἀξιοῦν-
τας τὸν[12] Ἐπικούρου λόγον[13] τοῦ[14] Πλάτωνος περὶ
ψυχῆς ῥᾴονας καὶ ἡδίους πρὸς θάνατον ἡμᾶς ποι-

---

[1] διαλυθὲν g : λυθὲν a.
[2] με a : μὲν g.
[3] ἐγγύς a : g omits.
[4] θανάτῳ a : θάνατον g.
[5] ἐπ' g : a omits.
[6] καὶ a : g omits.
[7] φαινεθ' g : φαινεσθ' a.
[8] προαπόλωλε a : ἀπόλωλε g.
[9] καὶ g : a omits.
[10] σοῦ Meziriacus (te Ferronus, t' Amyot) : οὐ a g.

treatment from the gods for all your piety ? You are deluded ; " what is blessed and imperishable is prey neither to feelings of wrath nor of favour." [a] You conceive of something after this life better than what you found in it ? You are deceived, " for what is dissipated has no sensation, and what has no sensation is nothing to us." ' [b] ' Then why, you knave, do you tell me to eat and rejoice ? ' ' Why else but because for you, who are labouring in the storm, shipwreck is imminent, " for surpassing pain leads straight to death." ' [c] Yet a voyager cast away when his vessel breaks up is kept from sinking by some hope of getting his person to land and swimming safely through ; but in these men's [d] philosophy the soul

Can find no egress from the hoary sea [e]

since she is at once annihilated and scattered, perishing before the body. Consequently she is overjoyed at receiving this most sapient and godlike doctrine, [f] that the end of her troubles is to be destroyed and perish and be nothing.

24. " As a matter of fact," he said, with a look at me, " it is foolish for us to include this point with the rest, since the other day we heard the able reply you gave to those who believe that Epicurus' theory of the soul makes us face death with greater composure

[a] *Cardinal Tenet* i.
[b] *Cardinal Tenet* ii.
[c] Frag. 448 (ed. Usener).
[d] *Cf.* Metrodorus, Frag. 38 (ed. Körte).
[e] Homer, *Od.* v. 410 ; alluded to in *Mor.* 594 A.
[f] Frag. 500 (ed. Usener).

---

[11] διαλεγομένου a : διαλεγομένους g.
[12] τὸν a : τῶν g (*sic*).   [13] λόγον a : λόγων g.
[14] τοῦ g : τοὺς a.

(1103) εἶν.''[1] ὑπολαβὼν οὖν[2] ὁ Ζεύξιππος, " εἶτα οὗτος,''
ἔφη, " δι' ἐκεῖνον ἀτελὴς ὁ λόγος ἔσται, καὶ φοβη-
θησόμεθα ταυτολογεῖν πρὸς Ἐπίκουρον[3] λέγοντες;''
" ἥκιστα,'' ἔφην ἐγώ·

" καὶ δὶς[4] γὰρ[5] ὃ δεῖ καλόν ἐστιν ἀκοῦσαι

1104 κατ'[6] Ἐμπεδοκλέα. πάλιν οὖν ὁ Θέων ἡμῖν παρα-
κλητέος· οὐ γὰρ ἀργὸν[7] οἶμαι παρεῖναι τοῖς τότε
λεχθεῖσιν, ἀλλὰ καὶ νέος ἐστὶ[8] καὶ οὐ δέδιε μὴ
λήθης εὐθύνας ὑπόσχῃ τοῖς νέοις.''

25. Καὶ ὁ Θέων ὥσπερ ἐκβιασθείς, " ἀλλ' εἰ
δοκεῖ ταῦτα,'' ἔφη, " ποιεῖν, οὐ μιμήσομαί σε, ὦ
Ἀριστόδημε· σὺ μὲν γὰρ ἐφοβήθης τὰ τούτου
λέγειν, ἐγὼ δὲ χρήσομαι τοῖς σοῖς. ὀρθῶς γάρ μοι
διαιρεῖν ἔδοξας[9] εἰς τρία γένη τοὺς ἀνθρώπους, τὸ
τῶν ἀδίκων καὶ πονηρῶν, δεύτερον δὲ τὸ τῶν πολλῶν καὶ ἰδιωτῶν, τρίτον δὲ τὸ τῶν ἐπιεικῶν καὶ
νοῦν ἐχόντων.

" Οἱ μὲν οὖν ἄδικοι καὶ πονηροὶ τὰς καθ' Ἅι-
Β δου[10] δίκας καὶ τιμωρίας δεδιότες καὶ φοβούμενοι

---

[1] πρὸς θάνατον ἡμᾶς ποιεῖν a : ἡμᾶς ποιεῖν πρὸς θάνατον g.
[2] οὖν a : g omits.
[3] ταυτολογεῖν πρὸς Ἐπίκουρον Wyttenbach : τὸ λόγιον πρὸς
ἐπίκουρον a ; πρὸς ἐπίκουρον τὸ λόγιον g.
[4] δὶς Schol. Plat. Gorg. 498 ε : δεῖ a ; δὴ g.
[5] γὰρ Schol. Plat. Gorg. 498 ε : παρ' a g.
[6] κατ' g : κατὰ τὸν a.
[7] ἀργὸν nos : αὐτὸν a g (Pohlenz would add παρέργως after
οἶμαι ; μόνον αὐτὸν Post).
[8] καὶ νέος ἐστὶ a : κενός ἐστι g.
[9] After ἔδοξας g breaks off in the middle of line 27 on
folio 217v (g has 30 lines a page).
[10] καθ' Ἅιδου Meziriacus : καθόλου a.

128

and serenity than Plato's." [a] Here Zeuxippus spoke up : " What ! Is the present discussion to remain incomplete because of the other, and are we to be afraid to repeat ourselves in reply to Epicurus of all people ? " " By no means," I said ; " as Empedocles[b] has it,

> Well may we hear the right word said again.

We must therefore once more call upon Theon ; for I do not think he was an idle auditor of what was said on that occasion ; he is also young and need not fear that the young men [c] will take him to task for lapses of memory."

25. To this Theon said, as though yielding to compulsion : " If it is settled then, I shall not imitate you, Aristodemus. For you were afraid [d] to repeat the arguments of our friend here, whereas I shall repeat yours. I thought your distinction of men into three classes [e] a good one—first evil-doers and the wicked, second the ordinary majority, and third the upright and intelligent.

" Now evil-doers and the wicked, dreading judgement and punishment in the world to come, and from

---

[a] This has been taken to refer to a lost work of Plutarch, such as those listed as No. 177 or 226 in the Catalogue of Lamprias. It is, however, unlikely that Plutarch would have repeated himself at such length in writing, and no known title of a lost work exactly fits the subject. He is probably publishing an earlier lecture as part of the present essay.

[b] Diels and Kranz, *Die Frag. d. Vorsokratiker*, Empedokles, B 25 ; *cf.* also Plato, *Gorgias*, 498 E—499 A and *Philebus*, 60 A.

[c] Students of the school, who are now present and who attended the lecture spoken of.

[d] *Cf.* 1103 E-F, *supra*.

[e] *Cf.* 1102 D, *supra*, and 1130 C-D, *infra*. The division is found in Plato, *Phaedo*, 89 E—90 A.

(1104) κακουργεῖν καὶ διὰ τοῦτο μᾶλλον ἡσυχίαν ἄγοντες
ἥδιον βιώσονται καὶ ἀταρακτότερον. οὐ γὰρ Ἐπίκουρος ἄλλῳ τινὶ τῆς ἀδικίας οἴεται δεῖν ἀπείργειν
ἢ φόβῳ κολάσεων. ὥστε καὶ προσεμφορητέον
ἐκείνοις[1] τῆς δεισιδαιμονίας καὶ κινητέον ἐπ' αὐτοὺς
ἅμα τὰ ἐξ οὐρανοῦ καὶ γῆς δείματα καὶ χάσματα[2]
καὶ φόβους καὶ ὑπονοίας εἰ μέλλουσιν ἐκπλαγέντες
ὑπὸ τούτων ἐπιεικέστερον ἔχειν καὶ πραότερον.
λυσιτελεῖ γὰρ αὐτοῖς τὰ μετὰ τὸν θάνατον φοβου-
μένοις μὴ ἀδικεῖν ἢ ἀδικοῦσιν ἐπισφαλῶς ἐν τῷ
βίῳ διάγειν καὶ περιφόβως.

26. '' Τοῖς δὲ πολλοῖς[3] καὶ ἄνευ φόβου περὶ τῶν
C ἐν Ἅιδου[4] παρὰ[5] τὸ μυθῶδες ἡ[6] τῆς ἀιδιότητος
ἐλπίς, καὶ ὁ πόθος τοῦ εἶναι, πάντων ἐρώτων πρε-
σβύτατος ὢν καὶ μέγιστος, ἡδοναῖς ὑπερβάλλει καὶ
γλυκυθυμίαις[7] τὸ παιδικὸν ἐκεῖνο δέος. ᾗ[8] καὶ
τέκνα καὶ γυναῖκα[9] καὶ φίλους ἀποβάλλοντες εἶναί
που μᾶλλον ἐθέλουσι καὶ διαμένειν κακοπαθοῦντας
ἢ παντάπασιν ἐξῃρῆσθαι καὶ διεφθάρθαι καὶ γεγονέναι τὸ μηδέν· ἡδέως δὲ τῶν ὀνομάτων τοῦ μεθ-
ίστασθαι τὸν θνήσκοντα καὶ μεταλλάττειν καὶ ὅσα
δηλοῖ μεταβολὴν ὄντα τῆς ψυχῆς οὐ φθορὰν τὸν
θάνατον ἀκροῶνται καὶ λέγουσιν οὕτως

αὐτὰρ ἐγὼ κἀκεῖθι φίλου μεμνήσομ' ἑταίρου

[1] ἐκείνης a[ac].
[2] χάσματα a : φάσματα Wyttenbach ; πλάσματα Post.
[3] πολλοῖς a : πολλοῖς ἱκανὴ Pohlenz.
[4] καὶ ἄνευ . . . Ἅιδου nos : καὶ ἄνευ . . . ἅδου ἡ a.
[5] παρὰ β : περὶ a.
[6] ἡ added by us.
[7] ἡδοναῖς . . . γλυκυθυμίαις Castiglioni : ἡδονῆς . . . γλυκυ-
θυμίας a.

that fear remaining more inactive, will enjoy for that reason a life of greater pleasure and less anxiety. For Epicurus [a] supposes that fear of punishment is the only motive to which we can properly appeal in deterring from crime. It follows that we should cram them even fuller of superstitious dread and bring to bear on them the joint array of celestial and terrestrial terrors and chasms [b] and alarms and apprehensions if they are to be shocked by all this into a state of greater honesty and restraint. For they are better off avoiding crime for fear of the next world than committing crimes and spending their lives in insecurity and apprehension.

26. " The great majority, however, have an expectation of eternity undisturbed by any myth-inspired fear of what may come after death ; and the love of being, the oldest and greatest of all our passions, is more than a counterpoise for that childish terror. Indeed when men have lost children, a wife, or friends, they would rather have them exist somewhere in hardship and survive than be utterly taken away and destroyed and reduced to nothing ; and they like to hear such expressions used of the dying as ' he is leaving us ' or ' going to dwell elsewhere ' and all that represent the soul as changing [c] but not perishing in death, and they talk like this :

> Nay even there I shall remember him [d]

[a] Frag. 534 (ed. Usener) ; *cf. Cardinal Tenets* xvii, xxxiv, xxxv.
[b] *Cf.* Colotes' attack on the myth in the *Republic* translated pp. 178 f., *infra.*   [c] *Cf.* Plato, *Apology*, 40 c.
[d] Homer, *Il.* xxii. 390. Achilles says of Patroclus:
> And if in Hades men forget the dead
> Nay even there I shall remember him.

---

[8] $\tilde{\eta} \beta^2$: $\tilde{\eta} a$.   [9] $\gamma\nu\nu\alpha\hat{\iota}\kappa a$ a : $\gamma\nu\nu\alpha\hat{\iota}\kappa a\varsigma$ Baxter.

(1104) καὶ

D   τί σοι πρὸς Ἕκτορ' ἢ γέροντ' εἴπω πόσιν;

ἐκ δὲ τούτου παρατροπῆς γενομένης καὶ ὅπλα καὶ
σκεύη καὶ ἱμάτια συνήθη τοῖς τεθνηκόσι καὶ ὡς ὁ
Μίνως τῷ Γλαύκῳ

Κρητικοὺς αὐλοὺς θανόντι[1] κῶλα ποικίλης νε-
βροῦ

συνθάπτοντες ἥδιον ἔχουσι. κἄν τι δόξωσιν αἰτεῖν
καὶ ποθεῖν ἐκείνους, χαίρουσιν ἐπιδιδόντες,[2] ὥσπερ
ὁ Περίανδρος τῇ γυναικὶ τὸν κόσμον ὡς δεομένῃ
καὶ ῥιγοῦν λεγούσῃ συγκατέκαυσεν. οἱ δὲ Αἰακοὶ
καὶ Ἀσκάλαφοι καὶ Ἀχέροντες οὐ πάνυ διαταράττουσιν, οἷς γε καὶ χοροὺς καὶ θέατρα καὶ μοῦσαν
E παντοδαπὴν ὡς ἡδόμενοι δεδώκασιν.[3]   ἀλλ' ἐκεῖνο
τοῦ θανάτου τὸ πρόσωπον ὡς φοβερὸν καὶ σκυθρω-
πὸν καὶ σκοτεινὸν ἅπαντες ὑποδειμαίνουσι, τὸ τῆς
ἀναισθησίας καὶ λήθης καὶ ἀγνοίας· καὶ πρὸς τὸ
' ἀπόλωλε ' καὶ τὸ ' ἀνῄρηται '[4] καὶ τὸ ' οὐκ ἔστι '

---

[1] θανόντι Reiske (θανοῦσι Rasmus) : θανούσης a.

[2] ἐπιδόντες a[ac].

[3] παντοδαπὴν ὡς ἡδόμενοι δεδώκασιν nos : ἡδομένοις παντοδαπὴν γενομένου δεδώκασιν a ; ἡδονῆς παντοδαπῆς γέμουσαν δεδώκασιν Meziriacus ;   ἡδονῆς παντοδαπῆς γενέτειραν ἀποδεδώ-
κασιν? Pohlenz ;   ὡς ἂν ἡδομένοις παντοδαπὴν γενομένου τούτου
δεδώκασιν Post.

[4] τὸ ἀνῄρηται A[a]E : τἀνῄρηται a (τ- possibly an after-
thought)A[1].

A PLEASANT LIFE IMPOSSIBLE, 1104

and

> What word from you to Hector shall I bring,
> Or to your aged husband ? [a]

Then a false turn is taken, and people feel easier
when they bury with the dead the arms and property
and clothes with which they were familiar, as Minos
buried with Glaucus

> The Cretan flutes,
> Bones of the dappled fawn. [b]

And if they imagine that the dead are asking them
for something that they miss, they gladly give it, as
Periander burnt all the finery for his dead wife in the
belief that she desired it and complained of being
cold. [c] The figures of Aeacus [d] and Ascalaphus [e] and
Acheron [f] can hardly be said to terrify them greatly,
since to these they have given the honour of choruses
and presentation in theatres and of elaborate music, [g]
taking pleasure, it would seem, in the giving. No ;
the countenance worn by death that dismays all men
as fearful, grim, and dark, is insensibility, oblivion,
and knowing nothing. Such expressions as ' he is
lost ' and ' he has perished ' and ' he is no more '

[a] Euripides, *Hecuba*, 422. Polyxena, about to be led off
and sacrificed, speaks to her mother Hecuba.

[b] Nauck, *Trag. Graec. Frag.*, Adesp. 419.

[c] Herodotus, v. 92η. 2-3.

[d] Grandfather of Ajax and Achilles ; after death a judge
of the dead.

[e] Son of Acheron ; punished for betraying Persephonê's
eating of the pomegranate seeds (*cf.* Ovid, *Metamorphoses*, v.
534-550 and Apollodorus, *Bibl.* i. 5. 3 with Frazer's note in
the L.C.L.).

[f] Eponym of the infernal river.

[g] Perhaps Plutarch is thinking of a dithyramb telling the
story of Persephonê : *cf.* Melanippides, Frag. 3 (D. Page,
Poetae Melici Graeci, No. 759).

133

(1104) ταράσσονται καὶ δυσανασχετοῦσι τούτων λεγο-
μένων·

> τὸ ἔπειτα κείσεται[1] βαθυδένδρῳ
> ἐν χθονὶ συμποσίων τε καὶ λυρᾶν ἄμοιρος
> ἰαχᾶς τε παντερπέος αὐλῶν

καὶ

> ἀνδρὸς δὲ ψυχὴ πάλιν ἐλθεῖν οὔτε λεϊστὴ
> οὔθ' ἑλετή, ἐπεὶ ἄρ κεν ἀμείψεται ἕρκος ὀδόντων.

(27.) ἦν[2] καὶ προσεπισφάττουσιν[3] οἱ ταυτὶ λέγοντες
' ἅπαξ ἄνθρωποι γεγόναμεν, δὶς δὲ οὐκ ἔστι γενέ-
σθαι· δεῖ δὲ τὸν αἰῶνα μηκέτ' εἶναι.'[4] καὶ γὰρ τὸ
F παρὸν ὡς μικρόν, μᾶλλον δὲ μηδ' ὁτιοῦν πρὸς τὸ
σύμπαν[5] ἀτιμάσαντες[6] ἀναπόλαυστον[7] προΐενται, καὶ
ὀλιγωροῦσιν ἀρετῆς καὶ πράξεως οἷον ἐξαθυμοῦντες
καὶ καταφρονοῦντες ἑαυτῶν ὡς ἐφημέρων καὶ ἀβε-
1105 βαίων καὶ πρὸς οὐθὲν ἀξιόλογον γεγονότων. τὸ
γὰρ ' ἀναισθητεῖν τὸ διαλυθὲν[8] καὶ μηδὲν[9] εἶναι
πρὸς ἡμᾶς τὸ ἀναισθητοῦν ' οὐκ ἀναιρεῖ τὸ τοῦ
θανάτου δέος ἀλλ' ὥσπερ ἀπόδειξιν αὐτοῦ προστί-
θησιν. αὐτὸ γὰρ τοῦτό ἐστιν ὃ δέδοικεν ἡ φύσις·

> ἀλλ' ὑμεῖς μὲν πάντες ὕδωρ καὶ γαῖα γένοισθε—

τὴν εἰς τὸ μὴ φρονοῦν μηδὲ αἰσθανόμενον διάλυσιν

---

[1] τὸ ἔπειτα κείσεται Pohlenz (ὡς τό, ἔπειτα κείσεται Dübner):
τὸ ἐπιτακήσεται a.
[2] ἦν Pohlenz (ἦ Baxter): ἦ a.
[3] προσεπισφάττουσιν a: προεπισφάττουσιν Pohlenz; προσδια-
στρέφουσιν? Westman. [4] εἶναι Baxter: ἰέναι a.
[5] σύμπαν Xylander: σύμπαντα a.
[6] ἀτιμάσαντες Cobet ι ἀτιμήσαντες a.
[7] ἀναπόλαυστον Wyttenbach: ἀναπόλαυστα a.

disturb them and these lines when quoted fill them
with uneasiness :

> Henceforth shall he lie
> In the deep roots of earth, and know no more
> Of banquets or the lyre or the sweet cry
> Of flutes [a]

and

> No raid or capture can bring back the life
> Once it has passed the barrier of the teeth [b]—

(27.) a life that is actually dealt the finishing blow by
those [c] who say : ' We men are born once ; there is no
second time ; we must forever be no more.' Indeed by
discounting the present moment as a minute fraction,
or rather as nothing at all, in comparison with all
time, men let it pass fruitlessly. They think poorly
of virtue and manly action ; they lose heart, you
might say, and despise themselves as creatures of a
day, impermanent, and born for no high end. For
the doctrine [d] that ' what is dissipated has no sensation, and what has no sensation is nothing to us ' does
not remove the terror of death, but rather confirms it
by adding what amounts to a proof. For this is the
very thing our nature dreads :

> May all of you be turned to earth and water— [e]

the dissolution of the soul into what has neither

---

[a] D. Page, *Poetae Melici Graeci*, Frag. 1009 (Adesp. 91).

[b] Homer, *Il.* ix. 408–409.

[c] Frag. 204 (ed. Usener) and *Gnom. Vat.* 14 ; *cf.* 1106 ꜰ, *infra.*

[d] Frag. 500 (ed. Usener) ; *cf. Cardinal Tenet* ii, quoted at 1103 ᴅ, *supra.*

[e] Homer, *Il.* vii. 99.

---

[8] ἀναισθητεῖν τὸ διαλυθὲν Usener (ἀναισθητεῖν τὸ λυθὲν Gata-
ker) : ἀναίσθητον καὶ λυθὲν a.   [9] μηδὲν a²AE : μηθὲν a¹.

(1105) τῆς ψυχῆς, ἣν Ἐπίκουρος εἰς κενὸν καὶ ἀτόμους
διασπορὰν ποιῶν ἔτι μᾶλλον ἐκκόπτει τὴν ἐλπίδα
τῆς ἀφθαρσίας, δι' ἣν ὀλίγου δέω λέγειν πάντας
εἶναι καὶ πάσας προθύμους τῷ Κερβέρῳ διαδάκνε-
σθαι καὶ φορεῖν εἰς τὸν τρητόν,[1] ὅπως ἐν τῷ εἶναι
B μόνον διαμένωσι μηδὲ ἀναιρεθῶσι. καίτοι ταῦτα
μέν, ὥσπερ ἔφην, οὐ πάνυ πολλοὶ δεδίασι, μητέρων
ὄντα καὶ τιτθῶν δόγματα καὶ λόγους μυθώδεις, οἱ
δὲ καὶ δεδιότες τελετάς τινας αὖ πάλιν καὶ καθαρ-
μοὺς οἴονται βοηθεῖν, οἷς ἁγνισάμενοι διατελεῖν ἐν
Ἅιδου παίζοντες καὶ χορεύοντες ἐν τόποις[2] αὐγὴν
καὶ πνεῦμα καθαρὸν καὶ φθόγγον ἔχουσιν. ἡ δὲ
τοῦ ζῆν στέρησις ἐνοχλεῖ καὶ νέους καὶ γέροντας·

> δυσέρωτες γὰρ φαινόμεθ' ὄντες
> τοῦδε,[3] ὅ τι τοῦτο[4] στίλβει κατὰ γῆν

ὡς Εὐριπίδης φησίν· οὐδὲ ῥᾳδίως οὐδὲ ἀλύπως
ἀκούομεν

> ὡς ἄρα εἰπόντα μιν τηλαυγὲς ἀμβρόσιον
> ἐλασίππου πρόσωπον[5]
> ἀπέλιπεν ἀμέρας.

---

[1] τρητόν Rasmus (τρητὸν πίθον Reiske) : ἄτρητον a.
[2] τόποις Wyttenbach : τοῖς a.
[3] τοῦδε σ² : τοῦ δὲ a.   [4] τοῦτο Euripides : τόδε a.
[5] πρόσωπον Wyttenbach : πρὸς τόπον a.

---

[a] Cf. Leutsch and Schneidewin, *Paroem. Gr.*, vol. i, p. 33
(Zenobius, *Cent.* ii. 6) and vol. ii, p. 154 (Macarius, *Cent.* iii.
16). The Danaids in Hades draw water in broken vessels
and carry it to a leaky jar.
[b] 1104 B-C, *supra.*
[c] Cf. Cicero, *Tusc. Disput.* i. 21 (48) and *De Nat. Deor.* ii.
2 (5).
[d] Cf. Plato, *Republic*, ii, 364 B—365 A, 366 A-B.

thought nor feeling ; and Epicurus, by making the dissolution a scattering into emptiness and atoms, does still more to root out our hope of preservation, a hope for which (I had almost said) all men and all women are ready to match their teeth against the fangs of Cerberus and carry water to the leaky urn,[a] if only they may still continue to be and not be blotted out. Yet such tales as these, as I said,[b] are not feared by very many, being the doctrine and fabulous argument of mothers and nurses [c] ; and even those who fear them hold that there is an answering remedy in certain mystic ceremonies and rituals of purification,[d] and that when cleansed by these they will pass their time in the other world in play and choral dancing in regions where there is radiance and a sweet breeze and a sound of voices.[e] Whereas privation of life is a gnawing thought to young as well as old :

> Smit with a painful love are we of this
> We know not what, this brightness here on earth

as Euripides [f] says ; and it is not calmly or without a pang that we give ear to this :

> Thus spoke he ; and the radiant face
> Ambrosial of the charioting day
> Departed from him.[g]

[e] *Cf.* a fragment of Plutarch *On the Soul* (vol. vii, p. 23. 7-14 Bern.). The experience of death is like initiation into a great mystery. "At first we wander and run about laboriously and make certain journeys in the dark that are disquieting and lead nowhere ; then before the actual consummation come all the terrors—we shiver and tremble and sweat and are thunderstruck ; but then a marvellous light meets us and pure regions and meadows with voices and dances and all the majesty of sacred recitals and holy visions ; . . ."

[f] *Hippolytus*, 193-194.

[g] Page, *Poetae Melici Graeci*, Frag. 1010 (Adesp. 92).

(1105)

C (28.) διὸ τῇ δόξῃ τῆς ἀθανασίας συναναιροῦσι τὰς
ἡδίστας ἐλπίδας καὶ μεγίστας τῶν πολλῶν.

" Τί δῆτα[1] τῶν ἀγαθῶν οἰόμεθα καὶ βεβιωκότων
ὁσίως καὶ δικαίως, οἷ[2] κακὸν μὲν οὐθὲν ἐκεῖ, τὰ δὲ
κάλλιστα καὶ θειότατα προσδοκῶσι; πρῶτον μὲν
γάρ, ὡς[3] ἀθληταὶ στέφανον οὐκ ἀγωνιζόμενοι[4] λαμβάνουσιν ἀλλὰ ἀγωνισάμενοι καὶ νικήσαντες, οὕτως[5]
ἡγούμενοι τοῖς ἀγαθοῖς τὰ νικητήρια τοῦ βίου
μετὰ τὸν βίον ὑπάρχειν θαυμάσιον οἷον φρονοῦσι
τῇ ἀρετῇ πρὸς ἐκείνας τὰς ἐλπίδας· ἐν αἷς ἐστι καὶ
τοὺς νῦν ὑβρίζοντας ὑπὸ πλούτου καὶ δυνάμεως
καὶ καταγελῶντας ἀνοήτως τῶν κρειττόνων ἐπ-
D ιδεῖν ἀξίαν δίκην τίνοντας. ἔπειτα τῆς ἀληθείας
καὶ θέας τοῦ ὄντος οὐδεὶς ἐνταῦθα τῶν ἐρώντων[6]
ἐνέπλησεν ἑαυτὸν ἱκανῶς, οἷον δι᾿ ὁμίχλης ἢ νέφους
τοῦ σώματος ὑγρῷ καὶ ταραττομένῳ τῷ λογισμῷ
χρώμενος, ἀλλ᾿ ὄρνιθος δίκην ἄνω βλέποντες ὡς
ἐκπτησόμενοι τοῦ σώματος εἰς μέγα τι καὶ λαμ-
πρόν, εὐσταλῆ καὶ ἐλαφρὰν ποιοῦσι τὴν ψυχὴν ἀπὸ
τῶν θνητῶν, τῷ φιλοσοφεῖν μελέτῃ χρώμενοι τοῦ
ἀποθνήσκειν, οὕτως μέγα τι καὶ τέλεον ὄντως ἀγαθὸν ἡγούμενοι[7] τὴν τελευτήν, ὡς βίον ἀληθῆ βιω-
σομένην ἐκεῖ τὴν ψυχήν, οὐχ ὕπαρ[8] νῦν[9] ζῶσαν,
E ἀλλ᾿ ὀνείρασιν ὅμοια πάσχουσαν. εἰ τοίνυν ' ἡδὺ

---

[1] δῆτα a : δὲ τὰ Kronenberg.
[2] οἳ added by Baxter (qui Ferronus).
[3] ὡς added by Pohlenz ; ὥσπερ or καθάπερ Castiglioni ;
ὥσπερ οἱ ? Westman.
[4] ἀγωνιζόμενοι Reiske : ἀγωνιζόμενοι οὐ a.
[5] οὕτως a : καὶ οὕτως Westman.
[6] ἐρώντων a[2]AE : ἐρώτων a[1].
[7] ἡγούμενοι nos : ἡγοῦμαι a (ἡγοῦνται β[288]).
[8] ὕπαρ ΛΕ : ἧπαρ a.
[9] νῦν Α[288]E : aA[1] omit.

(28.) Hence in abolishing belief in immortality they also abolish the pleasantest and greatest hopes of ordinary men.

" What then do we suppose they do to the pleasures of the good, whose lives have been just and holy, who look forward to nothing evil in that other world but instead to all that is most glorious and divine ? For in the first place, just as athletes receive the crown not while they are engaged in the contest [a] but when it is over and victory is won, so men who believe that the awards for victory in life await the good when life is done are inspired by their virtue to a most wonderful confidence [b] when they fix their eyes on these hopes, which include that of seeing at last the condign punishment of those who in their wealth and power are injurious and insolent now and who in their folly laugh all higher powers to scorn. In the next place no one impassioned for the truth and the vision of reality has ever been fully satisfied in this world, since the light of reason, veiled by the body as by a mist or cloud, is wavering and indistinct ; but like a bird [c] that gazes upward, they are ready to take wing from the body to some luminous expanse, and thus they lighten and disburden the soul of the gear of mortality, taking philosophy as an exercise in death.[d] They regard death as so great and so truly perfect a blessing since they hold that in that other world the soul will live a real life, whereas now it is not fully awake but is living instead in a kind of dream. If then ' the memory of a dead friend is

---

[a] Cf. *Mor.* 561 A.
[b] Cf. Plato and Pindar in *Republic*, i, 331 A.
[c] Cf. Plato, *Phaedrus*, 249 D 7 and the *Seventh Letter*, 348 A 1.
[d] Plato, *Phaedo*, 64 A 4-6, 67 D 7-10, E 4-5, 80 E 5—81 A 2.

(1105) πανταχόθεν ἡ φίλου μνήμη τεθνηκότος,' ὥσπερ
Ἐπίκουρος εἶπε, καὶ ἤδη νοεῖν πάρεστιν ἡλίκης
ἑαυτοὺς χαρᾶς ἀποστεροῦσι, φάσματα μὲν¹ καὶ
εἴδωλα τεθνηκότων ἑταίρων οἰόμενοι δέχεσθαι καὶ
θηρεύειν,² οἷς οὔτε νοῦς ἐστιν οὔτε αἴσθησις, αὐτοῖς
δὲ συνέσεσθαι πάλιν ἀληθῶς, καὶ τὸν φίλον πατέρα
καὶ τὴν φίλην μητέρα καί που γυναῖκα χρηστὴν
ὄψεσθαι μὴ προσδοκῶντες, μηδὲ ἔχοντες ἐλπίδα τῆς
ὁμιλίας ἐκείνης καὶ φιλοφροσύνης, ἣν ἔχουσιν οἱ τὰ
αὐτὰ Πυθαγόρᾳ καὶ Πλάτωνι καὶ Ὁμήρῳ περὶ ψυ-
F χῆς δοξάζοντες. ᾧ δὲ ὅμοιόν ἐστιν αὐτῶν τὸ πάθος
Ὅμηρος ὑποδεδήλωκεν, εἴδωλον τοῦ Αἰνείου κατα-
βαλὼν εἰς μέσον τοῖς μαχομένοις ὡς τεθνηκότος,
εἶτα ὕστερον αὐτὸν ἐκεῖνον ἀναδείξας

> ζωόν τε³ καὶ ἀρτεμέα προσιόντα
> καὶ μένος ἐσθλὸν ἔχοντα

τοῖς φίλοις·

> οἱ δὲ ἐχάρησαν

φησί, καὶ τὸ εἴδωλον μεθέμενοι περιέσχον αὐτόν.⁴
1106 οὐκοῦν καὶ ἡμεῖς τοῦ λόγου δεικνύοντος ὡς ἔστιν
ἐντυχεῖν⁵ ἀληθῶς τοῖς τεθνεῶσι καὶ τῷ φρονοῦντι
καὶ⁶ φιλοῦντι τοῦ φρονοῦντος αὐτοῦ καὶ φιλοῦντος

---

¹ μὲν added by Reiske.
² θηρεύειν a : θεωρεῖν Sandbach ; τηρεῖν? Pohlenz.
³ τε Homer : a omits.
⁴ μεθέμενοι περιέσχον αὐτόν Meziriacus : θέμενοι παρέχον
(-έσχον μ ; -εἶχον κ) ἑαυτόν a.

140

pleasant on every count' as Epicurus [a] said, we need no more to make us see the great delight that they renounce when they suppose that they can receive and capture the apparitions and likenesses [b] of dead companions—images that have neither mind nor feeling —but do not think they will meet once more those friends themselves, or ever again see a dear father or dear mother or perhaps a gentle wife, and have not even the hope of such company and welcome that they possess who share the views of Pythagoras [c] and Plato [d] and Homer [e] about the soul. There is a hint in Homer of the case in which they find themselves. He places on the ground between the contending armies a likeness of Aeneas, lying there as if dead,[f] only to present the real Aeneas later as

> Drawing near alive and sound of limb
> And breathing valour [g]

as he joins his friends. They were filled with joy,[h] he says, and let go the likeness to gather round the man himself. Then let us too, when reason shows that we can truly meet the dead and with the part of us that thinks and loves embrace and join the very part of man that thinks and loves, refuse to imitate those

[a] Frag. 213 (ed. Usener).
[b] That is, the films : cf. Lucretius, iv. 722-761.
[c] The doctrine of metempsychosis involves the survival of the soul.
[d] Cf. for instance Phaedo, 68 A, 106 E 9—107 A 1.
[e] Thus Achilles sees the soul of Patroclus (Il. xxiii. 65-107) and Odysseus that of his mother (Od. xi. 152-224).
[f] Il. v. 449-453.
[g] Il. v. 515-516.
[h] Il. v. 514.

---

[5] ἐντυχεῖν Basle edition of 1542 : εὐτυχεῖν a.
[6] φρονοῦντι καὶ added by Bern.

(1106) ἅψασθαι καὶ συγγενέσθαι, . . .[1] μὴ δυναμένους
μηδὲ ἀπορρῖψαι τὰ εἴδωλα πάντα καὶ τοὺς φλοιούς,[2]
ἐφ᾽[3] οἷς ὀδυρόμενοι καὶ κενοπαθοῦντες[4] διατελοῦσιν.

29. " Ἄνευ δὲ τούτων,[5] οἱ μὲν ἑτέρου βίου τὸν
θάνατον ἀρχὴν κρείττονος νομίζοντες, ἐάν τε ἐν
ἀγαθοῖς ὦσι μᾶλλον ἥδονται μείζονα προσδοκῶντες·
ἄν τε μὴ κατὰ γνώμην τῶν ἐνταῦθα τυγχάνωσιν οὐ
πάνυ δυσχεραίνουσιν, ἀλλ᾽ αἱ τῶν μετὰ τὸν θάνατον
B ἀγαθῶν καὶ καλῶν ἐλπίδες ἀμηχάνους ἡδονὰς καὶ
προσδοκίας ἔχουσαι πᾶν μὲν ἔλλειμμα πᾶν δὲ πρόσ-
κρουσμα τῆς ψυχῆς ἐξαλείφουσι καὶ ἀφανίζουσιν
ὥσπερ ἐν ὁδῷ, μᾶλλον δὲ ὁδοῦ παρατροπῇ βραχείᾳ,
ῥᾳδίως τὰ συντυγχάνοντα καὶ μετρίως φερούσης.
οἷς δὲ ὁ βίος εἰς ἀναισθησίαν περαίνει καὶ διάλυσιν,[6]
τούτοις ὁ θάνατος τῶν ἀγαθῶν[7] οὐ τῶν κακῶν
μεταβολὴν ἐπιφέρων, ἀμφοτέροις μέν ἐστι λυπηρός,
μᾶλλον δὲ[8] τοῖς εὐτυχοῦσιν ἢ τοῖς ἐπιπόνως ζῶσι·
τούτων μὲν γὰρ[9] ἀποκόπτει τὴν ἄδηλον ἐλπίδα τοῦ
πράξειν ἄμεινον, ἐκείνων δὲ βέβαιον ἀγαθόν, τὸ
ἡδέως ζῆν, ἀφαιρεῖται. καὶ καθάπερ οἶμαι τὰ μὴ
C χρηστὰ τῶν φαρμάκων ἀλλὰ ἀναγκαῖα,[10] κουφίζοντα
τοὺς νοσοῦντας ἐπιτρίβει καὶ λυμαίνεται τοὺς ὑγιαί-

---

[1] Here Ferronus supposes a lacuna. Bern. supplies χαίρειν ἐῶμεν τοὺς τοῦτο συμβαλέσθαι, Kronenberg μὴ μιμώμεθα τοὺς μεθέσθαι, Pohlenz (tentatively) τοσαύτην ἐλπίδα μὴ ἀφῶμεν διὰ τοὺς τοῦ ὄντος ἀντέχεσθαι, Post πειθόμεθα (or ὑπακούωμεν) ἐῶντες χαίρειν τοὺς μεθέσθαι.

[2] φλοιούς aA¹ : φίλους A²E β².

[3] ἐφ᾽ Wyttenbach : ἐν a.

[4] κενοπαθοῦντες Pohlenz : καινοπαθοῦντες a.

[5] τούτων Benseler : τούτου a.

[6] διάλυσιν Reiske (dissolutione Ferronus) : διαλύει a.

[7] τῶν ἀγαθῶν supplied by us; Wyttenbach supplies ἀλλὰ καὶ (Pohlenz drops καὶ) τῶν ἀγαθῶν ἀποβολήν after μεταβολήν.

142

who are unable to let go [a] or cast aside all ' likenesses '
whatever and the mere ' husks ' [b] over which they
keep up a lamentation wherein they take appearance
for reality.

29. " Quite apart from this, those who consider
death the beginning of a new and better life, get
greater pleasure in the midst of blessings as they
expect still greater ones, or if they do not obtain the
portion of blessings in this world that they could wish
are not overmuch embittered. Rather, their hopes
for a fullness of blessing and felicity after death bring
with them wonderful pleasures and expectations,
and erase and obliterate every deficiency and every
rebuff from the mind, which as if on a road, or rather
a short byway, accepts easily and calmly the chances
of the journey. To those [c] on the other hand who
hold that life comes in the end to insentience and
dissolution, death is painful whatever one's fortune,
since it brings a change from good, not from evil. It
is more painful, however, to the fortunate than to
those whose lives are hard ; for it debars the wretched
from the uncertain hope of better times, while it
robs the fortunate of a solid asset, his pleasant life.
The case, I think, is like that of medicines that are
not positively good, but are used under compulsion :
though they relieve the sick, they bring misery and

[a] The text is corrupt. The words " refuse to imitate " and
" to let go " translate conjectural supplements.
[b] *All* " likenesses," whether Homeric or Epicurean.
" Likeness " (eidôlon) is the Epicurean term for " film " ;
for " husk " *cf. cortex* (" bark ") in Lucretius, iv. 51.
[c] Frag. 500 (ed. Usener).

8 δὲ Bσ²: a omits.
9 γὰρ E²ᵐ ? σ²: a omits.
10 ἀλλὰ ἀναγκαῖα] Hartman would delete.

(1106) νοντας, οὕτως ὁ Ἐπικούρου λόγος τοῖς μὲν ἀθλίως
ζῶσιν οὐκ εὐτυχῆ τοῦ κακῶς πράσσειν[1] τελευτὴν
ἐπαγγέλλεται τὴν ἀναίρεσιν καὶ διάλυσιν[2] τῆς ψυχῆς,
τῶν δὲ φρονίμων καὶ σοφῶν καὶ βρυόντων ἀγαθοῖς
παντάπασι κολούει[3] τὸ εὔθυμον, ἐκ τοῦ ζῆν μακα-
ρίως εἰς τὸ μὴ ζῆν μηδὲ εἶναι καταυτρέφων.[4]
αὐτόθεν μὲν οὖν[5] ἐστι δῆλον ὡς ἀγαθῶν ἀποβολῆς
ἐπίνοια λυπεῖν[6] πέφυκεν ὅσον ἐλπίδες βέβαιοι καὶ
ἀπολαύσεις εὐφραίνουσι παρόντων. (30.) οὐ μὴν
D ἀλλὰ καὶ λέγουσιν αὐτοῖς[7] κακῶν ἀπαύστων καὶ[8]
ἀορίστων λυθεῖσαν ὑποψίαν ἀγαθὸν βεβαιότατον
καὶ ἥδιστον ἀπολιπεῖν τὴν ἐπίνοιαν τοῦ λελύσθαι[9]·
καὶ τοῦτο ποιεῖν τὸν Ἐπικούρου λόγον, ἱστάντα
τοῦ θανάτου τὸ δέος ἐν τῇ διαλύσει τῆς ψυχῆς.
εἴπερ οὖν ἥδιστόν ἐστιν ἀπαλλαγὴ προσδοκίας κακῶν ἀπείρων, πῶς οὐκ ἀνιαρὸν αἰωνίων ἀγαθῶν
ἐλπίδος[10] στερεῖσθαι καὶ τὴν ἀκροτάτην εὐδαιμονίαν
ἀποβαλεῖν; ἀγαθὸν μὲν γὰρ οὐδὲ ἑτέροις, ἀλλὰ
πᾶσι τοῖς οὖσι τὸ μὴ εἶναι παρὰ φύσιν καὶ ἀλλό-
τριον· ὧν δὲ ἀφαιρεῖ τὰ τοῦ βίου κακὰ τῷ τοῦ
θανάτου κακῷ, τὸ ἀναίσθητον ἔχουσι παραμύθιον
ὥσπερ ἀποδιδράσκοντες,[11] καὶ τοὐναντίον, οἷς ἐξ
E ἀγαθῶν εἰς τὸ μηδὲν μεταβολή, φοβερώτατον

---

[1] τοῦ κακῶς πράσσειν Pohlenz (μὲν, τοῦ δὲ κακῶς πράσσειν
ὅμως Reiske) : τοῖς δὲ κακῶς πράσσουσι a.
[2] ἀναίρεσιν καὶ διάλυσιν a : διάλυσιν καὶ ἀναίρεσιν X[8] (and so
Bern. and Pohlenz).
[3] κολούει Wyttenbach : κωλύει a.
[4] καταστρέφων Usener : καταστρέφον a.
[5] οὖν β[2] : a omits.
[6] λυπεῖν a : τοσοῦτον λυπεῖν ? Reiske.
[7] αὐτοῖς Stephanus : αὐτοῖς a (αὐτοὶ Reiske).
[8] καὶ Leonicus and Donatus Polus : a omits.

144

injury to the healthy. So the doctrine of Epicurus [a] promises the wretch no very happy relief from adversity, the extinction and dissolution of his soul; but from the prudent and wise and those who abound in all good things it quite eradicates all cheer by altering their condition from blissful living to not living or being at all. Now it is at once evident that the thought of losing good things is naturally painful to the same degree as the assured prospect or present enjoyment of them brings delight. (30.) Nevertheless they [b] assert that when the foreboding of incessant evils to which no period is appointed is dispelled they are left with a benefit that is in the highest degree assured and pleasant, the thought of release; and that this is done by Epicurus' doctrine when it terminates the fear of death with the dissolution of the soul. If then relief from expecting infinite woe is highly pleasant, how can it not be painful to be deprived of hope of everlasting weal and to lose a felicity beyond compare? For not to be is a boon to neither class of men; it is unnatural and inimical to everything that is. [c] Those from whom it takes the miseries of life by the misery of death can find comfort, like runaways, in eluding all sensation; whereas those on the contrary who pass from prosperity to nothing, see before them a most appalling issue, a point at which their present

[a] Frag. 500 (ed. Usener).
[b] Frag. 501 (ed. Usener); Metrodorus, Frag. 38 (ed. Körte).
[c] *Cf.* Cicero, *De Finibus*, v. 11 (31): " ab interitu naturam abhorrere."

---

[9] λελύσθαι a: λελύσεσθαι van Herwerden.
[10] ἐλπίδος Meziriacus: ἐλπίδα a.
[11] ἀποδιδράσκοντες Baxter (*subterfugissent* Xylander): ἀποδιδράσκοντα a.

PLUTARCH'S MORALIA

(1106) ὁρῶσι τέλος,[1] ἐν ᾧ παύσεται τὸ μακάριον. οὐ γὰρ
ὡς ἀρχὴν ἑτέρου[2] τὴν ἀναισθησίαν δέδιεν ἡ φύσις,
ἀλλ' ὅτι τῶν παρόντων ἀγαθῶν στέρησίς ἐστι. τὸ
γὰρ ' οὐ πρὸς ἡμᾶς ' παντὸς ἀναιρέσει τοῦ ἡμετέρου
γινόμενον ἤδη πρὸς ἡμᾶς ἐστι τῇ ἐπινοίᾳ, καὶ τὸ
ἀναίσθητον οὐ λυπεῖ τότε τοὺς μὴ ὄντας, ἀλλὰ
τοὺς ὄντας, εἰς τὸ μὴ εἶναι βαπτομένους[3] ὑπ' αὐτοῦ
καὶ μηδαμῶς ἐκδυσομένους.[4] ὅθεν οὐδὲ ὁ Κέρβε-
ρος οὐδὲ ὁ Κωκυτὸς ἀόριστον ἐποίησε τοῦ θανάτου
τὸ δέος, ἀλλὰ ἡ τοῦ μὴ ὄντος ἀπειλή, μεταβολὴν[5]
F εἰς τὸ εἶναι πάλιν οὐκ ἔχουσα τοῖς φθαρεῖσι· ' δὶς '
γὰρ ' οὐκ ἔστι γενέσθαι, δεῖ δὲ τὸν αἰῶνα μὴ εἶναι ' κατ' Ἐπίκουρον. εἰ γάρ ἐστι τὸ πέρας τὸ[6]
μὴ εἶναι, τοῦτο δὲ ἀπέραντον καὶ ἀμετάστατον,
εὕρηται κακὸν αἰώνιον ἡ τῶν ἀγαθῶν στέρησις
ἀναισθησίᾳ μηδέποτε παυσομένη.[7] καὶ σοφώτερος
Ἡρόδοτος εἰπὼν ὡς ' ὁ θεὸς γλυκὺν γεύσας τὸν
1107 αἰῶνα φθονερὸς ἐν αὐτῷ ὢν φαίνεται,'[8] καὶ μάλιστα
τοῖς εὐδαιμονεῖν δοκοῦσιν, οἷς δέλεάρ ἐστι λύπης
τὸ ἡδύ, γευομένοις ὧν στερήσονται. τίνα γὰρ
εὐφροσύνην ἢ ἀπόλαυσιν καὶ βρυασμὸν οὐκ ἂν ἐκ-
κρούσειε καὶ καταιγίσειεν[9] ἐμπίπτουσα συνεχῶς ἡ
ἐπίνοια[10] τῆς ψυχῆς ὥσπερ εἰς πέλαγος ἀχανὲς τὸ

---

[1] ὁρῶσιν τέλος Wyttenbach (ὁρῶσιν [or συνορῶσιν] ἑαυτοῖς
τέλος Reiske) : ὁρῶ ἐντελὲς a.
[2] ἑτέρου a : ἑτέρου κακοῦ Reiske.
[3] βαπτομένους Xylander : βλαπτομένους a.
[4] μηδαμῶς ἐκδυσομένους Pohlenz (μήπω ἐκδυσομένους Dübner) : μηδ' ὡς δυσομένους a.
[5] μεταβολὴν Ald.[2] and Meziriacus : μεταβαλεῖν a.
[6] τὸ πέρας τῶ (τῶ from τὸ aᶜ) aᵃᶜ : πέρας τῷ εἶναι τὸ Wyttenbach.
[7] ἀναισθησίᾳ . . . παυσομένῃ Emperius : ἀναισθησίαν . . .
παυσομένην a.

146

felicity will end. For human nature does not fear the loss of sensation as a beginning of something new, but as costing us the good which we now enjoy. For this ' nothing to us,' when achieved by the extinction of everything that is ours, is already ' something to us ' in our thoughts. And lack of sensation is no hardship to those who when the time comes no longer are, but it is to those who are, because it plunges them into non-being, from which they are never to emerge. Hence it is not Cerberus nor yet Cocytus that has set no period to the fear of death, but the threat of non-being, which allows those once dead no return to being, for ' there is no second birth ; we must forever be no more ' as Epicurus [a] says. For if the limit is non-being, and this has no limit and no exit, we discover that this loss of all good things is an evil that lasts forever, because it comes from an insentience that will never end. And Herodotus [b] was wiser who said that ' God, who has let us taste the sweetness of life, is seen herein to be envious,' and especially of men who are accounted happy, for all their pleasure is for them a lure to misery,[c] since what they taste will be taken from them. For what delight of the spirit or ' revelling ' [d] satisfaction would not be dashed and overwhelmed, in those who place all excellence and felicity in plea-sure, under the constant assaults of this thought—

[a] Frag. 204 (ed. Usener) ; cited also 1104 E, supra.
[b] vii. 46.
[c] R. M. Jones compares the language of Plato, Timaeus, 69 D : " pleasure, the greatest bait of evil . . . "
[d] Cf. 1098 B, supra.

---

[8] ὧν φαίνεται a : εὑρίσκεται ἐὼν Herodotus.
[9] καταιγίσειεν nos (καταποντίσειεν Pohlenz) : κατά γε a.
[10] ἡ ἐπίνοια σ² κ¹ : ἢ ἐπινοία a.

(1107) ἄπειρον ἐκχεομένης, τῶν ἐν ἡδονῇ τιθεμένων τὸ
καλὸν καὶ μακάριον; εἰ δὲ δὴ καὶ μετὰ ἀλγηδόνος,
ὥσπερ Ἐπίκουρος οἴεται, τοῖς πλείστοις ἀπόλλυσθαι συμβαίνει, παντάπασιν ἀπαρηγόρητός ἐστιν ὁ
τοῦ θανάτου φόβος, εἰς ἀγαθῶν στέρησιν διὰ κακῶν
ἄγοντος.

B   31. " Καὶ πρὸς ταῦτα μὲν οὐκ ἀποκαμοῦνται μαχόμενοι καὶ βιαζόμενοι πάντας ἀνθρώπους, ἀγαθὸν
μὲν ἡγεῖσθαι τὴν τῶν κακῶν ἀποφυγήν, κακὸν δὲ
μηκέτι νομίζειν τὴν τῶν ἀγαθῶν στέρησιν· ἐκεῖνο
δὲ ὁμολογοῦσι, τὸ μηδεμίαν ἐλπίδα μηδὲ χαρὰν
ἔχειν τὸν θάνατον ἀλλὰ ἀποκεκόφθαι πᾶν τὸ ἡδὺ
καὶ τὸ ἀγαθόν. ἐν ᾧ χρόνῳ πολλὰ καλὰ καὶ μεγάλα
καὶ θεῖα προσδοκῶσιν οἱ τὰς ψυχὰς ἀνωλέθρους
εἶναι διανοούμενοι καὶ ἀφθάρτους ἢ μακράς τινας
χρόνων περιόδους νῦν μὲν ἐν γῇ νῦν δὲ ἐν οὐρανῷ
περιπολούσας, ἄχρι[1] οὗ συνδιαλυθῶσι τῷ κόσμῳ,
μετὰ ἡλίου καὶ σελήνης εἰς πῦρ νοερὸν ἀναφθεῖσαι.

C τοιαύτην χώραν ἡδονῶν τοσούτων Ἐπίκουρος ἐκτέμνεται,[2] καὶ ἐπὶ[3] ταῖς ἐκ θεῶν ἐλπίσιν ὥσπερ
εἴρηται καὶ χάρισιν ἀναιρεθείσαις τοῦ[4] θεωρητικοῦ
τὸ φιλομαθὲς καὶ τοῦ πρακτικοῦ τὸ φιλότιμον ἀπο-
τυφλώσας εἰς στενόν τι κομιδῇ καὶ οὐδὲ καθαρὸν
τὸ ἐπὶ τῇ σαρκὶ τῆς ψυχῆς χαῖρον συνέστειλε καὶ
κατέβαλε τὴν φύσιν, ὡς μεῖζον ἀγαθὸν τοῦ τὸ
κακὸν φεύγειν οὐδὲν ἔχουσαν."

[1] ἄχρις a.
[2] ἐκτέμνεται a : ἀποτέμνεται β[288].
[3] ἐπὶ ταῖς Madvig : ταῖς a.
[4] τοῦ Madvig : ἐπὶ τοῦ a.

---

[a] Cf. 1130 ε, infra.   [b] Frag. 502 (ed. Usener).

of the soul spilt out into infinity as into some yawn-ing ocean ? [a] And if, as Epicurus [b] imagines, for most people the process of dying is attended with pain, the fear of death is quite beyond any comfort, since death ushers us through misery to loss of every good.

31. " And yet against these arguments they will never weary of contending with all men, trying to force them to hold the escape from evil a good, yet not also the loss of good things an evil.   This how-ever they concede : that death brings no hope or joy but means the severance of all that is pleasant and good. Whereas this space of time unfolds a multitude of noble prospects, magnificent and divine, to those who hold the soul to be imperishable and incorrupt-ible,[c] or else hold that for long cycles of time it roams now on earth, now in heaven, until it suffers dissolu-tion with the universe, when with the sun and moon it blazes into intellectual fire.[d] It is a space like this, with pleasures so ample, pleasures of such magnitude that the surgery of Epicurus [e] cuts out of our lives. Not content with removing all hope of help from Heaven and all bestowal of grace, as we said,[f] he kills the love of learning [g] in our soul and the love of honour [h] in our heart, and thus constricts our nature and casts it down into a narrow space indeed and not a clean one either, where the mind delights in no-thing but the flesh, as if human nature had no higher good than escape from evil."

[c] The Platonic view.
[d] The Stoic view.
[e] Frag. 418 (ed. Usener).
[f] Cf. chapters 21-23, supra.
[g] Cf. chapters 9-14, supra.
[h] Cf. chapters 15-19, supra.

REPLY TO COLOTES
IN DEFENCE OF THE
OTHER PHILOSOPHERS
(ADVERSUS COLOTEM)

INTRODUCTION

THE *Adversus Colotem* is a reply to Colotes' otherwise unknown book entitled " On the Point that Conformity to the Views of the Other Philosophers Actually Makes it Impossible to Live."

Colotes of Lampsacus presumably became a disciple of Epicurus when Epicurus held his school in that city (310–306 B.C.). We may suppose that Colotes was at least fourteen years old—the early age when Epicurus himself began the study of philosophy—in 306, and was thus born at the latest in 320. Epicurus' letter to him (1117 B-C) was probably written after Epicurus had left Lampsacus for Athens in 306— though it could have been written after a subsequent visit—and would indicate that Colotes' act of supplication had been performed a short while before, perhaps when he knew that Epicurus was leaving for good. The endearing form of the name—*Kolotaras* or *Kolotarion*—used by Epicurus, together with that presumably recent display of generous emotion, suggests that Colotes at the time of Epicurus' departure was very young.

In the book Colotes alludes to the views of Arcesilaüs, who became head of the Academy some time in the course of the olympiad 268–264. Arcesilaüs left no writings ; his fame rested on his lectures alone, and we may assume that when attacked by Colotes

153

he was already head of the Academy.[a] Colotes'
book, then, was not written before 268.[b] The Ptolemy
to whom it is addressed is therefore Ptolemy II,[c] who
succeeded Ptolemy I in 282 and died in 246. Perhaps the book was addressed to him when he was ally
of Athens in the Chremonidean war, which ended for
the city with its surrender to Antigonus Gonatas in
263-262.

Colotes may ultimately have directed the school
at Lampsacus ; we hear of a disciple, Menedemus,
whom he lost to the Cynics.[d] He favoured polemic
against Plato. We have fragments of *Replies* to
Plato's *Lysis* and *Euthydemus* [e] and of an attack on

[a] Plutarch (1121 E) says that Epicurus was jealous of
Arcesilaüs' fame. Epicurus died in 270, when Arcesilaüs
was about forty-five. It is likely that Arcesilaüs had distinguished himself before he became head of the Academy,
since the head was elected by the students (*Acad. Philos.
Index Herc.*, col. xviii [ed. Mekler, p. 67]). A regular attack
such as Colotes' implies a more than local reputation. It is in
any case intended to draw students from the Academy, and
to do that you attack the head.

[b] Colotes is not mentioned in Epicurus' will, and W. Crönert (*Kolotes und Menedemos* [Studien zur Palaeographie
und Papyruskunde, VI (Leipzig, 1906)], p. 11, note 42)
infers that he remained behind at Lampsacus. The present
book, in all probability aimed at an audience of young
Academics, was no doubt written during a visit to Athens.

[c] *Cf.* Crönert, *op. cit.*, p. 13. As Plutarch implies (1111 F),
Ptolemy II was no unlettered king : he was taught by Strato,
Philetas, and Zenodotus. For the dates of his reign see A. E.
Samuel, *Ptolemaic Chronology* (Munich, 1962), chapters i-ii.

[d] *Cf.* Crönert, *op. cit.*, p. 4.

[e] Published by Crönert (*op. cit.*, pp. 163-170) from Hercu-
lanean papyri. The reply to the *Lysis* is earlier than the reply
to the *Euthydemus*, which refers to it. In the reply to the
Lysis Zeno of Citium is mentioned, who died in 264-261. If
Colotes did not mention living scholarchs by name, neither
reply is earlier than that date. He appears to have imitated

154

the myth in the *Republic*.[a] Another title is uncertain.[b] The attack on the *Republic* left its mark. Colotes asks how it was possible for a dead man to come back to life.[c] Cicero and Plutarch both imitated the Platonic myth. Cicero's narrator appears in a dream, the *Somnium Scipionis*, and Plutarch's Aridaeus (*Mor.* 563 D) gives up only the intelligent part of his soul. In the present book Colotes deals with Democritus, Parmenides, Empedocles, Socrates, Melissus, Plato, Stilpon, and two contemporary schools identified by Plutarch as those of the Cyrenaics and of Arcesilaüs. Democritus has pride of place ; the rest are in chronological order.[d] The common complaint against all is that their doctrines make it impossible to deal with external objects [e] and so to live.

Metrodorus in the style of the title of the present book (see p. 164, note *a*, *infra*). Metrodorus also wrote replies to Platonic dialogues (the *Gorgias* and the *Euthyphro* [p. 546, ed. Körte]), and the language of his attack on Diogenes (1127 B-c) is like Colotes' heavy with polemical double meaning.

   [a] See Macrobius, *Comm. in* Somnium Scipionis, i. 1. 9–2. 4 and Proclus, *Comm. in Platonis* Rem Publicam, vol. ii, pp. 105. 23–106. 14, 109. 8-12, 111. 6-9, 113. 9-13, 116. 19-21, 121. 19-25 (ed. Kroll).

   [b] " On Laws and Opinion " ($\pi\epsilon\rho\grave{\iota}$ $\nu\acute{o}\mu\omega\nu$ $\kappa\alpha\grave{\iota}$ $\delta\acute{o}\xi\eta\varsigma$) in Crönert, *op. cit.*, p. 130, note 542. Unfortunately the two preceding lines of the papyrus (Philodemus, *On Flattery*) are imperfect and unintelligible. If the title is his it no doubt refers to Epicurus' urging Idomeneus not to live a slave to laws and men's opinions (1127 D ; Frag. 134, ed. Usener).

   [c] Proclus, *op. cit.*, vol. ii, p. 113. 12-13 ; also p. 116. 19-21.

   [d] Plutarch places Empedocles after Democritus and Plato after Parmenides ; he says nothing of Melissus' doctrine. Thus his order is : Democritus, Empedocles, Parmenides, Plato, Socrates, Stilpon, the Cyrenaics, and Arcesilaüs.

   [e] Democritus, Empedocles, and Socrates discredit the testimony of the senses about external objects ; Parmenides denies them ; Plato makes beliefs about them worthless,

155

PLUTARCH'S MORALIA

"The other philosophers" is a sweeping expression. Plutarch mentions nine as the targets of abuse [a]; Colotes dismissed Xenocrates and the Peripatetics as followers of Plato. To judge by Plutarch, Colotes did not mention Thales, Pythagoras, Heracleitus, Anaxagoras, the Cynics, or the Stoics. The book is an attack on Arcesilaüs. The other philosophers are singled out because the sceptics of the Academy regarded them as predecessors. Plutarch says (1121 F—1122 A) that the sophists of the day accused Arcesilaüs of fathering his scepticism on Socrates, Plato, Parmenides, and Heracleitus [b]; and Colotes asserts that he said nothing of his own but conveyed the notion that he did.[c] Socrates—the Platonic Socrates—is distinguished from Plato and

Stilpon makes useful statements about them impossible, and the Cyrenaics make no statements about them at all; and Arcesilaüs refuses to assent to anything. The final charge against Arcesilaüs, that he threatens to destroy all law, and thus to return man to primitive conditions which would be fatal, is the only one into which the impossibility of dealing with objects does not enter.

[a] At 1108 B Plutarch lists Socrates, Democritus, Plato, Stilpon, Empedocles, Parmenides, and Melissus; to these we must add the unnamed schools he mentions later (1120 C): the Cyrenaics and the Academy of Arcesilaüs. In this list the order is first the moralists, in chronological sequence, then the physicists in the order of Plutarch's reply (Melissus being merged with Parmenides). Plutarch is going on to praise the philosophers for their gift of the good life.

[b] Here cited in the order of the extent of their influence on Arcesilaüs. They recur at 1124 D in the chronological order Parmenides, Socrates, Heracleitus, Plato (Heracleitus being given the later dating).

[c] So Colotes would have it that Er is really Zoroaster: cf. Proclus on the *Republic* (ed. Kroll), vol. ii, p. 109. 8-12 and the note in J. Bidez and F. Cumont, *Les Mages hellénisés*, vol. ii (Paris, 1938), p. 160.

156

dealt with (to judge by Plutarch) at greater length ; the reason is that Plato is a dogmatist, whereas Socrates was almost a pure sceptic. Colotes here agrees with an Academic tradition that may go back to Arcesilaüs (*cf.* Cicero, *Acad. Post.* i. 4 [15-18]), as he does when he makes the Peripatetics followers of Plato.

It might well have seemed at the time that Arcesilaüs was carrying everything before him. Epicurus had died in 270. Strato had died in 270–268, and the Lyceum was headed by Lyco, an athlete and expert in the education of boys.

The very charge that Colotes brings against the philosophers, that they make it impossible to live, is a variant of the charge brought against the Sceptics, that they destroy our life.[a] It was not easy to attack Arcesilaüs on the ground of doctrine, as he had none (Cicero, *Acad. Pr.* ii. 6 [17]). But a man shows certain

---

[a] Diogenes Laert. ix. 104. Colotes also uses this variant (1119 c-d). Another variant is " confound our life " (1108 f), which Colotes may have got from Epicurus (*cf. Gnom. Vat.* 57 [Frag. 6. 56-57, ed. Arrighetti]). " Destroy " or " abolish " is *anairein*, literally " pick up," and hence " remove." Philosophers used the word of the operations of causes and reasoning. One opposite " removes " another, and a philosopher by his reasoning, or the reasoning itself, removes the thing disproved. The development was furthered by a common use of *tithenai* (sometimes *hypotithenai*), " lay down," originally used of laying down laws, to indicate a thesis or position that will be maintained throughout the subsequent reasoning. (Thus Plato speaks of " picking up " or " removing " the *hypotheses* " things laid down " in *Republic*, vii, 533 c 8.) As we lay down what was not there before, so we remove what was already there and take away the familiar and accepted. This is opposed to *apoleipein*, " to leave us with " something possessed and cherished. Thus to " destroy " our life is to use reasoning that leads to the impossibility of life (and particularly of civilized life) as we live it.

beliefs by the acts of his life. These can be shown to conflict with his professed uncertainty about the world around him (and Arcesilaüs spent his life attacking Zeno's criterion), since that uncertainty makes it impossible to live. The same objection can be made to the philosophers Arcesilaüs cited as his authorities. Cicero lists the following as authorities claimed by the Academics (*Acad. Pr.* ii. 5 [14]): Empedocles, Anaxagoras, Democritus, Parmenides, Xenophanes, Plato, and Socrates. Perhaps Anaxagoras and Xenophanes are missing from Colotes' attack because Anaxagoras was censured by Socrates, and Xenophanes' views were much like Parmenides'; whereas Melissus, Stilpon, and the Cyrenaics were dropped by Cicero's anti-Academic because they were not of the celebrity required for making his point, that the Academics, like subversive statesmen, hide behind the great names of the past.

Democritus was attacked in the Epicurean school, perhaps by Epicurus himself, for holding the view that the sense-qualities are human conventions, and only the atoms and the void are real, and thus making it impossible to live. Diogenes of Oenoanda (ii–iii century A.D.) says in his inscription :

> Democritus too erred in a fashion unworthy of himself when he said that the atoms alone exist in truth among realities, but everything else by convention. For according to your account, Democritus, far from discovering the truth, we shall not even be able to live, since we shall neither avoid fire nor a wound nor . . . [a]

[a] Frag. 7, col. ii. 2–iii. 1 (ed. Grilli). Here " not even live " is opposed to discovering the truth, perhaps because Democritus had said (Frag. B 117, ed. Diels-Kranz) " in reality we know nothing ; for truth is in the depths." It is likely that Colotes intended the same opposition (*cf.* R. Westman,

Hence Democritus' pride of place in Colotes' book : the Epicureans had first brought the objection against him. He was also the author of the most celebrated sceptical dictum, " no more this than that." We shall presently find another reason.

Two charges are brought against Democritus. First, by saying that each and every object is no more of one description than of another he has thrown our life into confusion. Second, the dictum that colour is a convention while the realities are the atoms and the void, contradicts our senses, and any-one putting this doctrine into practice could not con-ceive of even himself as a man or as alive. The dis-tinction that Colotes makes between the two sayings is that the first affects sense-objects, the second our-selves as well. This distinction can be traced through the rest of the polemic.[a]

In drawing this distinction between objects and ourselves Colotes is inspired by a distinction made

---

Plutarch gegen Kolotes [Helsingfors, 1955], pp. 97-98), and not (as one might suppose from the *Non Posse Suaviter Vivi Secundum Epicurum*) an opposition to living pleasantly. The Academics justified their wisdom—suspension of judge-ment—not so much by appealing to the resulting felicity (peace of mind) as to their duty as philosophers of assenting to nothing but the truth.

[a] He says in a question put to Empedocles (1112 D) " neither do we exist nor do we in living make use of other things." The " inhabited cities " of the attack on Parmenides include ourselves, and his " fire " and " water " are sense-objects. In the assault on Socrates the distinction is especially clear (1117 D, 1118 c). Plato holds it useless to consider horses horses and men men. The Platonic examples recur in the attack on Stilpon (" horseman " being substituted for " horse " for a polemical motive) and on the Cyrenaics. " Wall," " door," and " the man who suspends judgement " occur in the attack on Arcesilaüs.

by the Pyrrhonists. They said that Democritus destroyed both the *criterion* and the *phaenomena* :

> (The Sceptics hold that Democritus was one of them)
> when he expelled the qualities, where he says " cold is by
> convention, hot by convention, but the atoms and the void
> are in reality," and again " in reality we know nothing ;
> for truth is in the depths." (Diogenes Laertius, ix. 72.)
> Thus according to the Sceptics the phaenomenon is the
> criterion, as Aenesidemus says ; and so too says Epicurus.
> But Democritus says that none of the phaenomena is a
> criterion, and the phaenomena do not exist. (Diogenes
> Laertius, ix. 106.)
> But the Democritean philosophy is also said to have a
> community with the sceptical, since it is held to use the
> same material as we do. For from the fact that honey
> appears sweet to some and bitter to others, they say Demo-
> critus (Frag. A 134, ed. Diels-Kranz) reasoned that it is
> neither sweet nor bitter, and for this reason pronounced
> about it the words " no more this than that," a sceptical
> expression. Yet the Sceptics and the Democriteans use
> the phrase " no more this than that " in different ways.
> The Democriteans apply it to the phaenomenon's being
> neither whereas we apply it to not knowing whether some
> phaenomenon is both or neither. But the distinction be-
> tween us is most obvious when Democritus says (Frag.
> B 9, ed. Diels-Kranz) " in reality are the atoms and the
> void." For by " in reality " he means " in truth " ; and
> I think it is superfluous to remark that in saying that " in
> truth the atoms and the void are existent " he differs from
> us. (Sextus, *Outlines of Pyrrhonism*, i. 213-214.)[a]

Phaenomenon (" what appears ") can mean " what
seems (but is not necessarily) true " and " what is

---

[a] In the later work, *Against the Mathematicians* (vii. 135-
140) we find no mention of the " no more this than that " in
connexion with Democritus. No doubt Sextus or his authorities (like Plutarch) did not find it in their Democritus. So
Galen (*cf.* Democritus, Frag. A 49, ed. Diels-Kranz), like
Plutarch, speaks instead of the " aught " and " naught " in
connexion with the dictum about the conventional character
of the sense-qualities.

REPLY TO COLOTES

evidently true." What is evidently true is the sensation as fact; what seems—or only seems—true is sensation the report. The term criterion comes from the conflict of the Sceptics with the dogmatists, who asserted that there is something on which we can rely to determine truth. This thing is the criterion; and the dogmatists asserted that the sensation is such a criterion. Democritus abolishes this criterion. We taste honey in health and have the sensation " sweet." We taste it in illness and have the sensation " bitter." The sensation corresponding to the quality of the honey is as much the sensation " sweet " as it is the sensation " bitter "; or to put this in Democritus' language (which prepares us for the next dictum), is " no more this than that."

Democritus then abolishes the pretended original itself. There is no such external reality as " sweet " or " bitter "; there are only the atoms and the void. We prove a thing a mere linguistic or legal convention and not an eternal verity by confronting it with a conflicting law or linguistic expression of equal authority. The sensations " sweet " and " bitter " discredit each other as verities. They are conventions.

The formulation " is no more this than that " is designedly paradoxical when used of the sensation : it refers to the sensation as a report of the reality (and the report is no more " sweet " than " bitter "), and sounds as if it referred to the sensation as a fact (and the sensation " sweet " is certainly not " bitter," nor is the sensation " bitter " " sweet "). To treat sensation as a report involves a slight personification : sense speaks to us in the only language it knows, sensations. So the rival of sense, reason, speaks to us, but its language is more like the language of men. How does Democritus pass from " no more this than that " to the reality of the atoms and the void ? The first dictum discredits the report of sense, but not entirely : the two sensations agree in that each exists and each is one. Thus they report a single reality. If one, the reality cannot be both sweet and bitter. It is therefore neither. We must therefore consult reason, and treat that " sweet " and " bitter " not as a report, but as a product or result. It results from something done to us by a single external reality. If external, the reality must act on us by transmission. There must be something solid to strike us, and space for that something solid to come through. Reality is therefore body and void.

Then why did Epicurus, who accepted the teaching that the atoms and the void are real, disagree with the doctrine that sense-qualities are a human convention ? It would seem that Epicurus never treated sensation as something outside the physical world, reporting about it. He always treated sensation as a physical fact, a result of the impact of one set of atoms and void on another. He starts where Democritus left off. For him " sweet " names a certain configuration of atoms and void and the movement it imparts to another configuration of atoms and void in ourselves ; it does not name an intimate and unanalysable feeling.

Plutarch holds that the saying as it appears in Colotes—each and every *sense-object* is no more this than that (1108 F)—is a view held by Protagoras. We may suppose that Epicurus assailed it in this form, and in an attack on Protagoras. Epicurus said in a letter (Frag. 172, ed. Usener) that Protagoras

began as a " basket-carrier " (no doubt the basket
contained firewood : *cf.* Diogenes Laertius, iv. 3)
and " faggot-carrier." Democritus noticed an ingenious way he had of arranging the faggots, and
took him as his scribe ; then Protagoras taught
school in a village and finally embarked on a sophist's
career. This looks as if Epicurus regarded Protagoras
as a man who had rearranged Democritean " matter,"
copied it without understanding it fully, and propa-
gated it among the ignorant. Protagoras' most
famous dictum was " Man is the measure of all things ;
of things that are, that they are ; of things that are
not, that they are not." It is things that are " no
more this than that," and man the sensation who is
always true. The reality, instead of being neither
sweet nor bitter, is both, and thus has to be two
realities ; Democritus' contradictory sensation-report
ceases to be contradictory, since it now concerns two
separate realities, and the middleman, our informant
sense, who is placed by Democritus between the two
sensations and the reality, disappears to be replaced
by ourselves, a collective unit undistinguishable from
the two sensations. Thus we get Colotes' distinction between " things " (plural) and (a singular)
" man."

Things to be sure are for Colotes sense-objects and
not external qualities, but the shift was prepared by
Protagoras himself, who used the all-inclusive *chrêmata*
(" things ") in his dictum. In any case Colotes forces
it on his philosophers : thus he imports " objects "
into the first dictum of Democritus (1108 F) and *synkrisin* (a scientific synonym) into the second (1110 E) ;
he modifies the text of Empedocles (ἑκάστου 1111 F)
to force a parallel with Democritus ; and he foists

examples of objects on the Cyrenaics, who had used examples of qualities (1120 D-E).

Colotes has dealt with " things " in the first charge against Democritus ; he must therefore deal with " man " in the second. Yet there is nothing in the Protagorean dictum that suggests the use to which Colotes puts it. He says to his philosopher in effect : " You have made your world (largely by a process of removal) ; let us see you live in it." The distinction suited Colotes' purposes because it not only was made by the Epicureans [a] but can be seen in Arcesilaüs himself. Sextus (*Against the Mathematicians*, vii. 150-158) preserves a detailed argument of that philosopher against the Stoic criterion, " apprehension." When the criterion has been exploded Sextus adds (158) :

> But since the next point to be examined, as we saw, is the question of the conduct of life, and this is not usually presented without a criterion, on which the accreditation of felicity—that is, the goal of life—depends, Arcesilaüs says that the man who suspends judgement about everything will test his acts of choice and of avoidance—his actions in sum—by their reasonableness . . .

Colotes, a happy combination of caricaturist and Epicurean, likes to present his views in concrete terms. Without " apprehension " we cannot trust the senses, and without reliance on the senses we cannot know sense-qualities or sense-objects. Thus Arcesilaüs abolishes things. For " life " we substitute " living

---

[a] *Cf.* the title of a book of Metrodorus (Frag. 5, ed. Körte) : " On the Fact that the Cause which Depends on Ourselves is of Greater Effect in Producing Felicity than the Cause which Depends on Things (περὶ τοῦ μείζονα εἶναι τὴν παρ' ἡμᾶς αἰτίαν πρὸς εὐδαιμονίαν τῆς ἐκ τῶν πραγμάτων)." The title, we note, is in the style of Colotes' own.

man." To the polemical eye the world of Arcesilaüs himself falls into two parts, " things " and " man."

After citing or paraphrasing the erroneous doctrine Colotes follows with the attack. Here in the manner of Epicurean polemic the offender, like some student caught at fault, is scolded to his face. The attack, it appears, was not a carefully reasoned exposition of the Epicurean stand, but largely a series of caricatures, in which we see the philosopher or his adherent in the pretty pass to which his tenets lead him. This method of polemic was well suited to its audience, young visitors from the Academy, perhaps come to collect material for a disputation. They knew enough about the philosophers to be amused by the caricature, and were far better fortified against argument than against ridicule. The ridicule of Democritus, the Epicurean ancient, serves as a proem, and prepares them to accept the ridicule of Parmenides and Socrates, the venerables of the Academy.

We suppose that a list of predecessors of the sceptics, with citations or paraphrases of the views of each that impugned some form of knowledge, had been drawn up in the Academy in the time of Arcesilaüs and was known to Colotes and his audience. Such a collection lies behind most of the learning on this subject of Sextus, of Diogenes Laertius in the Life of Pyrrho, and of Cicero in his *Academics*. From it Colotes drew most of his knowledge of the views of the philosophers attacked. For Socrates he could add from his own reading ; for Empedocles from Hermarchus ; and he could have learned the views of Arcesilaüs from students who had deserted to the Garden.

165

In the following survey of Colotes' charges and
attack we supply the missing names, as Plutarch
often uses the equivalents of " he." The mss. leave
blanks where the archetype was illegible. Supplements of the blanks are enclosed in angular brackets ;
other conjectures are in parentheses.

1. Democritus

1108 f Colotes first charges Democritus with throwing
our life into confusion by saying that of objects each is no
more of this quality than of that.

1110 e The slime and the ⟨confusion ?⟩ into which
Colotes says those persons fall who say of objects " no
more this than that " . . .

Democritus had said " in reality we know nothing,
for truth lies in the depths " (Frag. b 117, ed. Diels-
Kranz). He meant submerged in the depth of the
sea, where we cannot reach or see it. But " depth "
suggests a bottom ; and Plato lets Socrates speak of
falling into a " depth " of nonsense and perishing
there (*Parmenides*, 130 d 7-8). Colotes lets the Democritean (and not Democritus himself, who is treated
more gently than Socrates) find his " truth " at the
bottom of a mud hole. Colotes may also be glancing
at Democritus' " dark and spurious (*skotiê*) " knowledge of the senses (Frag. b 11, ed. Diels-Kranz).
Thus Plato too speaks of the eye of the soul as buried
in barbaric slime (*Republic*, vii, 533 d 1).

1110 e Colotes says that the dictum " colour is by convention and sweet by convention " and a compound ⟨and
the rest⟩ by convention, " ⟨whereas the reality is the void⟩
and the atoms " is an attack by Democritus on the senses,
and a man adhering to this account and putting it to use
would not think of himself as even ⟨a man⟩ or as alive.

REPLY TO COLOTES

Colotes interpolates *synkrisin* (Epicurus' word for a compound of atoms) into the dictum and reverses the order of " atoms " and " void." " Compound " is an equivalent of *pragma* or " sense-object," and when you abolish these your first result is naturally a void. " Man " and " alive " are Colotes' way of speaking of the " life " that Democritus abolished. (Even the Pyrrhonists admitted that they were alive [Diogenes Laertius, ix. 103].) Democritus had said " man is what we all know " (Frag. B 165, ed. Diels-Kranz) ; he thus contradicts himself.

2. Parmenides

1113 F Colotes speaks of the shameful sophistries of Parmenides. By calling all things one Parmenides has somehow prevented us from living.

1114 B Parmenides for one has neither abolished fire nor water nor a precipice nor cities, as Colotes says, inhabited in Europe and Asia.

By making everything one Parmenides has obliterated his own elements (fire and earth : see Frags. A 23, 24, 35, ed. Diels-Kranz, and Diogenes Laert., ix. 21 ; they appear in Plutarch's answer as the light and the dark) and their mixtures (water is a mixture of fire and earth : Frag. A 35, ed. Diels-Kranz). And as he makes being uniform and continuous (Frag. B 8. 6, 23-24, ed. Diels-Kranz), there can be no such thing as even a singular precipice. Colotes may be thinking of the story that Pyrrho had to be kept by his pupils from walking over precipices (Diogenes Laertius, ix. 62).[a] The cities were probably suggested by Par-

---

[a] *Cf.* Aristotle, *Metaphysics*, Γ 4 (1008 b 16) and Lucretius, iv. 509.

menides' being a man of Elea, and are plural because Parmenides denied all plurality, not merely the collective. They are in Europe and Asia, and thus include not only Parmenides and Arcesilaüs but ourselves ; the audience were city folk.

1114 D Colotes says that Parmenides simply takes away all things by laying down one being.

The formulation is Platonic : the " laying down of one (as) being " is in the *Parmenides* (142 D 3-4). " Simply " in philosophy is " without qualification " ; it can also mean " at a single blow " and " like a simpleton." Parmenides " picks up " (the literal sense of " removes " or " takes away ") by laying down.

3. Empedocles

1111 F But Colotes fastens on Empedocles in turn (as) breathing the same doctrine [Frag. B 8, ed. Diels-Kranz] :

        This too I'll tell thee :
There is no nature of each mortal thing
Nor any lamentable brood of death ;
Mixture alone there is and dissolution
Of things commingled, and men call them nature.

I do not see wherein these words interfere with living . . .

1112 D How then did it enter Colotes' head to put to Empedocles such questions as this ? " Why do we weary ourselves in serious concern for ourselves, seeking certain objects and avoiding certain objects ? For neither do we exist nor do we in living make use of other things."

" Breathing "—that is, " inspired by "—is a thrust at Democritus, who said (Frag. B 18, ed. Diels-Kranz) " whatsoever a poet writes with the god within him and a holy breath (*hieron pneuma*) is very fine " ; Democritus, like Empedocles, is here no better than

a poet. " Why do we weary ourselves " has a certain
pathos that surprises in Colotes. The verb is literally
" pound " or " chop " without displacing ; the sense
of " wearying " comes from the soreness and debility
we get from such a pounding. In Frag. B 2. 6 (ed.
Diels-Kranz, cited by Sextus for Empedocles' distrust
of the senses) Empedocles says we are " driven all
over " : we are driven from one place to another, and
appear as plants, fish, men, or gods. The verb can
also mean " hammer " and " strike," but the object
is displaced : the horse moves on, the iron flattens,
the man goes into exile. Perhaps Colotes' " pound "
or " knock " is a malicious interpretation of this : we
let drive at ourselves and only get worn out for our
pains. And we certainly do " take ourselves seriously " when we imagine we are immortal. Colotes'
words " we exist " and " living " are double-edged.
According to Empedocles in each state our senses
are so restricted that they tell us nothing of the
others ; thus we confine " exist " and " live " to our
existence as men. But the elements that compose
us exist and are in a sense alive, as they constantly
seek or repel (this being Empedocles' Love and Strife
and Colotes' seeking and avoidance). Thus in the
conventional sense, we, as men, can be said to live
and die ; in the true sense we, as the elements, live
and exist forever. Colotes' words are subtle rather
than pathetic. " For neither do *we* exist "—it is the
elements that do so—" nor do we *live* "—that is, pass
through a human life that ends in death, a sense of
" live " rejected by Empedocles—" making use of
other things "—these in Empedocles are no more
" things " than we are " men." " Nature " was
understood by Colotes and his Academic source as

169

" reality " [a] in opposition to " appearance." The present fragment of Empedocles may have disappeared in Sextus because " nature " is open to the Aristotelian interpretation proposed by Plutarch, " generation," and on this interpretation the passage ceases to be relevant.

1113 A

When what is mixed ⟨comes to⟩ the light of day
As man or breed of beasts or plants or birds,
Men (speak) of birth ; but when they are dissolved
Of woful doom. They speak ⟨not⟩ as they should.
But I too speak as they do, by convention.

Though Colotes ⟨cited these lines himself⟩ he failed to see that Empedocles did not abolish men, beasts, plants, and birds . . .

1113 D

No sage in his prophetic soul would say
That while men live the thing that they call " life,"
So long they are, and suffer good and ill ;
But till the joining of their elements
And ⟨after⟩ dissolution men are nothing.

For these are not the words of one who denies the existence of men who have been born and are living, but rather of one who takes both the unborn and the already dead to exist. Yet Colotes has found no fault with this, but says that on Empedocles' view we shall never so much as fall ill or receive a wound.

Colotes takes Empedocles to hold that men are immortal ; and immortals are immune to disease and wounds. Disease, we may suppose, is from the inside, wounds are from the outside. Thus Empedocles' doctrine is in contradiction with itself (since in the first of the two quotations he abolished man) and with his life : he went mad, and was killed by the leap into Aetna.

[a] So too by Sextus (cf. Outlines of Pyrrhonism, i. 233) and so no doubt by Lacydes, of whom the Suda says s.v. ἔγραψε δὲ φιλόσοφα καὶ περὶ φύσεως.

REPLY TO COLOTES

4. Socrates

1108 b Colotes has a way of presenting Socrates with grass and asking how comes it that he puts his food in his mouth and not in his ear.

As Socrates was superior to the senses he cannot know grass from food; as he does not even know himself, he cannot tell his mouth from his ear. But perhaps Colotes made these remarks before he came to deal with Socrates' self-ignorance. In that case they may have been suggested by *Phaedo* 64 d 2-4, 65 b 1-7. If Socrates has such contempt for the pleasures of food and for the senses and the body, why does he bother to taste his food ? Why not put it in his ear, the channel of that " talk " or " argumentation " he esteems so highly (99 e 1—100 a 3) ? (So too with the " cloak " mentioned at 1117 f : if he cares so little for the comfort of a cloak (64 d 9) why wrap his cloak about himself and not put it around the column ?)

1116 f Colotes adds : " we shall dismiss this business of Chaerephon's as it is nothing but a cheap and sophistical tale."

Colotes turns Socrates' own language against him : " cheap " (*phortikos*) and " sophist " are no compliments in the Socratic dialogues. A moralist contradicts himself when his own statements are open to the strictures he passes on others.

1117 d Again Colotes, premising with these profound and noble truths, that " we eat food, not grass, and when rivers are high we cross by boat, but when they become fordable, on foot," follows up with this : " The fact is, Socrates, that your arguments were charlatans ; and what you said to people in your conversations was one thing, but what you actually did was something else again."

171

Crossing the river comes from a " conversation " well
known to Academic youth, the *Phaedrus* (242 A),[a]
where Socrates threatens to cross the Ilissus and is
prevented by his sign ; the grass from *Republic*, ix,
586 A 8, where Socrates uses " graze " of men. The
" swaggering arguments " (*alazones logoi*)—which
claim more than they can perform [b] —are those of
the *Phaedo* (92 D 2-4) [c] ; and the final comment, that
Socrates' acts did not tally with his words, puts a new
interpretation on the striking phrase : it is no longer
the talk, but Socrates, that is the charlatan. We have
no irony or ironist here.[d]

1117 F Let Colotes himself be asked those questions :
how comes it that he eats food and not grass, well suited
as he is for such provender, and drapes his cloak about his
person and not around the pillar ?

The second question was suggested by the death-
scene (*Phaedo*, 118 A) ; the prison doubtless had its
columns.

1118 A . . . if Colotes does not cross rivers on foot
when they are high and keeps out of the way of snakes
and wolves . . .

Colotes found the snake in *Republic*, ii, 358 B 3, the
wolf in *Republic*, i, 336 D 6-7.

[a] Noticed by von Arnim, *s.v.* " Kolotes " in Pauly-Wissowa, vol. xi (1921), col. 1121. 61.
[b] Colotes refers them to the discussion of the practice of
death (*Phaedo*, 64 B 8—69 E 5).
[c] The expression also occurs in *Lysis*, 218 D 2-3 and *Republic*, viii, 560 C 2.
[d] Cicero's anti-Academic says that Socrates' scepticism did
not represent his true belief, but was ironic (*Acad. Post.* i.
4 [16]). Colotes means that in spite of his talk of training
himself to do without the senses (*Phaedo*, 64 D 1—69 E 5)
Socrates relied on them to live. Epicurus (Frag. 231, ed.
Usener) censured Socrates for his irony.

REPLY TO COLOTES

1118 c But where Colotes resorts to downright ridicule and denigration of Socrates for seeking to discover what is man, and as Colotes says, for the " cocky " statement that he did not even know (himself) . . .

Sextus mentions Socrates' explicit confession that he did not know whether he was a man or something else (*Outlines of Pyrrhonism*, ii. 22 ; *Against the Mathematicians*, vii. 264). " Cocky " (*neanieuomenon*) is another Platonic word, used by Socrates in *Phaedrus*, 235 A 6 and *Gorgias*, 527 D 6.

5. Melissus

[Plutarch cites nothing of the attack.]

In vindicating Parmenides Plutarch no doubt considered that he had vindicated the follower as well.

6. Plato

1115 c But Plato asserts that horses are uselessly ⟨considered⟩ by us to be horses and men ⟨men⟩.

Colotes has *Phaedo*, 73 c 1—77 A 5 (*cf.* also 96 D 8—102 A 1) in mind ; the examples " horses " and " man " occur at 73 E 5-6 and 96 D 9-E 1. Plato does not make this assertion. It is an inference from his giving sense-objects that recall an idea the name of that idea and his saying that the sense-object is something else than the idea and need not even resemble it (74 c 4—75 A 1). Thus we learn nothing certain about the sense-object " horse " when it is called " horse," the name of the idea.

7. Stilpon

1119 c-D Colotes mentions one of the little verbal puzzles that Stilpon used to propound to the sophists . . . and

173

. . . assails Stilpon in high tragic style, saying that his
assertion that a thing cannot be predicated of something
else is the taking away of our life. " For how shall we
live if we cannot call a man good or a man a general, but
can only on one side call a man a man and on the other
good good and general general, or if we cannot speak of
ten thousand horse or a strong city, but only say that horsemen are horsemen and ten thousand ten thousand, and so
with the rest ? "

Plato makes it nugatory to consider a man a man ;
Stilpon holds it impossible to call him even that, if
subject and predicate indicate different things. In
his attack on the myth in the *Republic* Colotes cen-
sures Plato for taking a tragic tone ; Plutarch returns
the compliment. Colotes has taken his examples
from Stilpon's famous reply to Demetrius Poliorcetes,
who asked him after the sack of Megara (306 B.C.)
whether he had lost anything. Stilpon (who had
been plundered) replied that he had lost nothing of
his own, as he had observed no one making off with
his virtue.[a] The first " man " is Stilpon, and " good "
the character he has not lost ; the second " man "
and the " general " are Demetrius ; the " ten thousand horse " are his army ; and the " strong city " is
Megara. This time Stilpon loses his virtue.

[a] Epicurus (Frags. 173-175, ed. Usener) attacked Stilpon
for holding that the sage was content with himself and had
no need of a friend, presumably on the ground of this saying.
Some versions merely mention " what is mine " (*Mor.* 475 c
and Seneca, *De Constantia Sapientis,* 5. 6, *Ep.* 9. 18) ; others
mention only his " knowledge " (*Life of Demetrius,* chap.
ix. 9 [893 A] and Simplicius on the *Categories,* p. 403. 19 [ed.
Kalbfleisch]) or " education " (*Mor. 5 F*). For the fuller version see *Gnom. Vat.* 515 (ed. Sternbach).

REPLY TO COLOTES

8. The Cyrenaics

1120 c-d The Cyrenaics . . . thought that evidence derived from the senses was insufficient warrant for certainty about sense-objects . . ., admitting that external objects appear, but refusing to venture further and assert that they are. Therefore, says Colotes, they cannot live and cannot make use of sense-objects, and he adds in derision : " These people do not say that a man or horse or wall is, but say it is themselves who are ' walled,' ' horsed,' and ' humanized.' "

Colotes chooses unfair examples, says Plutarch ; the Cyrenaics said " sweetened." As in the attack on Democritus, Colotes replaces qualities with objects. Here the object-examples (" wall " from Arcesilaüs, " horse " and " man " from Plato) point up the absurdity.

9. Arcesilaüs

1108 d These people charge the other philosophers with using that wisdom of theirs to make it impossible to live . . .

" These people " are the Epicureans, represented by Colotes ; " the other philosophers " are the sceptics, represented by Arcesilaüs. The wisdom of that philosopher lay in suspending judgement, since the criterion had been discredited.[a] By this piece of wisdom he abolishes life.

[a] Sextus, *Against the Mathematicians*, vii. 155-157. Zeno held that the sage would never have opinions, but only knowledge, as opinions can be false, and it is disgraceful for a sage to err. Knowledge ultimately rests on sense-perception. The sense image can be rejected as untrue, or held weakly (and is then opinion), but when it is a true impression it is held firmly by reason and assented to (von Arnim, *Stoicorum Vet. Frag.* i, pp. 16-20). Arcesilaüs retained the description of the sage as one who knows for certain, but denied that any

1121 F For though Arcesilaüs said nothing of his own Colotes says that he gave the unlettered the impression and belief that he did—our critic, of course, is widely read himself and writes with a beguiling charm.

Arcesilaüs derives all his views from the " other philosophers " and is thus refuted already. The audience, lettered (unlike the Epicureans) and proud of it, is warned not to be taken in like their inferiors by literary graces. Arcesilaüs is in effect another poet ; his philosophy is so much music (*Phaedo*, 61 A 3-4).

1122 E But how comes it that the suspender of judgement does not run to a mountain but to the bath, and does not on rising pass to the wall but to the double door when he wishes to issue forth to market ?

" Run " suggests the " impulse " (*hormê*) on which Arcesilaüs relied, and perhaps a certain quickness in the man himself ; Numenius (in Eusebius, *Praep. Evang.* xiv. 5. 12 [part ii, p. 271. 20, ed. Mras]) calls him *itês* (" impetuous "). The bath and market may hint at a love of crowds or of high living ; men of Arcesilaüs' means commonly left marketing to the servants. The mountain is a private place, the bath a public one. Another sense of *epechein* (" suspend judgement," " hold back ") is hinted at here. Medical writers use it of various kinds of physical retention. To bring out this sense we should have to render " run *for* the mountain " and " *for* the bathhouse." Worse is to come. " Wall " is no doubt Arcesilaüs' own illustration, taken (like Aristotle's bronze sphere and Chrysippus' signet) from the scene of the lecture.

---

sensation was proof against error. The sage, therefore, avoiding precipitancy and error, withholds consent from the sense image.

REPLY TO COLOTES

It would be in Arcesilaüs' style to illustrate his polemic against the Stoic " apprehension " or " grasping " with an object that Zeno could not hold in his hand. (Zeno illustrated " apprehension " and the process of which it was a part by holding up his outstretched palm and closing his fingers on it, finally holding the clenched fist in the other hand [Cicero, *Acad. Pr.* ii. 47 (145)].) " Door " (plural in the Greek, since it has two wings) would as an example possess the same advantage ; indeed we may hazard the guess that Arcesilaüs would rise from his lecturer's seat, walk to the wall or door, and lay his hand against it in a counterpart of Zeno's gesture. In view, however, of a certain use of " wall " (Lucian, *Asinus*, 9 ; *cf.* Pollux, v. 21) and of " door " (Euripides, *Cyclops*, 502) we must suppose that Colotes is also pointing to Arcesilaüs' private life. (For " pass " *cf.* Aristotle, *Generation of Animals*, i. 17 [721 b 18], iv. 8 [776 b 29] ; for " issue forth " *cf. ibid.*, i. 5 [717 b 24].) There may even be a reference here to Theodotê and Phila (Diogenes Laertius, iv. 40). Such women might well be established near the market-place ; in any case they offered a market of their own. If the other reference is to Cleochares (*ibid.*, iv. 41) Colotes is raking up the distant past, as Demochares, the rival to whom Arcesilaüs once yielded precedence, died in 271–270, aged over eighty.

1122 F—1123 A " But it is impossible to refuse assent to plain evidence, for neither to deny nor to affirm things credited is more unreasonable than to deny them." (The MSS. give : " for to deny things accredited is more unreasonable than neither to deny nor to affirm them.")

Confronted with a conflict of views Arcesilaüs refused assent or denial to either, as either might be errone-

177

ous, and the sage does not err (Cicero, *Acad. Pr.* ii. 20 [66]). For the actions of daily life, however, a criterion was expected, and Arcesilaüs' was the " reasonable " (*eulogon* : *cf.* Sextus, *Against the Mathematicians*, vii. 158). The Epicurean objector here (probably Colotes himself) has this criterion in mind as his term " unreasonable " (*paralogos*) would indicate. In these daily decisions we are guided by accepted beliefs among other things, and *paralogos* means not only " unreasonable " but running counter to all normal expectation or custom. To suspend judgement is itself a most outlandish and unparalleled sort of thing, like the very actions that the " reasonable " is supposed to avoid.

1124 b And so this doctrine of retaining judgement is no myth, as Colotes thinks, or bait to attract froward or flighty youth . . .

Colotes knows Arcesilaüs' audience well ; it is his own. The word *lamyros* (" froward ") can mean " greedy " ; it is also used of women who invite advances. Like attracts like. " Flighty " or " precipitate " makes a neat point. Arcesilaüs suspended judgement, since assent would be precipitate and unworthy of a sage. The pupils may not be precipitate about assenting, but they are about acting.

In his commentary on the *Republic* Proclus cites Colotes' censure of the myth (vol. ii, p. 105. 23-106. 14, ed. Kroll) :

Colotes the Epicurean reproaches Plato, saying that he abandons scientific truth and dwells on falsehood by telling myths like a poet, and not presenting demonstrations like a man of science ; and that in contradiction with himself he abused the poets in the preliminaries to this discussion for inventing stories about the underworld that arouse terror and fill their hearers with the fear of death, and then

REPLY TO COLOTES

himself at the end transforms the philosophic Muse into a theatrical narration of myths about the world after death; for, says Colotes, the bellowing opening in that passage and the savage and fiery executioners of the tyrant and Tartarus and the rest—how do they leave tragedians any room for going further ? And his third objection is that such myths must have a good deal of purposelessness. For they are not adapted to the multitude, who cannot even see their meaning, and they are superfluous for the wise, who have no need of being made better by such terrors. Since then they [presumably, writers of myths] cannot find an answer to the question : for whom are they written ? they show that their exertions in the matter of telling myths are purposeless.

("Philosophic Muse" comes from the *Philebus* [67 B 6], though Colotes may also have had *Republic*, vi, 499 D 4 and *Phaedo*, 61 A 3-4 in mind.) Arcesilaüs' doctrine is a "myth" in part because of the poetry of his style (*cf. memousômenos*, 1121 F).

1124 D . . . as the book nears the end Colotes says : "The men who appointed laws and customs and established the government of cities by kings and magistrates brought human life into a state of great security and peace and delivered it from tumults. If somebody should take all this away we shall live a life of beasts and anyone who chances upon another will all but devour him."

The dogmatists had said that the Pyrrhonist would be capable of butchering his own father and eating the flesh (Diogenes Laertius, ix. 108). Epicurus did not go so far, we may suppose, in his picture of primitive life ; hence the qualification "all but." We have Plutarch's word for it that Colotes did not mention Arcesilaüs by name ; "somebody" has here the meaning "a certain somebody." Arcesilaüs is doing something that will nullify all law and custom, and this will end in a return to primitive conditions,

179

which for man in his present softened state will be
fatal. Thus Arcesilaüs destroys " life " in the sense
not only of civilization but of existence itself. We
are told that he introduced the practice of arguing
both sides of a question (Diogenes Laertius, iv. 28 ;
cf. Cicero, *Acad. Post.* i. 12 [45] and *Acad. Prior.* ii. 3
[7] with Reid's note). This was a way of enforcing
his view that affirmative and negative arguments on
any point are in even balance (1124 A). This con-
trasting of opposing views, for the purpose of winning
hearers from an attachment to either, could easily be
applied to legislation ; indeed the Pyrrhonists so
applied it (*cf.* Diogenes Laertius, ix. 83). The result
to be expected is the nullification of law. We shall
therefore be reduced to the condition of man before
the institution of laws and government. What this
was we may see from the account in the fifth book of
Lucretius : " Men were unable to keep in view a
common good nor had they the wit to observe custom
or law in their dealings with one another. Whatever
prize chance offered, each carried off, since each had
instinctively learned to use his strength and live for
himself " (958-961). In verses 1011-1027 Lucretius
says that this changed with the discovery of houses,
clothing and fire, and the establishment of marriage.
Love for wife and children softened men. Neighbours were now ready to become friends and avoid
mutual injury ; if most had not observed this compact the race would have perished. (That is, they
had been so far softened that a return to the earlier
state would have been fatal.) Then (1105-1150) the
more intelligent became kings and began to build
cities and citadels for their own security. Next kings
were overthrown through jealousy, and mob rule and

turbulence ensued. As a result people instituted magistracies held in rotation (thus avoiding the jealousy) and set up laws, since the race was worn out by unending hostilities.

We notice one slight discrepancy between Lucretius and Colotes. Lucretius lets kings precede magistrates, and come to power by their superior intelligence. Colotes makes both kings and magistrates a human institution. It may be that Lucretius or his source has abbreviated here, and mentioned only what happened in certain parts of the world, including most of Greece. Elsewhere kings survived, and contrived to make their office a legal one.

Colotes' work was short, probably in a single book, as it was read and answered in a single session of Plutarch's school. There was also time to hear the protests of an outsider, Heracleides [a]; and after the audience had dispersed, the circle around Plutarch—Theon, Aristodemus, and Zeuxippus—held under Theon's direction the discussion recorded in the *Non Posse Suaviter Vivi Secundum Epicurum*. Of the works that Plutarch presents as reports of lectures the *De Audiendis Poetis* occupies some twenty-three pages of the Frankfort edition, the *De Audiendo* eleven, the *De Capienda ex Inimicis Utilitate* six, the *Adversus Colotem* twenty. (The *Non Posse Suaviter Vivi Secundum Epicurum* covers about twenty-one.) It would take about an hour and a half to read the *Adversus Colotem*

---

[a] *Cf. Mor.* 1086 ε, *supra.* It is possible that the objections were actually made to the published book. Plutarch's exhaustion (*ibid.*, 1087 ᴀ) after the reply may have been real, but it allows the discussion in the *Non Posse Suaviter Vivi Secundum Epicurum* to be conducted in a gentler tone by the diffident Theon : thus Plutarch has taken account of Heracleides' protest.

aloud at the usual rate of delivery for a lecture. If Colotes' work was as long as Plutarch's reply, the session would have had to be of twice the usual length.

We pass to Plutarch's reply. After a short address to Saturninus, to whom the book is dedicated (as Colotes had dedicated his to Ptolemy II), Plutarch tells how his friends requested him to reply, after Aristodemus, alleging his anger, had refused. Plutarch is also afraid of appearing too angry, but will use the utmost freedom of language to defend the philosophers and the good life against the Epicureans.

The harmful Epicurean views run through their philosophy. Colotes, on the other hand, has taken isolated statements out of their context, which explained and supported them. Even so, most of the difficulties raised by Colotes will be found to apply to Epicurus himself.

Democritus is first attacked, his reward for being Epicurus' teacher. The first charge is due to a misunderstanding of what Democritus said. And in any case the doctrine attacked can be derived from various statements made by Epicurus himself, as (1) that all sense impressions are true ; (2) that sensation occurs when some of the components of a mixture penetrate passages in the sense organs that they exactly fit ; (3) that wine can either be heating or cooling ; (4) that colours are not intrinsic to bodies. The second charge is true, and applies even more obviously to Epicurus.

Plutarch passes to the attack on Empedocles, who denied that things have a " nature " or death ; there is nothing but a mixing and unmixing of components. If this means that life becomes impossible Epicurus

REPLY TO COLOTES

is liable to the same charge on the same grounds, indeed more liable, as Empedocles allowed his elements certain qualities beyond mere impenetrability and rigidity. If Empedocles merely objects to the use of the word " nature " for " a natural thing," the point is merely verbal and gives no occasion for Colotes' attack ; Epicurus himself would have had to admit that by " nature " he meant no more. Plutarch, however, believes that the interpretation of " nature " as birth is the correct one, and that Empedocles is merely denying generation from nothing.

Parmenides is now taken up. Plutarch does not deny the sophistries, but insists they are not shameful : they have had no harmful moral or religious consequences, and for one so ancient, Parmenides has done well. But he has called the universe one. So too does Epicurus ; and when he divides this singular universe into two, bodies and the void, and takes the void to be nothing, he leaves us with a unity (which Plutarch does not call by the plural " bodies " but by the singular " infinity "). The charge is not pressed ; Plutarch quickly adds that the Epicurean infinity and void lead nowhere, whereas Parmenides combines as elements the light and dark and produces a world. Parmenides is distinguishing between the world of the intelligible and the world of opinion or sensation, as Plato did even more distinctly in his theory of ideas.

We thus pass to Plato. Colotes shows his lack of instruction when he says that Aristotle and the Peripatetics followed the doctrines of Plato that are here impugned. What Plato is actually doing is to distinguish between the world of being, the exemplar,

183

and the world of becoming, the imitation; he is not doing away with the latter.

Socrates comes next. Plutarch first deals with the abuse. The charge of vulgarity is answered by citing choice samples of liberties taken by the Epicureans with religious terms and acts; and the charge of not living up to his doctrine by mentioning the heroic acts of Socrates' life. Socrates' treatment of the senses is defended by the Epicurean doctrine that only the sage is unalterably convinced of anything. Colotes was not reckoned a sage (like Metrodorus); how then can he put such trust in the senses? Actually our responses to appearances are not a matter of dogmas or reasoning at all, but are due to causes in which reason has no part.

Next Colotes ridicules Socrates for saying that he did not even know himself. Plutarch points out the source and shows the true sense of the remark from the context. Socrates is here asking " What is man ?," a question faced by many others, Epicurus included; Colotes never reached that stage. And granting it to be a foolish question, how does it prevent us from living?

Stilpon's denial of all but identical predication is taken by Plutarch as a jest, a puzzle presented to the sophists to solve. It does not make us live worse, like the Epicurean views that forbid us to attach to the gods the ancient epithets that describe their beneficence and concern, or the Epicurean denial of " meaning," which makes thought impossible.

Plutarch now attacks Colotes for not mentioning by name the two contemporary schools he assails, although he made free with the eminent names of the past; it must have been cowardice. (It was conven-

REPLY TO COLOTES

tional not to mention by name a contemporary you
were attacking, and as with other courtesies the
motives differed in different cases.) Plutarch identifies the first contemporary school as the Cyrenaics,
the second as the Academy of Arcesilaüs.

The first school (the Cyrenaics) refused to make
pronouncements about external objects, and confined
themselves to statements about their sensations.
Plutarch attacks Colotes for formulating this philosophy not in the words of the school, but in his own
comic neologisms (1120 D). Plutarch then shows that
the Epicureans similarly accept the impressions as
true but in the case of illusions deny the interpretation ; and when they use one act of sensation to con-
firm or discredit another they let opinion decide
about the truth, trusting fallible opinion more than
the " truthful " sensations.

Arcesilaüs is the last of the philosophers discussed.
Plutarch traces the attack on Arcesilaüs to Epicurus'
jealousy of him. The charge that Arcesilaüs said
nothing original is met with the charge of the sophists
of the day, who alleged that he fathered his views on
Socrates, Plato, Parmenides, and Heracleitus. Plutarch thanks Colotes for vindicating the doctrine as
an ancient tradition.

The doctrine of suspended judgement has not been
shaken by far more elaborate and philosophical assaults. Plutarch proceeds to expound it, and shows
that the Epicurean objection that we must " assent "
to plain evidence is inconsistent with one of their own
pronouncements, that we need no teacher—that is,
no intervention of reason—to tell us that pleasure is
good, but only to have sensation and be made of
flesh. We Academics do not distort sensation by

forcing assent on it ; we simply treat the irrational thing as its nature demands, that is, as irrational.

The charge that it is more " unreasonable " to withhold assent and denial from " plain evidence " [a] is met by examples of the Epicureans' treatment of " plain evidence." They deny the consensus of mankind when they deny religious beliefs and the natural affection of parent for child ; they deny our own feelings when they assert that there is no mean between pleasure and pain, and they deny the plain evidence that sensation can err when they call the phantoms of madness and illusion real. It is actually more reasonable to distrust all sensation than to trust such sensations as these, as we must if all sensations are equally true.

Finally Plutarch takes a statement that Colotes had directed against Arcesilaüs (whom he did not name) and presents it as a most damning indictment of the Epicureans themselves. Colotes had praised the institutors of laws and customs for rescuing us from turbulence and war, and added that anyone who set out to destroy all this would reduce us to bestial savagery. This Plutarch denies ; even without our laws the doctrines of Parmenides, Socrates, Heracleitus and Plato will preserve us from such a life. It is the Epicurean doctrines that make laws necessary.

---

[a] " Plain evidence " is the Epicurean term, which Plutarch treats as equivalent to " accredited beliefs " (*ta pepisteumena*). The sceptics asserted that they would take certain actions, in spite of their suspension of judgement. Sextus (*Outlines of Pyrrhonism*, i. 23) distinguishes four cases : (1) we are guided by our nature, (2) we are compelled by our experiences, (3) we follow habits and usages, and (4) we follow the teaching of the arts. Plutarch's examples of Epicurean disregard of " plain evidence " can all be easily brought under the first three.

REPLY TO COLOTES

And it is these doctrines that nullify the laws, and among them the religious beliefs of mankind. Plutarch then surveys the Epicurean views about law-givers and the Epicurean abstention from public office and contrasts the conduct of the other philosophers (omitting the Cyrenaics and Arcesilaüs, and compensating by the addition of Heracleitus and Melissus), and ends by saying that the Epicurean quarrel is not so much with the lawgivers whom they vilify as with law itself.

The titles, preserved in the catalogue of Lamprias, of nine lost works show Plutarch's continuing concern with the problems of Academic scepticism : Περὶ τῆς εἰς ἑκάτερον ἐπιχειρήσεως βιβλία ε′ (No. 45) " On Arguing Both Sides of a Question " in five books ; Περὶ τοῦ μίαν εἶναι τὴν ἀπὸ τοῦ Πλάτωνος Ἀκαδημίαν (No. 63) " On the Unity of the Academy Derived from Plato " ; Περὶ τῆς διαφορᾶς τῶν Πυρρωνείων καὶ Ἀκαδημαϊκῶν (No. 64) " On the Distinction Between the Pyrrhonists and Academics " ; Περὶ τοῦ μὴ μάχεσθαι τῇ μαντικῇ τὸν Ἀκαδημαϊκὸν λόγον (No. 131) " That the Reasoning of the Academics does not Conflict with Divination " ; Σχολαὶ Ἀκαδημαϊκαί (No. 134) " Academic Discussions " ; Περὶ τῶν Πύρρωνος δέκα τόπων [τρόπων ?] (No. 158) " On the Ten Modes of Pyrrhon " ; Περὶ Κυρηναίων [Κυρηναϊκῶν Bern.] (No. 188) " On the Cyrenaics " ; Εἰ ἄπρακτος ὁ περὶ πάντων ἐπέχων (No. 210) " Whether One who Suspends Judgement about Everything Will be Unable to Act " ; and Πῶς κρινοῦμεν τὴν ἀλήθειαν (No. 225) " How we shall Judge the Truth."

The dialogue is a companion piece to the *Non Posse Suaviter Vivi Secundum Epicurum.* Ziegler [a] dates it

---

[a] Pauly-Wissowa, vol. xxi. 1, *s.v.* " Plutarchos," coll. 762 f.

PLUTARCH'S MORALIA

by the dedication to Saturninus, who was identified by E. Bourget [a] as L. Herennius Saturninus, proconsul of Achaïa in 98–99. If we press the remarks at 1107 E, Saturninus was in a position of almost royal authority at the time of dedication.

The scene of the dialogue is Plutarch's school, no doubt at Chaeronea. If the scene had been Delphi, we should have expected some indication of this in at least one of the companion dialogues. The essay is No. 81 in the Catalogue of Lamprias.

Manuscripts E and B [b] alone preserve it entire. The Aldine was apparently printed from a lost twin of B. To these can be added MS. 517 of the library of St. Mark, which contains on fol. 67ᵛ passages from 1126 C, C-D, and 1125 D in the hand of Georgius Gemistus Plethon,[c] and MS. 429 of the State Library at Munich, which on fol. 119ᵛ contains part of 1126 B. Neither manuscript presents variants significant enough to determine the affiliation of the text. We have collated the Aldine directly; E, B, and the excerpts from photostats. We record all differences between E and B. The translation of Epicurus' endearments has been taken from Paul Shorey's personal copy of Bernardakis' edition.

To the translations the following may be added :

A. Ferronus, *Plutarchi Chaeronei in Coloten Liber Posterior*, Lugduni, 1555, pp. 9-75. (The " first book

[a] *De Rebus Delphicis Imperatoriae Aetatis* (Montpellier, 1905), p. 71.

[b] Traces of correction are found in B. Thus at 1120 E we have πρὸς E : τὸν B. The original had τὸν superscribed over πρὸς, meaning πρὸς τόν. At 1121 D we have προσελθοῦσι E : ἐλθοῦσι B. In the original προσα was expunged.

[c] *Cf.* Aubrey Diller in *Scriptorium*, viii (1954), pp. 123-127 and x (1956), pp. 27-41.

against Colotes " is the *Non Posse Suaviter Vivi Secundum Epicurum.*)

G. M. GRATII in *Opuscoli Morali, di Plutarco Cheronese* . . . Parte Seconda, Venice, 1598, pp. 317ᵛ-329.

A. G., "Against Colotes the Disciple and Favourite of Epicurus " in *Plutarch's Morals*, vol. v, Fifth edition, London, 1718, pp. 312-357.   The first edition is dated London, 1684.

J. J. HARTMAN in *De Avondzon des Heidendoms²*, part II, Leiden, 1912, pp. 240-252.   Only chapters 1-3 and 30-34 are translated.

O. APELT, *Plutarch, Moralische Schriften*, Bändchen I, Leipzig, 1926, pp. 1-55.

ΠΡΟΣ ΚΩΛΩΤΗΝ[1] ΥΠΕΡ ΤΩΝ
ΑΛΛΩΝ ΦΙΛΟΣΟΦΩΝ[2]

E   1. Κωλώτης, ὃν Ἐπίκουρος εἰώθει Κωλωταρᾶν[3]
ὑποκορίζεσθαι καὶ Κωλωτάριον, ὦ Σατορνῖνε,[4]
βιβλίον ἐξέδωκεν ἐπιγράψας περὶ τοῦ ὅτι κατὰ τὰ
τῶν ἄλλων φιλοσόφων δόγματα οὐδὲ ζῆν ἐστιν.
ἐκεῖνο μὲν οὖν Πτολεμαίῳ τῷ βασιλεῖ προσπεφώ-
νηται· ἃ δὲ ἡμῖν ἐπῆλθεν εἰπεῖν πρὸς τὸν Κωλώτην,
ἡδέως ἂν οἶμαί σε γεγραμμένα διελθεῖν, φιλόκαλον
καὶ φιλάρχαιον ὄντα καὶ τὸ μεμνῆσθαι καὶ διὰ
χειρῶν ἔχειν ὡς μάλιστα δυνατόν ἐστι τοὺς λόγους
τῶν παλαιῶν βασιλικωτάτην διατριβὴν ἡγούμενον.
   2. Ἔναγχος οὖν ἀναγινωσκομένου τοῦ συγγράμ-
F ματος εἷς τῶν ἑταίρων, Ἀριστόδημος ὁ Αἰγιεὺς
(οἶσθα γὰρ τὸν ἄνδρα τῶν ἐξ Ἀκαδημίας οὐ ναρθη-
κοφόρον ἀλλὰ ἐμμανέστατον ὀργιαστὴν Πλάτωνος),
οὐκ οἶδα ὅπως παρὰ τὸ εἰωθὸς ἐγκαρτερήσας
σιωπῇ καὶ παρασχὼν ἑαυτὸν ἀκροατὴν ἄχρι τέλους
κόσμιον, ὡς τέλος ἔσχεν ἡ ἀνάγνωσις, " εἶεν,"
ἔφη, " τίνα τούτῳ μαχούμενον ἀνίσταμεν ὑπὲρ τῶν

---

[1] Κωλώτην Bern. and two mss. in Treu's apparatus to the
Catalogue of Lamprias : κολ. EB passim.
[2] ὑπὲρ τῶν ἄλλων φιλοσόφων Catalogue of Lamprias : περὶ
τῶν ἄλλων φιλοσόφων E ; B omits.
[3] Κωλωταρᾶν Crönert : κολωτάραν EB.
[4] Σατορνῖνε Ald. : σατορνῖλε EB.

REPLY TO COLOTES IN DEFENCE OF
THE OTHER PHILOSOPHERS

1. Colotes, my dear Saturninus, whom Epicurus used to call affectionately his " Colly " and " Collikins," brought out a book entitled " On the Point that Conformity to the Doctrines of the Other Philosophers Actually Makes it Impossible to Live." This book he addressed to King Ptolemy; you, I think, would enjoy perusing a written account of the answer it occurred to me to make to Colotes, as you are a lover of all that is excellent and old and consider it a most royal occupation to recall and have in hand, so far as circumstances allow, the teachings of the ancients.

2. While the book was being read not long ago, one of our company, Aristodemus [b] of Aegium (you know the man : no mere thyrsus-bearer of Academic doctrine, but a most fervent devotee of Plato [c]), with unusual patience somehow managed to hold his peace and listen properly to the end. When the reading was over he said : " Very well ; whom do we appoint our champion to defend the philosophers against this

---

[a] Frag. 140 [a] (p. 346, ed. Usener).
[b] A speaker in the *Non Posse Suaviter Vivi Secundum Epicurum*; otherwise unknown.
[c] *Cf.* Plato, *Phaedo*, 69 c : " Many the thyrsus-bearers, few the bacchants."

191

(1107) φιλοσόφων; οὐ γὰρ ἄγαμαι τὸ¹ τοῦ Νέστορος,
ἑλέσθαι δέον ἐκ τῶν ἐννέα τὸν ἄριστον, ἐπὶ τῇ
τύχῃ ποιουμένου καὶ διακληροῦντος." "ἀλλὰ
ὁρᾷς," ἔφην, "ὅτι κἀκεῖνος ἐπὶ τὸν κλῆρον ἑαυτὸν
ἔταξεν, ὥστε τοῦ φρονιμωτάτου βραβεύοντος γενέσθαι τὸν κατάλογον,

1108   ἐκ δ' ἔθορε κλῆρος κυνέης ὃν ἄρ' ἤθελον αὐτοί,
Αἴαντος.

οὐ μὴν ἀλλ' εἰ σὺ προστάττεις ἑλέσθαι

πῶς ἂν ἔπειτ' Ὀδυσῆος² ἐγὼ θείοιο³ λαθοίμην;

ὅρα δὴ καὶ σκόπει πῶς ἀμυνῇ τὸν ἄνδρα." καὶ ὁ
Ἀριστόδημος, "ἀλλ' οἶσθα," ἔφη, "τὸ τοῦ Πλάτωνος, ὅτι τῷ παιδὶ χαλεπήνας οὐκ αὐτὸς ἐνέτεινε
πληγὰς ἀλλὰ Σπεύσιππον ἐκέλευσεν, εἰπὼν αὐτὸς
ὀργίζεσθαι. καὶ σὺ τοίνυν παραλαβὼν κόλαζε⁴ τὸν
ἄνθρωπον ὅπως βούλει· ἐγὼ γὰρ ὀργίζομαι."

Τὰ αὐτὰ δὴ καὶ τῶν ἄλλων παρακελευομένων
B "λεκτέον μέν," ἔφην, "ἄρα, φοβοῦμαι δὲ μὴ δόξω
καὶ αὐτὸς ἐσπουδακέναι μᾶλλον ἢ δεῖ πρὸς τὸ
βιβλίον ὑπ' ὀργῆς⁵ δι' ἀγροικίαν καὶ βωμολοχίαν
καὶ ὕβριν τοῦ ἀνθρώπου χόρτον τινὰ προβάλλοντος
συνήθως⁶ Σωκράτει καὶ πῶς εἰς τὸ στόμα τὸ σιτίον

¹ ἄγαμαι τὸ Cobet (ἄγαμαι Ald.² and Stephanus): ἄγαν followed by a blank of 4 letters EB.
² ὀδυσῆος E : ὀδυσσῆος B.
³ θείοιο B : θείοι E.
⁴ κόλαζε Reiske : κόμιζε EB.
⁵ ὑπ' ὀργῆς Wyttenbach : ὑπὲρ τῆς EB.
⁶ συνήθως nos : ἐσθήσεως Eᵃʳ (apparently) ; a blank of 3
letters in Fʳ, of 5 in B, followed by ἤσεως (δι' ἐρωτήσεως Pohlenz ; ἀντὶ σιτήσεως Bern.).

192

man ? For I hardly admire Nestor's plan [a] of leaving the matter to the chance of the lot when the thing to do was to choose the best of the nine." " But you observe," said I, " that he also appointed himself to cast the lots, so that the selection should take place under the direction of the most prudent [b] of the company, and

> Out of the helmet leapt the lot of Ajax,
> That all desired. [c]

But since you direct that a choice shall be made,

> How could I then forget godlike Odysseus ? [d]

Look to it then and consider what defence you will make against the man." Aristodemus replied : " But you know how Plato,[e] when incensed at his servant, did not beat him personally but told Speusippus to do it, saying that he himself was angry ; do you too then take the fellow in hand and chastise him as you please, since I am angry."

As the others seconded his request I said : " I see then that I must speak ; but I fear that I too shall appear to take the book more seriously than is proper, in resentment at the insolent rudeness of the scurrilous wag, who has a way of presenting Socrates with ' grass ' and asking how comes it that he puts his

[a] Homer, *Il.* vii. 170-181 ; *cf. Mor.* 544 D. Hector challenged the Greeks to single combat. Nine heroes volunteer, and Nestor selects the champion by lot. The scholiast answers an objection similar to Aristodemus'.

[b] Aristodemus is gently reminded that Plutarch is the director.

[c] Homer, *Il.* vii. 182-183.

[d] Homer, *Il.* x. 243 (and *Od.* i. 65) ; quoted also in *Mor.* 55 B.

[e] *Cf. Mor.* 10 D and 551 B with the note.

(1108) οὐκ εἰς τὸ οὖς ἐντίθησιν ἐρωτῶντος. ἀλλ' ἴσως ἂν
ἐπὶ τούτοις καὶ γελάσειέ τις ἐννοήσας τὴν Σωκράτους πραότητα καὶ χάριν·

> ὑπέρ γε μέντοι παντὸς Ἑλλήνων στρατοῦ

τῶν ἄλλων φιλοσόφων, ἐν οἷς Δημόκριτός εἰσι[1] καὶ
Πλάτων καὶ Στίλπων καὶ Ἐμπεδοκλῆς καὶ Παρμενίδης καὶ Μέλισσος οἱ κακῶς ἀκηκοότες, οὐ
μόνον

> αἰσχρὸν σιωπᾶν[2]

ἀλλ' οὐδὲ ὅσιον ἐνδοῦναί τι καὶ ὑφελέσθαι[3] τῆς
C ἄκρας ὑπὲρ αὐτῶν παρρησίας, εἰς τοῦτο δόξης
φιλοσοφίαν προαγαγόντων. καίτοι τὸ μὲν ζῆν οἱ
γονεῖς μετὰ τῶν θεῶν ἡμῖν ἔδωκαν, παρὰ δὲ τῶν
φιλοσόφων δίκης καὶ νόμου συνεργὸν οἰόμεθα λόγον
ἐπιθυμιῶν κολαστὴν λαβόντες εὖ ζῆν· τὸ δὲ εὖ ζῆν
ἐστι κοινωνικῶς ζῆν καὶ φιλικῶς καὶ σωφρόνως
καὶ δικαίως, ὧν οὐθὲν ἀπολείπουσιν οἱ περὶ γαστέρα
τἀγαθὸν εἶναι βοῶντες, οὐκ ἂν δὲ τὰς ἀρετὰς ὁμοῦ
πάσας τετρημένου χαλκοῦ πριάμενοι δίχα τῆς ἡδονῆς, πάσης πανταχόθεν ἐξελαθείσης· ἐνδεῖν δὲ
αὐτοῖς τὸν περὶ θεῶν καὶ ψυχῆς[4] λόγον ὡς ἡ μὲν

---

[1] εἰσι nos : ἐστι EB.
[2] αἰσχρὸν σιωπᾶν B : αἰσχρο followed by a blank of 4 letters
and πᾶν E.
[3] ὑφελέσθαι EB : ὑφίεσθαι Wyttenbach ; ὑφέσθαι a conjecture in the margin of Turnebus' Aldine.
[4] θεῶν καὶ ψυχῆς] ψυχῆς καὶ θεῶν E[ac].

---

[a] From the *Philoctetes* of Euripides : Nauck, *Trag. Graec.
Frag.*, Eur. 796. The verse runs :

> " It were shame
> To hold my peace and let barbarians speak."

194

food in his mouth and not in his ear. But this perhaps might even make you laugh when you think of
Socrates' unruffled wit ;

Yet in defence of all the Grecian host

—of all the other philosophers, among whom Democritus, Plato, Stilpon, Empedocles, Parmenides, and
Melissus are singled out for abuse—not only

Is silence shameful *

but to yield in the slightest and withhold the most
outspoken language would be downright impiety in
vindicating men who have brought philosophy to
such high repute. Consider : life was bestowed on
us by our parents with the aid of heaven ; but the
good life, in our view, we owe to the philosophers,
who gave us the reasoning that helps justice and law
in curbing our lusts ; and to live the good life is to
live a life of participation in society, of loyalty to
friends, of temperance and honest dealing. But none
of this is left to us *b* by those who keep shouting that
the good is to be found in the belly *c* ; that they would
not give a copper with a hole in it for all the virtues
in a lump apart from pleasure, supposing pleasure
totally banished from every one of them *d* ; and that
the account they need of the gods and of the soul is
an account that tells how the one is dissolved and

---

b The argument was used against the Academics : *cf.*
Cicero, *Acad. Pr.* ii. 10 (31) : by destroying apprehension
the Academics destroy philosophy and virtue and overthrow
the very foundations of our life.

c Metrodorus, Frag. 40 (ed. Körte) ; *cf.* 1125 A, *infra* and
1087 D and 1098 D, *supra.* Setting up pleasure as the end
is the ruin of the social virtues above all : *cf.* Cicero, *Acad.
Pr.* ii. 46 (140).

d Epicurus, Frag. 512 (ed. Usener).

(1108) ἀπόλλυται διαλυθεῖσα, τοῖς δὲ οὐθενὸς[1] μέλει τῶν
D καθ' ἡμᾶς. τοῖς μὲν γὰρ ἄλλοις φιλοσόφοις ἐγ-
καλοῦσιν οὗτοι διὰ τὸ σοφὸν ὡς τὸ ζῆν ἀναιροῦσιν,
ἐκεῖνοι δὲ τούτοις ὅτι ζῆν ἀγεννῶς[2] καὶ θηριωδῶς
διδάσκουσι.

3. " Καίτοι ταῦτα μὲν ἐγκέκραται τοῖς Ἐπικούρου λόγοις καὶ διαπεφοίτηκεν αὐτοῦ τῆς φιλο-
σοφίας· ὁ δὲ Κωλώτης ὅτι φωνάς τινας ἐρήμους
πραγμάτων ἀποσπῶν καὶ μέρη λόγων καὶ σπαρά-
γματα κωφὰ τοῦ[3] βεβαιοῦντος καὶ συνεργοῦντος
πρὸς νόησιν καὶ πίστιν ἕλκων ὥσπερ ἀγορὰν ἢ
πίνακα τεράτων συντίθησι τὸ βιβλίον, ἴστε δήπου
παντὸς μᾶλλον ὑμεῖς," ἔφην, " τὰ συγγράμματα
τῶν παλαιῶν διὰ χειρὸς ἔχοντες. ἐμοὶ δὲ δοκεῖ
καθάπερ ὁ Λυδὸς ἐφ' αὑτὸν ἀνοίγειν οὐ θύραν μίαν,
E ἀλλὰ ταῖς πλείσταις τῶν ἀποριῶν καὶ μεγίσταις
περιβάλλειν τὸν Ἐπίκουρον.

" Ἄρχεται γὰρ ἀπὸ Δημοκρίτου, καλὰ καὶ πρέ-
ποντα διδασκάλια κομιζομένου παρ' αὐτοῦ. καίτοι
πολὺν χρόνον αὐτὸς ἑαυτὸν ἀνηγόρευε Δημοκρίτειον
ὁ Ἐπίκουρος, ὡς ἄλλοι τε λέγουσι καὶ Λεοντεύς,
εἷς τῶν ἐπ' ἄκρον Ἐπικούρου μαθητῶν, πρὸς Λυ-
κόφρονα γράφων τιμᾶσθαί τέ φησι τὸν Δημόκριτον
ὑπὸ Ἐπικούρου διὰ τὸ πρότερον ἅψασθαι τῆς ὀρθῆς

---

[1] οὐθενὸς E : οὐδενὸς B.
[2] ἀγεννῶς EᶜB : ἀγενῶς Eᵃᶜ ?
[3] κωφὰ τοῦ EB : κωφὰ δίχα τοῦ Pohlenz ; κωφὰ λόγου or
κωφὰ λόγου τοῦ Post.

---

[a] Cf. Epicurus, Letter to Herodotus, 65.
[b] Cf. Epicurus, Frags. 361-364 (ed. Usener) ; Cardinal
Tenet i.
[c] Cf. Mor. 548 c.
[d] Cf. Mor. 520 c for the " freak market " at Rome.

perishes [a] and the others care nothing for our affairs.[b] Thus these people charge the other philosophers with making life impossible by their wisdom, whereas the other philosophers charge them with teaching us to live ignobly and like the brutes.

3. "Now these views permeate all of Epicurus' arguments and are found everywhere in his philosophy; but the case is otherwise with the views attacked. Colotes detaches certain sayings shorn of their real meaning and rips from their context mutilated fragments of argument,[c] suppressing all that confirmed them and contributed to comprehension and belief, piecing his book together like the freaks on display in a market [d] or depicted in a painting,[e] as you who are of this company are of course well aware," I said, "versed as you are in the writings of the ancients. As I see it, he is opening the door [f] to his own ruin, like the Lydian, and not just one door; no, most of his charges, and the gravest, demolish Epicurus.

"He begins with Democritus,[g] who thus receives for his teaching a handsome and appropriate fee. And this although Epicurus [h] long proclaimed himself a Democritean, as is attested among others by Leonteus, one of Epicurus' most devoted pupils, who writes to Lycophron that Democritus was honoured by Epicurus for having reached the correct ap-

[e] Cf. 1123 c, infra.
[f] Cf. Mor. 636 f. The proverb does not apparently occur elsewhere. The Lydian is no doubt Candaules: the door behind which he hid Gyges to see the queen disrobe was the same behind which she hid Gyges to murder his master (Herodotus, i. 9. 2, 12. 1).
[g] Diels and Kranz, Die Frag. der Vorsokratiker, Demokritos, A 53.
[h] Cf. Frag. 234 (ed. Usener) with the note.

(1108) γνώσεως, καὶ τὸ σύνολον τὴν πραγματείαν Δημοκρίτειον προσαγορεύεσθαι διὰ τὸ περιπεσεῖν αὐτὸν
πρότερον ταῖς ἀρχαῖς περὶ φύσεως.[1] ὁ δὲ Μητρόδωρος ἄντικρυς ἐν τῷ[2] περὶ φιλοσοφίας εἴρηκεν ὡς
F εἰ μὴ προκαθηγήσατο Δημόκριτος οὐκ ἂν προῆλθεν
Ἐπίκουρος ἐπὶ τὴν σοφίαν. ἀλλ᾽ εἰ κατὰ τὰ Δημοκρίτου δόγματα ζῆν οὐκ ἔστιν, ὡς οἴεται Κωλώτης, γελοῖος ἦν ἐπὶ τὸ μὴ ζῆν ἄγοντι Δημοκρίτῳ
κατακολουθῶν ὁ Ἐπίκουρος.

4. " Ἐγκαλεῖ δὲ αὐτῷ πρῶτον ὅτι τῶν πραγμάτων ἕκαστον εἰπὼν[3] οὐ μᾶλλον τοῖον ἢ τοῖον
1109 εἶναι συγκέχυκε τὸν βίον. ἀλλὰ τοσοῦτόν γε Δημόκριτος ἀποδεῖ τοῦ νομίζειν μὴ μᾶλλον εἶναι
τοῖον ἢ τοῖον τῶν πραγμάτων ἕκαστον ὥστε Πρω-
ταγόρᾳ τῷ σοφιστῇ τοῦτο εἰπόντι μεμαχῆσθαι καὶ
γεγραφέναι πολλὰ καὶ πιθανὰ πρὸς αὐτόν. οἷς
οὐδὲ ὄναρ ἐντυχὼν ὁ Κωλώτης ἐσφάλη περὶ λέξιν
τοῦ ἀνδρός, ἐν ᾗ διορίζεται μὴ μᾶλλον τὸ ' δὲν ' ἢ
τὸ ' μηδὲν ' εἶναι, ' δὲν ' μὲν ὀνομάζων τὸ σῶμα,
' μηδὲν ' δὲ τὸ κενόν, ὡς καὶ τούτου φύσιν τινὰ καὶ
ὑπόστασιν ἰδίαν ἔχοντος.

" Ὁ[4] δ᾽ οὖν δόξας τὸ ' μηδὲν μᾶλλον εἶναι τοῖον
ἢ τοῖον ' Ἐπικουρείῳ δόγματι κέχρηται τῷ ' πά-
B σας εἶναι τὰς δι᾽ αἰσθήσεως φαντασίας ἀληθεῖς.'

---

[1] περὶ φύσεως EᶜB (-σιν Eᵃᶜ ?): Hartman would delete ;
Goerbing would place the words before πραγματείαν, Westman after γνώσεως.
[2] ἐν τῷ added by Menagius.
[3] εἰπὼν Xylander : ἐπιὼν EB.
[4] ὁ B : ὃ E.

ᵃ Frag. 33 (ed. Körte).
ᵇ Diels and Kranz, *Die Frag. der Vorsokratiker*, Demokritos, B 156.

proach to knowledge before him, and that indeed his whole system was called Democritean because Democritus had first hit upon the first principles of natural philosophy. Metrodorus [a] states outright in his work *On Philosophy* that if Democritus had not shown the way Epicurus would not have attained to his wisdom. Yet if the principles of Democritus make it impossible to live, as Colotes supposes, Epicurus cuts a ridiculous figure as he follows in the footsteps of Democritus down the road to no more living.

4. " Colotes first charges him with asserting that no object is any more of one description than of another,[b] and thus throwing our life into confusion. But so far is Democritus from considering an object to be no more of one description than of another that he has attacked the sophist Protagoras [c] for making this assertion and set down many telling arguments against him. Colotes, who is innocent of the slightest acquaintance with them,[d] mistook an expression in which Democritus [e] lays it down that ' aught ' is no more real than ' naught,' using the term ' aught ' of body and ' naught ' of empty space, meaning that space like body has a real existence of its own.

" But whatever we think of that, whoever held that nothing is any more of one description than of another is following an Epicurean doctrine,[f] that all the impressions reaching us through the senses are true.

---

[c] *Cf.* Diels and Kranz, *Die Frag. der Vorsokratiker*, Protagoras, A 15.

[d] Literally " who had not read them even in a dream." For the phrase see W. Headlam on Herondas, i. 11, Solon, Frag. 25. 2-3 (ed. Diehl³), Simplicius on the *Physics* (p. 29. 2, ed. Diels), and Leutsch and Schneidewin, *Paroem. Gr.* ii, p. 576.

[e] *Cf.* Diels and Kranz, *Die Frag. der Vorsokratiker*, Demokritos, A 49.

[f] Epicurus, Frag. 250 (ed. Usener).

(1109) εἰ γὰρ δυοῖν λεγόντων τοῦ μὲν αὐστηρὸν εἶναι τὸν
οἶνον τοῦ δὲ γλυκὺν οὐδέτερος ψεύδεται τῇ αἰσθήσει, τί μᾶλλον ὁ οἶνος αὐστηρὸς ἢ γλυκύς ἐστι;
καὶ μὴν λουτρῷ γε τῷ αὐτῷ τοὺς μὲν ὡς θερμῷ
τοὺς δὲ ὡς ψυχρῷ χρωμένους ἰδεῖν ἐστιν· οἱ μὲν
γὰρ ψυχρὸν οἱ δὲ θερμὸν ἐπιβάλλειν κελεύουσι.
πρὸς δὲ Βερονίκην[1] τὴν Δηιοτάρου[2] τῶν Λακεδαι-
μονίων τινὰ γυναικῶν ἀφικέσθαι λέγουσιν· ὡς δὲ
ἐγγὺς ἀλλήλων προσῆλθον, εὐθὺς ἀποστραφῆναι
τὴν[3] μὲν τὸ μύρον ὡς ἔοικε τὴν δὲ τὸ βούτυρον
δυσχεράνασαν. εἴπερ οὖν μὴ μᾶλλόν ἐστιν ἡ ἑτέρα
τῆς ἑτέρας ἀληθὴς αἴσθησις, εἰκός ἐστι καὶ τὸ ὕδωρ
C μὴ μᾶλλον εἶναι ψυχρὸν ἢ θερμὸν καὶ τὸ μύρον καὶ
τὸ βούτυρον μὴ μᾶλλον εὐῶδες ἢ δυσῶδες· εἰ γὰρ
αὐτὸ τὸ[4] φαινόμενον ἕτερον ἑτέρῳ φάσκει τις, ἀμφότερα[5] εἶναι λέγων λέληθεν.

5. '' Αἱ δὲ πολυθρύλητοι[6] συμμετρίαι καὶ ἁρ-
μονίαι τῶν περὶ τὰ αἰσθητήρια πόρων αἵ τε πολυ-
μιξίαι τῶν σπερμάτων, ἃ δὴ πᾶσι χυμοῖς καὶ ὀ-
σμαῖς καὶ χρόαις[7] ἐνδιεσπαρμένα λέγουσιν ἑτέραν
ἑτέρῳ[8] ποιότητος κινεῖν αἴσθησιν, οὐκ ἄντικρυς εἰς
τὸ ' μὴ μᾶλλον ' τὰ πράγματα συνελαύνουσιν αὐτοῖς; τοὺς γὰρ οἰομένους ψεύδεσθαι τὴν αἴσθησιν
ὅτι τὰ ἐναντία πάθη γινόμενα τοῖς χρωμένοις ἀπὸ
D τῶν αὐτῶν ὁρῶσι παραμυθούμενοι διδάσκουσιν ὡς

___

[1] Βερονίκην nos : βερρονίκην EB (i.e., ρο was superscribed over βερνίκην or βερενίκην).

[2] Δηϊτάρου Rasmus (Deiotari Xylander ; Ἀντιπάτρου Reiske): δηϊταύρου EB.   [3] τὴν] τὸν B[ac?1?].

[4] αὐτὸ τὸ nos (τὸ αὐτὸ Wyttenbach): αὖ τὸ EB.

[5] ἀμφότερα EB : ἀμφότερον Benseler.

[6] πολυθρύλητοι Dübner : πολυθρύλητοι EB[r] (πολλυ- B[ar]).

[7] χρόαις nos : χροιαῖς EB.

[8] ἑτέρῳ E : ἑτέρας B (ἑτέρων Ald.).

200

For if one of two persons says that the wine is dry and the other that it is sweet, and neither errs in his sensation, how is the wine any more dry than sweet? Again, you may observe that in one and the same bath some treat the water as too hot, others as too cold, the first asking for the addition of cold water, the others of hot. There is a story that a Spartan lady came to visit Beronicê,[a] wife of Deiotarus.[b] No sooner did they come near each other than each turned away, the one (we are told) sickened by the perfume, the other by the butter. If then one sense-perception is no more true than another, we must suppose that the water is no more cold than hot, and that perfume or butter is no more sweet-smelling than ill-smelling; for he who asserts that the object itself is what appears one thing to one person and another to another has unwittingly said that it is both things at once.

5. "As for the old story of the 'right size' and 'perfect fit'[c] of the passages in the sense organs, and on the other hand the multiple mixture of the 'seeds' that they say are found dispersed in all savours, odours, and colours so as to give rise in different persons to different perceptions of quality, do not these theories actually compel objects in their view to be no more this than that? For when people take sensation to be deceptive because they see that the same objects have opposite effects on those resorting to it, these thinkers offer the reassuring explanation that since well-

---

[a] Otherwise unknown.

[b] Four Galatian kings or princes of the name are known. They belong to the first century B.C.

[c] Cf. Epicurus, *Letter to Herodotus*, 47, 49, 50, 53, *Letter to Pythocles*, 107, and Frag. 284 (ed. Usener). Körte assigns the whole of chapter 5 to Metrodorus (Frag. 1).

(1109) ἀναπεφυρμένων καὶ συμμεμιγμένων[1] ὁμοῦ τι[2] πάν
των, ἄλλου δὲ ἄλλῳ πεφυκότος ἐναρμόττειν, οὐκ
ἔστι τῆς αὐτῆς πᾶσι[3] ποιότητος ἐπαφὴ καὶ ἀντί
ληψις οὐδὲ πᾶσι τοῖς μέρεσι κινεῖ πάντας ὡσαύτως
τὸ ὑποκείμενον, ἀλλὰ ἐκείνοις ἕκαστοι μόνοις ἐντυγ
χάνοντες πρὸς ἃ σύμμετρον[4] ἔχουσι τὴν αἴσθησιν,
οὐκ ὀρθῶς διαμάχονται περὶ τοῦ χρηστὸν ἢ πονηρὸν
ἢ λευκὸν ἢ μὴ λευκὸν εἶναι τὸ πρᾶγμα, τὰς αὑτῶν
οἰόμενοι βεβαιοῦν αἰσθήσεις τῷ τὰς ἀλλήλων[5] ἀναι
ρεῖν· δεῖ δὲ αἰσθήσει μὲν μηδεμιᾷ μάχεσθαι[6]—
πᾶσαι γὰρ ἅπτονταί τινος, οἷον ἐκ πηγῆς τῆς
E πολυμιξίας ἑκάστη λαμβάνουσα τὸ πρόσφορον καὶ
οἰκεῖον—, ὅλου δὲ μὴ κατηγορεῖν ἁπτομένους με
ρῶν, μηδὲ τὸ αὐτὸ δεῖν οἴεσθαι[7] πάσχειν ἅπαντας,
ἄλλους κατ' ἄλλην ποιότητα καὶ δύναμιν αὐτοῦ
πάσχοντας.

"Ὥρα δὴ[8] σκοπεῖν τίνες μᾶλλον ἄνθρωποι τὸ
' μὴ[9] μᾶλλον ' ἐπάγουσι τοῖς πράγμασιν ἢ οἳ πᾶν
μὲν τὸ αἰσθητὸν κρᾶμα παντοδαπῶν ποιοτήτων
ἀποφαίνουσι

σύμμικτον ὥστε γλεῦκος ὑλιστήριον,[10]

ἔρρειν δὲ ὁμολογοῦσι τοὺς κανόνας αὐτοῖς καὶ

---

[1] συμμεμιγμένων E : συμμιγνυμένων B.
[2] τι E : τοι B (and so B at Mor. 579 c, 872 c, 1059 D, 1112 F, 1113 c, and 1125 D).
[3] πᾶσι added by Reiske after ἐπαφὴ, placed here by Pohlenz.   [4] ἃ σύμμετρον EB[1]γρ : ἀσύμμ. B[t].
[5] ἀλλήλων EB[t] : ἄλλων B[1ss,2]γρ.
[6] μηδεμιᾷ μάχεσθαι Dübner (μηδεμιᾷ διαμάχεσθαι Reiske) : μηδὲ διαμάχεσθαι EB.   [7] δεῖν οἴεσθαι E : οἴεσθαι δεῖν B.
[8] ὥρα δὴ Wyttenbach : ἆρα δὴ E ; ἆρα δεῖ B.

nigh everything is mixed and compounded with everything else, and since different substances are naturally
adapted to fit different passages, the consequence is
that everyone does not come into contact with and
apprehend the same quality, and again the object
perceived does not affect everyone in the same way
with every part. What happens instead is that
different sets of persons encounter only those components to which their sense organs are perfectly
adjusted, and they are therefore wrong when they
fall to disputing whether the object is good or bad
or white or not white, imagining that they are con-
firming their own perceptions by denying one another's. The truth of the matter is that no sense-perception should be challenged,[a] as all involve a contact
with something real, each of them taking from the
multiple mixture as from a fountain what agrees with
and suits itself; and we should make no assertions
about the whole when our contact is with parts, nor
fancy that all persons should be affected in the same
way, when different persons are affected by different
qualities and properties in the object.

" It is time to consider the question : who are more
chargeable with imposing on objects the doctrine
that nothing is more this than that, than those who
assert that every perceptible object is a blend of
qualities of every description,

> Mixed like the must entangled in the filter,[b]

and who confess that their standards would go glim-

---

[a] *Cf.* Epicurus, *Cardinal Tenets* xxiii and xxiv.
[b] Nauck, *Trag. Graec. Frag.*, Adesp. 420.

---

[9] μὴ E[c]B : μα E[ac] ?
[10] ὑλιστήριον Emperius : αὐλητήριον EB.

(1109) παντάπασιν οἴχεσθαι τὸ κριτήριον, εἴπερ[1] εἰλικρινὲς
αἰσθητὸν ὁτιοῦν καὶ μὴ πολλὰ ἕκαστον ἀπέλιπον.

6. '' Ὅρα δὲ[2] ἃ περὶ τοῦ οἴνου τῆς θερμότητος
ἐν τῷ Συμποσίῳ Πολύαινον[3] αὐτῷ[4] διαλεγόμενον
F Ἐπίκουρος πεποίηκε. λέγοντος γάρ, ' οὐ φὴς
εἶναι,[5] ὦ Ἐπίκουρε, τὰς ὑπὸ τοῦ οἴνου διαθερμα-
σίας; ', ὑπέλαβε, ' τί δεῖ[6] τὸ καθόλου θερμαντικὸν
ἀποφαίνεσθαι τὸν οἶνον εἶναι; ' καὶ μετὰ σμικρόν,
' φαίνεται μὲν γὰρ δὴ τὸ καθόλου οὐκ εἶναι θερμαν-
τικὸς ὁ οἶνος, τοῦδε δέ τινος ὁ τοσοῦτος εἶναι[7] θερ-
μαντικὸς ἂν ῥηθείη.' καὶ πάλιν αἰτίαν ὑπειπὼν
θλίψεις τε καὶ διασπορὰς ἀτόμων, ἑτέρων δὲ συμ-
1110 μίξεις καὶ παραζεύξεις αἰτιασάμενος ἐν τῇ πρὸς τὸ
σῶμα καταμίξει τοῦ οἴνου, ἐπιλέγει, ' διὸ δὴ καθόλου μὲν οὐ ῥητέον τὸν οἶνον εἶναι θερμαντικόν, τῆς
δὲ τοιαύτης φύσεως καὶ τῆς οὕτως διακειμένης θερμαντικὸν τὸν τοσοῦτον, ἢ τῇσδε τὸν τοσοῦτον εἶναι
ψυκτικόν. ἔνεισι γὰρ καὶ τοιαῦται ἐν τῷ τοιούτῳ
ἀθροίσματι φύσεις ἐξ ὧν ἂν ψυχρὸν συσταίη ἢ αἳ
ἂν παρὰ[8] ἑτέραις παραζυγεῖσαι ψυχρασίας φύσιν
ἀποτελέσειαν· ὅθεν ἐξαπατώμενοι οἱ μὲν ψυκτικὸν
τὸ καθόλου φασὶν εἶναι τὸν οἶνον οἱ δὲ θερμαντικόν.'

'' Ὁ δὴ λέγων ἐξηπατῆσθαι τοὺς πολλοὺς τὸ

[1] εἴπερ Emperius (ἄν, εἴπερ Madvig) : ἄπερ EB.
[2] δὲ E : δὴ B.
[3] Πολύαινον Turnebus, Xylander : πολύδινον EB.
[4] αὐτῷ Usener : αὐτῶ EB.
[5] φὴς εἶναι Basle edition of 1542 : φησὶν EB.
[6] τί δεῖ nos (τί δέ; τοῦτό σ' ἔπεισε Pohlenz ; τίς δὲ [reading

mering and the criterion of truth quite disappear if they permitted any sense-object whatsoever to be purely one thing and did not leave every one of them a plurality ?

6. " Consider the discussion that Epicurus in his *Symposium* [a] presents Polyaenus as holding with him about the heat in wine. When Polyaenus asks, ' Do you deny, Epicurus, the great heating effect of wine ? ', he replies, ' What need is there to generalize that wine is heating ? ' A little later he says, ' For it appears that it is not a general fact that wine is heating, but a given quantity of wine may be said to be heating for a given person.' Again, after assigning as one cause the crowding and dispersal of atoms, and as another, the mixture and alignment of these with others, when the wine is mingled with the body, he adds in conclusion,[b] ' Therefore one should not generalize that wine is heating, but only say that this amount is heating for this constitution in this condition, or that that amount is chilling for another. For in an aggregate such as wine there are also certain natural substances of such a sort that cold might be formed of them, or such that, when aligned with others, they would produce a real coolness. Hence, deceived by this, some generalize that wine is cooling, others that it is heating.'

" If then the man who asserts that the majority

---

[a] Frag. 58 (ed. Usener) ; *cf. Mor.* 652 A and the Aristotelian *Problems*, iii. 5 (871 a 28 ff.) and iii. 26 (874 b 23 ff.).

[b] Frag. 59 (ed. Usener).

ἀποφαίνεται] Usener ; τίς οὐ Basle edition of 1542 ; τίς οὖν ἀνάγκη Reiske) : τίς σε EB.

[7] εἶναι Basle edition of 1542 : εἰ EB.

[8] ἢ αἰ ἂν παρὰ nos : εἰ δέον γε EB (ἢ αἰ εἰς δέον γε Pohlenz ; ἢ αἰ γε Usener).

(1110)

B θερμαῖνον θερμαντικὸν ἢ τὸ ψῦχον ψυκτικὸν ὑπο-
λαμβάνοντας, εἰ μὴ νομίζοι τὸ μὴ μᾶλλον εἶναι
τοῖον ἢ τοῖον ἕκαστον ἀκολουθεῖν οἷς εἴρηκεν, αὐτὸς
ἐξηπάτηται.

" Προστίθησι δὲ ὅτι ' πολλάκις οὐδὲ ἦλθεν εἰς τὸ
σῶμα θερμαντικὴν ἐπιφέρων ἢ ψυκτικὴν δύναμιν ὁ
οἶνος, ἀλλὰ κινηθέντος τοῦ ὄγκου καὶ γενομένης
τῶν σωμάτων μεταστάσεως αἱ ποιοῦσαι τὸ θερμὸν
ἄτομοι νῦν μὲν συνῆλθον εἰς τὸ αὐτὸ καὶ παρέσχον
ὑπὸ πλήθους θερμότητα καὶ πύρωσιν τῷ σώματι,
νῦν δὲ ἐκπεσοῦσαι κατέψυξαν.'

7. " Ὅτι[1] δὲ τούτοις πρὸς πᾶν ἐστι[2] χρῆσθαι τὸ
καλούμενον καὶ νομιζόμενον πικρὸν γλυκὺ καθαρ-
τικὸν ὑπνωτικὸν φωτεινόν, ὡς οὐδενὸς ἔχοντος
C αὐτοτελῆ ποιότητα καὶ δύναμιν οὐδὲ δρῶντος μᾶλλον ἢ πάσχοντος ὅταν ἐγγένηται[3] τοῖς σώμασιν,
ἄλλην δὲ ἐν ἄλλοις διαφορὰν καὶ κρᾶσιν λαμβάνον-
τος, οὐκ ἄδηλόν[4] ἐστιν. αὐτὸς γὰρ οὖν Ἐπίκουρος[5]
ἐν τῷ δευτέρῳ τῶν πρὸς Θεόφραστον οὐκ εἶναι
λέγων τὰ χρώματα συμφυῆ τοῖς σώμασιν, ἀλλὰ
γεννᾶσθαι[6] κατὰ ποιάς τινας τάξεις καὶ θέσεις[7] πρὸς
τὴν ὄψιν, οὐ μᾶλλόν φησι κατὰ τοῦτον τὸν λόγον
ἀχρωμάτιστον σῶμα εἶναι ἢ[8] χρῶμα ἔχον.

" Ἀνωτέρω δὲ κατὰ λέξιν ταῦτα γέγραφεν·
' ἀλλὰ καὶ χωρὶς τούτου τοῦ μέρους οὐκ οἶδα ὅπως
δεῖ τὰ ἐν τῷ σκότει ταῦτα ὄντα φῆσαι χρώματα

---

[1] ὅτι Reiske : ἔτι ΕΒ.
[2] πρὸς πᾶν ἐστι Reiske : προεπανέστη ΕΒ.
[3] ἐγγένηται Reiske : ἐγγένωνται ΕΒ.
[4] ἄδηλον Reiske : ἄδηλός ΕΒ.
[5] ἐπίκουρος Ε : ὁ ἐπίκουρος Β.
[6] γεννᾶσθαι Ε : γενᾶσθαι Β.
[7] τάξεις καὶ θέσεις] θέσεις καὶ τάξεις Ε^ac.
[8] ἢ Ε^cΒ : Ε^ac omits.

are deceived in supposing that what heats is heating
or what cools is cooling should refuse to recognize
' Everything is no more this than that ' as a conclusion from his premises, he is himself deceived.

" He proceeds to add,[a] 'And often the wine does
not even possess the property of heating or cooling as
it enters the body. Rather, the bodily mass is so set
in motion that the corpuscles shift their position : the
heat-producing atoms are at one .time concentrated,
becoming numerous enough to impart warmth and
heat to the body, but at another time are driven out,
producing a chill.'

7. " It is not hard to see that this reasoning may
be applied to every object called or commonly held
to be bitter, sweet, cathartic, soporific, or luminous :
that none has a self-contained quality or potency or
is more active than passive on entering the body, but
acquires different properties as it blends with different
bodies. Accordingly Epicurus [b] himself in the second
book of his *Reply to Theophrastus*, when he says that
colours are not intrinsic to bodies but a result of
certain arrangements and positions relative to the
eye, is asserting by this reasoning that body is no
more colourless than coloured.

" Earlier in the work he writes word for word as
follows [c] : ' But even apart from the discussion on
this head, I do not see how one can say that these

    [a] Frag. 60 (ed. Usener).
    [b] Frag. 30 (ed. Usener). Epicurus was probably answering
Theophrastus' attack on the Democritean view of perceptible
qualities (*De Causis Plantarum*, vi. 2 ; *De Sensu*, 68-83
[where 72-82 deal with colour]). See Zeller, *Die Philosophie
der Griechen*, vol. ii. 2⁴, p. 853.
    [c] Frag. 29 (ed. Usener) ; *cf.* Lucretius, ii. 746-747, 795-
798.

(1110) ἔχειν. καίτοι πολλάκις ἀέρος ὁμοίως σκοτώδους
D περικεχυμένου οἱ μὲν αἰσθάνονται χρωμάτων διαφορᾶς[1] οἱ δὲ οὐκ αἰσθάνονται δι' ἀμβλύτητα τῆς
ὄψεως· ἔτι δὲ εἰσελθόντες εἰς σκοτεινὸν οἶκον οὐ-
δεμίαν ὄψιν χρώματος ὁρῶμεν, ἀναμείναντες δὲ
μικρὸν ὁρῶμεν.' οὐ μᾶλλον οὖν ἔχειν ἢ μὴ ἔχειν
χρῶμα ῥηθήσεται τῶν σωμάτων ἕκαστον. εἰ δὲ τὸ
χρῶμα πρός τι, καὶ τὸ λευκὸν ἔσται πρός τι καὶ
τὸ κυανοῦν, εἰ δὲ ταῦτα, καὶ τὸ γλυκὺ καὶ τὸ πι-
κρόν, ὥστε κατὰ πάσης ποιότητος ἀληθῶς τὸ μὴ
μᾶλλον εἶναι ἢ μὴ εἶναι κατηγορεῖσθαι· τοῖς γὰρ
οὕτω πάσχουσιν ἔσται τοιοῦτον, οὐκ ἔσται δὲ τοῖς
μὴ πάσχουσι.

E   " Τὸν οὖν βόρβορον καὶ τὸν τάραχον[2] ἐν ᾧ φησι
γίνεσθαι τοὺς τὸ ' μηδὲν μᾶλλον ' ἐπιφθεγγομένους
τοῖς πράγμασιν, ἑαυτοῦ κατασκεδάννυσι καὶ τοῦ
καθηγεμόνος ὁ Κωλώτης.

8.   " Ἆρα οὖν ἐνταῦθα μόνον ὁ γενναῖος

ἄλλων ἰατρὸς αὐτὸς ἕλκεσιν[3] βρύων

ἀναπέφηνεν; οὐ μὲν οὖν[4]· ἀλλ' ἔτι μᾶλλον ἐν τῷ
δευτέρῳ τῶν ἐπιτιμημάτων λέληθε τῷ Δημοκρίτῳ
τὸν Ἐπίκουρον ἐκ τοῦ ζῆν συνεξωθῶν. τὸ γὰρ
' νόμῳ χροιὴν εἶναι καὶ νόμῳ γλυκὺ ' καὶ νόμῳ

---

[1] διαφορᾶς Ald. : διαφορὰς EB.
[2] τάραχον Wyttenbach (πηλὸν Amyot ; τῦφον van Herwerden) : τ followed by a blank of 8 letters E, 6 B.
[3] ἕλκεσιν Nauck : ἕλκεσι EB.
[4] οὐ μὲν οὖν Bern. : οὔμενουν EB.

ᵃ For the inclusion of this sentence in the fragment of

objects in the dark have colour. True, it often happens that when objects are enveloped in air of the same degree of darkness, some people perceive a distinction of colour while others whose eyesight is weak do not ; again, on first entering a dark room we see no colour, but do so after waiting a short time.' *a* Therefore no body will any more be said to have colour than not. If colour is relative, white and blue *b* will be relative ; and if these, then also sweet and bitter, so that of every quality we can truly say, ' It is no more this than it is not this ' ; for to those affected in a certain way the thing will be this, but not to those not so affected.

"Accordingly the slime and confusion in which Colotes says those people become mired who say of things ' no more this than that ' are slime and confusion that he dumps on himself and his master.

8. " Is it here alone that our friend turns out to be a

Healer of others, full of sores himself ? *c*

Not at all ; in his second charge he fails even more signally to notice that along with Democritus he expels Epicurus from the company of the living. He says that Democritus' *d* words ' colour is by convention, sweet by convention,' a compound by convention,

---

Epicurus see R. Westman, *Plutarch gegen Kolotes : seine Schrift "Adversus Colotem" als philosophiegeschichtliche Quelle* (Acta Philosophica Fennica, Fasc. vii, 1955), Helsingfors, 1955, pp. 141-143.

b Plutarch is thinking of the colour of the sea : *cf.* Cicero, *Acad. Pr.* ii. 33 (105).

c Nauck, *Trag. Graec. Frag.*, Eur. 1086 ; quoted also in *Mor.* 71 F, 88 D, and 481 A.

d Diels and Kranz, *Die Frag. der Vorsokratiker*, Demokritos, A 49, B 9, 117, 125.

(1110) σύγκρισιν[1] καὶ τὰ ἄλλα, ' ἐτεῇ δὲ τὸ κενὸν καὶ[2] τὰς
ἀτόμους ' ἀντειρημένον[3] φησὶν ὑπὸ Δημοκρίτου
F ταῖς αἰσθήσεσι, καὶ τὸν ἐμμένοντα τῷ λόγῳ τούτῳ
καὶ χρώμενον οὐδ' ἂν αὐτὸν[4] ὡς ἄνθρωπός[5] ἐστιν
ἢ ζῇ διανοηθῆναι.

" Πρὸς τοῦτον ἀντειπεῖν μὲν οὐδὲν ἔχω τὸν λόγον, εἰπεῖν δὲ ὅτι ταῦτα τῶν Ἐπικούρου δογμάτων
οὕτως ἀχώριστά ἐστιν ὡς τὸ σχῆμα καὶ τὸ βάρος
αὐτοὶ τῆς ἀτόμου λέγουσι. τί γὰρ λέγει Δημόκριτος; οὐσίας ἀπείρους τὸ πλῆθος ἀτόμους τε καὶ
ἀδιαφθόρους,[6] ἔτι δὲ ἀποίους καὶ ἀπαθεῖς, ἐν τῷ
κενῷ φέρεσθαι διεσπαρμένας· ὅταν δὲ πελάσωσιν
1111 ἀλλήλαις ἢ συμπέσωσιν ἢ περιπλακῶσι φαίνεσθαι
τῶν ἀθροιζομένων τὸ μὲν ὕδωρ τὸ δὲ πῦρ τὸ δὲ
φυτὸν τὸ δὲ ἄνθρωπον, εἶναι δὲ πάντα[7] τὰς ἀτόμους
' ἰδέας ' ὑπ' αὐτοῦ καλουμένας, ἕτερον δὲ μηδέν·
ἐκ μὲν γὰρ τοῦ μὴ ὄντος οὐκ εἶναι γένεσιν, ἐκ δὲ
τῶν ὄντων μηδὲν ἂν γενέσθαι τῷ μήτε πάσχειν
μήτε μεταβάλλειν τὰς ἀτόμους ὑπὸ στερρότητος·
ὅθεν οὔτε χρόαν ἐξ ἀχρώστων οὔτε φύσιν ἢ ψυχὴν
ἐξ ἀποίων καὶ ἀπαθῶν[8] ὑπάρχειν. ἐγκλητέος οὖν
ὁ Δημόκριτος οὐχὶ τὰ συμβαίνοντα ταῖς ἀρχαῖς

---

[1] σύγκρισιν EB : πικρὸν Sandbach ; λευκὸν or ψυχρὸν
Reiske.
[2] ἐτεῇ δὲ τὸ κενὸν καὶ (to which ἅπασαν is prefixed by Westman, καὶ τὰ ἄλλα by us) supplied by Wyttenbach to fill a
blank of 25 letters in E, 26 in B.
[3] ἀντειρημένον nos : εἰρημένον EB.
[4] αὐτὸν Xylander : αὑτὸν EB.
[5] ἄνθρωπός supplied by Pohlenz (ἄνθρωπος ἢ ζῷόν ? nos) to fill
blank of 12 letters in E, 10 in B.
[6] ἀδιαφθόρους Emperius : διαφόρους EB.
[7] πάντα E : πάντας B or B¹.

and so the rest, 'what is real are the void and the atoms' are an attack on the senses; and that anyone who abides by this reasoning and puts it into practice could not even conceive of himself as a man [a] or as alive.

" I cannot deny the truth of this, but I can affirm that this view is as inseparable from Epicurus' as shape and weight are by their own assertion [b] inseparable from the atom. For what does Democritus [c] say? That entities infinite in number, indivisible and indestructible, destitute moreover of quality and incapable of modification, move scattered about in the void; that when they draw near one another or collide or become entangled the resulting aggregate appears in the one case to be water, in others fire, a plant, or a man, but that everything really *is* the indivisible 'forms,' as he calls them, and nothing else. For there is no generation from the non-existent, and again nothing can be generated from the existent, as the atoms are too solid to be affected and changed. From this it follows that there is no colour, since it would have to come from things colourless, and no natural entity [d] or mind, since they would have to come from things without qualities or the capacity to be affected. Democritus is therefore to be censured not for admitting the consequences that

---

[a] Cf. Aristocles in Eusebius, *Praep. Evang.* xiv. 19. 5.

[b] Frag. 275 (ed. Usener).

[c] Diels and Kranz, *Die Frag. der Vorsokratiker*, Demokritos, A 57.

[d] Literally " nature "; for the word *cf.* Aristotle, *On Democritus*, Frag. 1, p. 144. 23 (ed. Ross).

---

[8] ἀπαθῶν supplied by Turnebus (in his text), Vulcobius and Xylander (ἀψύχων Turnebus [in the margin], Amyot, and Westman) to fill a blank of 7 letters in E, 6 in B.

(1111)
B
ὁμολογῶν ἀλλὰ λαμβάνων ἀρχὰς αἷς ταῦτα συμβέβηκεν. ἔδει γὰρ ἀμετάβλητα μὴ θέσθαι τὰ πρῶτα,
θέμενον δὲ δὴ[1] συνορᾶν ὅτι ποιότητος οἴχεται πάσης
γένεσις· ἀρνεῖσθαι δὲ συνορῶντα τὴν ἀτοπίαν ἀναι-
σχυντότατον· ὥστ' ἀναισχυντότατα[2] ὁ Ἐπίκουρός
φησιν ἀρχὰς μὲν ὑποτίθεσθαι τὰς αὐτάς, οὐ λέγει[3]
δὲ ' νόμῳ χροιὴν ' καὶ γλυκὺ καὶ πικρὸν[4] καὶ τὰς
ἄλλας ποιότητας. εἰ μὲν οὖν τὸ ' οὐ λέγει '[5] τοιοῦ-
τόν ἐστιν ' οὐχ ὁμολογεῖ,' τῶν εἰθισμένων τι ποιεῖ·
καὶ γὰρ τὴν πρόνοιαν ἀναιρῶν εὐσέβειαν ἀπολιπεῖν
λέγει, καὶ τῆς ἡδονῆς ἕνεκα τὴν φιλίαν αἱρούμενος
ὑπὲρ τῶν φίλων τὰς μεγίστας ἀλγηδόνας ἀναδέχε-
σθαι, καὶ τὸ μὲν πᾶν ἄπειρον ὑποτίθεσθαι, τὸ δὲ
ἄνω καὶ κάτω μὴ ἀναιρεῖν. ἔστι δὲ οὐδὲ ἐν οἴνῳ
C καὶ γέλωτι πάνυ προσῆκον τὸ τοιοῦτον,[6] κύλικα
μὲν λαβόντα, καὶ πιεῖν ὅσον ἂν ἐθέλῃ καὶ ἀποδοῦναι
τὸ λεῖπον· ἐν δὲ τῷ λόγῳ μάλιστα δεῖ τοῦ σοφοῦ
τούτου μνημονεύειν ἀποφθέγματος, ' ὧν αἱ ἀρχαὶ
οὐκ ἀναγκαῖαι, τὰ τέλη ἀναγκαῖα.' οὐκ οὖν[7] ἀναγκαῖον ὑποθέσθαι, μᾶλλον δὲ ὑφελέσθαι[8] Δημοκρίτου,
ἀτόμους εἶναι τῶν ὅλων ἀρχάς· θεμένῳ δὲ τὸ δόγμα
καὶ καλλωπισαμένῳ ταῖς πρώταις πιθανότησιν

---

[1] δὲ δὴ Wyttenbach : δὲ μὴ ΕΒ (δέ πη Post).

[2] ἀναισχυντότατον· ὥστ' ἀναισχυντότατα nos (ἀναισχυντότατον·
ὥστ' ἀναισχυντότατον Pohlenz) : ἀναισχυντοτατ Ε (α τ [?] over
the third α and an apostrophe erased) ; ἀναισχυντότατα Β.

[3] λέγει Ε : λέγειν Β.

[4] πικρὸν nos : λευκόν ΕΒ.   [5] λέγει Ε : λέγειν Β.

[6] οὐδὲ . . . τοιοῦτον our supplement : οὓς followed by a
blank of 48 letters Ε, 37 Β.

[7] οὐκ οὖν Reiske : οὐκοῦν ΕΒ.

[8] ὑφελέσθαι Wyttenbach : ἀφελέσθαι ΕΒ.

---

[a] Plutarch's interpretation of 1108 ε, supra.

[b] Frag. 368 (ed. Usener).

flow from his principles, but for setting up principles that lead to these consequences. For he should
not have posited immutable first elements; having
posited them, he should have looked further and
seen that the generation of any quality becomes impossible. But to see the absurdity and deny it is the
purest effrontery. Epicurus accordingly acts with the
purest effrontery when he claims [a] to lay down the
same first principles, but nevertheless does not say
that ' colour is by convention ' and so the qualities
sweet, bitter and the rest. If ' does not say ' means
' does not admit ' it is so, he is following his familiar
practice ; thus he [b] does away with providence but
says he has left us with piety ; he [c] chooses friends
for the pleasure he gets, but says that he assumes the
greatest pains on their behalf ; and he [d] says that
while he posits an infinite universe he does not eliminate ' up ' and ' down.' Not even over the wine and in
carefree merriment is it exactly proper [e] to accept a
cup, drink only as much as you please, and hand back
the rest ; but above all in one's reasoning one should
remember this wise saying [f] : ' Where the beginning
is not forced on us, the conclusion is.' There was no
necessity to assume, or rather to filch from Democritus, the premise that the first elements of all things
are atoms. But once you have laid down the doctrine [g]
and made a fine showing with its initial plausibilities,

[c] Frag. 546 (ed. Usener). For pains endured for the sake
of friends cf. 1103 A, supra.

[d] Frag. 299 (ed. Usener).

[e] The words " Not even . . . proper " are a conjectural
supplement of a blank in the mss. In pledging a health (pro-
posis) the pledger drank from the cup and handed it to the
other, who was expected to drain the cup.

[f] We have not found the saying elsewhere.

[g] Frag. 288 (ed. Usener).

213

(1111) αὐτοῦ προσεκποτέον ἐστὶ τὸ δυσχερές, ἢ δεικτέον
ὅπως ἄποια σώματα παντοδαπὰς ποιότητας αὐτῷ
μόνῳ τῷ συνελθεῖν παρέσχεν. οἷον εὐθὺς τὸ καλούμενον θερμὸν ὑμῖν πόθεν ἀφῖκται καὶ πῶς ἐπιγέγονε
D ταῖς ἀτόμοις, αἳ[1] μήτε ἦλθον ἔχουσαι θερμότητα
μήτε ἐγένοντο θερμαὶ συνελθοῦσαι; τὸ μὲν γὰρ
ἔχοντος ποιότητα, τὸ δὲ πάσχειν πεφυκότος, οὐδέτερον δὲ ταῖς ἀτόμοις ὑπάρχειν φατὲ προσῆκον
εἶναι διὰ τὴν ἀφθαρσίαν.

9. " ' Τί οὖν; οὐχὶ καὶ Πλάτωνι συνέβαινε καὶ
Ἀριστοτέλει καὶ Ξενοκράτει χρυσὸν ἐκ μὴ χρυσοῦ
καὶ λίθον ἐκ μὴ λίθου καὶ τἄλλα γεννᾶν ἐκ τεσσάρων
ἁπλῶν καὶ πρώτων ἄπαντα;'[2] πάνυ μὲν οὖν· ἀλλ'
ἐκείνοις μὲν εὐθύς τε συνίασιν αἱ ἀρχαὶ πρὸς τὴν
ἑκάστου γένεσιν ὥσπερ συμβολὰς μεγάλας φέρου-
σαι τὰς ἐν αὐταῖς ποιότητας, καὶ ὅταν συνέλθωσιν
E εἰς τὸ αὐτὸ καὶ συμπέσωσι, ξηροῖς ὑγρὰ καὶ ψυχρὰ
θερμοῖς καὶ στερεὰ μαλθακοῖς, σώματα κινούμενα
παθητικῶς[3] ὑπ'[4] ἀλλήλων καὶ μεταβάλλοντα δι'
ὅλων, ἑτέραν ἀφ' ἑτέρας κράσεως συναποτίκτει
γένεσιν. ἡ δὲ ἄτομος αὐτή[5] τε καθ' ἑαυτὴν ἔρη-
μός ἐστι καὶ γυμνὴ πάσης γονίμου δυνάμεως, καὶ
πρὸς ἄλλην προσπεσοῦσα βρασμὸν ὑπὸ σκληρότητος
καὶ ἀντιτυπίας, ἄλλο δὲ οὐδὲν ἔσχεν οὐδὲ ἐποίησε
πάθος, ἀλλὰ παίονται καὶ παίουσι τὸν ἅπαντα χρό-

---

[1] αἱ Usener (εἰ Bern.) : ἂν EB.
[2] ἄπαντα Pohlenz : ἁπάντων EB.
[3] παθητικῶς Reiske : παθητικοῖς EB.
[4] ὑπ' Xylander : ἀπ' EB.   [5] αὐτή E : αὕτη B.

you must drain the disagreeable conclusions along with it,[a] or else show how bodies without quality have given rise to qualities of every kind by the mere fact of coming together. Take for example the quality called hot. How do you account for it ? From where has it come and how has it been imposed on the atoms, which neither brought heat with them nor became hot by their conjunction ? For the former implies the possession of quality, the latter the natural capacity to be affected, neither of which, say you, can rightly belong to atoms by reason of their indestructibility.

9. " ' What of it ? Did not Plato too and Aristotle and Xenocrates [b] find themselves producing gold from something not gold, stone from something not stone, and so with everything else, producing it from four simple and primary components ? '[c] Quite so ; but on their view the first principles, on coming together to generate this thing or that, come provided at the outset with their own qualities, no inconsiderable provision ; and when they meet and combine, wet with dry, cold with hot, and hard with soft, since they are bodies that interact on each other's qualities and that change throughout, they jointly bring into being a variety of objects corresponding to the variations in the mixture. Whereas an atom,[d] taken alone, is destitute and bare of any generative power, and when it collides with another is so hard and resistant that a shock ensues, but it neither suffers nor causes any further effect. Rather the atoms receive and inflict

---

[a] *Cf.* Aristophanes, *Plutus*, 1085 and *Mor.* 525 D with the note.
[b] Frag. 52 (ed. Heinze).
[c] The words of an imaginary adversary.
[d] Frag. 286 (ed. Usener).

(1111) νον, οὐχ ὅπως ζῷον ἢ ψυχὴν ἢ φύσιν ἀλλ' οὐδὲ
πλῆθος ἐξ ἑαυτῶν κοινὸν οὐδὲ σωρὸν ἕνα παλλο-
μένων ἀεὶ καὶ διισταμένων δυνάμεναι παρασχεῖν.
F   10.   " Ὁ δὲ Κωλώτης, ὥσπερ ἀγραμμάτῳ βασιλεῖ προσδιαλεγόμενος, πάλιν ἐξάπτεται τοῦ Ἐμπεδοκλέους ὡς[1] ταὐτὸ πνέοντος·

ἄλλο δέ τοι ἐρέω· φύσις οὐδενός ἐστιν ἑκάστου[2]
θνητῶν, οὐδέ τις οὐλομένη θανάτοιο γενέθλη[3]·
ἀλλὰ μόνον μῖξίς τε διάλλαξίς τε μιγέντων
ἔστι, φύσις δ' ἐπὶ τοῖς ὀνομάζεται ἀνθρώποισι.

ταῦτα ἐγὼ μὲν οὐχ ὁρῶ καθ' ὅ τι[4] πρὸς τὸ ζῆν ὑπ-
1112 εναντιοῦται[5] τοῖς ὑπολαμβάνουσι μήτε γένεσιν τοῦ
μὴ ὄντος εἶναι μήτε φθορὰν τοῦ ὄντος, ἀλλὰ ὄντων
τινῶν συνόδῳ πρὸς ἄλληλα τὴν γένεσιν, διαλύσει δὲ
ἀπ' ἀλλήλων τὸν θάνατον ἐπονομάζεσθαι. ὅτι γὰρ
ἀντὶ τῆς γενέσεως εἴρηκε τὴν φύσιν, ἀντιθεὶς τὸν
θάνατον αὐτῇ[6] δεδήλωκεν ὁ Ἐμπεδοκλῆς[7]· εἰ δὲ οἱ
μίξεις[8] τὰς γενέσεις τιθέμενοι τὰς δὲ φθορὰς δια-
λύσεις οὐ ζῶσιν οὐδὲ δύνανται ζῆν, τί ποιοῦσιν
ἕτερον οὗτοι; καίτοι ὁ μὲν Ἐμπεδοκλῆς τὰ στοιχεῖα κολλῶν καὶ συναρμόττων θερμότησι καὶ μαλα-
κότησι καὶ ὑγρότησι μῖξιν αὐτοῖς καὶ συμφυῖαν

___

[1] ὡς added by Pohlenz.
[2] ἑκάστου EB : ἐόντων Aristotle, *Metaphysics*, Δ 4 (1015 a 1);
ἁπάντων *Placita*.
[3] οὐλομένη θ. γενέθλη EB : οὐλομένου θ. τελευτή *Placita*.
[4] καθ' ὅτι Stephanus : καθότι EB.
[5] ὑπεναντιοῦται Basle edition of 1542 : ὑπεναντιοῦσθαι EB
(re vera).
[6] αὐτῇ Xylander, Stephanus : ἀστὴρ EB.
[7] ἐμπεδοκλῆς B : ἐμπεδοκλ followed by a blank of 2 letters
E.
[8] μίξεις E : μίξει B.

216

blows for all time, and so far are they from being able to produce an animal or mind or natural being [a] that they cannot even produce out of themselves a collective plurality or the unity of a heap in their constant shaking and scattering.

10. " But Colotes, as though addressing an unlettered king, fastens in turn on Empedocles [b] as one inspired with this same doctrine [c] :

> This too I'll tell thee :
> No nature is there of a mortal thing
> Nor any curst fatality of death.
> Mixture alone there is and dissolution
> Of things commingled, and men call them nature.

I for one do not see in what respect the words lead to any difficulty in living for those [d] who assume that there is neither generation of the non-existent nor destruction of the existent, but that ' generation ' is a name given to the conjunction of certain existents with one another, and ' death ' a name given to their separation. That he used ' nature ' in the sense of ' generation ' Empedocles has indicated by opposing death to it. But if those who say that generation is a mixture and death a dissolution do not and cannot live, what else do the Epicureans do ? Yet, when Empedocles cements and joins the elements together by the operation of heat, softness, and moisture he somehow opens the way for them to a ' mixture ' that

---

[a] Cf. Cicero, De Nat. Deor. i. 39 (110) : " quae etiam si essent [that is, individua corpora], quae nulla sunt, pellere se ipsa et agitari inter se concursu fortasse possent, formare, figurare, colorare, animare non possent." See also Sextus, Outlines of Pyrrhonism, iii. 187.

[b] Diels and Kranz, Die Frag. der Vorsokratiker, Empedokles, B 8.

[c] The view that qualities are conventional, and only the ultimate principles real.   [d] Frag. 283 (ed. Usener).

(1112)

B ἐνωτικὴν ἀμωσγέπως ἐνδίδωσιν, οἱ δὲ τὰς ἀτρέ-
πτους καὶ ἀσυμπαθεῖς ἀτόμους εἰς τὸ αὐτὸ συνελαύ-
νοντες ἐξ αὐτῶν μὲν οὐδέν, αὐτῶν δὲ πολλὰς ποιοῦσι
καὶ συνεχεῖς πληγάς. ἡ γὰρ περιπλοκὴ κωλύουσα
τὴν διάλυσιν μᾶλλον ἐπιτείνει τὴν σύγκρουσιν, ὥστε
μηδὲ μίξιν εἶναι μηδὲ κόλλησιν ἀλλὰ ταραχὴν καὶ
μάχην κατ᾽ αὐτοὺς τὴν¹ λεγομένην γένεσιν· εἰ² δὲ
ἀκαρὲς αἱ ἄτομοι προσπεσοῦσαι³ νῦν μὲν ἀπίασι διὰ
τὴν ἀντίκρουσιν, νῦν δὲ πρόσασι τῆς πληγῆς ἐκλυ-
θείσης, πλεῖον⁴ ἢ διπλάσιον χωρίς εἰσιν ἀλλήλων
χρόνον, οὐ ψαύουσαι καὶ πλησιάζουσαι, ὥστε μηδὲν
ἐξ αὐτῶν ἀποτελεῖσθαι μηδὲ ἄψυχον, αἴσθησις δὲ
C καὶ ψυχὴ καὶ νοῦς καὶ φρόνησις οὐδὲ βουλομένοις
ἐπίνοιαν δίδωσιν ὡς γένοιτ᾽ ἂν ἐν κενῷ καὶ ἀτόμοις,
ὧν οὔτε καθ᾽ ἑαυτὰ ποιότης ἐστὶν οὔτε πάθος ἢ
μεταβολὴ συνελθόντων, ἀλλ᾽ οὐδὲ συνέλευσις ἢ
σύγκρασιν ποιοῦσα καὶ μίξιν καὶ συμφυΐαν ἀλλὰ
πληγὰς καὶ ἀποπηδήσεις. ὥστε τοῖς τούτων⁵ δόγμασι τὸ ζῆν ἀναιρεῖται καὶ τὸ ζῷον εἶναι, κενὰς καὶ
ἀπαθεῖς καὶ ἀθέους καὶ ἀψύχους, ἔτι δὲ ἀμίκτους
καὶ ἀσυγκράτους ἀρχὰς ὑποτιθεμένοις. (11.) πῶς
οὖν ἀπολείπουσι φύσιν καὶ ψυχὴν καὶ ζῷον; ὡς
ὅρκον, ὡς εὐχήν, ὡς θυσίαν, ὡς προσκύνησιν, ῥήματι καὶ λόγῳ καὶ τῷ⁶ φάναι καὶ προσποιεῖσθαι
καὶ ὀνομάζειν ἃ ταῖς ἀρχαῖς καὶ τοῖς δόγμασιν
ἀναιροῦσιν.

¹ κατ᾽ αὐτοὺς τὴν F : καθ᾽ αὐτοὺς τὴν B re vera (καθ᾽ αὐτοὺς Aldine).
² εἰ Xylander : οἱ EB.
³ αἱ ἄτομοι προσπεσοῦσαι supplied by Westman to fill a blank of 20 letters in E, 18 in B.
⁴ πλεῖον EB : πλεῖον᾽ Usener.
⁵ τούτων E : τοιούτων B.   ⁶ τῷ E : τὸ B.

218

coalesces into a natural unity ; whereas those [a] who herd together unyielding and unresponsive atoms produce nothing out of them, but only an uninterrupted series of collisions among the atoms themselves. For the entanglement that prevents dissolution produces rather an intensification of the collisions, so that ' generation ' is by their account neither mixture nor cohesion, but confusion and conflict. On the other hand, if the atoms after an instant of collision rebound for a while from the impact, and for a while draw near when the blow is spent,[b] the time that they are separated from one another, without contact or proximity, is more than twice as long, so that nothing, not even an inanimate body, is produced out of them ; while perception, mind, intelligence and thought cannot so much as be conceived, even with the best of will, as arising among void and atoms, things which taken separately have no quality and which on meeting are not thereby affected or changed ; indeed even their meeting is not one that leads to fusion or mixture or coalescence, but only to shocks and rebounds.[c] Thus by the doctrines of these men life and living things are abolished, since the primal elements on their hypothesis are void, impassive, godless, and inanimate, and moreover incapable of mixture or fusion. (11.) Then how can they claim to leave room for a thing's nature, for mind, for a living being ? As they do for an oath, for prayer, for sacrifice, for worship : in their manner of speaking, in word, by affirmation, by pretending, by naming things that by their ultimate principles and tenets they abolish.

[a] Frag. 286 (ed. Usener).
[b] A blow could be overcome either by another blow or (as here) by the atom's own weight : Epicurus, *Letter to Herodotus*, 61.   [c] *Cf. Mor.* 921 D.

(1112)
D

" Εἰ[1] δὲ δὴ τὸ πεφυκὸς αὐτὸ φύσιν καὶ τὸ γε-
γονὸς γένεσιν ὀνομάζουσιν, ὥσπερ οἱ ξυλείαν[2] τὰ
ξύλα καὶ συμφωνίαν καλοῦντες ἐκφορικῶς τὰ συμ-
φωνοῦντα, πόθεν ἐπῆλθεν αὐτῷ τοιαῦτα προβάλ-
λειν ἐρωτήματα[3] τῷ Ἐμπεδοκλεῖ; ' τί κόπτομεν,'
φησίν, ' ἡμᾶς αὐτούς, σπουδάζοντες ὑπὲρ ἡμῶν
αὐτῶν καὶ ὀρεγόμενοί τινων πραγμάτων καὶ φυλατ-
τόμενοί τινα πράγματα; οὔτε γὰρ ἡμεῖς ἐσμεν οὔτε
ἄλλοις[4] χρώμενοι ζῶμεν.' ' ἀλλὰ θάρρει,' φαίη τις
ἄν, ' ὦ φίλον Κωλωτάριον· οὐδείς σε κωλύει σπου-
δάζειν ὑπὲρ σεαυτοῦ, διδάσκων ὅτι '' Κωλώτου
φύσις '' αὐτὸς ὁ Κωλώτης ἐστὶν ἄλλο δὲ οὐθέν,

E οὐδὲ χρῆσθαι τοῖς πράγμασι (τὰ δὲ πράγματα
ὑμῖν ἡδοναί εἰσιν)[5] ὑποδεικνύων ὡς οὐκ ἔστιν ἀμή-
των φύσις οὐδὲ ὀσμῶν οὐδὲ πλησιάσεως, ἄμητες
δέ εἰσι καὶ μύρα καὶ γυναῖκες.' οὐδὲ γὰρ ὁ γραμματικὸς λέγων τὸ ' βίην Ἡρακληείην '[6] αὐτὸν
εἶναι τὸν Ἡρακλέα,' οὐδὲ οἱ τὰς συμφωνίας καὶ
τὰς δοκώσεις[8] ἐκφορὰς μόνον εἶναι φάσκοντες οὐχὶ
καὶ φθόγγους καὶ δοκοὺς ὑπάρχειν λέγουσιν· ὅπου
καὶ ψυχήν τινες ἀναιροῦντες καὶ φρόνησιν οὔτε τὸ
ζῆν ἀναιρεῖν οὔτε τὸ φρονεῖν δοκοῦσιν. Ἐπικούρου

---

[1] εἰ Wyttenbach : οἱ EB.
[2] ξυλείαν van Herwerden : ξυλίαν EB.
[3] ἐρωτήματα E : ῥήματα B.
[4] οὔτε ἄλλοις EB : οὔτε τἀλλ' οἷς Post ; οὔτ' ἀλλ' οἷς Pohlenz.
[5] εἰσιν] Benseler would omit.
[6] Ἡρακληείην Bern. : ἡρακλείην EB (the same error occurs
at *Mor.* 944 F).

220

" But if by ' nature ' they merely mean a thing that naturally is and by ' generation ' a thing generated, just as by a mode of expression men call pieces of wood ' wood-cutting ' and concordant notes a ' concord,' what put it into Colotes' head to ask such questions of Empedocles as this ? ' Why do we wear ourselves out, taking ourselves seriously and seeking certain realities and avoiding others ? For neither do we exist nor in our lives make use of other realities.' ' Why never fear,' one might answer, ' my dearest Collikins ; no one keeps you from taking yourself seriously when he teaches that Colotes' " nature " is nothing but Colotes himself, or your dealing with " realities " (" realities "[a] for you and your company being pleasures) when he points out that there is no " nature " of cakes or odours or intercourse, but that there are cakes and perfumes and women.' No more does the grammarian who says that ' Heraclean might '[b] is Heracles himself ; nor do those who declare that ' concords ' and ' rafterings ' are mere forms of speech deny the existence of notes and rafters[c]— indeed we see that some people who abolish both mind and thought suppose that they abolish neither living nor thinking.[d] When Epicurus[e] says, ' the

---

[a] A play on *pragmata* (" realities " or " affairs ") ; the Epicureans rejected political activity.
[b] A stock example of periphrasis : *cf. Life and Poetry of Homer*, ii. 29.
[c] Sextus (*Outlines of Pyrrhonism*, iii. 99 and *Against the Mathematicians*, ix. 343) speaks of " rafterings " being nothing more than the things raftered.
[d] The Epicureans themselves : *cf.* 1112 b-c, *supra*.
[e] Frag. 76 (ed. Usener).

---

[7] After Ἡρακλέα Amyot would supply ἀναιρεῖ τὸν Ἡρακλέα.
[8] δοκώσεις EB[t] : δοκήσεις B[2?ss].

(1112) δὲ λέγοντος, ' ἡ τῶν ὄντων φύσις σώματά ἐστι καὶ
τόπος,' πότερον οὕτως ἀκούομεν[1] ὡς ἄλλο τι τὴν
F φύσιν παρὰ τὰ ὄντα βουλομένου λέγειν ἢ τὰ[2] ὄντα
δηλοῦντος ἕτερον δὲ μηθέν, ὥσπερ ἀμέλει καὶ κενοῦ
φύσιν αὐτὸ τὸ κενόν, καὶ νὴ Δία τὸ πᾶν[3] παντὸς
φύσιν ὀνομάζειν εἴωθε; κἂν εἴ τις ἔροιτο, ' τί λέγεις, ὦ Ἐπίκουρε; τὸ μέν τι[4] κενὸν εἶναι, τὸ[5] δὲ
φύσιν κενοῦ; ', ' μὰ Δία,' φήσει[6]· ' νενόμισται δέ
πως ἡ τοιαύτη τῶν ὀνομάτων ὁμιλία

νόμῳ δ' ἐπίφημι[7] καὶ αὐτός.'

τί οὖν ἕτερον ὁ Ἐμπεδοκλῆς πεποίηκεν διδάξας[8]
ὅτι φύσις παρὰ τὸ φυόμενον οὐθέν ἐστιν οὐδὲ θάνα-
1113 τος παρὰ τὸ θνῆσκον, ἀλλ' ὥσπερ οἱ ποιηταὶ πολλάκις ἀνειδωλοποιοῦντες λέγουσιν,

ἐν δ' Ἔρις, ἐν δὲ Κυδοιμὸς ὁμίλεον, ἐν δ' ὀλοὴ
Κήρ,[9]

οὕτως γένεσίν τινα καὶ φθορὰν καλοῦσιν οἱ πολλοὶ
ἐπὶ τοῖς συνισταμένοις καὶ διαλυομένοις; τοσοῦτον
δ'[10] ἐδέησε τοῦ κινεῖν τὰ ὄντα καὶ μάχεσθαι τοῖς
φαινομένοις ὥστε μηδὲ τὴν φωνὴν ἐκβαλεῖν ἐκ τῆς
συνηθείας, ἀλλ' ὅσον εἰς τὰ πράγματα βλάπτουσαν
ἀπάτην παρεῖχεν ἀφελὼν αὖθις ἀποδοῦναι τοῖς ὀνό-

---

[1] ἀκούομεν EB : ἀκούωμεν Hartman.
[2] ἢ τὰ Reiske (ἢ μόνα ταῦτα Pohlenz) : τὰ EB.
[3] τὸ πᾶν Stephanus (τὰ πάντα Ald.[2]) : τὸ πάντα EB.
[4] τι E : τοι B.
[5] τὸ Madvig : τὰ EB.
[6] φήσει EB[c] : φύσει B[ac].

nature of existing things is atoms and void,' do we
take him to mean that ' nature ' is distinct from
' existing things,' or simply to indicate ' existing
things ' and nothing more, just as it is his habit for
instance to use the expression 'the nature of void' for
' void ' and indeed ' the nature of the universe ' for
' the universe ' ? And if someone should ask, ' What
do you mean, Epicurus ? That here is one thing, the
" void," and there another, the " nature of void " ? ',
he would say, ' Certainly not ; such usage of terms
has somehow become conventional among men,

And I too speak as they do, by convention.' [a]

Then is this not precisely what Empedocles has done ?
He teaches that there is no such thing as nature
apart from what is naturally produced or death apart
from what dies, but that just as the poets often create
imaginary beings and say,

Here Tumult, Strife, and dismal Death attend, [b]

so it is common usage to give such names as ' generation ' and ' destruction ' to the things undergoing
combination or separation. So far was Empedocles
from upsetting the world and contradicting appearances that he did not even banish the expression
from common speech, but removed only the harmful
misunderstanding that it causes about the things
named and then restored to the terms their current

---

[a] See 1113 B, *infra*.
[b] Homer, *Il.* xviii. 535.

7 δ' ἐπίφημι Reiske : δὲ ἤ τί φημὶ EB.
8 διδάξας Basle edition of 1542 (νὴ Δία διδάξας Bern.) : ἤ
διδάξας EB.
9 ὀλοὴ κήρ Reiske from Homer : ὀλοὸν κῆρ EB.
10 δ' supplied by Pohlenz.

(1113) μασι τὸ νενομισμένον ἐν τούτοις·

> οἱ δ', ὅτε μὲν[1] κατὰ φῶτα μιγὲν φάος αἰθέρος
> ἵκῃ[2]
> ἢ κατὰ θηρῶν ἀγροτέρων γένος ἢ κατὰ θάμνων
> ἠὲ κατ' οἰωνῶν, τότε μὲν τὸ λέγουσι[3] γενέσθαι,
> B εὖτε δ' ἀποκρινθῶσι,[4] τὰ δ'[5] αὖ δυσδαίμονα πό-
> τμον·
> ᾗ θέμις[6] οὔ[7] καλέουσι, νόμῳ[8] δ' ἐπίφημι[9] καὶ
> αὐτός.

ταῦτ' αὐτὸς[10] ὁ Κωλώτης παραθέμενος οὐ συνεῖδεν[11] ὅτι φῶτας μὲν καὶ θῆρας καὶ θάμνους[12] καὶ οἰωνοὺς ὁ Ἐμπεδοκλῆς οὐκ ἀνήρηκεν, ἅ γέ φησι μιγνυμένων τῶν στοιχείων ἀποτελεῖσθαι, τοὺς δὲ τῇ συγκρίσει ταύτῃ καὶ διακρίσει ' φύσιν ' τινὰ καὶ ' πότμον δυσδαίμονα ' καὶ ' θάνατον ἀλοίτην '[13] ἐπικατηγοροῦντας ᾗ σφάλλονται διδάξας οὐκ ἀφείλετο τὸ χρῆσθαι ταῖς εἰθισμέναις φωναῖς περὶ αὐτῶν.

12. '' Ἐμοὶ μέντοι δοκεῖ μὴ τοῦτο κινεῖν τὸ ἐκ-
C φορικὸν ὁ Ἐμπεδοκλῆς ἀλλ', ὡς πρότερον εἴρηται, πραγματικῶς διαφέρεσθαι περὶ τῆς ἐξ οὐκ ὄντων γενέσεως, ἣν φύσιν τινὲς καλοῦσι· δηλοῖ δὲ μάλιστα

---

[1] ὅτε μὲν E : ὅτε B.
[2] μιγὲν φάος αἰθέρος ἵκῃ Mullach : μίγεν φὼς αἰθέρι followed by a blank of 7 letters E, 8 B (μιγέντ' εἰς αἰθέρ' ἵκωνται Diels).
[3] τὸ λέγουσι Reiske (τάδε [τόδε Bern.] φασὶ Xylander) : τὸν followed by a blank of 8 letters EB.
[4] ἀποκρινθῶσι Panzerbieter : ἀποκριθῶσι EB.
[5] τὰ δ' Stephanus (τὸ δ' Reiske) : τάδ' EB.
[6] ᾗ (or ἥ ; ἥ Diels) θέμις Mor. 820 F : εἶναι EB.

224

REPLY TO COLOTES, 1113

use in these lines :

> When what is mixed comes to the light of day
> As man or as a beast or plant or bird,
> Men say 'tis born ; but call the parts disjoined
> Unhappy fate. They speak not as they should.
> But I too speak as they do, by convention.[a]

Though Colotes cites these lines himself he fails to see that Empedocles did not abolish men, beasts, plants, and birds—since he says that they are produced by the mixture of the elements—but rather, once he had informed those who go further and use for this combination and separation the terms ' nature ' and ' unhappy fate ' and ' vengeful death '[b] how they go wrong, he did not disallow the use of the current expressions about them.

12. " Yet for my part I hold that Empedocles is not here bringing up a point about verbal expression but, as I said earlier,[c] is controverting a point of fact, generation from the non-existent, which some call ' nature.'[d] He shows this especially in the following

[a] Diels and Kranz, *Die Frag. der Vorsokratiker*, Empedokles, b 9. The last line is also quoted in *Mor.* 820 f.
[b] Diels and Kranz, *Die Frag. der Vorsokratiker*, Empedokles, b 10.
[c] 1113 a, *supra*.
[d] For " nature " in the sense of generation or genesis cf. Aristotle, *Metaphysics*, Δ 4 (1014 b 16-17) and Cherniss, *Aristotle's Criticism of Presocratic Philosophy* (Baltimore, 1935), p. 109, note 446.

---

[7] οὐ supplied by Meziriacus.
[8] καλέουσι, νόμῳ Reiske : καλέουσιν, ὅμως EB.
[9] ἐπίφημι Stephanus : ἐπιφημὶ EB.
[10] ταῦτ' αὐτὸς nos (ἃ Meziriacus ; ταῦτα Reiske) : EB omit.
[11] συνεῖδεν E : συνοῖδεν B.
[12] θάμνους E (not θάμνας) B.
[13] ἀλοίτην J. G. Schneider : ἀλοιτὴν EB.

(1113) διὰ τούτων τῶν ἐπῶν·

> νήπιοι· οὐ γάρ σφιν δολιχόφρονές εἰσι μέριμναι·
> οἵ[1] δὴ γίνεσθαι πάρος οὐκ ἐὸν ἐλπίζουσιν
> ἤ τι[2] καταθνήσκειν τε καὶ ἐξόλλυσθαι ἀπάντῃ.[3]

ταῦτα γὰρ τὰ ἔπη μέγα βοῶντός ἐστι τοῖς ὦτα
ἔχουσιν ὡς οὐκ ἀναιρεῖ γένεσιν ἀλλὰ τὴν ἐκ μὴ
ὄντος, οὐδὲ φθορὰν ἀλλὰ τὴν πάντῃ, τουτέστι τὴν
εἰς τὸ μὴ ὂν ἀπολλύουσαν. ἐπεὶ τῷ γε βουλομένῳ
μὴ ἀγρίως οὕτως μηδὲ ἠλιθίως ἀλλὰ πραότερον
D συκοφαντεῖν τὸ μετὰ ταῦτα ἐπὶ τοὐναντίον ἂν αἰτιά-
σασθαι παράσχοι, τοῦ Ἐμπεδοκλέους λέγοντος

> οὐκ ἂν ἀνὴρ[4] τοιαῦτα σοφὸς φρεσὶ[5] μαντεύσαιτο
> ὡς ὄφρα μέν τε βιῶσι, τὸ δὴ βίοτον καλέουσι,
> τόφρα μὲν οὖν εἰσιν καί σφιν[6] πάρα δεινὰ[7] καὶ
>   ἐσθλά,
> πρὶν δὲ πάγεν τε[8] βροτοὶ καὶ ἐπεὶ λύθεν,[9] οὐδὲν ἄρ'
>   εἰσί.

ταῦτα γὰρ οὐκ ἀρνουμένου μὴ εἶναι τοὺς γεγονότας
καὶ ζῶντάς ἐστιν, εἶναι δὲ μᾶλλον οἰομένου καὶ τοὺς
μηδέπω γεγονότας καὶ τοὺς ἤδη τεθνηκότας. ἀλλ'
ὅμως[10] ὁ Κωλώτης τοῦτο μὲν οὐκ ἐγκέκληκε, λέγει
δὲ κατ' αὐτὸν οὐδὲ[11] νοσήσειν ἡμᾶς οὐδὲ τραυματι-
σθήσεσθαι. καὶ πῶς ὁ πρὸ τοῦ βίου καὶ μετὰ τὸν
E βίον ἑκάστῳ λέγων παρεῖναι ' δεινὰ καὶ ἐσθλὰ '

---

[1] οἳ EB[lt]: αἱ B[ss].   [2] τι E: τοι B.
[3] ἀπάντῃ Xylander: πάντῃ EB.
[4] ἀνὴρ Stephanus, Xylander: ἀνὴρ φρεσὶ EB.
[5] φρεσὶ E[c]B: μαντεύσαιτο E[ac] apparently.
[6] εἰσὶν καί σφιν E: εἰσί καί σφι B.
[7] δεινὰ] δειλὰ Bergk.
[8] πάγεν τε Reiske: παγέντε EB.

226

lines [a] :

> Fools! For they have no thoughts that range afar
> Who look for birth of what was not before
> Or for a thing to die and wholly perish.

These are the words of one who says in ringing tones
to all who have ears to hear that he does not abolish
generation, but only generation from the non-existent ; nor abolish destruction, but only out and out
destruction, that is, the destruction that reduces to
non-existence. Indeed anyone who prefers a more
moderate sort of cavilling to that simple-minded
fierceness will find in the subsequent passage a
handle for the opposite charge. There Empedocles [b]
says :

> No sage in his prophetic soul would say
> That, while men live (this thing they call their ' life '),
> So long they are, and suffer good and ill ;
> But both before the joining of their frame,
> And once it is disjoined, why, they are nothing.

For these are not the words of one who denies the
existence of men who have been born and are living,
but rather of one who takes both the unborn and the
already dead to exist. Colotes, however, has found
no fault with this, but says that on Empedocles' view
we shall never so much as fall ill or receive a wound.
But how could one who says that before life and after
life each person suffers ' good and ill,' leave no suffer-

---

[a] Diels and Kranz, *Die Frag. der Vorsokratiker*, Empedokles, b 11.
[b] Diels and Kranz, *Die Frag. der Vorsokratiker*, Empedokles, b 15.

---

⁹ ἐπεὶ λύθεν Reiske (ὡς λύθεν Xylander) : λυθέντ' EB.
¹⁰ ὅμως Pohlenz : ὅλως EB.
¹¹ οὐδὲ Ald.², Basle edition of 1542 : οὐδὲν EB.

(1113) περὶ τοὺς ζῶντας οὐκ ἀπολείπει τὸ πάσχειν; τίσιν
οὖν ἀληθῶς ἔπεται τὸ μὴ τραυματίζεσθαι μηδὲ
νοσεῖν, ὦ Κωλῶτα; ὑμῖν τοῖς ἐξ ἀτόμου καὶ κενοῦ
συμπεπηγόσιν, ὧν οὐδετέρῳ μέτεστιν αἰσθήσεως.
καὶ οὐ τοῦτο δεινόν, ἀλλ᾽ ὅτι μηδὲ ἡδονὴν τὸ
ποιῆσον ὑμῖν ἐστι, τῆς μὲν ἀτόμου μὴ δεχομένης
τὰ ποιητικὰ τοῦ δὲ κενοῦ μὴ πάσχοντος ὑπ᾽ αὐτῶν.
13. " Ἐπεὶ δὲ ὁ μὲν Κωλώτης ἐφεξῆς τῷ Δημοκρίτῳ τὸν Παρμενίδην ἐβούλετο συγκατορύσ-
σειν, ἐγὼ δὲ ὑπερβὰς τὰ ἐκείνου τὰ τοῦ Ἐμπεδοκλέους προέλαβον[1] διὰ τὸ μᾶλλον ἀκολουθεῖν τοῖς
F πρώτοις ἐγκλήμασιν αὐτοῖς, ἀναλάβωμεν τὸν Παρμενίδην. ἃ μὲν οὖν αὐτόν φησιν αἰσχρὰ σοφίσματα
λέγειν ὁ Κωλώτης, τούτοις ἐκεῖνος ὁ ἀνὴρ οὐ φιλίαν
ἐποίησεν ἀδοξοτέραν, οὐ φιληδονίαν θρασυτέραν,
οὐ τοῦ καλοῦ τὸ ἀγωγὸν ἐφ᾽ ἑαυτὸ καὶ δι᾽ ἑαυτὸ
τίμιον ἀφεῖλεν, οὐ τὰς περὶ θεῶν δόξας συνετάραξε·
1114 τὸ δὲ πᾶν ἓν εἰπὼν οὐκ οἶδα ὅπως ζῆν ἡμᾶς κεκώλυ-
κε. καὶ γὰρ Ἐπίκουρος ὅταν λέγῃ τὸ πᾶν ἄπειρον
εἶναι καὶ ἀγένητον[2] καὶ ἄφθαρτον καὶ μήτε αὐξό-
μενον μήτε μειούμενον, ὡς περὶ[3] ἑνός τινος διαλέ-
γεται τοῦ παντός. ἐν ἀρχῇ δὲ τῆς πραγματείας
ὑπειπὼν τὴν τῶν ὄντων φύσιν σώματα εἶναι καὶ
κενόν, ὡς μιᾶς οὔσης εἰς δύο πεποίηται τὴν διαίρεσιν, ὧν θάτερον ὄντως μὲν οὐθέν ἐστιν, ὀνομάζεται δὲ ὑφ᾽ ὑμῶν ἀναφὲς καὶ κενὸν καὶ ἀσώματον·
ὥστε καὶ ὑμῖν ἓν τὸ πᾶν ἐστιν, εἰ μὴ βούλεσθε

---

[1] προέλαβον Wyttenbach : προσλαβὼν EB[188] ; συλλαβὼν B[14].
[2] ἀγένητον E : ἀγέννητον B.
[3] ὡς περὶ E : ὥσπερ B.

---

[a] Cf. Aristotle, Physics, i. 2 (185 a 9-10), i. 3 (186 a 6-7) ;
Eudemus, Frag. 43 (ed. Wehrli).

ing to the living ? Who is it, Colotes, who really find themselves impervious to wounds and disease ? You yourselves, compacted of atom and void, neither of which has any sensation. You may not object to this, but there is worse to come : there will be nothing to give you pleasure either, since your atom does not receive the causes of pleasure and your void does not respond to them.

13. " Since Colotes did his best to demolish Parmenides next after Democritus, whereas I skipped that passage and dealt first with his treatment of Empedocles because it has a better connexion with the first set of charges taken by themselves, let us now return to Parmenides. As for the ' shameful ' sophistries [a] that Colotes imputes to him, the great philosopher did not use them to lessen the high repute of friendship or to embolden the lust for pleasure ; he did not strip virtue of her native beauty or of being valued for her own sake ; he did not play havoc with our beliefs about the gods. Yet by saying that ' the universe is one ' [b] he has somehow prevented us from living. So Epicurus [c] too, when he says that ' the universe ' is infinite, ungenerated and imperishable, and subject neither to increase nor diminution, speaks of the universe as of some one thing. When he premises at the beginning of his treatise [d] that ' the *nature* of things *is* atoms and void,' he treats that nature as one, dividing it into two parts, one of them actually nothing, but termed by you and your company ' intangible,' ' empty,' and ' bodiless.' So that for you too the universe is one, unless you mean to

[b] *Cf.* Diels and Kranz, *Die Frag. der Vorsokratiker*, Parmenides, A 7, 8, 23 and 49.

[c] Frag. 296 (ed. Usener) ; *cf. Letter to Herodotus*, 41, 39.

[d] The thirty-seven books *On Nature* : Frag. 74 (ed. Usener).

(1114) κεναῖς φωναῖς περὶ κενοῦ χρῆσθαι, σκιαμαχοῦντες
πρὸς τοὺς ἀρχαίους.

" ' ' Ἀλλ' ἄπειρα νὴ Δία πλήθει τὰ σώματα κατὰ
B Ἐπίκουρόν ἐστι, καὶ γίνεται τῶν φαινομένων ἕκαστον ἐξ ἐκείνων.' ὅρα μὲν οἵας ὑποτίθεσθε πρὸς
γένεσιν ἀρχάς, ἀπειρίαν καὶ κενόν· ὧν τὸ μὲν ἄ-
πρακτον ἀπαθὲς ἀσώματον, ἡ δὲ ἄτακτος ἄλογος
ἀπερίληπτος, αὐτὴν[1] ἀναλύουσα καὶ ταράττουσα
τῷ μὴ κρατεῖσθαι μηδὲ ὁρίζεσθαι διὰ πλῆθος. ἀλλ'
ὅ γε Παρμενίδης οὔτε ' πῦρ ' ἀνήρηκεν οὔτε ' ὕδωρ '
οὔτε ' κρημνὸν ' οὔτε ' πόλεις,' ὥς φησι Κωλώτης,
' ἐν Εὐρώπῃ καὶ Ἀσίᾳ κατοικουμένας '· ὅς γε καὶ
διάκοσμον[2] πεποίηται, καὶ στοιχεῖα μιγνὺς τὸ λαμ-
πρὸν καὶ σκοτεινὸν ἐκ τούτων τὰ φαινόμενα πάντα
καὶ διὰ τούτων ἀποτελεῖ. καὶ γὰρ περὶ γῆς εἴρηκε
C πολλὰ καὶ περὶ οὐρανοῦ καὶ ἡλίου καὶ σελήνης καὶ
ἄστρων καὶ γένεσιν ἀνθρώπων ἀφήγηται[3] καὶ οὐδὲν
ἄρρητον, ὡς ἀνὴρ ἀρχαῖος ἐν φυσιολογίᾳ καὶ συν-
θεὶς γραφὴν ἰδίαν, οὐκ ἀλλοτρίαν διαφορῶν,[4] τῶν
κυρίων παρῆκεν.

" Ἐπεὶ δὲ καὶ Πλάτωνος καὶ Σωκράτους ἔτι
πρότερος συνεῖδεν ὡς ἔχει τι δοξαστὸν ἡ φύσις,
ἔχει δὲ καὶ νοητόν, ἔστι δὲ τὸ μὲν δοξαστὸν ἀβέβαιον καὶ πλανητὸν ἐν πάθεσι πολλοῖς καὶ μετα-
βολαῖς τῷ φθίνειν καὶ αὔξεσθαι καὶ πρὸς ἄλλον
ἄλλως ἔχειν καὶ μηδὲ ἀεὶ πρὸς τὸν αὐτὸν ὡσαύτως

---

[1] αὐτὴν B[c] : αὐτὴν EB[ac].
[2] διάκοσμον Turnebus : διὰ κόσμον EB.
[3] ἀφήγηται Wyttenbach : ἀφήρηται EB.
[4] ἀλλοτρίην διαφορῶν Apelt (ἀλλοτρίας διαφόρησιν Post) : ἀλλοτρίαν διαφορὰν EB.

use empty vocables about the empty void, shadow-boxing with the ancients.

" ' But for Epicurus,[a] ' you exclaim, ' the number of bodies is infinite and every single object in the world of sense is generated from them.' Observe right here the sort of first principles you people adopt to account for generation : infinity and the void—the void incapable of action, incapable of being acted upon, bodiless ; the infinite disordered, irrational, incapable of formulation, disrupting and confounding itself because of a multiplicity that defies control or limitation. But Parmenides for one has abolished neither ' fire ' nor ' water,' neither ' a precipice ' nor ' cities lying in Europe and Asia ' in Colotes' words, since he [b] has actually made a cosmic order, and by blending as elements the light and the dark produces out of them and by their operation the whole world of sense. Thus he has much to say about earth, heaven, sun, moon, and stars, and has recounted the genesis of man ; and for an ancient natural philosopher—who has put together a book of his own, and is not pulling apart the book of another—he has left nothing of real importance unsaid.

" But since even before Plato [c] and Socrates he saw that nature has in it something that we apprehend by opinion, and again something that we apprehend by the intellect, and that what belongs to the world of opinion is inconstant and passes through a wide range of accidents and changes, since for sensation it grows and decays and differs for different persons and is not, even for the same person, always the same :

[a] Frag. 269 (ed. Usener).
[b] Diels and Kranz, *Die Frag. der Vorsokratiker*, Parmenides, b 8. 53-61.
[c] *Cf.* Plato, *Tim.* 27 d—28 a.

(1114) τῇ αἰσθήσει, τοῦ νοητοῦ δὲ ἕτερον εἶδος, ἔστι γὰρ

οὐλομελές[1] τε καὶ ἀτρεμὲς ἠδ' ἀγένητον,[2]

D ὡς αὐτὸς εἴρηκε, καὶ ὅμοιον ἑαυτῷ καὶ μόνιμον ἐν τῷ εἶναι, ταῦτα συκοφαντῶν ἐκ τῆς φωνῆς ὁ Κωλώτης καὶ τῷ ῥήματι διώκων οὐ τῷ πράγματι τὸν λόγον ἁπλῶς φησι πάντα ἀναιρεῖν τῷ ἓν ὂν ὑποτίθεσθαι τὸν Παρμενίδην. ὁ δὲ ἀναιρεῖ μὲν οὐδετέραν φύσιν, ἑκατέρᾳ δὲ ἀποδιδοὺς τὸ προσῆκον εἰς μὲν τὴν τοῦ ἑνὸς καὶ ὄντος ἰδέαν τίθεται τὸ νοητόν, ὂν μὲν ὡς ἀΐδιον καὶ ἄφθαρτον, ἓν δὲ ὁμοιότητι πρὸς αὐτὸ καὶ τῷ μὴ δέχεσθαι διαφορὰν προσαγορεύσας, εἰς δὲ τὴν ἄτακτον καὶ φερομένην τὸ αἰσθητόν. ὧν καὶ κριτήριον ἰδεῖν[3] ἐστιν,

ἠμὲν[4] Ἀληθείης εὐπειθέος[5] ἀτρεκὲς ἦτορ,[6]

E τοῦ νοητοῦ καὶ κατὰ ταὐτὰ ἔχοντος ὡσαύτως ἁπτόμενον,

ἠδὲ[7] βροτῶν δόξας αἷς[8] οὐκ ἔνι[9] πίστις ἀληθὴς

---

[1] ἔστι γὰρ οὐλομελές EB (E has a marginal sign that indicates a quotation but does not tell where it begins; B has none). The verse of Parmenides begins with οὖλον μουνογενές in Clement and Simplicius, with μοῦνον μουνογενές in [Plutarch], *Strom.* Proclus cites οὐλομελές, omitting what precedes. Westman would read μοῦνόν τ' οὐλομελές in the line of Parmenides.

[2] ἀγένητον E (ἀγέννητον B) with the rest of the citations and Simplicius, *De Caelo*, and *Physics* (p. 120. 23, ed. Diels): ἀτέλεστον Simplicius elsewhere on the *Physics.*

[3] ἰδεῖν] ἴδιον Wyttenbach.

[4] ἠμὲν Rasmus (ἢ μὲν Xylander): ἡ μὲν EB.

[5] εὐπειθέος EB with Clement, Sextus, and Diogenes Laert.: εὐκυκλέος Simplicius; εὐφεγγέος Proclus.

whereas what belongs to the world of the intellect is another kind of thing, for it is

> Entire, unmoving, and unborn

to quote his own [a] words, and is like itself [b] and enduring in what it is,[c] Colotes quibbles about the language and attacks the manner of expression, not the matter, when he says that Parmenides makes a clean sweep of all things by laying down one as being. Parmenides [d] however abolishes neither the one world nor the other. He gives each its due, and puts what belongs to the world of the intellect under the head of ' one ' and ' being,' calling it ' being ' because it is eternal and imperishable, and ' one ' because it is uniform with itself and admits of no variation, while he puts what belongs to the world of sense under the head of disordered motion. Of these we may further observe the criteria :

> The unerring heart of most persuasive Truth,[e]

which deals with what is intelligible and forever unalterably the same,

> And man's beliefs, that lack all true persuasion [f]

[a] Diels and Kranz, *Die Frag. der Vorsokratiker*, Parmenides, B 8. 4.
[b] *Ibid.*, B 8. 22.
[c] *Ibid.*, B 8. 29-30.   [d] *Ibid.*, A 34.
[e] *Ibid.*, B 1. 29.
[f] *Ibid.*, B 1. 30.

---

[6] ἀτρεκὲς ἦτορ Xylander from Diogenes Laert. ix. 22 (ἀτρεμὲς ἦτορ the other citations) : ἀτρεκ followed by a blank of 7 letters EB.
[7] ἠδὲ Stephanus (ἢ δὲ Xylander) : ἡ δὲ EB.
[8] αἷς EB : ταῖς the other citations (τῆς Diogenes Laert.).
[9] οὐκ ἔνι EB and the other citations : οὐκέτι Diogenes Laert.

PLUTARCH'S MORALIA

(1114) διὰ τὸ παντοδαπὰς μεταβολὰς καὶ πάθη καὶ ἀνομοιότητας δεχομένοις ὁμιλεῖν πράγμασι. καίτοι πῶς ἂν ἀπέλιπεν αἴσθησιν καὶ δόξαν, αἰσθητὸν μὴ ἀπολιπὼν μηδὲ δοξαστόν; οὐκ ἔστιν εἰπεῖν. ἀλλ' ὅτι τῷ μὲν ὄντως ὄντι προσήκει διαμένειν ἐν τῷ εἶναι, ταῦτα δὲ νῦν μέν ἐστι νῦν δὲ οὐκ ἔστιν, ἐξίσταται δὲ ἀεὶ καὶ μεταλλάσσει τὴν φύσιν, ἑτέρας ᾤετο[1] μᾶλλον ἢ τῆς ἐκείνου τοῦ ὄντος ἀεὶ δεῖσθαι προσηγορίας. ἦν οὖν ὁ περὶ τοῦ ὄντος ὡς ἓν εἴη λόγος οὐκ ἀναίρεσις τῶν πολλῶν καὶ αἰσθητῶν, F ἀλλὰ δήλωσις αὐτῶν τῆς πρὸς τὸ νοητὸν διαφορᾶς. ἦν ἔτι μᾶλλον ἐνδεικνύμενος Πλάτων τῇ περὶ τὰ εἴδη πραγματείᾳ καὶ αὐτὸς ἀντίληψιν τῷ Κωλώτῃ παρέσχε.

14. "Διὸ καὶ τὰ πρὸς τοῦτον εἰρημένα δοκεῖ μοι λαβεῖν ἐφεξῆς. καὶ πρῶτόν γε τὴν ἐπιμέλειαν καὶ 1115 πολυμάθειαν τοῦ φιλοσόφου σκεψώμεθα, λέγοντος ὅτι τούτοις τοῖς δόγμασι τοῦ[2] Πλάτωνος ἐπηκολουθήκασιν Ἀριστοτέλης καὶ Ξενοκράτης καὶ Θεόφραστος καὶ πάντες οἱ Περιπατητικοί. ποῦ γὰρ ὢν τῆς ἀοικήτου τὸ βιβλίον ἔγραφες, ἵνα ταῦτα συντιθεὶς τὰ ἐγκλήματα μὴ τοῖς ἐκείνων συντάγμασιν ἐντύχῃς μηδὲ ἀναλάβῃς εἰς χεῖρας Ἀριστοτέλους τὰ περὶ οὐρανοῦ καὶ τὰ περὶ ψυχῆς, Θεοφράστου δὲ τὰ πρὸς τοὺς φυσικούς, Ἡρακλείδου[3] δὲ τὸν Ζωροάστρην, τὸ περὶ τῶν ἐν Ἅιδου, τὸ περὶ τῶν φυσικῶς ἀπορουμένων, Δικαιάρχου δὲ τὰ περὶ ψυχῆς, ἐν οἷς πρὸς τὰ κυριώτατα καὶ μέγιστα

---

[1] ᾤετο Wyttenbach (*statuit* Xylander) : ὥστε EB.
[2] τοῦ ; B omits.

because they consort with objects admitting all manner of changes, accidents, and irregularities. Yet how could he have left us with sensation and belief, if he had left us with no object of sensation and no object of belief ? The question is unanswerable. No, since what truly is should persevere in being, whereas these things, that meet the eye, now are, and now are not, forever abandoning their nature and taking on another, they required, so it seemed to him, a designation differing from that which is applied to the first, which always is. Thus his contention, that being is one, was no denial of the plural and perceptible, but an indication of their distinction from what is known by the mind. Plato too, in conveying this distinction even more clearly in his theory of ideas, has afforded Colotes an opening for attack.

14. " I therefore intend to deal next with the attack on Plato. And first let us consider the diligence and learning of our philosopher, who says that these doctrines of Plato were followed by Aristotle, Xenocrates, Theophrastus, and all the Peripatetics. In what wilderness did you write your book, that when you framed these charges you failed to look at their writings or take into your hands Aristotle's works *On the Heavens* and *On the Soul*, Theophrastus' *Reply to the Natural Philosophers*,[a] Heracleides'[b] *Zoroaster*, *On the Underworld*, and *Disputed Questions in Natural Philosophy*, and Dicaearchus'[c] *On the Soul*, in which they constantly differ with Plato, contra-

---

[a] See Regenbogen in Pauly-Wissowa, Suppl. vii (1955), col. 1539. 14-23.
[b] Frag. 68 (ed. Wehrli).
[c] Frag. 5 (ed. Wehrli).

---

[3] Ἡρακλείδου Reiske : ἡρακλείτου EB.

(1115)

B τῶν φυσικῶν ὑπεναντιούμενοι τῷ Πλάτωνι καὶ μαχόμενοι[1] διατελοῦσι; καὶ μὴν τῶν ἄλλων Περιπατητικῶν ὁ κορυφαιότατος Στράτων οὔτε Ἀριστοτέλει κατὰ πολλὰ συμφέρεται καὶ Πλάτωνι τὰς ἐναντίας ἔσχηκε δόξας περὶ κινήσεως, περὶ νοῦ καὶ περὶ ψυχῆς καὶ περὶ γενέσεως, τελευτῶν τε[2] τὸν κόσμον αὐτὸν οὐ ζῷον εἶναί φησι, τὸ δὲ κατὰ φύσιν ἔπεσθαι τῷ κατὰ τύχην· ἀρχὴν γὰρ ἐνδιδόναι τὸ αὐτόματον εἶτα οὕτως περαίνεσθαι τῶν φυσικῶν παθῶν ἕκαστον. τάς γε μὴν ἰδέας, περὶ ὧν ἐγκαλεῖ τῷ Πλάτωνι, πανταχοῦ κινῶν Ἀριστοτέλης καὶ πᾶσαν ἐπάγων ἀπορίαν αὐταῖς ἐν τοῖς ἠθικοῖς ὑπο-

C μνήμασιν, ἐν τοῖς φυσικοῖς, διὰ τῶν ἐξωτερικῶν διαλόγων, φιλονεικότερον ἐνίοις ἔδοξεν ἢ φιλοσοφώτερον ἔχειν τῷ δόγματι τούτῳ,[3] ὡς προθέμενος τὴν Πλάτωνος ὑπερείπειν[4] φιλοσοφίαν· οὕτω μακρὰν ἦν τοῦ ἀκολουθεῖν. τίνος οὖν εὐχερείας ἐστὶ τὰ δοκοῦντα τοῖς ἀνδράσι μὴ μαθόντα καταψεύδεσθαι τὰ μὴ δοκοῦντα, καὶ πεπεισμένον ἐλέγχειν ἑτέρους αὐτόγραφον ἐξενεγκεῖν ἀμαθίας ἔλεγχον καθ' αὑτοῦ καὶ θρασύτητος, ὁμολογεῖν Πλάτωνι φάσκοντα τοὺς διαφερομένους καὶ ἀκολουθεῖν τοὺς ἀντιλέγοντας;

---

[1] μαχόμενοι E : μαχούμενοι B.

[2] τε added by Pohlenz (δὲ by Wyttenbach).

[3] ἔχειν τῷ δόγματι τούτῳ Rose (place before φιλονεικότερον ? nos) : ἐκ τῶν δογμάτων τούτων EB (ἐκποιεῖν ἑαυτὸν τῶν δογμάτων τούτων Bignone; ἐκκρούειν τὴν πίστιν τῶν δογμάτων τούτων Pohlenz; κατακερτομεῖν τῶν δογμάτων τούτων Düring).

[4] ὑπερείπειν Reiske : ὑπεριδεῖν EB.

---

[a] Frag. 35 (ed. Wehrli) ; cf. Frag. 13.

dicting him about the most fundamental and far-reaching questions of natural philosophy ? Strato [a] indeed, foremost of the remaining Peripatetics, is on many points not in accord with Aristotle, and has adopted views the reverse of Plato's about motion and about intelligence, soul, and generation ; and he says in the end that the universe itself is not animate and that nature is subsequent to chance,[b] for the spontaneous initiates the motion, and only then are the various natural processes brought to pass. As for the ideas, for which our Epicurean denounces Plato, Aristotle,[c] who everywhere assails them and brings up against them every sort of objection in his treatises on ethics and on natural philosophy and in his popular dialogues, was held by some [d] to be more contentious than philosophical in his attitude to this doctrine and bent on undermining Plato's philosophy—so far was he from following him. How frivolous can a man be ! Not to inform himself of these men's views, then to father on them views that they did not hold, and in the conviction that he is exposing others to bring out in his own hand an exposure of his own ignorance and recklessness when he asserts that men who differ with Plato agree with him and that men who attack him are his followers !

<hr/>

[b] Cf. Plato, Laws, x, 888 E 5, 889 A, and the whole discussion that follows, especially 892 B-C, 896 E 8-9, 897 B, 898 C.

[c] For comments on this whole passage see I. Düring, Aristotle in the Ancient Biographical Tradition (Gothenburg, 1957), pp. 323-325.

[d] Cf. Aristotle, On Philosophy, Frag. 10 (ed. Ross): " . . . and in the dialogues he proclaims loudly and distinctly that he is unable to enter into this doctrine [of the ideas], even if someone should imagine that he is opposing it out of contentiousness " (. . . μὴ δύνασθαι τῷ δόγματι τούτῳ συμπαθεῖν, κἄν τις αὐτὸν οἴηται διὰ φιλονεικίαν ἀντιλέγειν).

(1115)   15. " ' 'Αλλὰ δὴ Πλάτων φησὶ τοὺς ἵππους ὑφ'
ἡμῶν ματαίως ἵππους εἶναι δοξάζεσθαι[1] καὶ τοὺς
D ἀνθρώπους ἀνθρώπους.'[2] καὶ ποῦ τοῦτο τῶν Πλάτωνος συγγραμμάτων ἀποκεκρυμμένον εὗρεν ὁ Κωλώτης; ἡμεῖς γὰρ ἐν πᾶσιν ἀναγινώσκομεν καὶ
τὸν ἄνθρωπον ἄνθρωπον καὶ τὸν ἵππον ἵππον καὶ
πῦρ τὸ πῦρ ὑπ' αὐτοῦ δοξαζόμενον· ᾗ καὶ δοξαστὸν
ὀνομάζει τούτων ἕκαστον. ὁ δ'[3] οἷα δὴ σοφίας οὐδ'
ἀκαρὲς ἀπέχων ὡς ἓν καὶ ταὐτὸν ἔλαβε[4] τὸ μὴ εἶναι
τὸν ἄνθρωπον καὶ τὸ εἶναι μὴ ὂν τὸν ἄνθρωπον.

" Τῷ Πλάτωνι δὲ θαυμαστῶς ἐδόκει διαφέρειν
τὸ μὴ εἶναι τοῦ μὴ ὂν εἶναι· τῷ μὲν γὰρ ἀναίρεσιν
οὐσίας πάσης, τῷ δὲ ἑτερότητα δηλοῦσθαι τοῦ
μεθεκτοῦ καὶ τοῦ μετέχοντος, ἣν οἱ μὲν ὕστερον εἰς
γένους καὶ εἴδους καὶ κοινῶς[5] τινων καὶ ἰδίως[6]
E λεγομένων ποιῶν διαφορὰν ἔθεντο μόνον, ἀνωτέρω
δὲ οὐ προῆλθον, εἰς λογικωτέρας ἀπορίας ἐμπε-
σόντες. ἔστι δὲ τοῦ μεθεκτοῦ πρὸς τὸ μετέχον
λόγος ὂν αἰτία τε πρὸς ὕλην ἔχει καὶ παράδειγμα
πρὸς εἰκόνα καὶ δύναμις πρὸς πάθος. ᾧ γε δὴ
μάλιστα τὸ καθ' αὑτὸ καὶ ταὐτὸν ἀεὶ διαφέρει τοῦ
δι' ἕτερον καὶ μηδέποτε ὡσαύτως ἔχοντος· ὅτι τὸ
μὲν οὔτε ἔσται ποτὲ μὴ ὂν οὔτε γέγονε καὶ διὰ
τοῦτο πάντως καὶ ὄντως ὄν ἐστι, τῷ[7] δὲ οὐδὲ ὅσον
ἀπ' ἄλλου συμβέβηκε μετέχειν τοῦ εἶναι βέβαιόν
ἐστιν, ἀλλ' ἐξίσταται δι' ἀσθένειαν, ἅτε τῆς ὕλης
περὶ τὸ εἶδος ὀλισθανούσης[8] καὶ πάθη πολλὰ καὶ

---

[1] δοξάζεσθαι added by us, λέγεσθαι by Madvig, and νομίζεσθαι (after ματαίως) by Reiske.
[2] ἀνθρώπους added by Reiske.
[3] ὁ δ' Stephanus : ὁδ' EB.   [4] ἔλαβε EᶜB : ὑπέλαβε Eᵃᶜ ?
[5] κοινῶς Pohlenz : κοινῶν EB.
[6] ἰδίως Pohlenz : ἰδίων EB.   [7] τῷ Reiske : τὸ EB.

238

15. " ' But Plato says that it is idle to regard horses as being horses and men men.' And where in Plato's writings did Colotes find this tucked away ? I for one in reading them find that he everywhere regards man as man, horse as horse, and fire as fire ; indeed this is why he terms each of them an ' object of opinion.' But our friend, as one separated from wisdom by not so much as a hair, took ' man is not ' to be one and the same as ' man is non-being.'

" But in Plato's view there is a world of difference between ' is not ' and ' is non-being,' for by the former is meant the denial of any kind of being, by the latter the otherness [a] of the participant and what it participates in, an otherness that later philosophers brought under the head of a mere difference of genus and species [b] or between characters shared and characters not shared,[c] and went no higher, as they became involved in problems more purely dialectical. The relation of the partaken in to the partaker is that of cause to matter, model to copy, power to effect. And it is chiefly by this relation that the absolute and always identical differs from what is caused by something else and is never in the same state. The former will never be non-being and has never come to be, and is therefore in the full and true sense ' being ' ; whereas the latter has no firm hold even on such participation in being as it incidentally has from something else, but is too weak to preserve its identity, inasmuch as matter sits loosely to its form and

---

[a] Cf. Plato, Sophist, 255 D-E, 258 D-E.
[b] As Aristotle.
[c] As the Stoics : cf. Mor. 1077 D and von Arnim, Stoicorum Vet. Frag. ii, Frags. 395 and 398.

---

[g] ὀλισθανούσης Bern. : ὀλισθαινούσης E.B.

(1115)

F μεταβολὰς ἐπὶ τὴν εἰκόνα τῆς οὐσίας, ὥστε κινεῖσθαι καὶ σαλεύεσθαι, δεχομένης.

" "Ωσπερ οὖν ὁ λέγων Πλάτωνα μὴ εἶναι τὴν εἰκόνα τὴν Πλάτωνος οὐκ ἀναιρεῖ τὴν ὡς εἰκόνος αἴσθησιν αὐτῆς καὶ ὕπαρξιν, ἀλλὰ ἐνδείκνυται καθ' αὐτό[1] τινος ὄντος καὶ πρὸς ἐκεῖνο ἑτέρου γεγονότος διαφοράν, οὕτως οὔτε φύσιν οὔτε χρῆσιν οὔτε αἴσθησιν ἀνθρώπων ἀναιροῦσιν οἱ κοινῆς τινος οὐσίας
1116 μετοχῇ καὶ ἰδέας[2] γινόμενον ἡμῶν ἕκαστον εἰκόνα τοῦ παρασχόντος τὴν ὁμοιότητα τῇ γενέσει προσαγορεύοντες. οὐδὲ[3] γὰρ ὁ πῦρ μὴ λέγων εἶναι τὸν πεπυρωμένον σίδηρον ἢ τὴν σελήνην ἥλιον, ἀλλὰ κατὰ Παρμενίδην

νυκτιφαὲς[4] περὶ γαῖαν ἀλώμενον ἀλλότριον φῶς,

ἀναιρεῖ σιδήρου χρῆσιν ἢ σελήνης φύσιν, ἀλλ' εἰ μὴ λέγοι[5] σῶμα μηδὲ πεφωτισμένον, ἤδη μάχεται ταῖς αἰσθήσεσιν, ὥσπερ ὁ σῶμα καὶ ζῷον καὶ γένεσιν καὶ αἴσθησιν μὴ ἀπολιπών. ὁ δὲ ταῦτα ὑπάρχειν τῷ[6] μετεσχηκέναι καὶ ὅσον ἀπολείπεται τοῦ ὄντος ἀεὶ καὶ τὸ εἶναι παρέχοντος αὐτοῖς ὑπονοῶν οὐ παρορᾷ τὸ αἰσθητὸν ἀλλ' οὐ[7] παρορᾷ τὸ νοητόν,
B οὐδὲ ἀναιρεῖ τὰ γινόμενα καὶ φαινόμενα περὶ ἡμᾶς τῶν παθῶν, ἀλλὰ ὅτι βεβαιότερα τούτων ἕτερα καὶ μονιμώτερα πρὸς οὐσίαν ἐστὶ τῷ μήτε γίνεσθαι μήτε ἀπόλλυσθαι μήτε πάσχειν μηθὲν ἐνδείκνυται

---

[1] αὐτό E : ἑαυτό B.
[2] καὶ ἰδέας Bern. (ἢ ἰδέας Reiske) : καὶ ἰδέα EB.
[3] οὐδὲ E : ὁ δὲ B.
[4] νυκτιφαὲς Scaliger : νυκτὶ φάος EB.
[5] λέγοι EB[t] : λέγει B[188].
[6] ὑπάρχειν τῷ Ald.[2], Leonicus : τῶ ὑπάρχειν EB.
[7] ἀλλ' οὐ Pohlenz : ἀλλὰ EB.

admits into its copy of being many effects and alterations that lead to movement and instability.

"As then one who says that Plato's image is not Plato does not deny the perception and existence of it as an image, but is pointing out the difference between what *is* in its own right and what has come into existence as something distinct from the former and relative to it, just so neither do those persons deny the reality or use or perception of men, who term each of us, coming into existence as we do through participation in a certain common being and form, an image of what imparted its likeness to our formation. No more indeed does he who denies that a lump of ignited iron is fire, or who says that moonlight is not sunshine, calling it instead in the words of Parmenides [a]

> A light of alien breed
> That gleams at night and roves around the earth,

abolish the use of iron or the reality of moonlight; only if he should deny that the one is a body and the other luminous, would he be at war with the senses, as he [b] was who left in the world no body, no animal, no generation, and no sense. But he who supposes that these things exist by participation and fall far short of what forever is and gives them their being, is not blind to what we see, but rather is not blind to what we know; he does not deny the world of becoming and of objects present to our senses, but points out to those who can follow that there are other things more stable than these and more enduring in being because they neither begin nor come to an end nor

[a] Diels and Kranz, *Die Frag. der Vorsokratiker*, Parmenides, B 14.
[b] Epicurus.

(1116) τοῖς ἑπομένοις καὶ διδάσκει καθ ρώτερον τῆς διαφορᾶς ἁπτόμενος τοῖς ὀνόμασι ⸱ὰ μὲν ὄντα τὰ δὲ
γινόμενα προσαγορεύειν. τοῦτο δὲ καὶ τοῖς νεωτέ-
ροις συμβέβηκε· πολλὰ γὰ⸱ καὶ μεγάλα πράγματα
τῆς τοῦ ὄντος ἀποστεροῦσι προσηγορίας, τὸ κενόν,
τὸν χρόνον, τὸν τόπον, ἁπλῶς τὸ τῶν λεκτῶν γένος,
ἐν ᾧ καὶ τἀληθῆ πάντα ἔνεστι. ταῦτα γὰρ ὄντα
μὲν μὴ εἶναι, τινὰ δὲ εἶναι λέγουσι, χρώμενοι δὲ
C αὐτοῖς ὡς ὑφεστῶσι καὶ ὑπάρχουσιν ἐν τῷ βίῳ καὶ
τῷ φιλοσοφεῖν διατελοῦσιν.

16. " Ἀλλ' αὐτὸν ἡδέως ἂν ἐροίμην τὸν κατή-
γορον εἰ τοῖς ἑαυτῶν πράγμασι τὴν διαφορὰν οὐκ
ἐνορῶσι ταύτην καθ' ἣν τὰ μὲν μόνιμα καὶ ἄτρεπτα
ταῖς οὐσίαις ἐστίν, ὡς λέγουσι καὶ τὰς ἀτόμους
ἀπαθείᾳ καὶ στερρότητι πάντα χρόνον ὡσαύτως
ἔχειν, τὰ δὲ συγκρίματα πάντα ῥευστὰ καὶ μετα-
βλητὰ καὶ γινόμενα καὶ ἀπολλύμενα εἶναι, μυρίων
μὲν εἰδώλων ἀπερχομένων ἀεὶ καὶ ῥεόντων, μυρίων
δὲ ὡς εἰκὸς ἑτέρων ἐκ τοῦ περιέχοντος ἐπιρρεόντων
καὶ ἀναπληρούντων τὸ ἄθροισμα ποικιλλόμενον ὑπὸ
τῆς ἐξαλλαγῆς ταύτης καὶ μετακεραννύμενον, ἅτε
D δὴ καὶ τῶν ἐν βάθει τοῦ συγκρίματος ἀτόμων οὐδέποτε λῆξαι κινήσεως οὐδὲ παλμῶν πρὸς ἀλλήλας[1]
δυναμένων, ὥσπερ αὐτοὶ λέγουσιν.

" Ἀλλ' ἔστι μὲν ἐν τοῖς πράγμασιν ἡ τοιαύτη
διαφορὰ τῆς οὐσίας· σοφώτερος δὲ τοῦ Πλάτωνος

---

[1] ἀλλήλας Usener : ἀλλήλα EB.

[a] The Stoics. Their theory of " incorporeals " is criticized
by Plutarch at *Mor.* 1074 D.

[b] " Something," the most inclusive Stoic term, comprises
the corporeal, which alone " is," and the four incorporeals ;
void, time, place, and the meaning of words. See M. Pohlenz, *Die Stoa*, vol. i, p. 64 ; vol. ii, p. 37.

suffer change ; and fixing the distinction more exactly by his use of terms he teaches them to call the one sort things that are and the other things that come to be. We find that the more recent philosophers [a] have also done the like ; they refuse to many important realities the name of being—the void, time, place, and the whole class of meanings without exception, which includes everything true. For these, they say, though they are not ' being,' are nevertheless ' something ' [b] ; and they continue to make use of them in their lives and their philosophy as real and substantial.

16. " But I should like to ask the very man who brings this indictment if his school [c] does not see this distinction in their own system, whereby some objects are enduring and unchanging in their being, just as atoms too in their doctrine are forever the same because they are too hard to be affected, while all aggregates of atoms are subjetc to flux and change and come into being and pass out of it,[d] as innumerable films leave them in a constant stream, and innumerable others, it is inferred, flow in from the surroundings and replenish the mass,[e] which is varied by this interchange and altered in its composition, since in fact even the atoms in the interior of the aggregate can never cease moving or vibrating against one another, as the Epicureans say themselves.[f]

" ' It is true,' you say, ' that this sort of difference in ways of being is found in the actual world. But

[c] Epicurus, Frag. 282 (ed. Usener).
[d] *Cf.* Lucretius, i. 464-482 and Diogenes of Oenoanda, Frag. 4. ii-iii (ed. Grilli).
[e] *Cf.* Epicurus, *Letter to Herodotus*, 48.
[f] *Cf.* Epicurus, *Letter to Herodotus*, 43, 50 ; Lucretius, ii. 95-111.

(1116) ὁ Ἐπίκουρος ᾗ πάντα ὁμοίως ὄντα προσαγορεύει,
τὸ ἀναφὲς κενὸν τὸ ἀντερεῖδον σῶμα τὰς ἀρχὰς τὰ
συγκρίματα, κοινῆς καὶ μιᾶς¹ ἡγούμενος οὐσίας
μετέχειν τὸ ἀίδιον τῷ γινομένῳ, τὸ ἀνώλεθρον τῷ
φθειρομένῳ, τὰς ἀπαθεῖς καὶ διαρκεῖς καὶ ἀμετα-
βλήτους καὶ μηδέποτε τοῦ εἶναι δυναμένας ἐκπε-
σεῖν φύσεις ταύταις αἷς² ἐν τῷ πάσχειν καὶ μετα-
Ε βάλλειν τὸ εἶναι, ταῖς μηδένα χρόνον ὡσαύτως
ἐχούσαις.' εἰ δὲ δὴ καὶ ὡς³ ἔνι μάλιστα διήμαρτε
τούτοις ὁ Πλάτων, ὀνομάτων ὤφειλε⁴ συγχύσεως
εὐθύνας ὑπέχειν τοῖς ἀκριβέστερον ἑλληνίζουσι τούτοις καὶ καθαρώτερον διαλεγομένοις, οὐχ ὡς ἀναιρῶν τὰ πράγματα καὶ τοῦ ζῆν ἐξάγων ἡμᾶς αἰτίαν
ἔχειν ὅτι τὰ γινόμενα γινόμενα⁵ καὶ οὐκ ὄντα, καθάπερ οὗτοι, προσηγόρευσεν.⁶

17. " Ἀλλ᾽ ἐπεὶ⁷ τὸν Σωκράτην μετὰ τὸν Παρμενίδην ὑπερέβημεν, ἀναληπτέος ἡμῖν ἐφεξῆς ὁ
περὶ τούτου λόγος.⁸ εὐθὺς οὖν τὸν ἀφ᾽ ἱερᾶς κεκίνη-
κεν ὁ Κωλώτης, καὶ διηγησάμενος ὅτι χρησμὸν ἐκ

¹ μιᾶς nos : μὴ δὲ ΕΒ.
² αἷς nos (ὧν Wyttenbach) : ὡς ΕΒ.
³ δὴ καὶ ὡς Wyttenbach : δικαίως ὡς ΕΒ.
⁴ ὤφειλε Dübner (ὠφείλει Turnebus ; ὀφείλει Ald.²) : ὦ
φίλε ΕΒ.
⁵ γινόμενα added by Bignone.
⁶ προσηγόρευσεν Stephanus : προσηγόρευσαν ΕΒ.
⁷ ἐπεὶ Β² Turnebus : ἐπὶ ΕΒ¹.
⁸ ἀναληπτέος (ἡμῖν added by us) ἐφεξῆς ὁ περὶ τούτου λόγος

Epicurus [a] shows himself a better philosopher than Plato in applying " being " to all alike, to the intangible void and resistant body and to the elements and their aggregates, holding that a common and single way of being is found in both the eternal and the generated, both the indestructible and the destructible, both the unaffected and enduring and changeless realities that can never be expelled from their being and those whose being lies in the fact that they are acted upon and changed and which never for an instant remain as they were.' Yet granting that Plato was entirely mistaken in this, it is for the crime of linguistic subversion that he should have been summoned to a rendering of accounts before these examiners whose Greek is more correct and style more pure [b] ; he should not have been charged with abolishing reality and ushering us out of this life because he styled a thing that becomes ' a thing that becomes,' and not like these people ' a thing that is.'

17. " But since after Parmenides we skipped Socrates, we must next take up the discussion of him. At the very outset Colotes throws in his reserves [c] : after relating that Chaerephon returned from Delphi

---

[a] Frag. 76 (p. 345, ed. Usener) ; cf. also the note to Frag. 74 (p. 124, ed. Usener).

[b] Epicurus' style was notoriously bad (cf. Usener, *Epicurea*, pp. 88-90, 343).

[c] For the proverb (literally " to move the piece from the sacred line ") cf. *Mor.* 783 B, 975 A, and Leutsch and Schneidewin, *Paroem. Graeci*, vol. i, p. 221 (Diogenianus, *Centuria*, iii. 36). It is derived from a game like draughts : see F. H. Colson, *Classical Review*, lvi (1942), p. 116.

Pohlenz : ἀναληπτέος (-οι B[ac]) followed by a blank of 35 letters E, 31 B.

(1116) Δελφῶν περὶ Σωκράτους ἀνήνεγκε Χαιρεφῶν ὃν
ἴσμεν ἅπαντες, ταῦτα ἐπείρηκε[1]· ' τὸ μὲν οὖν τοῦ
F Χαιρεφῶντος διὰ τὸ τελέως σοφιστικὸν καὶ φορτικὸν διήγημα εἶναι παρήσομεν.' φορτικὸς οὖν[2] ὁ
Πλάτων ὁ τοῦτον ἀναγράψας τὸν χρησμόν, ἵνα
τοὺς ἄλλους ἐάσω· φορτικώτεροι δὲ Λακεδαιμόνιοι
τὸν περὶ Λυκούργου χρησμὸν ἐν ταῖς παλαιοτάταις
ἀναγραφαῖς ἔχοντες· σοφιστικὸν δὲ ἦν διήγημα τὸ
τοῦ[3] Θεμιστοκλέους, ᾧ πείσας Ἀθηναίους τὴν πόλιν
ἐκλιπεῖν κατεναυμάχησε τὸν βάρβαρον· φορτικοὶ δὲ
1117 οἱ τῆς Ἑλλάδος νομοθέται τὰ μέγιστα καὶ πλεῖστα
τῶν ἱερῶν πυθόχρηστα[4] καθιστάντες. εἰ τοίνυν ὁ
περὶ Σωκράτους, ἀνδρὸς εἰς ἀρετὴν θεολήπτου γενομένου, χρησμὸς ἀνενεχθεὶς ὡς σοφοῦ φορτικὸς
ἦν καὶ σοφιστικός, τίνι προσείπωμεν ἀξίως ὀνόματι
τοὺς ὑμετέρους ' βρόμους ' καὶ ' ὀλολυγμοὺς ' καὶ
' κροτοθορύβους ' καὶ ' σεβάσεις '[5] καὶ ἐπιθειάσεις
αἷς προστρέπεσθε[6] καὶ καθυμνεῖτε τὸν ἐπὶ ἡδονὰς
παρακαλοῦντα συνεχεῖς καὶ πυκνάς; ὃς ἐν τῇ πρὸς
Ἀνάξαρχον ἐπιστολῇ ταυτὶ γέγραφεν, ' ἐγὼ δὲ ἐφ'

---

[1] ἐπείρηκε Meziriacus : ἀπείρηκε EB.
[2] οὖν EB[188] : γὰρ B[t] (γὰρ οὖν Aldine).
[3] τὸ τοῦ nos : τὸ EB.
[4] πυθόχρηστα Turnebus : πυθοχρησία E ; πυθοχρηστία B.
[5] σεβάσεις Turnebus : σοβάσεις EB.
[6] προστρέπεσθε Turnebus : προτρέπεσθε EB.

---

[a] A scholium to Aristophanes, Clouds, 144, gives it as

with the oracle about Socrates that we all know,[a] he comments : ' we shall dismiss this business of Chaerephon's, as it is nothing but a cheap and sophistical tale.' Then Plato was cheap, who recorded [b] this oracle, not to mention the rest ; the Lacedaemonians were cheaper still, who preserved in their most ancient records the oracle about Lycurgus [c]; that ' business ' of Themistocles [d] was a sophistical tale, which persuaded the Athenians to abandon the city and won victory over the barbarian at sea. Cheap too are the lawgivers of Greece who established the greater number of rites of worship, and these the most important, on the authority of Delphi. If then the oracle that was brought back about Socrates, a man who had become a zealot for virtue, calling him wise, was a cheap sophist's trick, what epithet do they deserve, your ' roars ' of ecstasy and ' cries of thanksgiving ' and tumultuous ' bursts of applause ' [e] and ' reverential demonstrations,' [f] all that apparatus of adoration that you people resort to in supplicating and hymning the man who summons you to sustained and frequent pleasures ? A man who in the letter to Anaxarchus [g] can pen such words as these :

follows (cf. H. W. Parke and D. E. Wormell, *The Delphic Oracle*, vol. ii [Oxford, 1956], no. 420, p. 170) :

> σοφὸς Σοφοκλῆς, σοφώτερος δ' Εὐριπίδης,
> ἀνδρῶν δὲ πάντων Σωκράτης σοφώτατος.

> Great wisdom is by Sophocles possessed ;
> Still greater wisdom has Euripides ;
> But Socrates is wisest of mankind.

[b] *Apology*, 21 A.
[c] Herodotus, i. 65. 3.
[d] Herodotus, vii. 143 ; Plutarch, *Life of Themistocles*, chap. x. 1-3 (116 D-E).
[e] Frag. 143 (ed. Usener).
[f] 1117 B, *infra*.
[g] Frag. 116 (ed. Usener).

247

PLUTARCH'S MORALIA

(1117) ἡδονὰς συνεχεῖς παρακαλῶ καὶ οὐκ ἐπ' ἀρετάς,
κενὰς καὶ ματαίας καὶ ταραχώδεις ἐχούσας τῶν
B καρπῶν τὰς ἐλπίδας.' ἀλλ' ὅμως ὁ μὲν Μητρόδωρος τὸν Τίμαρχον παρακαλῶν φησι ' ποιήσωμέν
τι καλὸν ἐπὶ καλοῖς, μόνον οὐ καταδύντες ταῖς
ὁμοιοπαθείαις καὶ ἀπαλλαγέντες ἐκ τοῦ χαμαὶ βίου
εἰς τὰ 'Επικούρου ὡς ἀληθῶς θεόφαντα ὄργια.'
Κωλώτης δὲ αὐτὸς ἀκροώμενος 'Επικούρου φυσιο-
λογοῦντος ἄφνω τοῖς γόνασιν αὐτοῦ προσέπεσε,
καὶ ταῦτα γράφει σεμνυνόμενος αὐτὸς 'Επίκουρος·
' ὡς σεβομένῳ γάρ σοι τὰ τότε ὑφ' ἡμῶν λεγόμενα
προσέπεσεν ἐπιθύμημα ἀφυσιολόγητον τοῦ[1] περι-
πλακῆναι ἡμῖν γονάτων ἐφαπτόμενον καὶ πάσης
τῆς εἰθισμένης ἐπιλήψεως γίνεσθαι κατὰ τὰς σε-
C βάσεις τινῶν[2] καὶ λιτάς· ἐποίεις οὖν,' φησί, ' καὶ
ἡμᾶς ἀνθιεροῦν σὲ αὐτὸν[3] καὶ ἀντισέβεσθαι.' συγ-
γνωστὰ νὴ Δία τοῖς λέγουσιν ὡς παντὸς[4] ἂν πρίαιν-

---

[1] τοῦ Emperius : τὸ EB.
[2] τινῶν Hirzel (τιμίων ? Post) : τιμῶν EB.
[3] σὲ αὐτὸν Usener : σεαυτὸν EB.
[4] παντὸς Xylander, Meziriacus : πάντες EB.

---

[a] Where anticipation is not disappointed by the event, and the event does not lead to unpleasantness.

[b] Frag. 38 (ed. Körte).

[c] Perhaps religious language : cf. the Spartan prayer, that the gods grant τὰ καλὰ ἐπὶ τοῖς ἀγαθοῖς (Alcibiades II, 148 c).

[d] With Epicurus. " Sinking away " implies retiring into seclusion from surrounding dangers, and like " communion " was probably suggested by mystic rites.

[e] Statues of gods were supplicated in this way, as by the chorus of maidens in the Seven Against Thebes of Aeschylus : cf. 95-96, 185, 211-212, 258.

[f] Frag. 141 (ed. Usener).

> But I for my part summon you to sustained pleasures [a] and not to virtues, which fill us with hopes of future recompense that are fond and foolish and fatal to our peace of spirit.

These are his words ; and yet Metrodorus [b] for one can use the following language in a summons to Timarchus :

> Let us crown an auspicious beginning with an auspicious end, [c] all but sinking away by a communion of experience [d] and exchanging this earthbound life for the holy mysteries of Epicurus, which are in very truth the revelation of a god.

Colotes himself, for another, while hearing a lecture of Epicurus on natural philosophy, suddenly cast himself down before him and embraced his knees [e] ; and this is what Epicurus [f] himself writes about it in a tone of solemn pride : ' You, as one revering my remarks on that occasion, were seized with a desire, not accounted for on scientific lines,[g] to embrace me by clasping my knees and lay hold of me to the whole extent of the contact that is customarily established in revering and supplicating certain personages.[h] You therefore caused me,' he says, ' to consecrate you in my turn and demonstrate my reverence.' [i] My word ! We can pardon those who say that they

---

[g] R. Westman (*Plutarch gegen Kolotes*, pp. 27-31) interprets " not accounted for by my lecture on natural philosophy." In any case such an isolated gesture of supplication is wrong, as it proceeds from a belief that the gods can be moved, and that Epicurus is a god of popular belief.

[h] The gods and deified monarchs in particular.

[i] The " consecration " (actually bestowed in the letter) takes the form of pointing out the only way for a man to be divine : to enjoy the felicity of a god. Colotes had merited such " consecration " by his reverence for the philosophical truth, not by his mistaken gesture. Though " imperishable " he still " goes about " very much a mortal.

(1117) τὸ τῆς ὄψεως ἐκείνης εἰκόνα γεγραμμένην θεάσασθαι, τοῦ μὲν προσπίπτοντος εἰς γόνατα καὶ περιπλεκομένου, τοῦ δὲ ἀντιλιτανεύοντος καὶ ἀντιπροσκυνοῦντος. οὐ μέντοι τὸ θεράπευμα τοῦτο, καίπερ εὖ τῷ Κωλώτῃ συντεθέν, ἔσχε καρπὸν ἄξιον· οὐ γὰρ ἀνηγορεύθη σοφὸς ἀλλὰ μόνον, ' ἄφθαρτός μοι περιπάτει,' φησί, ' καὶ ἡμᾶς ἀφθάρτους διανοοῦ.' (18.) τοιαῦτα μέντοι ῥήματα καὶ κινήματα καὶ πάθη συνειδότες αὐτοῖς[1] ἑτέρους φορτικοὺς ἀποκαλοῦσι.

D   " Καὶ δῆτα καὶ προθεὶς ὁ Κωλώτης τὰ σοφὰ ταῦτα καὶ καλὰ περὶ τῶν αἰσθήσεων, ὅτι ' σιτία προσαγόμεθα καὶ οὐ χόρτον, καὶ τοὺς ποταμούς, ὅταν ὦσι μεγάλοι, πλοίοις διαπερῶμεν, ὅταν δὲ εὐδιάβατοι γένωνται, τοῖς ποσίν,' ἐπιπεφώνηκεν· ' ἀλλὰ γὰρ ἀλαζόνας ἐπετήδευσας λόγους, ὦ Σώκρατες· καὶ ἕτερα μὲν διελέγου τοῖς ἐντυγχάνουσιν, ἕτερα δὲ ἔπραττες.' πῶς γὰρ οὐκ ἀλαζόνες οἱ Σωκράτους λόγοι μηδὲν αὐτοῦ[2] εἰδέναι φάσκοντος ἀλλὰ μανθάνειν ἀεὶ καὶ ζητεῖν τὸ ἀληθές; εἰ δὲ τοιαύταις, ὦ Κωλῶτα, Σωκράτους φωναῖς περιέπεσες οἵας Ἐπίκουρος γράφει πρὸς Ἰδομενέα·
E   ' πέμπε οὖν ἀπαρχὰς ἡμῖν εἰς τὴν τοῦ ἱεροῦ σώματος θεραπείαν ὑπέρ τε αὐτοῦ καὶ τέκνων· οὕτω γάρ

---

[1] αὐτοῖς B : αὐτοῖς E.
[2] αὐτοῦ EB : αὐτὸς nos ; αὐτὸν Post.

---

[a] Metrodorus was the only one besides himself that Epicurus proclaimed a " sage ": cf. Cicero, De Fin. ii. 3 (7) and Seneca, Ep. 18. 9.

[b] Cf. Epicurus' letter to his mother (Frag. 65. 29-40, ed. Arrighetti) : " . . . For these things that I gain are nothing small or of little force, things of a sort that make my state equal to a god's, and show me as a man who not even by his

would pay any price to see a painting of that scene, one kneeling at the feet of the other and embracing his knees while the other returns the supplication and worship. Yet that act of homage, though skilfully contrived by Colotes, bore no proper fruit : he was not proclaimed a sage.[a] Epicurus merely says : ' Go about as one imperishable in my eyes, and think of me as imperishable too.' [b] (18.) Yet with such language, postures, and emotions on their conscience they dub others cheap.

"Again Colotes, after laying down these profound and noble truths about the senses, that ' we eat food, not grass, and when rivers are high we cross by boat, but when they have become fordable, we cross them on foot,' follows up with this : ' The fact is, Socrates, that your arguments were charlatans ; what you said to people in your dialogues was one thing, but what you actually did was something else again.' How oould Socrates' conversations be anything but charlatanism when he said that he knew nothing himself but was always learning and searching for the truth ! But if, Colotes, you had met with expressions of Socrates' such as Epicurus [c] pens in a letter to Idomeneus

> So send us for the care of our sacred [d] person an offering of first-fruits on behalf of yourself and your children— for thus I am moved to speak,

mortality falls short of the imperishable and blessed nature. For while I am alive, I know joy to the same degree as the gods." What is imperishable has no disease or trouble (cf. Lucretius, iii. 484-486, Colotes, 1113 D, supra)—and we may infer, no pain of body or mind— ; and whether the time is infinite or finite the pleasure is the same (Cardinal Tenet xix).

[c] Frag. 130 (ed. Usener).

[d] For Idomeneus see on 1127 D, infra. As we may infer from the term " first-fruits," used for example of the yearly offerings sent by many cities to Eleusis, he contributed

251

(1117) μοι λέγειν ἐπέρχεται,' τίσιν ἂν ῥήμασιν ἀγροικοτέ-
ροις ἐχρήσω; καὶ μὴν ὅτι Σωκράτης ἄλλα μὲν
ἔλεγεν ἄλλα δὲ ἔπραττε, θαυμαστῶς μαρτυρεῖ σοι
τὰ ἐπὶ Δηλίῳ, τὰ ἐν Ποτιδαίᾳ, τὰ ἐπὶ τῶν τριά-
κοντα, τὰ πρὸς Ἀρχέλαον, τὰ πρὸς τὸν δῆμον, ἡ
πενία, ὁ θάνατος· οὐ γὰρ ἄξια ταῦτα τῶν Σωκρα-
τικῶν λόγων. ἐκεῖνος ἦν, ὦ μακάριε, κατὰ Σωκράτους ἔλεγχος ἕτερα μὲν[1] λέγοντος ἕτερα δὲ
πράττοντος, εἰ τὸ ἡδέως ζῆν τέλος ἐκθέμενος οὕτως ἐβίωσε. (19.) ταῦτα μὲν οὖν πρὸς τὰς βλασφημίας.

F   " Ὅτι δὲ οἷς ἐγκαλεῖ περὶ τῶν ἐναργῶν[2] ἔνοχος
αὐτός ἐστιν οὐ συνεῖδεν.[3] ἓν γάρ ἐστι τῶν Ἐπικούρου δογμάτων τὸ μηδὲν ἀμεταπείστως πεπεῖσ-
θαι μηδένα πλὴν τὸν σοφόν. ἐπεὶ τοίνυν ὁ Κωλώτης οὐκ ἦν σοφὸς οὐδὲ μετὰ τὰς σεβάσεις ἐκείνας,
ἐρωτάσθω πρῶτος[4] ἐκεῖνα τὰ ἐρωτήματα, πῶς σιτία
προσάγεται καὶ οὐ χόρτον ἐπιτήδειος ὤν, καὶ τὸ
ἱμάτιον τῷ σώματι καὶ οὐ τῷ κίονι περιτίθησι,
μήτε ἱμάτιον εἶναι τὸ ἱμάτιον μήτε σιτίον τὸ σιτίον
1118 ἀμεταπείστως πεπεισμένος. εἰ δὲ καὶ ταῦτα πράτ-
τει καὶ τοὺς ποταμούς, ὅταν ὦσι μεγάλοι, ποσὶν
οὐ διέρχεται, καὶ τοὺς ὄφεις φεύγει καὶ τοὺς λύ-
κους, μηδὲν εἶναι τούτων οἷον φαίνεται πεπεισμένος

---

[1] μὲν B : E omits.   [2] ἐναργῶν E : ἐναγῶν B.
[3] συνεῖδεν E : συνοῖδεν B.
[4] ἐρωτάσθω πρῶτος nos : ἐρωτάτω πρῶτον EB (Bern. adds
ἑαυτὸν).

---

regularly to the support of Epicurus. Since first fruits were
offered to a god, and the support was for Epicurus' bodily
needs, we have the expression " sacred person."
   [a] Cf. Life of Alcibiades, chap. vii. 6 (195 A) and Plato,
Symposium, 220 E 7—221 C 1.

to what more unmannerly terms could you have resorted ? Indeed your charge that Socrates said one thing and did another is most wonderfully borne out by what he did at Delium,[a] at Potidaea,[b] under the Thirty,[c] by his bearing toward Archelaüs [d] and before the assembly at Athens,[e] and by his poverty and death. For nothing in all this could ever match his talk. The only thing that could really, my blissful innocent, have damned Socrates for belying his precepts by his practice, is this : if he had set up pleasure as the supreme good and then lived as he did. (19.) So much in reply to the abuse.

" Colotes has not seen that he is himself liable to his charge of distrusting the plain evidence of the senses. For it is one of Epicurus' tenets [f] that none but the sage is unalterably convinced of anything. Now since Colotes was no sage, not even after that demonstration of reverence, let him be the first to whom these questions of his are put : How comes it that he eats food and does not eat grass (well suited as he is to such provender) and wraps his cloak about himself and not around the pillar, though he is not unalterably convinced that either the cloak is a cloak or that the food is food ? But if he not only does all this, but also does not cross rivers on foot when they are high and keeps out of the way of snakes and wolves, not from an unalterable conviction that any of these things is such as it appears, but

[b] Cf. Life of Alcibiades, chap. vii. 4-5 (194 E) and Plato, Symposium 220 D 5-E 7.

[c] Cf. Plato, Apology, 32 c 3-D 8.

[d] Cf. Frag. xviii. 15 (vol. vii, p. 117. 14-19, ed. Bern.).

[e] Cf. Plato, Apology, 32 A 9-c 3.

[f] Frag. 222 (ed. Usener). The Academics used the same argument against the Stoics : cf. Cicero, Acad. Pr. ii. 47 (145).

(1118) ἀμεταπείστως ἀλλὰ πράττων ἔκαστα κατὰ τὸ φαινόμενον, οὐδὲ Σωκράτει δήπουθεν ἐμποδὼν ἦν ἡ
περὶ τῶν αἰσθήσεων δόξα τοῦ χρῆσθαι τοῖς φαινομένοις ὁμοίως. οὐ γὰρ Κωλώτῃ μὲν ὁ ἄρτος ἄρτος
ἐφαίνετο καὶ χόρτος ὁ χόρτος ὅτι τοὺς ' διοπετεῖς '
ἀνεγνώκει Κανόνας, ὁ δὲ Σωκράτης ὑπὸ ἀλαζονείας
ἄρτου μὲν ὡς χόρτου, χόρτου δὲ ὡς ἄρτου, φαντα-
B σίαν ἐλάμβανε. δόγμασι γὰρ ἡμῶν καὶ λόγοις
οὗτοι χρῶνται βελτίοσιν οἱ σοφοί, τὸ δ' αἰσθάνεσθαι
καὶ τυποῦσθαι πρὸς τὰ φαινόμενα κοινόν ἐστι πάθος
ἀλόγοις περαινόμενον αἰτίαις. ὁ δὲ τὰς αἰσθήσεις
λόγος ἐπαγόμενος ὡς οὐκ ἀκριβεῖς οὐδὲ ἀσφαλεῖς
πρὸς πίστιν οὔσας οὐκ ἀναιρεῖ τὸ φαίνεσθαι τῶν
πραγμάτων ἡμῖν ἔκαστον, ἀλλὰ χρωμένοις κατὰ
τὸ φαινόμενον ἐπὶ τὰς πράξεις ταῖς αἰσθήσεσι τὸ
πιστεύειν ὡς ἀληθέσι πάντῃ καὶ ἀδιαπτώτοις οὐ
δίδωσιν αὐταῖς· τὸ γὰρ ἀναγκαῖον ἀρκεῖ καὶ χρειῶ-
δες ἀπ' αὐτῶν, ὅτι βέλτιον ἔτερον οὐκ ἔστιν· ἦν δὲ
ποθεῖ φιλόσοφος ψυχὴ λαβεῖν ἐπιστήμην περὶ ἑκάστου καὶ γνῶσιν οὐκ ἔχουσι.

20. '' Περὶ μὲν οὖν τούτων καὶ πάλιν ὁ Κωλώτης
C εἰπεῖν παρέξει, ταῦτα πολλοῖς ἐγκεκληκώς. ἐν οἷς
δὲ κομιδῇ διαγελᾷ καὶ φλαυρίζει τὸν Σωκράτην
ζητοῦντα τί ἄνθρωπός ἐστι καὶ νεανιευόμενον, ὡς
φησιν, ὅτι μηδὲ αὐτὸς αὐτὸν[1] εἰδείη, δῆλος μέν
ἐστιν αὐτὸς οὐδέποτε πρὸς τούτῳ γενόμενος. ὁ δὲ

---

[1] αὐτὸν added by Pohlenz.

a See Usener, Epicurea, p. 104. 25-26, 27-28.
b Cf. Cicero, Acad. Pr, ii. 32 (103).
c Cf. Plato, Phaedo 64 e 1, 67 a 4.

in each instance guided by the appearance, then surely Socrates too was not precluded by his views about the senses from dealing with appearances in the same way. For reading the heaven-sent [a] *Canons* did not make bread appear bread to Colotes and grass appear grass, whereas Socrates' charlatanism gave bread to him the appearance of grass and grass the appearance of bread. For it is only in doctrine and argument that these sages have the advantage over the rest of us ; to perceive with the senses and to receive impressions when confronted with appearances happens to everyone, since it is the work of causes that have nothing to do with reasoning. The inductive argument by which we conclude that the senses are not accurate or trustworthy does not deny that an object presents to us a certain appearance, but forbids us, though we continue to make use of the senses and take the appearance as our guide in what we do, to trust them as entirely and infallibly true.[b] For we ask no more of them than utilitarian service in the unavoidable essentials,[c] since there is nothing better available ; but they do not provide the perfect knowledge and understanding of a thing that the philosophical soul longs to acquire.[d]

20. " Now of these matters Colotes will give us occasion to speak again,[e] as he has brought these charges against many. We pass to the downright derision and scurrility of his attack on Socrates for seeking to discover what man is and ' flaunting ' (as Colotes puts it) the boast that he did not even know himself.[f] In all this we can see that Colotes for his part had never given himself to the problem. Whereas

---

[d] *Cf.* Plato, *Phaedo*, 65 A 10–c 3, c 11–d 2, E 4, 66 B 6-7, E 2-3, 68 A 1-2.   [e] 1120 F—1121 E, 1123 B—1124 B, *infra.*
   [f] Plato, *Phaedrus*, 230 A.

(1118) Ἡράκλειτος ὡς μέγα τι καὶ σεμνὸν διαπεπρα-
γμένος, ' ἐδιζησάμην,' φησίν, ' ἐμεωυτόν,'[1] καὶ τῶν
ἐν Δελφοῖς γραμμάτων θειότατον ἐδόκει τὸ ' γνῶθι
σαυτόν,' ὃ δὴ καὶ Σωκράτει τῆς[2] ἀπορίας καὶ ζητή-
σεως ταύτης ἀρχὴν ἐνέδωκεν, ὡς Ἀριστοτέλης ἐν
τοῖς Πλατωνικοῖς εἴρηκε· Κωλώτῃ δὲ γελοῖον δο-
D κεῖ. τί οὖν οὐ καταγελᾷ καὶ τοῦ καθηγεμόνος
τοῦτο αὐτὸ πράττοντος ὁσάκις γράφοι καὶ διαλέ-
γοιτο περὶ οὐσίας ψυχῆς καὶ τοῦ ἀθρόου τῆς κατ-
αρχῆς;[3] εἰ γὰρ τὸ ἐξ ἀμφοῖν, ὡς ἀξιοῦσιν αὐτοί,
σώματος τοιοῦδε καὶ ψυχῆς, ἄνθρωπός ἐστιν, ὁ
ζητῶν ψυχῆς φύσιν ἀνθρώπου ζητεῖ φύσιν ἐκ τῆς
κυριωτέρας ἀρχῆς. ὅτι δὲ αὕτη λόγῳ δυσθεώρητος
αἰσθήσει δὲ ἄληπτός ἐστι, μὴ παρὰ Σωκράτους,
σοφιστοῦ καὶ ἀλαζόνος ἀνδρός, ἀλλὰ παρὰ τῶν
σοφῶν τούτων λάβωμεν, οἳ μέχρι τῶν περὶ σάρκα
τῆς ψυχῆς δυνάμεων, αἷς θερμότητα καὶ μαλακό-
τητα καὶ τόνον παρέχει τῷ σώματι, τὴν οὐσίαν
E συμπηγνύντες αὐτῆς[4] ἔκ τινος θερμοῦ καὶ πνευ-
ματικοῦ καὶ ἀερώδους οὐκ ἐξικνοῦνται πρὸς τὸ
κυριώτατον ἀλλὰ ἀπαγορεύουσι· τὸ γὰρ ᾧ κρίνει

---

[1] ἐμεωϋτόν B : ἐμὲ ὠϋτόν E.
[2] τῆς added by Pohlenz.
[3] καταρχῆς] προκαταρχῆς Crönert.   [4] αὐτῆς] αὐτοῖς E[ac].

---

[a] Diels and Kranz, *Die Frag. der Vorsokratiker*, Hera-
kleitos, B 101.
[b] *Cf.* Plato, *Apology*, 21 B 7-8, 22 A 4, 23 B 5, 29 C 7.
[c] Frag. 1 (ed. Rose) ; *On Philosophy*, Frag. 1 (ed. Ross).
[d] Frag. 314 (ed. Usener).
[e] The " aggregate " may be the body (so Westman, *op.
cit.* p. 231), body and soul, or the complex of four components
that constitutes the soul (*cf.* 1118 E, *infra*). " Initiation "
may refer to initiating the movement of the soul. The Epicurean Zeno of Sidon wrote a book Περὶ παρεγκλίσεως καὶ

Heracleitus [a] said as of some great and lofty achievement ' I searched myself out '; and ' Know Thyself ' was held to be the most godlike of the Delphic inscriptions, being moreover the command that set Socrates to wondering and inquiring so,[b] as Aristotle[c] has said in his Platonic writings. Colotes, however, finds the question absurd. Why then does he not deride his master [d] too, who did this very thing as often as he wrote or spoke about the constitution of the soul and the ' initiation of the aggregate '? [e] For if (as they themselves hold) the combination of the two parts, a body of a certain description and a soul, is man,[f] then one who seeks to discover the nature of soul is seeking to discover the nature of man, starting from the more important source. And that the soul is hard to apprehend by reason and cannot be discerned by sense let us not learn from Socrates, that sophist and charlatan,[g] but from these sages, who get as far as those powers of the soul that affect the flesh, by which it imparts warmth and softness and firmness to the body, when they manufacture its substance by combining their own varieties of heat, gas and air,[h] but quit before they reach the seat of power. For that whereby it judges, remembers, loves, and hates—in

τῆς τοῦ ἀθρόου προκαταρχῆς " On the Swerve and the Original Initiation of the Aggregate " (Crönert, op. cit. p. 23).

[f] Westman (op. cit. p. 158), points out that this is a reference to the definition (Epicurus, Frag. 310, ed. Usener) " man is such a conformation as this together with animateness " (ἄνθρωπός ἐστι τοιουτονὶ μόρφωμα μετ' ἐμψυχίας). The definition evidently corrects Democritus' " man is what we all know " (Frag. в 165, ed. Diels-Kranz).

[g] Cf. Arrian, Epicteti Diss. ii. 20. 23 (Usener, Epicurea, p. 246. 34).

[h] Cf. Lucretius, iii. 231-236 and R. Heinze, T. Lucretius Carus De Rerum Natura Buch III (Leipzig, 1926), pp. 42 f.

PLUTARCH'S MORALIA

(1118) καὶ μνημονεύει καὶ φιλεῖ καὶ μισεῖ, καὶ ὅλως τὸ
φρόνιμον καὶ λογιστικὸν ἔκ τινός φασιν¹ ' ἀκατ-
ονομάστου ' ποιότητος ἐπιγίνεσθαι. καὶ ὅτι μὲν
αἰσχυνομένης ἐστὶν ἀγνοίας τουτὶ τὸ ' ἀκατονό-
μαστον ' ἐξομολόγησις οὐκ ἔχειν ὀνομάσαι φα-
σκόντων ὃ μὴ δύνανται καταλαβεῖν, ἴσμεν· ' ἐχέτω
δὲ συγγνώμην ' καὶ τοῦτο, ὡς λέγουσι. φαίνεται
γὰρ οὐ φαῦλον οὐδὲ ῥᾴδιον οὐδὲ τοῦ τυχόντος εἶναι
καταμαθεῖν ἀλλὰ ἐνδεδυκὸς ἀπόρῳ τινὶ τόπῳ καὶ
F δεινῶς ἀποκεκρυμμένον, ᾧ γε ὄνομα μηδὲν ἐν τοσούτοις πρὸς δήλωσιν οἰκεῖόν ἐστιν. οὐ Σωκράτης
οὖν ἀβέλτερος, ὅστις εἴη ζητῶν ἑαυτόν, ἀλλὰ πάντες
οἷς ἔπεισί τι τῶν ἄλλων πρὸ τούτου ζητεῖν ὅ τι²
τὴν γνῶσιν ἀναγκαίαν ἔχον οὕτως εὑρεθῆναι χαλε-
πόν ἐστιν. οὐ γὰρ ἂν ἐλπίσειεν ἑτέρου λαβεῖν ἐπιστήμην ὃν διαπέφευγε τῶν ἑαυτοῦ τὸ κυριώτατον
καταλαβεῖν.

21. ' Ἀλλὰ διδόντες αὐτῷ τὸ μηδὲν οὕτως ἄ-
χρηστον εἶναι μηδὲ φορτικὸν ὡς τὸ ζητεῖν αὐτόν,
1119 ἐρώμεθα τίς αὕτη τοῦ βίου σύγχυσίς ἐστιν ἢ πῶς
ἐν τῷ ζῆν οὐ δύναται διαμένειν ἀνὴρ ὅτε τύχοι πρὸς
ἑαυτὸν ἀναλογιζόμενος, ' φέρε τίς ὢν οὗτος ὃ³ ἐγὼ
τυγχάνω; πότερον ὡς κρᾶμα, τὸ μεμιγμένον ἔκ τε
τῆς ψυχῆς καὶ τοῦ σώματος, ἢ μᾶλλον ἡ ψυχὴ τῷ
σώματι χρωμένη, καθάπερ ἱππεὺς ἀνὴρ ἵππῳ χρώμενος, οὐ τὸ ἐξ ἵππου καὶ ἀνδρός; ἢ τῆς ψυχῆς τὸ

¹ φασιν Pohlenz : φησὶν EB.
² ὅ τι nos : ὅτι EB.
³ ὃ B : ὅ E.

ᵃ Frag. 314 (ed. Usener) ; cf. Lucretius, iii. 241-245.
ᵇ Cf. Diogenes Laert. x. 118 : the Epicureans hold that
258

short its thinking and reasoning faculty—is added to
these, they [a] say, from a quality ' that has no name.'
This talk of the thing ' that has no name ' is, we know,
a confession of embarrassed ignorance : what they
cannot make out they assert that they cannot name.
But let this too ' be excused,' [b] as they say. For the
thing is evidently nothing ordinary, nor its understanding easy and a matter for common capacities ;
it has burrowed into some impenetrable nook [c] and
lies most cunningly concealed, if indeed no word in
the whole range of language is suited to express it.
Then Socrates was not a fool in this endeavour to discover who he was ; the fools are all those who take it
into their heads to give priority to some other question over this, to which the answer must be found, and
yet it is so difficult to find. For no one can hope to
attain to the understanding of anything else when
knowledge of that, which of all he owns comes first
and foremost, has eluded his grasp.[d]

21. " Still, conceding to him that nothing is so
frivolous or cheap as the quest for knowledge of oneself, let us ask him how it can lead to the collapse
of this life of ours, or how a man cannot continue to
live who at some moment or other falls to reasoning
with himself ' Let me see now, what am I in fact, this
thing called I ? Am I like a blend, the combination of
this soul with this body ? Or am I rather my soul
using my body, as a horseman is a man using a horse,
not a compound of horse and man ? Or is each of us

the sage will not punish slaves, but will feel pity and excuse
a good one.   [e] *Cf.* Plato, *Sophist*, 239 c 5-7.
  [d] *Cf.* Plato, *Phaedrus*, 229 E 5—230 A 1: " I have not yet
been able, as the inscription at Delphi has it, to know myself.
Thus it appears to me absurd, when you are still ignorant of
this, to examine what belongs to others."

(1119) κυριώτατον, ᾧ φρονοῦμεν καὶ λογιζόμεθα καὶ πράττομεν, ἕκαστος ἡμῶν ἐστι, τὰ δὲ λοιπὰ καὶ ψυχῆς μόρια πάντα καὶ σώματος ὄργανα τῆς τούτου δυνάμεως; ἢ τὸ παράπαν οὐκ ἔστιν οὐσία ψυχῆς ἀλλ'
B αὐτὸ τὸ σῶμα κεκραμένον ἔσχηκε[1] τὴν τοῦ φρονεῖν καὶ ζῆν δύναμιν;' ἀλλὰ τούτοις μὲν οὐκ ἀναιρεῖ τὸν βίον ὁ Σωκράτης, ἃ δὴ πάντες οἱ φυσικοὶ ζητοῦσιν, ἐκεῖνα δὲ ἦν τὰ ἐν Φαίδρῳ δεινὰ καὶ ταρακτικὰ τῶν πραγμάτων, αὐτὸν[2] οἰομένου δεῖν ἀναθεωρεῖν ' εἴτε Τυφῶνός ἐστι θηρίον πολυπλοκώτερον καὶ μᾶλλον ἐπιτεθυμμένον[3] εἴτε θείας τινὸς καὶ ἀτύφου μοίρας φύσει μετέχον.' ἀλλὰ τούτοις γε τοῖς ἐπιλογισμοῖς οὐ τὸν βίον ἀνῄρει, τὴν δὲ ἐμβροντησίαν ἐκ τοῦ βίου καὶ τὸν τῦφον[4] ἐξήλαυνε καὶ τὰς ἐπαχθεῖς καὶ ὑπερόγκους κατοιήσεις[5] καὶ μεγαλαυχίας. ταῦτα
C γὰρ ὁ Τυφῶν ἐστιν, ὃν πολὺν ὑμῖν[6] ἐνεποίησεν[7] ὁ καθηγεμὼν καὶ θεοῖς πολεμῶν καὶ θείοις ἀνδράσι.

22. " Μετὰ δὲ Σωκράτην καὶ Πλάτωνα προσμάχεται Στίλπωνι· καὶ τὰ μὲν ἀληθινὰ δόγματα καὶ

---

[1] ἔσχηκε placed here in E : before δύναμιν in B.
[2] αὐτὸν E : αὐτὸν B.
[3] ἐπιτεθυμμένον Reiske (from *Phaedrus*, 230 A 4) : ἐπιτεθυμένον E ; ἐπιτεθειμένον B.
[4] τῦφον Dübner : τύφον EB.
[5] κατοιήσεις E : κατοικήσεις B.
[6] ὑμῖν EB^c (υ in an erasure in B).
[7] ἐνεποίησεν E : ἐποίησεν B.

---

[a] *Cf.* Aristotle, *Protrepticus*, Frag. 6 (ed. Ross) ; *Eth. Nic.* ix. 4 (1166 a 22-23) ; *Metaphysics*, H 3 (1043 a 34-37, b 2-4, 10-13). The view that a man is his soul is found in the *Phaedo*, 115 c-E; *cf.* also L. Alfonsi, " L' Assioco pseudoplatonico," in *Studi Mondolfo* (Bari, 1950), p. 266.
[b] *Cf.* Plato, *Phaedo*, 85 E—86 D ; Dicaearchus, Frag. 7-12 (ed. Wehrli) ; Galen, *De naturalibus facultatibus*, i. 12 (vol. ii, pp. 27-28, ed. Kuehn, p. 120. 22-25, ed. Helmreich) ; and

not the soul, but the chief part of the soul, by which
we think and reason and act, all the other parts of
soul as well as of body being mere instruments of its
power ? [a] Or is there no substance of soul at all, and
has the body unaided acquired by its composition the
power of thought and life ? ' [b] But it is not with these
questions (you say), to which all students of natural
philosophy seek an answer, that Socrates abolishes
the possibility of living ; it is the enormities in the
Phaedrus [c] that make a chaos of our lives, where he
believes that he ought to consider himself to see
' whether he is a beast more intricate and puffed
up than Typhon, or whether by nature he enjoys a
lot that is divine and free from the fumes of infatua-
tion.' [d] But he did not surely by these reflexions
make life impossible ; he cleared it rather of the
crack-brained vapourings of folly and delusion—of
the ponderous load of silly conceits and noisy boast-
ing. For this is what Typhon signifies, and your
master [e] has implanted plenty of him in you with his
war against the gods and godlike men.

22. " After Socrates and Plato he assails Stilpon,
and without setting down the man's real teaching

De moribus animae chap. iv (vol. iv, p. 782, ed. Kuehn, p. 44,
ed. von Mueller); Heracleides, Frag. 72 (ed. Wehrli).

[c] 230 A.

[d] Typhon (the " smoulderer ") is described (under the
name Typhoeus) by Hesiod in the *Theogony*, 820-861) as a
son of Gaia with a hundred serpent's heads who was smitten
by Zeus' thunderbolt and when he fell filled the valleys of
Aetna with the flame. Plutarch plays on his dazed stupor
when smitten, on his loud and varied voices, and on his (and
the mountain's) weight and size : Plato on his half-serpentine
shape (" intricate " renders *polyplokōteron*, literally " with
more folds "); both play on his vanity (in attacking the gods)
and on his vapourings (*typhos* is both smoke and vanity).

[e] Frag. 558 (ed. Usener).

PLUTARCH'S MORALIA

(1119) τοὺς λόγους τοῦ ἀνδρός, οἷς ἑαυτόν τε κατεκόσμει
καὶ πατρίδα καὶ φίλους καὶ τῶν βασιλέων τοὺς περὶ
αὐτὸν σπουδάσαντας, οὐ[1] γέγραφεν, οὐδὲ ὅσον ἦν
φρόνημα τῇ ψυχῇ μετὰ πρᾳότητος καὶ μετριοπα-
θείας, ὧν δὲ παίζων καὶ χρώμενος γέλωτι[2] πρὸς
τοὺς σοφιστὰς λογαρίων προύβαλλεν[3] αὐτοῖς, ἑνὸς
μνησθεὶς καὶ πρὸς τοῦτο μηδὲν εἰπὼν[4] μηδὲ λύσας
τὴν πιθανότητα τραγῳδίαν ἐπάγει τῷ Στίλπωνι καὶ
D τὸν βίον ἀναιρεῖσθαί φησιν ὑπ' αὐτοῦ λέγοντος
ἕτερον ἑτέρου μὴ[5] κατηγορεῖσθαι. ' πῶς γὰρ βιω-
σόμεθα μὴ λέγοντες ἄνθρωπον ἀγαθὸν μηδὲ ἄνθρωπον στρατηγὸν ἀλλὰ ἄνθρωπον ἄνθρωπον καὶ χωρὶς
ἀγαθὸν ἀγαθὸν καὶ στρατηγὸν στρατηγόν, μηδὲ
ἱππεῖς μυρίους μηδὲ πόλιν ἐχυράν, ἀλλὰ ἱππεῖς
ἱππεῖς καὶ μυρίους μυρίους καὶ τὰ ἄλλα[6] ὁμοίως; '
τίς δὲ διὰ ταῦτα χεῖρον ἐβίωσεν ἀνθρώπων; τίς
δὲ τὸν λόγον ἀκούσας οὐ συνῆκεν ὅτι παίζοντός
ἐστιν εὐμούσως ἢ γύμνασμα τοῦτο προβάλλοντος
ἑτέροις διαλεκτικόν; οὐκ ἄνθρωπον, ὦ Κωλῶτα,
μὴ λέγειν ἀγαθὸν οὐδὲ ἱππεῖς μυρίους δεινόν ἐστιν,
E ἀλλὰ τὸν θεὸν μὴ λέγειν θεὸν μηδὲ νομίζειν, ὃ
πράττετε ὑμεῖς, μήτε Δία Γενέθλιον μήτε Δήμητρα[7]
Θεσμοφόρον εἶναι μήτε Ποσειδῶνα Φυτάλμιον[8]
ὁμολογεῖν ἐθέλοντες. οὗτος ὁ χωρισμὸς τῶν ὀνομάτων πονηρός ἐστι καὶ τὸν βίον ἐμπίπλησιν ὀλι-

---

[1] οὐ Stegmann : οὔτε EB.   [2] γέλωτι E : B omits it here.
[3] προύβαλλεν E : προύβαλε γέλωτι B.
[4] πρὸς τοῦτο μηδὲν εἰπὼν E : μηδὲν εἰπὼν πρὸς τοῦτο B.
[5] μὴ Turnebus : ἄλλη EB.   [6] τὰ ἄλλα E : τἆλλα B.
[7] Δήμητρα Usener : δήμητραν EB.
[8] φυτάλμιον E : φοιτάλμιον B.

---

[a] Demetrius Poliorcetes and Ptolemy Soter (Diogenes
Laert. ii. 115).

262

and thought, which brought distinction to himself, his country, his friends, and the kings [a] who valued him, or his high mettle, joined with gentleness and equanimity,[b] Colotes mentions one of the little puzzles that Stilpon used to propound to the sophists to tease and have his sport with them, and without meeting the challenge or detecting and exposing the fallacy assails Stilpon in the highflown language of the stage, saying that he robs us of our life by the assertion that one thing cannot be predicated of another. ' For how shall we live if we cannot call a man good or a man a general, but can only on one side call a man a man, and on the other good good and general general, or if we cannot speak of ten thousand horse or a strong city, but only say that horsemen are horsemen and ten thousand ten thousand, and so with the rest ? ' What man's life was ever the worse for Stilpon's remark ? Who that heard it did not recognize it as a pretty piece of foolery or a dialectical exercise propounded for others to solve ? What is grave, Colotes, is not to refuse to call a man good or horsemen ten thousand, it is to refuse to call or believe a god a god, and this is what you and your company do, who will not admit [c] that Zeus is 'Author of the Race,' [d] Demeter ' Giver of Laws,' [e] or Poseidon ' Guardian of Growth.' [f] It is this disjoining of one word from another that works harm and fills your

[b] See the apophthegms in *Mor.* 468 A and 475 C (*cf.* also 5 F) and the *Life of Demetrius*, chap. ix. 8-10 (893 A-B).

[c] The Epicureans held that the gods do not concern themselves with man ; Epicurus (*Letter to Herodotus*, 77) warns against using names of the gods that are inconsistent with their blessed state.

[d] *Cf. Mor.* 766 C.

[e] *Cf. Mor.* 994 A.

[f] *Cf. Mor.* 158 E, 451 C, 675 F, and 730 D.

(1119) γωρίας ἀθέου καὶ θρασύτητος ὅταν τὰς συνεζευ-
γμένας τοῖς θεοῖς προσηγορίας ἀποσπῶντες συναναιρῆτε[1] θυσίας, μυστήρια, πομπάς, ἑορτάς. τίνι γὰρ
προηρόσια[2] θύσομεν, τίνι σωτήρια; πῶς δὲ φωσ-
φόρεια, βακχεῖα, προτέλεια γάμων ἄξομεν, μὴ
τελείους[3] ἀπολιπόντες μηδὲ βακχεῖς καὶ φωσφόρους
F καὶ προηροσίους[4] καὶ σωτῆρας; ταῦτα γὰρ ἅπτεται
τῶν κυριωτάτων καὶ μεγίστων ἐν πράγμασιν ἔχοντα
τὴν ἀπάτην οὐ περὶ φωνάς τινας οὐδὲ λεκτῶν σύνταξιν οὐδὲ ὀνομάτων συνήθειαν· ὡς εἴ γε καὶ ταῦτα
τὸν βίον ἀνατρέπει, τίνες μᾶλλον ὑμῶν πλημμελοῦσι
περὶ τὴν διάλεκτον, οἳ τὸ τῶν λεκτῶν γένος, οὐσίαν
τῷ λόγῳ παρέχον,[5] ἄρδην ἀναιρεῖτε, τὰς φωνὰς καὶ
τὰ τυγχάνοντα μόνον ἀπολιπόντες, τὰ δὲ μεταξὺ
σημαινόμενα πράγματα, δι' ὧν γίνονται μαθήσεις,
1120 διδασκαλίαι, προλήψεις, νοήσεις, ὁρμαί, συγκατα-
θέσεις, τὸ παράπαν οὐδὲ εἶναι λέγοντες;

23. " Οὐ μὴν ἀλλὰ τὸ ἐπὶ[6] τοῦ Στίλπωνος τοιοῦ-

---

[1] συναναιρῆτε Usener : συναναιρεῖτε ΕΒ.
[2] προηρόσια Xylander, Reiske : προτέλεια ΕΒ.
[3] τελείους added by Reiske, who also suggests γαμηλίους.
[4] προηροσίους Reiske : προηρεσίους ΕΒ.
[5] παρέχον Usener : παρέχοντες ΕΒ.
[6] ἐπὶ Basle edition of 1542 : 'πὶ ΕΒ.

---

[a] The sacrifice was offered to Demeter and Persephonê to
ensure the growth of the crops : cf. L. Deubner, Attische
Feste (Berlin, 1932), pp. 68 f.
[b] For festivals of this name cf. A. Mommsen, Feste der
Stadt Athen (Leipzig, 1898), p. 408, note 5, and M. P.
Nilsson, Griechische Feste (Leipzig, 1906), pp. 34 f.
[c] Nothing is known of this festival : cf. M. P. Nilsson, op.
cit. p. 469.
[d] Cf. M. P. Nilsson, op. cit. pp. 306 f. ; L. Deubner, op.
cit. p. 149.
[e] A sacrifice preceding the marriage ceremony.

lives with a godless negligence and recklessness, when you tear away from the gods the appellations attached to them and by that single act annihilate all sacrifices, mysteries, processions and festivals. To whom shall we offer the Sacrifice Before the Ploughing,[a] the Sacrifice for Deliverance ?[b] How shall we hold the ceremonies of the Bearing of Light,[c] of the Revels,[d] and of the Prenuptial Rites,[e] if we leave ourselves no Lady of Nuptials,[f] no Reveller,[g] no Bearer of Light,[h] no Guardian of the Ploughing,[i] and no Deliverer ?[j] These views affect matters of the highest and gravest import, and the error in them involves reality, not a set of vocables or the conjunction of meanings[k] or the accepted usage of words ; indeed if mere linguistic confusion of this sort is ruinous to our lives, what school is more at fault in its views about language than yours,[l] who make a clean sweep of the whole category of meanings, which impart to discourse its substantial reality, and leave us with nothing but vocables and facts, when you say that the intermediate objects of discourse, the things signified, which are the means of learning, teaching, conception, understanding, appetition, and assent, do not exist at all ?

23. " Stilpon's point however is this : if we

[f] The word *teleios* (literally " fulfiller ") is added by Reiske. Hera had the epithet as presiding over marriages.

[g] An epithet or name of Dionysus.

[h] An epithet of Hecatê and Artemis.

[i] An epithet of Demeter (*cf. Mor.* 158 E).

[j] An epithet of Zeus (*cf. Mor.* 1049 A, 1076 B) and many other gods.

[k] *Cf.* 1116 B, *supra*. The Stoics held that meanings constitute a distinct kind of incorporeal entity between words and corporeal objects.

[l] Frag. 259 (ed. Usener).

(1120) τόν ἐστιν· εἰ περὶ ἀνθρώπου τὸ ἀγαθὸν ἢ[1] περὶ
ἵππου τὸ τρέχειν κατηγοροῦμεν, οὔ φησι ταὐτὸν
εἶναι τῷ[2] περὶ οὗ κατηγορεῖται τὸ κατηγορούμενον, ἀλλ᾽ ἕτερον[3] μὲν ἀνθρώπῳ τοῦ τί ἦν εἶναι τὸν
λόγον, ἕτερον δὲ τῷ ἀγαθῷ· καὶ πάλιν τὸ ἵππον
εἶναι τοῦ τρέχοντα εἶναι διαφέρειν.[4] ἑκατέρου γὰρ
ἀπαιτούμενοι τὸν λόγον οὐ τὸν αὐτὸν ἀποδίδομεν
ὑπὲρ ἀμφοῖν. ὅθεν ἁμαρτάνειν τοὺς ἕτερον ἑτέρου
κατηγοροῦντας ὡς ὂν ἀμφοῖν τὸ εἶναι ταὐτόν.[5] εἰ
μὲν γὰρ ταὐτόν ἐστι τῷ ἀνθρώπῳ τὸ ἀγαθὸν καὶ
τῷ ἵππῳ τὸ τρέχειν, πῶς καὶ σιτίου καὶ φαρμάκου
B τὸ ἀγαθὸν καὶ νὴ Δία πάλιν λέοντος καὶ κυνὸς τὸ
τρέχειν κατηγοροῦμεν; εἰ[6] δ᾽ ἕτερον, οὐκ ὀρθῶς
ἄνθρωπον ἀγαθὸν καὶ ἵππον τρέχειν λέγομεν. εἴπερ
οὖν[7] ἐν τούτοις ἐξέπαιξε[8] πικρῶς ὁ Στίλπων, τῶν
ἐν ὑποκειμένῳ καὶ καθ᾽ ὑποκειμένου λεγομένων μηδεμίαν ἀπολιπὼν συμπλοκὴν πρὸς τὸ ὑποκείμενον,
ἀλλὰ ἕκαστον αὐτῶν, εἰ μὴ κομιδῇ ταὐτὸν ᾧ συμβέβηκε λέγεται, μηδὲ ὡς συμβεβηκὸς οἰόμενος δεῖν
περὶ αὐτοῦ λέγεσθαι, φωναῖς τισι δυσκολαίνων καὶ
πρὸς τὴν συνήθειαν ἐνιστάμενος, οὐ τὸν βίον ἀναιρῶν οὐδὲ τὰ πράγματα δῆλός ἐστι.

---

[1] περὶ ἀνθρώπου τὸ ἀγαθὸν ἢ supplied by us.
[2] τῷ Turnebus : τὸ EB.
[3] After ἕτερον Madvig would add οὐδ᾽ εἰ περὶ ἀνθρώπου τὸ
ἀγαθὸν εἶναι, ἀλλ᾽ ἕτερον.
[4] εἶναι διαφέρειν EB[188] : διαφέρειν εἶναι B[t].
[5] ὡς ὂν ἀμφοῖν τὸ (ὡς ὂν τὸ τί ἦν Warmington) εἶναι ταὐτόν
our supplement of a blank of 26 letters in E, 30 in B.
[6] κατηγοροῦμεν; εἰ Wyttenbach (κατηγορούμενον; εἰ Reiske) :
κατηγορούμεν and a blank of 2 letters E ; κατηγοροῦμεν and a
blank of 1 letter B[ac] ; κατηγορούμενον B[c].
[7] οὖν E : B omits.
[8] ἐξέπαιξε nos : ἐξαιμάξει EB.

predicate good of man or running of a horse, the predicate (he maintains) is not the same as the subject, but the formula that defines the essence of man is one thing, while that which defines the essence of good is something else again ; and again to be a horse differs from to be running, for when asked for a definition we do not give the same formula for each. Therefore they err who predicate one thing of another, as if the essence of both were the same. For if good is the same as man, and running the same as horse, how comes it that we also predicate good of food and of medicine, or again (for that matter) running of a lion and of a dog ? But if they are different, we err when we say that a man is good and that a horse runs. If Stilpon then has here produced a biting piece of mockery, forbidding us to couple *a* things inherent in and predicated of a subject *b* with that subject, in the belief that none of them, unless completely identical with the thing of which it is an accident, should be expressed as an accident of it either, he is evidently making difficulties with certain vocables and raising objections against common usage,*c* but he is not annihilating our life or the realities of which we speak.

---

a For this sense of " coupling " (*symplokē*) *cf. Categories*, 2 (1 a 16-19) and Plato, *Sophist*, 262 c 6. " Running " and " horse " are examples taken from *Categories*, 2 (1 a 18, b 5).

b For the distinction *cf. Categories*, 2 (1 a 20–b 9). What inheres in a substance and is predicated of it is an accident : *cf.* Pseudo-Archytas, p. 28. 10 (ed. Nolle).

c Plutarch's solution is that Stilpon does not deny the connexion that exists between an accident and its substance, but objects to expressing it by means of " certain vocables," that is, the verb " is," which is properly restricted to the predication of essential attributes. *Cf.* Aristotle, *Physics*, i. 2 (185 b 25-32).

(1120) 24. " Γενόμενος δ' οὖν ὁ Κωλώτης ἀπὸ τῶν
C παλαιῶν τρέπεται πρὸς τοὺς καθ' ἑαυτὸν φιλοσό-
φους, οὐδενὸς τιθεὶς ὄνομα· καίτοι καλῶς εἶχε καὶ
τούτους ἐλέγχειν ἐπ' ὀνόματος ἢ μηδὲ τοὺς πα-
λαιούς. ὁ δὲ τὸν Σωκράτην καὶ τὸν Πλάτωνα καὶ
τὸν Παρμενίδην τοσαυτάκις θέμενος ὑπὸ τὸ γρα-
φεῖον δῆλός ἐστιν ἀποδειλιάσας πρὸς τοὺς ζῶντας,
οὐ μετριάσας ὑπ' αἰδοῦς, ἣν τοῖς κρείττοσιν οὐκ
ἔνειμε. βούλεται δὲ προτέρους μέν, ὡς ὑπονοῶ,
τοὺς Κυρηναϊκοὺς ἐλέγχειν, δευτέρους δὲ τοὺς περὶ
Ἀρκεσίλαον Ἀκαδημαϊκούς. οὗτοι γὰρ ἦσαν οἱ
περὶ πάντων ἐπέχοντες· ἐκεῖνοι δὲ τὰ πάθη καὶ τὰς
φαντασίας ἐν αὐτοῖς τιθέντες οὐκ ᾤοντο τὴν ἀπὸ
D τούτων πίστιν εἶναι διαρκῆ πρὸς τὰς ὑπὲρ τῶν
πραγμάτων καταβεβαιώσεις, ἀλλ' ὥσπερ ἐν πολιορ-
κίᾳ τῶν ἐκτὸς ἀποστάντες εἰς τὰ πάθη κατέκλεισαν
αὐτούς, τὸ 'φαίνεται' τιθέμενοι, τὸ δ' 'ἐστὶν' μὴ[1]
προσαποφαινόμενοι περὶ τῶν ἐκτός.

" Διὸ φησιν αὐτοὺς ὁ Κωλώτης μὴ δύνασθαι ζῆν
μηδὲ χρῆσθαι τοῖς πράγμασιν· εἶτα κωμῳδῶν,
' οὗτοι,' φησίν, ' ἄνθρωπον εἶναι καὶ ἵππον καὶ τοῖχον οὐ λέγουσιν, αὐτοὺς δὲ τοιχοῦσθαι καὶ ἱπποῦσθαι καὶ ἀνθρωποῦσθαι,' πρῶτον αὐτοῖς ὥσπερ οἱ
συκοφάνται κακούργως χρώμενος τοῖς ὀνόμασιν·
ἕπεται μὲν γὰρ ἀμέλει καὶ ταῦτα τοῖς ἀνδράσιν,
E ἔδει δὲ ὡς ἐκεῖνοι διδάσκουσι δηλοῦν τὸ γινόμενον.

---

[1] μὴ Dübner's supplement of a blank of two letters in E.;
there is no blank in B (μηκέτι Reiske).

[a] Frag. I в 69 (ed. Giannantoni) ; Frag. 218 (cd. Manne-
bach).

REPLY TO COLOTES, 1120

24. " At all events after finishing with the ancients
Colotes addresses himself to the philosophers of his
own time, mentioning no names, though the proper
course would have been to name these men too in
his refutation, or not to name the ancients either.
He who so often let drop from his pen the names of
Socrates, Plato, and Parmenides evidently lost heart
when he came to face the living ; he did not moderate
his tone because he was respectful, or he would have
shown the same respect to their betters. He intends,
I suspect, to refute the Cyrenaics first, and second
the Academy of Arcesilaüs. For this second school
were those who withheld judgement on everything ;
whereas the first,[a] placing all experiences and impressions within themselves, thought that evidence derived from them was insufficient warrant for certainty
about reality and withdrew as in a siege from the
world about them and shut themselves up in their
responses,—admitting that external objects ' appear,' but refusing to venture further and pronounce
the word ' are.'

" Therefore, says Colotes, they cannot live and
cannot cope with the world around them, and he
proceeds to add in derision : ' This set do not say
that a man or horse or wall is, but say that it is themselves who are " walled," " horsed," and " manned." '
In the first place, like a pettifogger, he is unfair in
the very terms he uses.[b] To be sure these consequences among the rest follow from the tenets of the
school ; yet he should have presented the results as the
school presents them in its teaching. For the terms

[b] Colotes uses such comic neologisms as τοιχοῦσθαι " turn
wall," ἱππποῦσθαι " turn horse," and ἀνθρωποῦσθαι " turn man,"
instead of adopting the Cyrenaic illustrations, " sweetened "
and the rest, as Plutarch does in the next sentence.

269

(1120) γλυκαίνεσθαι γὰρ λέγουσι καὶ πικραίνεσθαι καὶ
ψύχεσθαι καὶ θερμαίνεσθαι[1] καὶ φωτίζεσθαι καὶ
σκοτίζεσθαι, τῶν παθῶν τούτων ἑκάστου τὴν ἐνάργειαν[2] οἰκείαν ἐν αὑτῷ[3] καὶ ἀπερίσπαστον ἔχοντος·
εἰ δὲ γλυκὺ τὸ μέλι καὶ πικρὸς ὁ θαλλὸς καὶ ψυχρὰ
ἡ χάλαζα καὶ θερμὸς ὁ ἄκρατος καὶ φωτεινὸς ὁ
ἥλιος[4] καὶ σκοτεινὸς ὁ τῆς νυκτὸς ἀήρ, ὑπὸ πολλῶν
ἀντιμαρτυρεῖσθαι καὶ θηρίων καὶ σπερμάτων[5] καὶ
ἀνθρώπων, τῶν μὲν δυσχεραινόντων τὸ μέλι,[6] τῶν
δὲ προσιεμένων τὴν θαλλίαν καὶ ἀποκαομένων ὑπὸ
τῆς χαλάζης καὶ καταψυχομένων ὑπὸ οἴνου καὶ
F πρὸς[7] ἥλιον ἀμβλυωττόντων καὶ νύκτωρ βλεπόντων.
ὅθεν ἐμμένουσα τοῖς πάθεσιν ἡ δόξα διατηρεῖ τὸ
ἀναμάρτητον, ἐκβαίνουσα δὲ καὶ πολυπραγμονοῦσα
τῷ κρίνειν καὶ ἀποφαίνεσθαι περὶ τῶν ἐκτὸς αὑτήν
τε πολλάκις ταράσσει καὶ μάχεται πρὸς ἑτέρους
ἀπὸ τῶν αὐτῶν ἐναντία πάθη καὶ διαφόρους φαντασίας λαμβάνοντας.

25. " Ὁ δὲ Κωλώτης ἔοικε τὸ αὐτὸ πάσχειν
τοῖς νεωστὶ γράμματα μανθάνουσι τῶν παίδων, οἳ
τοὺς χαρακτῆρας ἐν τοῖς πυξίοις ἐθιζόμενοι λέγειν,
ὅταν ἔξω γεγραμμένους ἐν ἑτέροις ἴδωσιν, ἀμφι-
1121 γνοοῦσι καὶ ταράττονται. καὶ γὰρ οὗτος, οὓς ἐν

----

[1] καὶ ψύχεσθαι καὶ θερμαίνεσθαι added by Reiske.
[2] ἐνάργειαν Pohlenz : ἐνέργειαν EB.
[3] αὑτῷ Bᶜ : αὐτῷ EBᵃᶜ.
[4] καὶ φωτεινὸς ὁ ἥλιος added by Madvig.
[5] σπερμάτων nos : πραγμάτων EB.
[6] τὸ μέλι supplied by Xylander to fill a blank of 6 letters
in E, 9 in B.
[7] πρὸς E : τὸν B.

they use are ' sweetened,' ' turned bitter,' ' chilled,'
' heated,' ' illumined,' and ' darkened,' each of these
experiences possessing within itself, intrinsic and un-
challenged, the manifest character that guarantees
its truth ; whereas the view that honey is sweet, the
foliage of the olive bitter, hail cold, neat wine heating,
sunlight luminous, and night air dark, encounters
evidence to the contrary from many witnesses—
animals, grains, and men alike ; for to some honey
is disagreeable,[a] some will feed on olive leaves,[b] some
are scorched [c] by hail, some chilled by wine,[d] and
some that in sunlight are purblind see well at night.
Accordingly when opinion keeps within the bounds of
our responses it continues free from error ; but when
it strays beyond and meddles with judgements and
pronouncements about external matters, it is forever
getting embroiled with itself and falling into conflict
with others in whom the same matters give rise to
contrary experiences and dissimilar impressions.

25. " It would appear that Colotes is in the pre-
dicament of boys who have just begun to read : they
are accustomed to reciting the characters written on
their tablets, but are perplexed and at a loss when
they see characters outside the tablets and written
on other objects. So with him : the reasoning that

---

[a] As to the jaundiced, who find it bitter (Sextus, *Outlines of Pyrrhonism*, i. 211).

[b] As goats : *cf.* Sophocles, Frag. 502 (ed. Pearson, with the note) and Diogenes Laert. ix. 80 ; for sheep *cf.* Aristotle, *History of Animals*, viii. 10 (596 a 25) ; for calves, Theocritus, iv. 44-45.

[c] For grain scorched by cold *cf.* the Aristotelian *Problems*, xxiii. 34 (935 a 19, 24-25). Theophrastus restricts the word to the shrivelling of the leaves of trees by cold winds : *cf. Hist. Plant.* iv. 14. 11-12, *De Causis Plant.* ii. 1. 6, v. 12. 2-6.

[d] *Cf.* 1109 E—1110 B, *supra.*

(1121) τοῖς Ἐπικούρου γράμμασιν ἀσπάζεται καὶ ἀγαπᾷ
λόγους, οὐ συνίησιν οὐδὲ γινώσκει λεγομένους ὑφ'
ἑτέρων. οἱ¹ γὰρ εἰδώλου προσπίπτοντος ἡμῖν περι-
φεροῦς, ἑτέρου δὲ κεκλασμένου, τὴν μὲν αἴσθησιν
ἀληθῶς τυποῦσθαι λέγοντες, προσαποφαίνεσθαι δὲ
οὐκ ἐῶντες ὅτι στρογγύλος ὁ πύργος ἐστίν, ἡ δὲ
κώπη κέκλασται, τὰ πάθη τὰ αὐτῶν καὶ τὰ φαντά-
σματα βεβαιοῦσι, τὰ δὲ² ἐκτὸς οὕτως ἔχειν ὁμολογεῖν
οὐκ ἐθέλουσιν· ἀλλ' ὡς ἐκείνοις τὸ ἱπποῦσθαι καὶ
τὸ τοιχοῦσθαι λεκτέον, οὐχ ἵππον οὐδὲ τοῖχον,
B οὕτως ἄρα τὸ στρογγυλοῦσθαι καὶ τὸ σκαληνοῦσθαι
τὴν ὄψιν, οὐ σκαληνὸν οὐδὲ στρογγύλον ἀνάγκη
τούτοις τὴν κώπην καὶ³ τὸν πύργον λέγειν· τὸ γὰρ
εἴδωλον ὑφ' οὗ πέπονθεν ἡ ὄψις κεκλασμένον ἐστίν,
ἡ κώπη δὲ ἀφ' ἧς τὸ εἴδωλον οὐκ ἔστι κεκλασμένη.
διαφορὰν οὖν τοῦ πάθους πρὸς τὸ ὑποκείμενον ἐκτὸς
ἔχοντος, ἢ μένειν ἐπὶ τοῦ πάθους δεῖ τὴν πίστιν ἢ
τὸ εἶναι τῷ φαίνεσθαι προσαποφαινομένην ἐλέγχε-
σθαι. τὸ δὲ δὴ βοᾶν αὐτοὺς καὶ ἀγανακτεῖν ὑπὲρ
τῆς αἰσθήσεως οὐ λεγούσης⁴ τὸ ἐκτὸς εἶναι θερμόν,
C ἀλλὰ τὸ ἐν αὐτῇ πάθος γέγονε τοιοῦτον, ἆρ' οὐ

¹ οἱ E : εἰ B.   ² δὲ E : δ' B.
³ τούτοις τὴν κώπην καὶ added by Pohlenz (τὴν κώπην καὶ
Dübner ; τὴν κώπην is inserted after σκαληνὸν by Reiske).
⁴ οὐ λεγούσης nos : οὐ λέγουσι EB (ὡς οὐ λέγουσι Wyttenbach).

ᵃ Frag. 252 (ed. Usener).
ᵇ The Epicurean theory that vision is due to the impinge-
ment on the eye of films sent out by the visible object is set
forth in Epicurus' *Letter to Herodotus*, 46-48 and Lucretius,
iv. 29-352.
ᶜ For the Epicurean explanation of optical illusions see
Frag. 247 (ed. Usener) and Lucretius, iv. 353-468. The distant square tower seen as round and the straight oar seen as

he accepts with satisfaction when he finds it in the writings of Epicurus [a] he neither understands nor recognizes when it is used by others. For the school that asserts that when a round film [b] impinges on us, or in another case a bent one, the imprint is truly received by the sense, but refuses to allow us to go further and affirm that the tower is round or that the oar is bent,[c] maintains the truth of its experiences and sense impressions, but will not admit that external objects correspond ; and as surely as that other school must speak of ' being horsed ' and ' walled,' but not of a horse or wall, so this school of theirs is under the necessity of saying that the eye is rounded or be-angled, and not that the oar is bent or the tower round, for it is the film producing the effect in the eye that is bent, whereas the oar is not bent from which the film proceeded. Thus, since the effect produced on the senses differs from the external object, belief must stick to the effect or be exposed as false if it proceeds to add ' it is ' to ' it appears.' That vociferous and indignant protest of theirs in defence of sensation, that it does not assert the external object to be warm, the truth being merely that the effect produced in sensation has been of this kind—,[d] is it not the same as the statement [e] about

bent where it touches the water are stock examples : they appear as illustrations in Diogenes Laert. ix. 85 and Sextus, *Outlines of Pyrrhonism*, i. 118-119. *Cf.* also Lucretius, iv. 353-363, 438-442, 501 f. ; Cicero, *Acad. Pr.* ii. 7 (19), 25 (79) with Reid's note ; for the tower *cf.* also Euclid, *Optics*, Prop. 9.

[d] Plutarch is careful not to let the Epicurean sensation say anything : it is *alogos* (Sextus, *Against the Mathematicians*, vii. 210, viii. 9), that is, irrational, and unlike opinion, can make no statements, but only occur.

[e] Of the Cyrenaics : *cf.* 1120 E, *supra*.

(1121) ταὐτόν ἐστι τῷ λεγομένῳ περὶ τῆς γεύσεως ὅτι τὸ
ἐκτὸς οὗ φησιν εἶναι γλυκύ, πάθος δέ τι καὶ κίνημα
περὶ αὐτὴν γεγονέναι τοιοῦτον; ὁ δὲ λέγων ἀνθρω-
ποειδῆ φαντασίαν λαμβάνειν, εἰ δὲ ἄνθρωπός ἐστι
μὴ αἰσθάνεσθαι, πόθεν εἴληφε τὰς ἀφορμάς; οὐ
παρὰ τῶν λεγόντων καμπυλοειδῆ φαντασίαν λαμβάνειν, εἰ δὲ καμπύλον ἐστὶ μὴ προσαποφαίνεσθαι
τὴν ὄψιν μηδ' ὅτι στρογγύλον, ἀλλά τι φάντασμα
περὶ αὐτὴν καὶ τύπωμα στρογγυλοειδὲς γέγονε;
" ' Νὴ Δία,' φήσει τις· ' ἀλλ' ἐγὼ τῷ πύργῳ
προσελθὼν καὶ τῆς κώπης ἁψάμενος ἀποφανοῦμαι
τὴν μὲν εὐθεῖαν εἶναι, τὸν δὲ πολύγωνον, ἐκεῖνος δέ,
κἂν ἐγγὺς γένηται, τὸ δοκεῖν καὶ τὸ φαίνεσθαι,
πλέον δὲ οὐδὲν ὁμολογήσει.' ναὶ μὰ Δία σοῦ γε
D μᾶλλον, ὦ βέλτιστε, τὸ ἀκόλουθον ὁρῶν καὶ φυλάτ-
των, τὸ πᾶσαν εἶναι φαντασίαν ὁμοίως ἀξιόπιστον
ὑπὲρ ἑαυτῆς, ὑπὲρ ἄλλου δὲ μηδεμίαν ἀλλὰ ἐπίσης
ἔχειν. σοὶ δὲ οἴχεται τὸ πάσας ὑπάρχειν ἀληθεῖς,
ἄπιστον δὲ καὶ ψευδῆ μηδεμίαν, εἰ ταύταις μὲν οἴει
δεῖν προσαποφαίνεσθαι περὶ τῶν ἐκτός, ἐκείναις[1] δὲ
πλὴν αὐτοῦ[2] τοῦ πάσχειν πλέον οὐδὲν ἐπίστευες.
εἰ μὲν γὰρ ἐπίσης ἔχουσιν ἐγγύς τε[3] γενόμεναι καὶ
μακρὰν οὖσαι πρὸς πίστιν, ἢ πάσαις δίκαιόν ἐστιν
ἢ μηδὲ ταύταις ἔπεσθαι τὴν προσαποφαινομένην τὸ

---

[1] ἐκείναις Basle edition of 1542 : ἐκεῖνος EB.
[2] πλὴν αὐτοῦ Pohlenz' supplement of a blank of 10 letters
in E., 5 in B.
[3] τε added by Reiske.

---

[a] The Epicureans held that a judgement about a distant
view can be proved or refuted by a closer view : *cf.* Sextus,
274

taste : it does not assert that the external object is sweet—there has merely occurred in the taste an effect and movement of this kind ? A man says, ' I receive an impress of humanity, but I do not perceive whether a man is there.' Who put him in the way of such a notion ? Was it not the school who assert that they receive an impress of curvature, but that their sight does not go beyond to pronounce that the thing is curved or yet that it is round ; there has merely occurred in it an appearance and impress of rotundity ?

" ' Exactly,' someone [a] will say ; ' but for my part I shall go up to the tower and I shall feel the oar, and thereupon I shall pronounce the oar straight and the tower angular ; but this other fellow even at close quarters will grant only that he has this " view " and that there is this " appearance," but will grant nothing more.' Exactly, my good friend, since he is a better hand than you at noticing and holding to the consequences of his doctrine—that every sensation is equally trustworthy when it testifies in its own behalf, but none when it testifies in behalf of anything else, but all are on the same footing. And here is an end to your tenet that all sensations are true and none untrustworthy or false, if you think it proper for one set of them to proceed to make assertions about external objects, whereas you refused to trust the others in anything beyond the experience itself. For if they are on the same footing of trustworthiness whether they come close or are at a distance, it is only fair to confer on all the power of adding the judgement ' it is ' or else to deny it to the former as

Against the Mathematicians, vii. 211, 215-216 and Diogenes Laert. x. 34.

(1121) εἶναι κρίσιν· εἰ δὲ γίνεται διαφορὰ τοῦ πάθους
ἀποστᾶσι καὶ προσελθοῦσι,[1] ψεῦδός ἐστι τὸ μήτε
E φαντασίαν μήτε αἴσθησιν ἑτέρας[2] ἑτέραν ἐναργεστέ-
ραν ὑπάρχειν, καθάπερ ἃς λέγουσιν ἐπιμαρτυρήσεις
καὶ ἀντιμαρτυρήσεις οὐθέν εἰσι πρὸς τὴν αἴσθησιν
ἀλλὰ πρὸς τὴν δόξαν· ὥστε εἰ ταύταις[3] ἑπομένους
ἀποφαίνεσθαι περὶ τῶν ἐκτὸς κελεύουσι, τῆς δόξης
κρίμα τὸ εἶναι, τῆς δ' αἰσθήσεως πάθος τὸ φαινόμενον ποιοῦντες, ἀπὸ τοῦ πάντως ἀληθοῦς τὴν κρίσιν ἐπὶ τὸ διαπῖπτον πολλάκις μεταφέρουσιν. (26.)
ἀλλὰ ταῦτα μὲν ὅσης ἐστὶ μεστὰ ταραχῆς καὶ μάχης
πρὸς ἑαυτά, τί δεῖ λέγειν ἐν τῷ παρόντι;

" Τοῦ δὲ Ἀρκεσιλάου τὸν Ἐπίκουρον οὐ μετρίως
ἔοικεν ἡ δόξα παραλυπεῖν[4] ἐν τοῖς τότε χρόνοις μά-
F λιστα τῶν φιλοσόφων ἀγαπηθέντος. μηθὲν γὰρ
αὐτὸν ἴδιον λέγοντά φησιν ὑπόληψιν ἐμποιεῖν καὶ
δόξαν ἀνθρώποις ἀγραμμάτοις, ἅτε δὴ πολυγράμ-
ματος αὐτὸς ὢν καὶ μεμουσωμένος. ὁ δὲ Ἀρκεσί-
λαος τοσοῦτον ἀπέδει τοῦ καινοτομίας τινὰ δόξαν
ἀγαπᾶν καὶ ὑποποιεῖσθαί τι[5] τῶν παλαιῶν ὥστε
ἐγκαλεῖν τοὺς τότε σοφιστὰς ὅτι προστρίβεται Σω-
1122 κράτει καὶ Πλάτωνι καὶ Παρμενίδῃ καὶ Ἡρα-

[1] προσελθοῦσι Ε : ελθοῦσι Β.
[2] ἑτέρας added after ἑτέραν by Meziriacus ; placed here
by Bern.
[3] εἰ ταύταις Reiske : ἐπ' αὐταῖς ΕΒ.
[4] παραλυπεῖν ΕΒ[2] : παραλιπεῖν Β[1].
[5] τι added by Reiske.

---

[a] Cf. Usener, Epicurea, p. 181, note on Frag. 247 ; Sextus,
Against the Mathematicians, vii. 212 ; Diogenes Laert. x. 34.
[b] Frag. 239 (ed. Usener ; cf. his note on p. 348. 14).
[c] Colotes.

well. Whereas if there is a difference in the effect produced on the observer when he stands at a distance and when he is close at hand, it is false to say that no impression and no sensation has in its stamp of reality a better warrant of truth than another. So too the ' testimony in confirmation ' and ' testimony in rebuttal ' [a] of which they speak has no bearing on the sensation but only on our opinion of it ; so if they tell us to be guided by this testimony when we make statements about external objects, they appoint opinion to pass the verdict ' it is ' and sense to undergo the experience ' it seems,' and thus transfer the decision from what is unfailingly true to what is often wrong. (26.) But what need to dwell at present on all the confusion and internal inconsistency of their position ?

" The reputation of Arcesilaüs, the best loved among the philosophers of the time, would appear to have annoyed Epicurus [b] mightily. Thus he [c] says that although this philosopher said nothing new,[d] he gave the unlettered the impression and belief that he did—our critic of course is widely read himself and writes with a beguiling charm. But so far was Arcesilaüs from cherishing any reputation for novelty or laying claim to any ancient doctrine as his own, that the sophists [e] of the day accused him of foisting his own views about the suspension of judgement and the impossibility of infallible apprehension on Socrates, Plato, Parmenides, and Heracleitus, who had precious

---

[d] Arcesilaüs brought the same charge against Zeno : Cicero, *Acad. Pr.* ii. 6 (16).

[e] No doubt the Theodoreans and Bion : *cf.* Bignone, *L'Aristotele perduto e la formazione filosofica di Epicuro* (Florence, 1936), vol. i. 46, note 1, who compares Numenius in Eusebius, *Praep. Evang.* xiv. 6. 6 (ii, p. 274. 7, ed. Mras).

(1122) κλείτω τὰ περὶ τῆς ἐποχῆς δόγματα καὶ τῆς
ἀκαταληψίας οὐδὲν δεομένοις, ἀλλὰ οἷον ἀναγωγὴν
καὶ βεβαίωσιν αὐτῶν εἰς ἄνδρας ἐνδόξους ποιού-
μενος. ὑπὲρ μὲν οὖν τούτου Κωλώτῃ χάρις καὶ
παντὶ τῷ τὸν Ἀκαδημαϊκὸν λόγον ἄνωθεν ἥκειν εἰς
Ἀρκεσίλαον ἀποφαίνοντι.

"Τὴν δὲ περὶ πάντων ἐποχὴν οὐδ' οἱ πολλὰ
πραγματευσάμενοι καὶ κατατείναντες εἰς τοῦτο
συγγράμματα καὶ λόγους ἐκίνησαν· ἀλλὰ ἐκ τῆς
Στοᾶς αὐτῇ[1] τελευτῶντες ὥσπερ Γοργόνα τὴν ἀ-
B πραξίαν ἐπάγοντες ἀπηγόρευσαν, ὡς πάντα πειρῶσι
καὶ στρέφουσιν αὐτοῖς οὐχ ὑπήκουσεν ἡ ὁρμὴ γενέσθαι συγκατάθεσις οὐδὲ τῆς ῥοπῆς ἀρχὴν ἐδέξατο
τὴν αἴσθησιν,[2] ἀλλ' ἐξ ἑαυτῆς ἀγωγὸς ἐπὶ τὰς
πράξεις ἐφάνη, μὴ δεομένη τοῦ προστίθεσθαι. νό-
μιμοι γὰρ οἱ πρὸς ἐκείνους ἀγῶνές εἰσι, καὶ

ὁπποῖόν[3] κ' εἴπῃσθα ἔπος, τοῖόν κ' ἐπακούσαις·

---

[1] αὐτῇ Pohlenz : αὐτῆς EB.
[2] αἴσθησιν EB : πρόσθεσιν Pohlenz.
[3] ὁπποῖόν Homer : ὁποῖον EB.

---

[a] Perhaps a reference to Antiochus of Ascalon : see
A.J.P., vol. lxxvii (1956), p. 74. Among the Stoics Chrysippus (cf. Diogenes Laert. vii. 198 " Reply to Arcesilaüs'
Little Method. One Book ") and Antipater devoted themselves to refuting the Academics : cf. Mor. 1057 A.

[b] A bugbear that turned men to stone. For the view that
Academic scepticism petrifies its adherents, making them
stone dead intellectually and stonily impervious to shame see
Arrian, Epicteti Diss. i. 5. 1-3 ; Cicero glances at the shame-
lessness in Ad Fam. ix. 8. 1.

[c] For this argument see Cicero, Acad. Pr. ii. 8 (25) and
Diogenes Laert. ix. 107. For the title of a lost work of Plutarch (No. 210 in the Catalogue of Lamprias) dealing with
the argument see Introduction, p. 187.

little need of such a gloss ; but Arcesilaüs wished to certify his views, as it were, by this appeal to highly respected names. So for his sake we are thankful to Colotes and everyone who shows that the Academic reasoning came to Arcesilaüs as an ancient tradition.

" The view that we should suspend judgement about everything was not shaken even by those [a] who undertook elaborate investigations and composed lengthy and argumentative treatises to refute it, but these men at last brought up against it from the Stoa like some Gorgon's head [b] the argument from total inaction [c] and gave up the battle.[d] For in spite of all their probing and wrenching, impulse refused to turn into assent [e] or accept sensation [f] as what tips the scale [g] ; it was seen instead to lead to action on its own initiative, requiring no approval from other quarters. For debates with those opponents are conducted according to rule, and

As you have spoken, so will you be answered [h] ;

[d] On the uselessness of arguing with the Academics see Cicero, *Acad. Pr.* ii. 10 (32) and Arrian, *Epicteti Diss.* i. 5. 2.

[e] The Stoics considered assent (*synkatathesis*) requisite to all action : *cf.* Cicero, *Acad. Pr.* ii. 8 (24-25), 12 (38-39), 19 (62). It is this " added " element that the Academics reject : *cf.* Cicero, *Acad. Post.* i. 11 (40) ; Sextus, *Outlines of Pyrrhonism*, i. 222.

[f] " Sensation " (*aisthêsis*) is used by the Stoics for apprehension (the word implies assent) through the senses : *cf.* Cicero, *Acad. Post.* i. 11 (41) and von Arnim, *Stoicorum Vet. Frag.* i, Frag. 62, ii, Frags. 71-75.

[g] For the image of the scales, which is here implied, see 1122 c, *infra*.

[h] Homer, *Il.* xx. 250. Diogenes Laertius (ix. 73) says that some cited the line to show that Homer was a Sceptic, and meant that to any statement is opposed another statement of equal force.

279

(1122) Κωλώτῃ δὲ οἶμαι τὰ περὶ ὁρμῆς καὶ συγκαταθέσεως ὄνῳ λύρας ἀκρόασιν εἶναι. λέγεται δὲ τοῖς συνεπομένοις καὶ ἀκούουσιν ὅτι τριῶν περὶ τὴν ψυχὴν κινημάτων ὄντων, φανταστικοῦ καὶ ὁρμητικοῦ καὶ συγκαταθετικοῦ, τὸ μὲν φανταστικὸν οὐδὲ βουλο-

C μένοις ἀνελεῖν ἐστιν, ἀλλὰ ἀνάγκη προεντυγχάνοντας τοῖς πράγμασι τυποῦσθαι καὶ πάσχειν ὑπ' αὐτῶν, τὸ δὲ ὁρμητικὸν ἐγειρόμενον ὑπὸ τοῦ φανταστικοῦ πρὸς τὰ οἰκεῖα πρακτικῶς κινεῖ[1] τὸν ἄνθρωπον, οἷον ῥοπῆς ἐν τῷ ἡγεμονικῷ καὶ νεύσεως γινομένης. οὐδὲ τοῦτο οὖν ἀναιροῦσιν οἱ περὶ πάντων ἐπέχοντες, ἀλλὰ χρῶνται τῇ ὁρμῇ φυσικῶς ἀγούσῃ πρὸς τὸ φαινόμενον οἰκεῖον. τί οὖν φεύγουσι μόνον; ᾧ μόνῳ ψεῦδος ἐμφύεται καὶ ἀπάτη, τὸ δοξάζειν καὶ προπίπτειν[2] τὴν συγκατάθεσιν, εἶξιν οὖσαν ὑπὸ ἀσθενείας τῷ φαινομένῳ, χρήσιμον δὲ οὐδὲν ἔχουσαν. ἡ γὰρ πρᾶξις δυοῖν δεῖται, φαν-

---

[1] κινεῖ Stephanus : κινεῖν EB.
[2] προπίπτειν Salmasius : προσπίπτειν EB.

---

[a] Cf. von Arnim, Stoicorum Vet. Frag. ii, Frag. 74, iii, Frags. 169 and 177 (Mor. 1057 A-B).

[b] A proverb : cf. Leutsch and Schneidewin, Paroem. Gr. i, p. 291 (Diogenianus, Cent. vii. 33 with the note), ii, p. 193 (Macarius, Cent. vi. 38) ; Proverbia Alexandrina (ed. Crusius), no. 33 ; Philodemus, Rhet. iv, col. 28ᵃ (vol. i, p. 209, ed. Sudhaus) ; Galen, De Animae Passionibus, i. 2 (vol. v. 64, ed. Kühn, p. 50. 8, ed. Marquardt).

[c] Cf. Sextus, Outlines of Pyrrhonism, i. 22 : ἐν πείσει γὰρ καὶ ἀβουλήτῳ πάθει κειμένη [sc. ἡ φαντασία] ἀζήτητός ἐστιν (" since it [the sense-impression] is a matter of being affected and of an experience with which our will will have nothing to do, it is not an object of inquiry ").

[d] For the Stoic metaphor of the tilting cf. Cicero, Acad.

whereas this talk of impulse and assent [a] gets from Colotes, I fancy, the response that a performance on the lyre gets from an ass.[b] For those who follow and have ears to hear the argument runs like this.

" ' The soul has three movements : sensation, impulse, and assent.

" ' Now the movement of sensation cannot be eliminated, even if we would ; instead, upon encountering an object, we necessarily receive an imprint and are affected.[c]

" ' Impulse, aroused by sensation, moves us in the shape of an action directed towards a suitable goal : a kind of casting weight has been put in the scale of our governing part, and a directed movement is set afoot.[d] So those who suspend judgement about everything do not eliminate this second movement either, but follow their impulse, which leads them instinctively to the good presented by sense.

" ' Then what is the only thing that they avoid ? That only in which falsity and error can arise, namely forming an opinion and thus interposing rashly [e] with our assent, although such assent is a yielding to appearance that is due to weakness [f] and is of no use whatever. For two things are requisite for action :

Pr. ii. 12 (38) and von Arnim, *Stoicorum Vet. Frag.* ii, Frag. 988 (p. 288. 25).

[e] The sceptics accused the dogmatists of rashness of assent: *cf.* Diogenes Laert. ix. 74 ; Sextus, *Against the Mathematicians,* ix. 49 ; Cicero, *Acad. Post.* i. 12 (45), *Acad. Pr.* ii. 20 (66) with Reid's note.

[f] Zeno called opinion (as opposed to knowledge) a weak and false assent or apprehension (von Arnim, *Stoicorum Vet. Frag.* i, Frags. 67-69). Plutarch finds that the weakness lies in assenting at all (*cf.* Chrysippus in *Mor.* 1057 b). " Opinion " to both is a belief held as certainly true that can nevertheless be false. It is not a belief that the holder recognizes may be wrong.

D τασίας τοῦ οἰκείου καὶ πρὸς τὸ φανὲν οἰκεῖον ὁρμῆς,
ὧν οὐδέτερον τῇ ἐποχῇ μάχεται. δόξης γάρ, οὐχ
ὁρμῆς οὐδὲ φαντασίας ὁ λόγος ἀφίστησιν. ὅταν
οὖν φανῇ τὸ[1] οἰκεῖον, οὐθὲν δεῖ πρὸς τὴν ἐπ' αὐτὸ
κίνησιν καὶ φορὰν δόξης, ἀλλὰ ἦλθεν εὐθὺς ἡ ὁρμή,
κίνησις οὖσα καὶ φορὰ τῆς ψυχῆς.

27. " Καὶ μὴν αὐτῶν γε τούτων[2] ὡς[3] ' αἴσθησιν
ἔχειν δεῖ καὶ σάρκινον εἶναι, καὶ φανεῖται ἡδονὴ
ἀγαθόν ' · οὐκοῦν καὶ τῷ ἐπέχοντι ἀγαθὸν φανεῖται·
καὶ γὰρ αἰσθήσεως μετέχει καὶ σάρκινός ἐστι, καὶ
λαβὼν ἀγαθοῦ φαντασίαν ὀρέγεται καὶ ὁρμᾷ, πάντα
πράττων ὅπως οὐ διαφεύξεται αὐτόν,[4] ἀλλ' ὡς
ἀνυστὸν ἀεὶ συνέσται τῷ οἰκείῳ, φυσικαῖς οὐ γεω-
E μετρικαῖς ἑλκόμενος ἀνάγκαις. ἄνευ διδασκάλου
γὰρ αὐτὰ προκαλεῖται τὰ καλὰ ταῦτα καὶ λεῖα καὶ
προσηνῆ κινήματα τῆς σαρκός, ὡς αὐτοί φασιν
οὗτοι, καὶ τὸν πάνυ μὴ φάσκοντα μηδὲ ὁμολογοῦντα
κάμπτεσθαι καὶ μαλάσσεσθαι τούτοις.

" ' ' Ἀλλὰ πῶς οὐκ εἰς ὄρος ἄπεισι τρέχων ὁ
ἐπέχων ἀλλὰ εἰς βαλανεῖον, οὐδὲ πρὸς τὸν τοῖχον

---

[1] After τὸ we omit ἡδύ.
[2] αὐτῶν γε τούτων EB : αὐτό γε τοῦτο Usener ; αὐτῶν γε
τούτων ἀκούομεν βοώντων Pohlenz.
[3] ὡς EB : καὶ τὸ ' καὶ or τὸ ' καὶ ? nos.
[4] αὐτόν EB : Benseler would omit.

---

[a] Cf. 1118 A-B, supra.
[b] Cf. Mor. 1057 A ; Sextus, Against the Mathematicians,
vii. 30 ; Cicero, De Nat. Deor. i. 37 (104) with Pease's note.
[c] Cf. Usener, Epicurea, p. 279, note on Frag. 411.
[d] The phrase comes from Plato, Republic, v, 458 D.
[e] Frag. 411 (ed. Usener). Perhaps the only part of this
statement that is Epicurean is " no teacher is needed " and
" movements of the flesh," the rest being Plutarch's rendition

sense must present a good, and impulse must set out for the good so presented ; and neither of these conflicts with suspension of judgement.[a] For the argument detaches us from opinion, not from impulse or sensation. So, once something good for us is perceived, no opinion is required to set us moving and keep us going in its direction ; the impulse comes directly, and is a movement initiated and pursued by the soul.'[b]

27. "Now the Epicureans themselves maintain that ' you need but have sensation and be made of flesh, and sense will present pleasure to you as good.'[c] Therefore it will also present a good to the man who suspends judgement, since he is both endowed with sensation and made of flesh. On receiving from sense this presentation of a good he reaches out for it by impulse, bending every effort to prevent its escape and to have with him always as far as possible what is good for him, being ruled by laws of his nature and not of geometrical proof.[d] For no teacher is needed ; by themselves these glorious smooth and agreeable movements of the flesh (as they themselves assert)[e] call to action even one who stoutly denies and refuses to acknowledge that he unbends and turns soft in response to them.

" ' But how comes it that the man who suspends judgement does not go dashing off to a mountain instead of to the bath, or why does he not get up and

of the following view (Sextus, *Against the Mathematicians*, xi. 96) : " . . . some of the Epicurean sect are in the habit of saying . . . that naturally and without teaching the animal avoids pain and seeks pleasure ; for at birth, and before it becomes a slave to matters of opinion, as soon as it is struck by the unfamiliar chill of the air, it wails and screams [*cf.* Empedocles, Frag. в 118 Diels-Kranz]."

(1122) ἀλλὰ πρὸς τὰς θύρας ἀναστὰς βαδίζει βουλόμενος
εἰς ἀγορὰν προελθεῖν· ' τοῦτο ἐρωτᾶς ἀκριβῆ τὰ
αἰσθητήρια λέγων εἶναι καὶ τὰς φαντασίας ἀληθεῖς; ὅτι φαίνεται δήπουθεν αὐτῷ βαλανεῖον οὐ τὸ
F ὄρος ἀλλὰ τὸ βαλανεῖον, καὶ θύρα οὐχ ὁ τοῖχος
ἀλλὰ ἡ θύρα, καὶ τῶν ἄλλων ὁμοίως ἕκαστον. ὁ
γὰρ τῆς ἐποχῆς λόγος οὐ παρατρέπει τὴν αἴσθησιν
οὐδὲ τοῖς ἀλόγοις πάθεσιν αὐτοῖς καὶ κινήμασιν
ἀλλοίωσιν ἐμποιεῖ διαταράττουσαν τὸ φανταστικόν,
ἀλλὰ τὰς δόξας μόνον ἀναιρεῖ, χρῆται δὲ τοῖς ἄλλοις ὡς πέφυκεν.

" ' 'Ἀλλὰ ἀδύνατον τὸ μὴ συγκατατίθεσθαι τοῖς
1123 ἐναργέσι· τοῦ[1] γὰρ ἀρνεῖσθαι τὰ πεπιστευμένα τὸ[1]
μήτε ἀρνεῖσθαι μήτε τιθέναι παραλογώτερον.' τίς[2]
οὖν κινεῖ τὰ πεπιστευμένα καὶ μάχεται τοῖς ἐναρ-
γέσιν; οἱ μαντικὴν ἀναιροῦντες καὶ πρόνοιαν ὑπάρχειν θεῶν μὴ φάσκοντες μηδὲ τὸν ἥλιον ἔμψυχον
εἶναι μηδὲ τὴν σελήνην, οἷς πάντες ἄνθρωποι θύουσι
καὶ προσεύχονται καὶ σέβονται. τὸ δὲ φύσει περι-
έχεσθαι τὰ τεκόντα τῶν γεννωμένων[3] οὐχὶ πᾶσι
φαινόμενον ἀναιρεῖτε; τὸ δὲ πόνου καὶ ἡδονῆς μηδὲν εἶναι μέσον οὐκ ἀποφαίνεσθε παρὰ τὴν πάντων
αἴσθησιν, ἥδεσθαι τὸ μὴ ἀλγεῖν καὶ πάσχειν τὸ μὴ
πάσχειν[4] λέγοντες;
28. " 'Ἀλλ' ἵνα τἆλλα ἐάσω, τί μᾶλλον ἐναργὲς
B οὕτως ἐστὶ καὶ πεπιστευμένον ὡς τὸ[5] παρορᾶν καὶ

---

[1] τοῦ . . . τὸ Shorey : τὸ . . . τοῦ EB.
[2] τίς Stephanus : τί EB.
[3] γεννωμένων Rasmus : γειναμένων EB.
[4] πάσχειν Bignone : a blank of 7 letters E, 5 B.
[5] ὡς τὸ Ald.[2], Stephanus, Xylander : ὥστε EB.

---

[a] Cf. Cicero, Acad. Pr. ii. 12 (38).

walk to the wall instead of the door when he wishes
to go out to the market-place ? ' You ask this when
you hold that the sense organs are accurate and sense
images true ? Why, because what appears to him
to be a bath is not the mountain but the bath, and
what appears to him to be a door is not the wall
but the door, and so with everything else. For the
doctrine of suspension of judgement does not deflect
sensation or introduce into the non-rational affections
and movements themselves a change that disturbs the
presentation of sense images ; it is only our opinions
that it eliminates, whereas it deals with the other
parts in accordance with their natural uses.

" ' But it is impossible to refuse assent to plain
evidence,[a] since neither to deny nor to affirm the
accepted is more unreasonable than to deny it.' Then
who is it that upsets accepted beliefs and comes in
conflict with the plainest facts ? It is those [b] who
reject divination and deny that there exists a divine
providence or that the sun and moon are living beings,
to whom sacrifice and prayer and reverence is offered
up by all mankind. Do you people [c] not dismiss
the instinctive love of parents for their offspring,
a fact accepted by all? And do you[d] not, in defi-
ance of the experience of all mankind, affirm the absence of any mean between pain and pleasure when
you say that it is a pleasure to feel no pain,[e] in
other words that not to be acted upon is to be acted
upon ?

28. " But leaving aside other instances, what is
more plainly evident in this way and more accepted

[b] Frags. 368, 342 (ed. Usener).
[c] Frag. 528 (ed. Usener) ; cf. 1100 D, supra.
[d] Frag. 420 (ed. Usener).
[e] Cf. Cicero, De Fin. ii. 3-5 (9-17).

(1123) παρακούειν ἐν πάθεσιν ἐκστατικοῖς καὶ μελαγχολι-
κοῖς ὄντα, ὅταν ἡ διάνοια τοιαῦτα πάσχῃ καὶ
ταράττηται·

αἱ δέ[1] με δᾳδοφόροι μελανείμονες ὄμμα πυροῦσι
καὶ

πῦρ πνέουσα καὶ φόνον
πτεροῖς ἐρέσσει[2] μητέρ'[3] ἀγκάλαις ἐμὴν
ἔχουσα;

ταῦτα μέντοι καὶ πολλὰ τούτων ἕτερα τραγικώτερα
τοῖς Ἐμπεδοκλέους ἐοικότα τεράσμασιν[4] ὧν κατα-
γελῶσιν, ' εἰλίποδ' ἀκριτόχειρα '[5] καὶ ' βουγενῆ ἀνδρόπρωρα '[6] καὶ τίνα γὰρ οὐκ ὄψιν ἢ φύσιν ἔκφυλον
εἰς τὸ αὐτὸ συνενεγκόντες ἐκ τῶν ἐνυπνίων καὶ τῶν
C παρακοπῶν οὐδὲν εἶναί φασι παρόραμα τούτων
οὐδὲ ψεῦδος οὐδὲ ἀσύστατον, ἀλλὰ φαντασίας ἀληθεῖς ἁπάσας καὶ σώματα καὶ μορφὰς ἐκ τοῦ περιέχοντος ἀφικνουμένας. εἶτα ἔστι τι τῶν ὄντων
ἀδύνατον ἐπισχεῖν, εἰ ταῦτα πιστεύεσθαι δυνατόν
ἐστιν; ἃ γὰρ οὐδεὶς σκευοποιὸς ἢ πλάστης θαυ-
μάτων ἢ γραφεὺς δεινὸς ἐτόλμησε μῖξαι πρὸς
ἀπάτην εἰκάσματα καὶ παίγνια, ταῦτα ὑπάρχειν
ἀπὸ σπουδῆς τιθέμενοι, μᾶλλον δὲ ὅλως εἰ ταῦτα
μὴ ὑπάρχοι πίστιν οἴχεσθαι καὶ βεβαιότητα καὶ

---

[1] αἱ δέ E : αἰ δέ B.
[2] πῦρ—ἐρέσσει supplied by us in a blank of 35-30 letters.
[3] μητέρ' Euripides : μητέρα EB.
[4] τεράσμασιν EB[1t] (in E with a triangle of points over the
first σ) : τεράτεσι B[2mg].
[5] εἰλίποδ' ἀκριτόχειρα Emperius : εἰλίποδα κριτόχειρα EB.
[6] ἀνδρόπρωρα EB[1ss] : ἀνδράπρωρα B[1t].

than that one possessed by wild or sombre madness
has illusions of sight and hearing, when his mind is
affected and distracted by phantoms such as these :

> These woman shapes with torches in their hand
> And robed in dusky black, inflame my vision [a]

and

> Breathing fire and blood
> She plies her wings, my mother in her arms ? [b]

These and many of another stagier variety, resem-
bling the Empedoclean [c] monsters that they [d] deride

> With lurching ox-feet, random arms

and

> Ox-creatures, fronted like a man

and—but what phantom or prodigy do they omit ?—
all of these they [e] assemble from dreams and delirium and say that none is an optical illusion or false
or unsubstantial, but all are true impressions, bodies
and shapes that reach us from the surrounding air.
That being the case, is there anything in the world
about which it is impossible to suspend judgement,
when such things as these can be accepted as real ?
Things that no artful joiner, puppet-maker, or painter
ever ventured to combine for our entertainment into
a likeness to deceive the eye, these they seriously
suppose to exist, or rather they assert that, if these
did not exist, there would be an end of all assurance

---

[a] That is, the Furies : cf. Callimachus, Frag. anon. 387
(ed. Schneider ; not in Pfeiffer).

[b] Euripides, Iphigeneia among the Taurians, 288-290.

[c] Diels and Kranz, Die Frag. der Vorsokratiker, Empedokles, в 60 and в 61. 2.

[d] The Epicureans : cf. Lucretius, v. 878-924.

[e] Frag. 254 (ed. Usener).

PLUTARCH'S MORALIA

(1123) κρίσιν ἀληθείας φάσκοντες, αὐτοὶ καταβάλλουσιν
εἰς ἀφασίαν πάντα πράγματα· καὶ ταῖς κρίσεσι φό-
D βους καὶ ταῖς πράξεσιν ὑποψίας ἐπάγουσιν, εἰ τὰ
πραττόμενα καὶ νομιζόμενα καὶ συνήθη καὶ ἀνὰ
χεῖρας ἡμῖν ἐπὶ τῆς αὐτῆς φαντασίας καὶ πίστεως
ὀχεῖται τοῖς μανικοῖς καὶ ἀτόποις καὶ παρανόμοις
ἐκείνοις φάσμασιν. ἡ γὰρ ἰσότης ἣν ὑποτίθενται
πᾶσι τῶν νενομισμένων ἀφίστησι μᾶλλον ἢ προστίθησι τοῖς παραλόγοις τὴν πίστιν. ὅθεν ἴσμεν οὐκ
ὀλίγους τῶν φιλοσόφων ἥδιον ἂν θεμένους τὸ μηδεμίαν ἢ τὸ[1] πάσας ἀληθεῖς εἶναι τὰς φαντασίας,
καὶ μᾶλλον ἂν οἷς ὕπαρ ἐντυγχάνουσι[2] διαπιστή-
σαντας ἀνθρώποις καὶ πράγμασι καὶ λόγοις ἁπλῶς
ἅπασιν ἢ μίαν ἐκείνων ἀληθῆ καὶ ὑπάρχουσαν
E εἶναι φαντασίαν πεισθέντας ἃς[3] λυττῶντες ἢ κορυ-
βαντιῶντες ἢ κοιμώμενοι λαμβάνουσιν.[4] ἃ τοίνυν
ἔστι μὲν ἀναιρεῖν ἔστι δ' ὡς οὐκ ἔστιν,[5] οὐκ ἔστιν
ἐπέχειν περὶ αὐτῶν, εἰ μηδὲν ἄλλο, τήν γε διαφω-
νίαν ταύτην λαβόντας αἰτίαν ἀποχρῶσαν ὑπονοίας
πρὸς τὰ πράγματα καὶ οὐδὲ οὕτως ὡς[6] ὑγιὲς οὐδέν,

[1] ἢ τὸ Dübner : ἤτοι EB.
[2] ὕπαρ ἐντυγχάνουσι Pohlenz (ὕπαρ παρατυγχάνουσι Kronenberg) : οὐ παρατυγχάνουσι EB.
[3] ἃς added in Basle edition of 1542.
[4] λαμβάνουσιν B : λαμβάνωσιν E.
[5] οὐκ ἔστιν our addition ; κριτήριον ἀποδέχεσθαι, πῶς ἀσφαλέ-
στερον Pohlenz.
[6] οὐδὲ οὕτως ὡς nos : οὐδὲ οὕτως E ; οὕτως B.

a Cf. Epicurus, Letter to Herodotus, 51-52, Cardinal Tenets
xxiii and xxiv, Frag. 253 (ed. Usener ; cf. Frag. 251 and
p. 349. 6-8) ; Diogenes Laert. x. 32 ; Cicero, De Fin. i. 7
(22), Acad. Pr. ii. 25 (79) with Reid's note.

and certainty and judgement about truth [a] ; and by
taking this stand they themselves reduce the world
to the state where nothing is asserted or denied,[b]
bring fear into our decisions and misgiving into our
acts as we reflect that action, accepted belief, and
the familiar [c] and daily business of our lives rest on
the same footing of confidence in sensation as those
shapes of madness and whimsy that defy all custom
and law. For by putting all in the same boat [d] their
theory does more to estrange [e] us from established
beliefs than to convince us that the grotesques are
real. Hence not a few philosophers, we know, would
prefer the position that no appearance is true to the
position that all are true, and would rather give up
confidence at one sweep in all men, things, and statements encountered in their waking moments than
trust as true and real a single one of these appearances that come to us in delirium or ecstasy or sleep.
If then it is possible to deny appearances, and in a
way impossible to do so, is it not possible to suspend
judgement about them if for no other reason than
because of this conflict of views ? Is that not reason
enough to make us regard the world about us with
suspicion,—not that we actually take it to be completely crazy, but only conclude that there is no end

[b] For *aphasia* (used by Timon : *cf.* A 2 p. 176. 7 and B 9.
2, ed. Diels) as a withdrawal from assertion and denial *cf.*
Sextus, *Outlines of Pyrrhonism*, i. 192.

[c] The Academics were accused of abolishing the familiar
or customary : *cf.* Cicero, *Acad. Pr.* ii. 13 (42) and 27 (87)
with Reid's notes. In *Mor.* 1036 c Plutarch turns the argument against the Stoics, as here he turns it against the
Epicureans.

[d] Frag. 251 (ed. Usener) ; *cf.* 1124 B, *infra*.

[e] For *apostasis* (detachment) as a Sceptic term *cf.* Sextus,
Outlines of Pyrrhonism, i. 192.

(1123) ἀσάφειαν δὲ καὶ ταραχὴν ἔχοντα[1] πᾶσαν; ταῖς
μέν γε περὶ κόσμων ἀπειρίας[2] καὶ ἀτόμων φύσεως
καὶ ἀμερῶν καὶ παρεγκλίσεων διαφοραῖς, εἰ καὶ
πάνυ πολλοὺς διαταράττουσιν, ἔνεστιν ὅμως παρα-
μυθία τὸ μηδὲν ἐγγὺς εἶναι, μᾶλλον δὲ ὅλως ἐπέκεινα τῆς αἰσθήσεως ἀπῳκίσθαι τῶν ζητουμένων
F ἕκαστον· ἡ δ' ἐν ὀφθαλμοῖς[3] αὕτη καὶ ἀκοαῖς καὶ
χερσὶν ἀπιστία καὶ ἄγνοια καὶ ταραχὴ περὶ τὰ
αἰσθητὰ καὶ τὰς φαντασίας, εἴτε ἀληθεῖς εἰσιν εἴτε
ψευδεῖς, τίνα δόξαν οὐ σαλεύει; ποίαν δὲ οὐκ ἄνω
καὶ κάτω ποιεῖ συγκατάθεσιν καὶ κρίσιν; εἰ γὰρ
οὐ κραιπαλῶντες οὐδὲ φαρμακῶντες ἄνθρωποι καὶ
παρακόπτοντες ἀλλὰ νήφοντες καὶ ὑγιαίνοντες καὶ
γράφοντες περὶ ἀληθείας καὶ κανόνων καὶ κριτη-
1124 ρίων ἐν τοῖς ἐναργεστάτοις πάθεσι καὶ κινήμασι τῆς
αἰσθήσεως ἢ τὸ ἀνύπαρκτον ἀληθὲς ἢ ψεῦδος καὶ
ἀνύπαρκτον ἡγοῦνται τὸ ἀληθές, οὐκ εἰ περὶ πάντων ἡσυχάζουσιν, ἀλλ' εἴ τισιν ὅλως ἄνθρωποι[4]
συγκατατίθενται, θαυμάζειν ἄξιον· οὐδὲ ἄπιστον,
εἰ μηδεμίαν κρίσιν ἔχουσι περὶ τῶν φαινομένων,
ἀλλ' εἰ τὰς ἐναντίας ἔχουσι, τοῦ γὰρ ἐναντία λέγειν
ἀλλήλοις καὶ ἀντικείμενα τὸ μηδέτερον, ἀλλὰ ἐπέχειν περὶ τῶν ἀντικειμένων ἧττον ἄν τις θαυμάσειεν.
ὁ γὰρ μήτε[5] τιθεὶς μήτε ἀρνούμενος ἀλλὰ ἡσυχάζων
καὶ τῷ τιθέντι τὴν δόξαν ἧττον μάχεται τοῦ ἀρνουμένου καὶ τῷ ἀρνουμένῳ τοῦ τιθέντος. εἰ δὲ περὶ

---

[1] ἔχοντα Wyttenbach : ἔχοντας EB.
[2] ἀπειρίας EB[r] : ἀπειρίαις B[ar].
[3] ὀφθαλμοῖς E : ὀφθαλμαῖς B.
[4] ἄνθρωποι Emperius : ἀνθρώποις EB.
[5] μήτε Stegmann : μὴ EB.

---

[a] Cf. Lucretius, ii. 216-220.

to the doubt and confusion that it begets? Disagreement whether there are an infinite number of universes, whether there are in nature indivisible bodies that have no parts, and about the swerve,[a] though it disturbs very many, is yet attended with this comfort, that none of these matters touches us nearly, or rather that these questions in each case lie quite beyond the range of sense. Whereas this distrust and uncertainty and perplexity about our eyes, our hearing, and our hands, when we question the objects and images of sense and wonder whether they are true or false—what faith does it leave unshaken? What act of assent and judgement does it not turn topsy-turvy? For if men not sodden with drink or confused by strong medicine and out of their right minds, but sober and in perfect health, writing books on truth and norms and standards of judgement, if such men suppose in the presence of the plainest and most vivid responses and movements of the senses that the non-existent is true or that the true is false and non-existent, we may well wonder, not that men withhold assent altogether, but that things exist to to which they assent at all; and what is hard to take is not their passing no judgement on appearances, but their passing contrary judgements. Compared with this making of statements clean contrary to each other and equal in the scales,[b] a refusal to make a statement either way, and suspension of judgement about the opposing arguments is less surprising. For one who neither affirms nor denies, but holds his peace, is less at odds with the affirmer of the view than is the denier, and with the denier than is the

[b] The Sceptics spoke of a counterpoise of equal and conflicting statements: cf. Sextus, *Outlines of Pyrrhonism*, i. 12, *Against the Mathematicians*, viii. 363.

291

(1124)

B τούτων δυνατόν ἐστιν ἐπέχειν, οὐδὲ περὶ τῶν ἄλλων
ἀδύνατον, κατά γε ὑμᾶς αἴσθησιν αἰσθήσεως καὶ
φαντασίαν φαντασίας οὐδ' ὁτιοῦν διαφέρειν ἡγου-
μένους.

29. " Οὐ μῦθος οὖν οὐδὲ θήρα μειρακίων λαμυρῶν[1] καὶ προπετῶν ὁ περὶ τῆς ἐποχῆς λόγος ἐστίν,
ὡς οἴεται Κωλώτης, ἀλλὰ ἕξις ἀνδρῶν καὶ διάθεσις
φυλάττουσα τὸ ἀδιάπτωτον καὶ μὴ προϊεμένη[2] ταῖς
διαβεβλημέναις οὕτω καὶ δυστατούσαις[3] αἰσθήσεσι
τὴν κρίσιν μηδὲ συνεξαπατωμένη τούτοις οἳ τὰ
φαινόμενα τῶν ἀδήλων πίστιν ἔχειν φάσκουσιν,
ἀπιστίαν τοσαύτην καὶ ἀσάφειαν ἐν τοῖς φαινομένοις
ὁρῶντες. ἀλλὰ μῦθος μέν ἐστιν ἡ ἀπειρία καὶ τὰ
C εἴδωλα, προπέτειαν δὲ καὶ λαμυρίαν ἐμποιεῖ νέοις
ὁ περὶ Πυθοκλέους οὔπω γεγονότος ὀκτωκαίδεκα
ἔτη γράφων οὐκ εἶναι φύσιν ἐν ὅλῃ τῇ Ἑλλάδι
ἀμείνω καὶ τερατικῶς αὐτὸν εὖ ἀπαγγέλλειν, καὶ
πάσχειν αὐτὸς τὸ[4] τῶν γυναικῶν, εὐχόμενος ἀνε-
μέσητα πάντα εἶναι[5] καὶ ἀνεπίφθονα τὰ τῆς[6] ὑπερ-
βολῆς τοῦ νεανίσκου· σοφισταὶ δέ εἰσι καὶ ἀλαζόνες
οἱ πρὸς ἄνδρας ἐλλογίμους οὕτως ἀσελγῶς καὶ
ὑπερηφάνως γράφοντες. καίτοι Πλάτων καὶ Ἀριστοτέλης καὶ Θεόφραστος καὶ Δημόκριτος ἀντειρή-
κασι τοῖς πρὸ αὑτῶν· βιβλίον δὲ τοιαύτην ἐπιγραφὴν

---

[1] λαμυρῶν Bern. : λαμύρων EB.
[2] προϊεμένη Wyttenbach : προσιεμένη EB.
[3] δυστατούσαις EB : δυσσυστατούσαις ?
[4] αὐτὸς τὸ Madvig : αὐτὸ τὸ Eᶜ ; αὐτὸ EᵃᶜB.
[5] πάντα εἶναι E : εἶναι πάντα B.
[6] τὰ τῆς Emperius : τῆς EB.

---

[a] Frag. 251 (ed. Usener).
[b] Cf. Plato, *Phaedo*, 67 E 6-7, 68 A 2
[c] Frag. 263 (ed. Usener).

affirmer. And if it is possible to withhold judgement about these sensations, it is not impossible to withhold it about others as well, at least on the principles of your school,[a] who set one act or image of sensation on exactly the same footing as another.

29. "And so this doctrine of withholding judgement is no idle tale, as Colotes thinks, or bait to fill the lecture hall with froward and flighty youth ; it is a settled state and attitude of grown men that preserves them from error and refuses to abandon judgement to anything so discredited[b] and incoherent as the senses or to be deluded as these people[c] are deluded who call the seen the evidence of things unseen although they observe that appearances are so untrustworthy and ambiguous. No ; the idle tale is their infinity and their films ; the young are made flighty and froward by the one[d] who writes of Pythocles, not yet eighteen, that in all of Greece there is no one more gifted and that his powers of expression are a prodigy, who writes that he himself is moved to pray as the women do—that all that superiority of talent may not bring down on the young man's head the jealousy and resentment of heaven[e] ; and the sophists and charlatans are those who[f] in their disputes with eminent men write with such shameless arrogance. It is true that Plato, Aristotle, Theophrastus and Democritus disputed against those who preceded them ; but no one else ever had the temerity

[d] Frag. 161 (ed. Usener) ; *cf.* Frag. 165 and Philodemus, *On Death*, iv, col. xii. 32.

[e] Early brilliance presages an early death : *cf.* Quintilian, *Education of the Orator*, vi proem. 10. We doubtless are told that Pythocles was not yet eighteen because he never reached that age.

[f] Frag. 237 (ed. Usener).

PLUTARCH'S MORALIA

(1124) ἔχον ὁμοῦ πρὸς ἅπαντας οὐδεὶς ἄλλος ἐξενεγκεῖν
ἐτόλμησεν.

D   30. " Ὅθεν ὥσπερ οἱ περὶ[1] τὸ θεῖον πλημμελή-
σαντες ἐξαγορεύων τὰ ἑαυτοῦ κακὰ τελευτῶντος
ἤδη τοῦ βιβλίου φησὶν ὅτι ' τὸν βίον οἱ νόμους
διατάξαντες καὶ νόμιμα καὶ τὸ βασιλεύεσθαι τὰς
πόλεις καὶ ἄρχεσθαι καταστήσαντες εἰς πολλὴν
ἀσφάλειαν καὶ ἡσυχίαν ἔθεντο καὶ θορύβων ἀπήλ-
λαξαν· εἰ δέ τις ταῦτα ἀναιρήσει, θηρίων βίον βιω-
σόμεθα καὶ ὁ προστυχὼν τὸν ἐντυχόντα[2] μονονοὺ
κατέδεται.' τοῦτο γὰρ ὁ Κωλώτης αὐταῖς λέξεσιν
ἐκπεφώνηκεν, οὐ δικαίως οὐδὲ ἀληθῶς. ἂν γὰρ
ἀνελών τις τοὺς νόμους τὰ Παρμενίδου καὶ Σωκράτους καὶ Ἡρακλείτου καὶ Πλάτωνος ἀπολίπῃ δό-
E γματα, πολλοῦ δεήσομεν ἀλλήλους κατεσθίειν καὶ
θηρίων βίον ζῆν· φοβησόμεθα γὰρ τὰ αἰσχρὰ καὶ
τιμήσομεν ἐπὶ τῷ καλῷ δικαιοσύνην, θεοὺς ἄρχον-
τας ἀγαθοὺς καὶ δαίμονας ἔχειν τοῦ βίου φύλακας
ἡγούμενοι καὶ τὸν ὑπὲρ γῆς καὶ ὑπὸ γῆν χρυσὸν
ἀρετῆς ἀντάξιον μὴ τιθέμενοι καὶ ποιοῦντες ἑκου-
σίως διὰ τὸν λόγον, ᾗ φησι Ξενοκράτης, ἃ νῦν
ἄκοντες[3] διὰ τὸν νόμον. πότε οὖν ἔσται θηριώδης
καὶ ἄγριος καὶ ἄμικτος ἡμῶν ὁ βίος; ὅταν ἀναιρεθῶσι[4] μὲν οἱ νόμοι, μένωσι δὲ οἱ πρὸς ἡδονὴν παρα-
καλοῦντες λόγοι, πρόνοια δὲ θεῶν μὴ νομίζηται,
σοφοὺς δὲ ἡγῶνται τοὺς τῷ καλῷ προσπτύοντας,

[1] περὶ E : B omits.   [2] ἐντυχόντα E : ἐντυγχάνοντα B.
[3] ἄκοντες E : ἀκούοντες B.
[4] ἀναιρεθῶσι Xylander : αἱρεθῶσι EB.

[a] For such public confession see F. Cumont, *Les Religions
orientales dans le paganisme romain* (fourth edition, Paris,
1929), p. 36 with notes 40 and 41 (pp. 218-219) and *Mor.*
566 f with the note.

294

to publish a book with such a title, an attack on all his predecessors lumped together.

30. " Hence, like some offender against heaven, he publicly proclaims his own misdeeds [a] when he says as the book nears its end : ' The men who appointed laws and usages and established the government of cities by kings and magistrates brought human life into a state of great security and peace and delivered it from turmoil. But if anyone takes all this away, we shall live a life of brutes, and anyone who chances upon another will all but devour him.' For this is Colotes' public declaration in his own words, and it is dishonest and untrue. For if someone takes away the laws, but leaves us with the teachings of Parmenides, Socrates, Heracleitus and Plato, we shall be very far from devouring one another and living the life of wild beasts ; for we shall fear all that is shameful and shall honour justice for its intrinsic worth, holding that in the gods we have good governors [b] and in the daemons protectors [c] of our lives, accounting all ' the gold on earth and under it a poor exchange for virtue,' [d] and doing freely at the bidding of our reason, as Xenocrates [e] says, what we now do perforce at the command of the law. Then when will our life be that of a beast, savage and without fellowship ? When the laws are swept away, but the arguments that summon us to a life of pleasure are left standing, when the providence of heaven is not believed in,[f] and when men take for sages those who

[b] *Cf.* Plato, *Phaedo*, 63 A 9.

[c] *Cf.* Hesiod, *Works and Days*, 253.

[d] Plato, *Laws*, v, 728 A 4-5 (where there is an allusion to Homer, *Il.* ix. 401).

[e] Frag. 3 (ed. Heinze) ; *cf.* also *Mor.* 446 E.

[f] Frag. 368 (ed. Usener) ; *cf.* 1117 A, *supra*.

PLUTARCH'S MORALIA

(1124) ἂν ἡδονὴ μὴ προσῇ, χλευάζωσι δὲ ταῦτα καὶ γελῶσιν

F   ἔστιν[1] Δίκης ὀφθαλμός, ὃς τὰ πάνθ' ὁρᾷ

καὶ

πέλας[2] γὰρ ἐστὼς ὁ θεὸς ἐγγύθεν βλέπει[3]

καὶ

ὁ μὲν θεός, ὥσπερ δὴ καὶ ὁ παλαιὸς λόγος, ἀρχήν τε καὶ μέσα καὶ τελευτὴν ἔχων τοῦ παντὸς εὐθείᾳ[4] περαίνει κατὰ φύσιν περιπορευόμενος· τῷ δ' ἕπεται Δίκη, τῶν ἀπολειπομένων τιμωρὸς τοῦ θείου νόμου.

1125 οἱ γὰρ τούτων καταφρονοῦντες ὡς μύθων καὶ περὶ γαστέρα τἀγαθὸν ἡγούμενοι καὶ τοὺς ἄλλους πόρους δι' ὧν ἡδονὴ παραγίνεται, νόμου δέονται καὶ φόβου καὶ πληγῆς καὶ βασιλέως τινὸς καὶ ἄρχοντος ἐν χειρὶ τὴν δίκην ἔχοντος, ἵνα μὴ τοὺς πλησίον κατεσθίωσιν ὑπὸ λαιμαργίας ἀθεότητι θρασυνομένης.

"Καὶ γὰρ ὁ τῶν θηρίων βίος τοιοῦτός ἐστιν ὅτι τῆς ἡδονῆς οὐδὲν ἐπίσταται κάλλιον οὐδὲ δίκην θεῶν οἶδεν οὐδὲ σέβεται τῆς ἀρετῆς τὸ κάλλος, ἀλλ'

---

[1] ἔστιν Stephanus : ἔστι EB.
[2] πέλας EB : πόρρω Stobaeus, i. 3. 42. 1.
[3] βλέπει EB : κλύει Stobaeus, i. 3. 42. 1.
[4] εὐθείᾳ A^cO^c of Plato [εὐθεια A, εὐθεῖα O] : εὐθεῖα EB.

---

[a] Frag. 512 (ed. Usener) ; cf. 1129 B, infra.
[b] Nauck, Trag. Graec. Frag., Adespota, 421 ; cf. Mor. 161 F.
[c] Nauck, Trag. Graec. Frag., Adespota, 490. 2 ; cf. Menander, Frag. 683. 12 (ed. Körte²).

296

' spit on excellence, unless pleasure attends it '[a] and who scoff and jeer at such words as these :

> An eye there is of Justice, that sees all [b]

and

> For God looks closely, ever standing near [c]

and

> God, even as the ancient account relates, holding the beginning, middle, and end of the universe, proceeds directly, as is his nature, in his round ; upon him follows Justice, who visits with punishment all who fall short of the divine law.[d]

For it is men who look with contempt on all these things as old wives' tales [e] and think that our good is to be found in the belly and the other passages by which pleasure makes her entry [f]—it is these who stand in need of law, fear, blows and some king or magistrate wth justice in his strong right arm [g] to deter them from proceeding to devour their neighbours when their ravening appetite, prompted by their godlessness, casts off restraint.

" Indeed wild animals lead the kind of life that they do because they have no knowledge of anything higher than pleasure, no conception of a divine justice,[h] and no reverence for the intrinsic worth of

[d] Plato, *Laws*, iv, 715 E—716 A, quoted also in *Mor.* 601 B and 781 F.

[e] *Cf. Mor.* 420 B.

[f] Epicurus, Frag. 409 (ed. Usener) ; Metrodorus, Frag. 7. 40 (ed. Körte) ; *cf.* 1087 D, 1108 C, *supra*.

[g] *Cf.* Hesiod, *Works and Days*, 189 and 192, and Plato, *Theaetetus*, 172 E 6.

[h] *Cf.* Hesiod, *Works and Days*, 277-278. Epicurus (*Cardinal Tenet* xxxii) had said that for those animals that were unable to make a compact neither to injure nor be injured by one another there is no justice or injustice.

(1125) εἴ τι θαρραλέον αὐτοῖς ἢ πανοῦργον ἢ δραστήριον
ἐκ φύσεως ἔνεστι, τούτῳ πρὸς ἡδονὴν σαρκὸς καὶ
ἀποπλήρωσιν ὀρέξεως χρῆται, καθάπερ οἴεται δεῖν
B ὁ σοφὸς Μητρόδωρος λέγων τὰ καλὰ πάντα καὶ
σοφὰ καὶ περιττὰ τῆς ψυχῆς ἐξευρήματα τῆς κατὰ
σάρκα ἡδονῆς ἕνεκα καὶ τῆς ἐλπίδος τῆς ὑπὲρ
ταύτης συνεστάναι καὶ πᾶν εἶναι κενὸν ἔργον ὃ μὴ
εἰς τοῦτο κατατείνει. τούτοις τοῖς διαλογισμοῖς καὶ
φιλοσοφήμασιν ἀρθέντων τῶν[1] νόμων ὄνυχες λύκων
ἐνδέουσι καὶ ὀδόντες λεόντων καὶ γαστέρες βοῶν
καὶ τράχηλοι καμήλων. καὶ ταῦτα τὰ πάθη καὶ τὰ
δόγματα λόγων καὶ γραμμάτων ἀπορίᾳ τὰ θηρία
βρυχήμασι καὶ χρεμετισμοῖς καὶ μυκήμασι δηλοῖ,[2]
καὶ πᾶσα φωνὴ γαστρός ἐστιν αὐτοῖς καὶ σαρκὸς
C ἡδονὴν ἀσπαζομένη[3] καὶ σαίνουσα παροῦσαν ἢ μέλ-
λουσαν, εἰ μή τι φύσει φιλόφωνόν ἐστι καὶ κωτίλον.[4]
    31. " Οὐδεὶς οὖν ἔπαινος ἄξιος ἂν γένοιτο τῶν
ἐπὶ ταῦτα τὰ πάθη τὰ θηριώδη νόμους θεμένων καὶ
πολιτείας καὶ ἀρχὰς καὶ νόμων διάταξιν. ἀλλὰ
τίνες εἰσὶν οἱ ταῦτα συγχέοντες καὶ καταλύοντες
καὶ ἄρδην ἀναιροῦντες; οὐχ οἱ πολιτείας ἀφι-
στάντες αὐτοὺς καὶ τοὺς πλησιάζοντας; οὐχ οἷ[5] τὸν
τῆς ἀταραξίας στέφανον ἀσύμβλητον εἶναι ταῖς
μεγάλαις ἡγεμονίαις λέγοντες; οὐχ οἱ τὸ βασι-
λεύειν ἁμαρτίαν καὶ διάπτωσιν ἀποφαίνοντες καὶ
γράφοντες αὐταῖς λέξεσιν ὅτι ' λέγειν δεῖ πῶς[6]

---

[1] ἀρθέντων τῶν Bern. (ἀναιρεθέντων τῶν Madvig): ἀρθέντων EB.

[2] μυκήμασι δηλοῖ Reiske's supplement of a blank of 12-15 letters in E, 10 in B : ὑλαγμοῖς βοᾷ Bignone.

[3] ἀσπαζομένη Stephanus : ἀσπαζομένης EB.

[4] κωτίλον B : κωτίλον E.

[5] πολιτείας through οὐχ οἷ] B omits.

[6] After πῶς Meziriacus would add τις.

virtue ; they use instead whatever natural gifts they have of boldness, cunning, or industry to get pleasure of the flesh and satisfaction of appetite. And the sage Metrodorus [a] thinks that this is as it should be, when he says that all the wonderful, ingenious and brilliant inventions of the mind have been contrived for the sake of the pleasure of the flesh or for the sake of looking forward to it, and that any accomplishment that does not lead to this end is worthless. Get rid of all law by such reasoning and philosophy and what is lacking ? A wolf's claws, a lion's fangs, an ox's belly, and a camel's neck. Again, it is these feelings and these doctrines that the brutes for want of speech and writing express by roars and whinnies and lowings ; and every sound they utter serves to welcome and fawn upon present or future pleasure of the belly and the flesh, except for the few who have an inborn love of song and chatter.[b]

31. " No praise accordingly can ever do justice to the men who dealt with these brutish feelings by establishing laws and with them states and governments and a system of legislation. But who are the men that nullify these things, overthrowing the state and utterly abolishing the laws ? Is it not those who withdraw themselves and their disciples from participation in the state ? Is it not those [c] who say that the crown of an untroubled spirit is a prize beyond all comparison with success in some great command ? Is it not those who say that to be king is a fault and a mistake ? Who write in these very words [d] : ' We

[a] Frag. 6 (ed. Körte) ; cf. Usener, *Epicurea*, p. 278, note to Frag. 409. *Cf.* also 1087 D, *supra*.

[b] *Cf.* 1091 C-D, *supra*.

[c] Frag. 556 (ed. Usener ; cf. also Frag. 8).

[d] Frag. 554 (ed. Usener).

299

(1125) ἄριστα τὸ τῆς φύσεως τέλος συντηρήσει καὶ πῶς τις ἑκὼν εἶναι μὴ πρόσεισιν ἐξ ἀρχῆς ἐπὶ τὰς τῶν πληθῶν ἀρχάς '· καὶ ἔτι ταῦτα πρὸς ἐκείνοις·

D ' οὐδὲν οὖν ἔτι δεῖ τοὺς Ἕλληνας σώζειν οὐδὲ ἐπὶ σοφίᾳ στεφάνου παρ' αὐτῶν τυγχάνειν, ἀλλ' ἐσθίειν καὶ πίνειν, ὦ Τιμόκρατες, ἀβλαβῶς τῇ σαρκὶ καὶ κεχαρισμένως ';

" Ἀλλὰ μὴν ἧς γε καὶ Κωλώτης ἐπαινεῖ διατά- ξεως τῶν νόμων πρῶτόν ἐστιν ἡ περὶ θεῶν δόξα καὶ μέγιστον, ᾗ καὶ Λυκοῦργος Λακεδαιμονίους καὶ Νομᾶς Ῥωμαίους καὶ Ἴων ὁ παλαιὸς Ἀθη- ναίους καὶ Δευκαλίων Ἕλληνας ὁμοῦ τι[1] πάντας καθωσίωσαν, εὐχαῖς καὶ ὅρκοις καὶ μαντεύμασι καὶ φήμαις ἐμπαθεῖς πρὸς τὰ θεῖα δι' ἐλπίδων ἅμα καὶ φόβων καταστήσαντες. εὕροις δ' ἂν ἐπιὼν πόλεις

E ἀτειχίστους, ἀγραμμάτους, ἀβασιλεύτους, ἀοίκους, ἀχρημάτους, νομίσματος μὴ δεομένας,[2] ἀπείρους θεάτρων καὶ γυμνασίων· ἀνιέρου δὲ πόλεως καὶ ἀθέου, μὴ χρωμένης εὐχαῖς μηδὲ ὅρκοις μηδὲ μαν- τείαις μηδὲ θυσίαις ἐπ' ἀγαθοῖς μηδὲ ἀποτροπαῖς κακῶν οὐδείς ἐστιν οὐδὲ ἔσται γεγονὼς θεατής· ἀλλὰ πόλις[3] ἄν μοι δοκεῖ μᾶλλον ἐδάφους χωρὶς ἢ πολιτεία τῆς περὶ θεῶν δόξης ὑφαιρεθείσης[4] παντά- πασι σύστασιν λαβεῖν ἢ λαβοῦσα τηρῆσαι. τοῦτο μέντοι τὸ συνεκτικὸν ἁπάσης κοινωνίας καὶ νομο- θεσίας ἔρεισμα καὶ βάθρον οὐ κύκλῳ περιιόντες οὐδὲ κρύφα καὶ δι' αἰνιγμάτων, ἀλλὰ τὴν πρώτην

F τῶν κυριωτάτων δοξῶν προσβαλόντες[5] εὐθὺς ἀνα-

---

[1] τι E : τοι B and Plethon's paraphrase.
[2] δεομένας Basle edition of 1542 : δεομένους EB.
[3] πόλις Turnebus ; μόλις EB.
[4] ὑφαιρεθείσης E°B (α- E^{ac}) : ἐναιρεθείσης Ald.

300

must proceed to tell how a person will best uphold the purpose of his nature and how of his own free will he is not to present himself for public office at all.' They go even further, and add to these sentiments the following [a] : ' So we are not called upon to be saviours of the Greeks or to receive from them any crown for wisdom, but to eat and drink, my dear Timocrates, in a way that will do the flesh no hurt and gratify it.'

"Again the very legislation that Colotes praises provides first and foremost for our belief in the gods, a faith whereby Lycurgus made the Spartans a dedicated people, Numa the Romans, Ion of old the Athenians, and Deucalion well-nigh the whole Greek nation, using hope as well as fear to establish in them by means of prayers, oaths, oracles and omens, a lively sense of the divine. In your travels you may come upon cities without walls, writing, king, houses or property, doing without currency, having no notion of a theatre or gymnasium ; but a city without holy places and gods, without any observance of prayers, oaths, oracles, sacrifices for blessings received or rites to avert evils, no traveller has ever seen or will ever see. No, I think a city might rather be formed without the ground it stands on than a government, once you remove all religion from under it, get itself established or once established survive.[b] Now it is this belief, the underpinning and base that holds all society and legislation together, that the Epicureans, not by encirclement or covertly in riddles, but by launching against it the first of their most Cardinal

[a] Metrodorus, Frag. 41 (ed. Körte) ; *cf.* 1098 c-d, *supra.*
[b] *Cf.* Cicero, *De Nat. Deor.* i. 2 (4) with Pease's note.

[5] προσβαλόντες Apelt : προσλαβόντες EB.

PLUTARCH'S MORALIA

(1125) τρέπουσιν. εἶθ' ὥσπερ ὑπὸ Ποινῆς ἐλαυνόμενοι
δεινὰ ποιεῖν ὁμολογοῦσι συγχέοντες τὰ νόμιμα καὶ
τὰς διατάξεις τῶν νόμων ἀναιροῦντες, ἵνα μηδὲ
συγγνώμης τύχωσι. τὸ μὲν γὰρ ἁμαρτάνειν περὶ
δόξαν, εἰ καὶ μὴ σοφῶν,[1] ὅμως ἀνθρώπινόν ἐστι·
τὸ δὲ ἐγκαλεῖν ἑτέροις ἅπερ αὐτοὶ πράττουσι πῶς
ἄν τις εἴποι[2] φειδόμενος τῶν ἀξίων ὀνομάτων;

1126   32. "Εἰ γὰρ πρὸς Ἀντίδωρον ἢ Βίωνα τὸν σοφιστὴν γράφων ἐμνήσθη νόμων καὶ πολιτείας καὶ δια-
τάξεως, οὐκ ἄν τις εἶπεν αὐτῷ

'μέν', ὦ ταλαίπωρ',[3] ἀτρέμα[4] σοῖς ἐν δεμνίοις

περιστέλλων τὸ σαρκίδιον, ἐμοὶ δὲ περὶ τούτων
οἰκονομικῶς καὶ πολιτικῶς βεβιωκότες ἐγκαλεί-
τωσαν'· εἰσὶ δὲ οὗτοι πάντες οἷς Κωλώτης λελοιδόρηκεν. ὧν Δημόκριτος μὲν παραινεῖ τήν τε
πολεμικὴν τέχνην μεγίστην οὖσαν ἐκδιδάσκεσθαι
καὶ τοὺς πόνους διώκειν, ἀφ' ὧν τὰ μεγάλα καὶ
λαμπρὰ γίνεται[5] τοῖς ἀνθρώποις· Παρμενίδης δὲ
B τὴν ἑαυτοῦ πατρίδα διεκόσμησε νόμοις ἀρίστοις,
ὥστε τὰς ἀρχὰς καθ' ἕκαστον ἐνιαυτὸν ἐξορκοῦν
τοὺς πολίτας ἐμμενεῖν[6] τοῖς Παρμενίδου νόμοις·

[1] σοφῶν E : σοφῶν B.
[2] εἴποι B : εἴπῃ E.
[3] μένε ὦ ταλαίπωρε EB.
[4] ἀτρέμα E : ἀτρέμας B.
[5] γίνεται E : γίνονται B.
[6] ἐμμενεῖν Diels (ἦ μὴν ἐμμενεῖν van Herwerden) : ἐμμένειν EB.

[a] *Cardinal Tenet* i. The first four were the most cardinal :
cf. Westman, *op. cit.*, p. 230.
[b] Attacked by Epicurus : cf. B. A. Müller in Pauly-
Wissowa, Supp. iii (1918), coll. 120-121.

Tenets,[a] proceed directly to demolish. Then as if driven by some vengeful Fury they confess that in upsetting established observances and sweeping aside the ordinances of the laws they are committing a grave offence, as if on purpose to make it impossible to pardon them. For to be wrong in a belief is a failing, if not of sages, yet of men ; but to accuse others of doing what you are guilty of yourselves— how is that to be described without a generous expenditure of the strong language that it deserves ?

32. " For if he had brought up this matter of laws and government and ordinances in a book directed against Antidorus [b] or the sophist Bion,[c] no one would have retorted [d]

' Poor wretch, lie quiet in your coverlets [e]

wrapping cozily your bit of flesh, and let me see such charges brought by men who have shown by their lives that they can manage a household and serve the state.' But all that Colotes has abused are just such men. Democritus [f] urges us to seek instruction and mastery in the art of war, since it is of the first importance, and to pursue strenuous labours, which are for mankind the path to greatness and renown. Parmenides [g] appointed for his native city the best of laws, so that every year the citizens bind the magistrates by oath to abide by Parmenides' laws. Empe-

---

[c] See Bion's own account of his early career in Diogenes Laert. iv. 46-47.

[d] As Plutarch is doing now.

[e] Euripides, *Orestes*, 258 (said to Orestes, who is mad and raving) ; quoted also in *Mor.* 465 c, 501 c, and 788 f.

[f] Diels and Kranz, *Die Frag. der Vorsokratiker*, Demokritos, b 157 ; *cf.* 1100 c, *supra*.

[g] *Ibid.*, Parmenides, a 12.

(1126) Ἐμπεδοκλῆς δὲ τούς τε πρώτους τῶν πολιτῶν
ὑβρίζοντας καὶ διαφοροῦντας τὰ κοινὰ ἐξήλεγξε[1]
τήν τε χώραν ἀπήλλαξεν ἀκαρπίας καὶ λοιμοῦ δια-
σφάγας ὄρους ἀποτειχίσας δι' ὧν ὁ νότος εἰς τὸ
πεδίον ὑπερέβαλλε· Σωκράτης δὲ μετὰ τὴν κατα-
δίκην φυγῆς αὐτῷ μεμηχανημένης ὑπὸ τῶν φίλων
οὐκ ἐχρήσατο, τοὺς νόμους βεβαιῶν, ἀλλὰ ἀδίκως
ἀποθανεῖν εἵλετο μᾶλλον ἢ σωθῆναι παρανόμως·
Μέλισσος δὲ τῆς πατρίδος στρατηγῶν Ἀθηναίους
κατεναυμάχησε· Πλάτων δὲ καλοὺς μὲν ἐν γράμ-
C μασι λόγους περὶ νόμων καὶ πολιτείας ἀπέλιπε,
πολὺ δὲ κρείττονας ἐνεποίησε τοῖς ἑταίροις,[2] ἀφ'
ὧν Σικελία διὰ Δίωνος ἠλευθεροῦτο καὶ Θρᾴκη διὰ
Πύθωνος καὶ Ἡρακλείδου Κότυν ἀνελόντων, Ἀθηναίων δὲ Χαβρίαι στρατηγοὶ καὶ Φωκίωνες ἐξ
Ἀκαδημίας ἀνέβαινον. Ἐπίκουρος μὲν γὰρ εἰς
Ἀσίαν ἐξέπεμπε τοὺς Τιμοκράτει λοιδορησομένους
τῆς[3] βασιλικῆς ἐξελὼν[4] αὐλῆς τὸν ἄνθρωπον ὅτι
Μητροδώρῳ προσέκρουσεν ἀδελφὸς ὤν, καὶ ταῦτα
ἐν τοῖς βιβλίοις γέγραπται τοῖς[5] ἐκείνων· Πλάτων
δὲ τῶν ἑταίρων ἐξαπέστειλεν Ἀρκάσι μὲν Ἀρι-
στώνυμον διακοσμήσοντα τὴν πολιτείαν, Ἠλείοις δὲ

---

[1] ἐξήλεγξε Westman : ἐξελέγξας EB.
[2] ἑταίροις B[188] : ἑτέροις EB[t].
[3] Before τῆς Usener omits καί.
[4] ἐξελὼν Wyttenbach (ἐξελῶντας Madvig) : ἐξελὼν EB.
[5] τοῖς B : τῆς E.

---

[a] Diels and Kranz, *Die Frag. der Vorsokratiker*, Empedokles, A 14 ; *cf. Mor.* 515 c.
[b] As related in Plato's *Crito* ; *cf. Mor.* 581 c.
[c] *Cf. Life of Pericles*, chaps. xxvi–xxvii (166 C-E) and Diels
and Kranz, *Die Frag. der Vorsokratiker*, Melissos, A 3.

docles [a] convicted the foremost men of his city of
flouting the laws and plundering the public funds,
and delivered the land from sterility and plague by
walling up clefts in the mountain through which the
south wind spilled over into the plain. Socrates after
condemnation refused the opportunity of escape that
his friends had contrived for him,[b] thus upholding
the laws, and preferred an unjust death to an unlawful
escape. Melissus [c] led his country's forces and defeated the Athenians at sea. And though Plato [d]
left us in his writings an admirable philosophy of laws
and of the state, the philosophy that he implanted in
his disciples was more admirable by far, a philosophy
that brought freedom to Sicily through Dion,[e] and to
Thrace through Python [f] and Heracleides,[g] the slayers
of Cotys, while at Athens such generals as Chabrias and
Phocion [h] came up from the Academy. Thus while
Epicurus [i] sends people off to Asia to rail at Timocrates, meaning to drive the man from court because
he had fallen out with Metrodorus, whose brother
he was—and this is published in their books—Plato
sent one disciple, Aristonymus, to the Arcadians to
reform their constitution, another, Phormio,[j] to the

[d] R. M. Jones, *The Platonism of Plutarch* (Menasha,
1916), p. 139, notes the reference to Plato, *Phaedrus*, 275-
276.

[e] These happenings were roughly contemporary. Cotys
was killed in 359 ; Dion set out for Sicily in 357 ; Chabrias
is first heard of as general in 390–389, last in 357–356 ; and
Phocion (born 402–401, executed in 318) was forty-five times
general, beginning not later than 365–364.

[f] Cf. *Mor.* 542 E, 816 E.

[g] Cf. F. Wehrli, *Herakleides Pontikos*, p. 62, note to Frag.
11.

[h] Cf. *Life of Phocion*, chap. iv. 2 (743 c).

[i] Cf. Usener, *Epicurea*, p. 123. 22 ; Körte, *Metrodori
Epicurei Fragmenta*, p. 555.   [j] Cf. *Mor.* 805 D.

(1126)
D Φορμίωνα, Μενέδημον[1] δὲ Πυρραίοις. Εὔδοξος δὲ
Κνιδίοις καὶ Ἀριστοτέλης Σταγειρίταις, Πλάτωνος
ὄντες συνήθεις, νόμους ἔγραψαν· παρὰ δὲ Ξενοκρά-
τους Ἀλέξανδρος ὑποθήκας ᾔτησε περὶ βασιλείας·
ὁ δὲ πεμφθεὶς πρὸς Ἀλέξανδρον ὑπὸ τῶν ἐν Ἀσίᾳ
κατοικούντων Ἑλλήνων καὶ μάλιστα διακαύσας
καὶ παροξύνας ἅψασθαι τοῦ πρὸς τοὺς βαρβάρους
πολέμου Δήλιος ἦν Ἐφέσιος, ἑταῖρος Πλάτωνος.
Ζήνων τοίνυν ὁ Παρμενίδου γνώριμος ἐπιθέμενος
Δημύλῳ[2] τῷ τυράννῳ καὶ δυστυχήσας περὶ τὴν
πρᾶξιν ἐν πυρὶ τὸν Παρμενίδου λόγον ὥσπερ χρυσὸν
ἀκήρατον καὶ δόκιμον παρέσχε, καὶ ἀπέδειξεν ἔρ-
E γοις ὅτι τὸ αἰσχρὸν ἀνδρὶ μεγάλῳ φοβερόν ἐστιν,
ἀλγηδόνα δὲ παῖδες καὶ γύναια καὶ γυναίων ψυχὰς
ἔχοντες ἄνδρες δεδίασι· τὴν γὰρ γλῶτταν αὑτοῦ[3]
διατραγὼν[4] τῷ τυράννῳ προσέπτυσεν.

33. " Ἐκ δὲ τῶν Ἐπικούρου λόγων καὶ δογμάτων οὐ λέγω τίς τυραννοκτόνος ἢ τίς ἀριστεὺς ἢ
τίς νομοθέτης ἢ τίς ἄρχων ἢ βασιλέως σύμβουλος
ἢ δήμου προστάτης ἢ βεβασανισμένος ὑπὲρ τῶν
δικαίων ἢ τεθνηκώς, ἀλλὰ τίς τῶν σοφῶν ἔπλευσεν
ὑπὲρ τῆς πατρίδος, ἐπρέσβευσεν, ἀνήλωσε; ποῦ γέγραπται πολιτικὴ πρᾶξις ὑμῖν; καίτοι ὅτι Μητρό-

---

[1] μενέδημον B : μελέδημον E, Marc. Gr. 517.
[2] Δημύλῳ Basle edition of 1542 : διμύλῳ EB.
[3] αὑτοῦ Stephanus, Xylander : αὐτοῦ EB.
[4] διατραγὼν van Herwerden : διατρώγων EB.

---

[a] Cf. Wilamowitz, Antigonos von Karystos (Berlin, 1881),
pp. 86 f.
[b] For this passage see the references in I. Düring, Aristotle in the Ancient Biographical Tradition (Gothenburg,
1957), p. 292.

REPLY TO COLOTES, 1126

Eleans, and a third, Menedemus,[a] to the Pyrrhaeans. Eudoxus drew up laws for the Cnidians, Aristotle [b] for the Stagirites ; both were men of Plato's company. Alexander applied to Xenocrates [c] for rules of royal government ; and the emissary sent to Alexander by the Greeks of Asia, who more than any other kindled his ardour and spurred him on to take up the war against the barbarians, was Delius [d] of Ephesus, a follower of Plato. Thus Zeno,[e] the disciple of Parmenides, after an unsuccessful attempt upon the life of the tyrant Demylus, revealed when tried in the fire that the teaching of Parmenides in his heart was like the purest gold and equal to the proof,[f] and demonstrated by the evidence of deeds that what a great man fears is shame, whereas pain is feared by children and weak women and men with such women's souls, for he bit off his tongue and spat it in the tyrant's face.

33. "But what has proceeded from Epicurus' philosophy and maxims ? I do not ask what slayer of tyrants or what champion in battle or what lawgiver or governor or adviser of kings or leader of his people or who that in a just cause has endured torment or death, I simply ask : Who of the sages ever took ship in his country's interests, went on an embassy, or expended a sum of money ? [g] Where in your writings is there any mention of an act of public service ? Yet

---

[c] Cf. R. Heinze, *Xenokrates* (Leipzig, 1892), p. 158.

[d] Perhaps the Dias of Philostratus, *Lives of the Sophists*, i. 3 (485-486).

[e] Diels and Kranz, *Die Frag. der Vorsokratiker*, Zenon, A 7 ; cf. *Mor.* 505 D, 1051 c. The shame would have been the betrayal of his accomplices.

[f] Cf. Plato, *Republic*, vi, 503 A.

[g] Cf. *Mor.* 1033 B-c for a similar criticism of the Stoics.

(1126) δωρος εἰς Πειραιᾶ κατέβη σταδίους τεσσαράκοντα
F Μιθρῇ¹ τινι Σύρῳ τῶν βασιλικῶν συνειλημμένῳ
βοηθήσων, πρὸς πάντας ἐγράφετο² καὶ πάσας³ ἐπι-
στολαῖς, μεγαληγορῶντος Ἐπικούρου καὶ σεμνύ-
νοντος ἐκείνην τὴν ὁδόν. τί οὖν εἴ τι τοιοῦτον
ἐπέπρακτο αὐτοῖς οἷον Ἀριστοτέλει, τὴν πατρίδα
κτίσαι⁴ διεφθαρμένην ὑπὸ Φιλίππου, Θεοφράστῳ δὲ
δὶς ἐλευθερῶσαι τυραννουμένην; οὐκ ἐπιλιπεῖν ἔδει
πρότερον φέροντα βύβλους⁵ τὸν Νεῖλον ἢ τούτους
ἀποκαμεῖν γράφοντας περὶ αὐτῶν;⁶ καὶ οὐ τοῦτο
1127 δεινόν ἐστιν, ὅτι τοσούτων ὄντων φιλοσόφων μόνοι
σχεδὸν ἀσύμβολοι τῶν ἐν ταῖς πόλεσιν ἀγαθῶν
κοινωνοῦσιν, ἀλλ' ὅτι καὶ τραγῳδιῶν ποιηταὶ καὶ
κωμῳδιῶν ἀεί τι πειρῶνται χρήσιμον παρέχεσθαι
καὶ λέγειν ὑπὲρ νόμων καὶ πολιτείας, οὗτοι δέ, κἂν
γράφωσι, γράφουσι περὶ πολιτείας ἵνα μὴ πολι-
τευώμεθα, καὶ περὶ ῥητορικῆς ἵνα μὴ ῥητορεύωμεν,
καὶ περὶ βασιλείας ἵνα⁷ φεύγωμεν τὸ συμβιοῦν βα-
σιλεῦσι· τοὺς δὲ πολιτικοὺς ἄνδρας ἐπὶ γέλωτι καὶ
καταλύσει τῆς δόξης ὀνομάζουσι⁸ μόνον ὡς⁹ τὸν
Ἐπαμεινώνδαν, ἐσχηκέναι τι λέγοντες ἀγαθὸν καὶ

¹ Μιθρῇ Usener : μίθρη EB.
² ἐγράφετο Reiske : ἐγράφέ τε EB.
³ πάσας Rasmus : πάσαις EB.
⁴ κτίσαι EBᶜ : κτῆσαι Bᵃᶜ.
⁵ βύβλους van Herwerden : βίβλους EB.
⁶ αὐτῶν EB : αὑτῶν Stephanus (defended by Post).
⁷ After ἵνα the Basle edition of 1542 omits μή.
⁸ ὀνομάζουσι Amyot : ὀνόμασι EB.
⁹ μόνον ὡς Pohlenz (μόνον Amyot ; ὡς Dübner) : μόνοις EB.

ᵃ Test. 14, p. 567 (ed. Körte).
ᵇ About five miles.
ᶜ A minister of Lysimachus who early befriended Epicurus and continued friendly to the school. Presumably his

when Metrodorus [a] went down to the Peiraeus, a distance of some forty stades,[b] to help one Mithres,[c] a Syrian, a royal officer who had been arrested, letters went out to everyone, men and women alike, with Epicurus' [d] solemn glorification of that journey. Well, what would have happened if they had done as great a thing as Aristotle, who restored his native city which Philip had destroyed,[e] or Theophrastus, who twice delivered his from tyrants ? Would not the supply of papyrus have had to run out through over-cropping of the Nile before these men would have wearied of writing about it ? What is grave is not so much that among so many philosophers these alone (one might say) enjoy the advantages of civilized life without paying their share ; it is that poets, both tragic and comic, are always trying to convey some useful lesson and take the side of law and government ; whereas these men, if they write about such matters at all, write on government [f] to deter us from taking part in it, on oratory [g] to deter us from public speaking, and about kingship [h] to make us shun the company of kings.[i] They [j] mention statesmen only to deride them and belittle their fame, for instance Epameinondas, who they say had but one good thing

---

arrest occurred after the defeat and death of Lysimachus (281 B.C.). See W. Liebich, *Aufbau, Absicht und Form der Pragmateiai Philodems* (Berlin-Steglitz, 1960), p. 95, note 1.

[d] Frag. 194 (ed. Usener) ; *cf.* 1097 B, *supra*.

[e] *Cf.* 1097 B, *supra* and the *Vita Marciana* of Aristotle, 17 (p. 100, ed. Düring ; line 83, ed. Gigon).

[f] Frag. 8 (ed. Usener) ; *cf.* Frag. 525.

[g] *Cf.* Usener, *Epicurea*, p. 109. 17 ; Diogenes of Oenoanda, Frag. 54 (p. 93, ed. Grilli).

[h] Frag. 6 (ed. Usener).

[i] *Cf.* Seneca, *Ep.* 22. 5.

[j] Frag. 560 (ed. Usener).

(1127) τοῦτο δὲ μικκόν,[1] οὑτωσὶ τῷ ῥήματι φράζοντες,
B αὐτὸν δὲ σιδηροῦν σπλάγχνον ἀποκαλοῦντες καὶ
πυνθανόμενοι τί παθὼν ἐβάδιζε διὰ τῆς Πελοποννή-
σου μέσης καὶ οὐ πιλίδιον ἔχων οἴκοι καθῆτο,[2] δη-
λαδὴ περὶ τὴν τῆς γαστρὸς ἐπιμέλειαν ὅλος καθε-
στώς. ἃ δὲ Μητρόδωρος ἐν τῷ περὶ φιλοσοφίας
ἐξορχούμενος πολιτείαν γέγραφεν οὐκ ᾤμην δεῖν
παρεῖναι· λέγει δὲ ὅτι ʻ τῶν σοφῶν τινες ὑπὸ δαψι-
λείας τύφου οὕτως[3] καλῶς ἐνεῖδον τὸ ἔργον αὐτῆς
ὥστε οἴχονται φερόμενοι πρὸς τὰς αὐτὰς Λυκούργῳ
καὶ Σόλωνι ἐπιθυμίας κατὰ τοὺς περὶ βίων λόγους
καὶ ἀρετῆς.ʼ τῦφος οὖν ἦν καὶ δαψίλεια τύφου τὸ
ἐλευθέρας εἶναι τὰς Ἀθήνας τήν τε[4] Σπάρτην εὐνο-
C μεῖσθαι καὶ τοὺς νέους μὴ θρασύνεσθαι, μηδ' ἐξ
ἑταιρῶν παιδοποιεῖσθαι μηδὲ πλοῦτον καὶ τρυφὴν
καὶ ἀσέλγειαν ἄρχειν ἀλλὰ νόμον καὶ δικαιοσύνην
ἐν ταῖς πόλεσιν· αὗται γὰρ ἦσαν ἐπιθυμίαι Σόλωνος.
καὶ λοιδορῶν ὁ Μητρόδωρος ἐπιλέγει τοῖς εἰρημένοις ʻ διὸ καὶ καλῶς ἔχει τὸν ἐλεύθερον ὡς ἀληθῶς γέλωτα γελάσαι ἐπί τε δὴ πᾶσιν ἀνθρώποις

---

[1] μικκὸν Stephanus : μίκκον EB.
[2] καθῆτο Leonicus : κάθητο EB.   [3] οὕτως E : οὕτω B.
[4] τήν τε Pohlenz (τε καὶ τὴν or καὶ τὴν Ald.[2]) : τε τὴν EB.

---

[a] In the Greek mikkon, Boeotian for mikron, " small."
Even the one good thing about him, his abstention from unnecessary pleasures, was an example of the Boeotian insensibility.
[b] That is, lacking ordinary human sensibility to hardship.
[c] The great Peloponnesian campaign of 370–369 took
place in winter.   [d] Frag. 31 (ed. Körte).
[e] Plato, Diogenes (the Cynic), and Zeno (of Citium) took
Lycurgus' state as model for their Republics (Life of Lycurgus,
chap. xxxi. 2 [59 A]). Metrodorus has the Republic ascribed
to Diogenes in mind, as is shown by his mention of " conceit " and " prodigality."

310

about him, and even that ' sma' '[a] (for this is their
expression), and dubbing the man himself ' iron-
guts '[b] and asking what possessed him to go walking
across the Peloponnese and not sit at home with a
nice felt cap on his head,[c] wholly concerned (we must
suppose) with the care and feeding of his belly. And
Metrodorus'[d] frivolous dismissal of the state in his
work *On Philosophy* should not, I believe, be allowed
to pass unnoticed. ' Certain sages,'[e] he says, ' in
their prodigality of conceit, have been so well able
to detect the function of the state that in their discourse about ways of life and about virtue they go
flying off after the same desires as Lycurgus and
Solon.' Then it was conceit and prodigality of conceit,
this notion that Athens should be free,[f] and Sparta
ruled by law and order[g] with the young men knowing
their place[h]—and that we should not take harlots
for mothers of our children[i] and that wealth, luxury,
and brutal licence should not prevail in our cities, but
law and justice,[j] for these were among the desires of
Solon. And to the remarks quoted Metrodorus[k] adds
this piece of abuse : ' It is therefore fitting to burst
into the laughter of one truly free at all men[l] and

[f] *Cf. Life of Solon*, chap. xv. 6 (86 E).
[g] *Cf. Life of Lycurgus*, chap. v. 4 (42 B).
[h] A reference to the strict Lycurgan education of the young.
[i] *Cf.* 1098 B, *supra*; Metrodorus' union with Leontion was fruitful. For Solon's law, which dispensed the son of a hetaera from supporting his father, *cf. Life of Solon*, chap. xxii. 4 (90 E).
[j] *Cf. Life of Solon*, chapters xiii-xvi (84 F—87 D).
[k] Frag. 32 (ed. Körte).
[l] Diogenes laughs at men for not having the hardihood of animals (*cf.* Dio Chrysostom, *Or.* vi. 13-34) ; Diogenes alone is free (*ibid.* 34).

(1127) καὶ ἐπὶ τοῖς Λυκούργοις τούτοις καὶ Σόλωσιν.'
ἀλλ' οὐκ ἐλεύθερος οὗτος, ὦ Μητρόδωρε,[1] ἐστὶν
ἀλλ' ἀνελεύθερος καὶ ἀνάγωγος καὶ οὐδὲ μάστιγος
ἐλευθέρας δεόμενος, ἀλλὰ τῆς ἀστραγαλωτῆς ἐκείνης ᾗ[2] τοὺς Γάλλους πλημμελοῦντας ἐν τοῖς Μητρῴοις κολάζουσιν.

D   34. " "Ὅτι δὲ οὐ νομοθέταις ἀλλὰ νόμοις ἐπολέ-
μουν ἔξεστιν ἀκούειν Ἐπικούρου· ἐρωτᾷ γὰρ αὐτὸν[3]
ἐν ταῖς διαπορίαις εἰ πράξει[4] τινὰ ὁ σοφὸς ὧν οἱ
νόμοι ἀπαγορεύουσιν, εἰδὼς ὅτι λήσει, καὶ ἀπο-
κρίνεται· ' οὐκ εὔοδον τὸ ἁπλοῦν ἐπικατηγόρημα,'[5]
τουτέστι, ' πράξω μέν, οὐ βούλομαι δὲ ὁμολογεῖν.'
πάλιν δὲ οἶμαι γράφων πρὸς Ἰδομενέα διακελεύεται
' μὴ νόμοις καὶ δόξαις δουλεύοντα ζῆν, ἐφ' ὅσον ἂν
μὴ τὴν διὰ τοῦ πέλας ἐκ πληγῆς ὄχλησιν παρα-
σκευάζωσιν.' εἴπερ οὖν οἱ νόμους καὶ πολιτείας
ἀναιροῦντες τὸν βίον ἀναιροῦσι τὸν ἀνθρώπινον,

E   Ἐπίκουρος δὲ καὶ Μητρόδωρος τοῦτο ποιοῦσι,

---

[1] μητρόδωρε E : μητρόδωρ' B.   [2] ᾗ Turnebus : ἢ EB.
[3] αὐτὸν Stephanus : αὐτὸν EB.
[4] εἰ πράξει E : εἰς πρᾶξιν B.
[5] ἐπικατηγόρημα EB : ἐστι κατηγόρημα Stephanus.

---

[a] Apuleius (*Metamorphoses*, viii. 28) describes a celebration where a Gallus (a self-castrated devotee of the Great
Mother) accuses himself of sins and then punishes himself
with a whip loaded with knucklebones. Plutarch may have
in mind some saying of Arcesilaüs. Asked why men leave
the other schools for the Epicurean, but never the Epicurean,
he said : " Men become Galli, but Galli never become men "
(Diogenes Laert. iv. 43). Again he said of a student overbold
in disputation, " Will not someone check him with a knuckle ? "
(*ibid.* 34). Plato compares a long-winded answerer to a
bronze vessel that keeps booming when struck until it is
silenced by putting the hand to it (*Protagoras*, 329 A).
" Knuckle " can also mean this sort of loaded whip.

more particularly at these Lycurguses and Solons.' Such laughter is not that of a free man, Metrodorus, but servile and ill-bred, and it does not even call for a freeman's lash but for that loaded knout which punishes the Galli for their sins at the rites of the Great Mother.[a]

34. "That their war, moreover, was not with lawgivers but with laws we may learn from Epicurus,[b] who asks himself in the *Disputed Questions* whether the sage who knows that he will not be found out will do certain things that the laws forbid. He answers, 'the unqualified predication is not free from difficulty' —that is, 'I shall do it, but I do not wish to admit it.' Again—in a letter [c] to Idomeneus, I believe—he calls upon him 'not to live in servitude to laws and men's opinions, as long as they refrain from making trouble in the form of a blow administered by your neighbour.' [d] If, then, to abolish laws and governments is to abolish humane living, and if Epicurus and Metro-

[b] Frag. 18 (ed. Usener). The question was no doubt suggested by the reason Epicurus gave for observing justice or the compact neither to injure nor be injured : there is no assurance of not being found out, and the fear of punishment is an evil (*Cardinal Tenets* xxxiv, xxxv). Suppose the fear of detection removed : will the sage disobey the laws ? The answer was probably on the lines of *Cardinal Tenet* xxxviii : when the advantage that is promoted by the rule ceases to exist, what was just before ceases to be just. It is no doubt this kind of law, that enforces what has ceased to be just, that the sage will violate when assured of impunity.

[c] Frag. 134 (ed. Usener).

[d] According to Seneca, *Ep.* 21. 3, Idomeneus held a position of high importance under a strict government. Epicurus is saying that Idomeneus is not to take his legal duties and high standing so seriously that he becomes a slave to them ; and " neighbour " may well be a covert way of referring to Lysimachus. His seat, Lysimacheia, was a little over twenty miles from Lampsacus, where Idomeneus lived.

(1127) τοὺς μὲν συνήθεις ἀποτρέποντες τοῦ τὰ κοινὰ πράττειν, τοῖς δὲ πράττουσιν ἀπεχθανόμενοι, τοὺς δὲ
πρώτους καὶ σοφωτάτους τῶν νομοθετῶν κακῶς
λέγοντες, τῶν δὲ νόμων παρακελευόμενοι περιφρο-
νεῖν, ἐὰν μὴ προσῇ φόβος πληγῆς καὶ κολάσεως,
οὐκ οἶδα τί τηλικοῦτο κατέψευσται τῶν ἄλλων ὁ
Κωλώτης ἡλίκον ἀληθῶς τῶν Ἐπικούρου λόγων
καὶ δογμάτων κατηγόρηκεν.''

dorus do just this when they *a* dissuade their followers from public service and quarrel with those engaged in it, and again when they speak despitefully of the earliest and wisest lawgivers *b* and recommend contempt for law if it is not supported by the fear of a blow or punishment, I know of no false charge directed by Colotes against the others so grave as his true arraignment of Epicurus' philosophy and teaching."

a 1125 c, *supra.*   *b* 1127 b-c, *supra.*

IS "LIVE UNKNOWN" A
WISE PRECEPT?
(AN RECTE DICTUM SIT LATENTER
ESSE VIVENDUM)

INTRODUCTION

THE seventh of the Epicurean *Cardinal Tenets* states :
" Some persons have wished to gain fame and celebrity, thinking that in this way they would acquire
security from other men. If, then, the life of such
men is secure, they have achieved the good of their
nature ; but if their life is not secure, they do not
possess the end that they originally sought in conformity with the requirements of their nature."
Similarly, in a passage preserved by Plutarch (*Mor.*
37 A), Epicurus says : " Happiness and blessedness
are not found in the amount of one's wealth or the
eminence of one's position or in office or authority,
but in absence of pain and calmness of feeling and in
a disposition of mind that marks the limits of what is
natural." [a] The Epicurean maxim, " Live unknown,"
was no doubt an expression of this rejection of the
desire for pre-eminence.[b]

Plutarch attacks the maxim in a number of ways :
(1) Epicurus was dishonest in saying it, for his motive
was a desire for fame (chap. i) ; (2) the concealment
of one's vices prevents their cure, the concealment
of one's virtues renders them useless to others (chaps.
ii-iii) ; (3) whereas sensual gratification requires

---

[a] *Cf.* also Lucretius, ii. 1-14, iii. 59-73 ; Diogenes of
Oenoanda, Frag. xxiv, coll. ii. 3-iii. 1 (ed. Grilli) ; and *Gnom.
Vat.* 67 and 81.

[b] See C. Bailey, *The Greek Atomists and Epicurus* (Oxford,
1928), p. 516.

darkness, virtuous conduct deserves to be exhibited for all to see (chap. iv) ; (4) recognition provides the occasion and the incentive for action, while obscurity dulls body and mind (chaps. iv-v) ; (5) man by his very nature seeks the light ; that is, man desires to know and to be known (chap. vi) ; and (6) those who have won fame for virtuous activity are rewarded after death, whereas the oblivion that follows on inaction is a punishment (chap. vii).

There is no clear evidence of date of composition. Pohlenz [a] would date the essay earlier than the *Adversus Colotem* and the *Non Posse Suaviter Vivi Secundum Epicurum* ; G. M. Lattanzi [b] would put it later. K. Ziegler [c] sees in the abrupt beginning and the presence of hiatus indications that it is an unfinished sketch.

The essay is translated in the versions of all the *Moralia* listed in vol. I (pp. xxviii-xxx) ; *cf.* also vol. VII (pp.x-xi). Of translations not mentioned or not specified there, we add the following :

D. ERASMUS, " Num recte dictum sit, λάθε βιώσας, id est, sic vive ut nemo te sentiat vixisse." In *Opuscula Plutarchi nuper traducta.* Erasmo Rot. interprete, Basle, 1514. We have consulted this version in the Paris edition of 1544 (pp. 185-187).

GIOVANNI TARCAGNOTTA, " Se è ben detto vivi sì, che niuno il sappia." In *Opuscoli Morali di Plutarco* . . . Venice, 1598 (Part I), pp. 609-612.

[a] *Plutarchi Moralia*, vol. vi. 2 (Leipzig, 1952), p. 123.
[b] " La composizione del *De Latenter Vivendo* di Plutarco," *Rivista di Filologia e di Istruzione Classica*, vol. lx (1932), pp. 332-337.
[c] Pauly-Wissowa, vol. xxi. 1 (1951), col. 766. See also the comment of Pohlenz in *Plutarchi Moralia*, vol. iii (Leipzig, 1929), p. xvii.

PLUTARCH'S MORALIA

Marcello Adriani, " Se è ben detto vivi sì che niun
lo sappia." In *Opusculi di Plutarco volgarizzati da
Marcello Adriani* . . . Tomo quarto, Milan, 1827,
pp. 571-578.
Charles Whitaker, " Whether 'twere rightly said,
Live Conceal'd." In *Plutarch's Morals* : Trans-
lated from the Greek by Several Hands. Vol.
III[5], London, 1718, pp. 35-42.
A. R. Shilleto, " Whether ' Live Unknown ' be a
Wise Precept." In *Plutarch's Morals* . . . Lon-
don, 1898, pp. 373-378.
J. J. Hartman, " Het boekje over de vraag : Of het
en goede leer is ' Leef onopgemerkt.' " In *De
Avondzon des Heidendoms*[2], Tweede Deel, Leyden,
1912, pp. 233-238.
O. Apelt, " Ob es eine richtige Vorschrift sei : Lebe
im Verborgenen." In *Plutarch, Moralische
Schriften* I, Leipzig, 1926, pp. 111-118.
W. P. Theunissen, " Of de uitspraak : ' Leef in het
verborgene ' juist is." In *Plutarchus, Een bloem-
lezing uit zijn geschriften*, Haarlem, 1950, pp.
309-313.
Felicità Portalupi, *Plutarco De latenter vivendo*. Tra-
duzione e note (Università di Torino, Pubblica-
zioni della Facoltà di Magistero, 22). Turin,
1961.

Twenty-five mss. of the *De latenter vivendo* are
known to us : LCy HUαnBrAγπσκτβμςδEψ g cd.
Seven are independent, and are related as shown in
the diagram on the following page. ms. d derives
from c ; the rest derive from α, a copy of U. Their
relations are the same as in the *Non Posse Suaviter
Vivi Secundum Epicurum*. C² used a ms. allied to A, and
is not cited ; ψ is a copy of Stephanus' edition. The
320

six excerpts in ϛ, adding up in all to about 36 lines of Pohlenz' text, are most closely related to μ and the Aldine, as in the *De Fato* and the *Consolatio ad Uxorem.*

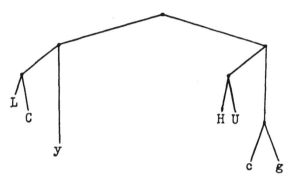

The essay is No. 178 in the Catalogue of Lamprias.

ΕΙ ΚΑΛΩΣ ΕΙΡΗΤΑΙ ΤΟ ΛΑΘΕ ΒΙΩΣΑΣ[1]

1128 1. Ἀλλ' οὐδὲ ὁ[2] τοῦτο εἰπὼν λαθεῖν ἠθέλησεν·
B αὐτὸ γὰρ τοῦτο εἶπεν ἵνα μὴ λάθῃ, ὥς τι φρονῶν
περιττότερον ἐκ τῆς εἰς ἀδοξίαν προτροπῆς δόξαν
ἄδικον ποριζόμενος·

μισῶ σοφιστὴν ὅστις οὐχ αὑτῷ σοφός.

τοὺς μὲν γὰρ περὶ Φιλόξενον τὸν Ἐρύξιδος[3] καὶ
Γνάθωνα τὸν Σικελιώτην ἐπτοημένους περὶ τὰ ὄψα
λέγουσιν ἐναπομύττεσθαι[4] ταῖς παροψίσιν ὅπως
τοὺς συνεσθίοντας διατρέψαντες[5] αὐτοὶ μόνοι τῶν
παρακειμένων ἐμφορηθῶσιν· οἱ δὲ ἀκράτως[6] φιλό-
δοξοι καὶ κατακόρως διαβάλλουσιν ἑτέροις τὴν
δόξαν ὥσπερ ἀντερασταῖς ἵνα τυγχάνωσιν αὐτῆς
ἀνανταγωνίστως, καὶ ταὐτὸ[7] τοῖς ἐρέσσουσιν ποι-
C οῦσιν[8]· ὡς γὰρ ἐκεῖνοι πρὸς τὴν πρύμναν ἀφορῶντες

---

[1] εἰ καλῶς εἴρηται τὸ λάθε βιώσας y HU (with an erasure of 25 letters in the preceding line) g c : L is illegible ; C omits for the rubricator ; περὶ τοῦ λάθε βιώσας Catalogue of Lamprias. [2] ὁ LCy HU : g c omit.

[3] Ἐρύξιδος] εὐρύξιδος L?Cy[1].

[4] ἐναπομύττεσθαι g c : ἐναμύττεσθαι L?Cy (ἐνά- H)U.

[5] διατρέψαντες HU[1] g c : διαστρέψαντες (L illegible) Cy U[2].

[6] ἀκράτως HU[1] g c : ἀκρατῶς LCy U[2].

[7] ταὐτὸ HU (L illegible ; ταὐτὸν C ; ταυτον y) : ταυτὰ g ; ταυτὶ c.

[8] ποιοῦσιν] (L illegible) C[1]y omit.

IS "LIVE UNKNOWN" A WISE
PRECEPT?

1. But not even the author [a] of the precept wished to be unknown, as he made this very statement to escape from being unknown, dishonestly courting fame as a person of no ordinary wisdom by his advice to seek obscurity :

> I hate the sage who recks not his own rede. [b]

Now Philoxenus [c] son of Eryxis and Gnathon [d] of Sicily were so excited about fine food that (it is said) they blew their noses on the dainties to discourage the other banqueters and so be the only ones to stuff themselves with the food on the table. So those with an inordinate and unrelieved appetite for fame disparage fame to others, their rivals as it were in love, in order to secure it without competition. [e] Herein they operate like oarsmen : for as rowers face the stern of the ship, yet by their efforts add to the

[a] Epicurus ; cf. Frag. 551 (ed. Usener).
[b] Euripides, Frag. 905 (Nauck, *Trag. Graec. Frag.*, p. 652) ; also quoted in the *Life of Alexander*, chap. liii. 2 (695 c).
[c] Cf. *Mor.* 668 c and Frag. 25. 2 (vol. vii, p. 132. 2, ed. Bern.).
[d] Cf. *Mor.* 707 E.
[e] On Epicurus' thirst for fame cf. 1100 A-c, *supra*.

(1128) τῆς νεὼς τῇ κατὰ πρῷραν ὁρμῇ[1] συνεργοῦσιν ὡς
ἂν[2] ἐκ τῆς ἀνακοπῆς περίρροια[3] καταλαμβάνουσα
συνεπωθῇ[4] τὸ πορθμεῖον, οὕτως οἱ τὰ τοιαῦτα παρ-
αγγέλματα διδόντες ὥσπερ ἀπεστραμμένοι τὴν
δόξαν διώκουσιν.[5] ἐπεὶ τί λέγειν[6] ἔδει τοῦτο,[7] τί
δὲ[8] γράφειν καὶ γράψαντα ἐκδιδόναι πρὸς τὸν μετὰ
ταῦτα χρόνον, εἰ λαθεῖν ἐβούλετο τοὺς ὄντας ὁ μηδὲ
τοὺς ἐσομένους;

2. Ἀλλὰ τοῦτο[9] μὲν αὐτὸ τὸ[10] πρᾶγμα πῶς οὐ
πονηρόν· λάθε βιώσας—ὡς τυμβωρυχήσας;[11] ἀλλ'
αἰσχρόν ἐστι τὸ ζῆν, ἵνα ἀγνοῶμεν πάντες; ἐγὼ δ'
D ἂν εἴποιμι μηδὲ κακῶς βιώσας λάθε, ἀλλὰ γνώ-
σθητι, σωφρονίσθητι, μετανόησον· εἴτε ἀρετὴν ἔ-
χεις, μὴ γένῃ ἄχρηστος, εἴτε κακίαν, μὴ μείνῃς
ἀθεράπευτος.

Μᾶλλον δὲ διελοῦ[12] καὶ διόρισον τίνι τοῦτο προστάττεις. εἰ μὲν ἀμαθεῖ καὶ πονηρῷ καὶ ἀγνώμονι,[13] οὐθὲν[14] διαφέρεις τοῦ λέγοντος, '' λάθε καὶ
πυρέττων, λάθε[15] φρενιτίζων,[16] μὴ γνῶ σε ὁ[17] ἰατρός·

---

[1] τῇ . . . ὁρμῇ g : τὴν . . . ὁρμὴν (L illegible)Cy HU
c(with odd -ὴν²).

[2] συνεργοῦσιν ὡς ἂν (L illegible)Cy U² g c : ὡς συνεργοῦσιν
ὅσον HU¹.

[3] περίρροια y HU g c (-αν [L illegible]C¹) : παλίρροια van
Herwerden.   [4] συνεπωθῇ LCy U² g : -εῖ HU¹ c.

[5] διώκουσιν LCy HU : δι and a blank of 5 letters g ; διω
and a blank of 6 letters c.   [6] λέγειν LCy HU g : λέγεις c.

[7] τοῦτο LCy HU : τὸ g ; c omits in a blank of 4 letters.

[8] δὲ] δεῖ g.   [9] τοῦτο] τούτῳ Post.

[10] τὸ y HU g c : LC omit.

[11] τυμβωρυχήσας y U² g c : τυμβορυχήσας LC HU¹.

[12] διελοῦ LCy H²ᵐU g c : H¹ omits.

[13] ἀγνώμονι LC¹y : ἀνοήτῳ HU g c.

[14] οὐθὲν LC HU g : οὐδὲν y c.

[15] λάθε HU g : λάθε καὶ LCy c.

[16] φρενιτίζων y (-νη- LC HU) : φροντίζων g c.

forward push of the prow, inasmuch as the eddy of
the water from their backdrive whirls about, over-
takes the vessel and helps to drive it forward [a]; just
so people who offer recommendations of this kind
pursue fame, you might say, with their backs turned
to it. For what need was there for him to say this,
what need to write it and then publish it for the years
to come, if he wanted to be unknown to the people
of his day, this man who did not even want to be
unknown to posterity? [b]

2. But surely the thing he speaks of must itself be
evil: " Keep your life unknown"—as you would your
grave-robbing? Why, is life a shameful thing, that
none of us should know about it? My own advice
would be : do not even let your evil living be
unknown, but be known for what you are, be chas-
tened, reconsider. If you have virtues, don't fail to
make yourself useful ; if you have vices, don't neglect
the cure.

Better still, distinguish and define the sort of person
to whom you address this command. If you speak
so to one who is foolish, vicious and unfeeling, you are
no better than one who says, " Let your fever too be
unknown, your madness ; don't let the physician

---

[a] This explanation was suggested by the theory of *anti-
peristasis*, which accounts for an object (for example a stone
when thrown) continuing to move after losing contact with the
mover : the air in front of the object is pushed onward, and
imparts a push to other air, and finally to the air which closes
behind the object and thus pushes it forward. *Cf.* Plato,
Tim. 58 E—59 A, Aristotle, *Physics*, iv. 8 (215 a 14 ff.), and
Simplicius, *ad loc.* (p. 668. 25–669. 2, ed. Diels).

[b] *Cf.* Cicero, *Pro Archia*, 11 (26) : " Ipsi illi philosophi
etiam in eis libellis quos de contemnenda gloria scribunt
nomen suum inscribunt."

---

[17] γνῶ σε ὁ LCy HU g : γνώσεται c.

(1128) ἴθι ῥίψας ποι κατὰ σκότους¹ σεαυτόν, ἀγνοούμενος²
τοῖς³ πάθεσιν. καὶ σὺ ἴθι τῇ κακίᾳ νόσον ἀνήκεστον
νοσῶν καὶ ὀλέθριον,⁴ ἀποκρύπτων τοὺς φθόνους,
τὰς δεισιδαιμονίας, ὥσπερ τινὰς σφυγμούς, δεδιὼς
E παρασχεῖν τοῖς νουθετεῖν καὶ ἰᾶσθαι δυναμένοις."
οἱ δὲ σφόδρα παλαιοὶ καὶ τοὺς νοσοῦντας φανερῶς⁵
παρεῖχον⁶· τούτων⁷ δὲ ἕκαστος εἴ τι πρόσφορον
ἔχοι, παθὼν αὐτὸς⁸ ἢ παθόντα θεραπεύσας, ἔφραζε⁹
τῷ δεομένῳ· καὶ τέχνην οὕτω φασὶν¹⁰ ἐκ πείρας
συνερανιζομένην¹¹ μεγάλην γενέσθαι. ἔδει δὴ¹² καὶ
τοὺς νοσώδεις βίους καὶ τὰ τῆς ψυχῆς¹³ παθήματα
πᾶσιν ἀπογυμνοῦν, καὶ ἅπτεσθαι καὶ λέγειν ἕκαστον
ἐπισκοποῦντα τὰς διαθέσεις· '' ὀργίζῃ ''· τοῦτο
'' φύλαξαι ''¹⁴· '' ζηλοτυπεῖς ''· ἐκεῖνο '' ποίησον ''·
'' ἐρᾷς· κἀγώ ποτ' ἠράσθην ἀλλὰ μετενόησα.'' νῦν
δὲ ἀρνούμενοι ἀποκρυπτόμενοι περιστέλλοντες ἐμ-
βαθύνουσι τὴν κακίαν ἑαυτοῖς.

F   3. Καὶ μὴν εἴ γε¹⁵ τοῖς χρηστοῖς λανθάνειν καὶ
ἀγνοεῖσθαι παραινεῖς, Ἐπαμεινώνδᾳ λέγεις, '' μὴ
στρατήγει,'' καὶ Λυκούργῳ, '' μὴ νομοθέτει,'' καὶ

¹ σκότους Castiglioni : σκότου.
² L breaks off before |νος.
³ τοῖς nos (αὐτοῖς Jacobs ; ὁμοῦ τοῖς Bern.) : που τοῖς C
HU g c ; σὺν τοῖς y.
⁴ ὀλέθριον Cy HU g : ἀλλότριον c.
⁵ φανερῶς] φανεροὺς yᵗ y²ᵐ ; φανερῶς πᾶσι Post.
⁶ παρεῖχον nos : προσεῖχον Cᶜ (from προτεῖχον ; προσεῖχεν
y²ᵐ) HU : ἐποίουν yᵗ ; προσῆγον g c (προῆγον Kronenberg ;
Pohlenz suggests πρὸ θυρῶν ἐκθέντες [or προθέντες εἰς τὰς
ὁδοὺς] ἐπισκοπεῖν τοῖς παριοῦσι παρεῖχον).
⁷ τούτων] τούτοις ?
⁸ αὐτὸς Cy HU c : g omits.
⁹ ἔφραζε Cy HU g : ἔφραξε c.
¹⁰ φασὶν yᶜ U² g c (φησὶν HU¹) : φανερὰν C¹y²ᶜ ?
¹¹ συνερανιζομένην Reiske : συνεργαζομένην.

find you out[a]; go fling yourself down somewhere in
the dark, where you and your ailments will be unknown."—" You too go ahead, afflicted by your vice,
a desperate and deadly disease, hiding your fits of
envy and superstition, as you might some throbbing
inflammation, because you dread to submit them to
those who can warn and heal." In very ancient times
the sick themselves were submitted to public inspec-
tion,[b] and everyone who knew of anything serviceable,
having been a sufferer himself or tended one, informed the man who needed help ; and in this way,
it is said, a great art arose, assembled from the experience of many different people. Now it would be well
if the same were done with lives that are diseased
and with the disorders of the mind : that they were
laid bare for all to see, and each observer should
handle the ailing part and say as he considered the
patient's condition : " Your trouble is anger ; take
this precaution " ; " You suffer from jealousy ; I
prescribe that remedy ; " " You are in love ; I once
succumbed to love myself, but I recognized my mistake." As it is, when they deny, conceal and disguise
their disorders they are embedding their vices deeper
in themselves.

3. On the other hand, if it is to the good that you
tender this advice to be unnoticed and unknown, you
are telling Epameinondas not to be general, Lycurgus

---

[a] *Cf. Mor.* 81 f—82 a and 518 c-d.
[b] *Cf.* Herodotus, i. 197 ; Strabo, iii, p. 155 C ; Maximus
of Tyre, vi. 2 (p. 67. 11-19, ed. Hobein) ; Servius on the
Aeneid, xii. 395 ; Isidore, *Etym.* x. 72.

---

[12] δὴ C¹ y HU : δὲ g c.
[13] ψυχῆς] H¹ or ᵃᶜ omits.
[14] φύλαξαι Cy HUᶜ (-αι rewritten) : φύλαξον Uᵃᶜ ᶻ g c.
[15] γε y : τε C HU g c.

(1128) Θρασυβούλῳ[1], " μὴ τυραννοκτόνει," καὶ Πυθαγόρᾳ, " μὴ παίδευε," καὶ Σωκράτει, " μὴ διαλέγου," καὶ σεαυτῷ πρώτον, Ἐπίκουρε, " μὴ γράφε τοῖς ἐν Ἀσίᾳ φίλοις μηδὲ τοὺς[2] ἀπ' Αἰγύπτου ξενολόγει

1129 μηδὲ τοὺς Λαμψακηνῶν ἐφήβους[3] δορυφόρει μηδὲ διάπεμπε βίβλους πᾶσι καὶ πάσαις ἐπιδεικνύμενος τὴν σοφίαν μηδὲ διατάσσου περὶ ταφῆς." τί γὰρ αἱ κοιναὶ τράπεζαι; τί δὲ αἱ τῶν ἐπιτηδείων καὶ καλῶν[4] σύνοδοι; τί δὲ αἱ τοσαῦται μυριάδες στίχων ἐπὶ Μητρόδωρον, ἐπὶ Ἀριστόβουλον, ἐπὶ Χαιρέδημον γραφόμεναι καὶ συνταττόμεναι[5] φιλοπόνως ἵνα μηδὲ[6] ἀποθανόντες λάθωσιν, ἵν' ἀμνηστίαν[7] νομοθετῇς ἀρετῇ[8] καὶ ἀπραξίαν τέχνῃ καὶ σιωπὴν φιλοσοφίᾳ καὶ λήθην εὐπραγίᾳ;

4. Εἰ[9] δὲ ἐκ τοῦ βίου καθάπερ ἐκ συμποσίου φῶς
B ἀναιρεῖς τὴν γνῶσιν, ὡς[10] πάντα ποιεῖν[11] πρὸς ἡδονὴν ἐξῇ[12] λανθάνουσιν,[13] " λάθε βιώσας."[14] πάνυ μὲν οὖν, ἂν[15] μεθ' Ἡδείας[16] βιοῦν μέλλω τῆς ἑταίρας καὶ

---

[1] θρασυβούλῳ U g c (θρασυβούλλωι H) : θρασύλῳ C[1] : θρασύλλῳ y.

[2] τοὺς y : τοῖς C HU g c.

[3] ἐφήβους Cy HU g : ἐφήμους c.

[4] καλῶν] φίλων ? Wilamowitz.

[5] συνταττόμεναι Cy HU c : συντασσόμεναι g.

[6] μηδὲ HU g c : μὴ C[1]y.

[7] ἵν' ἀμνηστίαν y : ἵν' ἀμνηστία C ; ἵνα (an erasure of three letters) μνηστεία H ; ἵναμνηστεία U[1] (ἵν' ἀμνηστεία U[2]) ; ἵναμνηστεία g c.

[8] ἀρετῇ H[r] : ἀρετὴν Cy H[ar]U g c.   [9] εἰ] τί y.

[10] ὡς Dübner : ᾧ Cy U[2] ; ὣ U[1] ; ὃ g c U[2ss?] ; H omits.

[11] ποιεῖν Cy U[c] : ποιεῖ HU[ac] g c.

[12] πρὸς ἡδονὴν ἐξῇ Pohlenz : πρὸς ἡδονὴν ἐξ ἡδονῆς Cy U[2] ; πρὸς ἡδονὴν ἐξηδον and a blank of 2 letters HU[1] ; πρὸς ἡδονὴν g c.

[13] λανθάνουσι Cy HU (Pohlenz adds λέγε μοι) : λανθάνουσαν g c.   [14] λάθε βιώσας Cy HU : g c omit.

to frame no laws, Thrasybulus to slay no tyrants, Pythagoras not to teach, Socrates not to converse, and yourself to begin with, Epicurus, not to write to your friends in Asia,[a] not to enlist recruits from Egypt,[b] not to cultivate the youth of Lampsacus, not to circulate books [c] to every man and every woman in which you advertise your wisdom, and not to leave instructions about funeral ceremonies. For what else is the meaning of the common meals ? Of the meetings of your friends and of the fair ? [d] Of the tens of thousands of lines written to honour Metrodorus, Aristobulus, Chaeredemus,[e] and composed with no small labour so that even after death these men may escape oblivion—that you should lay down the law that virtue shall not be spoken of, that skill shall be idle, philosophy silent, and services forgotten ?

4. If you remove publicity from our life as you might the illumination from a drinking party, so that every pleasure may freely be indulged without detection—" live unknown." Yes indeed, if I am to live with Hedeia the courtesan and end my days with

---

[a] Frag. 107 (ed. Usener).   [b] Frag. 106 (ed. Usener).

[c] Cf. Usener, Epicurea, p. 87. 23-28.

[d] Cf. Epicurus' will (Frag. 217, ed. Usener), which provides that sums shall be devoted " for the customary celebration of my birthday every year on the tenth of Gamelion and for the meeting that takes place on the twentieth of every month of those engaged with me in philosophy in memory of Metrodorus and myself . . ."

[e] Epicurus' brothers, Aristobulus and Chaeredemus, predeceased him, as did Metrodorus. The works entitled Metrodorus (in five books), Aristobulus, and Chaeredemus were written in their honour.

---

[15] ἂν Cy HU c : g omits.

[16] μεθ' ἡδείας U² g c : μετ' ἰδίας Cy¹ (μεθ' ἰδίας y² H ; μετίδίας U¹ ?).

PLUTARCH'S MORALIA

(1129) Λεοντίῳ συγκαταζῆν[1] καὶ " τῷ καλῷ προσπτύειν "
καὶ τἀγαθὸν " ἐν σαρκὶ καὶ γαργαλισμοῖς " τίθε-
σθαι· ταῦτα δεῖται[2] σκότους[3] τὰ τέλη,[4] ταῦτα
νυκτός, ἐπὶ ταῦτα τὴν λήθην καὶ τὴν ἄγνοιαν. ἐὰν[5]
δέ τις ἐν μὲν φυσικοῖς θεὸν ὑμνῇ[6] καὶ δίκην καὶ
πρόνοιαν, ἐν δὲ ἠθικοῖς νόμον καὶ κοινωνίαν καὶ
πολιτείαν, ἐν δὲ πολιτείᾳ τὸ καλὸν ἀλλὰ μὴ τὴν
χρείαν, διὰ τί λάθῃ[7] βιώσας; ἵνα μηδένα παιδεύσῃ,
μηδενὶ[8] ζηλωτὸς[9] ἀρετῆς μηδὲ παράδειγμα καλὸν
γένηται; εἰ Θεμιστοκλῆς Ἀθηναίους ἐλάνθανεν, οὐκ
C ἂν ἡ Ἑλλὰς ἀπεώσατο[10] Ξέρξην· εἰ Ῥωμαίους[11] Κά-
μιλλος, οὐκ ἂν ἡ Ῥώμη πόλις ἔμεινεν· εἰ Δίωνα
Πλάτων, οὐκ ἂν ἠλευθερώθη[12] ἡ[13] Σικελία. ὡς γὰρ[14]
οἶμαι τὸ φῶς οὐ μόνον φανεροὺς ἀλλὰ καὶ χρησίμους
καθίστησιν ἡμᾶς ἀλλήλοις, οὕτως ἡ γνῶσις οὐ μόνον
δόξαν ἀλλὰ καὶ πρᾶξιν ταῖς ἀρεταῖς δίδωσιν. Ἐπαμεινώνδας γοῦν εἰς[15] τεσσαρακοστὸν ἔτος ἀγνοηθεὶς
οὐδὲν ὤνησε Θηβαίους· ὕστερον δὲ πιστευθεὶς καὶ
ἄρξας τὴν μὲν πόλιν ἀπολλυμένην ἔσωσεν, τὴν δ'
Ἑλλάδα δουλεύουσαν[16] ἠλευθέρωσεν, καθάπερ ἐν
φωτὶ τῇ δόξῃ τὴν ἀρετὴν ἐνεργὸν ἐπὶ καιροῦ παρα-

---

[1] συγκαταζῆν] συνκαταζῆν HU[1].
[2] δεῖται HU g c : δὴ τοῦ Cy.
[3] σκότους Cy HU : g c omit.
[4] τέλη Cy HU : μέλη g c.
[5] ἐὰν C HU g c : ἂν y.
[6] θεὸν ὑμνῇ C HU g c : ὑμνεῖ θεὸν y.
[7] λάθῃ C HU g c : λάθοι y ; μὴ λάθῃ U[ar].
[8] μηδενὶ Cy HU : ἢ μηδενὶ g c.
[9] ζηλωτὸς g c : ζῆλος Cy HU.
[10] ἀπεώσατο HU g c : ἀτιώσατο C[ac] ; ἀπώσατο C[c]y.
[11] ῥωμαίους Cy (ρ- HU[1]) U[2] g ; ῥωμαῖος c.
[12] ἠλευθερώθη Cy HU g : ἐλευθερώθη c.
[13] ἡ C HU g c : y omits.
[14] ὡς γὰρ Pohlenz : ὥσπερ C[1]y HU[1] g c ; ὥσπερ δὲ U[2]a.

Leontion [a] and " spit on noble action " [b] and place
the good in the " flesh " [c] and in " titillations " [d];
these rites require darkness, these require night, and
for these let us have concealment and oblivion. But
take one who in natural philosophy extols God and
justice and providence, in ethics law and society and
participation in public affairs, and in political life the
upright and not the utilitarian act,[e] what need has
he to live unknown ? In order to educate no one and
become for no one an inspirer of virtuous emulation
or a noble example ? If Themistocles had been unknown at Athens, Greece would not have repelled
Xerxes ; if Camillus had been unknown at Rome,
Rome would not have remained a city ; if Plato had
been unknown to Dion, Sicily would not have been set
free : just as light makes us not only visible but also
useful to one another, so being known lends to our
virtues not only renown but also the means of action.
Take Epameinondas, who until his fortieth year was
unrecognized and so of no benefit to the Thebans ;
later, once trust and office had been conferred on him,
he preserved his city from present ruin and delivered
Greece from subjection. His fame was the light in
which he put his virtue to work when the crisis came.

[a] Concubine (Diogenes Laert. x. 23) or wife (Seneca,
Frag. 45 [ed. Haase ; Usener, *Epicurea*, p. 98. 8]) of Metrodorus.
[b] Frag. 512 (ed. Usener).
[c] In the extant fragments Epicurus always adds the mental pleasure of anticipation : *cf. Cardinal Tenet* xx, *Gnom.
Vat.* 33.
[d] Frags. 412, 413 (ed. Usener).
[e] Epicurus, Frag. 524 (ed. Usener).

---

¹⁵ εἰς Cy U g c : ἐκ H.
¹⁶ δουλεύουσαν HU g c : δουλεύσασαν Cy.

(1129) σχόμενος·

   λάμπει[1] γὰρ ἐν χρείαισιν[2] ὥσπερ εὐγενὴς[3]
D   χαλκός, χρόνῳ δ᾽ ἀργῆσαν ἤμυσεν

οὐ μόνον[4] στέγος,[5] ὥς φησι Σοφοκλῆς, ἀλλὰ καὶ
ἦθος ἀνδρός, οἷον εὐρῶτα καὶ γῆρας ἐν ἀπραξίᾳ δι᾽
ἀγνοίας ἐφελκόμενον. ἡσυχία δὲ κωφὴ καὶ βίος[6]
ἑδραῖος ἐπὶ[7] σχολῆς ἀποκείμενος οὐ σώματα μόνον[8]
ἀλλὰ καὶ ψυχὰς[9] μαραίνει· καὶ καθάπερ τὰ λανθά-
νοντα τῶν ὑδάτων τῷ περισκιάζεσθαι καὶ καθῆσθαι
μὴ ἀπορρέοντα σήπεται, οὕτω τῶν ἀκινήτων βίων,
ὡς ἔοικεν, ἄν τι χρήσιμον ἔχωσιν μὴ ἀπορρεόντων
μηδὲ πινομένων φθείρονται καὶ ἀπογηράσκουσιν αἱ
σύμφυτοι δυνάμεις.

   5. Οὐχ ὁρᾷς ὅτι νυκτὸς μὲν[10] ἐπιούσης τά τε σώματα δυσεργεῖς βαρύτητες ἴσχουσι[11] καὶ τὰς ψυχὰς
E ὄκνοι καταλαμβάνουσιν ἀδρανεῖς, καὶ συσταλεὶς ὁ[12]
λογισμὸς εἰς αὑτὸν[13] ὥσπερ πῦρ ἀμαυρὸν ὑπὸ ἀργίας
καὶ κατηφείας μικρὰ[14] διεσπασμέναις[15] πάλλεται
φαντασίαις, ὅσον αὐτὸ τὸ ζῆν τὸν ἄνθρωπον ὑποσημαίνων,[16]

---

   [1] λάμπει Cy U² : λάμπεις HU¹ g c.
   [2] χρείαισιν A²E : χρείαις ἵν᾽ Cy HU g c.
   [3] εὐγενὴς Cy HU g c : εὐπρεπὴς Mor. 788 в, 792 л.
   [4] δ᾽ ἀργῆσαν ἤμυσεν οὐ μόνον margin of an Aldine at the
University of Illinois Library : διαργήσας (διαρκέσας y¹)
ἤμυνε θυμὸν ἂν (y omits ἂν).
   [5] στέγος C HU : y omits ; στέγης g c.
   [6] βίος Cy U g c : βίαιως H.

332

For not only a " house," as Sophocles [a] says,

> grows bright with use, like noble bronze ;
> Disused, it leans at last to ruin.

It is the same with a man's character, which in the inaction of obscurity collects something like a clogging coat of mould. A repose of which nothing is heard and a life stationary and laid away in leisure withers not only the body but the mind ; just as pools [b] concealed by overshadowing branches and lying still with no outflow putrefy, so too, it would appear, with quiet lives : as nothing flows from them of any good they have in them and no one drinks of the stream, their inborn powers lose their prime of vigour and fall into decay.

5. Do you not observe how at the onset of night a slow heaviness comes over the body and an inert reluctance over the mind, while our reason, withdrawing into itself like a dim fire, is so indolent and subdued that it flickers in scattered little fits of fancy just enough to indicate that the man is alive ; but when the rising sun

---

[a] Sophocles, Frag. 780 (Nauck, *Trag. Graec. Frag.*, p. 314) ; Frag. 864 (ed. Pearson) ; quoted also in *Mor.* 788 B and 792 A. For the sense of " noble " see E. Fraenkel on Aeschylus, *Agamemnon*, 391.

[b] *Cf. Mor.* 725 D, 957 D.

---

[7] ἐπὶ Cy HU g : ἀπὸ c.
[8] σώματα μόνον Cy : μόνον σώματα HU c ; μόνον σῶμα g.
[9] ψυχὰς Cy HU : ψυχὴν g c.   [10] μὲν] y omits.
[11] βαρύτητες ἴσχουσι] βαρύτατοι c.
[12] ὁ] g omits.
[13] αὐτὸν y U² c : αὐτὸν C HU¹ ; ἑαυτὸν g.
[14] μικρὰ Cy HU : μακρὰ g c (μακρὰν Reiske ; εἰς μικρὰ ?).
[15] διεσπασμέναις Cy HU g : διεσπασμένας c.
[16] ὑποσημαίνων HU g c : ὑποσημαίνειν C¹y.

(1129) ἦμος[1] δ' ἠπεροπῆας[2] ἀπεπτοίησεν[3] ὀνείρους

ὁ ἥλιος ἀνασχὼν καὶ[4] καθάπερ εἰς ταὐτὸ συμμίξας
ἐπέστρεψε καὶ συνώρμησεν τῷ φωτὶ τὰς πράξεις[5]
καὶ τὰς νοήσεις τὰς ἁπάντων, ὥς φησι Δημόκριτος,
" νέα[6] ἐφ' ἡμέρῃ φρονέοντες " [7] ἄνθρωποι, τῇ πρὸς
ἀλλήλους ὁρμῇ[8] καθάπερ ἀρτήματι[9] συντόνῳ σπασθέντες[10] ἄλλος ἀλλαχόθεν ἐπὶ τὰς πράξεις ἀνίστανται;[11]

6. Δοκῶ δὲ ἐγὼ καὶ τὸ ζῆν αὐτὸ καὶ ὅλως τὸ
F φῦναι καὶ μετασχεῖν ἀνθρώπῳ[12] γενέσεως εἰς γνῶσιν
ὑπὸ θεοῦ δοθῆναι. ἔστι δὲ[13] ἄδηλος καὶ ἄγνωστος
ἐν τῷ παντὶ[14] πόλῳ[15] κατὰ[16] μικρὰ καὶ σποράδην
φερόμενος· ὅταν δὲ γένηται, συνερχόμενος αὐτῷ
καὶ λαμβάνων μέγεθος ἐκλάμπει καὶ καθίσταται
δῆλος ἐξ ἀδήλου καὶ φανερὸς ἐξ ἀφανοῦς. οὐ[17] γὰρ
εἰς οὐσίαν ὁδὸς[18] ἡ γένεσις,[19] ὥς ἔνιοι λέγουσιν, ἀλλ'
οὐσίας εἰς γνῶσιν· οὐ γὰρ ποιεῖ τῶν γινομένων
1130 ἕκαστον ἀλλὰ δείκνυσιν, ὥσπερ οὐδὲ[20] ἡ φθορὰ τοῦ
ὄντος ἄρσις εἰς τὸ[21] μὴ ὄν ἐστιν, ἀλλὰ μᾶλλον εἰς
τὸ ἄδηλον ἀπαγωγὴ τοῦ διαλυθέντος. ὅθεν δὴ τὸν

---

[1] ἦμος Cy U[2] g c : ἥμος HU[1].
[2] δ' ἠπεροπῆας Etym. Magnum : δὲ στεροπῆας Cy U[2] ; δὴ
(from δὲ δὴ) στεροπήας H[c] ; δὴ στεροπῆας U[1] ; δ' ὑπεροπῆας g c.
[3] ἀπεπτοίησεν HU : ἀπεποίησεν C[1] g c ; ἃ πεποίηκεν y[2] (ἃ
πέποιηκεν y[1]).   [4] καὶ] y omits.   [5] πράξεις] πράσεις y.
[6] νέα C g c : νέᾳ y HU (νέα νέη Post).
[7] φρονέοντες Wyttenbach (from Mor. 655 D, 722 D) : τρέ-
φοντες.   [8] τῇ . . . ὁρμῇ] τὴν . . . ὁρμὴν y.
[9] ἀρτήματι HU g c : ἀρτήματα C[1] ; ἀρτύματα y.
[10] συντόνῳ σπασθέντες Reiske : συντόνως (and so yσt) πλα-
σθέντες (-ας C[1]).   [11] ἀνίστανται y HU g c : ἀνίσταται C[1].
[12] ἀνθρώπῳ Wyttenbach : ἀνθρώπων Cy HU g c ; ἄνθρωπον
σ[288].   [13] δὲ Cy HU g : δὲ καὶ c.
[14] παντὶ] H[t] omits (supplied by H[188]).

Startles to flight the hypocritic dreams [a]

and, as it were, blends doing and thinking in one and all into a single whole, as its light calls them to attention and imparts a common motion, then, as Democritus [b] says, " with a new mind for the new day," all men, drawn by mutual attraction as by a strong bond, arise from their separate slumbers to engage in their tasks ?

6. I hold that life itself and indeed a man's very birth and becoming are a gift of God to make him known. So long as man moves about in small and scattered particles in the great vault of the universe, he remains unseen and unrecognized, but once brought into being, as he joins with himself and acquires a certain magnitude, he stands out conspicuous, and from unseen and unnoticed takes his place noticed and seen. For to become is not to pass into being,[c] as some say, but to pass from being to being known ; for generation does not create the thing generated but reveals it, just as destruction is not the transfer of what is to what is not, but rather the removal from our sight of what has suffered dissolution. This

[a] Cf. Callimachus, Frag. Anon. 93, p. 723 (ed. Schneider) ; rejected by Pfeiffer.

[b] Frag. в 158 (Diels and Kranz, Frag. der Vorsokratiker, ii, p. 175) ; quoted also in Mor. 655 D and 722 D.

[c] Cf. the Platonic Definitions, 411 A : " becoming is a movement into being ; a partaking of being ; a proceeding into being " ; Aristotle, Topics, vi. 2 (139 b 20) : " becoming is a bringing into being " (where the definition is attacked) ; Aristotle, Metaphysics, Γ 2 (1003 b 7).

---

[15] πόλω g c : πολλῷ Cy HU.
[16] κατὰ r t : καὶ κατά.   [17] οὐ Cy HU : καὶ g c.
[18] οὐσίαν ὁδὸς H[c] (οὐσίαν ὁδὸν H[ac])U² (οὐσίας οδον U¹) g c : οὐσίας ὁδὸν C¹y.   [19] γένεσις Turnebus : γνῶσις.
[20] οὐδὲ] δὲ g.   [21] τὸ] τι y.

(1130) μὲν ἥλιον Ἀπόλλωνα κατὰ τοὺς πατρίους καὶ παλαιοὺς θεσμοὺς[1] νομίζοντες Δήλιον καὶ Πύθιον
προσαγορεύουσι· τὸν δὲ τῆς ἐναντίας κύριον[2] μοίρας,
εἴτε θεὸς εἴτε δαίμων ἐστίν,[3] ὀνομάζουσιν, ὡς ἂν
εἰς[4] ἀιδὲς[5] καὶ ἀόρατον ἡμῶν[6] ὅταν διαλυθῶμεν[7]
βαδιζόντων[8]

νυκτὸς ἀιδνᾶς ἀεργηλοῖό θ'[9] ὕπνου κοίρανον.

οἶμαι δὲ καὶ τὸν ἄνθρωπον αὐτὸν οὑτωσὶ φῶτα
καλεῖν τοὺς παλαιοὺς ὅτι τοῦ γινώσκεσθαι καὶ
γινώσκειν ἑκάστῳ διὰ συγγένειαν ἔρως ἰσχυρὸς
B ἐμπέφυκεν. αὐτήν τε[10] τὴν ψυχὴν ἔνιοι τῶν φιλοσόφων φῶς εἶναι τῇ οὐσίᾳ νομίζουσιν, ἄλλοις τε χρώμενοι τεκμηρίοις καὶ ὅτι τῶν ὄντων μάλιστα τὴν
μὲν[11] ἄγνοιαν ἡ ψυχὴ δυσανασχετεῖ καὶ πᾶν τὸ ἀφεγ-
γὲς ἐχθαίρει[12] καὶ ταράττεται περὶ[13] τὰ σκοτεινά,
φόβου[14] καὶ ὑποψίας ὄντα πλήρη πρὸς αὐτήν, ἡδὺ δὲ
αὐτῇ[15] καὶ ποθεινὸν οὕτω τὸ[16] φῶς ἐστιν ὥστε μηδ'[17]
ἄλλῳ τινὶ[18] τῶν φύσει τερπνῶν ἄνευ φωτὸς ὑπὸ
σκότους χαίρειν,[19] ἀλλὰ τοῦτο πᾶσαν ἡδονὴν καὶ

---

[1] θεσμοὺς] θεοὺς H.   [2] κύριον Cy HU : g omits ; καὶ c.
[3] ἐστὶν C[1]y HUa[1] : ἐστὶν ἄδην a²⁸⁸ AE g c.
[4] εἰς HUart U² g c : C[1]y U^r omit.
[5] ἀιδὲς C[1] (ἀηδὲς H^ac) : ἀειδὲς H^cU g c.
[6] ἡμῶν C HU g c : y omits.
[7] διαλυθῶμεν HU g c : διαλυθῶσι C[1] (-ιν y).
[8] βαδιζόντων] βαδιζόντων ἡμῶν C[1]y.
[9] ἀεργηλοῖό θ' U²a^cAE : ἀεργήλοις θ' C[1] H(a- U[1]) ; ἀεργή-
λην θ' y ; ἀεργηλοῖσθ' g c.
[10] αὐτήν τε HU g (αὐτὴν τὲ C c) : αὐτὴν δὲ y.
[11] μὲν] y[1] omits.
[12] ἐχθαίρει Wyttenbach : ἐξαιρεῖ Cy HU g c.
[13] περὶ our addition (πρὸς Reiske, διὰ Pohlenz).
[14] φόβου] καὶ φόβου y.
[15] αὐτῇ HU g c : C[1]y omit, Cy having αὐτῇ after φῶς below.
[16] τὸ Cy U²a : HU[1] g c omit.

is why the sun,[a] which by old traditional ordinances is held to be Apollo, is called Delian and Pythian [b] ; while the lord of the opposite realm, whether god or daemon, is called

> The Prince of viewless night and idle sleep [c]

from the notion that on dissolution we pass to the *aïdes* or unseen.[d] Indeed I imagine that the ancients called man *phôs* [e] because from our kinship with one another a strong love is implanted in each of us of being known and of knowing. And some philosophers [f] believe that the soul itself is in its substance light, appealing among other proofs to the fact that the soul finds ignorance the most vexatious of all things and hates everything unilluminated and is disturbed by all that is dark, which to her is full of fear and mistrust, whereas light is so agreeable to her when present and so missed when absent that in the dark without light she has no pleasure even in the other naturally pleasant things, while the addition of light, as of some universal condiment, renders every pleasure

[a] The sun is lord of the world of Becoming : Plato, *Rep.* vi, 508-509.

[b] *Delios* is here derived from *dêlos* (plain to see), for which cf. *Mor.* 394 A, and *Pythios* from *punthanomai* (ascertain) : cf. Cornutus, *Theologiae Graecae Compendium*, p. 67. 2-3, 10-11 (ed. Lang).

[c] D. Page, *Poetae Melici Graeci*, Frag. 996 (Frag. Adesp. 78).

[d] For this etymology of Hades see Plato, *Cratylus*, 403 A, 404 B.

[e] Cf. for this etymology of *phôs* (wight) from *phôs* (light) *Etym. Magnum, s.v.* (804. 28-30).

[f] Cf. Heracleides, Frag. 100 (ed. Wehrli) and *Mor.* 281 B.

17 μηδ' C : μὴ δι' y ; μηδὲ HU g c.
18 ἄλλῳ τινὶ y : ἄλλό τι C HU g c.
19 χαίρειν C¹y^t HU¹ g c : θέλειν y^{aγρ} U²a.

(1130) πᾶσαν διατριβὴν καὶ ἀπόλαυσιν,[1] ὥσπερ τι κοινὸν[2] ἥδυσμα καταμιγνύμενον, ἱλαρὰν[3] ποιεῖ καὶ φιλάνθρωπον. ὁ δὲ εἰς τὴν ἄγνοιαν αὐτὸν ἐμβάλλων[4] καὶ σκότος[5] περιαμπισχόμενος καὶ κενοταφῶν τὸν C βίον ἔοικεν αὐτὴν βαρύνεσθαι τὴν γένεσιν καὶ ἀπαυδᾶν πρὸς τὸ εἶναι.

7. Καίτοι τῆς γε δόξης καὶ τοῦ εἶναί φασιν[6] εὐσεβῶν χῶρον,[7]

τοῖσι[8] λάμπει[9] μὲν[10] μένος[11] ἀελίου[12]
τὰν ἐνθάδε[13] νύκτα κάτω
φοινικορόδοις[14] ἐνὶ[15] λειμώνεσσιν,[16]

καὶ τοῖσιν ἀκάρπων μὲν ἀνθηρῶν δὲ[17] καὶ συσκίων[18] δένδρων ἄνθεσιν τεθηλὸς ἀναπέπταται πεδίον, καὶ ποταμοί τινες ἄκλαυστοι[19] καὶ λεῖοι διαρρέουσιν, καὶ διατριβὰς ἔχουσιν ἐν μνήμαις καὶ λόγοις τῶν γεγονότων καὶ ὄντων παραπέμποντες αὐτοὺς[20] καὶ συνόντες. ἡ δὲ τρίτη τῶν ἀνοσίως βεβιωκότων

---

[1] διατριβὴν καὶ ἀπόλαυσιν] ἀπόλαυσιν καὶ διατριβὴν y.
[2] κοινὸν] καινὸν g.   [3] ἱλαρὰν Reiske : ἱλαρὸν (ἱ-C[1] H).
[4] ἐμβάλλων Bern. : ἐμβαλὼν.   [5] σκότος] σκότους H.
[6] εἶναί φασιν Fr. Jacobs (ἐπαίνου κάθοδον εἶναί φασιν εἰς Post) : εἶναι φύσιν.
[7] χῶρον] χώρων Cy.   [8] τοῖσι] τοῖσιν HU.
[9] λάμπει U[2]a (and Mor. 120 c): λάμπεν HU[1]; λάμπε Cy g c.
[10] μὲν] added from Mor. 120 c.   [11] μένος] μὲν ὡς H.
[12] ἀελίου] ἡλίου C[1]y[1].   [13] ἐνθάδε Mor. 120 c : ἐνθένδε.
[14] φοινικορόδοις] φοινοκορόδοιο c.
[15] ἐνὶ Bern. (τ᾽ ἐνὶ Boeckh ; τε Mor. 120 c) : ἐν.
[16] λειμώνεσσιν C (-σσι U c; χειμώνεσσι y[t] [λει- y[288]]): λειμώνεσιν H (-εσι g).   [17] δὲ added by Wilamowitz.
[18] συσκίων Ruhnken : σκυθίων.
[19] ἄκλαυστοι HUa g cd : ἄπαυστοι C[1]y[1] ; ἄκλαυτοι y[2γρ]Λ[2]E.
[20] αὐτοὺς Xylander : αὐτούς.

and every pastime and enjoyment cheerful and agreeable.[a] But he who casts himself into the unknown state and wraps himself in darkness and buries his life in an empty tomb would appear to be aggrieved at his very birth and to renounce the effort of being.

7. Yet to fame and to being belongs, they say, a place reserved for pious dead :

> For some the sun shines bright below, while here
> Is night, on meadows red with roses [b] ;

and before others [c] spreads a great and flowery plain with trees which, though sterile,[d] are abloom with varicoloured blossoms and cast a thick shade, and certain rivers attended by no sound of lamentation flow smoothly past,[e] while those who dwell there pass their time together recalling and speaking of the past and present. But the third path [f] is the way

---

[a] *Cf.* Aristotle, *Protrepticus*, Frag. 9 (ed. Ross) and 1093 A, *supra*.

[b] Pindar, Frag. 129 (ed. Snell), 135 (ed. Turyn) ; *cf. Mor.* 120 c. These are presumably the Islands of the Blest.

[c] This is presumably the habitation of the good. The spreading plain and the rivers suggest it is not an island ; the shade, that there is light.

[d] Trees of the underworld are sterile : *cf.* the scholiasts (BQ and HTV) on Homer, *Odyssey*, x. 510.

[e] Thus the habitations of the blest and of the good are no places of unending night, like the place in the *Odyssey* (xi. 14-22), nor are they covered with pale asphodel, nor have they rivers ablaze with fire (like Pyriphlegethon) or noisy with the tumult of waters (*Odyssey*, x. 515) or like Cocytus and Acheron associated with grief and lamentation.

[f] For the three roads *cf.* Wilamowitz, *Pindaros*, pp. 497, 499 ; Varro in Servius on the *Georgics*, i. 34 ; Pindar, *Ol.* ii. 57 ff. ; Reiner, *Die rituelle Totenklage* (Tübinger Beiträge, 30, p. 83). See also R. M. Jones, *The Platonism of Plutarch*, pp. 66-67 ; Wehrli, *Herakleides Pontikos*, p. 92 ; Bignone, *L'Aristotele perduto*, vol. ii, p. 599.

(1130)
D καὶ παρανόμως[1] ὁδός ἐστιν, εἰς[2] ἔρεβός τι[3] καὶ βάρα-
θρον ὠθοῦσα[4] τὰς ψυχάς

> ἔνθεν τὸν ἄπειρον[5] ἐρεύγονται[6] σκότον
> βληχροὶ δνοφερᾶς νυκτὸς ποταμοί[7]

δεχόμενοι καὶ ἀποκρύπτοντες ἀγνοίᾳ καὶ λήθῃ τοὺς
κολαζομένους. οὐ γὰρ οὐδὲ[8] γῦπες κειμένων ἐν
γῇ[9] τῶν πονηρῶν κείρουσιν ἀεὶ[10] τὸ ἧπαρ (κατα-
κέκαυται γὰρ ἢ κατασέσηπεν), οὐδὲ βαρῶν τινων
ἀχθοφορίαι θλίβουσι καὶ καταπονοῦσι τὰ σώματα
τῶν κολαζομένων—

> οὐ γὰρ ἔτι σάρκας τε[11] καὶ ὀστέα ἶνες ἔχουσιν

οὐδέ ἐστιν ὑπόλειμμα σώματος τοῖς τεθνηκόσι τιμωρίας ἀπέρεισιν[12] ἀντιτύπου δέξασθαι δυνάμενον—
E ἀλλ' ἐν κολαστήριον ὡς ἀληθῶς τῶν κακῶς βιωσάν-
των, ἀδοξία καὶ ἄγνοια[13] καὶ παντελῶς[14] ἀφανισμός,
αἴρων εἰς τὸν ἀμειδῆ ποταμὸν ἀπὸ[15] τῆς Λήθης καὶ[16]
καταποντίζων[17] εἰς ἄβυσσον καὶ ἀχανὲς πέλαγος,
ἀχρηστίαν καὶ ἀπραξίαν πᾶσάν τε[18] ἄγνοιαν καὶ
ἀδοξίαν συνεφελκόμενον.[19]

---

[1] παρανόμως Hartman : παρανόμων.
[2] εἰς] C[1] omits.   [3] τι (τις C[ac])] τε g.
[4] ὠθοῦσα] ὠθεῖσα y.   [5] ἄπειρον] ἄπορον y.
[6] ἐρεύγονται] ἐρεύγεται y.
[7] ποταμοὶ] ποταμὸν g.
[8] οὐ γὰρ οὐδὲ Stegmann : οὐ γὰρ οὔτε (οὔτε γὰρ y).
[9] γῇ] τῇ γῇ Cy.
[10] κείρουσιν ἀεὶ] ἀεὶ κείρουσιν y.   [11] τε] H omits.
[12] ἀπέρεισιν μ[288] and Wyttenbach : αἵπερ εἰσὶν (-ιν H).
[13] ἀδοξία καὶ ἄγνοια HU g c : ἀγνωσία καὶ ἀδοξία Cy[1] (ἀγνωσία καὶ ἀδοξία καὶ ἄγνοια y[2]).
[14] παντελῶς] παντελὴς Turnebus.
[15] ἀπὸ] ὑπό τε Post.   [16] καὶ added by Reiske.
[17] καταποντίζων U[2]u : καταποντίζει C[1]y HU[1] g c.

taken by those who have lived a life of impiety and crime ; it thrusts their souls into a pit of darkness

> Whence sluggish streams of murky night belch forth
> The dark that has no bourne,[a]

as they receive into their waters those sentenced to punishment and engulf them in obscurity and oblivion. For no vultures tear forever at the liver of the wicked as they lie stretched on the ground [b]— since it has been consumed in fire [c] or has rotted away —nor does the bearing of any heavy burden crush and wear out the bodies of those punished,[d]

> for their sinews
> No longer hold together flesh and bone,[e]

and the dead have no remnant of the body that could sustain the weight of crushing punishment. No, there is in truth but one penalty for those who have lived ill : obscurity, oblivion, and utter effacement, which carries them off from Lethê to the joyless river [f] and plunges them into a bottomless and yawning ocean,[g] an ocean that sucks into one abyss all failure to serve or to take action and all that is inglorious and unknown.

[a] Pindar, Frag. 130 (ed. Snell), 135 (ed. Turyn) ; cf. Mor. 17 c.
[b] The punishment of Tityos : cf. Odyssey, xi. 576-581.
[c] Cf. Odyssey, xi. 220-221.
[d] The punishment of Sisyphus : cf. Odyssey, xi. 593-600.
[e] Odyssey, xi. 219.
[f] From Lethê (suggested by láthe [" be unknown "] in the precept) the follower of the precept passes to joylessness (that is, he is deprived of the pleasures of the active life) and ultimately to complete oblivion.
[g] Cf. 1107 A, supra.

---

[18] πᾶσαν τὲ C¹y : πᾶσαν HU ; καὶ πᾶσαν g c.
[19] συνεφελκόμενον] ἐφελκόμενον Hac.

ON MUSIC
(DE MUSICA)

INTRODUCTION

FEW scholars would now ascribe the dialogue *De Musica* to Plutarch. The style shows little of Plutarch's manner or skill or powers of assimilation, and where it is not a tissue of excerpts is awkward and incorrect.

Wilamowitz [a] suggests that Planudes was the first to ascribe the dialogue to Plutarch. Of the spurious writings that Planudes included in his edition all but the *De Musica* and the *De Vita et Poesi Homeri* were taken from various collections of Plutarch's essays.[b] Planudes' sources for the two exceptions are lost or unknown. Each of the two was no doubt originally anonymous. Plutarch's name, it would seem (we do not yet have a critical edition), does not appear in the non-Planudean MSS. of the *De Vita et Poesi Homeri*; and in the oldest MSS. of the *De Musica* (M and V) it was inserted by a later hand. This absence of a name was an invitation to supply one, and the parallel with the *Life of Phocion* in the first sentence was enough to suggest that of Plutarch.

The occasion of the dialogue is a feast on the second

---

[a] *Griechische Verskunst* (Berlin, 1921), pp. 76-77, note 3.

[b] He found the *De Liberis Educandis* (2) and the *Placita Philosophorum* (51) in M; the *Consolatio ad Apollonium* (22) in a lost relation of v; the *De Fato* (37) in a lost relation of the second part of X; and the *Decem Oratorum Vitae* (63) in some lost relation of F. The *Regum et Imperatorum Apophthegmata* (59) and *Parallela Graeca et Romana* (61) always occur with works of Plutarch.

day of the Saturnalia ; thus the dialogue is a *Symposium*, and enjoys the liberties of the genre. The scene is unknown ; it is not Alexandria, for otherwise the epithet "Alexandrian " applied to Soterichus (1131 c) would be hard to explain. The Roman Saturnalia had been adopted by Greeks by the time of Lucian. The latest authority cited (1132 F) is Alexander Polyhistor, born about 100 B.C.

There are three speakers : Onesicrates, the host and preceptor, who opens and closes the discussion ; Lysias, an executant employed by Onesicrates ; and Soterichus of Alexandria. Among the unnamed guests must be counted another member of the school, the narrator.

The introduction places interest in music in the broader context of a zeal for instruction and devotion to culture ($\pi\alpha\iota\delta\epsilon\acute{\iota}a$). Even the feast of the Saturnalia, it appears, is to be spent in intellectual pursuits. Onesicrates, who had invited to the feast men learned in music, reminds them in his opening statement that on the preceding day they had enquired into grammar ; he now selects music as a fitting sequel. He asks first for an historical account of the origin of music, its progress, and its most famous practitioners ; and second for a discussion of the ends that it serves (1131 B-E).

Lysias undertakes to relate the early history of music. He begins by pointing to the large number of treatises on ancient music and their lack of agreement. As if to prove his point, he first takes from Heracleides information about the origin of singing to the cithara, the accomplishments of certain early composers, and perhaps also the names of the earliest nomes sung to the cithara and the auloi. He deals

345

with singing to the cithara and singing to the auloi together, although he evidently gives the preference to his own instrument, the cithara. Next he passes to auletic. He then draws from Alexander of Aetolia and others quite different information that in part supplements, in part conflicts with the material from Heracleides (1131 F—1133 B).

Leaving these problems unresolved, Lysias proceeds with greater confidence to trace the history of singing to the cithara in the period after Terpander, and to discuss the origin of certain nomes for the auloi. There follow names of persons who instituted musical performances at certain cities, with brief mention of the musical forms in which they composed. Next comes an account of the origin of the enharmonic genus. Lysias concludes with some remarks on innovations in rhythm, drawing a contrast between those innovations that were compatible with the ancient dignity of music and those that led to its corruption. Having thus prepared the way for the second of Onesicrates' two topics, the ends that music serves, he calls on Soterichus to continue the discussion (1133 B—1135 D).

Before dealing with the ends Soterichus eliminates the corruptions. Music once had a majesty and nobility that has now been lost, but that might, with the right education, be regained. The original majesty came from Apollo, its inventor, who was " graced with every virtue." The corruption came with the introduction of modes suited to lamentation and other unmanly emotions. Plato is Soterichus' authority for the rejection of these effeminate modes ; Aristoxenus is his authority for the historical details of their adoption (1135 E—1136 E).

ON MUSIC

The critical judgement that thus confines music to prescribed limits is not, Soterichus insists, based on ignorance of what it rejects ; it is an informed judgement. Plato was well acquainted with the modes and their uses. He preferred the Dorian to the Lydian, Mixolydian, and Ionian because he judged the majestic Dorian proper for warlike and temperate men. So too the simple majesty of ancient music was the result not of ignorance but of choice (1136 ε—1138 c).

As for Plato, his familiarity with harmonics is evident in the account of the creation of the soul in the *Timaeus* ; and Aristotle, his disciple, held harmony to be celestial and divine ; even the senses by which harmony is perceived are celestial.

The concern of the ancients for education in music is thus fully justified. They held music to be useful on every occasion, but especially in facing the dangers of war and at athletic contests. Still earlier they employed it wholly in honouring the gods and educating the young. To-day it is quite otherwise ; the educational use of music has been supplanted by the music of the theatre (1138 c—1140 F).

Is music then to resist all change, and so escape corruption ? Did not even the ancients innovate ? Soterichus' reply is that the innovations introduced by the ancients were not of a kind to destroy the majesty of music ; but that Lasus of Hermionê, Melanippides, and others of more recent times changed the character of music and corrupted it (1140 F—1142 A).

Soterichus (following Aristoxenus, who drew upon Plato's programme for making rhetoric an art) now discusses in some detail the knowledge and training required for a true musician. In their preference for

majestic and simple music the ancients recognized
that the end of music is moral character, not the
mere pleasure of the ear. Pythagoras went so far as
to deny to the ear any part in the judgement of music,
saying that its excellence lies entirely in the intelligible proportions of the scale. But our contemporaries
have dulled both ear and mind (1142 B—1145 D).

The proper employment of music, Soterichus concludes, may be learned from Homer. Those who
cultivate it for its nobility reflect this nobility in all
their actions and are of service to their fellow men.
Music is man's means of expressing his gratitude to
God, and of purifying his soul (1145 D—1146 D).

In his closing speech Onesicrates makes two further
points : music is of service at banquets as an antidote
to wine, and God followed musical harmony in ordering the heavens. The meeting ends with a paean
and libations to the gods (1146 D—1147 A).

When the speakers allude to " modern " music and
to " men of our times," the reference is undoubtedly
(except at 1140 c) to the fourth or third century B.C.
Yet the mention (1132 F) of Alexander, a polymath
of the first century B.C.,[a] has led scholars to suppose
that our author had before him a compilation made
in Roman times.[b]

---

[a] Other sources mentioned by name are earlier : Glaucus
of Italy (1132 E, 1133 F) belongs to the fifth century ; Anticleides (1136 A) to the fourth ; Istrus (1136 A) and Dionysius
Iambus (1136 c) to the third.

[b] F. Lasserre, *Plutarque, De la musique* (Olten and Lausanne, 1954), pp. 101 f., suggests as the immediate source the
younger Dionysius of Halicarnassus (second century A.D.),
who wrote thirty-six books on music and was still an authority
in Byzantine times. R. Westphal, *Plutarch, Über die Musik*
(Breslau, 1865), p. 16, had supposed him to be the immediate
source of chapters xv-xvii.

Weil and Reinach [a] (who knew nothing of a Planudean edition) divided the manuscripts of the *De Musica* into the *Codices Plutarchiani* and the *Codices Musici*, a division retained (with some modification) by Ziegler [b] and Lasserre. Our own division is into M V α W aN vq, α being the source of the rest of the Planudeans.[c]

Thirty-nine mss. of the *De Musica* are known to us : MeJfZx VhPSbFT αεoAγπσκτβμλδRjkE WD aGN vsqu. All are derivative but M V α W aN vq. The derivative mss. are related as follows :

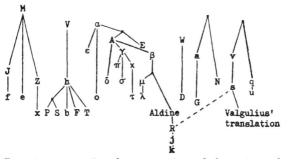

Our stemma omits the connexion of the principal mss. ; the variants are indecisive and show extensive crossing. We could dispense with aN, vq, and α ;

[a] H. Weil and T. Reinach, *Plutarque, De la musique* (Paris, 1900), p. xlvi.

[b] *Plutarchi Moralia*, vol. vi. 3 (Leipzig, 1953 ; second edition, 1959). In the second edition, pp. vii-x, Ziegler distinguishes *Plutarchei*, *Musici*, and *Platonici*.

[c] One *Plutarchianus* (Urbinas 99 ; not mentioned by previous editors) has a non-Planudean text ; three *Musici* (Vaticanus 221, Barberinianus 265, and Rossianus 977) descend from the Planudean edition by way of the Aldine of 1509.

PLUTARCH'S MORALIA

they tell us nothing about the archetype that is not known from M, V, and W.

The dialogue has often been translated apart from the *Moralia* :

Plutarchi Chaeronei Philosophi Clarissimi Musica, Carolo Valgulio Brixiano interprete. Published at Brescia in 1507. We use the reprint in *Opuscula Plutarchi* (Paris, 1526), foll. 108ᵛ-115ʳ.

P. J. BURETTE. Πλουτάρχου διάλογος περὶ μουσικῆς. Dialogue de Plutarque sur la musique, traduit en françois. Avec des remarques. Par M. Burette. *Memoires de Litterature*, tirez des registres de l'Academie Royale des Inscriptions et Belles Lettres. . . . Tome dixième. A Paris . . . M. DCCXXXVI pp. 111-310. The same author publishes in the eighth volume of the same series (1733) an " Examen du traité de Plutarque sur la musique " (pp. 27-44), " Observations touchant l'histoire litteraire du dialogue de Plutarque sur la musique " (pp. 44-62), and "Analyse du dialogue de Plutarque sur la musique " (pp. 80-96) ; in the thirteenth volume (1740) " Suite des remarques " (pp. 173-316) ; in the fifteenth (1743) " Suite " (pp. 293-394) ; in the seventeenth (1751) " Fin " (pp. 31-60) and " Dissertation-épilogue, comparaison de la théorie de l'ancienne musique et de la moderne " (pp. 61-126).

J. H. BROMBY. *The* Περὶ Μουσικῆς *of Plutarch Translated*. Chiswick, 1822.

Plutarchi de Musica edidit Ricardus Volkmann. Leipzig, 1856.

Plutarch über die Musik von Rud. Westphal. Breslau, 1865.

ON MUSIC

Plutarque De la Musique Περὶ μουσικῆς. Édition critique et explicative par Henri Weil et Th. Reinach. Paris, 1900.

G. SKJERNE, *Plutarks Dialog om Musiken.* Copenhagen, 1909.

N. N. TOMASOV, *Plutarkh O Muzyka.* Perevod s grečeskogo N. N. Tomasova . . . Petersburg, 1922.

F. LASSERRE, *Plutarque, De la musique.* Olten and Lausanne, 1954.

The work is not mentioned in the Catalogue of Lamprias.

ΠΕΡΙ ΜΟΥΣΙΚΗΣ[1]

B   1. Ἡ μὲν Φωκίωνος τοῦ χρηστοῦ γυνὴ κόσμον
αὐτῆς ἔλεγεν εἶναι τὰ Φωκίωνος στρατηγήματα·
ἐγὼ δὲ κόσμον ἐμὸν οὐ μόνον ἴδιον ἀλλὰ γὰρ καὶ
κοινὸν τῶν οἰκείων πάντων ἡγοῦμαι τὴν τοῦ ἐμοῦ
διδασκάλου περὶ λόγους σπουδήν. τῶν μὲν γὰρ
στρατηγῶν τὰ ἐπιφανέστατα κατορθώματα σωτη-
ρίας μόνον οἴδαμεν τῆς ἐκ τῶν παραχρῆμα κινδύνων
αἴτια γιγνόμενα[2] στρατιώταις ὀλίγοις ἢ πόλει μιᾷ
ἢ κἂν ἑνί τινι ἔθνει, βελτίους δ᾽ οὐδαμῶς ποιοῦντα
C οὔτε τοὺς στρατιώτας οὔτε τοὺς πολίτας, ἀλλ᾽ οὐδὲ
τοὺς ὁμοεθνεῖς· τὴν δὲ παιδείαν, οὐσίαν[3] εὐδαι-
μονίας οὖσαν αἰτίαν τ᾽ εὐβουλίας, οὐ μόνον ἐστὶν
εὑρεῖν ἢ οἴκῳ ἢ πόλει ἢ ἔθνει χρησίμην, ἀλλὰ παντὶ
τῷ τῶν ἀνθρώπων γένει. ὅσῳ οὖν ἡ ἐκ παιδείας
ὠφέλεια μείζων πάντων στρατηγημάτων, τοσούτῳ
καὶ ἡ περὶ αὐτῆς μνήμη ἀξία σπουδῆς.

2. Τῇ γοῦν[4] δευτέρᾳ τῶν Κρονίων ἡμέρᾳ ὁ καλὸς
Ὀνησικράτης ἐπὶ τὴν ἑστίασιν ἄνδρας μουσικῆς

---

[1] περὶ μουσικῆς M[1aΓ] (π[ερὶ] μ[ουσικῆς]) a : πλουτάρχου περὶ
μουσικῆς V[2] W a(τοῦ πλ.)N vq ; [περὶ] μου[σι]κ[ῆς] πλο[υ]-
τάρχ[ου] M[2aΓ] ; M[2Γ] V[1] omit.   [2] γιγνόμενα] γινόμενα aN.
[3] οὐσίαν] οὐσίας M.   [4] γοῦν (γοῦν W)] οὖν vq.

[a] This was his appellation : cf. Life of Phocion, chap. x. 4
(746 c) ; Dio Chrysostom, lxxiii. 7 ; Aelian, V.H. iii. 47,
xii. 43.

ON MUSIC

1. THE wife of Phocion the Good [a] said that his feats of generalship were her adornment [b]; for my part I hold that not only my own adornment, but that of all my friends as well, is my preceptor's zeal for letters. For we know that whereas the most brilliant successes of generals end merely in preserving from momentary dangers a few soldiers, a single city, or at most a single nation, but in no wise make better men of those soldiers or citizens or yet of those fellow nationals, culture, on the other hand, which is the substance of felicity and the source of good counsel,[c] can be found useful not merely to a family or a city or a nation, but to the whole human race. The greater benefit conferred by culture in comparison with all military exploits is the measure of the value that belongs to the discussion of it.

2. Thus on the second day of the Saturnalia [d] the noble Onesicrates had invited to his feast men learned

---

[b] Cf. *Life of Phocion*, chap. xix. 4 (750 D) and Stobaeus, vol. iii, p. 267. 4-7 (ed. Hense).

[c] The points that " culture " leads to good counsel and is better than military victory were taken from the praise of rhetoric : cf. the preface to the *Rhetoric to Alexander*. For *logoi* (discourse) as responsible for the greatest blessings cf. Isocrates, *Or*. iii. 5, and for their relation to good counsel, *Or*. iii. 8.

[d] The festival of the Saturnalia at this time lasted seven days, beginning December 17.

(1131) ἐπιστήμονας παρακεκλήκει· ἦσαν δὲ Σωτήριχος
'Αλεξανδρεὺς καὶ Λυσίας εἷς τις[1] τῶν σύνταξιν παρ᾿
αὑτοῦ λαμβανόντων. ἐπεὶ δὲ τὰ νομιζόμενα συντε-
D τέλεστο, " τὸ μὲν αἴτιον τῆς ἀνθρώπου φωνῆς,"
ἔφη, " ὅ τι ποτ᾿ ἐστίν, ὦ ἑταῖροι, νῦν ἐπιζητεῖν οὐ
συμποτικόν, σχολῆς γὰρ νηφαλιωτέρας δεῖται τὸ
θεώρημα· ἐπεὶ δ᾿ ὁρίζονται τὴν φωνὴν οἱ ἄριστοι
γραμματικοὶ ἀέρα πεπληγότα αἰσθητὸν ἀκοῇ,
τυγχάνομέν τε χθὲς ἐζητηκότες περὶ γραμματικῆς
ὡς τέχνης ἐπιτηδείου γράμμασι[2] τὰς φωνὰς δημι-
ουργεῖν καὶ ταμιεύειν τῇ ἀναμνήσει, ἴδωμεν τίς
μετὰ ταύτην δευτέρα πρέπουσα φωνῇ ἐπιστήμη.
οἶμαι δὲ ὅτι μουσική· ὑμνεῖν γὰρ εὐσεβὲς καὶ προη-
γούμενον ἀνθρώποις τοὺς χαρισαμένους αὐτοῖς μόνοις τὴν ἔναρθρον φωνὴν θεούς· τοῦτο δὲ καὶ
Ὅμηρος ἐπεσημήνατο ἐν οἷς λέγει

E   οἱ δὲ πανημέριοι μολπῇ θεὸν ἱλάσκοντο
    καλὸν ἀείδοντες παιήονα, κοῦροι 'Αχαιῶν,
    μέλποντες ἑκάεργον· ὁ δὲ φρένα τέρπετ᾿ ἀκούων.

ἄγε δή, ὦ μουσικῆς θιασῶται, τίς πρῶτος ἐχρήσατο
μουσικῇ ἀναμνήσατε τοὺς ἑταίρους,[3] καὶ τί εὗρεν
πρὸς αὔξησιν ταύτης ὁ χρόνος, καὶ τίνες γεγόνασιν
εὐδόκιμοι τῶν τὴν μουσικὴν ἐπιστήμην μεταχειρι-
σαμένων· ἀλλὰ μὴν καὶ εἰς πόσα καὶ εἰς τίνα[4] χρή-

---

[1] τις] vq omit.
[2] γράμμασι van Herwerden : γραμμαῖς.
[3] ἑταίρους (-αῖ- v^{ac})] ἑτέρους V W^{ac}.
[4] πόσα καὶ εἰς τίνα] τίνα καὶ εἰς πόσα v.

---

[a] Cf. Donatus, Ars Gram., p. 367. 5 (vol. iv, ed. Keil) and
Marius Victorinus, Ars Gram., p. 4. 13 (vol. vi, ed. Keil).
The definition is Stoic : cf. Diogenes Laert. vii. 55.

[b] Phônê (" vocal utterance ") can also mean " word,"

in music ; these were Soterichus of Alexandria and Lysias, one of his pensioners. At the close of the customary ceremonies Onesicrates said : " To inquire at present into the theory of the human voice, my friends, would be out of place in a convivial gathering, as that problem requires leisure of a soberer kind. But since the best grammarians define vocal sound as ' beaten air perceptible to hearing,' [a] and it happens that we yesterday inquired into grammar as an art adapted to the production of vocal utterances [b] and their preservation for recollection by means of letters,[c] let us consider what second science, coming after grammar, is concerned with the voice. I take it to be music. For it is an act of piety and a principal concern of man to sing hymns to the gods, who have granted articulate speech [d] to him alone ; Homer [e] moreover adverted to this in the words :

> The Greeks made supplication to the god
> All day in beauteous song, chanting a paean,
> Hymning the Archer ; he, well pleased, gave ear.

Come then, you votaries of music, and recall to the company who first employed it, what inventions time has brought to its advancement, and who among those who practised the science of music have won renown [f] ; and tell further the number and nature of

spoken or written. " Words " consist of " letters " (or sounds), and our author speaks of this composition of words as a production of them from their elements.

[c] In Greek grammar " letters " are not only the signs of the alphabet but the sounds that the signs represent.

[d] *Cf.* Marius Victorinus, *Ars Grammatica*, p. 4. 17-19 (vol. vi, ed. Keil), who divides " articulate voice " into that found in music and that found in ordinary speech.

[e] *Iliad*, i. 472-474, cited again at 1146 c, *infra*.

[f] These points are dealt with in the speech of Lysias, who mentions the first two at 1135 D, *infra*.

(1131) σιμον τὸ ἐπιτήδευμα." ταῦτα μὲν εἶπεν ὁ διδάσκαλος.

F 3. Ὁ δὲ Λυσίας ὑπολαβών, " παρὰ πολλοῖς,"
ἔφη, " ἐζητημένον πρόβλημα[1] ἐπιζητεῖς, ἀγαθὲ
Ὀνησίκρατες. τῶν τε γὰρ Πλατωνικῶν οἱ πλεῖστοι
καὶ τῶν ἀπὸ τοῦ Περιπάτου φιλοσόφων οἱ ἄριστοι
περί τε τῆς ἀρχαίας μουσικῆς συντάξαι ἐσπούδασαν
καὶ περὶ τῆς παρ' αὐτοῖς[2] γεγενημένης παραφθορᾶς[3]·
ἀλλὰ γὰρ καὶ γραμματικῶν καὶ ἁρμονικῶν οἱ ἐπ'
ἄκρον παιδείας ἐληλακότες πολλὴν σπουδὴν περὶ
τοῦτο[4] πεποίηνται· πολλὴ γοῦν ἡ τῶν συντεταχότων
διαφωνία.

" ' Ἡρακλείδης δ' ἐν τῇ Συναγωγῇ τῶν ἐν μουσικῇ[5] τὴν κιθαρῳδίαν καὶ[6] τὴν κιθαρῳδικὴν ποίησιν
πρῶτόν φησιν Ἀμφίονα[7] ἐπινοῆσαι τὸν Διὸς καὶ
1132 Ἀντιόπης, τοῦ πατρὸς δηλονότι διδάξαντος αὐτόν.
πιστοῦται δὲ τοῦτο ἐκ τῆς ἀναγραφῆς τῆς ἐν Σικυῶνι[8] ἀποκειμένης δι' ἧς τάς τε[9] ἱερείας τὰς ἐν
Ἄργει καὶ τοὺς ποιητὰς καὶ τοὺς μουσικοὺς ὀνομάζει.

" Κατὰ δὲ τὴν αὐτὴν ἡλικίαν καὶ Λίνον τὸν ἐξ
Εὐβοίας θρήνους πεποιηκέναι λέγει καὶ Ἄνθην τὸν

---

[1] πρόβλημα] τὸ πρόβλημα W.
[2] παρ' αὐτοῖς nos : αὐτοῖς M V a W[188] aN vq ; αὐτῆς W[t].
[3] παραφθορᾶς M a (-ὰς W) aN v[1]q : παραφορᾶς V v[2t].
[4] τοῦτο] τούτων N.
[5] ἐν μουσικῇ M[2] (-ῇ from -ῃ) V a W aN vq : διαλαμψάντων
ἐν μ. Bergk ; περὶ μουσικῆς Voss ; εὐδοκιμησάντων ἐν μ. Weil
and Reinach ; εὑρημάτων ἐν μ. Lasserre.
[6] τὴν κιθαρῳδίαν καὶ] W omits.
[7] ἀμφίονα V[c] a[c] W aN vq : ἀμφίνοα M ; ἀμφίωνα V[ac] (?)
a[ac] (?).
[8] σικυῶνι a[c] N[2] : σικυῶνι M V a[ac] W aN[1] : σικυόνι vq.
[9] τάς τε] τάς τε τὰς V.

the ends that the cultivation of music serves." [a] Thus spoke our preceptor.

3. " Many," Lysias replied, " have sought to answer the question you raise, most excellent Onesicrates. Thus most of the Platonists [b] and the best of the Peripatetics [c] have devoted their efforts to the composition of treatises on ancient [d] music and its corruption in their own day ; furthermore, the most learned grammarians [e] and students of harmonics [f] have also devoted much study to the subject. Thus there is abundant lack of unison in the authorities.

" Heracleides [g] in his *Collection* says that the first invention in music was that of singing to the cithara and of poetry thus sung, and that it was made by Amphion,[h] son of Zeus and Antiopê, evidently taught by his sire. This is attested by the document preserved at Sicyon,[i] which provided Heracleides with the names of the priestesses at Argos, the composers, and the musicians.

" In the same period furthermore (he says) Linus of Euboea composed dirges, Anthes of Anthedon in

[a] These points are dealt with by Soterichus.

[b] The Platonists cited are Plato himself and Heracleides.

[c] The Peripatetics cited are Aristotle, Heracleides, and Aristoxenus.

[d] "Ancient" music was the music that prevailed before the innovations of Lasus and the rest.

[e] The grammarians cited are Glaucus, Dionysius Iambus, Anticleides, Istrus, and Alexander Polyhistor.

[f] The " harmonicists " are cited at 1134 D ; *cf.* also 1143 E-F.

[g] Frag. 157 (ed. Wehrli).

[h] *Cf.* Pliny, *N.H.* vii. 204 ; Pausanias, ix. 5. 8 ; *Suda, s.v.* ; and Julian, *Ep.* 30 (vol. i. 2, p. 57 Bidez ; p. 36 Bidez-Cumont).

[i] *Die sikyonische Anagraphe*, Frag. 1, ed. Jacoby (*Frag. d. gr. Hist.* iii B 550, p. 536).

(1132) ἐξ Ἀνθηδόνος τῆς Βοιωτίας ὕμνους καὶ Πίερον[1]
τὸν ἐκ Πιερίας τὰ περὶ τὰς Μούσας ποιήματα·
ἀλλὰ καὶ Φιλάμμωνα[2] τὸν Δελφὸν Λητοῦς τε
πλάνας[3] καὶ Ἀρτέμιδος καὶ Ἀπόλλωνος γένεσιν
δηλῶσαι ἐν μέλεσι καὶ χοροὺς πρῶτον περὶ τὸ ἐν
Δελφοῖς ἱερὸν στῆσαι· Θάμυριν δὲ τὸ γένος Θρᾷκα[4]
B εὐφωνότερον καὶ ἐμμελέστερον πάντων τῶν τότε
ᾆσαι, ὡς ταῖς Μούσαις κατὰ τοὺς ποιητὰς εἰς
ἀγῶνα καταστῆναι· πεποιηκέναι δὲ τοῦτον ἱστορεῖ-
ται Τιτάνων πρὸς τοὺς θεοὺς πόλεμον· γεγονέναι δὲ
καὶ Δημόδοκον Κερκυραῖον παλαιὸν μουσικόν, ὃν
πεποιηκέναι Ἰλίου τε πόρθησιν καὶ Ἀφροδίτης καὶ
Ἡφαίστου γάμον· ἀλλὰ μὴν καὶ Φήμιον Ἰθακήσιον
νόστον τῶν[5] ἀπὸ Τροίας μετ' Ἀγαμέμνονος ἀνα-
κομισθέντων ποιῆσαι.

"Οὐ λελυμένην δὲ εἶναι τῶν προειρημένων τὴν
C τῶν ποιημάτων λέξιν καὶ μέτρον οὐκ ἔχουσαν, ἀλλὰ
καθάπερ[6] Στησιχόρου τε καὶ τῶν ἀρχαίων μελοποιῶν, οἳ ποιοῦντες ἔπη τούτοις μέλη περιετίθεσαν·
καὶ γὰρ τὸν Τέρπανδρον ἔφη κιθαρῳδικῶν[7] ποιητὴν
ὄντα νόμων κατὰ νόμον ἕκαστον τοῖς ἔπεσιν τοῖς
ἑαυτοῦ καὶ τοῖς Ὁμήρου μέλη περιτιθέντα ᾄδειν ἐν
τοῖς ἀγῶσιν· ἀποφῆναι δὲ τοῦτον λέγει ὀνόματα
πρῶτον τοῖς κιθαρῳδικοῖς νόμοις· ὁμοίως δὲ Τερπάνδρῳ Κλονᾶν, τὸν πρῶτον συστησάμενον τοὺς
αὐλῳδικοὺς νόμους καὶ τὰ προσόδια, ἐλεγείων τε

[1] πίερον V : πίεριον.
[2] φιλάμμωνα] Φιλάμμονα Hatzidakis (cf. Hesiod, Frag. 111 [ed. Rzach] and Rhesus, 916).
[3] πλάνας added by Weil and Reinach.
[4] θρᾷκα V a aN vq: θραϊκὰ M ; θρᾷκα (from θράκα) καὶ Wᶜ.
[5] τῶν] τὸν M V.
[6] After καθάπερ Wyttenbach would add ἤ, Ziegler τὴν.

Boeotia hymns, and Pierus of Pieria his poems on the
Muses ; again Philammon of Delphi gave an account
in music of the wanderings of Leto and of the birth
of Artemis and Apollo, and was the first to set up
choruses [a] at the Delphic shrine ; Thamyris, a native
of Thrace, sang with the most beautiful and melodious
voice of all men of that time, so that (as the poets [b]
say) he engaged in a contest with the Muses, and it
is recorded that he composed a *War of the Titans With
the Gods* ; and there was also an ancient musician,
Demodocus of Corcyra, who composed a *Sack of Troy* [c]
and a *Marriage of Aphroditê and Hephaestus* [d] ; and
again Phemius of Ithaca composed a *Return of the
Heroes* who set out for home from Troy with Agamemnon.[e]

" In the compositions of these men the words were
not in free rhythms and lacking in metre, but were
like those of Stesichorus and the ancient lyric poets,
who composed dactylic hexameters and set them to
music ; thus he says that Terpander also, who was a
composer of nomes sung to the cithara, set to music
in each nome hexameters [f] of his own and Homer's
and sang them in the contests ; and he asserts that
Terpander was the first to give names [g] to nomes
sung to the cithara, and that like Terpander Clonas,
the first to construct nomes and processionals sung to

[a] *Cf.* Pherecydes, Frag. 120, ed. Jacoby (*Frag. d. gr.
Hist.*, Erster Teil [Neudruck, 1957], p. 92).
[b] *Cf.* Homer, *Iliad*, ii. 594-600.
[c] *Cf.* Homer, *Odyssey*, viii. 499-520.
[d] *Cf.* Homer, *Odyssey*, viii. 266-366.
[e] *Cf.* Homer, *Odyssey*, i. 325-327.
[f] *Cf.* Proclus, *Chrest.* 45 (320 b 5-6, ed. Bekker).
[g] *Cf.* 1132 D, *infra*.

---

[7] κιθαρῳδικῶν] -ὸν M N.

(1132) καὶ ἐπῶν ποιητὴν γεγονέναι, καὶ Πολύμνηστον τὸν
Κολοφώνιον τὸν μετὰ τοῦτον γενόμενον τοῖς αὐτοῖς
χρήσασθαι ποιήμασιν.

D   4. " Οἱ δὲ νόμοι οἱ κατὰ τούτους, ἀγαθὲ Ὀνησίκρατες, ἦσαν¹ Ἀπόθετος, Ἔλεγοι, Κωμάρχιος,
Σχοινίων, Κηπίων τε καὶ Δεῖος² καὶ Τριμελής³·
ὑστέρῳ δὲ χρόνῳ καὶ τὰ Πολυμνάστια⁴ καλούμενα
ἐξευρέθη. οἱ δὲ τῆς κιθαρῳδίας νόμοι πρότερον οὐ⁵
πολλῷ χρόνῳ τῶν αὐλῳδικῶν κατεστάθησαν ἐπὶ
Τερπάνδρου· ἐκεῖνος γοῦν⁶ τοὺς κιθαρῳδικοὺς πρό-
τερος⁷ ὠνόμασεν, Βοιώτιόν τινα καὶ Αἰόλιον Τρο-
χαῖόν τε καὶ Ὀξὺν Κηπίωνά τε καὶ Τερπάνδρειον
καλῶν, ἀλλὰ μὴν καὶ Τετραοίδιον. πεποίηται δὲ
τῷ Τερπάνδρῳ καὶ προοίμια κιθαρῳδικὰ ἐν ἔπεσιν.

E ὅτι δὲ οἱ κιθαρῳδικοὶ νόμοι οἱ πάλαι ἐξ ἐπῶν συν-
ίσταντο Τιμόθεος ἐδήλωσεν· τοὺς γοῦν⁸ πρώτους
νόμους ἐν ἔπεσι διαμιγνύων διθυραμβικὴν λέξιν
ᾖδεν, ὅπως μὴ εὐθὺς φανῇ παρανομῶν εἰς τὴν ἀρ-
χαίαν μουσικήν.

¹ Before ἦσαν we delete αὐλῳδικοί.
² τε καὶ δεῖος is corrupt. Τενέδιος Amyot ; τε καὶ Λύδιος
Salmasius ; τε καὶ Λεῖος Wyttenbach ; τε καὶ Τεῖος Burette ;
Ἐπικήδειος Westphal.   ³ τριμελής] Τριμερής Xylander.
⁴ Πολυμνάστια] Πολυμνήστεια van Herwerden (πολυμνίστια s).
⁵ οὐ added by Weil and Reinach.   ⁶ γοῦν] οὖν vq.
⁷ πρότερος] πρότερον ε.   ⁸ γοῦν] οὖν vq.

ᵃ " Reserved," " stored away," or " secret." Cf. Pollux,
iv. 65, 79, and 1133 A, infra.
ᵇ " Songs " or " laments."
ᶜ " Of the leader of the revels."
ᵈ " Cable." Burette compares Hesychius σχοινίνην φωνήν·
τὴν σαθρὰν καὶ διερρωγυῖαν " Reedy voice : feeble and broken."
Perhaps we should rather compare Pindar's σχοινοτένειά τ'
ἀοιδὰ διθυράμβων (frag. 86 [ed. Turyn], 70 b [ed. Snell]) " rope-
like song of the dithyramb," that is, loose and long.

the auloi, was a poet of elegiac and hexameter verse, and that Polymnestus of Colophon, who flourished later, employed the same metres.

4. " The nomes in the style of these last, most excellent Onesicrates, were as follows : the Apothetos,[a] Elegoi,[b] Comarchios,[c] Schoinion,[d] Cepion,[e] . . . ,[f] and Trimeles [g] ; later the so-called Polymnestian pieces were invented. The nomes sung to the cithara were established in Terpander's days, somewhat earlier than those sung to the auloi ; thus he gave names to these before the others had received their names, calling them [h] Boeotian and Aeolian, Trochaios [i] and Oxys,[j] Cepion and Terpandrean, and furthermore Tetraoidios.[k] Terpander also composed preludes sung to the cithara in hexameters. That the ancient nomes sung to the cithara were in hexameters was shown by Timotheüs, as he sang his first nomes in heroic hexameters, with a mixture of the diction of the dithyramb, in order not to display at the start any violation of the laws of ancient music.

[e] Named from Cepion or Capion, disciple of Terpander (cf. 1133 c, infra).

[f] The Greek is corrupt.

[g] " Three-membered " or " three-tuned."

[h] Cf. Pollux, iv. 65 : " The nomes of Terpander named from his national origin are the Aeolian and Boeotian ; those named from the rhythms are the Orthios <from the orthios foot ⏑ ‐́ ‐́> and the Trochaios ; those from the mode are the Oxys and Tetraoidios ; and those from himself and his favourite are the Terpandrean and Capion." Suda, s.v. ὄρθιος νόμος says there were seven nomes for singing to the cithara. Under the next entry he mentions the Orthios and the Trochaios, named by Terpander from the rhythm ; and under the entry νόμος he mentions further the Tetradios and Oxys.

[i] " Trochaic."

[j] " High-Pitched."   [k] " Four-Songed."

361

(1132) '' "Εοικεν δὲ κατὰ τὴν τέχνην τὴν κιθαρῳδικὴν
ὁ Τέρπανδρος διενηνοχέναι· τὰ Πύθια γὰρ τετράκις
ἑξῆς νενικηκὼς ἀναγέγραπται. καὶ τοῖς χρόνοις δὲ
σφόδρα παλαιός ἐστιν· πρεσβύτερον γοῦν[1] αὐτὸν
Ἀρχιλόχου ἀποφαίνει Γλαῦκος ὁ ἐξ Ἰταλίας ἐν
συγγράμματί τινι τῷ[2] περὶ τῶν ἀρχαίων ποιητῶν τε
καὶ μουσικῶν· φησὶν γὰρ αὐτὸν δεύτερον γενέσθαι
F μετὰ τοὺς πρώτους ποιήσαντας αὐλῳδίαν.

5. '' Ἀλέξανδρος δ' ἐν τῇ Συναγωγῇ τῶν περὶ
Φρυγίας κρούματα Ὄλυμπον ἔφη πρῶτον εἰς τοὺς
Ἕλληνας κομίσαι, ἔτι δὲ καὶ τοὺς Ἰδαίους Δα-
κτύλους· Ὕαγνιν δὲ πρῶτον αὐλῆσαι, εἶτα τὸν τούτου υἱὸν Μαρσύαν, εἶτα Ὄλυμπον· ἐζηλωκέναι δὲ
τὸν Τέρπανδρον Ὁμήρου μὲν τὰ ἔπη, Ὀρφέως δὲ
τὰ μέλη. ὁ δὲ Ὀρφεὺς οὐδένα φαίνεται μεμιμη-
μένος, οὐδεὶς γάρ πω γεγένητο εἰ μὴ οἱ τῶν αὐλῳδικῶν[3] ποιηταί· τούτοις δὲ κατ' οὐθὲν τὸ Ὀρφικὸν
1133 ἔργον ἔοικεν. Κλονᾶς δὲ ὁ τῶν αὐλῳδικῶν νόμων

---

[1] γοῦν] οὖν v[c]q ; δὲ v[ac].   [2] τῷ] Post would omit.
[3] αὐλῳδικῶν] αὐλητικῶν Westphal ; αὐλῳδικῶν νόμων Bergk.

---

[a] Frag. 2, ed. Müller (*Frag. Hist. Graec.*, vol. ii, p. 23).
[b] E. Hiller (*Rhein. Mus.* xli [1886], p. 408) finds this sentence difficult, since Orpheus (a singer to the cithara) must
have come after the first composers of music sung to the auloi.
He therefore supposes that our author has confused Terpander and Orpheus.
[c] Frag. 77, ed. Jacoby (*Frag. d. gr. Hist.*, iii A 273, p.
109).
[d] *Cf.* Clement, *Strom.* i. 16. 76. 6 (vol. ii, p. 50. 1, ed.
Stählin) ; *Anecd. Oxon.* (ed. Cramer), vol. iv, p. 400. 19 ;
Suda, s.v. Ὄλυμπος 2 (vol. iii, p. 522. 22, ed. Adler).
[e] For Hyagnis as inventor of the auloi or of the auletic art
cf. Dioscorides in the *Anth. Pal.* ix. 340 ; the Marmor Parium,
19 (which gives the date 1505/4 B.C.) ; and Nonnus, *Dion.*
xli. 374. Aristoxenus (Fr g. 78, ed. Wehrli), the Marmor

" Terpander appears to have been eminent as an executant in singing to the cithara ; thus it is recorded that he won four successive victories at the Pythian games. He belongs furthermore to the remotest times ; thus Glaucus [a] of Italy in a book *On the Ancient Poets and Musicians* makes him older than Archilochus, saying that Terpander came second after the first composers of music sung to the auloi.[b]

5. " Alexander [c] in his *Notices on Phrygia* said that Olympus first brought the music of the auloi to the Greeks,[d] but that the Idaean Dactyls did so too ; that Hyagnis [e] was the first to play the auloi and that his son Marsyas [f] came next, and after him Olympus ; and that [g] Terpander took as his models the hexameters of Homer and the music of Orpheus. But Orpheus evidently imitated no predecessor, as there were none as yet,[h] unless it was composers of songs for the auloi,[i] and Orpheus' work resembles theirs in no way. Clonas, the composer of nomes sung to

Parium, and the Anonymus Bellermanni, 28 speak of Hyagnis as inventor of the Phrygian *harmonia*.

[f] For Marsyas as son of Hyagnis *cf.* Antipater or Philippus in the *Anth. Pal.* ix. 266 ; Apuleius, *Flor.* 3 ; Nonnus, *Dion.* x. 233 ; the scholiast on Aeschylus, *Persians*, 939 Wecklein, 940 Dähnhardt [or Jacoby, *Frag. d. gr. Hist.*, Domitius Kallistratos, iii B 433. 3, p. 334] ; the scholiast on the Platonic *Minos*, 318 B ; and Tzetzes, *Chil.* i. 15.

[g] This clause, as Westphal saw, comes not from Alexander but from Glaucus. Hiller (*Rhein. Mus.* xli [1886], pp. 403 f.) supposes that our author, using a compiler who cited Alexander, has been careless with the syntax.

[h] The source takes Orpheus to be the first singer to the cithara (*cf. Orphicorum Frag.*, Testim. 56-58, ed. Kern), taught by Apollo. Thus there were no preceding singers to the cithara for him to imitate.

[i] Hiller (*Rhein. Mus.* xli [1886], p. 406) supposes that the source here (Glaucus) is thinking of Ardalus (*cf.* 1133 A, *infra*).

(1133) ποιητής, ὁ ὀλίγῳ ὕστερον Τερπάνδρου γενόμενος, ὡς μὲν Ἀρκάδες λέγουσιν, Τεγεάτης ἦν, ὡς δὲ Βοιωτοί, Θηβαῖος. μετὰ δὲ Τέρπανδρον καὶ Κλονᾶν Ἀρχίλοχος παραδίδοται γενέσθαι. ἄλλοι δέ τινες τῶν συγγραφέων Ἄρδαλόν φασι Τροιζήνιον πρότερον Κλονᾶ τὴν αὐλῳδικὴν συστήσασθαι μοῦσαν· γεγονέναι δὲ καὶ Πολύμνηστον ποιητήν, Μέλητος τοῦ Κολοφωνίου υἱόν, ὃν Πολυμνηστίους[1] νόμους ποιῆσαι. περὶ δὲ Κλονᾶ[2] ὅτι τὸν Ἀπόθετον νόμον καὶ Σχοινίωνα πεποιηκὼς εἴη μνημονεύουσιν οἱ ἀναγεγραφότες. τοῦ δὲ Πολυμνήστου
B καὶ Πίνδαρος καὶ Ἀλκμὰν οἱ τῶν μελῶν ποιηταὶ ἐμνημόνευσαν. τινὰς δὲ τῶν νόμων τῶν κιθαρῳδικῶν τῶν ὑπὸ Τερπάνδρου πεποιημένων Φιλάμμωνά[3] φασι τὸν ἀρχαῖον τὸν Δελφὸν συστήσασθαι.

6. " Τὸ δ' ὅλον ἡ μὲν κατὰ Τέρπανδρον κιθαρῳδία καὶ μέχρι τῆς Φρύνιδος ἡλικίας παντελῶς ἁπλῆ τις οὖσα διετέλει· οὐ γὰρ ἐξῆν τὸ παλαιὸν οὕτως ποιεῖσθαι τὰς κιθαρῳδίας ὡς νῦν οὐδὲ μεταφέρειν τὰς ἁρμονίας καὶ τοὺς ῥυθμούς· ἐν γὰρ τοῖς νόμοις ἑκάστῳ διετήρουν τὴν οἰκείαν τάσιν. διὸ
C καὶ ταύτην ἐπωνυμίαν εἶχον· νόμοι γὰρ προσηγορεύθησαν ἐπειδὴ οὐκ ἐξῆν παραβῆναι τὸ[4] καθ' ἕκαστον νενομισμένον εἶδος τῆς[5] τάσεως. τὰ γὰρ

---

[1] Πολυμνηστίους nos (ἄλλους τε καὶ Πολυμνηστίους Pohlenz) : πολύμνηστόν τε καὶ πολυμνήστην.
[2] κλονᾶ V a W a v²q : κλοναὶ M ; κλονᾶν N ; κλεονᾶ v¹.
[3] φιλάμμωνα M V a Wᶜ aN vq : φιλάμονα Wᵃᶜ : φιλάμιμονα J s and Hatzidakis.

the auloi who lived shortly after Terpander, was according to the Arcadians a man of Tegea, according to the Boeotians, of Thebes. After Terpander and Clonas Archilochus is reported to have lived. But certain other writers say that Ardalus [a] of Troezen elaborated songs to the auloi before Clonas, and that there was also a poet Polymnestus, son of Meles of Colophon, who composed Polymnestian nomes. Of Clonas our authors record that he composed in the Apothetos nome and the Schoinion.[b] Polymnestus is mentioned by the lyric poets Pindar [c] and Alcman.[d] And some of the nomes for singing to the cithara in which Terpander composed were, it is said, first developed by the ancient Philammon of Delphi.[e]

6. " In short, the style of singing to the cithara instituted by Terpander continued to be quite simple down to the period of Phrynis [f] ; for in ancient times it was not permitted to sing to the cithara as at present or to modulate from one harmony or rhythm to another, for in each nome the tuning appropriate to it was observed throughout. This indeed is the reason for the name : they were called *nomoi* [g] because it was forbidden to violate the accepted tuning that prevailed in each. Thus the performers, after

---

[a] *Cf.* Pliny, *N.H.* vii. 204 : " cum tibiis canere voce Troezenius Ardalus [*Harduinus* ; dardanus mss.] instituit."

[b] *Cf.* Pollux, iv. 79 : " To Clonas again belong the nomes for the auloi Apothetos and Schoinion."

[c] Frag. 218 (ed. Turyn), 188 (ed. Snell).

[d] Frag. 145 (Page, *Poet. Mel. Gr.* p. 79).

[e] *Cf. Suda, s.v.* Τέρπανδρος.

[f] *Cf.* Pollux, iv. 66 and Proclus, *Chrest.* 46.

[g] That is, " nomes " or " laws " : *cf.* Plato, *Laws*, vii, 799 E 10—800 A 7 and Aristides Quintilianus, *De Musica*, ii. 6 (p. 67, ed. Meibom ; p. 59, ed. Winnington-Ingram).

---

[4] τὸ added by von Arnim.   [5] τῆς] vq omit.

(1133) πρὸς τοὺς θεοὺς ὡς βούλονται ἀφοσιωσάμενοι, ἐξέ-
βαινον εὐθὺς ἐπί τε τὴν Ὁμήρου καὶ τῶν ἄλλων
ποίησιν. δῆλον δὲ τοῦτ' ἔστιν διὰ τῶν Τερπάνδρου
προοιμίων. ἐποιήθη δὲ καὶ τὸ σχῆμα τῆς κιθάρας
πρῶτον κατὰ Κηπίωνα τὸν Τερπάνδρου μαθητήν,
ἐκλήθη δὲ Ἀσιὰς διὰ τὸ κεχρῆσθαι τοὺς Λεσβίους
αὐτῇ κιθαρῳδούς, πρὸς τῇ Ἀσίᾳ κατοικοῦντας.
D τελευταῖον δὲ Περίκλειτόν φασι κιθαρῳδὸν νικῆσαι
ἐν Λακεδαίμονι Κάρνεια,[1] τὸ γένος ὄντα Λέσβιον·
τούτου δὲ τελευτήσαντος τέλος λαβεῖν Λεσβίοις[2] τὸ
συνεχὲς τῆς κατὰ τὴν κιθαρῳδίαν διαδοχῆς. ἔνιοι
δὲ πλανώμενοι νομίζουσι κατὰ τὸν αὐτὸν[3] χρόνον
Τερπάνδρῳ Ἱππώνακτα γεγονέναι· φαίνεται δὲ
Ἱππώνακτος καὶ Περίκλειτος ὢν πρεσβύτερος.

7. " Ἐπεὶ δὲ τοὺς αὐλῳδικοὺς νόμους καὶ κιθαρῳδικοὺς ὁμοῦ τοὺς ἀρχαίους ἐμπεφανίκαμεν, μετα-
βησόμεθα ἐπὶ μόνους[4] τοὺς αὐλητικούς.[5] λέγεται
γὰρ τὸν προειρημένον Ὄλυμπον, αὐλητὴν ὄντα τῶν[6]
ἐκ Φρυγίας, ποιῆσαι νόμον αὐλητικὸν εἰς Ἀπόλλωνα
τὸν καλούμενον Πολυκέφαλον· εἶναι δὲ τὸν Ὄλυμ-

---

[1] κάρνεια a[2] s : καρνία M V a[1] W (-ᾳ a)N v[1]q ; κάρνια v[2].
[2] λεσβίοις] λεσβίους v.
[3] αὐτὸν added by D[2] and Wyttenbach.
[4] μόνους] Ziegler would omit.
[5] αὐλητικούς Volkmann : αὐλῳδικούς.
[6] τῶν] τὸν M W ; q[ac] omits.

---

[a] Cf. Duris of Samos, Frag. 81, ed. Jacoby (Frag. d. gr.
Hist. ii A 76, p. 156).
[b] Jerome assigns Hipponax to the twenty-third Olympiad
(688–685 B.C.) [see Eusebius, Chron. ii. 85, ed. Schoene :
" Hipponax notissimus redditur "]. Athenaeus (xiv, 635 e-f)
puts a victory of Terpander's in the twenty-sixth Olympiad.

discharging their duty to the gods (which they did
as they pleased), passed at once to the poetry of
Homer and the rest. This can be seen in Terpander's
preludes. Again, the cithara was first given its form
in the days of Cepion, Terpander's disciple. It was
called the Asian cithara because it was used by the
Lesbian singers to the cithara, who live near Asia.[a]
The series closes, they say, with the singer to the
cithara Pericleitus, a native of Lesbos, who won a
victory at the Carneian festival in Sparta. With his
death the unbroken succession of singers to the cithara
at Lesbos came to an end. Some authorities [b] mis-
takenly suppose Hipponax to be a contemporary of
Terpander. But even Pericleitus is evidently more
ancient than Hipponax.

7. " Now that I have given an account of the
ancient nomes sung to the auloi as well as of those
sung to the cithara, I shall pass to instrumental music
for the auloi alone. The aforesaid Olympus,[c] an
aulete from Phrygia, is said to have composed a nome
for the auloi in honour of Apollo, the so-called Many-
Headed nome.[d] (This Olympus the authorities say

[c] Cf. 1132 F, supra.
[d] Cf. Pindar, *Pythian Odes*, xii : Athena invents the art
of playing the auloi in order to imitate the lament of the
Gorgons for Medusa, and calls her music the nome of many
heads. Pindar hints at the reason for the name in the second
strophe : Perseus heard the lament poured forth from under
the heads of maidens and of dreadful serpents. Nonnus
(*Dionysiaca*, xl. 231) puts the number of serpents involved at
two hundred, no doubt counting a hundred for each Gorgon.
The scholiasts on Pindar, *Pythian Odes*, xii. 39a (vol. ii, p.
268. 10-15, ed. Drachmann) present two other explanations :
the chorus that followed the lead of the aulete consisted of
fifty men ; and that " heads " are preludes ; hence the song
(which Olympus is said to have invented) consisted of many
preludes.

(1133)

E πον τοῦτόν φασιν ἕνα τῶν[1] ἀπὸ τοῦ πρώτου Ὀλύμπου τοῦ[2] Μαρσύου, πεποιηκότος εἰς τοὺς θεοὺς τοὺς
νόμους· οὗτος γὰρ παιδικὰ γενόμενος Μαρσύου καὶ
τὴν αὔλησιν μαθὼν παρ' αὐτοῦ, τοὺς νόμους τοὺς
ἁρμονικοὺς ἐξήνεγκεν εἰς τὴν Ἑλλάδα οἷς νῦν
χρῶνται οἱ Ἕλληνες ἐν ταῖς ἑορταῖς τῶν θεῶν.
ἄλλοι δὲ Κράτητος εἶναί φασιν τὸν[3] Πολυκέφαλον
νόμον, γενομένου μαθητοῦ Ὀλύμπου· ὁ δὲ Πρατίνας
Ὀλύμπου φησὶν εἶναι τοῦ νεωτέρου τὸν νόμον
τοῦτον.

" Τὸν δὲ καλούμενον Ἁρμάτιον νόμον λέγεται
ποιῆσαι ὁ πρῶτος Ὄλυμπος, ὁ Μαρσύου μαθητής.[4]
F τὸν δὲ Μαρσύαν φασί τινες Μάσσην καλεῖσθαι, οἱ
δ' οὔ,[5] ἀλλὰ Μαρσύαν, εἶναι δ' αὐτὸν Ὑάγνιδος[6]
υἱὸν τοῦ πρώτου εὑρόντος τὴν αὐλητικὴν τέχνην.
ὅτι δ' ἐστὶν Ὀλύμπου ὁ Ἁρμάτιος νόμος ἐκ τῆς
Γλαύκου ἀναγραφῆς τῆς ὑπὲρ τῶν ἀρχαίων ποιητῶν
μάθοι ἄν τις, καὶ ἔτι γνοίη ὅτι Στησίχορος ὁ
Ἱμεραῖος[7] οὔτε Ὀρφέα οὔτε Τέρπανδρον οὔτε Ἀρχίλοχον[8] οὔτε Θαλήταν ἐμιμήσατο, ἀλλ' Ὄλυμπον,
χρησάμενος τῷ Ἁρματίῳ νόμῳ καὶ τῷ κατὰ δά-
κτυλον εἴδει, ὅ[9] τινες ἐξ Ὀρθίου νόμου φασὶν εἶναι.

---

[1] ἕνα τῶν (ἕνα τῶν M, with a stroke over -a indicating a proper name)] ἕνα τὸν W ; ἔνατον Weil and Reinach.

[2] Meziriacus would add μαθητοῦ τοῦ after τοῦ. But cf. Ἀριστοτέλης ὁ Πλάτωνος at 1139 B, infra.

[3] τὸν] vq omit.

[4] ὁ πρ. Ὀλ. ὁ Μ. μ.] τὸν πρῶτον ὄλυμπον τὸν μ. μαθητὴν vq.

[5] οὔ (οὖ W)] οὔκ ? Bern.

[6] ὑάγνιδος a aN : ὑαγνίδου M V v¹q ; ὑαγνιδοῦ W ; ὑα-γνίδος v²ᵗ.

[7] ἱμεραῖος aN vq : ει- M W ; εἰ- V ; εἰ- a.

[8] ἀρχίλοχον Z¹ᵗ v²ᵐ (as Meziriacus had conjectured) : ἀντί-λοχον.

[9] ὅ a (as Amyot had conjectured) : οἵ (αἵ οἱ vᵃᶜ).

368

was a descendant of the elder Olympus, the disciple of Marsyas, who had composed his nomes in honour of the gods ; for this elder Olympus, who had been the favourite of Marsyas, from whom he learned to play the auloi, brought to Greece the enharmonic nomes which the Greeks now perform at the festivals of the gods.) Others say that the Many-Headed nome is a composition of Crates,[a] who had been a disciple of Olympus ; Pratinas [b] however asserts that this nome belongs to Olympus the younger.

" The so-called Chariot nome [c] is said to have been composed by the elder Olympus, the disciple of Marsyas. Some say that Marsyas was called Masses, others deny this and say his name was Marsyas, and that he was son of Hyagnis, who first invented the art of playing the auloi. That the Chariot nome is by Olympus one might gather from Glaucus' [d] account of the ancient poets, and one might further discover that Stesichorus of Himera imitated not Orpheus or Terpander or Archilochus or Thaletas, but Olympus, and made use of the Chariot nome and the dactylic rhythm, which some assert is derived from the Orthios

[a] Otherwise unknown.

[b] Frag. 6 (Page, *Poet. Mel. Gr.*, p. 369).

[c] The grammarians explain the name in a number of ways, as might be expected when there were no words accompanying the music. Thus the *Etymologicum Magnum* (145. 25-47) and the scholia on Euripides, *Orestes*, 1384 present the following explanations of the name : (1) from the chariot which dragged the body of Hector ; (2) from the chariot conveying the Mother of the Gods ; (3) from the chariot conveying brides at weddings ; (4) from a Boeotian Harmateus, who composed it as a nome of Athena ; (5) from the strong and rapid motion of a chariot ; (6) from the high thin sound of chariot axles ; (7) from the Phrygian word for " war " ; (8) from the music played when the stallion covered the mare.

[d] Frag. 3, ed. Müller (*Frag. Hist. Graec.* ii, p. 23).

(1133) ἄλλοι δέ τινες ὑπὸ Μυσῶν εὑρῆσθαι τοῦτον τὸν
νόμον· γεγονέναι γάρ τινας ἀρχαίους αὐλητὰς Μυ-
σούς.

8. " Καὶ ἄλλος δ' ἐστὶ ἀρχαῖος νόμος καλού-
1134 μενος Κραδίας, ὅν φησι Ἱππῶναξ Μίμνερμον
αὐλῆσαι. ἐν ἀρχῇ γὰρ ἐλεγεῖα μεμελοποιημένα οἱ
αὐλῳδοὶ ᾖδον· τοῦτο δὲ δηλοῖ ἡ τῶν Παναθηναίων[1]
γραφὴ ἡ περὶ τοῦ μουσικοῦ ἀγῶνος. γέγονε δὲ καὶ
Σακάδας[2] Ἀργεῖος ποιητὴς μελῶν τε καὶ ἐλεγείων
μεμελοποιημένων· ὁ δ' αὐτὸς καὶ αὐλητὴς[3] ἀγαθὸς
καὶ τὰ Πύθια τρὶς νενικηκὼς ἀναγέγραπται. τούτου καὶ Πίνδαρος μνημονεύει· τόνων γοῦν[4] τριῶν
ὄντων κατὰ Πολύμνηστον καὶ Σακάδαν, τοῦ τε
Δωρίου[5] καὶ Φρυγίου καὶ Λυδίου, ἐν ἑκάστῳ τῶν
B εἰρημένων τόνων στροφὴν[6] ποιήσαντά φασιν τὸν
Σακάδαν διδάξαι ᾄδειν τὸν χορὸν Δωριστὶ μὲν τὴν
πρώτην, Φρυγιστὶ δὲ τὴν δευτέραν, Λυδιστὶ δὲ τὴν
τρίτην· καλεῖσθαι δὲ Τριμελῆ[7] τὸν νόμον τοῦτον διὰ
τὴν μεταβολήν. ἐν δὲ τῇ ἐν[8] Σικυῶνι ἀναγραφῇ
τῇ περὶ τῶν ποιητῶν Κλονᾶς εὑρετὴς ἀναγέγραπται
τοῦ Τριμελοῦς[10] νόμου.

9. " Ἡ μὲν οὖν πρώτη κατάστασις τῶν περὶ τὴν
μουσικὴν ἐν τῇ Σπάρτῃ, Τερπάνδρου καταστήσαν-

---

[1] Παναθηναίων] παρ' ἀθηναίων V a.
[2] Σακάδας] ὁ σακάδας G ; Σακάδας ὁ Westphal.
[3] αὐλητὴς Wyttenbach : ποιητὴς.
[4] γοῦν] οὖν νq.   [5] Δωρίου] δωριένο M.
[6] στροφὴν Dübner : στροφὰν (-ᾶν N a^{ac}).
[7] Τριμελῆ Burette : τριμερῆ (-ῆ M ; -εῖ W).
[8] ἐν] N omits.   [9] σικυῶνι εA² s : σικύωνι (κύωνι V).
[10] Τριμελοῦς Burette : τριμερούς.

---

[a] " Of the fig-branch." Cf. Hesychius, s.v. : " a nome
played on the auloi over the human scapegoats that are escorted out, whipped with fig-branches and fig-leaves."

nome. Others say that this nome was a Mysian invention, there having been certain ancient auletes who were Mysians.

8. " There is another ancient nome called Cradias,[a] which Hipponax [b] says Mimnermus performed on the auloi (for at first singers to the auloi sang elegiac verse set to music : this is shown by the inscription concerning the musical contest at the Panathenaic festival).[c] Sacadas of Argos was also a composer of music and of elegiac verse set to music ; he was furthermore an excellent aulete and is recorded to have won three victories at the Pythian games.[d] Pindar [e] also mentions him. Thus, there being three systems of tuning in the time of Polymnestus and Sacadas, the Dorian, the Phrygian, and the Lydian, they say that Sacadas composed a strophe in each, and taught the chorus to sing the first in the Dorian, the second in the Phrygian, and the third in the Lydian ; and that this nome was called Trimeles [f] because of the modulation. It is recorded however in the document at Sicyon [g] that deals with the poets that Clonas invented the Trimeles nome.

9. " Now music was first organized [h] at Sparta, under the direction of Terpander ; for its second

[b] Frag. 96 (Bergk, *Poet. Lyr. Gr.*⁴, vol. ii, p. 492) ; Frag. 153 (ed. Masson).

[c] *Cf. Life of Pericles*, chap. xiii. 11 (160 B), Aristotle, *Constitution of Athens*, 60. 1 ; see also J. A. Davison, " Notes on the Panathenaea," *J.H.S.* lxxviii (1958), pp. 39-40.

[d] *Cf.* Pausanias, x. 7. 4.

[e] Frag. 72 (ed. Turyn), 269 (ed. Snell).

[f] " Three-membered " or " three-aired."

[g] *Die sikyonische Anagraphe*, Frag. 2, ed. Jacoby (*Frag. d. gr. Hist.* iii B 550, p. 536).

[h] *Cf.* Plato, *Laws*, vii, 802 A, who speaks of the " establishing " (καθίστασθαι) of songs and dances.

371

(1134) τος, γεγένηται· τῆς δὲ[1] δευτέρας Θαλήτας[2] τε ὁ
Γορτύνιος καὶ Ξενόδαμος ὁ Κυθήριος καὶ Ξενό-
κριτος[3] ὁ Λοκρὸς καὶ Πολύμνηστος ὁ Κολοφώνιος
C καὶ Σακάδας ὁ Ἀργεῖος μάλιστα αἰτίαν ἔχουσιν
ἡγεμόνες γενέσθαι· τούτων γὰρ εἰσηγησαμένων τὰ[4]
περὶ τὰς Γυμνοπαιδίας τὰς ἐν Λακεδαίμονι λέγεται
κατασταθῆναι καὶ[5] τὰ περὶ τὰς Ἀποδείξεις τὰς ἐν
Ἀρκαδίᾳ τῶν[6] τε ἐν Ἄργει τὰ Ἐνδυμάτια καλούμενα. ἦσαν δὲ οἱ μὲν[7] περὶ Θαλήταν τε καὶ Ξενόδαμον καὶ Ξενόκριτον[8] ποιηταὶ παιάνων, οἱ δὲ περὶ
Πολύμνηστον τῶν ὀρθίων καλουμένων, οἱ δὲ περὶ
Σακάδαν ἐλεγείων. ἄλλοι δὲ Ξενόδαμον ὑπορχη-
μάτων ποιητὴν γεγονέναι φασὶ καὶ οὐ παιάνων,
καθάπερ Πρατίνας· καὶ αὐτοῦ δὲ τοῦ Ξενοδάμου
ἀπομνημονεύεται ᾆσμα ὅ ἐστιν φανερῶς ὑπόρχημα.
D κέχρηται δὲ τῷ γένει τῆς ποιήσεως ταύτης καὶ Πίνδαρος. ὁ δὲ παιὰν ὅτι διαφορὰν ἔχει πρὸς τὰ ὑπορχήματα τὰ Πινδάρου ποιήματα δηλώσει· γέγραφεν
γὰρ καὶ Παιᾶνας καὶ Ὑπορχήματα.

10. " Καὶ Πολύμνηστος δὲ αὐλῳδικοὺς νόμους
ἐποίησεν· εἰ[9] δὲ τῷ Ὀρθίῳ νόμῳ ἐν[10] τῇ μελοποιίᾳ
κέχρηται, καθάπερ οἱ ἁρμονικοί φασιν, οὐκ ἔχομεν[11]
ἀκριβῶς εἰπεῖν· οὐ γὰρ εἰρήκασιν οἱ ἀρχαῖοί τι περὶ
τούτου. καὶ περὶ Θαλήτα δὲ τοῦ Κρητὸς εἰ παιάνων
γεγένηται ποιητὴς ἀμφισβητεῖται. Γλαῦκος γὰρ
μετ' Ἀρχίλοχον φάσκων γεγενῆσθαι Θαλήταν,
μεμιμῆσθαι μὲν[12] αὐτόν φησι τὰ Ἀρχιλόχου μέλη,

---

[1] δὲ] a[1] omits ; a[2] inserts it after δευτέρας.
[2] Θαλήτας] θαλέτας v[1].
[3] Ξενόκριτος] ξενόκροτος a.   [4] τὰ] τὰς a[1] q[ar].
[5] καὶ π[2]μ (as Hiller had conjectured) : the rest omit.
[6] τῶν] τόν M.   [7] μὲν] a omits.
[8] Ξενόκριτον] ξενόκρατον N.   [9] εἰ Volkmann : ἐν.

organization Thaletas of Gortyn, Xenodamus of Cythera, Xenocritus of Locri, Polymnestus of Colophon, and Sacadas of Argos are said to have been chiefly responsible, since it was at their suggestion that the festival of the Gymnopaediae at Lacedaemon was instituted and so too the Apodeixeis [a] in Arcadia and the so-called Endymatia [b] at Argos. Thaletas, Xenodamus, and Xenocritus were composers of paeans, Polymnestus of so-called orthian pieces, and Sacadas of elegiacs. Others, like Pratinas,[c] assert that Xenodamus was a composer not of paeans but of hyporchemes [d]; and of Xenodamus himself a song is preserved which is evidently a hyporcheme. Pindar too employed this kind of composition. That there is a difference between the paean and the hyporcheme will be seen from Pindar's works, as he composed both *Paeans* [e] and *Hyporchemes.*[f]

10. " Polymnestus too composed nomes sung to the auloi, but whether he employed the Orthios nome in his music, as the writers on harmonics assert, we are unable to say definitely, as on this point the ancients are silent. Whether Thaletas of Crete composed paeans is also disputed. Thus Glaucus,[g] who asserts that Thaletas is later than Archilochus, says that he imitated Archilochus' music, but expanded it to

---

[a] That is, " Exhibitions " ; otherwise unknown.
[b] That is, " Festival of Apparelling " ; otherwise un-known.
[c] Frag. 6 (Page, *Poet. Mel. Gr.*, No. 713).
[d] A choral song accompanied by dancing and pantomimic action.   [e] Frags. 41-81 (ed. Turyn), 52-70 (ed. Snell).
[f] Frags. 117-125 (ed. Turyn), 105-117 (ed. Snell).
[g] Frag. 4, ed. Müller (*Frag. Hist. Graec.* ii, p. 24).

---

[10] ἐν added by Volkmann.
[11] After χομεν Volkmann omits δ'.   [12] μέν] N omits.

(1134) ἐπὶ δὲ τὸ μακρότερον ἐκτεῖναι, καὶ παίωνα[1] καὶ
Ε κρητικὸν ῥυθμὸν εἰς τὴν μελοποιίαν ἐνθεῖναι[2]· οἷς
᾽Αρχίλοχον μὴ κεχρῆσθαι, ἀλλ᾽ οὐδὲ ᾽Ορφέα οὐδὲ
Τέρπανδρον· ἐκ γὰρ τῆς ᾽Ολύμπου αὐλήσεως Θαλήταν φασὶν ἐξειργάσθαι ταῦτα καὶ δόξαι ποιητὴν
ἀγαθὸν γεγονέναι.[3] περὶ δὲ Ξενοκρίτου,[4] ὃς ἦν τὸ
γένος ἐκ Λοκρῶν τῶν ἐν ᾽Ιταλίᾳ, ἀμφισβητεῖται εἰ
παιάνων ποιητὴς γέγονεν· ἡρωικῶν γὰρ ὑποθέσεων
F πράγματα ἐχουσῶν ποιητὴν γεγονέναι φασὶν αὐτόν·
διὸ καί τινας διθυράμβους καλεῖν αὐτοῦ τὰς ὑποθέ-
σεις· πρεσβύτερον δὲ τῇ ἡλικίᾳ φησὶν ὁ Γλαῦκος
Θαλήταν Ξενοκρίτου[5] γεγονέναι.

11. ‘ ῎Ολυμπος δέ, ὡς ᾽Αριστόξενός φησιν, ὑπο-
λαμβάνεται ὑπὸ τῶν μουσικῶν τοῦ ἐναρμονίου γένους εὑρετὴς γεγενῆσθαι· τὰ γὰρ πρὸ ἐκείνου πάντα
διάτονα καὶ χρωματικὰ ἦν. ὑπονοοῦσιν δὲ τὴν
εὕρεσιν τοιαύτην τινὰ γενέσθαι· ἀναστρεφόμενον
τὸν ῎Ολυμπον ἐν τῷ διατόνῳ καὶ διαβιβάζοντα[6] τὸ
μέλος πολλάκις ἐπὶ τὴν διάτονον παρυπάτην, τοτὲ
μὲν ἀπὸ τῆς παραμέσης, τοτὲ[7] δὲ ἀπὸ τῆς μέσης,
καὶ παραβαίνοντα τὴν διάτονον λιχανόν, καταμαθεῖν τὸ κάλλος τοῦ ἤθους, καὶ οὕτως τὸ ἐκ τῆς
1135 ἀναλογίας συνεστηκὸς σύστημα θαυμάσαντα καὶ

---

[1] παίωνα (Παιῶνα van Santen) : μάρωνα (κάρωνα V).
[2] ἐνθεῖναι (-ῆναι V W)] ἐκθεῖναι vq.
[3] γεγονέναι] εἶναι v.
[4] ξενοκρίτου v[2] : -οκράτου M V[r?] a[1],[3] N ; -οκράτους V[ar?]
a[2]A a v[1] q ; -ουκράτου W.
[5] ξενοκρίτου Basle edition of 1542 : ξενοκράτου (-ους vq).
[6] διαβιβάζοντα (-βηβ- v)] ἐμβιβάζοντα N.
[7] τοτὲ . . . τοτὲ aN E : τότε . . . τότε.

---

[a] The paean is ∪∪∪– or –∪∪∪, the cretic –∪–. Com-
374

greater length, and also used in his music the paeonic and cretic rhythms,[a] which Archilochus had not employed, nor had Orpheus either or Terpander ; for Thaletas is said to have developed them from the aulos music of Olympus and so gained the reputation of an excellent composer. With regard to Xenocritus, a Locrian from Italy, it is disputed whether he composed paeans, for it is said that he composed on heroic themes involving action. Hence some call his pieces dithyrambs. Glaucus [b] says that Thaletas was older than Xenocritus.

11. " Olympus, as Aristoxenus [c] says, is supposed by the musical experts to have been the inventor of the enharmonic genus, all music before him having been diatonic or chromatic. They suspect that the discovery took place as follows. Olympus was moving about in the diatonic genus,[d] frequently making the melody pass to the diatonic parhypatê, sometimes from the paramesê and sometimes from the mesê ; and when he skipped the diatonic lichanos he saw the beauty of the resulting character, and hence, conceiving an admiration for the set of intervals constructed on the analogy of this omission, adopted it,

mentators have suggested that by paeon may here be meant the paeon epibatos ($-\ -\ -$) and by cretic the ditrochee.
  [b] Frag. 4, ed. Müller (*Frag. Hist. Graec.* ii, p. 24).
  [c] Frag. 83 (ed. Wehrli) ; Testim. 98 (ed. da Rios).
  [d] The following diagram may be helpful (the asterisk indicates that the note is raised a quarter of a tone) :

diatonic	Olympus	enharmonic
b = paramesê	b = paramesê	b = paramesê
a = mesê	a = mesê	a = mesê
G = lichanos		
F = parhypatê	F = parhypatê	F = lichanos
E = hypatê	E = hypatê	E* = parhypatê
		E = hypatê

(1135) ἀποδεξάμενον, ἐν τούτῳ ποιεῖν ἐπὶ τοῦ Δωρίου
τόνου· οὔτε γὰρ τῶν τοῦ διατόνου ἰδίων οὔτε τῶν
τοῦ χρώματος ἅπτεσθαι, ἀλλὰ οὐδὲ τῶν τῆς ἁρμονίας. εἶναι δ' αὐτῷ τὰ πρῶτα τῶν ἐναρμονίων
τοιαῦτα. τιθέασιν γὰρ τούτων πρῶτον τὸ σπονδεῖον,[1] ἐν ᾧ οὐδεμία τῶν διαιρέσεων τὸ ἴδιον ἐμφαίνει, εἰ μή τις εἰς τὸν συντονώτερον σπονδεια-
σμὸν βλέπων[2] αὐτὸ τοῦτο διάτονον εἶναι ἀπεικάσει.[3]
δῆλον δ' ὅτι καὶ ψεῦδος καὶ ἐκμελὲς θήσει ὁ τοιοῦτο
τιθείς· ψεῦδος μὲν[4] ὅτι διέσει ἔλαττόν ἐστι τόνου
τοῦ περὶ τὸν ἡγεμόνα κειμένου, ἐκμελὲς δὲ ὅτι καὶ
B εἴ τις ἐν τῇ τοῦ τονιαίου δυνάμει τιθείη τὸ τοῦ
συντονωτέρου σπονδειασμοῦ ἴδιον συμβαίνοι ἂν δύο
ἑξῆς τίθεσθαι δίτονα,[5] τὸ μὲν ἀσύνθετον, τὸ δὲ
σύνθετον· τὸ γὰρ ἐν ταῖς μέσαις ἐναρμόνιον πυκνὸν
ᾧ νῦν χρῶνται οὐ δοκεῖ τοῦ ποιητοῦ εἶναι. ῥᾴδιον
δ' ἐστὶ συνιδεῖν ἐάν τις ἀρχαϊκῶς τινος αὐλοῦντος

---

[1] τὸ σπονδεῖον κ (as Westphal had conjectured ; τὸν σπον-
δειασμὸν Volkmann) : τὸν σπονδεῖον (τὸν σπονδείων qᵃᶜ).
[2] βλέπων] ἀποβλέπων vq[1].
[3] ἀπεικάσει V[1] Wᵃᶜ Nᵃᶜ vq : -ση.
[4] μὲν] v omits.
[5] δίτονα Meziriacus : διάτονα.

---

[a] That is, the tetrachord aGFE is diatonic; the tetrachord
aFE*E is enharmonic, and Olympus used the trichord aFE.
The three notes of this trichord are common to the diatonic,
the enharmonic, and the tonic chromatic tetrachords. Clement
(Strom. i. 16. 76. 5 [vol. ii, p. 49. 18 f., ed. Stählin]) credits
Agnis [that is, Hyagnis] with the discovery of the trichord
and the diatonic harmonia.
[b] R. P. Winnington-Ingram (" The Spondeion Scale,"
Class. Quart. xxii [1928], p. 85) takes the higher Spondeion
to be EF AB C* (the asterisk indicates that the note is raised
a quarter of a tone) ; this we express as EFabc[x].

composing in this set of intervals in the Dorian mode,
for it had no connection with the distinctive features
of the diatonic or of the chromatic genus, or indeed
of those of the enharmonic.ᵃ Such were his first enharmonic compositions. Thus, of these the authorities put the Spondeion ᵇ first, in which none of the
three genera shows its peculiar nature. (That is, if
you do not, with the upper notes ᶜ of the Spondeion
in mind, conjecture that just this portion is diatonic.
But it is clear that such an identification is both false
and contrary to the rules of music : false, because
the Spondeion interval is less by a diesis than the
tone situated next to the leading note ᵈ ; and contrary to the rules because if you set down the peculiar
nature of the upper notes of the Spondeion as residing
in the effect of the interval of a tone, the result would
be the placing in sequence of two ditones, the one
simple, the other compound.ᵉ) For the enharmonic
pycnon ᶠ which is now in use in the middle tetrachord
is not held to be the work of the composer. It is easy
to see this if you hear a performer play the auloi in

ᶜ That is, abc*.
ᵈ The leading note is the mesê, a ; the tone next to it, a-b.
But the next interval in the upper part of the Spondeion
scale is not b-c♯ (a full tone like a-b) but b-c*, a quarter of a
tone less.
ᵉ The two ditones are F-a and a-c♯. The first is simple,
as no note of the scale intervenes ; the second compound, as
b intervenes between a and c♯. Aristoxenus (*Harm.* iii. 64)
forbids two consecutive ditones.
ᶠ The tetrachord, comprising the interval of a fourth, is
divided into three intervals, bounded by four notes. When
the two smaller intervals added together are smaller than the
remaining interval they are called a *pyknon* or " condensa-
tion." In an enharmonic pycnon the two intervals are of a
quarter-tone each, and the remaining interval is a ditone.
In the middle tetrachord the enharmonic pycnon is EE*F.

(1135) ἀκούσῃ· ἀσύνθετον[1] γὰρ βούλεται εἶναι καὶ τὸ ἐν
ταῖς μέσαις ἡμιτόνιον.

"Τὰ μὲν οὖν πρῶτα τῶν ἐναρμονίων τοιαῦτα·
ὕστερον δὲ τὸ ἡμιτόνιον διῃρέθη ἔν τε τοῖς Λυδίοις
καὶ ἐν τοῖς Φρυγίοις. φαίνεται δ' Ὄλυμπος αὐξή-
σας μουσικὴν τῷ ἀγένητόν τι καὶ ἀγνοούμενον ὑπὸ
τῶν ἔμπροσθεν εἰσαγαγεῖν, καὶ ἀρχηγὸς γενέσθαι
τῆς Ἑλληνικῆς καὶ καλῆς μουσικῆς.

12. "Ἔστι δέ τις καὶ περὶ τῶν ῥυθμῶν[2] λόγος·
C γένη γάρ τινα καὶ εἴδη ῥυθμῶν προσεξευρέθη, ἀλλὰ
μὴν καὶ μελοποιῶν τε καὶ ῥυθμοποιῶν.[3] προτέρα
μὲν γὰρ ἡ Τερπάνδρου καινοτομία καλόν τινα τρόπον εἰς τὴν μουσικὴν εἰσήγαγεν· Πολύμνηστος δὲ
μετὰ τὸν Τερπάνδρειον τρόπον καινῷ[4] ἐχρήσατο,
καὶ αὐτὸς μέντοι ἐχόμενος τοῦ καλοῦ τύπου, ὡσαύτως[5] δὲ καὶ Θαλήτας καὶ Σακάδας· καὶ γὰρ οὗτοι
κατά γε τὰς ῥυθμοποιίας καινοί,[6] οὐκ ἐκβαίνοντες
μέντοι[7] τοῦ καλοῦ τύπου. ἔστι δὲ καί[8] τις Ἀλ-
κμανικὴ καινοτομία καὶ[9] Στησιχόρειος, καὶ αὐταί[10]

---

[1] ἀσύνθετον] σύνθετον W.   [2] τῶν ῥυθμῶν] τὸν ῥυθμὸν W.
[3] μελοποιῶν τε καὶ ῥυθμοποιῶν a[c:2:88] N (N omits τε) : μελοποιῶν τε καὶ ῥυθμοποιῶν.   [4] καινῷ Westphal : καὶ ᾧ.
[5] ὡσαύτως (ὡς αὔτως a)] αὔτως M (V with a space of 2-3
letters [indicating a paragraph or a lacuna] preceding).
[6] καινοί Weil and Reinach : ἱκανοί.
[7] μέντοι Wyttenbach : μὲν.   [8] καί added by Ziegler.
[9] καὶ aN v[c] or [2]: the rest omit.   [10] αὐταὶ Dübner : αὗται.

---

[a] The ditone (F-a) in the middle tetrachord (E-a) is admittedly incomposite ; and even the semitone (E-F), when
treated in the old-fashioned way, has no intervening note.
It is possible to translate " for even in the middle tetrachord
the semitone . . ." with Weil and Reinach. This implies
that in the upper tetrachord the semitone is *a fortiori* incomposite. In that case the author does not have abc* in mind
as part of the scale he is talking about.

the old-fashioned way; for even the semitone in the middle tetrachord is intended to be incomposite.[a]

"Such then were the earliest enharmonic compositions. Later the semitone was divided in both the Lydian and the Phrygian pieces. Olympus, it is seen, advanced music by introducing what had never been done before and what was unknown to his predecessors, and thus became the founder of music of the Hellenic and lofty style.

12. "There is also something to say about the rhythms, for certain additional genera and species of rhythm were invented, and indeed of melodic and rhythmic composition. Thus the originality of Terpander[b] had preceded the rest in introducing a certain noble style into music; while Polymnestus, after the introduction of the Terpandrian style, employed a new one, although he too remained faithful to the lofty manner; so too did Thaletas[c] and Sacadas, these also, at least in the conduct of rhythm, being innovators, but nevertheless not departing from the lofty manner. There is also some originality in Alcman and again in Stesichorus,[d] though their

[b] See 1140 F, infra.

[c] Cf. 1134 E, supra. Strabo too (x. 480) speaks of his use of cretic rhythms.

[d] The following metres are termed Stesichorean:

– ∪ ∪ – ∪ ∪ – ∪ – ∪ – ∪ Marius Plotius Sacerdos (Keil, *Gramm. Lat.* vi. 543. 26).

– ∪ ∪ – ∪ ∪ – ∪ ∪ – ∪ Servius (Keil, iv. 461. 2).

– ∪ ∪ – ∪ ∪ – ∪ ∪ – ∪ ∪ – ∪ ∪ – ∪ Servius (Keil, iv. 461. 20).

∪ ∪ – ∪ ∪ – ∪ ∪ – ∪ ∪ – ∪ ∪ – ∪ ∪ – Servius (Keil, iv. 462. 20).

– ∪ – – – ∪ – – – ∪ – – Schol. Pind. *Ol.* 3 (vol. i, p. 105. 4, 12, ed. Drachmann).

Even more are called Alcmanic:

– ∪ ∪ – ∪ ∪ – ∪ Servius (Keil, *Gramm. Lat.* iv. 460. 21).

– ∪ ∪ – ∪ ∪ – ∪ ∪ – Hephaestion, p. 376. 11 (ed. Consbruch); Servius (Keil, iv. 460. 25).

(1135) οὐκ ἀφεστῶσαι τοῦ καλοῦ. Κρέξος δὲ καὶ Τιμόθεος καὶ Φιλόξενος καὶ οἱ κατὰ ταύτην τὴν[1] ἡλικίαν
γεγονότες ποιηταὶ φορτικώτεροι καὶ φιλόκαινοι γεγόνασιν, τὸ[2] φιλάνθρωπον καὶ θεματικὸν νῦν ὀνο-
D μαζόμενον διώξαντες[3]· τὴν γὰρ ὀλιγοχορδίαν[4] καὶ
τὴν ἁπλότητα καὶ σεμνότητα τῆς μουσικῆς παντελῶς ἀρχαϊκὴν εἶναι συμβέβηκεν.

13. " Εἰρηκὼς κατὰ δύναμιν περί τε τῆς πρώτης
μουσικῆς καὶ τῶν πρῶτον εὑρόντων αὐτήν, καὶ ὑπὸ
τίνων κατὰ χρόνους ταῖς προσεξευρέσεσιν ηὔξηται,[5]
καταπαύσω τὸν λόγον καὶ παραδώσω τῷ ἑταίρῳ
Σωτηρίχῳ, ἐσπουδακότι οὐ μόνον περὶ μουσικὴν
ἀλλὰ καὶ περὶ τὴν ἄλλην ἐγκύκλιον παιδείαν· ἡμεῖς
γὰρ μᾶλλον χειρουργικῷ μέρει τῆς μουσικῆς ἐγγε-
γυμνάσμεθα." ὁ μὲν Λυσίας ταῦτ' εἰπὼν κατέ-
παυσε τὸν λόγον.

E 14. Σωτήριχος δὲ μετὰ τοῦτον ὧδέ πως ἔφη·
" ὑπὲρ σεμνοῦ ἐπιτηδεύματος καὶ θεοῖς μάλιστα
ἀρέσκοντος, ὠγαθὲ Ὀνησίκρατες, τοὺς λόγους ἡμᾶς
προετρέψω ποιήσασθαι. ἀποδέχομαι μὲν οὖν τῆς
συνέσεως τὸν διδάσκαλον Λυσίαν, ἀλλὰ μὴν καὶ τῆς

---

[1] κατὰ ταύτην τὴν (or κατὰ τὴν αὐτὴν) Wyttenbach : κατ'
αὐτὴν τὴν (κατ' αὐτοὺς [from -ῳ] τὴν Wac).
[2] τὸ Ziegler : τόν.
[3] διώξαντες] ἐκδιώξαντες aNd (in an omission in N1).
[4] ὀλιγοχορδίαν Valgulius : ὀλιγοχορείαν (-χορίαν Vac al·ss
[ιαν ss.] Nc ; -χροείαν Nac).   [5] ηὔξηται] ηὔξηνται V1.

‒∪∪‒∪∪‒∪∪‒∪∪ Marius Victorinus (Keil, vi. 73. 12, 115.
    9) ; Servius (Keil, iv. 460. 30).
‒∪∪‒∪∪‒∪∪‒∪∪‒ Servius (Keil, iv. 460. 32).
‒∪∪‒∪∪‒∪∪‒∪∪‒‒ Servius (Keil, iv. 461. 17).

innovations do not desert the noble manner. But Crexus, Timotheüs, Philoxenus, and the composers of that time had a streak of coarseness in them and were fond of novelty, aiming at the manner that is now called " popular " and " mercenary " [a]; thus restriction to a few notes and simplicity and grandeur in music has come to be quite obsolete.

13. " Now that I have spoken, so far as my ability allows, of the earliest music and its first inventors and told who advanced it in the course of time by new inventions, I shall end my talk and make way for my friend Soterichus, a student not only of music but of the whole round of the liberal arts ; my own training has rather been in the part of music that deals with execution." With this Lysias concluded his speech.

14. After him Soterichus spoke to this effect : " It is a high pursuit and one especially pleasing to the gods, most excellent Onesicrates, that you have urged us to discuss. Now I commend our preceptor Lysias for his discernment,[b] and again for the powers

---

∪–∪–∪–∪–∪– Marius Plotius Sacerdos (Keil, vi. 521. 1) ; Servius (Keil, iv. 458. 16).

–∪–∪–∪–∪ Servius (Keil, iv. 459. 17).

∪∪–∪∪–∪∪–∪∪–∪ Servius (Keil, iv. 462. 10).

∪∪–∪∪–∪∪–∪∪–∪∪–∪ Servius (Keil, iv. 462. 18).

∪∪–∪∪–∪∪–∪∪–∪∪–∪∪– Servius (Keil, iv. 462 24).

∪∪– –∪∪– –∪∪– –∪∪– – Servius (Keil, iv. 464. 25).

[a] " Thematikon " ; see Pollux, iii. 153 : " The so-called sacred contests, where the prize was only a crown, were called ' stephanitai ' and ' phyllinai ' (crown and leaf contests) ; while the so-called ' thematikoi ' [literally ' deposit '] contests were for money," and compare I. Düring in *Gnomon*, xxvii (1955), p. 435.

[b] Lysias has the right taste in music ; *cf.* συνετοί at 1142 E, *infra*.

PLUTARCH'S MORALIA

(1135) μνήμης ἧς¹ ἐπεδείξατο περί τε τοὺς εὑρετὰς τῆς
F πρώτης μουσικῆς καὶ περὶ τοὺς τὰ τοιαῦτα συγγε-
γραφότας· ὑπομνήσω δὲ τοῦθ' ὅτι τοῖς ἀναγεγραμ-
μένοις μόνοις² κατακολουθήσας πεποίηται τὴν
δεῖξιν. ἡμεῖς δ' οὐκ ἄνθρωπόν τινα παρελάβομεν
εὑρετὴν τῶν τῆς μουσικῆς ἀγαθῶν, ἀλλὰ τὸν πά-
σαις³ ἀρεταῖς κεκοσμημένον θεὸν Ἀπόλλωνα. οὐ⁴
γὰρ Μαρσύου ἢ Ὀλύμπου ἢ Ὑάγνιδος ὥς τινες
οἴονται εὕρημα ὁ αὐλός, μόνη δὲ κιθάρα Ἀπόλλωνος, ἀλλὰ καὶ αὐλητικῆς καὶ κιθαριστικῆς εὑρετὴς
ὁ θεός. δῆλον δὲ ἐκ τῶν χορῶν καὶ τῶν θυσιῶν
ἃς προσῆγον μετὰ αὐλῶν τῷ θεῷ καθάπερ ἄλλοι τε
1136 καὶ Ἀλκαῖος ἔν τινι τῶν ὕμνων ἱστορεῖ. καὶ ἡ
ἐν Δήλῳ δὲ⁵ τοῦ ἀγάλματος αὐτοῦ ἀφίδρυσις ἔχει
ἐν μὲν τῇ δεξιᾷ τόξον, ἐν δὲ τῇ ἀριστερᾷ Χάριτας,
τῶν τῆς μουσικῆς ὀργάνων ἑκάστην τι ἔχουσαν· ἡ
μὲν γὰρ λύραν κρατεῖ, ἡ δὲ αὐλούς, ἡ δ' ἐν μέσῳ
προσκειμένην⁶ ἔχει τῷ στόματι σύριγγα· ὅτι δ'
οὗτος οὐκ ἐμὸς ὁ λόγος,⁷ Ἀντικλείδης⁸ καὶ Ἴστρος
ἐν ταῖς Ἐπιφανείαις περὶ τούτων ἀφηγήσαντο.
οὕτως δὲ παλαιόν ἐστι τὸ ἀφίδρυμα τοῦτο ὥστε⁹
τοὺς ἐργασαμένους αὐτὸ τῶν¹⁰ καθ' Ἡρακλέα Με-
ρόπων φασὶν εἶναι. ἀλλὰ μὴν καὶ τῷ κατακομί-
ζοντι παιδὶ τὴν Τεμπικὴν δάφνην εἰς Δελφοὺς

---

¹ ἧς M : ἦν. ² μόνοις] μόνον aN.
³ πάσαις M V : πάσαις ταῖς.
⁴ οὐ Stegmann : οὔτε. ⁵ δὲ] τὲ vq.
⁶ προσκειμένην Turnebus : προκειμένην (κειμένην N¹).
⁷ After λόγος Ziegler supposes a lacuna. But cf. a similar
construction with ὅτι at 1139 B.
⁸ Ἀντικλείδης Valesius (Ἀντικλείδης ἐν τοῖς Δηλιακοῖς Weil
and Reinach) : ἀντικλῆς (-ῆς a).
⁹ ὥστε a² aN s : the rest omit.
¹⁰ αὐτὸ τῶν (-τὸ τῶν aᶜ in an erasure)] ἀπὸ τῶν vq.

of memory that he has displayed with regard to the inventors of the earliest music and to those who have written on the theme ; but I will remind you that in this display he has confined himself to written accounts. I, on the other hand, have learned that the inventor of the blessings of music was not a man, but one graced with every virtue, the god Apollo. For the aulos is no invention of Marsyas or Olympus or Hyagnis, as some suppose [a] (only the cithara being Apollo's), but the god is the inventor both of the music of the aulos and of that of the cithara. This is shown by the choruses and sacrifices presented to the god to the accompaniment of auloi, as is recorded among others by Alcaeus [b] in one of his hymns. Again, the statue of the god at Delos holds a bow in the right hand, and Graces in the left, [c] each of them holding a musical instrument, one a lyre, another auloi, and the one in the middle has pipes of Pan at her lips. That this is no tale of my own devising [d] is shown by what is told of this by Anticleides [e] and by Istrus in his *Epiphanies.* [f] So ancient is the statue that it is said to be the work of the Meropes of Heracles' time. Again, the boy who fetches the laurel from Tempê

[a] *Cf.* 1133 ғ, *supra.*

[b] Frag. 3 (Bergk, *Poet. Lyr. Gr.*[4] iii, p. 147) ; Frag. 307 (Lobel and Page, *Poet. Lesb. Frag.*, p. 259).

[c] *Cf.* Pausanias, ix. 35. 3, with Frazer's commentary.

[d] An echo of Euripides' *Melanippê* (Nauck, *Trag. Graec. Frag.*, Eur. 484. 1) :

κοὐκ ἐμὸς ὁ μῦθος ἀλλὰ τῆς μητρὸς πάρα

" Not mine the tale, but told me by my mother."

[e] Frag. 14, ed. Jacoby (*Frag. d. gr. Hist.* ii в 140, p. 802).

[f] Frag. 52, ed. Jacoby (*Frag. d. gr. Hist.* iii в 334, p. 182). The full title was *Epiphanies of Apollo* ; *cf.* Harpocration, *s.v.* φαρμακός and Photius, *Lex.*, *s.v.* τριττύαν.

(1136) παρομαρτεῖ αὐλητής· καὶ τὰ ἐξ Ὑπερβορέων δὲ
B ἱερὰ μετὰ αὐλῶν καὶ συρίγγων καὶ κιθάρας εἰς τὴν
Δῆλόν φασι τὸ παλαιὸν στέλλεσθαι. ἄλλοι δὲ καὶ
αὐτὸν τὸν θεὸν φασιν αὐλῆσαι, καθάπερ ἱστορεῖ ὁ
ἄριστος μελῶν ποιητὴς Ἀλκμάν· ἡ δὲ Κόριννα καὶ
διδαχθῆναί φησιν τὸν Ἀπόλλω[1] ὑπ᾽ Ἀθηνᾶς αὐλεῖν.
⌈ σεμνὴ οὖν κατὰ πάντα ἡ μουσική, θεῶν εὕρημα
⌊ οὖσα.

15. '' Ἐχρήσαντο δ᾽ αὐτῇ οἱ παλαιοὶ κατὰ τὴν
ἀξίαν, ὥσπερ καὶ τοῖς ἄλλοις ἐπιτηδεύμασιν πᾶσιν·
οἱ δὲ νῦν τὰ σεμνὰ αὐτῆς παραιτησάμενοι ἀντὶ τῆς
ἀνδρώδους ἐκείνης καὶ θεσπεσίας καὶ θεοῖς φίλης
κατεαγυῖαν καὶ κωτίλην εἰς τὰ θέατρα εἰσάγουσιν.
τοιγάρτοι Πλάτων ἐν τῷ τρίτῳ τῆς Πολιτείας δυσ-
C χεραίνει τῇ τοιαύτῃ μουσικῇ· τὴν γοῦν[2] Λύδιον ἁρμονίαν παραιτεῖται, ἐπειδὴ ὀξεῖα καὶ ἐπιτήδειος
πρὸς θρῆνον. ᾗ[3] καὶ τὴν πρώτην σύστασιν αὐτῆς
φασι θρηνώδη τινὰ γενέσθαι. Ὄλυμπον γὰρ πρῶτον Ἀριστόξενος ἐν τῷ πρώτῳ περὶ μουσικῆς ἐπὶ
τῷ Πύθωνί φησιν ἐπικήδειον αὐλῆσαι Λυδιστί.
εἰσὶν δ᾽ οἱ Μελανιππίδην τούτου τοῦ μέλους ἄρξαι
φασίν. Πίνδαρος δ᾽ ἐν Παιᾶσιν ἐπὶ τοῖς Νιόβης[4]
γάμοις φησὶν Λύδιον ἁρμονίαν πρῶτον διδαχθῆναι,
ἄλλοι δὲ Τόρηβον[5] πρῶτον τῇ ἁρμονίᾳ χρήσασθαι,
καθάπερ Διονύσιος ὁ Ἴαμβος ἱστορεῖ.

---

[1] Ἀπόλλω] -ωνα V[ar] ? AE W[ac]D (as at 1135 F, supra).
[2] γοῦν] οὖν νq.   [3] ᾗ] ἢ M ; ἢ V.
[4] τοῖς Νιόβης] τοις νιόβης M ; τῆς νιόβης V a[1]A[1] a[ac] ? ;
τοῖς τῆς νιόβης νq.
[5] Τόρηβον] Τόρρηβον Volkmann.
[6] τῇ] ταύτῃ τῇ Weil and Reinach.

---

[a] Frag. 51 (Page, *Poet. Mel. Gr.*, p. 49).
[b] Frag. 15 (Page, *Poet. Mel. Gr.*, p. 339).

to Delphi is accompanied by an aulete, and it is said that the sacred objects sent by the Hyperboreans were in ancient times conducted to Delos to the music of auloi, of pipes of Pan, and of the cithara. Others say that the god himself played the auloi, as Alcman,[a] that admirable composer, records ; while Corinna [b] even says that Apollo was taught the auloi by Athena. Thus music is in every way a noble pursuit, being an invention of the gods.

15. " In their cultivation of music the ancients respected its dignity, as they did in all other pursuits ; while the moderns have rejected its graver parts, and instead of the music of former days, strong, inspired, and dear to the gods, introduce into the theatres an effeminate twittering. Hence Plato in the third book of the *Republic* [c] shows distaste for such music ; thus he rejects the Lydian mode, since it is high-pitched and appropriate to lamentation. Indeed it is said to have been first composed as a dirge. For Aristoxenus in his first book *On Music* [d] says that Olympus was the first to perform on the auloi a lament for the Python in the Lydian mode ; while some say that Melanippides [e] originated this kind of composition. Pindar [f] says in his *Paeans* that the Lydian mode was first presented at the wedding of Niobê, while others, as Dionysius Iambus [g] records, assert that Torebus was the first to use this mode.

[c] 398 D 8–E 8.
[d] Frag. 80 (ed. Wehrli) ; Testim. 105 (ed. Da Rios).
[e] Frag. A 3 (ed. del Grande) ; *cf.* Bergk, *Poet. Lyr. Gr.*[4] iii, pp. 592 f.
[f] Frag. 75 (ed. Turyn) ; *cf.* the note on *Paean* xiii (Frag. 52 n.) in Snell's edition.
[g] A teacher of Aristophanes of Byzantium.

(1136)   16. " Καὶ ἡ Μιξολύδιος δὲ παθητική τίς ἐστιν,
τραγῳδίαις ἁρμόζουσα.   'Αριστόξενος δέ φησιν
D Σαπφὼ πρώτην[1] εὕρασθαι[2] τὴν Μιξολυδιστί, παρ'
ἧς τοὺς τραγῳδοποιοὺς μαθεῖν· λαβόντας γοῦν[3]
αὐτὴν[4] συζεῦξαι τῇ Δωριστί, ἐπεὶ ἡ μὲν τὸ μεγαλο-
πρεπὲς καὶ ἀξιωματικὸν ἀποδίδωσιν, ἡ δὲ τὸ
παθητικόν, μέμικται δὲ διὰ τούτων τραγῳδία.   ἐν
δὲ τοῖς ἱστορικοῖς οἱ ἁρμονικοὶ[5] Πυθοκλείδην φασὶ[6]
τὸν αὐλητὴν εὑρετὴν αὐτῆς γεγονέναι, αὖθις[7] δὲ
Λαμπροκλέα τὸν 'Αθηναῖον συνιδόντα ὅτι οὐκ ἐνταῦθα ἔχει τὴν διάζευξιν ὅπου σχεδὸν ἅπαντες
ᾤοντο, ἀλλ' ἐπὶ τὸ ὀξύ, τοιοῦτον αὐτῆς ἀπεργάσα-
σθαι τὸ σχῆμα οἷον τὸ ἀπὸ παραμέσης ἐπὶ[8] ὑπάτην
E ὑπατῶν.   ἀλλὰ μὴν καὶ τὴν 'Επανειμένην Λυδιστί,
ἥπερ[9] ἐναντία τῇ Μιξολυδιστί, παραπλησίαν οὖσαν
τῇ 'Ιάδι, ὑπὸ Δάμωνος εὑρῆσθαί φασι τοῦ 'Αθη-
ναίου.
        17. " Τούτων δὴ τῶν ἁρμονιῶν τῆς μὲν θρηνῳ-
δικῆς τινος οὔσης, τῆς δ' ἐκκελυμένης, εἰκότως ὁ
Πλάτων παραιτησάμενος αὐτὰς τὴν Δωριστὶ ὡς
πολεμικοῖς ἀνδράσιν καὶ σώφροσιν ἁρμόζουσαν
F εἵλετο, οὐ μὰ Δία ἀγνοήσας, ὡς 'Αριστόξενός φησιν

---

[1] πρώτην] πρῶτον V[1].   [2] εὕρασθαι] εὑρᾶσθαι M.
    [3] γοῦν] οὖν νq.   [4] αὐτὴν Ziegler : αὐτούς.
        [5] οἱ ἁρμονικοὶ nos : τοῖς ἁρμονικοῖς.
            [6] φασὶ] φησὶ Wyttenbach.
    [7] αὖθις Westphal : λύσις.   [8] ἐπὶ] ἐπὶ τὴν νq.
        [9] ἥπερ s and Wyttenbach : εἴπερ.

---

    [a] Frag. 81 (ed. Wehrli) ; Testim. 106 (ed. Da Rios).
    [b] Frag. A 2 (ed. del Grande).
    [c] As we pass from the paramesê (b) to the hypatê hypatôn
(B) we find that the disjunction is between b and a, and that
the remaining notes belong to two conjunct tetrachords, that

16. " The Mixolydian mode is also emotional, and suited to tragedy. Aristoxenus[a] says that Sappho was the first to invent the Mixolydian and that the tragedians learned it from her ; thus when they took it over they combined it with the Dorian, since the Dorian produces the effect of grandeur and dignity, the other, that of passion, and tragedy is a blend of the two. In their historical accounts the writers on harmonics say that the inventor was Pythocleides the aulete, and that later Lamprocles[b] of Athens, observing that it does not have its disjunction at the point where nearly everyone had supposed, but at the upper part, shaped it to resemble the passage from the paramesê to the hypatê hypatôn.[c] They say further that the lower-pitched Lydian, which is the opposite of the Mixolydian and similar to the Ionian, was invented by Damon of Athens.

17. "As of these modes the one is of a plaintive sort, the other enervated, Plato[d] naturally rejected them and chose the Dorian as proper for warlike and temperate men.[e] It was not due, I assure you, to the mistake (as Aristoxenus[f] asserts in his second

of the middle notes (a-E) and that of the lower notes (E-B). Weil and Reinach suppose that previously the Mixolydian, true to its name, had been a scale with one Dorian tetrachord (semitone, tone, tone in the ascending order in the diatonic genus) and one Lydian (tone, tone, semitone). As disjunction at the upper extremity is excluded, the possible combinations of Dorian (D), Lydian (L) and the disjunction (d) are dDL, DdL, dLD, LdD. Of these they eliminate DdL and dLD as not euphonious, and prefer LdD to dDL.

[d] Cf. *Republic*, iii, 398 ε 2 for the Mixolydian and ε 10 for the low-pitched Lydian.

[e] Cf. *Republic*, iii, 399 α 6–β 3 (the music of warlike and violent action) and 399 β 3–c 1 (that of temperate and voluntary action), summed up at 399 c 1-4.

[f] Frag. 82 (ed. Wehrli) ; Testim. 108 (ed. Da Rios).

(1136) ἐν τῷ δευτέρῳ τῶν Μουσικῶν, ὅτι καὶ ἐν ἐκείναις
τι χρήσιμον ἦν πρὸς πολιτείαν φυλακικήν[1]· πάνυ
γὰρ προσέσχεν τῇ μουσικῇ ἐπιστήμῃ Πλάτων,
ἀκουστὴς γενόμενος Δράκοντος[2] τοῦ Ἀθηναίου καὶ
Μετέλλου[3] τοῦ Ἀκραγαντίνου. ἀλλ' ἐπεί, ὡς
προείπομεν, πολὺ τὸ σεμνόν ἐστιν ἐν τῇ Δωριστί,
ταύτην προυτίμησεν[4]· οὐκ ἠγνόει δὲ ὅτι πολλὰ
Δώρια[5] Παρθένεια[6] Ἀλκμᾶνι ἀλλά[7] καὶ Πινδάρῳ
καὶ Σιμωνίδῃ καὶ Βακχυλίδῃ πεποίηται, ἀλλὰ μὴν
καὶ ἔτι[8] Προσόδια καὶ Παιᾶνες, καὶ μέντοι ὅτι[9] καὶ
τραγικοὶ οἶκτοί ποτε ἐπὶ τοῦ Δωρίου τρόπου ἐμελῳ-
1137 δήθησαν καί τινα ἐρωτικά. ἐξήρκει δ' αὐτῷ τὰ εἰς
τὸν Ἄρη[10] καὶ Ἀθηνᾶν καὶ τὰ σπονδεῖα· ἐπιρρῶσαι
γὰρ ταῦτα ἱκανὰ ἀνδρὸς σώφρονος ψυχήν· καὶ περὶ
τοῦ Λυδίου[11] δὲ οὐκ ἠγνόει καὶ περὶ τῆς Ἰάδος·
ἠπίστατο γὰρ ὅτι ἡ τραγῳδία ταύτῃ τῇ μελοποιίᾳ
κέχρηται.

18. " Καὶ οἱ παλαιοὶ δὲ πάντες οὐκ ἀπείρως ἔ-
χοντες πασῶν τῶν ἁρμονιῶν ἐνίαις ἐχρήσαντο. οὐ
γὰρ ἡ ἄγνοια τῆς τοιαύτης στενοχωρίας καὶ ὀλιγο-
χορδίας αὐτοῖς αἰτία γεγένηται, οὐδὲ δι' ἄγνοιαν οἱ
περὶ Ὄλυμπον καὶ Τέρπανδρον καὶ οἱ ἀκολουθή-

---

[1] φυλακικήν] φυλακήν v.
[2] Δράκοντος] Δάμωνος Wyttenbach.
[3] Μετέλλου] Μεγίλλου Cobet.
[4] προυτίμησεν) προητίμησεν M.
[5] δώρια a a[2] : δωρεια M ; δώρεια V a[1]N vq ; δωρεία W.
[6] After Παρθένεια (unaccented in M) Burette omits ἀλλά,
for which Wyttenbach conjectures ἅμα or μέλη.
[7] ἀλλά our supplement.   [8] ἔτι a : ὅτι.
[9] ὅτι] a[1] omits.   [10] Ἄρη] ἄρῃ M ; ἄρην vq.
[11] Λυδίου] Αἰολίου Weil and Reinach.

---

[a] 1136 D, supra.
[b] Cf. Frag. 16 (Page, Poet. Mel. Gr., p. 36).

book *On Music*) of assuming that the other two were
of no use to a state controlled by Guardians, for Plato
had studied the science of music with great care,
receiving instruction from Dracon of Athens and
Metellus of Agrigentum.   No, he preferred the
Dorian because, as I said earlier,[a] it has a preponder-
ance of noble gravity.   Yet he knew very well that
many Dorian Maiden Songs had been composed by
Alcman,[b] and others by Pindar, Simonides, and Bacchylides ; so too had Processionals and Paeans [c] ;
certainly he knew too that even lamentations in
tragedy had been set to the Dorian mode as well as
certain love songs.   But he was content with songs
to Ares and Athena [d] and with Spondeia,[e] as these
are well fitted to fortify the spirit of a temperate man.
Nor was he ignorant either of the Lydian or the
Ionian mode, for he knew that tragedy employed
such music.

18. " So too with all the ancients : it was not because they had never heard of the various modes that
they employed only a few.   No, it was not to ignorance that such restriction of range and confinement to
a few notes was due, nor was it from ignorance that
Olympus and Terpander and those who followed in

---

[c] For Bacchylides' Paeans *cf.* Frags. 4-6 (ed. Snell), for his
Processionals, Frags. 11-13 (ed. Snell) ; for Pindar's Paeans
cf. for instance Frag. 42 (ed. Turyn), for his Processionals,
Frags. 101, 102, 104 (ed. Turyn), and for his Maiden Songs,
Frags. 110, 116 (ed. Turyn).

[d] Weil and Reinach (p. 72) suppose that the nome of Ares
(1141 B, *infra*) and that of Athena (1143 B, *infra*) are meant.
These were both auletic, and it is probable that the nome of
Athena was in the Phrygian mode (*ibid.*).   Perhaps our
author is indeed excerpting unskilfully.   But Ares and
Athena are eminently warlike, whereas Athena is at the same
time temperate, and as such, they are suitably addressed by
warlike and temperate music.   [e] That is, " libation songs."

(1137)

B σαντες τῇ τούτων προαιρέσει περιεῖλον τὴν πολυ-
χορδίαν τε καὶ ποικιλίαν. μαρτυρεῖ γοῦν[1] τὰ Ὀλύμπου τε καὶ Τερπάνδρου ποιήματα καὶ τῶν τούτοις
ὁμοιοτρόπων πάντων· τρίχορδα γὰρ ὄντα καὶ ἁπλᾶ,
διαφέρει τῶν ποικίλων καὶ πολυχόρδων, ὡς μηδένα
δύνασθαι μιμήσασθαι τὸν Ὀλύμπου τρόπον, ὑστερίζειν δὲ τούτου τοὺς[2] ἐν τῷ πολυχόρδῳ τε καὶ πολυ-
τρόπῳ καταγινομένους.[3]

19. " Ὅτι δὲ οἱ παλαιοὶ οὐ δι' ἄγνοιαν ἀπείχοντο
τῆς τρίτης ἐν τῷ σπονδειάζοντι τρόπῳ φανερὸν
ποιεῖ ἡ ἐν τῇ κρούσει γενομένη[4] χρῆσις· οὐ γὰρ ἂν
ποτε αὐτῇ πρὸς τὴν παρυπάτην κεχρῆσθαι συμφώνως, μὴ γνωρίζοντας τὴν χρῆσιν, ἀλλὰ δῆλον ὅτι τὸ
C τοῦ κάλλους ἦθος[5] ὃ γίνεται ἐν τῷ σπονδειακῷ
τρόπῳ διὰ τὴν τῆς τρίτης ἐξαίρεσιν, τοῦτ' ἦν τὸ
τὴν αἴσθησιν αὐτῶν ἐπάγον ἐπὶ τὸ διαβιβάζειν τὸ
μέλος ἐπὶ τὴν παρανήτην.

" Ὁ αὐτὸς δὲ λόγος καὶ περὶ τῆς νήτης· καὶ γὰρ
ταύτῃ πρὸς[6] μὲν τὴν κροῦσιν ἐχρῶντο, καὶ πρὸς

---

[1] γοῦν] οὖν vq.
[2] δὲ τούτου τοὺς Bern. (δ' αὐτοῦ τοὺς Wyttenbach): δὲ
τούτους.
[3] καταγινομένους] -γεν- N.
[4] γενομένη] γιν- aN.
[5] κάλλους (κάλους V) ἦθος] ἤθους κάλλος Laloy.
[6] πρὸς] κατὰ Westphal.

---

[a] The three notes are those of the tetrachord in the gapped
scales, as in the Spondeion of Olympus (1134 F—1135 B,
supra). Cf. T. Reinach, La Musique grecque (Paris, 1926),
p. 16 and note.
[b] Presumably the tritê of the disjunct tetrachord, b* in the
enharmonic genus (c in the diatonic). In this paragraph

the way these men had chosen eschewed multiplicity of notes and variety. Witness the compositions of Olympus and Terpander and of all the composers who resemble them. These compositions, although confined to three notes [a] and simple, are better than those that make use of variation and many notes, so that no one is able to copy the style of Olympus, and all the composers of music of many notes and a variety of scales are his inferiors.

19. " That ignorance does not explain the failure of the ancients to employ the tritê [b] in libation airs is evident from their use of it in the accompaniment ; for they would never have employed it to make a concord [c] with the parhypatê if they had been ignorant of its use. No ; it is evident that the noble moral character produced in the libation airs by the elimination of the tritê [d] was what led their ear to let the melody pass to the paranetê.

" The same holds for the netê : this too they employed in the accompaniment, both as a note dis-

---

and the two following we assume that the source had in mind the Dorian mode and the enharmonic genus. The following diagram may be convenient :

Disjunct tetrachord	netê	e
	paranetê	e
	tritê	b*
	paramesê	b
Middle tetrachord	mesê	a
	lichanos	F
	parhypatê	E*
	hypatê	E

[c] The tritê is a fifth above the parhypatê.

[d] To eliminate the tritê in a Dorian enharmonic scale is to pass (reading down) from eeb*b to eeb. This result is exactly equivalent in the tetrachord of the disjunct notes to Olympus's omission of the diatonic lichanos in the tetrachord of the middle notes : aFE.

(1137) παρανήτην διαφώνως καὶ πρὸς μέσην συμφώνως[1]· κατὰ δὲ τὸ μέλος οὐκ ἐφαίνετο αὐτοῖς οἰκεία εἶναι τῷ σπονδειακῷ τρόπῳ.

" Οὐ μόνον δὲ τούτοις ἀλλὰ καὶ τῇ[2] συνημμένων[3] νήτῃ οὕτω κέχρηνται πάντες· κατὰ μὲν γὰρ τὴν

D κροῦσιν αὐτὴν διεφώνουν πρός τε παρανήτην[4] καὶ πρὸς παραμέσην[5] καὶ πρὸς λιχανόν· κατὰ δὲ τὸ μέλος κἂν αἰσχυνθῆναι τὸν χρησάμενον[6] ἐπὶ τῷ γινομένῳ δι' αὐτὴν ἤθει. δῆλον δ' εἶναι καὶ ἐκ τῶν Φρυγίων ὅτι οὐκ ἠγνόητο ὑπ'[7] Ὀλύμπου τε καὶ τῶν ἀκολουθησάντων ἐκείνῳ· ἐχρῶντο γὰρ αὐτῇ οὐ μόνον κατὰ τὴν κροῦσιν ἀλλὰ καὶ κατὰ τὸ μέλος ἐν τοῖς Μητρῴοις καὶ ἐν ἄλλοις[8] τισὶν τῶν Φρυγίων.

" Δῆλον δὲ καὶ τὸ[9] περὶ τῶν ὑπάτων, ὅτι οὐ δι' ἄγνοιαν ἀπείχοντο ἐν τοῖς Δωρίοις τοῦ τετραχόρδου τούτου· αὐτίκα ἐπὶ τῶν λοιπῶν τόνων ἐχρῶντο,

---

[1] διαφώνως . . . συμφώνως Burette : διαφώνων (with a sign of corruption by v[288,m] ; διὰ φώνω W) . . . συμφώνων.
[2] τῇ] τῶν aN ; τῆς v[ac] ?
[3] συνημμένων aN : -ου (συνημένου a[1]).
[4] διεφώνουν πρός τε παρανήτην] v omits.
[5] After παραμέσην Meziriacus would add καὶ συνεφώνουν πρός τε μέσην.
[6] τὸν χρησάμενον Ziegler : τῷ χρησαμένῳ.
[7] ἠγνόητο ὑπ' Burette : ἠγνόει τοῦ (ἠγνόσι τοῦ v [with a sign of corruption by v[2:m] ; ἠγνόητο τοῦ s).
[8] ἄλλοις added here by Weil and Reinach ; after τισιν by Westphal.　　　[9] τό] N omits (π- in an erasure) ; τῶ vq.

---

[a] The Greeks did not recognize the major third as a concord.

cordant with the paranetê and ^a as concordant with the mesê ; but in the melody they did not feel that it was suitable to libation airs.

" Not these notes alone, but also the netê of the conjunct tetrachord ^b was treated in this way by all : in the accompaniment they used it as discordant with the paranetê, the paramesê, and the lichanos ^c ; but in the melody the user would actually have felt ashamed at the moral character resulting from this note. It is also clear from the pieces in the Phrygian mode that Olympus and his followers were not ignorant of it ; for they used it not only in the accompaniment but also in the melody in the songs in honour of the Mother of the Gods and in certain other Phrygian compositions.

"Again the case of the lowest tetrachord is also clear : they did not omit it in the Dorian pieces through ignorance (since they employed it in the other modes, obviously with full knowledge of it),

^b The following diagram (Dorian enharmonic) may be convenient :

			Disjunct	netê	e
Conjunct	netê	d		paranetê	c
	paranetê	a♯		tritê	b*
	tritê	a*		paramesê	b
Middle	mesê	a			
	lichanos	F			
	parhypatê	E*			
Lowest	hypatê	E			
	lichanos	C			
	parhypatê	B*			
	hypatê	B			

^c The netê of the conjunct tetrachord (d) is two tones above the paranetê of the same tetrachord (a), one tone above the paranetê of the disjunct tetrachord (c), a tone and a half above the paramesê (b), and four tones and a half above the lichanos (F).

(1137)
E δηλονότι εἰδότες· διὰ δὲ τὴν τοῦ ἤθους φυλακὴν ἀφῄρουν ἐπὶ τοῦ Δωρίου τόνου, τιμῶντες τὸ καλὸν αὐτοῦ.

20. " Οἷόν τι καὶ ἐπὶ τῶν τῆς τραγῳδίας ποιητῶν· τῷ γὰρ χρωματικῷ γένει καὶ τῷ πυκνῷ[1] τραγῳδία μὲν οὐδέπω καὶ τήμερον κέχρηται, κιθάρα[2] δέ, πολλαῖς γενεαῖς πρεσβυτέρα τραγῳδίας οὖσα, ἐξ ἀρχῆς ἐχρήσατο. τὸ δὲ χρῶμα ὅτι πρεσβύτερόν ἐστιν τῆς ἁρμονίας σαφές. δεῖ γὰρ δηλονότι κατὰ τὴν τῆς ἀνθρωπίνης φύσεως ἔντευξιν καὶ χρῆσιν τὸ πρεσβύτερον λέγειν· κατὰ γὰρ αὐτὴν τὴν τῶν γενῶν φύσιν οὐκ ἔστιν ἕτερον ἑτέρου πρεσβύτερον. εἰ οὖν τις Αἰσχύλον ἢ Φρύνιχον φαίη δι'
F ἄγνοιαν ἀπεσχῆσθαι τοῦ χρώματος ἆρά γε οὐκ ἂν ἄτοπος εἴη; ὁ γὰρ αὐτὸς καὶ Παγκράτην ἂν εἴποι ἀγνοεῖν τὸ χρωματικὸν γένος, ἀπείχετο γὰρ καὶ οὗτος ὡς ἐπὶ τὸ πολὺ τούτου, ἐχρήσατο δ' ἔν τισιν. οὐ δι' ἄγνοιαν οὖν δηλονότι, ἀλλὰ διὰ τὴν προαίρεσιν ἀπείχετο· ἐζήλου γοῦν, ὡς αὐτὸς ἔφη, τὸν Πινδάρειόν τε καὶ Σιμωνίδειον τρόπον καὶ καθόλου τὸ[3] ἀρχαῖον καλούμενον ὑπὸ τῶν νῦν.

21. " Ὁ αὐτὸς δὲ λόγος καὶ περὶ Τυρταίου τε τοῦ Μαντινέως καὶ Ἀνδρέα[4] τοῦ Κορινθίου καὶ Θρασύλλου τοῦ Φλιασίου καὶ ἑτέρων πολλῶν, οὓς πάντας[5] ἴσμεν διὰ προαίρεσιν ἀπεσχημένους χρώματός τε καὶ μεταβολῆς καὶ πολυχορδίας καὶ ἄλλων
1138 πολλῶν ἐν μέσῳ ὄντων ῥυθμῶν τε καὶ ἁρμονιῶν καὶ

---

[1] καὶ τῷ πυκνῷ nos : καὶ τῷ ῥυθμῷ (καὶ τῷ ἐναρμονίῳ Valgulius : καὶ τῷ πρὸς τοῦτο ῥυθμῷ Westphal) ; Weil and Reinach would omit.

[2] κιθάρα (-ᾳ ε)] κιθαρῳδία Bury.

[3] τὸ] τὸν Turnebus.

[4] ἀνδρέα] -έου vq.   [5] πάντας] -ες vq.

but wishing to preserve the moral character, they cut off the lowest tetrachord in the Dorian mode out of regard for the dignity of that mode.

20. " So too with the tragic poets : to the present day tragedy has never employed the chromatic genus with its pycnon,[a] whereas the music of the cithara, which is many generations older than tragedy, has done so from the outset. That the chromatic genus is older than the enharmonic is clear ; for we must evidently use the expression ' older ' of what our human nature has earlier hit upon and employed, since when we consider the genera in their own essential character no one genus is older than another. If then someone should assert that Aeschylus or Phrynichus avoided the chromatic genus through ignorance, that would surely be nonsense, would it not ? It would be the same as saying that Pancrates [b] was ignorant of the chromatic genus, since he, too, for the most part avoided it ; yet he did use it in a few compositions. Evidently then his avoidance was due not to ignorance, but to choice, for as he said himself, he was an admirer of the style of Pindar and Simonides and, to sum up, of what is nowadays called old-fashioned.

21. " The same applies to Tyrtaeus of Mantinea, Andreas of Corinth, Thrasyllus of Phlius, and many more. All, we know, avoided on principle the chromatic genus, modulation, multiplicity of notes, and many other things—rhythms, scales, styles of poetical or musical composition and rendition—that were

---

[a] As there was an enharmonic that lacked the pycnon (cf. 1135 B, supra, with the notes) it may have seemed proper to the source our author is following here (Aristoxenus ?) to add " with the pycnon." The MSS. read " and its rhythm."

[b] Otherwise unknown.

(1138) λέξεων καὶ[1] μελοποιίας καὶ ἑρμηνείας. αὐτίκα
Τηλεφάνης ὁ Μεγαρικὸς οὕτως ἐπολέμησεν[2] ταῖς
σύριγξιν ὥστε τοὺς αὐλοποιοὺς οὐδ᾽[3] ἐπιθεῖναι πώ-
ποτε εἴασεν ἐπὶ τοὺς αὐλούς, ἀλλὰ καὶ τοῦ Πυθικοῦ
ἀγῶνος μάλιστα διὰ ταῦτ᾽[4] ἀπέστη. καθόλου δ᾽ εἴ
τις τῷ μὴ χρῆσθαι τεκμαιρόμενος καταγνώσεται
τῶν μὴ χρωμένων ἄγνοιαν, πολλῶν ἄν τι φθάνοι
καὶ τῶν νῦν καταγινώσκων, οἷον τῶν μὲν Δωριω-
B νείων[5] τοῦ Ἀντιγενειδείου[6] τρόπου καταφρονούντων
ἐπειδήπερ οὐ χρῶνται αὐτῷ, τῶν δ᾽ Ἀντιγενειδείων[7]
τοῦ Δωριωνείου[8] διὰ τὴν αὐτὴν αἰτίαν, τῶν δὲ
κιθαρῳδῶν τοῦ Τιμοθείου[9] τρόπου· σχεδὸν γὰρ
ἀποπεφοιτήκασιν εἴς τε τὰ καττύματα[10] καὶ εἰς τὰ
Πολυείδου ποιήματα.

" Πάλιν δ᾽ αὖ εἴ τις καὶ περὶ τῆς ποικιλίας ὀρθῶς
τε καὶ ἐμπείρως ἐπισκοποίη, τὰ τότε καὶ τὰ νῦν
συγκρίνων, εὕροι ἂν ἐν χρήσει οὖσαν καὶ τότε τὴν
ποικιλίαν. τῇ γὰρ περὶ τὰς ῥυθμοποιίας ποικιλίᾳ
οὔσῃ[11] ποικιλωτέρᾳ ἐχρήσαντο οἱ παλαιοί· ἐτίμων
γοῦν[12] τὴν ῥυθμικὴν ποικιλίαν, καὶ τὰ[13] περὶ τὰς

----

[1] καὶ] κατὰ Westphal.
[2] ἐπολέμησεν M^c (-σε the rest): -σαν M^{ac}.
[3] οὐδ᾽] οὐκ v^1.
[4] ταῦτ᾽] τοῦτ᾽ Weil and Reinach.
[5] δωριωνείων vq^c: -ίων.
[6] ἀντιγενειδείου W^{ac} N^{ac} Crönert (Hermes, xxxvii [1902], p. 225): -νιδείου.
[7] ἀντιγενειδείων Ziegler: -ιδείων (-ιδίων W).
[8] δωριωνείου vq: -ωνίου (-ώνου N^{ac}).
[9] τιμοθείου a q: -θείου (-θέου v).
[10] καττύματα PS a^2 W s: καταττύματα.
[11] ποικιλίᾳ οὔσῃ] Weil and Reinach would omit ποικιλίᾳ, Ziegler would omit οὔσῃ.
[12] γοῦν] οὖν vq.
[13] τὰ] M omits; τῇ W.

396

current at the time. Take Telephanes of Megara.
So hostile was he to the *syrinx* [a] of the aulos that he
never even permitted the aulos-makers to add it to
his instruments ; indeed it was mainly on this account
that he refused to perform at the Pythian games. In
short, if ignorance is to be imputed to anyone who
does not follow a certain practice, that will involve
you in a hasty verdict against many moderns [b]—as
against the school of Dorion,[c] since (holding it in contempt) they do not employ the style of Antigeneidas [d] ; against the school of Antigeneidas in turn,
who on the same ground do not employ the manner
of Dorion ; and against the singers to the cithara who
have no use for the style of Timotheüs, for they have
to all intents abandoned it for the ' patches ' [e] and
the compositions of Polyeidus.

"Again, take also the matter of complexity and
study it properly and with a thorough acquaintance
with the subject, comparing the compositions of a
former day with those of the present, and you will
find that complexity was current in those days too.
Thus in the conduct of the rhythm the ancients employed a complexity greater than that in use today,
for they set great store on complexity in rhythm.
Further, the interplay of the accompaniment was

[a] A device for raising the pitch of the aulos. For the nature
of the device *cf.* 1. Düring, *Ptolemaios und Porphyrios* (Göte-
borgs Högskolas Årsskrift, vol. xl, No. 1 [1934]), pp. 172 f.
and K. Schlesinger, *The Greek Aulos* (London, 1939), p. 54.
In non-technical Greek *syrinx* is a whistling or a tube.

[b] The words are those of the source, perhaps Aristoxenus,
who flourished about 320 B.C.

[c] An aulete at the court of Philip of Macedon.

[d] A Theban aulete who flourished about 400–370 B.C.

[e] Literally a sole stitched on a shoe. The musical meaning
has not been ascertained.

(1138) κρουσματικὰς[1] δὲ διαλέκτους τότε ποικιλώτερα ἦν·
C οἱ μὲν γὰρ νῦν φιλομελεῖς,[2] οἱ δὲ τότε φιλόρρυθμοι.[3]

" Δῆλον οὖν ὅτι οἱ παλαιοὶ οὐ δι᾽ ἄγνοιαν ἀλλὰ
διὰ προαίρεσιν ἀπείχοντο τῶν κεκλασμένων μελῶν.
καὶ τί θαυμαστόν; πολλὰ γὰρ καὶ ἄλλα τῶν κατὰ
τὸν βίον ἐπιτηδευμάτων οὐκ ἀγνοεῖται μὲν ὑπὸ τῶν
μὴ[4] χρωμένων, ἀπηλλοτρίωται δὲ αὐτῶν, τῆς χρείας
ἀφαιρεθείσης διὰ τὸ εἰς ἔνια ἀπρεπές.

22. " Δεδειγμένου[5] δὲ ὅτι[6] ὁ Πλάτων οὔτε ἀγνοίᾳ
οὔτε ἀπειρίᾳ τὰ ἄλλα παρῃτήσατο, ἀλλ᾽ ὡς οὐ πρέ-
ποντα τοιαύτῃ πολιτείᾳ, δείξομεν ἑξῆς ὅτι ἔμπειρος
ἁρμονίας ἦν. ἐν γοῦν[7] τῇ ψυχογονίᾳ τῇ ἐν τῷ
Τιμαίῳ τήν τε περὶ τὰ μαθήματα καὶ μουσικὴν
D σπουδὴν ἐπεδείξατο ὡδέ πως·

καὶ μετὰ ταῦτα συνεπλήρου[8] τά τε διπλάσια
καὶ τὰ[9] τριπλάσια διαστήματα, μοίρας τε[10] ἐκεῖθεν
ἀποτέμνων καὶ τιθεὶς εἰς τὸ μεταξὺ τούτων·
ὥστε ἐν ἑκάστῳ διαστήματι δύο εἶναι μεσότητας.

ἁρμονικῆς γὰρ ἦν[11] ἐμπειρίας τοῦτο τὸ προοίμιον,
ὡς αὐτίκα δείξομεν. τρεῖς εἰσιν μεσότητες αἱ
πρῶται, ἀφ᾽ ὧν λαμβάνεται πᾶσα μεσότης, ἀριθμη-
τική, ἁρμονική, γεωμετρουμένη.[12] τούτων[13] ἡ μὲν

---

[1] κρουσματικὰς] κρουματικὰς vq (all have κρουμάτων at
1142 в).
[2] φιλομελεῖς Bergk (modos . . . amplectebantur Valgulius): φιλομαθεῖς.
[3] φιλόρρυθμοι a[2] aN[c]: φιλόρυθμοι.
[4] μὴ added by Westphal; add γε instead?
[5] δεδειγμένου M V a W: -ον aN; -ων vq (all put a stop
after this word, none before).
[6] δὲ ὅτι Dübner (δὴ ὅτι Wyttenbach): ὅτι δὲ.
[7] γοῦν] οὖν v[2]q (a[ac] omits).

then more varied, as moderns like music for the tune, whereas the ancients were interested in the beat.

" It is clear then that the ancients abstained from overmodulated music not from ignorance but on principle. Need this surprise us ? Thus there are many other practices of daily life that are not unknown to those who do not adopt them but are regarded as unacceptable, their utility being cancelled by their unsuitability for certain ends.

22. " I have shown that Plato rejected other forms of music not through ignorance or unfamiliarity, but because they were not suited to his kind of state. I shall next show that he was acquainted with harmonics. Thus in the passage of the *Timaeus* [a] that deals with the creation of the soul he shows his study of mathematics and music in the words that follow :

> And thereafter he filled out the double and triple intervals, cutting off portions from that source and inserting them into the interstices of these ; and the result was the presence of two means in each interval.

These introductory remarks rest on an acquaintance with harmonic science, as I proceed to show. There are three primary means, and from them all means are derived [b] : the arithmetic, the harmonic, and that obtained geometrically. Of these means the first

---

[a] 35 c 2—36 A 3.
[b] For other means see Sir T. L. Heath, *A History of Greek Mathematics* (Oxford, 1921), vol. i, pp. 86-89.

---

[8] καὶ μετὰ ταῦτα συνεπλήρου] μετὰ δὲ ταῦτα συνεπληροῦτο Plato.
[9] τὰ] Plato omits.
[10] τε] ἔτι Plato.
[11] ἦν ἐμπ. (and so a[c])] ἐμπ. ἦν vq ; a[ac] omits ἦν.
[12] γεωμετρουμένη] γεωμετρικὴ W[ac] ?
[13] τούτων] τούτω MW.

(1138) ἴσῳ ἀριθμῷ ὑπερέχει καὶ ὑπερέχεται,[1] ἡ δὲ ἴσῳ
λόγῳ, ἡ δὲ οὔτε λόγῳ οὔτε ἀριθμῷ. ὁ τοίνυν
Πλάτων τὴν ψυχικὴν ἁρμονίαν τῶν τεσσάρων στοιχείων καὶ τὴν αἰτίαν τῆς[2] πρὸς ἄλληλα ἐξ ἀνομοίων
E συμφωνίας δεῖξαι ἁρμονικῶς βουληθείς, ἐν ἑκάστῳ
διαστήματι δύο μεσότητας ψυχικὰς ἀπέφηνε κατὰ
τὸν μουσικὸν λόγον. τῆς γὰρ διὰ πασῶν ἐν μουσικῇ συμφωνίας δύο διαστήματα μέσα εἶναι συμβέβηκεν, ὧν τὴν ἀναλογίαν δείξομεν. ἡ μὲν γὰρ διὰ
πασῶν ἐν διπλασίονι[3] λόγῳ θεωρεῖται· ποιήσει δ'
εἰκόνος χάριν τὸν διπλάσιον λόγον κατ' ἀριθμὸν τὰ
F ἓξ καὶ τὰ δώδεκα· ἔστι δὲ τοῦτο τὸ διάστημα ἀπὸ
ὑπάτης μέσων ἐπὶ νήτην διεζευγμένων. ὄντων οὖν
τῶν ἓξ καὶ τῶν[4] δώδεκα ἄκρων, ἔχει ἡ μὲν ὑπάτη
μέσων τὸν τῶν[5] ἓξ ἀριθμόν,[6] ἡ δὲ νήτη διεζευ-

---

[1] ὑπερέχει καὶ ὑπερέχεται] ὑπερέχει v[ac]; ὑπερέχεται v[c]; περι-
έχεται s.   [2] τῆς] τὴν M N.   [3] διπλασίονι] -ωνι M.
[4] τῶν added by γE.   [5] τὸν τῶν] τούτων M.
[6] ἀριθμόν] -ῶν M.

---

[a] This is the arithmetic mean. Thus 9 is such a mean between 12 and 6, as $12 - 9 = 3$ and $9 - 6 = 3$.

[b] The harmonic mean. Thus 8 is such a mean between 12
and 6, as $12 - 8 = 4$, a third of 12, and $8 - 6 = 2$, a third of 6.

[c] The geometric mean. If one extreme is twice the other,
both being integers (2a and a), the mean is $a\sqrt{2}$, and thus
must be represented by a line, as it is not a true number and
cannot (being " irrational ") enter into a ratio.

[d] The four elements are the four fixed notes of the octave.
These are represented by the numbers 6, 8, 9, and 12 :

Middle tetrachord	hypatê	E	6
	mesê	a	8
Disjunct tetrachord	paramesê	b	9
	netê	e	12

Each number illustrates one of the four kinds distinguished
by Plato (cf. Laws, vii, 819 B) and the Pythagoreans (cf.

exceeds the one extreme and is exceeded by the other by the same number,[a] the next by the same ratio,[b] and the last by neither a ratio nor by a number.[c] So Plato, wishing to show in terms of the science of harmonics the harmony of the four elements in the soul[d] and the cause of the concord of dissimilars with one another, presents in each interval two means of the soul, in accordance with the ratio of music. For it so happens that in music the consonance of the octave has two mean intervals.[e] The progression that they constitute I shall proceed to show. Now the consonance of the octave is seen to be in the duple ratio[f]; and this ratio, expressed in numbers, is illustrated by six and twelve, and the interval is that from the hypatê of the middle tetrachord to the netê of the disjunct tetrachord. Six then and twelve being the extremes, the hypatê of the middle tetrachord is represented by the number six, the netê of

Nicomachus, *Introduction to Arithmetic*, i. 8-10 [pp. 14-25, ed. Hoche] ; Theo of Smyrna, *On the Mathematics Useful for Reading Plato*, pp. 21. 20-24, 25. 5-26. 13 [ed. Hiller]; see also Philolaüs, Frag. в 5 [Diels and Kranz, *Frag. der Vorsokratiker*, i, p. 408]) : 9 is odd, and the rest represent the three kinds of even number. Thus 8 can be halved, and the halves halved, and the process can be repeated until unity is reached ; 6 can be halved only once, when an odd number is reached and the process cannot be repeated ; while 12 can be halved, and the halves halved, but here the process must end, as an odd number is reached. Thus 8 represents pure evenness, 9 pure oddness, and 6 and 12 varying degrees of intermixture. The odd represents limit, the even the unlimited : *cf.* 1139 F—1140 A, *infra*.

[e] The author means that the interval of the octave (12 : 6) is composed of the intervals 12 : 9 and 9 : 6 or 12 : 8 and 8 : 6. These he oddly terms " mean intervals."

[f] " Duple," " sesquialteran," " sesquitertian," and " sesquioctavan " render the Pythagorean names of the ratios that we should call 2 : 1, 3 : 2, 4 : 3, and 9 : 8.

(1138) γμένων τὸν τῶν δώδεκα. λαβεῖν δὴ[1] λοιπὸν χρὴ
πρὸς τούτοις ἀριθμοὺς τοὺς μεταξὺ πίπτοντας, ὧν[2]
ὁ μὲν ἐπίτριτος, ὁ δὲ ἡμιόλιος φανήσεται· εἰσὶν δὲ
ὅ[3] τῶν ὀκτὼ καὶ τῶν ἐννέα· τῶν γὰρ ἓξ τὰ μὲν ὀκτὼ
ἐπίτριτα, τὰ δὲ ἐννέα ἡμιόλια. τὸ μὲν ἓν ἄκρον
τοιοῦτο, τὸ δ' ἄλλο τὸ[4] τῶν δώδεκα τῶν μὲν ἐννέα
1139 ἐπίτριτα, τῶν δ' ὀκτὼ ἡμιόλια. τούτων οὖν τῶν
ἀριθμῶν ὄντων μεταξὺ τῶν ἓξ καὶ τῶν δώδεκα,
καὶ τοῦ διὰ πασῶν διαστήματος ἐκ τοῦ διὰ τεττάρων[5] καὶ τοῦ διὰ πέντε συνεστῶτος, δῆλον ὅτι ἕξει
ἡ μὲν μέση τὸν τῶν ὀκτὼ ἀριθμόν, ἡ δὲ παραμέση
τὸν τῶν ἐννέα. τούτου γενομένου ἕξει ἡ ὑπάτη
πρὸς μέσην[6] ὡς παραμέση πρὸς νήτην διεζευγμένων[7]· ἀπὸ γὰρ ὑπάτης[8] μέσων διὰ τεττάρων[9] ἐπὶ
μέσην, ἀπὸ δὲ παραμέσης ὡσαύτως[10] ἐπὶ νήτην
διεζευγμένων.[11,12] ἡ αὐτὴ δὲ ἀναλογία καὶ ἐπὶ τῶν
B ἀριθμῶν εὑρίσκεται· ὡς γὰρ ἔχει τὰ ἓξ πρὸς τὰ
ὀκτώ, οὕτως τὰ ἐννέα πρὸς τὰ δώδεκα· καὶ ὡς ἔχει
τὰ ἓξ πρὸς τὰ ἐννέα, οὕτως τὰ ὀκτὼ πρὸς τὰ δώ-
δεκα· ἐπίτριτα γὰρ τὰ μὲν ὀκτὼ τῶν ἔξ, τὰ δὲ
δώδεκα τῶν ἐννέα, ἡμιόλια δὲ[13] τὰ μὲν ἐννέα τῶν ἔξ,
τὰ δὲ δώδεκα τῶν ὀκτώ. ἀρκέσει τὰ εἰρημένα εἰς
τὸ ἐπιδεδειχέναι ἣν εἶχεν περὶ τὰ μαθήματα σπουδὴν καὶ ἐμπειρίαν Πλάτων.
    23. " "Οτι δὲ σεμνὴ ἡ ἁρμονία καὶ θεῖόν τι καὶ

---

[1] δὴ] δὲ v.   [2] After ὧν we omit οἱ ἄκροι.
[3] ὁ] ὡς W.   [4] τὸ] τῶ M.
[5] διὰ τεττάρων (-ετά- α)] διατεσσάρων M ; διὰ τεσσάρων V.
    [6] μέσην] τὴν μέσην N.
    [7] διεζευγμένων M E s : -ου.
[8] ὑπάτης aN v[2] Valgulius : παρυπάτης.
[9] διὰ τεττάρων V a aN vq (διατεττάρων W) : διὰ τεσσάρων M.
    [10] ὡσαύτως added by Weil and Reinach.
    [11] διεζευγμένων A[288]E s : -ου.

the disjunct tetrachord by the number twelve. It
remains to obtain in addition to these the numbers
that fall between, so that one of these shall have the
sesquitertian ratio, the other the sesquialteran.[a]
These are eight and nine, for eight has the sesquitertian ratio to six, nine the sesquialteran. Such then
are the ratios involving the one extreme. The other,
represented by the number twelve, has the sesquitertian ratio to nine, the sesquialteran to eight. Since
these are the numbers intermediate between six and
twelve, and since the interval of the octave is composed of the interval of the fourth and that of the
fifth, it is evident that the mesê will be represented
by the number eight, the paramesê by the number
nine. When this is done the hypatê will have the
same ratio to the mesê as the paramesê to the netê
of the disjunct tetrachord, since the interval from the
hypatê of the middle tetrachord to the mesê is a
fourth and so too the interval from the paramesê to
the netê of the disjunct tetrachord. The same proportion is found in the numbers as well; for six is to
eight as nine to twelve, and again six is to nine as
eight to twelve, since eight has the sesquitertian
ratio to six and twelve has it to nine, whereas nine has
the sesquialteran ratio to six and twelve has it to
eight. What has been said will suffice to show Plato's
study and knowledge of mathematics.

23. " That harmony is august and a thing divine

[a] The ratio can only be with the lesser extreme, 6, since
the terms sesquialteran and sesquitertian imply the ratio of
a larger number with a smaller.

[12] After διεζευγμένων Weil and Reinach omit διὰ πασῶν (διὰ
τεττάρων v[2] and Valgulius; διὰ τεττάρων· δῆλον δ' ὅτι καὶ ἀπὸ
ὑπάτης μέσων ἐπὶ νήτην διεζευγμένου, διὰ πασῶν aN).
[13] ἡμιόλια δὲ] ἡμιόλιά τε aN.

(1139) μέγα 'Αριστοτέλης ὁ Πλάτωνος[1] ταυτὶ λέγει·

'Η δὲ ἁρμονία[2] ἐστὶν οὐρανία, τὴν φύσιν ἔχουσα
θείαν καὶ καλὴν καὶ δαιμονίαν. τετραμερὴς δὲ
τῇ δυνάμει πεφυκυῖα, δύο μεσότητας ἔχει, ἀριθμητικήν[3] τε καὶ ἁρμονικήν, φαίνεταί τε τὰ μέρη
αὐτῆς[4] καὶ τὰ μεγέθη καὶ αἱ ὑπεροχαὶ κατ' ἀριθμὸν καὶ ἰσομετρίαν· ἐν γὰρ δυσὶ τετραχόρδοις
ῥυθμίζεται τὰ μέλη.

C ταῦτα μὲν τὰ ῥητά.[5]

'' Συνεστάναι δὲ αὐτῆς τὸ σῶμα ἔλεγεν ἐκ μερῶν
ἀνομοίων, συμφωνούντων μέντοι πρὸς ἄλληλα, ἀλλὰ
μὴν καὶ τὰς μεσότητας αὐτῆς κατὰ τὸν ἀριθμητικὸν
λόγον συμφωνεῖν. τὸν γὰρ νέατον πρὸς τὸν ὕπατον
ἐκ διπλασίου λόγου ἡρμοσμένον τὴν διὰ πασῶν
συμφωνίαν ἀποτελεῖν. ἔχει γάρ, ὡς προείπομεν,

---

[1] Πλάτωνος] πλατωνικὸς vq.
[2] ἁρμονία—ἁρμονία] ἁρμονία M.
[3] ἀριθμητικήν] τὴν ἀριθμητικήν vq.
[4] αὐτῆς] ταὐτὰ (cf. Plato, Tim. 32 A 6)?
[5] ῥητά] ῥήματα V.

---

[a] Aristotle, *Eudemus*, Frag. 47 (ed. Rose), *On Philosophy*,
Frag. 25 (ed. Ross). *Cf.* M. T. Cardini in *La Parola del
Passato*, vol. xvii (1962), pp. 300-312.
[b] The world soul contains the ratios or intervals of music
(Plato, *Timaeus*, 35 B—36 B), and the world or heaven is a god
(*ibid.* 34 B 1).
[c] The parts are the four terms, which can be represented
by the numbers 6, 8, 9, and 12. I. Düring (*Gnomon*, vol. xxvii
[1955], p. 435) takes the parts to be the tone, fourth, fifth, and
octave. '' Harmonia '' also means octave, and the phrase
'' in its operation '' includes the means with the '' parts,'' for
which *cf.* note h, *infra*.
[d] The magnitudes are the intervals (1) 12 : 8, 8 : 6, and (2)
12 : 9, 9 : 6. The excesses of (1) are 12 − 8 (a third of 12)

and great is remarked by Aristotle, the disciple of Plato, in these words [a] :

> Harmony is celestial, since its nature is divine, noble, and wonderfully wrought.[b] Being in its operation naturally quadripartite,[c] it has two means, arithmetic and harmonic, and its parts and magnitudes and excesses[d] are manifested in conformity with number [e] and equality of measure ; for melodies are given their form in the range of two tetra-chords.[f]

Such are his actual words.

" He said that its body [g] was constituted of parts dissimilar, yet concordant with one another,[h] and that furthermore its means were concordant in conformity with arithmetical ratio.[i] Thus the highest note, attuned to the lowest in the duple ratio, produces the concord of the octave. For as we said earlier,[j] har-

and $8-6$ (a third of 6), and show equality of measure ; the excesses of (2) are $12-9$ and $9-6$, or three, and show equality of number.

[e] To conform to number is to be expressible as integral numbers or in terms of them. Thus the geometrical mean between 6 and 12 is excluded, as it is not a number in the Pythagorean sense, being irrational.

[f] The middle (E–a) and the disjunct (b–e).

[g] As Plato distinguishes between a soul of the universe and the body enveloped by it (*cf. Timaeus*, 34 B 10—35 A 1), so here a distinction is apparently drawn between harmony itself (a set of ratios) and its body, consisting of sounds.

[h] *Cf.* 1138 D, *supra* : " concord of dissimilars." *Cf.* Philolaüs, Frag. B 6 (Diels and Kranz, *Die Frag. der Vorsokratiker*, i, p. 409. 2-9) and Plato, *Symposium*, 187 A-B. The dissimilars are the high-pitched and low-pitched. These correspond to the netê and hypatê ; hence " parts " earlier in the sentence is contrasted to the " means."

[i] Arithmetic ratio is one that can be expressed as holding between one integer and another ; *cf.* Nicomachus, *Introduction to Arithmetic*, i. 5. 1 (p. 11. 5-10, ed. Hoche).

[j] 1138 F, *supra*.

(1139) τὸν νέατον δώδεκα μονάδων, τὸν δὲ ὕπατον ἕξ, τὴν
δὲ παραμέσην συμφωνοῦσαν πρὸς ὑπάτην καθ᾽[1]
ἡμιόλιον λόγον ἐννέα μονάδων· τῆς δὲ μέσης[2] ὀκτὼ
εἶναι μονάδας ἐλέγομεν. συγκεῖσθαι δὲ διὰ τούτων
τῆς μουσικῆς τὰ κυριώτατα διαστήματα συμβαίνει,
τό τε διὰ τεσσάρων, ὅ ἐστι κατὰ τὸν ἐπίτριτον
D λόγον, καὶ τὸ διὰ πέντε, ὅ ἐστι κατὰ τὸν ἡμιόλιον
λόγον,[3] καὶ τὸ διὰ πασῶν, ὅ ἐστι κατὰ τὸν[4] διπλά-
σιον· ἀλλὰ γὰρ καὶ τὸν ἐπόγδοον σώζεσθαι, ὅς ἐστι
κατὰ τὸν τονιαῖον λόγον. ταῖς αὐταῖς δ᾽ ὑπεροχαῖς
ὑπερέχειν καὶ ὑπερέχεσθαι τῆς ἁρμονίας τὰ μέρη
ὑπὸ τῶν μερῶν καὶ τὰς μεσότητας ὑπὸ τῶν μεσοτήτων[5] κατά τε τὴν ἐν ἀριθμοῖς ὑπεροχὴν καὶ κατὰ
τὴν γεωμετρικὴν δύναμιν συμβαίνει. ἀποφαίνει
γοῦν αὐτὰς Ἀριστοτέλης τὰς δυνάμεις ἐχούσας
τοιαύτας, τὴν μὲν νεάτην τῆς μέσης τῷ τρίτῳ μέρει
E τῷ αὑτῆς ὑπερέχουσαν, τὴν δὲ ὑπάτην ὑπὸ τῆς
μέσης[6] ὑπερεχομένην ὁμοίως, ὡς γίνεσθαι[7] τὰς ὑπεροχὰς τῶν πρός τι· τοῖς γὰρ αὐτοῖς μέρεσιν ὑπερέχουσι καὶ ὑπερέχονται (τοῖς γοῦν[8] αὐτοῖς λόγοις
οἱ[9] ἄκροι τῆς μέσης καὶ παραμέσης ὑπερέχουσι καὶ
ὑπερέχονται, ἐπιτρίτῳ καὶ ἡμιολίῳ). τοιαύτη δὴ
ὑπεροχή ἐστιν ἡ ἁρμονική. ἡ δὲ τῆς νεάτης ὑπερ-

---

[1] καθ᾽ E aN v² : πρὸς καθ᾽.   [2] μέσης] μόνης v¹.
[3] λόγον] vq omit.   [4] τὸν] τὸ a.
[5] μερῶν . . . μεσοτήτων] μεσοτήτων . . . μερῶν Weil and
Reinach.
[6] μέσης Weil and Reinach : παραμέσης.
[7] γίνεσθαι] γίγνεσθαι vq.
[8] γοῦν] οὖν q (in an omission in v).
[9] οἱ A²E aN : the rest omit.

---

[a] 1139 A, supra.
[b] The mss. have paramesê, perhaps added by the compiler ; thus it occurs in the interpolation pointed out in the

ON MUSIC, 1139

mony has its highest note of twelve units, its lowest
of six, and its paramesê, which is concordant with the
hypatê in the sesquialteran ratio, of nine units ; and
we said [a] that there were eight units in the mesê.
These ratios, it so happens, enter into the principal
intervals of music : the fourth (which follows the sesquitertian ratio), the fifth (which follows the sesquialteran), and the octave (following the duple) ; indeed
the sesquioctavan is also accounted for, as it is the ratio
found in the tone. And it turns out that the parts and
means of harmony exceed and are exceeded by one
another by the same differences both when reckoned
in numbers and in terms of geometrical relation.
Thus Aristotle assigns to the means the following
properties : the netê exceeds the mesê by a third
part of itself, and the hypatê is exceeded by the mesê
in the same way.[b] Thus the excesses are relative,
for it is by the same submultiples that the exceeding
and being exceeded take place [c] (since it is in the
same ratios that the extremes exceed and are exceeded by the mesê and the paramesê, the sesquitertian and the sesquialteran).[d] Such then is the harmonic exceeding and being exceeded. The difference

next note but one. The subject here is the *harmonic* mean,
represented by the mesê or the number eight, while the
extremes are represented by the netê and hypatê or by the
numbers 12 and 6.

[c] One extreme (the netê, 12) exceeds the mesê or " mean "
(8) by 4, which is one third of 12, while the other extreme, the
hypatê (6) is exceeded by the mesê by 2, which is one third of
the hypatê. The interpolator (perhaps the compiler himself)
who read paramesê above thought of the hypatê (6) as being
exceeded by the paramesê (9) by 3, which is a third of 9.

[d] The words in parentheses are an interpolation, probably
by the compiler. The paramesê has no place in the discussion
of the *harmonic* mean.

407

(1139) οχὴ καὶ ἡ[1] τῆς μέσης κατ' ἀριθμητικὸν λόγον ἴσῳ
μέρει[2] τὰς ὑπεροχὰς ἐμφαίνουσιν. (ὡσαύτως καὶ
F ἡ παραμέση τῆς ὑπάτης· τῆς γὰρ μέσης ἡ παραμέση[3] κατὰ τὸν ἐπόγδοον λόγον ὑπερέχει· πάλιν ἡ
νεάτη τῆς ὑπάτης διπλασία ἐστίν, ἡ δὲ παραμέση
τῆς ὑπάτης ἡμιόλιος, ἡ δὲ μέση ἐπίτριτος πρὸς
ὑπάτην ἥρμοσται.) καὶ τοῖς μὲν μέρεσι καὶ τοῖς
πλήθεσι καὶ κατὰ 'Αριστοτέλη[4] ἡ ἁρμονία οὕτως
ἔχουσα πέφυκεν.

24. '' Συνέστηκε δὲ φυσικώτατα ἔκ τε τῆς ἀπεί-
ρου καὶ περαινούσης καὶ ἐκ τῆς ἀρτιοπερίσσου
φύσεως καὶ αὐτὴ καὶ τὰ μέρη αὐτῆς πάντα. αὐτὴ
μὲν γὰρ ὅλη ἀρτία ἐστί, τετραμερὴς οὖσα τοῖς
ὅροις· τὰ δὲ μέρη αὐτῆς[5] καὶ οἱ λόγοι ἄρτιοι καὶ
1140 περισσοὶ καὶ[6] ἀρτιοπέρισσοι. τὴν μὲν γὰρ νεάτην
ἔχει ἀρτίαν ἐκ δώδεκα μονάδων, τὴν δὲ παραμέσην
περισσὴν ἐξ ἐννέα μονάδων, τὴν δὲ μέσην[7] ἀρτίαν
ἐξ ὀκτὼ μονάδων, τὴν δὲ ὑπάτην ἀρτιοπέρισσον ἐξ
μονάδων οὖσαν. οὕτω δὲ πεφυκυῖα αὐτή τε καὶ τὰ
μέρη αὐτῆς πρὸς ἄλληλα ταῖς ὑπεροχαῖς τε καὶ
τοῖς λόγοις, ὅλη τε ὅλη[8] καὶ τοῖς μέρεσι συμφωνεῖ.

---

[1] ἡ added by Bern. [2] μέρει] πλήθει ?
[3] παραμέση—παραμέση] παραμέση M V.
[4] ἀριστοτέλη V a¹ W N (M and a omit the termination) :
-ην a²AE vq. [5] αὐτῆς] αὐτοῖς M.
[6] καὶ] N omits. [7] μέσην] παρὰ μέσην W.
[8] ὅλη τὲ ὅλη aNᶜ (-η from -ει) vq : ὅλη τε ὅλη A (τὲ E) ;
ὅλη τε (or τὲ) ὅλη (ὅ- W).

---

[a] The arithmetic mean or " mesê " between 12 and 6 is 9 ;
and it is represented by the paramesê, and not by the note
called mesê. We assume that the words rendered " the
difference of the netê and that of the arithmetical mesê "
mean " the difference of the netê from the arithmetical mesê
and that of the arithmetical mesê from the hypatê."

of the netê and that of the arithmetical mesê " present on the other hand remainders that are equal. (So too does that of the paramesê and hypatê ; for the paramesê exceeds the mesê in the sesquioctavan ratio, and again the netê exceeds the hypatê in the duple ratio, the paramesê the hypatê in the sesquialteran, and the mesê the hypatê in the sesquitertian.) [b] Such then according to Aristotle as well is the constitution of harmony both in the matter of submultiples and of numerical amounts.

24. " Harmony and all its parts are composed in their ultimate substance of the natures of the Unlimited, of Limit, and of the Even-odd.[c] Thus harmony [d] itself, taken as a whole, is even, having four terms [e] ; whereas its constituents and ratios are even, odd, and even-odd. Thus it has an even [f] netê, of twelve units, but an odd paramesê, of nine ; again an even mesê, of eight units, and an even-odd hypatê, of six. Since harmony itself is of this structure, and since its constituents have this natural relation to one another in their numerical differences and their ratios, harmony is concordant with itself as a whole and with its parts.

[b] This is another interpolation, perhaps by the compiler himself. The interpolator took the arithmetical " mesê " (" mean ") to be the note actually called " mesê " (" middle ").
[c] According to the Pythagoreans even belongs to the Unlimited, odd to Limit : cf. Aristotle, *Physics*, iii. 4 (203 a 10-15).
[d] The Pythagoreans used " harmony " of the octave ; cf. Philolaüs, Frag. B 6 (Diels and Kranz, *Frag. der Vorsokratiker*, i, p. 409. 10).
[e] The netê (12), paramesê (9), mesê (8), and hypatê (6).
[f] One would expect " odd-even " ; cf. Nicomachus, *Introduction to Arithmetic*, i. 10.

(1140) 25. " Ἀλλὰ μὴν καὶ αἱ αἰσθήσεις αἱ[1] τοῖς σώμασιν ἐγγιγνόμεναι[2] διὰ τὴν ἁρμονίαν, αἱ μὲν οὐράνιαι,[3]
θεῖαι οὖσαι, μετὰ θεοῦ τὴν αἴσθησιν παρεχόμεναι
B τοῖς ἀνθρώποις, ὄψις τε καὶ ἀκοή, μετὰ φωνῆς καὶ
φωτὸς τὴν ἁρμονίαν ἐπιφαίνουσι· καὶ[4] ἄλλαι δὲ
αὐταῖς ἀκόλουθοι, ᾗ αἰσθήσεις, καθ' ἁρμονίαν συν-
εστᾶσιν· πάντα γὰρ καὶ αὐταὶ ἐπιτελοῦσιν οὐκ ἄνευ
ἁρμονίας,[5] ἐλάττους μὲν ἐκείνων οὖσαι, οὐκ ἄπο δ'
ἐκείνων· ἐκεῖναι γὰρ ἅμα θεοῦ παρουσίᾳ παραγιγνό-
μεναι[6] τοῖς σώμασιν κατὰ λογισμὸν ἰσχυράν τε καὶ
καλὴν φύσιν ἔχουσι.[7]

26. " Φανερὸν οὖν ἐκ τούτων ὅτι τοῖς παλαιοῖς
τῶν Ἑλλήνων εἰκότως μάλιστα πάντων ἐμέλησε
πεπαιδεῦσθαι μουσικήν. τῶν γὰρ νέων τὰς ψυχὰς
ᾤοντο δεῖν διὰ μουσικῆς πλάττειν τε καὶ ῥυθμίζειν
ἐπὶ τὸ εὔσχημον, χρησίμης δηλονότι τῆς μουσικῆς
C ὑπαρχούσης πρὸς πάντα καιρὸν καὶ[8] πᾶσαν ἐσπου-
δασμένην πρᾶξιν, προηγουμένως δὲ πρὸς τοὺς πολεμικοὺς κινδύνους. πρὸς οὓς οἱ μὲν αὐλοῖς ἐχρῶντο,
καθάπερ Λακεδαιμόνιοι,[9] παρ' οἷς τὸ καλούμενον

---

[1] αἱ] ἐν V v (ἃν ᵍᵃᶜ).   [2] ἐγγιγνόμεναι] -γιν- N.
[3] After οὐράνιαι Thurot would add καί.
[4] After καί Rose would add αἱ.
[5] ἄνευ ἁρμονίας] ἃν εὐαρμονίας M.
[6] παραγιγνόμεναι] -γιν- a a ; -γεν- N.
[7] ἔχουσι] -ιν vᵗ ; -αι vˡˢˢ (now struck out).
[8] καιρὸν καί] καὶ a.
[9] Λακεδαιμόνιοι] λακεδαιμόνιοις M.

---

[a] Cf. Aristotle, Eudemus, Frag. 48 (ed. Rose), On Philosophy, Frag. 24 (ed. Ross): "And Proclus would have it that
the celestial bodies have only sight and hearing, as does Aristotle ; for alone of the senses they have those that contribute
to well-being, but not to being, while the other senses contribute to being . . ."

25. " Again, of the senses which are engendered in our bodies because of harmony those that are celestial,[a] sight and hearing, being divine [b] and having God as helper in providing men with sensation, reveal this harmony [c] to the accompaniment of sound and light ; and other senses too that come in their train are by virtue of being senses composed in conformity with a harmony. For these senses also in all of their effects have some harmony,[d] and while inferior to the first are not severed from them.[e] For the first, as they appear in our bodies along with the presence of God by way of reasoning,[f] have a powerful and noble nature.

26. " It is evident then from this that the ancients among the Greeks were with good reason concerned above all with training in music. For they thought that the minds of the young should be moulded and modulated by music to a pattern of graceful bearing,[g] since music is helpful for every occasion and all serious activity, but especially for meeting the perils of war. In meeting these some employed auloi, like the Lacedaemonians,[h] among whom the so-called Air of

---

[b] Cf. Aristoxenus ap. Philodemus, De Musica, iii, Frag. 76. 15-19 (p. 54, cd. Kemke ; p. 116, ed. van Krevelen) ; Aristoxenus, Frag. 73 (ed. Wehrli).

[c] Cf. Plato, Timaeus, 47 B 5–D 7.

[d] For proportion in sensation cf. Aristotle, De Anima, iii. 2. 9 (426 a 27–b 7).

[e] The Greek in this paragraph is often strange and very probably corrupt.

[f] That is, their cause is intelligence, not necessity : cf. e.g. Plato, Timaeus, 47 E 3-5.

[g] Cf. Plato, Republic, iii, 401 D 8.

[h] Cf. Life of Lycurgus, chap. xxii. 4-5 (53 E-F) and Aulus Gellius, Attic Nights, i. 11. 1.

(1140) Καστόρειον[1] ηὐλεῖτο μέλος ὁπότε τοῖς πολεμίοις ἐν
κόσμῳ προσῄεσαν μαχεσόμενοι.[2] οἱ δὲ καὶ πρὸς
λύραν ἐποίουν τὴν πρόσοδον τὴν πρὸς τοὺς ἐναν-
τίους, καθάπερ ἱστοροῦνται μέχρι πολλοῦ χρήσασθαι τῷ τρόπῳ τούτῳ τῆς ἐπὶ τοὺς πολεμικοὺς[3]
κινδύνους ἐξόδου Κρῆτες. οἱ δ' ἔτι καὶ καθ'
ἡμᾶς σάλπιγγιν[4] διατελοῦσιν χρώμενοι. Ἀργεῖοι
δὲ πρὸς τὴν τῶν Σθενείων τῶν καλουμένων παρ'
αὐτοῖς πάλην[5] ἐχρῶντο τῷ αὐλῷ· τὸν δὲ ἀγῶνα
τοῦτον ἐπὶ Δαναῷ μὲν τὴν ἀρχὴν τεθῆναί φασιν,
D ὕστερον δὲ ἀνατεθῆναι Διὶ Σθενίῳ.[6] οὐ μὴν ἀλλὰ
ἔτι[7] καὶ νῦν τοῖς πεντάθλοις νενόμισται προσαυλεῖ-
σθαι,[8] οὐδὲν μὲν κεκριμένον οὐδ' ἀρχαῖον, οὐδ'
οἷον ἐνομίζετο παρὰ τοῖς ἀνδράσιν ἐκείνοις ὥσπερ
τὸ ὑπὸ[9] Ἱέρακος πεποιημένον πρὸς τὴν ἀγωνίαν
ταύτην ὃ ἐκαλεῖτο Ἐνδρομή· ὅμως δὲ καὶ εἰ
ἀσθενές τι καὶ οὐ κεκριμένον, ἀλλ' οὖν προσ-
αυλεῖται.[10]

27. " Ἐπὶ μέντοι τῶν ἔτι ἀρχαιοτέρων οὐδὲ
εἰδέναι φασὶ τοὺς Ἕλληνας τὴν θεατρικὴν μοῦσαν,
ὅλην δὲ αὐτοῖς τὴν ἐπιστήμην πρός τε θεῶν τιμὴν
καὶ τὴν τῶν νέων παίδευσιν παραλαμβάνεσθαι, μηδὲ
E τὸ παράπαν ἤδη θεάτρου παρὰ τοῖς ἀνδράσιν ἐκείνοις κατεσκευασμένου, ἀλλὰ ἔτι τῆς μουσικῆς ἐν
τοῖς ἱεροῖς ἀναστρεφομένης,[11] ἐν οἷς τιμήν τε τοῦ

---

[1] Καστόρειον] καστώριον Μ[ac]; κασόριον V[ac].

[2] μαχεσόμενοι] μαχόμενοι W.

[3] πολεμικοὺς] πολεμικοῦ M ; W omits.

[4] σάλπιγγι (-ιν M)] σάλπιγξι V a[ac].

[5] πάλην aN : πάλιν.   [6] Σθενίῳ] -είω N[1].

[7] ἔτι] καὶ ἔτι a[ar] ? v.

[8] προσαυλεῖσθαι] προαυλεῖσθαι v[c] (from -λῆ-)q.

Castor was played on the auloi whenever in well-ordered ranks they advanced to fight the enemy. Others marched to battle to the music of the lyre ; thus the Cretans [a] are on record as having long maintained this practice when setting out to face the perils of war. Others again even in our day maintain the use of trumpets.[b] The Argives played the aulos at the wrestling match belonging to the festival called by them the Stheneia. It is said that the contest was originally instituted in honour of Danaüs, and was later consecrated to Zeus Sthenius. Nay even now it is the rule to conduct the pentathlic contests to the sound of the aulos. The music, to be sure, is in this case nothing distinguished or in the classic style, nor like the pieces that were the rule among the men of old, such as Hierax's [c] composition for this contest which was called Endromê [d] ; yet feeble and undistinguished though the music is, the aulos is nevertheless played.

27. " Certainly in still more ancient times the Greeks, it is said, did not even know of the music of the theatre, and for them the whole of this science was handed down for the purpose of honouring the gods or educating the young. No theatre at all had as yet even been set up among the men of those days ; rather music still had its abode in temples, where it

[a] *Cf.* Aulus Gellius, *Attic Nights*, i. 11. 6.
[b] Presumably the Romans are meant.
[c] *Cf.* Pollux, iv. 79.
[d] Weil and Reinach suggest that the word may refer to the run up to the long jump. It means " launching " or " charge."

---

[9] τὸ ὑπὸ] τοῦ α.
[10] προσαυλεῖται] προαυλεῖται vq.
[11] ἀναστρεφομένης (-ατρ- v)| -οις V.

(1140) θείου διὰ ταύτης ἐποιοῦντο καὶ τῶν ἀγαθῶν ἀνδρῶν
ἐπαίνους· εἰκὸς δὲ εἶναι, ὅτι[1] τὸ θέατρον ὕστερον
καὶ τὸ θεωρεῖν πολὺ πρότερον ἀπὸ τοῦ θεοῦ τὴν
προσηγορίαν ἔλαβεν. ἐπὶ μέντοι τῶν καθ' ἡμᾶς
χρόνων τοσοῦτον ἐπιδέδωκεν τὸ τῆς διαφθορᾶς[2]
εἶδος ὥστε τοῦ μὲν παιδευτικοῦ τρόπου μηδεμίαν
F μνείαν μηδὲ ἀντίληψιν εἶναι, πάντας δὲ τοὺς μουσικῆς ἁπτομένους πρὸς τὴν θεατρικὴν προσκεχω-
ρηκέναι[3] μοῦσαν.

28. '' Εἴποι τις ἄν[4]· ' ὦ τᾶν, οὐδὲν οὖν ὑπὸ[5] τῶν
ἀρχαίων προσεξεύρηται καὶ κεκαινοτόμηται;' φημὶ καὶ αὐτὸς ὅτι προσεξεύρηται, ἀλλὰ μετὰ τοῦ
σεμνοῦ καὶ πρέποντος. οἱ γὰρ ἱστορήσαντες τὰ
τοιαῦτα Τερπάνδρῳ μὲν τήν τε Δώριον νήτην προσ-
ετίθεσαν, οὐ χρησαμένων αὐτῇ τῶν ἔμπροσθεν
κατὰ τὸ μέλος· καὶ τὸν Μιξολύδιον δὲ τόνον ὅλον
προσεξευρῆσθαι λέγεται, καὶ τὸν τῆς ὀρθίου μελῳ-
δίας τρόπον τὸν κατὰ τοὺς ὀρθίους πρός τε τῷ
ὀρθίῳ καὶ τὸν σημαντὸν[6] τροχαῖον. ἔτι[7] δέ, καθάπερ Πίνδαρός φησι, καὶ τῶν σκολιῶν μελῶν Τέρπανδρος εὑρετὴς ἦν· ἀλλὰ μὴν καὶ Ἀρχίλοχος τὴν

---

[1] εἶναι ὅτι Ald.[2] Xylander : ὅτι (ε omits) εἶναι (ὅτι καὶ
Dübner).
[2] διαφθορᾶς M a (-ὰς W) a q : διαφορᾶς V N v.
[3] προσκεχωρηκέναι] κεχωρηκέναι V.
[4] εἴποι τις ἄν nos : εἴποι τις (ἴσως δ' ἂν εἴποι τις Bern. ; καὶ
μὴν ἂν εἴποι τις or τί δ' ἂν εἴποι τις Ziegler).
[5] ὑπὸ] ἀπὸ vq.
[6] πρός τε τῷ ὀρθίῳ καὶ τὸν σημαντὸν Rossbach : π. τὸν ὄρθιον
σημαντὸν (π. τ. ὄρθιον [end of line] -σημαντον M ; π. τ. ὄρθιον
σήμαντον V ; π. τ. ὀρθιοσήμαντον W).
[7] ἔτι (praeterea Valgulius) Wyttenbach : εἰ.

was used in worship and in the praise of good men.[a] This they say is likely, since the word *theatron* [b] at a later time, and the word *theórein* [c] much earlier, were derived from *theos*.[d] But in our own day the decadent kind has made such progress that there is no talk or notion of an educational use, and all who engage in music have entered the service of the music of the theatre.

28. " Here someone might ask : ' You mean then, my friend, that the ancients made no new inventions and introduced no innovations ? ' I too say that new inventions were made, but without derogating from nobility and decorum. Thus those who have looked into these matters assign to Terpander the invention of the Dorian netê [e] (his predecessors having made no use of it in the melody) ; and it is said that he invented the whole Mixolydian mode and the style of orthian melody which uses the orthios foot,[f] and in addition to this foot that he also invented the marked trochee.[g] Again, as Pindar [h] says, Terpander was also the inventor of the music of scolia. Further, Archilochus invented a new rhythmical system, that

---

[a] *Cf.* Plato, *Republic*, x, 607 A and *Laws*, vii, 801 E.

[b] " Theatre."

[c] " To be a spectator," especially at a religious ceremony. The etymology is attacked by Philodemus, *De Musica*, iv, col. 4. 40–col. 5. 12 ; *cf.* also i, Frag. 23. For this etymology of *theóros* (" spectator ") *cf. Etym. Mag.* 448. 42 and *Etym. Gud.* 260. 41.

[d] " God."

[e] *Cf.* [Aristotle], *Problems*, xix. 32 (920 a 14-18).

[f] The orthios has an arsis of four morae and a thesis of eight (Aristides Quintilianus, *De Mus.* i. 16 [p. 37, ed. Meibom ; p. 36. 3-4, ed. Winnington-Ingram]).

[g] The marked trochee has a thesis of eight morae and an arsis of four (Aristides Quintilianus, *De Mus.* i. 16).

[h] *Cf.* Frag. 129 (ed. Turyn), 125-126 (ed. Snell).

(1140) τῶν τριμέτρων[1] ῥυθμοποιίαν προσεξεῦρεν καὶ τὴν
1141 εἰς τοὺς οὐχ ὁμογενεῖς ῥυθμοὺς ἔντασιν καὶ τὴν
παρακαταλογὴν καὶ τὴν περὶ ταῦτα κροῦσιν· πρώτῳ
δὲ αὐτῷ τά τε ἐπῳδὰ καὶ τὰ τετράμετρα καὶ τὸ
κρητικὸν[2] καὶ τὸ προσοδιακὸν ἀποδέδοται καὶ ἡ
τοῦ ἡρῴου[3] αὔξησις, ὑπ᾽ ἐνίων δὲ καὶ τὸ ἐλεγεῖον,
πρὸς δὲ τούτοις ἥ τε τοῦ ἰαμβείου[4] πρὸς τὸν ἐπι-
βατὸν παίωνα ἔντασις καὶ ἡ τοῦ ηὐξημένου ἡρῴου
εἴς τε τὸ προσοδιακὸν καὶ τὸ[5] κρητικόν. ἔτι δὲ
τῶν ἰαμβείων[6] τὸ τὰ μὲν λέγεσθαι παρὰ τὴν κροῦσιν, τὰ δὲ ᾄδεσθαι, Ἀρχίλοχόν φασι καταδεῖξαι,
εἶθ᾽ οὕτω χρήσασθαι τοὺς τραγικοὺς ποιητάς·
B Κρέξον δὲ λαβόντα εἰς διθύραμβον ἀγαγεῖν.[7] οἴονται
δὲ καὶ τὴν κροῦσιν τὴν ὑπὸ τὴν ᾠδὴν τοῦτον πρῶτον εὑρεῖν, τοὺς δὲ ἀρχαίους πάντας[8] πρόσχορδα[9]
κρούειν.

29. " Πολυμνήστῳ[10] δὲ τόν θ᾽ Ὑπολύδιον νῦν

---

[1] τριμέτρων] μέτρων aN.
[2] Κρητικὸν Burette (προκρητικὸν Ritschl) : προκριτικὸν.
[3] ἡρῴου Salmasius : πρώτου.
[4] ἰαμβείου M a[c] N[1] vq : -ίου.
[5] τὸ π. καὶ τὸ s : τὸν π. καὶ τὸν.
[6] ἰαμβείων M a[c] vq : -ίων.
[7] διθύραμβον ἀγαγεῖν Lasserre : διθύραμβον (διθυράμβων Volkmann ; δι[δυ ν]σύλλαβον vq) χρήσασθαι (χρῆσιν Λ[2]) ἀγαγεῖν
(διθυράμβων [-ου] χρήσασθαι ἀγωγήν ;).
[8] πάντας] πάντα Westphal.
[9] πρόσχορδα] πρόσχονδρα W ; πρόσχόρδα v ; πρόχορδα q[188].
[10] Πολυμνήστῳ Weil and Reinach : πολυμνάστω.

---

[a] That is, the iambic trimeter. Perhaps the term rhyth-
mopoeia (rendered " rhythmical system ") is intended to ex-
clude the use of occasional iambic trimeters in the *Margites*,
ascribed to Homer : Archilochus composed whole poems in
iambic trimeters.

of the trimeter,[a] the combination of rhythms of different genera,[b] and the declamation with its instrumental accompaniment ; and he is the first to be credited with epodes,[c] tetrameters,[d] the cretic,[e] the prosodiac,[f] and the augmented dactylic hexameter [g] (some add the elegiac couplet), and again with the combination of iambic verse with the paeon epibatos [h] and that of the augmented dactylic hexameter with the prosodiac and the cretic.[i] Further they say that Archilochus introduced for iambics the mixed recitation of some and singing of others, both to an accompaniment, and that the tragic poets followed him in this, while Crexus took it over and applied it to the dithyramb. And it is thought that he first invented the accompaniment that is of higher pitch than the song, whereas his predecessors had all let the accompaniment follow the melody.

29. " To Polymnestus is ascribed the mode now

[b] Thus he combined dactyls (a rhythm of the " equal genus," thesis and arsis being of the same length) with trochees (which belong to the " duple genus," where the thesis is twice the length of the arsis) in such a line as ◡ – ◡ ◡ – ◡ ◡ – ◡ | – ◡ – ◡ – ◡ .

[c] An *epodos* is a verse of different rhythm or length coming after (literally " singing after ") another verse with which it forms a distich. The elegiac couplet is an instance ; hence its attribution to Archilochus.

[d] That is, the trochaic tetrameter.

[e] Perhaps here the ditrochee (as found in the ithyphallic) ; possibly the foot – ◡ – which when prefixed to the iambic trimeter turns it into a trochaic tetrameter.

[f] Perhaps the rhythm ◡ – ◡ ◡ – ◡ ◡ – ◡ .

[g] No doubt the verse – ◡ ◡ – ◡ ◡ – ◡ ◡ – ◡ ◡ | – ◡ – ◡ – ◡ .

[h] Perhaps here – ◡ ◡ – ◡ ◡ – . Archilochus combines it with iambics in such verses as – ◡ ◡ – ◡ ◡ – | ◡ – ◡ – ◡ – ◡ – and ◡ – ◡ – ◡ – ◡ -- | – ◡ ◡ – ◡ ◡ .--.

[i] No such combination is found among the fragments of Archilochus.

PLUTARCH'S MORALIA

(1141) ὀνομαζόμενον τόνον ἀνατιθέασιν, καὶ τὴν ἔκλυσιν
καὶ τὴν ἐκβολὴν πολὺ μείζω πεποιηκέναι φασὶν
αὐτόν. καὶ αὐτὸν δὲ τὸν[1] Ὄλυμπον ἐκεῖνον, ᾧ δὴ
τὴν ἀρχὴν τῆς Ἑλληνικῆς τε καὶ νομικῆς μούσης
ἀποδιδόασιν, τό τε τῆς ἁρμονίας γένος ἐξευρεῖν
φασιν καὶ τῶν ῥυθμῶν τόν τε προσοδιακόν,[2] ἐν ᾧ
ὁ τοῦ Ἄρεως[3] νόμος, καὶ τὸν χορεῖον, ᾧ πολλῷ
κέχρηται ἐν τοῖς Μητρῴοις· ἔνιοι δὲ καὶ τὸν βακ-
χεῖον Ὄλυμπον οἴονται εὑρηκέναι. δηλοῖ[4] δ᾽ ἕκαστον τῶν ἀρχαίων μελῶν ὅτι ταῦτα οὕτως ἔχει.

C " Λᾶσος[5] δὲ ὁ Ἑρμιονεὺς εἰς τὴν διθυραμβικὴν
ἀγωγὴν μεταστήσας τοὺς ῥυθμούς, καὶ τῇ τῶν
αὐλῶν πολυφωνίᾳ κατακολουθήσας, πλείοσί[6] τε
φθόγγοις καὶ διερριμμένοις[7] χρησάμενος, εἰς μετά-
θεσιν τὴν προϋπάρχουσαν ἤγαγεν μουσικήν.[8]

30. " Ὁμοίως δὲ καὶ Μελανιππίδης ὁ μελοποιὸς
ἐπιγενόμενος οὐκ ἐνέμεινεν[9] τῇ προϋπαρχούσῃ μουσικῇ, ἀλλ᾽ οὐδὲ Φιλόξενος οὐδὲ[10] Τιμόθεος· οὗτος
γάρ, ἑπταφθόγγου τῆς λύρας ὑπαρχούσης ἕως εἰς
Τέρπανδρον[11] τὸν Ἀντισσαῖον, διέρριψεν εἰς πλείονας
φθόγγους. ἀλλὰ γὰρ καὶ αὐλητικὴ ἀπὸ[12] ἁπλου-

1 δὲ τὸν a[2] W a vq : δὲ τὸν δὲ τὸν M V a[1] (the second δε
unaccented) ; τὸν N.
2 προσοδιακόν] προσοδικῶν W[1] (-ὸν W[2]).
3 Ἄρεως] ἄρεος aN.
4 δηλοῖ Wyttenbach : δῆλον.
5 Λᾶσος Volkmann : λάσος.
6 πλείοσί] πλείοσί V[r].
7 διερριμμένοις a[2] aN vq : -ιμέ- M V a[1] W.
8 τὴν πρ. ἤγαγε (-εν M) μ.] τὴν μ. πρ. ἤγαγεν aN[2] ; τῆς μουσικῆς πρ. ἤγαγεν N[1].
9 ἐνέμεινε (-εν W)] ἐνέμεινεν ἐν M.
10 οὐδὲ D v[2] Ald.[2] : ὁ δὲ.
11 Τέρπανδρον] Ἀριστοκλείδην Τερπάνδρειον Westphal.
12 ἀπὸ] v omits.
418

called Hypolydian, and it is said that he greatly increased the *eclysis* and the *ecbolê*.[a] Again, the great Olympus himself, who is credited with having initiated Greek and nomic music, is said to have invented the enharmonic genus and among rhythms the prosodiac [b] (in which the nome of Ares is composed) and the choree,[c] which he largely employed in his compositions in honour of the Great Mother; some think that Olympus also invented the bacchius.[d] The various pieces of ancient music all show the truth of this.

" Lasus of Hermionê,[e] by altering the rhythms to the tempo of the dithyramb, and by taking the extensive range [f] of the auloi as his guide and thus using a greater number of scattered notes,[g] transformed the music that had heretofore prevailed.

30. " Similarly Melanippides [h] the composer, who flourished later, did not stick to the traditional music, nor yet Philoxenus or Timotheüs; for Timotheüs broke up the seven notes which the lyre had had as far back as the time of Terpander of Antissa,[i] increasing their number. Indeed aulos-playing as well

---

[a] *Cf.* Aristides Quintilianus, *De Mus.* i. 10 (p. 28, ed. Meibom; p. 28. 4-6, ed. Winnington-Ingram): "The lowering of pitch by three non-composite dieses [that is, quarter tones] was called *eclysis*, the raising of the pitch by the same interval was called *spondeiasmos*, and the raising of the pitch by five dieses *ecbolê*." *Cf.* also Bacchius, *Isagogê*, 37, 41-42.

[b] See the note on 1141 A, *supra*.

[c] Different authors apply the name to – ◡ and ◡ ◡ ◡ .

[d] Different authors apply the name to – – ◡, ◡ – – , – ◡ ◡ –, ◡ – – ◡, and ◡ ◡ – –.

[e] Frag. A 10 (ed. del Grande).

[f] *Cf.* Plato, *Republic*, iii, 399 D 3-5.

[g] No doubt the notes filled the gaps in the old scales.

[h] Frag. A 4 (ed. del Grande).

[i] Frag. 5 (Bergk, *Poet. Lyr. Gr.*⁴ iii, p. 11).

(1141) στέρας εἰς ποικιλωτέραν μεταβέβηκεν μουσικήν· τὸ
γὰρ παλαιόν, ἕως εἰς Μελανιππίδην τὸν τῶν διθυράμβων ποιητήν, συμβεβήκει τοὺς αὐλητὰς παρὰ
D τῶν ποιητῶν λαμβάνειν τοὺς μισθούς, πρωταγωνι-
στούσης δηλονότι τῆς ποιήσεως, τῶν δ' αὐλητῶν
ὑπηρετούντων[1] τοῖς διδασκάλοις· ὕστερον δὲ καὶ
τοῦτο διεφθάρη, ὡς καὶ Φερεκράτη[2] τὸν κωμικὸν
εἰσαγαγεῖν τὴν Μουσικὴν[3] ἐν γυναικείῳ σχήματι
ὅλην κατῃκισμένην τὸ σῶμα· ποιεῖ δὲ τὴν Δικαιοσύνην διαπυνθανομένην τὴν αἰτίαν τῆς λώβης καὶ
τὴν Ποίησιν λέγουσαν

> Λέξω μὲν[4] οὐκ ἄκουσα· σοί τε γὰρ κλύειν
> ἐμοί τε λέξαι μῦθος[5] ἡδονὴν ἔχει.
> ἐμοὶ γὰρ ἦρξε τῶν κακῶν Μελανιππίδης,
> E ἐν τοῖσι πρῶτος[6] ὃς λαβὼν ἀνῆκέ με
> χαλαρωτέραν[7] τ'[8] ἐποίησε χορδαῖς δώδεκα.
> ἀλλ' οὖν ὅμως οὗτος μὲν ἦν ἀποχρῶν ἀνὴρ
> ἔμοιγε πρὸς τὰ νῦν κακά.[9]
> Κινησίας δέ μ'[10] ὁ κατάρατος Ἀττικὸς
> ἐξαρμονίους καμπὰς ποιῶν[11] ἐν ταῖς στροφαῖς[12]

---

[1] ὑπηρετούντων] ὑπηρέτουν τῶν M ; ὑπηρετόντων vq[1?ac?].
[2] Φερεκράτη] -ην N vq.
[3] τὴν Μουσικὴν] τὸν μουσικὸν M[ac].
[4] λέξω μὲν (λέξωμεν N)] λέγω μὲν V.
[5] μῦθος Weil and Reinach (μῦθον Kock) : θυμός.
[6] πρῶτος Meineke : πρώτοις.
[7] χαλαρωτέραν (and so V[2])] χαλαιωτέραν M V[c] (from σχ-).
[8] τ'] N vq omit.
[9] Bothe supplies πρὶν ἔνδεκ' οὐσῶν before ἀλλ', omitting
οὖν ; Kock suggests εἰς τὴν τέχνην before ἔμοιγε, but prints a
lacuna instead ; Düring supposes a lost remark by Justice
after κακά.
[10] μ' added by Meineke.

passed from simpler to more complex music. For formerly, up to the time of the dithyrambic poet Melanippides, it had been the custom for the auletes to receive their pay from the poets, <u>the words</u> evidently playing the major role, and the auletes subordinating themselves to <u>the authors</u> of them ; but later this practice also was lost. Thus Pherecrates the comic poet introduces Music in the guise of a woman whose whole person has been brutally mauled; and he lets Justice ask how she came to suffer such an outrage. Poetry replies [a] :

> Then gladly will I speak ; you in the hearing
> Will find your pleasure, in the telling I.
> My woes began with Melanippides.
> He was the first who took and lowered me,
> Making me looser with his dozen strings.
> Yet after all I found him passable
> Compared with what I suffer now.
> But the Athenian, curst Cinesias,
> Producing off-key shifts [b] in every movement [c]

[a] From the *Cheiron* of Pherecrates : Frag. 145 (Kock, *Comicorum Atticorum Fragmenta*, vol. i, p. 188 ; Edmonds, *Fragments of Attic Comedy*, vol. i, p. 262). Perhaps the author introduced this comic fragment and the next to lend to his " symposium " the element of playfulness and comedy that the literary symposium was supposed to join with seriousness : *cf.* Josef Martin, *Symposion. Die Geschichte einer literarischen Form* (Paderborn, 1931), pp. 2-18.
For the interpretation of the fragment see I. Düring, " Studies in Musical Terminology in 5th-Century Literature," *Eranos*, vol. xliii (1945), pp. 176-197.

[b] I. Düring interprets *kampê* (literally a " bend," here rendered " shift ") as a modulation.

[c] *Strophai* (literally " turns " or " twists," here rendered " movement ") has presumably also a musical sense, perhaps that of " stanzas."

---

[11] ποιῶν Vt a² aN vq : ποιως M a¹ ? W ; ποιῶς V¹⁸⁸.
[12] στροφαῖς a² aN q : τροφαῖς.

(1141)
F

ἀπολώλεχ᾽[1] οὕτως ὥστε τῆς ποιήσεως
τῶν διθυράμβων καθάπερ ἐν ταῖς ἀσπίσιν
ἀριστέρ᾽ αὐτοῦ φαίνεται τὰ δεξιά.
ἀλλ᾽ οὖν[2] ἀνεκτὸς[3] οὗτος ἦν ὅμως ἐμοί.[4]
Φρῦνις[5] δ᾽ ἴδιον στρόβιλον ἐμβαλών τινα
κάμπτων με καὶ στρέφων ὅλην διέφθορεν,
ἐν πενταχόρδοις[6] δώδεχ᾽ ἁρμονίας ἔχων.
ἀλλ᾽ οὖν ἔμοιγε χοῦτος ἦν ἀποχρῶν ἀνήρ·
εἰ[7] γάρ τι[8] κἀξήμαρτεν αὖθις[9] ἀνέλαβεν.
ὁ δὲ Τιμόθεός μ᾽,[10] ὦ φιλτάτη, κατορώρυχεν
καὶ διακέκναικ᾽[11] αἴσχιστα.[12]—Ποῖος οὑτοσὶ
ὁ[13] Τιμόθεος;—Μιλήσιός τις πυρρίας.

1142

κακά μοι παρέσχεν οἷς[14] ἅπαντας[15] οὓς λέγω
παρελήλυθ᾽[16] ἐπάγων[17] ἐκτραπέλους[18] μυρμηκιάς.[19]
κἂν ἐντύχῃ πού μοι[20] βαδιζούσῃ μόνῃ
ἀπέλυσε κἀνέλυσε[21] χορδαῖς[22] δώδεκα.

---

[1] ἀπολώλεχ᾽ Meineke : ἀπολώλεκέ με.
[2] οὖν Wyttenbach : οὐκ.
[3] ἀνεκτὸς Emperius : ἂν εἴποις.
[4] ὅμως ἐμοί Wyttenbach : ὅμως ὅμως (ὅμως v).
[5] Φρῦνις Runkel : φρύνις.
[6] πενταχόρδοις vq : πενταχόρδαις (no accent in V aN) M a¹A¹ W ; πέντε χορδαῖς a²A²E.
[7] εἰ β : ἦν M V W] ἦν a aN vq.
[8] τι] τις M.
[9] αὖθις a²AE s : αὖτις (αὖτις U¹ᵃᶜ?).
[10] μ᾽ s : με.
[11] διακέκναικ᾽ v (no accent) q : διακέκναιχ᾽.
[12] αἴσχιστα (αι- W)] αἴσχισται Vᶜ aᵃʳ.
[13] ὁ added by Meineke.
[14] οἷς Wilamowitz : οὗτος (Lloyd-Jones would place οὗτος before κακά, reading παρέσχ(ε)).
[15] ἅπαντας] πάντας Jacobs.

Has so undone me that his dithyrambs
Like objects mirrored in a polished shield
Show his dexterity to be left-handed.
Yet still and all I could put up with him.
But Phrynis had a screwbolt all his own [a]
And bent and twisted me to my perdition ;
His pentachords would play a dozen keys. [b]
Yet him too in the end I could accept,
For he recovered later when he slipped.
But Oh ! my dear, Timotheüs is murder,
Mayhem and outrage !—And who is the man ?
—A redhead [c] from Miletus. He's been worse
Than all the other fellows put together ;
His notes crawl up and down the scale like ants, [d]
And when he finds me on a walk alone [e]
He tears [f] and breaks [g] me with his dozen strings.

[a] Literally a " pine-cone." Düring suggests that it was a mechanical device for raising or lowering the pitch.

[b] Instead of the trichords of Olympus or the tetrachords of Aristoxenus we here have pentachords, that is, five notes in the range of a musical fourth.

[c] Pyrrhias (redhead) was a slave's name. Cf. also [Aristotle,] Physiognomonica 6 (812 a 16) : " Redheads are great rascals ; this is explained by reference to the fox."

[d] Cf. Aristophanes, Thesmophoriazusae, 100, where Agathon is said to be humming " ant's paths." Perhaps when the great gaps in the earlier scales were broken down the movement from one note to the next was felt to be so slight as to resemble the crawling of an ant.

[e] That is, not accompanied by words or the dance.

[f] Cf. apolelumena (" set free ") in Aristides Quintilianus (De Musica, i. 29) of metres lacking responsion.

[g] Aneluse " broke up " is perhaps to break up larger intervals into smaller ones.

---

[16] παρελήλυθ' δ² (-θεν s): παρελήλυθε (-εν M V W) παρελήλυθ'.

[17] ἐπάγων Lloyd-Jones (ἐσάγων Weil and Reinach): ἄγων.

[18] ἐκτραπέλους (and so q¹⁸⁸)] εὐ- qᵗ.

[19] μυρμηκιάς Meineke : -ίας.

[20] μοι] μὴ vq.

[21] ἀπέλυσε κἀνέλυσε] ἀπέδυσε κἀνέδυσε Wyttenbach.

[22] χορδαῖς] χορδάς J and Wyttenbach.

(1142) καὶ Ἀριστοφάνης ὁ κωμικὸς μνημονεύει Φιλοξένου
καί φησιν ὅτι εἰς τοὺς κυκλίους χοροὺς τοιαῦτα[1]
μέλη εἰσηνέγκατο. ἡ δὲ Μουσικὴ λέγει ταῦτα·

> ἐξαρμονίους ὑπερβολαίους τε ἀνοσίους
> καὶ νιγλάρους, ὥσπερ τε τὰς ῥαφάνους ὅλην
> καμπῶν[2] με κατεμέστωσε.

καὶ ἄλλοι δὲ κωμῳδοποιοὶ ἔδειξαν τὴν ἀτοπίαν τῶν
B μετὰ ταῦτα τὴν μουσικὴν κατακεκερματικότων.

31. "Ὅτι δὲ παρὰ τὰς ἀγωγὰς καὶ τὰς μαθήσεις
διόρθωσις ἢ διαστροφὴ γίνεται δῆλον Ἀριστόξενος
ἐποίησεν. τῶν γὰρ κατὰ τὴν αὑτοῦ[3] ἡλικίαν φησὶν
Τελεσίᾳ τῷ Θηβαίῳ συμβῆναι νέῳ μὲν ὄντι τρα-
φῆναι ἐν τῇ καλλίστῃ μουσικῇ καὶ μαθεῖν ἄλλα τε
τῶν εὐδοκιμούντων καὶ δὴ καὶ τὰ Πινδάρου τά τε
Διονυσίου τοῦ Θηβαίου καὶ τὰ Λάμπρου καὶ τὰ
Πρατίνου καὶ τῶν λοιπῶν ὅσοι τῶν λυρικῶν ἄνδρες
ἐγένοντο ποιηταὶ κρουμάτων ἀγαθοί· καὶ αὐλῆσαι
C δὲ καλῶς καὶ περὶ τὰ λοιπὰ μέρη τῆς συμπάσης
παιδείας ἱκανῶς διαπονηθῆναι· παραλλάξαντα δὲ
τὴν τῆς ἀκμῆς ἡλικίαν οὕτω σφόδρα ἐξαπατηθῆναι
ὑπὸ τῆς σκηνικῆς τε καὶ ποικίλης μουσικῆς[4] ὡς
καταφρονῆσαι τῶν καλῶν ἐκείνων ἐν οἷς ἀνετράφη,

---

[1] τοιαῦτα our supplement : Westphal would supply μονῳ-
δικὰ, Weil and Reinach would add προβατίων αἰγῶν τε.
[2] καμπῶν Elmsley (κάμπων PS ; s omits) : κάμπτων.
[3] αὑτοῦ Wyttenbach (ἑαυτοῦ T) : αὐτοῦ.
[4] μουσικῆς] μούσης a.

---

[a] Frag. 641 (ed. Kock). Weil and Reinach suppose that
the allusion is to *Plutus*, 293-294.
[b] Frag. A 15 (ed. del Grande).
[c] For these see A. W. Pickard-Cambridge, *Dithyramb,
Tragedy and Comedy* (Oxford, 1927), pp. 48-49.
[d] This seems to mean (if the text is sound our author is an

Further, Aristophanes [a] the comic poet mentions Philoxenus [b] and says that he introduced this kind of music into the cyclic choruses.[c] Music speaks as follows [d] :

> . . . damnable and off-key treble quavers
> Infecting me with wrigglers like a cabbage.[e]

Other comic poets as well have demonstrated the absurdity of those who since then have minced our music fine.[f]

31. " That success or failure in music depends on one's training and instruction is shown by Aristoxenus.[g] Thus he says that of his contemporaries Telesias [h] of Thebes had in youth been brought up on the finest kind of music, and had been taught among other approved compositions those of Pindar, Dionysius [i] of Thebes, Lamprus,[j] Pratinas, and those other lyric poets who had shown themselves excellent composers for the cithara ; and that he also performed well on the auloi, and had laboured to good purpose in the other branches of the musical art ; but when past his prime he had been so taken in by the elaborate music of the theatre that he lost interest in the noble works on which he had been reared, and set to

unskilful excerptor) that Music (in the fragment of Pherecrates) speaks as follows (of Philoxenus).

[e] *Kampón* are either " turns " (modulations) in music or " cabbage-worms," named from the bend they make in crawling (*cf.* " bend-worms," " loopers ").

[f] That is, they introduced smaller intervals.

[g] Frag. 76 (ed. Wehrli) ; Testimonium 26 (ed. da Rios).

[h] Otherwise unknown.

[i] Probably the celebrated musician who taught Epaminondas the playing of the cithara and singing to it (Nepos, *Epam.* 2. 1).

[j] Mentioned by Plato (*Menexenus*, 236 A).

(1142) τὰ Φιλοξένου δὲ καὶ Τιμοθέου ἐκμανθάνειν καὶ τούτων αὐτῶν τὰ ποικιλώτατα καὶ πλείστην ἐν αὐτοῖς[1] ἔχοντα καινοτομίαν· ὁρμήσαντά τε ἐπὶ τὸ ποιεῖν μέλη καὶ διαπειρώμενον ἀμφοτέρων τῶν τρόπων, τοῦ τε Πινδαρείου καὶ τοῦ[2] Φιλοξενείου, μὴ δύνασθαι κατορθοῦν ἐν τῷ Φιλοξενείῳ γένει· γεγενῆσθαι δὲ αἰτίαν τὴν ἐκ παιδὸς καλλίστην ἀγωγήν.

32. " Εἰ οὖν τις βούλεται μουσικῇ καλῶς καὶ
D κεκριμένως χρῆσθαι, τὸν ἀρχαῖον ἀπομιμείσθω τρόπον, ἀλλὰ μὴν καὶ τοῖς ἄλλοις αὐτὴν μαθήμασιν ἀναπληρούτω, καὶ φιλοσοφίαν ἐπιστησάτω παιδαγωγόν· αὕτη γὰρ ἱκανὴ κρῖναι τὸ μουσικῇ πρέπον μέτρον καὶ τὸ χρήσιμον. τριῶν γὰρ ὄντων μερῶν εἰς ἃ διῄρηται τὴν καθόλου διαίρεσιν ἡ πᾶσα μουσική, διατόνου, χρώματος, ἁρμονίας, ἐπιστήμονα χρὴ εἶναι τῆς τούτοις χρωμένης ποιήσεως τὸν μουσικῇ προσιόντα καὶ τῆς ἑρμηνείας τῆς τὰ πεποιημένα παραδιδούσης ἐπήβολον.[3]

" Πρῶτον μὲν οὖν κατανοητέον ὅτι πᾶσα μάθησις
E τῶν περὶ τὴν[4] μουσικὴν ἐθισμός[5] ἐστιν οὐδέπω προσ-

---

[1] αὐτοῖς Z Eᶜ : αὐτοῖς.
[2] τοῦ aN : the rest omit.
[3] ἐπήβολον (-πι- Vᵃᶜ)] ἐπίβολον v.
[4] τὴν] a omits.
[5] ἐθισμός] ἐθιμός M ; ἔθιμός N.

ᵃ In chapters 32-36 our author's source, Aristoxenus, makes extensive use of Plato's programme for a scientific rhetoric (*Phaedrus*, 268 ʟ 1—274 ʙ 5). The various musical disciplines correspond to Plato's necessary preliminaries (*Phaedrus*, 268

learning by heart the works of Philoxenus and Timotheüs, and even of these choosing the pieces most complex and full of innovation. Yet when he set out to compose music and tried his hand at both manners of composition, Pindar's and Philoxenus', he found himself unable to achieve success in the latter ; and the reason was his excellent training from boyhood.

32.[a] "And so if one wishes to cultivate music nobly and with discrimination, one should copy the ancient manner. But one should not stop here ; one should supplement it with the disciplines,[b] and take philosophy [c] for guide in youth, since philosophy is competent to decide the point to which the various skills can be employed so as to be appropriate to the musical art, and thus determine the whole question of their use.[d] Thus music in general has three main divisions —the diatonic, chromatic, and enharmonic genera—, and anyone entering a course of study in music should have learned the kinds of composition that employ these three and have acquired facility in interpreting the pieces so composed.

" Now first it must be understood that all the instruction given in music is a mere habituation which has not yet advanced to any insight into the reason

E 5-6, 269 A 2-3, B 7-8). The art (of music or rhetoric) combines the products of the various disciplines or the necessary preliminaries so that they are appropriate to one another and to the whole speech or composition, and aims to produce a moral character (in the case of music), or persuasion or virtue (in the case of rhetoric).

[b] *Cf.* Plato, *Phaedrus*, 268 E 6, 269 B 8.

[c] *Cf.* Plato, *Phaedrus*, 269 E 4—270 A 8.

[d] *Cf.* Plato's example of the would-be musician who can produce the highest and lowest possible notes (268 D 7-E 1) and his words " to what extent " (268 B 7-8). For " appropriate " *cf.* 268 D 5.

(1142) εἰληφὼς τὸ τίνος ἕνεκα τῶν διδασκομένων ἕκαστον
τῷ μανθάνοντι μαθητέον ἐστίν. μετὰ δὲ τοῦτο ἐν-
θυμητέον ὅτι πρὸς τὴν τοιαύτην ἀγωγήν τε καὶ
μάθησιν οὐδέπω προσάγεται τρόπων ἐξαρίθμησις·
ἀλλὰ οἱ μὲν πολλοὶ εἰκῇ μανθάνουσιν ὃ ἂν τῷ διδά-
σκοντι ἢ[1] τῷ μανθάνοντι ἀρέσῃ, οἱ δὲ συνετοὶ τὸ
εἰκῇ ἀποδοκιμάζουσιν, ὥσπερ Λακεδαιμόνιοι τὸ
παλαιὸν καὶ Μαντινεῖς καὶ Πελληνεῖς· ἕνα γάρ τινα
τρόπον ἢ παντελῶς ὀλίγους ἐκλεξάμενοι οὓς ᾤοντο
F πρὸς τὴν τῶν ἠθῶν ἐπανόρθωσιν ἁρμόττειν, ταύτῃ[2]
τῇ μουσικῇ ἐχρῶντο.

33. '' Φανερὸν δ' ἂν γένοιτο εἴ τις ἑκάστην ἐξετάζοι[3] τῶν ἐπιστημῶν τίνος ἐστὶ θεωρητική· δῆλον
γὰρ ὅτι ἡ μὲν ἁρμονικὴ γενῶν τε τῶν τοῦ ἡρμοσμένου καὶ διαστημάτων καὶ συστημάτων καὶ φθόγγων καὶ τόνων καὶ μεταβολῶν συστηματικῶν ἐστιν
γνωστική· πορρωτέρω δὲ οὐκέτι ταύτῃ προελθεῖν[4]
οἷόν τε. ὥστ' οὐδὲ ζητεῖν παρὰ ταύτης τὸ δια-
γνῶναι δύνασθαι πότερον οἰκείως εἴληφεν ὁ ποιητής,
ὅμοιον εἰπεῖν[5] ἐν Μυσοῖς,[6] τὸν Ὑποδώριον τόνον
ἐπὶ τὴν ἀρχὴν ἢ τὸν[7] Μιξολύδιόν τε καὶ Δώριον ἐπὶ
τὴν ἔκβασιν ἢ τὸν Ὑποφρύγιόν τε καὶ Φρύγιον ἐπὶ
τὸ μέσον.[8] οὐ γὰρ διατείνει ἡ ἁρμονικὴ πρω-

[1] ἢ| ἦ M. [2] ταύτῃ Weil and Reinach : αὐτῇ.
[3] ἐξετάζοι Pohlenz : ἐξετάζοιτο.
[4] προελθεῖν aN[ac] : προσελθεῖν.
[5] ὅμοιον εἰπεῖν] Cf. Aristoxenus, cited by Porphyry on
Ptolemy's *Harmonics*, p. 79. 16 (ed. Düring), Menander,
Ἐπιτρέποντες, 730, Chrysippus, Frag. 892 (*Stoicorum Vet.
Frag.* ii, p. 243. 32, ed. von Arnim), Diodorus, ii. 58, and
Diogenes Laert. vii. 105.
[6] ἐν Μυσοῖς Bergk : ἐν μούσοις (no accent a ; ἐν μουσικοῖς
vq[185] ; ἐν μούσαις q[t]).

why each detail is a necessary part of what the student must learn.[a] We must next observe that to achieve this sort of training and instruction no recourse has so far been made to the enumeration [b] of the modes. Instead the majority learn at random whatever happens to strike the fancy of master or pupil, while the discerning reject such lack of system, as did in ancient times the Lacedaemonians and the men of Mantineia and Pellenê. For these made a choice of some single mode or else a very small number of them, which in their belief tended to the formation of character, and cultivated this music and no other.

33. This will become clear if we pass in review the various disciplines and note the province of each. Thus take harmonics. It is evident that it studies the genera of movement in pitch, its intervals, its sets of tetrachords, its notes and modes and the modulations from one set of tetrachords to another ; and further than this harmonics cannot proceed. Hence we may not go on to ask it to determine whether the composer (in the *Mysians* [c] for instance) acted with propriety in taking the Hypodorian mode for the overture of the piece or the Mixolydian and Dorian for the finale or the Hypophrygian and Phrygian for the central part. For the science of harmonics does

---

[a] *Cf.* Plato, *Phaedrus*, 270 b 5-6, 270 d 9—271 c 1.
[b] *Cf.* Plato, *Phaedrus*, 270 d 6, 273 e 1.
[c] *Cf.* Aristotle, *Politics*, vii. 7 (1342 b 7-12) : " Thus the dithyramb is admittedly held to belong to the Phrygian mode. Of this the experts in the subject give many examples, among them telling how Philoxenus attempted to compose a dithyramb, the *Mysians* [Μυσοὺς Schneider; μύθους], in the Dorian mode, and was unable to do so, the very nature of the genre forcing him back into the suitable mode, the Phrygian."

---

7 τὸν] τὴν a v.   8 τὸ μέσον Volkmann : τὴν μέσην.

(1142) γματεία¹ πρὸς τὰ τοιαῦτα, προσδεῖται δὲ πολλῶν
1143 ἑτέρων· τὴν γὰρ τῆς οἰκειότητος δύναμιν ἀγνοεῖ.
οὔτε γὰρ τὸ χρωματικὸν γένος οὔτε τὸ ἐναρμόνιον
ἥξει ποτὲ ἔχον τὴν τῆς οἰκειότητος δύναμιν τελείαν²
καὶ καθ’ ἣν τὸ τοῦ πεποιημένου μέλους³ ἦθος ἐπι-
φαίνεται, ἀλλὰ τοῦτο τοῦ τεχνίτου ἔργον. φανερὸν
δὴ ὅτι ἑτέρα τοῦ συστήματος ἡ φωνὴ τῆς ἐν τῷ
συστήματι⁴ κατασκευασθείσης μελοποιίας, περὶ ἧς
οὐκ ἔστι⁵ θεωρῆσαι τῆς ἁρμονικῆς πραγματείας.

" Ὁ αὐτὸς δὲ λόγος καὶ περὶ τῶν ῥυθμῶν⁶·
οὐθεὶς⁷ γὰρ ῥυθμὸς τὴν τῆς τελείας οἰκειότητος
B δύναμιν ἥξει ἔχων ἐν αὑτῷ⁸· τὸ γὰρ οἰκείως ἀεὶ
λεγόμενον πρὸς ἦθός τι βλέποντες λέγομεν.

" Τούτου δέ φαμεν αἰτίαν εἶναι⁹ σύνθεσίν τινα ἢ
μῖξιν ἢ ἀμφότερα. οἷον Ὀλύμπῳ τὸ ἐναρμόνιον
γένος ἐπὶ Φρυγίου τόνου τεθὲν παίωνι ἐπιβατῷ
μιχθέν· τοῦτο γὰρ τῆς ἀρχῆς τὸ ἦθος ἐγέννησεν ἐπὶ
τῷ τῆς Ἀθηνᾶς νόμῳ· προσληφθείσης γὰρ μελοποιίας καὶ ῥυθμοποιίας, τεχνικῶς τε μεταληφθέν-
τος τοῦ ῥυθμοῦ μόνον αὐτοῦ καὶ γενομένου τροχαίου
ἀντὶ παίωνος, συνέστη τὸ Ὀλύμπου ἐναρμόνιον

---

¹ ἡ ἁρμονικὴ πραγματεία Burette (place after τοιαῦτα ?) :
τῇ ἁρμονικῇ πραγματείᾳ.
² τελείαν] τελείας ? (cf. τῆς τελείας οἰκειότητος infra).
³ μέλους aN : μέλος.   ⁴ συστήματι] διαστήματι V.
⁵ οὐκ ἔστι] οὐκ ἔτι M.
⁶ τῶν ῥυθμῶν] τόν ῥυθμόν M.
⁷ οὐθεὶς] οὐδεὶς V¹ᵃᵃ.
⁸ αὑτῷ s (ἑαυτῷ εΕ aN) : αὐτῷ.   ⁹ εἶναι] a omits.

ᵃ Cf. Plato, Phaedrus, 270 B 4—271 C 4, where the steps
necessary if one is to apply discourse and lawful practices to
the mind by art, and not by mere habituation, and thus
impart persuasion and virtue, are described.
ᵇ Cf. Plato, Phaedrus, 270 D 9—271 A 1.

not extend to such questions but requires many supplements, since it is blind to the significance of propriety. For neither the chromatic nor the enharmonic genus ever brings with it an understanding of the full scope of propriety, that makes clear the moral character of the music that has been composed. This instead is the function of the possessor of the art.[a] It is thus evident that the sound of a scale and that of the melody composed in it are two distinct matters, and that it is not the province of harmonics to study the latter.

" The same holds of rhythms as well. No rhythm brings with it an understanding of the meaning of propriety in its fullest sense ; for whenever we use the term ' propriety ' we always have in mind some moral character.[b]

" This moral character is produced, we assert, by some manner of combining elements or of blending them or of both.[c] Take Olympus : the enharmonic genus is put in the Phrygian key and blended with the paeon epibatos.[d] It is this that engendered the moral character of the opening of the nome of Athena; for when you add to this the conduct of the melody and the conduct of the rhythm, and when you skilfully modulate the rhythm by itself so that it changes to trochee from paeon,[e] the whole thus constituted is Olympus' enharmonic genus. Furthermore you may

[c] Perhaps " blend " refers to the union of melodic and rhythmical elements, whereas " combination " refers to the building of larger musical or rhythmical complexes from smaller.

[d] The foot – – – – – (with the thesis on the first, third, and fourth syllables).

[e] Probably to the marked trochee (thesis of eight times, arsis of four) from the paion epibatos.

(1143) γένος. ἀλλὰ μὴν καὶ τοῦ ἐναρμονίου γένους καὶ
τοῦ Φρυγίου τόνου διαμενόντων καὶ πρὸς τούτοις
τοῦ συστήματος παντός, μεγάλην ἀλλοίωσιν ἔσχη-
C κεν τὸ ἦθος· ἡ γὰρ καλουμένη ἁρμονία ἐν τῷ τῆς
Ἀθηνᾶς νόμῳ πολὺ διέστηκε κατὰ[1] τὸ ἦθος τῆς
ἀναπείρας. εἰ οὖν προσγένοιτο τῷ τῆς μουσικῆς
ἐμπείρῳ τὸ κριτικόν, δῆλον ὅτι οὗτος ἂν εἴη ὁ
ἀκριβὴς ἐν μουσικῇ· ὁ γὰρ εἰδὼς τὸ Δωριστὶ ἄνευ
τοῦ κρίνειν ἐπίστασθαι τὴν τῆς χρήσεως αὐτοῦ
οἰκειότητα οὐκ εἴσεται ὃ ποιεῖ· ἀλλ' οὐδὲ τὸ ἦθος
σώσει· ἐπεὶ καὶ περὶ αὐτῶν τῶν Δωρίων μελοποιῶν
ἀπορεῖται πότερόν ἐστιν διαγνωστικὴ ἡ ἁρμονικὴ
πραγματεία καθάπερ τινὲς οἴονται τῶν Δωρίων ἢ
οὔ.

" Ὁ αὐτὸς δὲ λόγος καὶ περὶ τῆς ῥυθμικῆς ἐπι-
D στήμης πάσης· ὁ γὰρ εἰδὼς τὸν παίωνα τὴν τῆς
χρήσεως αὐτοῦ οἰκειότητα οὐκ εἴσεται διὰ τὸ αὐτὴν
μόνην εἰδέναι τὴν τοῦ παίωνος ξύνθεσιν[2]· ἐπεὶ καὶ
περὶ αὐτῶν τῶν παιωνικῶν ῥυθμοποιῶν ἀπορεῖται
πότερόν ἐστι διαγνωστικὴ ἡ ῥυθμικὴ[3] πραγματεία
τούτων καθάπερ[4] τινές φασιν, ἢ[5] οὐ διατείνει μέχρι
τούτου.

" Ἀναγκαῖον οὖν δύο τοὐλάχιστον γνώσεις ὑπάρχειν τῷ μέλλοντι διαγνώσεσθαι τό τε οἰκεῖον καὶ τὸ
ἀλλότριον· πρῶτον μὲν τοῦ ἤθους οὗ ἕνεκα ἡ σύνθεσις γεγένηται, ἔπειτα τούτων ἐξ ὧν ἡ σύνθεσις.
ὅτι μὲν οὖν οὔθ' ἡ ἁρμονικὴ οὔθ' ἡ ῥυθμικὴ[6] οὔτε
E ἄλλη οὐδεμία τῶν καθ' ἓν μέρος λεγομένων αὐτάρ-

---

[1] κατὰ] a omits.
[2] ξύνθεσιν Wyttenbach : ξύνοισιν (ξύνεσιν V aN vq).
[3] ῥυθμικὴ] ῥυθμητικὴ M W.   [4] καθάπερ] ἢ καθάπερ aN.

keep the enharmonic genus and the Phrygian key, and the whole set of tetrachords to boot, but still find that the moral character has undergone a great alteration. Thus the so-called ' harmonia ' in the nome of Athena differs greatly in character from the introduction. It is clear then that to familiarity with music you must add the ability to judge, and only then will you have your musical expert. For one who knows the Dorian mode without the skill to pass judgement on whether it belongs here or there will not know what effect he is producing ; in fact he will not even preserve the moral character of the mode. Indeed the question is raised about compositions in the Dorian mode themselves whether the science of harmonics (as some think) can tell one piece from another or not.

" The same holds for the whole science of rhythm as well : for one who knows the paeon will not know when it is appropriately used, since all he knows is how the paeon is put together. Indeed in the case of compositions in the paeonic rhythm the question is raised whether rhythmics (as some assert) can tell them apart or whether it does not cover so much ground.

" Hence if you are to distinguish the appropriate from the inappropriate you must have knowledge of at least two things : first of the moral character at which the composition is directed, and second of the elements out of which it has been composed. These remarks, then, suffice to show that neither harmonics nor rhythmics nor any of the recognized special studies is competent unaided both to know the moral

---

⁵ ἤ vq : the rest omit.
⁶ οὔθ᾽ ἡ ῥυθμικὴ] V omits.

(1143) κης αὐτὴ καθ᾽ αὑτὴν καὶ τοῦ ἤθους εἶναι γνωστικὴ[1] καὶ τῶν ἄλλων κριτική, ἀρκέσει τὰ εἰρημένα.

34. '' Τριῶν δ᾽ ὄντων[2] γενῶν εἰς ἃ διαιρεῖται τὸ ἡρμοσμένον, ἴσων τοῖς τε τῶν συστημάτων μεγέ-θεσι καὶ ταῖς τῶν φθόγγων δυνάμεσιν, ὁμοίως δὲ καὶ ταῖς τῶν τετραχόρδων, περὶ ἑνὸς μόνου οἱ παλαιοὶ ἐπραγματεύσαντο, ἐπειδήπερ οὔτε περὶ χρώματος οὔτε περὶ διατόνου οἱ[3] πρὸ ἡμῶν ἐπεσκό-πουν, ἀλλὰ περὶ μόνου τοῦ ἐναρμονίου, καὶ αὖ τού-του[4] περὶ ἕν τι μέγεθος συστήματος, τοῦ καλου-μένου διὰ πασῶν. περὶ μὲν γὰρ[5] τῆς χρόας διεφέ-ροντο, περὶ δὲ τοῦ μίαν εἶναι μόνην[6] αὐτὴν τὴν
F ἁρμονίαν σχεδὸν πάντες συνεφώνουν. οὐκ ἂν οὖν ποτε συνίδοι τὰ περὶ τὴν ἁρμονικὴν πραγματείαν ὁ μέχρι αὐτῆς τῆς γνώσεως ταύτης προεληλυθώς,[7] ἀλλὰ δηλονότι[8] ὁ[9] παρακολουθῶν ταῖς τε κατὰ μέρος ἐπιστήμαις καὶ τῷ συνόλῳ σώματι τῆς μου-σικῆς καὶ ταῖς τῶν μερῶν μίξεσί τε καὶ συνθέσεσιν. ὁ γὰρ μόνον ἁρμονικὸς περιγέγραπται τρόπῳ τινί.

'' Καθόλου μὲν οὖν εἰπεῖν ὁμοδρομεῖν δεῖ τήν τε αἴσθησιν καὶ τὴν διάνοιαν ἐν τῇ κρίσει τῶν τῆς

---

[1] καὶ τοῦ ἤθους εἶναι γνωστικὴ nos : τοῦ ἤθους εἶναι καὶ γνω-στικὴ.   [2] ὄντων] ὄντων τῶν M.   [3] οἱ] M omits.
[4] αὖ τούτου V a W^c vq : αὐτοῦ τοῦ M (αὐτοῦ τοῦ W^{ac}) ; αὐ-τοῦ τούτου aN.   [5] γὰρ] a omits.
[6] μόνην] a omits.   [7] προεληλυθώς] προσεληλυθὼς M.
[8] δηλονότι M aN (δηλονότι W ; δῆλον ὅτι V a) : δῆλον ὡς vq.
[9] ὁ added by Weil and Reinach.

---

[a] In all three genera the notes have the same names and the same sequence, though the two internal notes of the tetrachord (the '' moveable '' notes) would hardly to our feeling have the same values.
[b] In all three genera the tetrachords have the same names and the same sequence.

character and to pass judgement on the other elements that enter into the composition.

34. " Of the three genera into which musical movement is divided, all of them equal in range and in the value of their notes,[a] as well as of their tetrachords,[b] the ancients studied only one, the enharmonic, our predecessors never considering either the chromatic or the diatonic,[c] and again in this they considered only the one range, that of the so-called octave.[d] For as to its shading they differed; but that ' harmony '[e] itself was but one all we may say agreed.[f] Hence no one could ever embrace the whole subject of harmonics who had advanced no farther than this knowledge; this can evidently be done only by one who can follow[g] not only the particular studies but the whole body of music and the blends and combinations of its elements, for one who knows harmonics and nothing else is in a fashion circumscribed.

" Thus, to speak in the broadest terms, the ear and the mind must keep abreast of each other when we pass judgement on the various elements in

[c] *Cf.* Aristoxenus, *Harm.* i. 2 and Proclus' comments (*On Plato's Timaeus*, iii, 192 A, vol. ii, p. 169, ed. Diehl). Perhaps Aristoxenus here is making an inference from the Greek instrumental notation, which was evidently devised for the enharmonic genus.

[d] " So-called " because octave in Greek (*dia pasôn*) is literally " through all the strings."

[e] " Harmony " can also mean " the enharmonic genus." Here it is used in both senses: all agreed that " harmony " was enharmonic and nothing else.

[f] Aristoxenus, Testim. 99 (ed. da Rios).

[g] With this discussion of " following " *cf.* ἐπακολουθεῖν in Plato, *Phaedrus*, 271 E 1 and the whole passage 271 D 7— 272 B 2. The whole notion of a laggard or over-hasty perception may have been suggested by Plato's ὀξέως at *Phaedrus* 271 E 1.

1144 μουσικῆς μερῶν, καὶ μήτε προάγειν, ὃ ποιοῦσιν αἱ
προπετεῖς τε καὶ φερόμεναι τῶν αἰσθήσεων, μήτε
ὑστερίζειν, ὃ ποιοῦσιν αἱ βραδεῖαί τε[1] καὶ δυσκίνη-
τοι. γίνεται δέ ποτε ἐπί τινων αἰσθήσεων καὶ τὸ
συγκείμενον ἐκ τοῦ συναμφοτέρου, καὶ ὑστεροῦσιν
αἱ αὐταὶ καὶ προτεροῦσιν διά τινα φυσικὴν ἀνω-
μαλίαν. περιαιρετέον οὖν τῆς μελλούσης ὁμοδρομεῖν αἰσθήσεως ταῦτα.

35. '' Ἀεὶ[2] γὰρ ἀναγκαῖον τρία ἐλάχιστα εἶναι τὰ
πίπτοντα ἅμα εἰς τὴν ἀκοήν, φθόγγον τε καὶ χρόνον
καὶ συλλαβὴν ἢ γράμμα. συμβήσεται δὲ ἐκ μὲν
τῆς[3] κατὰ τὸν φθόγγον πορείας τὸ ἡρμοσμένον
γνωρίζεσθαι, ἐκ δὲ τῆς κατὰ χρόνον τὸν ῥυθμόν, ἐκ
B δὲ τῆς κατὰ γράμμα ἢ συλλαβὴν τὸ λεγόμενον·
ὁμοῦ δὲ προβαινόντων ἅμα τὴν τῆς αἰσθήσεως ἐπι-
φορὰν ἀναγκαῖον ποιεῖσθαι. ἀλλὰ μὴν κἀκεῖνο
φανερόν, ὅτι οὐκ ἐνδέχεται, μὴ δυναμένης τῆς
αἰσθήσεως χωρίζειν ἕκαστον τῶν εἰρημένων, παρ-
ακολουθεῖν τε δύνασθαι τοῖς καθ' ἕκαστα καὶ συνορᾶν τό θ' ἁμαρτανόμενον ἐν ἑκάστῳ αὐτῶν καὶ τὸ
μή. πρῶτον οὖν περὶ συνεχείας γνωστέον. ἀναγκαῖον
γάρ ἐστιν ὑπάρχειν τῇ κριτικῇ δυνάμει συνέχειαν·
τὸ γὰρ εὖ καὶ τὸ ἐναντίως οὐκ ἐν ἀφωρισμένοις
τοῖσδέ τισι γίνεται φθόγγοις ἢ χρόνοις ἢ γράμμασιν,
ἀλλ' ἐν συνεχέσιν· ἐπειδὴ μῖξίς τίς ἐστιν τῶν[4] κατὰ
C τὴν χρῆσιν ἀσυνθέτων μερῶν. περὶ μὲν οὖν τῆς
παρακολουθήσεως τοσαῦτα.

[1] τε] vq omit.
[2] ἀεί v : αἰεί.   [3] μὲν τῆς] τῆς μὲν a.
[4] Volkmann would transpose τῶν after χρῆσιν ; Weil and
Reinach would delete it.

        [a] That is, the " mora " or rhythmical unit.
436

a musical composition ; the ear must not outstrip the mind, as happens when sensibilities are hasty and in headlong motion, nor yet lag behind, as happens when sensibilities are sluggish and inert. In some the ear even suffers from a combination of the two failings, and is both too slow and too fast, owing to some unevenness of constitution. All this must be eliminated if the ear is to keep step with the mind.

35. " For three smallest components must always simultaneously strike the ear : the note, the time,[a] and the syllable or sound.[b] From the course of the notes we recognize the structure of the scale ; from that of the times, the rhythm ; and from that of the sounds or syllables, the words of the song. As the three proceed in concert we must follow all with the ear simultaneously. Yet it is also evident that unless the ear can isolate [c] each of the three, it is impossible to follow the details of the three movements and observe the beauties and faults in each. Before we can do this we must know about continuity. Indeed, continuity is required for the exercise of critical judgement, since beauty and the opposite do not arise in this or that isolated note or time or speech-sound, but in the series, as they are a blend of the smallest elements in an actual composition. So much for the subject of following.

[b] Literally " letter." The grammarians used the word not only of the letters of the alphabet but of the sounds represented by them. The word *syllabē* (syllable) is literally " a taking together " ; it therefore could not properly be used of such a syllable as the *a-* in *a-ri-ston*, which contains a single sound. To include such a syllable (in our sense of the word) the author adds " or sound."

[c] That is, isolate the note from the continuum of notes, the time from that of times, and the syllable from that of syllables.

(1144) 36. " Τὸ δὲ μετὰ τοῦτο ἐπισκεπτέον ὅτι οἱ μου
σικῆς ἐπιστήμονες πρὸς τὴν κριτικὴν πραγματείαν
οὐκ εἰσὶν αὐτάρκεις. οὐ γὰρ οἷόν τε τέλεον γενέ
σθαι μουσικόν τε καὶ κριτικὸν ἐξ αὐτῶν τῶν δο
κούντων εἶναι μερῶν τῆς ὅλης μουσικῆς οἷον ἔκ τε
τῆς τῶν ὀργάνων ἐμπειρίας καὶ τῆς περὶ τὴν ᾠδήν,
ἔτι δὲ τῆς περὶ τὴν αἴσθησιν συγγυμνασίας (λέγω
δὲ τῆς συντεινούσης εἰς τὴν τοῦ ἡρμοσμένου ξύνεσιν
καὶ ἔτι τὴν¹ τοῦ ῥυθμοῦ)· πρὸς δὲ τούτοις ἔκ τε τῆς
ῥυθμικῆς καὶ τῆς ἁρμονικῆς πραγματείας καὶ τῆς
D περὶ τὴν κροῦσίν τε καὶ λέξιν θεωρίας, καὶ εἴ τινες
ἄλλαι τυγχάνουσιν λοιπαὶ οὖσαι.

" Δι' ἃς δ' αἰτίας οὐχ οἷόν τ' ἐξ αὐτῶν τούτων
γενέσθαι κριτικὸν πειρατέον καταμαθεῖν. πρῶτον
ἐκ τοῦ ἡμῖν ὑποκεῖσθαι τὰ μὲν τῶν κρινομένων
τέλεια, τὰ δ' ἀτελῆ· τέλεια μὲν αὐτό τε τῶν ποιη
μάτων ἕκαστον, οἷον τὸ ᾀδόμενον ἢ αὐλούμενον ἢ
κιθαριζόμενον καὶ ἡ² ἑκάστου αὐτῶν³ ἑρμηνεία,
οἷον ἥ τε αὔλησις καὶ ἡ ᾠδὴ καὶ τὰ λοιπὰ τῶν
τοιούτων· ἀτελῆ δὲ τὰ πρὸς ταῦτα συντείνοντα καὶ
τὰ τούτων ἕνεκα γινόμενα· τοιαῦτα δὲ τὰ μέρη τῆς
E ἑρμηνείας. δεύτερον ἐκ τῆς ποιήσεως· ὡσαύτως
γὰρ καὶ αὐτὴ⁴ ὑπόκειται.

" Κρίνειε⁵ γὰρ ἄν τις ἀκούων αὐλητοῦ πότερόν
ποτε συμφωνοῦσιν οἱ αὐλοὶ ἢ οὔ, καὶ πότερον ἡ

¹ τὴν] vq omit.
² καὶ ἡ Westphal : ἢ ἡ (ἢ N v).
³ αὐτῶν Volkmann : αὐτοῦ.
⁴ αὐτή W a : αὐτη M ; αὕτη V N ; αὐτὴ a.
⁵ ὑπόκειται. κρίνειε Lasserre (ὑπόκειται. οὐ μόνον κρίνειε
Weil and Reinach) : ὑποκρίνειε M V a ; between ὑπο and
κρίνειε W aN have a blank (of 6 letters in W a, of 4 in N).

ᵃ That is, music as understood in Aristoxenus' day.

438

36. " We must next observe that experts in music [a] are not thereby equipped with all that is needed for the exercise of critical judgement. For it is impossible to become a thoroughly rounded musician and critic merely from knowing the various branches that are taken to constitute the whole of music, for example from facility in the use of musical instruments and facility in singing, and again from the training of the ear (I mean the training that aims at the recognition of notes and again of rhythm), nor yet in addition to these from the disciplines of rhythmics and harmonics and the theory of accompaniment and verbal expression, and from any other studies there may be.

" The reasons that make it impossible to be a good critic from possessing these alone we must endeavour to see clearly. In the first place there is a distinction in the matters on which we pass judgement : some are ends in themselves, some not. Such an end are (1) each separate piece of music taken by itself, as the piece sung or played on the auloi or on the cithara, and (2) the performance by the artists of each such piece, as playing it on the auloi, singing it, and the rest. Not ends in themselves are the matters that contribute to these ends and that are brought in only to serve them. Examples are the various particulars of the interpreter's art. In the second place there is composition of the piece ; for the same distinction also applies here.

" Thus if you hear an aulete you can pass judgement whether the two auloi are concordant or not, and whether the discourse [b] of the instrument is dis-

[b] So literally. The word, evidently technical, occurs at 1138 B, *supra*, and in Aristotle, *De Anima*, ii. 8 (420 b 8).

(1144) διάλεκτος σαφὴς ἢ τοὐναντίον· τούτων δ' ἕκαστον
μέρος ἐστὶ τῆς αὐλητικῆς ἑρμηνείας,[1] οὐ μέντοι
τέλος, ἀλλ' ἕνεκα τοῦ τέλους γινόμενον· παρὰ ταῦτα
γὰρ αὖ καὶ τὰ τοιαῦτα πάντα κριθήσεται τὸ τῆς
ἑρμηνείας ἦθος, εἰ[2] οἰκεῖον ἀποδίδοται τῷ παραδοθέντι[3] ποιήματι, ὃ μεταχειρίσασθαι καὶ ἑρμηνεῦσαι
ὁ ἐνεργῶν βεβούληται.[4] ὁ αὐτὸς δὲ λόγος καὶ ἐπὶ
τῶν παθῶν τῶν ὑπὸ τῆς ποιητικῆς σημαινομένων
ἐν τοῖς ποιήμασιν.

F   37. "Ἅτε οὖν ἠθῶν μάλιστα φροντίδα πεποιη-
μένοι οἱ παλαιοὶ τὸ σεμνὸν καὶ ἀπερίεργον τῆς
ἀρχαίας μουσικῆς προετίμων. Ἀργείους μὲν γὰρ
καὶ κόλασιν ἐπιθεῖναί ποτέ φασι τῇ εἰς τὴν μουσικὴν παρανομίᾳ,[5] ζημιῶσαί τε τὸν ἐπιχειρήσαντα[6]
πρῶτον τοῖς[7] πλείοσιν τῶν ἑπτὰ χρήσασθαι παρ'
αὐτοῖς χορδῶν καὶ παραμιξολυδιάζειν ἐπιχειρήσαντα.

"Πυθαγόρας δ' ὁ σεμνὸς ἀπεδοκίμαζεν τὴν κρίσιν τῆς μουσικῆς τὴν διὰ τῆς αἰσθήσεως· νῷ γὰρ
ληπτὴν τὴν ταύτης ἀρετὴν ἔφασκεν εἶναι. τοιγάρτοι τῇ μὲν ἀκοῇ οὐκ ἔκρινεν αὐτήν, τῇ δὲ ἀναλογικῇ
1145 ἁρμονίᾳ· αὔταρκές τ' ἐνόμιζεν μέχρι τοῦ διὰ πασῶν
στῆσαι τὴν τῆς μουσικῆς ἐπίγνωσιν.

38. "Οἱ δὲ νῦν τὸ μὲν κάλλιστον τῶν γενῶν,

----

[1] δεύτερον through ἑρμηνείας] vq omit.   [2] εἰ] ἢ M^ac.
[3] παραδοθέντι aN : παραποδοθέντι M V nq ; παραποιηθέντι a;
παραποθέντι W.
[4] βεβούληται] βούλεται v¹ (βούληται v²).
[5] παρανομίᾳ] παρανομίαν M N.

tinct or the reverse. Each of these matters forms
a part of the art of performing on the auloi. Yet
neither is an end, but only a means to encompass the
end. For above and beyond all this and everything
else of this sort judgement will be passed on the moral
character of the interpretation—whether the performer has given the traditional piece he has chosen
to execute and interpret the moral character that
belongs to it. The same holds of the feelings indicated in the various pieces by the art of the composer.[a]

37. " Thus the men of old, whose chief concern was
with character, preferred the majesty and directness
that we find in ancient music. Indeed the Argives
are said on one occasion to have imposed a penalty on
the violation of musical style, fining the performer
who first tried in their city to use more than the seven
traditional strings and modulate to the Mixolydian
mode.[b]

" The grave Pythagoras rejected the judging of
music by the sense of hearing, asserting that its excellence must be apprehended by the mind. This is why
he did not judge it by the ear, but by the scale based
on the proportions, and considered it sufficient to
pursue the study no further than the octave.

38. " Our contemporaries however have entirely

[a] Cf. Plato, Phaedrus, 268 c 5–d 5, 269 a 2.
[b] Weil and Reinach take the word παραμιξολυδιάζειν
(which occurs nowhere else) to mean depart from the Mixolydian scale. It would appear easier to suppose that the
Argives (or Spartans, of whom the same story is told elsewhere) were attached to the Dorian mode, and refused to
allow departure from it in the course of performing the same
piece.

---

[6] ἐπιχειρήσαντα] Volkmann would delete.
[7] τοῖς] ταῖς Volkmann ; Weil and Reinach would delete.

(1145) ὅπερ μάλιστα διὰ σεμνότητα παρὰ τοῖς ἀρχαίοις
ἐσπουδάζετο, παντελῶς παρῃτήσαντο, ὥστε μηδὲ
τὴν τυχοῦσαν ἀντίληψιν τῶν ἐναρμονίων διαστημάτων τοῖς πολλοῖς ὑπάρχειν. οὕτως δὲ ἀργῶς διά-
κεινται καὶ ῥαθύμως ὥστε μηδ' ἔμφασιν νομίζειν
παρέχειν καθόλου τῶν ὑπὸ τὴν αἴσθησιν πιπτόν-
των τὴν ἐναρμόνιον δίεσιν, ἐξορίζειν δ' αὐτὴν ἐκ
τῶν μελῳδημάτων, πεφλυαρηκέναι τε λέγειν[1] τοὺς
δοξάζοντάς[2] τι περὶ τούτου καὶ τῷ γένει τούτῳ
B κεχρημένους. ἀπόδειξιν δ' ἰσχυροτάτην τοῦ τἀληθῆ
λέγειν φέρειν οἴονται μάλιστα μὲν τὴν αὐτῶν[3]
ἀναισθησίαν, ὡς πᾶν ὅ τι περ ἂν αὐτοὺς ἐκφύγῃ
τοῦτο καὶ δὴ πάντως ἀνύπαρκτον ὂν παντελῶς καὶ
ἄχρηστον· εἶτα καὶ τὸ μὴ δύνασθαι ληφθῆναι διὰ
συμφωνίας τὸ μέγεθος, καθάπερ τό τε ἡμιτόνιον
καὶ τὸν τόνον καὶ τὰ λοιπὰ δὲ τῶν τοιούτων διαστημάτων. ἠγνοήκασιν δ' ὅτι καὶ τὸ[4] τρίτον μέγεθος οὕτως ἂν καὶ τὸ πέμπτον ἐκβάλλοιτο[5] καὶ τὸ
ἕβδομον· ὧν τὸ μὲν τριῶν, τὸ δὲ πέντε, τὸ δὲ ἑπτὰ
διέσεών ἐστι· καὶ καθόλου πάνθ' ὅσα περιττὰ φαί-
C νεται[6] τῶν διαστημάτων ἀποδοκιμάζοιτ' ἂν ὡς
ἄχρηστα παρόσον οὐδὲν αὐτῶν διὰ συμφωνίας
λαβεῖν ἐστιν· ταῦτα δ' ἂν εἴη ὅσα ὑπὸ τῆς ἐλαχίστης
διέσεως μετρεῖται περισσάκις. οἷς ἀκολουθεῖν ἀνάγκη καὶ τὸ μηδεμίαν τῶν τετραχορδικῶν διαιρέσεων
χρησίμην εἶναι πλὴν μόνον[7] ταύτην δι' ἧς πᾶσιν
ἀρτίοις χρῆσθαι διαστήμασι συμβέβηκεν· αὕτη δ'

---

[1] τε λέγειν Weil and Reinach : δὲ vq ; τε.
[2] δοξάζοντάς W : δόξαντάς (δοξάσαντάς Bern., διδάξαντάς
Ziegler).
[3] αὐτῶν Z a^c s : αὑτῶν.　　　　[4] τὸ] vq omit.
[5] ἐκβάλλοιτο (and so V^188)] ἐκβάλοιτο V^1t.
[6] περιττὰ φαίνεται] φαίνεται περιττὰ M.

abandoned the noblest of the genera, which owing to its majesty was preferred by the ancients; and in consequence the great majority have not the most ordinary apprehension of enharmonic intervals. So lazy and supine are they that they conceive that of matters decided by the ear the enharmonic diesis [a] is quite imperceptible, and banish it from singing; and say that all who hold any views on the point or who have employed this genus have done something meaningless. They think the strongest demonstration of the truth of their view is in the first place their own dullness of ear, as if everything that escaped them must surely be entirely non-existent and incapable of employment; and next the fact that the interval cannot be obtained by means of concords, as we can obtain the semitone, the tone, and the other intervals of this kind.[b] They are unaware that the third, fifth, and seventh magnitudes [c] would also be rejected on these terms, the first containing three dieses, the next five, and the last seven; and in general all intervals that turned out to be odd would be rejected as incapable of being used, since none of them can be obtained by means of concords. This would amount to all intervals that are odd multiples of the smallest diesis. A consequence is that no division of the tetrachord can be used except one in which the intervals are all even multiples of the die-

---

[a] A quarter tone.
[b] A tone can be obtained by subtracting a fourth from a fifth, a semitone by subtracting two tones from a fourth.
[c] The first magnitude would be the smallest interval, the diesis of a quarter tone; the next would be two such dieses or a semitone; and so on.

---

[7] μόνον] μόνην a² s.

(1145) ἂν εἴη ἥ τε τοῦ συντόνου¹ διατόνου καὶ ἡ τοῦ τονιαίου χρώματος.

39. '' Τὸ δὲ τὰ τοιαῦτα λέγειν τε καὶ ὑπολαμβάνειν οὐ μόνον τοῖς φαινομένοις ἐναντιουμένων ἐστὶν ἀλλὰ καὶ αὐτοῖς² μαχομένων. χρώμενοι γὰρ αὐτοὶ τοιαύταις τετραχόρδων μάλιστα φαίνονται

D διαιρέσεσιν ἐν αἷς τὰ πολλὰ τῶν διαστημάτων ἤτοι περιττά ἐστιν ἢ ἄλογα³· μαλάττουσι γὰρ ἀεὶ⁴ τάς τε λιχανοὺς καὶ τὰς παρανήτας. ἤδη δὲ καὶ τῶν ἑστώτων τινὰς παρανιᾶσι φθόγγων, ἀλόγῳ τινὶ διαστήματι προσανιέντες αὐτοῖς τάς τε τρίτας καὶ τὰς παρανήτας, καὶ τὴν τοιαύτην εὐδοκιμεῖν μάλιστά πως οἴονται τῶν συστημάτων χρῆσιν ἐν ᾗ τὰ πολλὰ τῶν διαστημάτων ἐστὶν ἄλογα, οὐ μόνον⁵ τῶν κινεῖσθαι πεφυκότων φθόγγων, ἀλλὰ καί τινων ἀκινήτων ἀνιεμένων, ὡς ἔστι δῆλον τοῖς αἰσθάνεσθαι τῶν τοιούτων δυναμένοις.

40. '' Χρῆσιν δὲ μουσικῆς⁶ προσήκουσαν ἀνδρὶ ὁ

E καλὸς⁷ Ὅμηρος ἐδίδαξεν. δηλῶν⁸ γὰρ ὅτι ἡ μουσικὴ πολλαχοῦ χρησίμη τὸν Ἀχιλλέα πεποίηκε τὴν ὀργὴν πέττοντα τὴν πρὸς τὸν Ἀγαμέμνονα διὰ μουσικῆς ἧς⁹ ἔμαθεν παρὰ τοῦ σοφωτάτου Χείρωνος·

¹ καὶ omitted after συντόνου by Burette.
² αὐτοῖς εΕ s (ἑαυτοῖς aN) : αὐτοῖς.
³ ἄλογα Meziriacus : ἀνάλογα.
⁴ ἀεὶ νq : αἰεί.   ⁵ μόνον] μόνων V aᵇ˙ᶜ ?
⁶ μουσικῆς] νq omit.

⁷ ἀνδρὶ ὁ καλὸς] ἀνδριοκαλο M.
            ωσ
⁸ δηλῶν] δῆλον M.   ⁹ ἧς] ἦν νq.

ᵃ Semitone, tone, tone. *Cf.* Aristoxenus, *Harm.* ii. 51 (ed. Meibom ; p. 64. 11-13 [ed. da Rios]).

sis ; and the only such tetrachords are that of the sharp diatonic genus [a] and that of the tonic chromatic genus.[b]

39. " To express and entertain such views is not only to fly in the face of the facts but to be inconsistent with oneself. For these people are themselves observed to make the greatest use of the sort of division of the tetrachord where most of the intervals are either odd multiples of the diesis or else irrational, for they always flatten the lichanoi and the paranetai.[c] They have even gone so far as to flatten some of the stable notes,[d] at the same time flattening along with them by an irrational interval the tritai [e] and paranetai as well, and they fancy that the treatment of the set of tetrachords is somehow the most creditable in which the greater number of intervals are irrational, not only the moveable notes but even some of the stable ones being flattened, as is evident to all who have an ear for such matters.

40. " The employment of music that is fitting for a man may be learned from our noble Homer. To show that music is useful in many circumstances he gives us Achilles in the poem digesting his anger against Agamemnon by means of music, which he learned from the most wise Cheiron :

[b] Semitone, semitone, tone and a half. *Cf.* Aristoxenus, *Harm.* ii. 51 (ed. Meibom ; p. 63. 14-16 [ed. da Rios]).

[c] The lichanos and paranetê are the second highest notes in the tetrachords where they occur. The lichanos is the next highest note of the middle tetrachord (E-a) and of the lowest tetrachord (B-E) ; the paranetê of the rest (disjunct b-e, conjunct a-d, and excess e-a').

[d] The stable notes bound the tetrachord, which covers the interval of a fourth.

[e] The tritê is the next lowest note of the disjunct, conjunct, and excess tetrachords.

(1145) τὸν δ' εὗρον (φησίν) φρένα τερπόμενον φόρμιγγι
λιγείῃ
καλῇ δαιδαλέῃ· περὶ δ' ἀργύρεον ζυγὸν ἦεν·
τὴν ἄρετ' ἐξ ἐνάρων πόλιν Ἠετίωνος ὀλέσσας[1]·
τῇ ὅ γε θυμὸν ἔτερπεν, ἄειδε δ' ἄρα κλέα ἀνδρῶν.

μάθε, φησὶν Ὅμηρος, πῶς δεῖ μουσικῇ χρῆσθαι·
κλέα γὰρ ἀνδρῶν ᾄδειν καὶ πράξεις ἡμιθέων ἔπρε-
F πεν Ἀχιλλεῖ τῷ Πηλέως τοῦ δικαιοτάτου. ἔτι δὲ
καὶ τὸν καιρὸν τῆς χρήσεως τὸν ἁρμόττοντα διδάσκων Ὅμηρος ἀργοῦντι γυμνάσιον ἐξεῦρεν ὠφέλι-
μον καὶ ἡδύ. πολεμικὸς γὰρ ὢν καὶ πρακτικὸς ὁ
Ἀχιλλεύς, διὰ τὴν γενομένην αὐτῷ πρὸς τὸν Ἀγαμέμνονα μῆνιν οὐ μετεῖχεν τῶν κατὰ τὸν[2] πόλεμον
κινδύνων. ᾠήθη οὖν Ὅμηρος πρέπον εἶναι τὴν
ψυχὴν τοῖς καλλίστοις τῶν μελῶν παραθήγειν τὸν
ἥρωα ἵν' ἐπὶ τὴν μετὰ μικρὸν αὐτῷ γενησομένην
ἔξοδον παρεσκευασμένος ᾖ[3]· τοῦτο δὲ ἐποίει δηλονότι[4] μνημονεύων τῶν πάλαι πράξεων. τοιαύτη ἦν
1146 ἡ ἀρχαία μουσικὴ καὶ εἰς τοῦτο χρησίμη. Ἡρακλέα
τε γὰρ ἀκούομεν κεχρημένον μουσικῇ καὶ Ἀχιλλέα
καὶ πολλοὺς ἄλλους, ὧν παιδευτὴς ὁ σοφώτατος
Χείρων παραδέδοται, μουσικῆς τε ἅμα ὢν καὶ
δικαιοσύνης καὶ ἰατρικῆς διδάσκαλος.
   41. " Καθόλου δὲ ὅ γε νοῦν ἔχων οὐ τῶν ἐπιστημῶν ἂν[5] ἔγκλημα δήπου[6] θείη εἴ τις αὐτὸς[7] μὴ
κατὰ τρόπον χρῷτο, ἀλλὰ τῆς τῶν χρωμένων κα-

---

[1] ὀλέσσας εΑ²Ε aᵃʳ s : ὀλέσας (ὠλέσας N).
[2] τῶν (τὸν N) κατὰ τὸν] τὸν Wᵃᶜ ; τῶν Wᶜ ; τῶν (τὼν vᵃᶜ)
κατὰ vq.
[3] ᾖ] εἴη Μ.
[4] δηλονότι (δηλονότι Μ ; δῆλον ὅτι V a)] δῆλον ὡς nq.
[5] ἂν added by Ziegler.

And him they found delighting in a lyre
Clear and of curious make, with silver yoke,
Won in the pillage of Eëtion's city;
In this he joyed, singing heroic lays.[a]

See, Homer tells us, the proper way of employing music: for to sing the praise of heroes and the prowess of demigods befitted Achilles, son of the most righteous Peleus.[b] Homer furthermore teaches us the suitable occasion for such employment, presenting it as a beneficial and pleasant exercise for one reduced to inaction. For though a warrior and a man of action, Achilles was taking no part in the fighting of the war, because he was wroth with Agamemnon. Homer believed, we gather, that it was fitting for the hero to whet his spirit on the noblest music, in order to be prepared for the sally into battle that was shortly to follow. That is obviously what he was doing when he rehearsed feats of long ago. Such was the music of olden times and that is what it was used for. For we are told that Heracles, Achilles and many others had recourse to music, and their trainer, as tradition has it, was the paragon of wisdom Cheiron, instructor not only in music, but in justice [c] and medicine as well.

41. "Surely in no case would the man of sense impute the blame to a science when someone by his own act misuses it; he would consider that the

[a] *Iliad*, ix. 186-189.
[b] Peleus had resisted the advances of Hippolytê (or Astydameia), wife of Acastus; for this he was rewarded with the hand of the goddess Thetis.
[c] *Cf.* Homer, *Iliad*, xi. 830-832, where Patroclus is said to have learnt medicines from Achilles, who was taught by Cheiron, the most just of the centaurs.

<hr>

[6] δήπου] ποῦ v.   [7] αὐτὸς] αὐταῖς aN.

(1146) κίας ἴδιον εἶναι τοῦτο νομίσειεν. εἰ γοῦν[1] τις τὸν
παιδευτικὸν τῆς μουσικῆς τρόπον ἐκπονήσας τύχοι
ἐπιμελείας τῆς προσηκούσης ἐν τῇ τοῦ παιδὸς
B ἡλικίᾳ, τὸ μὲν καλὸν ἐπαινέσει τε καὶ ἀποδέξεται,
ψέξει δὲ τὸ ἐναντίον ἔν τε τοῖς ἄλλοις καὶ ἐν τοῖς
κατὰ μουσικήν, καὶ ἔσται ὁ τοιοῦτος καθαρὸς πάσης
ἀγεννοῦς[2] πράξεως, διὰ μουσικῆς τε τὴν μεγίστην
ὠφέλειαν καρπωσάμενος ὄφελος ἂν μέγα γένοιτο
αὑτῷ τε καὶ πόλει, μηθενὶ μήτε ἔργῳ μήτε λόγῳ
χρώμενος ἀναρμόστῳ, σῴζων ἀεὶ[3] καὶ πανταχοῦ τὸ
πρέπον καὶ σῶφρον καὶ κόσμιον.

42. '' Ὅτι δὲ καὶ ταῖς[4] εὐνομωτάταις τῶν πόλεων
ἐπιμελὲς[5] γεγένηται φροντίδα ποιεῖσθαι τῆς γεν-
ναίας μουσικῆς πολλὰ μὲν καὶ ἄλλα μαρτύρια παρα-
θέσθαι ἐστίν, Τέρπανδρον δ' ἄν τις παραλάβοι τὸν
τὴν γενομένην ποτὲ παρὰ Λακεδαιμονίοις στάσιν
C καταλύσαντα, καὶ Θαλήταν[6] τὸν Κρῆτα, ὅν φασι
κατά τι πυθόχρηστον Λακεδαιμονίους παραγενό-
μενον διὰ μουσικῆς ἰάσασθαι ἀπαλλάξαι τε τοῦ
κατασχόντος λοιμοῦ[7] τὴν Σπάρτην, καθάπερ φησὶν
Πρατίνας. ἀλλὰ γὰρ καὶ Ὅμηρος τὸν κατασχόντα
λοιμὸν τοὺς Ἕλληνας παύσασθαι λέγει διὰ μου-
σικῆς· ἔφη γοῦν

---

[1] εἰ γοῦν Weil and Reinach : εἶτ' (εἶτ' V v) οὖν.
[2] ἀγεννοῦς] ἀγενοῦς W N.
[3] ἀεὶ nos : αἰεί.
[4] ταῖς] ἐν ταῖς aN.
[5] ἐπιμελὲς] ἐπιμελεὺς v[1]q.
[6] θαλήταν] θελήσαντα V.
[7] λοιμοῦ] λιμοῦ M[ac].

---

[a] Cf. Plato, Gorgias, 456 D 5–E 2 and Isocrates, Nicocles
(Or. 3), 3–4.
[b] Plato, Republic, iii, 401 E 1—402 A 4.

defective character of the one who so used it was to blame.[a] Thus if one who has been diligent in the study of music for its value as education has received the proper attention while a boy, he will commend and embrace what is noble, and censure the contrary [b] not only in music, but in all other matters as well. Such a man will have no taint of ungenerous action, and as he has by way of music reaped the highest advantage, he will be of the greatest service to himself and to his country,[c] avoiding any inharmonious clash either in deed or in word, everywhere [d] and always upholding the seemly, the temperate and the well-ordered.[e]

42. " That furthermore the best regulated states have taken care to concern themselves with music of the grand style we could show by citing many examples, especially Terpander, who settled the civil strife that had broken out in Lacedaemon,[f] and the Cretan Thaletas, who is said in accordance with a Delphic oracle [g] to have visited Lacedaemon and by means of music to have brought health to the people, delivering Sparta, as Pratinas [h] asserts, from the pestilence that had broken out there. Indeed Homer too says that the pestilence that attacked the Greeks came to an end by music. These are his words [i] :

[c] Plato, *Republic*, iii, 413 E 5.

[d] Plato, *Republic*, iii, 402 c 2-6.

[e] Plato, *Republic*, iii, 403 A 7-8.

[f] *Cf.* Philodemus, *De Musica*, i, Frag. 30. 31-35 (p. 18, ed. Kemke; pp. 40 f., ed. van Krevelen); Diodorus, viii. 28; Zenobius, *Cent.* v. 9 (Leutsch and Schneidewin, *Paroem. Gr.* i, p. 118).

[g] *Cf.* H. W. Parke and D. E. W. Wormell, *The Delphic Oracle*, vol. ii, no. 223, p. 92.

[h] Frag. 6 (Page, *Poet. Mel. Gr.*, p. 369).

[i] *Iliad*, i. 472-474.

(1146)   οἱ δὲ πανημέριοι μολπῇ θεὸν ἱλάσκοντο
         καλὸν ἀείδοντες παιήονα, κοῦροι Ἀχαιῶν,
         μέλποντες ἑκάεργον· ὁ δὲ φρένα τέρπετ' ἀκούων.

τούτους τοὺς στίχους, ἀγαθὲ διδάσκαλε, κολοφῶνα
τῶν περὶ τῆς¹ μουσικῆς λόγων² πεποίημαι, ἐπεὶ
φθάσας σὺ τὴν μουσικὴν δύναμιν διὰ τούτων προ-
απέφηνας ἡμῖν· τῷ γὰρ ὄντι τὸ πρῶτον αὐτῆς καὶ
D κάλλιστον ἔργον ἡ εἰς τοὺς θεοὺς εὐχάριστός³ ἐστιν
ἀμοιβή, ἑπόμενον δὲ⁴ τούτῳ καὶ δεύτερον τὸ τῆς
ψυχῆς καθάρσιον⁵ καὶ ἐμμελὲς καὶ ἐναρμόνιον σύστημα."

Ταῦτ' εἰπὼν ὁ Σωτήριχος, " ἔχεις," ἔφη, " τοὺς
ἐπικυλικείους⁶ περὶ μουσικῆς⁷ λόγους, ἀγαθὲ διδάσκαλε."

43. Ἐθαυμάσθη μὲν οὖν ὁ Σωτήριχος ἐπὶ τοῖς
λεχθεῖσι· καὶ γὰρ ἐνέφαινε διὰ τοῦ προσώπου καὶ
τῆς φωνῆς τὴν περὶ μουσικὴν σπουδήν. ὁ δ' ἐμὸς
διδάσκαλος, " μετὰ τῶν ἄλλων," ἔφη, " καὶ τοῦτο
ἀποδέχομαι ἑκατέρου ὑμῶν,⁸ ὅτι τὴν τάξιν ἑκάτερος
τὴν⁹ αὐτὸς αὑτοῦ ἐφύλαξεν· ὁ μὲν γὰρ Λυσίας ὅσα
μόνον χειρουργοῦντι κιθαρῳδῷ προσῆκεν εἰδέναι
E τούτοις ἡμᾶς εἱστίασεν¹⁰· ὁ δὲ Σωτήριχος ὅσα καὶ
πρὸς ὠφέλειαν καὶ πρὸς θεωρίαν, ἀλλὰ γὰρ καὶ
δύναμιν καὶ χρῆσιν μουσικῆς συντείνει διδάσκων
ἡμᾶς ἐπεδαψιλεύσατο. ἐκεῖνο δ' οἶμαι ἑκόντας
αὐτοὺς ἐμοὶ καταλελοιπέναι· οὐ γὰρ καταγνώσομαι
αὐτῶν δειλίαν ὡς αἰσχυνθέντων κατασπᾶν μουσικὴν

---

¹ τῆς] V aN omit.
² τῶν . . . λόγων] τὸν . . . λόγον Mᵃᶜ ; τὸν . . . λόγων Wᵃᶜ.
³ εὐχάριστός] εὐχάριτός Mᶜ(a from ρ) aᵃᶜ.
⁴ δὲ] a¹ vq omit.

⁵ καθάρσιον] καθάρσιος M aᵃᶜ W (-ι).

> The Greeks made supplication to the god
> All day in beauteous song, chanting a paean,
> Hymning the Archer; he, well pleased, gave ear.

With these verses, most excellent preceptor, I conclude my speech on music, since you used them at the outset [a] to reveal to us its power. For in very truth its first and noblest office is the grateful return of thanks to the gods; while next in order and second in importance is that of composing the soul in purity,[b] in sureness of tone, and in harmony."

Soterichus then said : " You now have, most excellent preceptor, my speech on music, delivered over the cups."

48. Soterichus was admired for his speech; indeed, both in his expression and in his voice, he had shown how devoted he was to music. My preceptor said : " This too, among the rest, I observe with satisfaction in what you each have done : each has observed his station. Thus Lysias has regaled us only with what it becomes a practising singer to the cithara to know; while Soterichus has also lavished upon us instruction in what pertains to the benefit to be gained from music and to its theoretical aspect, not omitting, however, its effect and its employment. The one thing that they have left for me to say was left, I believe, on purpose; for I will not think so poorly of their courage as to suppose that they were ashamed to bring music down to the level of our

---

[a] At 1131 E, *supra*.
[b] For purification by music *cf.* Aristotle, *Politics*, viii. 7 (1341 b 38-40, 1342 a 4-16).

---

[6] ἐπικυλικείους Hemsterhusius : ἐπικυλικίους (ἐπικυκλίους M).

[7] περὶ μουσικῆς] vq omit.　　　[8] ὑμῶν] ἡμῶν M.

[9] τὴν] vq omit.　　　[10] εἰστίασεν] ἱστίασεν V a[1]A[1] W.

(1146) εἰς τὰ συσσίτια· εἰ γάρ που καὶ[1] χρησίμη καὶ παρὰ
πότον, ὡς[2] ὁ καλὸς Ὅμηρος ἀπέφηνεν·

F   μολπή,

γάρ πού φησιν,

    ὀρχηστύς τε, τὰ γάρ τ' ἀναθήματα[3] δαιτός.

καί μοι μηδεὶς ὑπολαβέτω ὅτι πρὸς τέρψιν μόνον
χρησίμην ᾠήθη μουσικὴν Ὅμηρος διὰ τούτων· ἀλλὰ
γὰρ βαθύτερός ἐστι νοῦς ἐγκεκρυμμένος τοῖς ἔπεσιν.
εἰς γὰρ ὠφέλειαν καὶ βοήθειαν τὴν μεγίστην τοῖς
τοιούτοις[4] καιροῖς παρέλαβεν μουσικήν, λέγω δὲ εἰς
τὰ δεῖπνα καὶ τὰς συνουσίας τῶν ἀρχαίων. συνέ-
βαινεν γὰρ εἰσάγεσθαι μουσικὴν ὡς ἱκανὴν ἀντισπᾶν
καὶ πραΰνειν τὴν τοῦ οἴνου ὑπόθερμον δύναμιν,
καθάπερ[5] πού φησιν καὶ ὁ ὑμέτερος[6] Ἀριστόξενος·
ἐκεῖνος γὰρ ἔλεγεν εἰσάγεσθαι μουσικὴν παρόσον ὁ
μὲν οἶνος σφάλλειν πέφυκεν τῶν ἄδην[7] αὐτῷ χρησα-
1147 μένων τά τε σώματα καὶ τὰς διανοίας, ἡ δὲ μουσικὴ
τῇ περὶ αὑτὴν[8] τάξει τε καὶ συμμετρίᾳ εἰς τὴν ἐναν-
τίαν κατάστασιν ἄγει τε καὶ πραΰνει. παρὰ τοῦτον
οὖν τὸν καιρὸν ὡς βοηθήματι τῇ μουσικῇ τοὺς
ἀρχαίους φησὶ κεχρῆσθαι Ὅμηρος.

44. '' Ἀλλὰ δὴ καὶ τὸ μέγιστον ὑμῖν,[9] ὦ ἑταῖροι,
καὶ μάλιστα σεμνοτάτην ἀποφαῖνον μουσικὴν παρα-
λέλειπται. τὴν γὰρ τῶν ὄντων φορὰν καὶ τὴν τῶν

    [1] καί] W aN omit.
    [2] παρὰ πότον ὡς Bryan (in conviviis Valgulius; aux festins,
comme Amyot): παρατετονως M V a W (-ὡς a)N; παραγεγονὼς
v^cq^t (παραγεγωνὼς v^ac); παρατετονὼς εἶχεν q^2·88.
    [3] ἀναθήματα] ἀναθύματα V.
    [4] τοῖς τοιούτοις Ziegler: αὐτοῖς M a; ἐν τοῖς V aN vq; τὰ
τοῖς W.

banquets. For here, if anywhere, music is of service, over the cups, as the noble Homer [a] declared ; there is a passage where he says

> Song and the dance, the graces of a feast.

And let no one, I pray, suppose that in these words Homer means that music ministers only to pleasure ; no, the verse conceals a deeper sense. It was for a most important service and remedial effect that Homer included music on such occasions, that is, at the meals and social gatherings of the ancients. For it is a fact that music was there introduced for its efficacy in counteracting and soothing the heat latent in wine, as your favourite Aristoxenus [b] somewhere says, for it was he who said that music was introduced forasmuch as wine makes the bodies and minds of those who overindulge in it disorderly, while music by its order and balance brings us to the opposite condition and soothes us. Hence Homer asserts that the ancients employed music as a remedy to meet this issue.

44. " But in fact, my friends, the greatest consideration, one that particularly reveals music as most worthy of all reverence, has been omitted. It is that the revolution of the universe [c] and the courses

---

[a] *Odyssey*, i. 152.
[b] Frag. 122 (ed. Wehrli) ; Testim. 27 (ed. Da Rios).
[c] Literally τὰ ὄντα, " the things which are." For this use of the expression *cf.* Aristotle, *Metaphysics*, A 5 (986 a 2) and Alexander on the passage (p. 41. 13, ed. Hayduck).

---

[5] καθάπερ] καθά vq.
[6] ὑμέτερος] ἡμέτερος M[1] vq.
[7] ἅδην M W (ἅδην V α aN ; ᾅδην A) : ᾅδειν vq.
[8] αὐτὴν Westphal : αὑτήν.
[9] ὑμῖν Turnebus (*a nobis* Valgulius) : ὑμῶν.

(1147) ἀστέρων κίνησιν οἱ περὶ Πυθαγόραν καὶ Ἀρχύταν
καὶ Πλάτωνα καὶ οἱ λοιποὶ τῶν ἀρχαίων φιλοσόφων
οὐκ ἄνευ μουσικῆς γίγνεσθαι καὶ συνεστάναι ἔφα-
σκον· πάντα γὰρ καθ' ἁρμονίαν ὑπὸ τοῦ θεοῦ κατ-
εσκευάσθαι φασίν. ἄκαιρον δ' ἂν εἴη νῦν ἐπεκτεί-
νειν[1] τοὺς περὶ τούτου λόγους, ἀνώτατον δὲ καὶ
μουσικώτατον τὸ[2] παντὶ τὸ[3] προσῆκον μέτρον ἐπι-
τιθέναι."

Ταῦτ' εἰπὼν ἐπαιώνισε, καὶ σπείσας[4] τῷ Κρόνῳ
καὶ τοῖς τούτου παισὶν[5] θεοῖς πᾶσι καὶ Μούσαις,
ἀπέλυσεν τοὺς ἑστιωμένους.[6]

[1] ἐπεκτείνειν] ἀπεκτείνειν a ; ὑπεκτείνειν N.
[2] τὸ] τῷ νq.　　　　　　　　　[3] τὸ] M omits.
[4] σπείσας] σπίσας V a¹ W.
[5] παισὶ (-σὶν Ma) : παισὶ σὺν W.
[6] No subscription M V a¹A¹ W νq ; πλουτάρχου περὶ μουσικῆς aN² ; περὶ μουσικῆς a²A²E.

of the stars are said by Pythagoras,[a] Archytas, Plato, and the rest of the ancient philosophers not to come into being or to be maintained without the influence of music ; for they assert that God has shaped all things in a framework based on harmony.[b] It is no time now, however, to expatiate further on this subject. Nothing is more important or more in the spirit of music than to assign to all things their proper measure."

With these words he intoned the paean, and after offering libations to Cronos, to all the gods his children, and to the Muses, he dismissed the banqueters.

[a] Cf. Aristotle, On the Pythagoreans, Frag. 203 (ed. Rose), 13 (ed. Ross).
[b] Cf. Plato, Cratylus, 405 c 6–D 3.

INDEX

[An index to the entire *Moralia* will be published in the final volume of the LCL edition. See also W. C. Helmbold and E. N. O'Neil, *Plutarch's Quotations* (Philological Monograph, XIX), Baltimore, 1959.]

INDEX

INDEX

INDEX

several kings of Galatia ; 1st cent. B.C.

Delian, 337 : epithet of Apollo

Delium, 253 : a temple in Boeotia, scene of the Athenian defeat of 424 B.C.

Delius, 307 : of Ephesus, a follower of Plato ; 4th cent. B.C.

Delos, 383, 385 : an island in the Aegean

Delphi, 245, 247, 359, 365, 385

Delphic, 257, 359, 449

Demeter, 263, 265

Demetrius Poliorcetes, cf. 262, note a : king of Macedon and famous as a general ; 337/6–283 B.C.

Democritean, 197, 199

Democritus, 103, 105, 195–217, 229, 293, 303, 335 : of Abdera, a philosopher ; 5th cent. B.C.

Demodocus, 359 : a bard in the *Odyssey*

Demylus, 307 : a tyrant defied by Zeno of Elea ; 5th cent. B.C.

Description of the World, 61 : title of a work by Eudoxus

Deucalion, 301 : a mythological figure

diatonic genus, 375, 377, 427, 435, 445

Dicaearchus, 71, 79, 235 : a pupil of Aristotle

diesis, 377, 443, 445 : a musical interval, reckoned by Aristoxenus as a quarter tone

Diodotus, 75 : unidentified

Diogenes, 121 ; cf. 311 : of Sinopê, the Cynic ; circa 400/390–328/3 B.C. ; for the *Republic* ascribed to him see 310, note d

Dion, 85, 305, 331 : of Syracuse, friend and pupil of Plato assassinated in 354 B.C.

Dionysia, 93 : festival of Dionysus

Dionysius, 45 : the Elder, tyrant of Syracuse from 405 to 367 B.C.

Dionysius, 85 : the Younger, tyrant of Syracuse circa 367–357, 347–344 B.C.

Dionysius, 425 : of Thebes, a musician ; 4th cent. B.C.

Dionysius Iambus, 385 : a historian ; 3rd cent. B.C.

dioptra, 63 : an optical instrument

Dioscuri, 123, 125 : the divine twins, Castor and Pollux

Disputed Questions, 73 : title of a work by Epicurus

Disputed Questions in Natural Philosophy, 235 : title of a work by Heracleides Ponticus

dithyramb, 361, 375, 417–423

ditone, 377

Dorian (mode in music), 371, 377, 387, 389, 393, 395, 415, 429, 433

Dorian Maiden Songs, 389

Dorion, 397 : an aulete at the court of Philip of Macedon ; 4th cent. B.C.

Dracon, 389 : Athenian musician, teacher of Plato

EËTION, 447 : king of Thebê and father of Andromachê

Egypt, 329

Eleans, 307

elegiac verse, 361, 371, 373, 417

Elegoi, 361 : a musical nome

elements, 213, 217, 219, 225, 231, 245, 401, 431–437

Empedoclean monsters, 287

Empedocles, 129, 195, 217–229, 303 ; quoted, 129, 217, 223, 225, 227, 287 : of Agrigentum, a philosopher ; circa 500–circa 430 B.C.

Endromê, 413 : part of an athletic contest

Endymatia, 373 : a festival at Argos

enharmonic genus, 81, 375–379, 395, 419, 427, 431–435, 443

Epameinondas, 91 (with note c), 93, 99, 101, 309, 327, 331 : Theban general ; circa 420–362 B.C.

Ephesus, 307

Epicurus, 15–331 passim ; quoted, 37, 47, 53, 87, 127, 135, 139, 147, 205, 207, 221, 229, 249, 251, 297, 299, 301, 313 ; cf. 29, note c ; 43, note b : founder of the Epicurean school ; 341–270 B.C.

460

INDEX

461

INDEX

Heracleides, 17, 305 : of Aenus, pupil of Plato and slayer of Cotys

Heracleides Ponticus, 71, 235, 357 : a pupil of Plato ; 4th cent. B.C.

Heracleitus, 39, 257, 277, 295 : of Ephesus, a philosopher ; 6th cent. B.C.

Heracles, 221, 383, 447 : a mythical hero

Hermionê, 419 : a city in the Peloponnese

Hermogenes, 123 : a speaker in Xenophon's *Symposium*

Herodotus, 59, 91, 147 ; quoted, 91, 123, 147 ; *cf.* 133, 197, note *f* : of Halicarnassus, the famous historian ; 5th cent. B.C.

Hesiod, quoted, 31 ; *cf.* 97, note *b* ; 297, note *g* : of Ascra in Boeotia, a didactic poet ; 8th cent. B.C.

hexameter verse, 359, 361, 363, 417

Hierax, 413 : an early musician

Hieron, 75 : tyrant of Gela and Syracuse ; died 467/6 B.C.

Hieronymus, 79 : of Rhodes, a Peripatetic philosopher ; 3rd cent. B.C.

Himera, 369 : a city in Sicily

Hipparchia, 17 : a Cynic philosopher, wife of Crates ; 4th cent. B.C.

Hipparchus, 69 : mathematician and astronomer ; *circa* 190-120 B.C.

Hippocrates, 41, 101 : the famous physician ; 5th cent. B.C.

Hipponax, 367, 371 : of Ephesus, an iambic poet ; 6th cent. B.C.

Hismenias, 77 : of Thebes, a flute-player ; 4th cent. B.C.

history, pleasures of, 57-61, 69, 71

Homer, 19, 61, 71, 77, 141, 355, 359, 363, 367, 445-449, 453 ; quoted (*Iliad*), 41, 99, 131, 135, 141, 193, 223, 279, 355, 447, 451, *cf.* 59 ; (*Odyssey*), 19, 21, 29, 31, 97, 127, 341, 453

Hyagnis, 363, 369, 383 : a musician, father of Marsyas

Hyampolis, 103 : a city of Phocis

hypatê, 401, 403, 407, 409 : a note of the scale

hypatê hypatôn, 387 : the lowest note of the lowest tetrachord

Hyperboreans, 385 : a mythical northern race

Hypodorian mode, 429

Hypolydian mode, 419

Hypophrygian mode, 429

hyporcheme, 373

Hyrcanians, 109 : a people dwelling on the southern shore of the Caspian

IAMBIC VERSE, 417

Iambus : see Dionysius Iambus

Idaean Dactyls, 363

ideas, theory of, 235, 237

Idomeneus, 251, 313 : a follower of Epicurus

instrumental music, 367

intellectual life, 31 ; pleasures of, 57-83

intervals (musical), 375, 377, 399-403, 407, 429, 443, 445

Ion, 301 : eponymous ancestor of the Ionians

Ionian mode, 387, 389

Ismenias : see Hismenias

Istrus, 383 : author of a work entitled *Epiphanies of Apollo* ; 3rd cent. B.C.

Italy, 363, 375

Ithaca, 29, 359

JUSTICE (a deity), 297

KINDLY, 121 : a divine epithet

LACEDAEMON, 373, 449 ; see also Sparta

Lacedaemonians, 247, 411, 429

Lachares, 45 : Athenian general, for a short time tyrant of Athens ; early 3rd cent. B.C.

Lady of Nuptials, 265 : an epithet of Hera

Laïs, 99 : a famous courtesan ; early 4th cent. B.C.

Lamprocles, 387 : of Athens, a musician ; early 5th cent. B.C.

Lamprus, 425 : a musician ; 5th cent. B.C.

Lampsacus, 45, 329 : a city on the Hellespont

INDEX

entangle the different senses of *harmonia, tasis, tonos* and *tropos* or of the Greek adverbs *Doristi, Lydisti, Phrygisti* etc. in the translation. In Aristoxenus a precise distinction can be found; but in the earlier writers the words appear to have been used rather loosely. See also scale

modulation, 365, 371, 395, 429, 431, 441

Mother of the Gods, 393; see also Great Mother

Muse(s), 65, 75, 77, 359, 455

Museum, the, 75: a centre of learning established by Ptolemy I at Alexandria

music, 71-79, 123, 133, 353-455 *passim*; pleasures of, 73-77

Mysians, 371

Mysians, 429: title of a dithyramb composed by Philoxenus

NANARUS, 75: satrap of Babylon

natural philosophy, 53, 105, 199, 235, 237, 249, 261; *cf.* 231

nature, 217, 221-225, 229, 231, 235, 237, 257, 261, 283, 291, 301

Neocles, 39, 89, 105: brother of Epicurus

Nestor, 193: king of Pylos in the Homeric poems

netê, 391, 393, 401, 403, 407, 409, 415: a note of the scale

Nicias, 63: an Athenian painter; 4th cent. B.C.

Nicidion, 89: a member of Epicurus' school

Nile, 309

Niobê, 385: daughter of Tantalus "no more this than that," 199-209

nome, 359-373, 419, 431, 433: a musical form

Notices on Phrygia, 363: title of a work by Alexander Polyhistor

Numa, 301: early king of Rome

OCTAVE, 401-407, 435, 441

Odysseus, 61, 193: a leader of the Greeks at Troy

Oedipus the King, cf. 59: a tragedy by Sophocles

Olympia, 107: a sanctuary of Zeus in Elis; scene of the Olympic festival, which occurred every four years and traditionally began in 776 B.C.

olympiads, 27

Olympus, 363, 367, 369, 375, 379, 383, 385, 389-393, 419, 431: a legendary Phrygian aulete

Olympus, 369: the Younger; also a legendary figure

On Kingship, 75: title of a work by Epicurus

On Music, 385, 389: title of a work by Aristoxenus

On Poems, 69: title of a work by Metrodorus

On the Ancient Poets and Musicians, 363: title of a work by Glaucus

On the Heavens, 235: title of a work by Aristotle

On the Highest Good, 45: title of a work by Aristotle

On the Soul, 235: title of works by Aristotle and Dicaearchus

Onesicrates, 353-357, 361, 381: a speaker in the *De Musica*

opinion, 231, 239, 271, 277, 281-285, 313; see also belief

oracle(s), 107, 247, 449

Orpheus, 363, 369, 375: a legendary Thracian musician

orthios, 415: a metrical foot

Orthios nome, 369, 373

Oxys nome, 361

PAEAN(S), 355, 373, 375, 389, 451, 455

paeon, 431, 433; *cf.* 375: a metrical foot

paeon epibatos, 417, 431: a metrical foot

Pan, 123; pipes of, 383, 385

Panathenaic festival, 371

Pancrates, 305: a composer

Pantheia, 61: a personage in Xenophon's *Education of Cyrus*

paramesê, 375, 387, 393, 403, 407, 409: a note of the scale

paranetê, 391, 393, 445: a note of the scale

parhypatê, 375, 391: a note of the scale

Parmenides, 195, 229-235, 241,

INDEX

245, 269, 277, 295, 303, 307 : of Elea, a philosopher ; 5th cent. B.C.

Peiraeus, 309 : harbour city of Athens

Peleus, 447 : father of Achilles

Pella, 79 : a city in Macedonia

Pellenê, 429 : a city of Achaia

Pelopidas, 91, 103 : Theban statesman and general ; circa 410–364 B.C.

Peloponnese, 311

pentachord, 423 : an arrangement of five notes in the range of a musical fourth

Periander, 133 : ruler of Corinth circa 625–585 B.C.

Pericleitus, 367 : of Lesbos, a citharode ; later than Terpander and earlier than Hipponax

Peripatetics, 235, 237, 357 ; cf. 47 : followers of Aristotle

Persian history, 61

Phaeacian good cheer, 61

Phaedrus, 261 : title of a work by Plato

Phaëthon, 67 : son of Helios and Clymenê

Phanias, 87 : a Peripatetic philosopher ; 4th cent. B.C.

Phemius, 359 : a bard in the Odyssey

Pherecrates, 421 : a writer of Old Comedy ; 5th cent. B.C.

Pherecydes, 39 : of Syros, a writer on cosmogony and theogony ; 6th cent. B.C.

Philammon, 359, 365 : of Delphi, an early musician

Philip I, 309 : king of Macedon 359–336 B.C.

Philip, 63 : of Opus, mathematician and astronomer ; 4th cent. B.C.

Philoctetes, 25 : one of the Greek leaders on the expedition to Troy

Philoxenus, 101 : Alexander the Great's admiral

Philoxenus, 381, 419, 425, 427 : of Cythera, a dithyrambic poet ; 435–379 B.C.

Philoxenus, 323 : a glutton

Phlius, 395 : a city in the Peloponnese

Phocion, 99, 305, 353 : Athenian general and statesman ; 402–318 B.C.

Phocis, 103 : a district in north central Greece

Phoebus, 93 ; see also Apollo

Phormio, 123 : a Spartan, visited by the Dioscuri

Phormio, 305 : a pupil of Plato

Phrygia, 363, 367

Phrygian (mode in music), 371, 379, 393, 429-433

Phrynichus, 395 : Athenian tragic poet ; 6th to 5th cent. B.C.

Phrynis, 365, 423 : a musician, of Mytilenê ; flourished circa 450 B.C.

Pieria, 359

Pierians, 77 ; see also Muses

Pierus, 359 : of Pieria, a legendary musician

Pindar, 121, 123, 365, 371, 373, 385, 389, 395, 415, 425, 427 ; quoted, 77, 121, 339, 341 : lyric poet ; 518-438 B.C.

pipes of Pan, 383, 385

Plataea, 91 : a city of Boeotia, scene of the Greek victory over the Persians in 479 B.C.

Plato, 49, 59, 69, 85, 129, 141, 191-195, 215, 231, 235-247, 261, 269, 277, 293, 295, 305, 307, 331, 385-389, 399-405, 455 ; quoted, 17, 119, 121, 261, 295, 297, 399 ; cf. 37, note d : 139, notes b-d ; 282, note d : Athenian philosopher ; circa 427-347 B.C.

Platonic writings of Aristotle, 257

Platonists, 357

pleasure, 15-149 passim, 195, 229, 247, 249, 253, 283, 285, 295-299, 329, 337, 421, 453

Plutarch's school, cf. 15-23, 109, 127, 129, 191

poetic inventions, 57

poetry, 71, 73, 367

poets, 41, 309, 359, 369, 371, 395, 421 ; comic, 421, 425 ; lyric, 359, 365, 425 ; tragic, 395, 417

Polyaenus, 39, 93, 123, 205 : a follower of Epicurus

Polyeidus, 397 : a musician

Polymnestian, 361, 365

INDEX

Polymnestus, 361, 365, 371, 373, 379, 417 : of Colophon, an early musician
Poseidon, 263
Potidaea, 253 : a city on the isthmus of Pallenê
Pratinas, 369, 373, 425, 449 : of Phlius, lyric and dramatic poet : 6th to 5th cent. B.C.
preludes, 361, 367
Prenuptial rites, 265
Processionals, 359, 389
prosodiac, 417, 419 : a metrical foot
Protagoras, 17, 199 : of Abdera, a Sophist ; 5th cent. B.C.
proverbs, 19, 21, 27, 45, 245, 281
providence, 53, 107, 109, 113, 117, 121, 213, 285, 295, 331
Ptolemy I, 63, 75 ; *cf.* 262, note *a* : Soter, ruler of Egypt from 323 to 282 B.C.
Ptolemy II, 191 ; *cf.* 154 : Philadelphus, sole ruler of Egypt from the death of Ptolemy Soter until 246 B.C.
pycnon, 377, 395 : the name of two intervals in the tetrachord when their sum is less than the remaining interval
Pyrrhaeans, 307 : the people of Pyrrha, a city of Lesbos
Pyrson, 111 : a friend of Epicurus
Pythagoras, 17, 67, 141, 329, 441, 455 : a philosopher ; 6th cent. B.C.
Pythia, 123 : priestess of Apollo at Delphi
Pythian, 337 : epithet of Apollo
Pythian games, 363, 371, 397
Pythocleides, 387 : an aulete, teacher of Lamprocles ; late 6th cent. B.C.
Pythocles, 69, 293 : a follower of Epicurus
Python, 305 : a follower of Plato
Python, 385 : a fabulous serpent

REPLIES, 93 : title of a work by Metrodorus
Reply to the Natural Philosophers, 235 : title of a work by Theophrastus
Reply to the Sophists, 47 : title of a work by Metrodorus

Reply to Theophrastus, 207 : title of a work by Epicurus
Republic 385 : title of a work by Plato
Return of the Heroes, 359 : title given to the song of Phemius (*Odyssey*, i. 325-327)
Reveller, 265 : an epithet of Dionysus
Revels (a festival), 265
rhythm(s), 79, 359, 365, 369, 375, 379, 395, 397, 415-419, 431, 433, 437, 439
Romans, 301
Rome, 91, 331

Sacadas, 371, 373, 379 : of Argos, a musician ; 6th cent. B.C.
Sack of Troy, 359 : title given to the song of Demodocus (*Odyssey*, viii. 499-520)
sage, the, 29, 33, 71, 73, 103, 105, 251-257, 295, 299, 303, 307, 311, 313, 323
Salamis, 103 : an island off Attica ; scene of the naval victory of 480 B.C.
Samians, 75
Sappho, 387 : of Lesbos, a poetess ; 7th to 6th cent. B.C.
Sardanapalus, 75 : king of Assyria ; 7th cent. B.C.
Sardonic laughter, 91
Saturnalia, 353
Saturnalian feast, 93
Saturninus, 191 ; *cf.* 188 : L. Herennius Saturninus, proconsul of Achaia, A.D. 98-99
scale (musical), 365, 391, 395, 415, 431, 437, 441. See also mode
Schoinion, 361, 365 : a musical nome
Scyths, 77, 109
semitone, 379, 443
sensation, 127, 135, 145, 147, 201, 229, 231, 235, 273-285, 289, 293, 411
sense(s), 83, 199, 231, 233, 241, 251-257, 273, 277, 281, 283, 291, 293, 411, 441
sense-object, 205, 291
sense organs, 203, 285
Sicily, 85, 305, 323, 331
Sicyon, 357, 371 : a city in the Peloponnese

466

INDEX

Simonides, 75, 389, 395 : of Ceos, lyric poet ; *circa* 556–468 B.C.

Socrates, 17, 123, 193, 195, 231, 245, 247, 251–261, 269, 277, 295, 305, 329 : Athenian philosopher, 469–399 B.C.

Solon, 311, 313 : Athenian legislator and poet ; 638–560 (?) B.C.

sophist, 247, 257, 263, 277, 293, 303

sophistries, 229

Sophocles, 63, 71, 107, 123, 333 ; quoted, 59, 63, 107, 333 : Athenian tragic poet ; 495–406 B.C.

Sositheüs, 111 : a friend of Epicurus

Soterichus, 355, 381, 451 : of Alexandria, a speaker in the *De Musica*

Sparta, 91, 311, 367, 371, 449 ; see also Lacedaemon

Spartan(s), 201, 301 ; *cf.* 119, note *b* ; see also Lacedaemonians

Speusippus, 193 : Plato's successor as head of the Academy ; died 339 B.C.

Spondeion (scale), 377 ; (libation song), 389 ; *cf.* 391, 393

Stagirites, 307 : the people of Stagira, Aristotle's native city

Stesichorus, 359, 369, 379 : lyric poet ; 6th cent. B.C.

Stheneia, 413 : an Argive festival

Sthenius, 413 : an epithet of Zeus

Stilpon, 195, 261–267 : of Megara, a philosopher ; late 4th cent. B.C.

Stoa, 279 ; *cf.* 242, note *a* : a school of philosophy

Strato, 237 : succeeded Theophrastus as head of the Lyceum in 287 B.C. ; died 270/68 B.C.

Strife (personified), 223

style, 81, 361, 365, 379, 391, 395, 397, 413, 415, 441, 449

superstition, 55, 109–113, 119, 131

suspension of judgement, 277–293

swerve (of atoms), 291

Symposium, 205 : title of a work by Epicurus

Syracusans, 45

Syrian, 85, 309

syrinx, 79, 397 : a device for raising the pitch of the aulos

TEGEA, 365 : a city in the Peloponnese

Telephanes, 397 : of Megara, an aulete ; 4th cent. B.C.

Telesias, 425 : of Thebes, a musician ; 4th cent. B.C.

Tempê, 383 : a narrow valley in Thessaly

Terpander, 359–371, 375, 379, 389, 391, 415, 419, 449 : of Antissa, an early musician

Terpandrean nome, 361

Terpandrean style, 379

tetrachord, 377, 393, 395, 401–405, 429, 433, 435, 443, 445 : four notes in the range of a musical fourth

tetrameter, 417 : a metrical line

Tetraoidios, 361 : a musical nome

text newly emended, 18, 24, 30, 44, 54, 60, 76, 78, 84, 88, 96, 108, 114, 120, 128, 130, 132, 138, 142, 146, 192, 194, 200, 204, 210, 212, 238, 244, 246, 252, 258, 266, 270, 272, 282, 286, 288, 326, 336, 356, 360, 364, 386, 388, 394, 402, 414, 422 (Lloyd-Jones), 424, 434, 448 ; new readings suggested also at 26 (Post), 44, 106 (Post), 108 (Post), 128 (Post), 130 (Post), 132 (Post), 196 (Post), 210, 220 (Post), 230 (Post), 236, 248 (Post), 250, 266 (Warmington), 282, 292, 324 (Post), 334 (Post), 340 (Post), 362 (Post), 422 (Lloyd-Jones), 430

Thaletas, 369, 373, 375, 379, 449 : of Gortyn, a musician ; 7th cent. B.C.

Thamyras or Thamyris, 63, 359 : a legendary musician of Thrace

Thasian wine, 35, 87

Thebans, 103, 331

Thebê, 61 : wife of Alexander of Pherae ; 4th cent. B.C.

Thebes, 99, 365, 425 ; a city of Boeotia

Themistocles, 87, 103, 247, 331 : Athenian statesman in the period of the Persian wars

Theodoreans, *cf.* 277, note *e* :

INDEX

followers of Theodorus, a sophist of the 3rd cent. B.C.

Theon, 17-23, 31, 85, 109, 129 : a member of Plutarch's school

Theophrastus, 17, 77, 79, 87, 207, 235, 293, 309 : of Eresus ; succeeded Aristotle (322 B.C.) as head of the Lyceum ; died 287 B.C.

Theopompus, 61 : of Chios, a historian ; 4th cent. B.C.

Thirty, the, 253 : oligarchic rulers of Athens, 404-403 B.C.

Thrace, 305, 359

Thrasonides, 75 : a character in a comedy by Menander

Thrasybulus, 91, 329 : Athenian general and statesman who put down the Thirty Tyrants ; died 388 B.C.

Thrasyleon, 75 : a character in a comedy by Menander

Thrasyllus, 395 : of Phlius, a musician

Timarchus, 249 : invited by Metrodorus to join the Epicurean school

Timocleia, 61 : a noble Theban lady ; 4th cent. B.C.

Timocrates, 95, 301, 305 : brother of the Epicurean Metrodorus

Timotheüs, 361, 381, 397, 419, 423, 427 : of Miletus, a dithyrambic poet ; 5th to 4th cent. B.C.

Titans, 359

tone, 377, 407, 443 : a musical interval

Torebus, 385 : an early musician, perhaps to be identified with the Lydian king of that name

tragedy, 387, 389, 395

Trimeles, 361, 371 : a musical nome

trimeter, 417 : a metrical line

tritê, 391, 445 : a note of the musical scale

Trochaios, 361 : a musical nome

trochee, 415, 431 : a metrical foot

Troezen, 365 : a city in the Peloponnese

Troy, 359

trumpets, 413

Truth (personified), 233

Tumult (personified), 223

Typhon, 261 : a mythological monster

tyrant(s), 27, 87, 115, 307, 309, 329

Tyrtaeus, 395 : of Mantinea, a musician ; 4th cent. B.C.

UNIVERSE, 213, 223, 229, 237, 291, 297, 335, 453

Visit to the Dead, 63 : a painting by Nicias

void, the, 211, 219, 223, 229, 231, 243, 245

War of the Titans with the Gods, 359 : title of a composition by Thamyris

wine, 31-35, 73, 93, 95, 99, 117, 201, 205, 207, 213, 271, 453

Xenocrates, 215, 235, 295, 307 : successor of Speusippus (339 B.C.) as head of the Academy ; died 314 B.C.

Xenocritus, 373, 375 : of Locri, an early musician

Xenodamus, 373 : of Cythera, an early musician

Xenophon, 61, 81 ; *cf.* 105 ; quoted, 123 f. : Athenian historian ; *circa* 430–*circa* 354 B.C.

Xerxes I, 331 : king of Persia from 485 to 465 B.C. ; defeated by Themistocles at Salamis, 480 B.C.

Zeno, 307 : of Elea, pupil of Parmenides ; 5th cent. B.C.

Zeus, 77, 121, 123, 263, 265, 357, 413

Zeuxippus, 15, 19, 31, 109, 129 : a member of Plutarch's school

Zoroaster, 235 : title of a work by Heracleides Ponticus